THE POLITICS OF
CULTURAL PLURALISM

CRAWFORD YOUNG

The University of Wisconsin Press

Framingham State College
Framingham, Ma

Published 1976

The University of Wisconsin Press
114 North Murray Street
Madison, Wisconsin 53715

The University of Wisconsin Press, Ltd.
1 Gower Street
London WC1E 6HA

Copyright © 1976
The Regents of the University of Wisconsin System
All rights reserved

Printings 1976, 1979

Printed in the United States of America

ISBN 0-299-06740-8 cloth, 0-299-06744-0 paper
LC 74-27318

Contents

JF
60
Y67
1979

List of Maps

List of Tables

Preface

This volume appears almost exactly a decade after the commitment was made to undertake the study, in late 1965. With such an elephantine gestation period, the work has accumulated an enormous number of debts to those who have nurtured it in one way or another during its embryonic state. Indeed, if all were to find explicit acknowledgment, this preface would rival the book itself in unwieldy length.

Initial paternity must be attributed to James S. Coleman, then my department chairman at Makerere University College in Uganda, more recently as Rockefeller Foundation representative in central Africa an associate in the development of social science at the Université Nationale du Zaire. The study became orphaned from the comparative politics series for which it was initially recruited; by the time it actually took shape, it diverged in length and format from the initial design. However, without this original stimulus to undertake the project, it would never have appeared.

Ford and Rockefeller have become best known as a presidential ticket, but I prefer to think of them as an eleemosynary partnership. The final intensive research, and above all the drafting of this manuscript, were accomplished during a year of research time generously provided by a Ford Foundation Faculty Fellowship during 1972-73, a program whose subsequent demise I greatly regret. Earlier, generous support from the Ford Foundation for my doctoral dissertation research during 1961-63 provided the opportunity for collection of data which served not only for my thesis, but for portions of this manuscript. My research in Uganda, during a year as visiting professor 1965-66, was supported by the Rockefeller Foundation; although my primary focus was a quite different topic, part of the material for the Uganda case study which figures in this study was acquired, thanks to this support.

The University of Wisconsin at Madison has contributed in many ways to this endeavor. Most of the ideas in this work have emerged in interaction with its students in courses and seminars. A particularly stimulating association with my colleagues Charles Anderson and Fred von der Mehden led to a first formulation of some of the hypotheses developed at greater length here in our collective work, *Issues of Political Development*. My colleagues in comparative politics have contributed far more than they realize in myriad encounters over the years of association since 1963, as concepts have slowly taken form. I wish to record my particular gratitude to Fred Hayward, Dennis Dresang, James Scott, Donald Emmerson, Henry Hart, Jan Vansina, Alex Wilde, Michael Schatzberg, Okello Oculi, Ilona Fabian, Mark Francillon, Murray Edelman, and Thomas Turner (plus, of course, the anonymous readers of the university Press) for their perceptive critique of portions or all of the manuscript. I hasten to exercise in their behalf the author's constitutional prerogative to grant full and unconditional pardon for errors of fact or judgment which may subsist.

No work of this size could have been undertaken unaided. Over the years, a series of particularly able research assistants have helped in innumerable ways. I acknowledge with particular gratitude the labors of Cathy Newbury, Nzongola Ntalaja, Thomas Turner, John Borneman, Mohammed Kismadi, and Sherryl Sundell, and the University of Wisconsin Graduate School Research Committee for making their assistance possible. Our miraculous Department Secretary, Elizabeth Pringle, was left with the chore of seeing through the final stages of manuscript typing when I evaporated in September 1973 for a two-year visiting appointment with the Université Nationale du Zaire. For the typing, I am indebted to Elizabeth Corbett, Susan B. Anthony, Sharon Bessette, and Marilyn Henry. The mammoth task of indexing was cheerfully undertaken by Elizabeth Diez.

For the maps, I am indebted to the University of Wisconsin Cartographic Laboratory, a labor performed with the dispatch and excellence which has long been its hallmark. My particular gratitude needs to be recorded to the University of Wisconsin Press, for its remarkably expeditious service at all stages.

Countless are the anonymous contributors who have shared their thoughts with me over the years. Particular note should be made of the students at the Université Nationale du Zaire; I used the draft manuscript as the basis for a course in political sociology in 1973-74, and found their reactions to the theses propounded especially stimulating.

Finally, my special thanks go to my wife and daughters, to whom this book is dedicated. Their moral support, and above all their patience and forbearance on the many occasions when these labors conflicted with family obligations, have contributed more than they will ever know.

Crawford Young

Madison, Wisconsin
15 September 1974

THE POLITICS OF CULTURAL PLURALISM

1 The Enduring Challenge Of Diversity

Are you a Mumbala or a Mupende?[1]

—Angry policeman to the author, Idiofa, southwest
Zaire, April 1962

The policeman's peremptory query remains vivid; indeed, it is a haunting epitaph to millions who have perished in communal strife since he spoke. The question went to the heart of an aspect of Zaire politics which I found particularly perplexing and elusive: defining the role and scope of ethnicity as a determinant of behavior and conflict. Extant paradigms of nationalist politics offered no conceptual basis for incorporating into the pattern of explanation a factor whose central importance was reconfirmed by daily observation.

The policeman was too distraught for me to feel prudent an exploration of the full meaning of his question, or even to explain my inability to respond within the categories offered. In reflecting afterwards on his intent, it seemed obvious enough that he sought to place a stranger within the social code which then dominated conflict in Idiofa. "Pende" stood for one of the dominant local groups; "Mbala" was a more imprecise term which denoted several neighboring groups, joined in the policeman's social perceptions as a single hostile configuration. At a moment of relatively high polarization, a participant is likely to find no cognitive space for neutral men. Thus, the need to place a stranger on one side or the other of the battlelines has some social logic after all, no matter how bizarre it seemed on first hearing.

Yet it is worth lingering another moment over the many implications of the interpellation. Pende and Mbala were not historical enemies whose endemic strife had only been temporarily halted by the enforced truce of colonial rule; chroniclers who visited this area in the nineteenth century make no mention of any such conflict. Ambitious young men from both groups during the colonial period sought urban employment in the regional center of Kikwit, or in the nearest major city of Kinshasa (then Leopold-

1. Hereafter, we will observe the growing convention of dropping the singular (Mu) and plural (Ba) prefixes of ethnic groups of the Bantu linguistic family. The policeman would not have dreamed of taking such liberties with the language; we have preserved his usage.

3

ville); they competed for places in the district secondary schools. However, before the coming of politics in 1959 no one would have thought that Pende-Mbala rivalry was a critical factor in the district.

Political mobilization was swift and massive in 1960.[2] Mass sentiment was expressed as aggressive, belligerent animosity to the colonizer and his system. Only very close scrutiny into the internal factions of the regional party and voting patterns would reveal the first signs of ethnic tensions, inter alia, between Pende and Mbala.[3]

However, the issue context rapidly altered after independence. The Belgians were greatly reduced in visibility. Contrary to expectations, independence had not raised the level of rural well-being; indeed, it had deteriorated. Discontent again stalked the land and cried out for the identification of new social enemies. For many, only politicians and civil servants had benefitted from independence. The Africanization of many posts made the Pende aware that they had fewer educated sons to fill them than did some other groups, which came to be lumped as Mbala. Government was presumed to control the critical vehicles of group (and individual) mobility, above all the distribution of schools—and Mbala were believed to have gained control of provincial institutions. The danger to the ethnic community was clear and present. The angry tone of the policeman's question presaged the bloody rebellion in which the Pende heavily participated in early 1964.[4]

Ethnic reality, of course, was far more complex than suggested. Idiofa was not really a Pende town, but rather was in the midst of the neighboring Mbunda. The latter are not closely related to the Pende in language and culture, but did share the sense of social disadvantage, suspicion of the Mbala, and, when the hour of rebellion struck, participation in the armed struggle. Thus, the policeman's Pende-Mbala formulation of the contours of conflict was fully intelligible.

Were the reader to visit Idiofa today, he would be most unlikely to encounter such a question—any more than he would have had he visited in 1960—or 1900. These labels would not be especially useful as a cognitive map to politics in the Mobutist era. They are yesterday's scorecards of

2. So striking was it that it became the basis for Herbert Weiss's "rural radicalism" thesis, that nationalism is to be understood not as agitational activism by an urban new elite, but rather as political leaders buffeted by enormous radicalizing pressures from their rural constituents; see *Political Protest in the Congo* (Princeton: Princeton University Press, 1967).

3. Ibid., pp. 160-80, 287-90; Benoit Verhaegen, *Rébellions au Congo* (Brussels: Centre de Recherche et d'Information Socio-Politiques, 1966), I, 50-65.

4. The causes of the Kwilu rebellion were, of course, far more complex than implied in this digression, in which only one aspect is discussed. See in particular the outstanding account in Verhaegen, *Rébellions au Congo*, I, 9-185.

collective alignment. Filed, but not obliterated, they are, of course, still terms which designate recognizable ethnic communities. They may—or may not—re-emerge tomorrow.

We have dwelt at length on what was, after all, a very banal encounter because it does suggest many of the themes we wish to explore in this study. In most of the developing world, identity patterns derived from shared language, culture, religion, or caste which are not coterminous with the territorial unit of sovereignty have been important, often crucial determinants of political alignments and conflict. The power of the communal factor in politics was seriously underestimated at the time of independence, both by scholars and statesmen. Only gradually did this dimension of political development begin to receive the attention its evident importance merited. As studies began to accumulate and political leaders experimented with various formulas for coping with this challenge, awareness has slowly grown of its enormous complexity. The identity groups existed at widely varying levels of intensity of collective awareness. Further, close inspection reveals that many widely used communal labels cover multiple layers of self-consciousness; it proves far from clear what the appropriate unit of analysis is. The definition of groups is in constant flux; any theory of ethnic conflict must incorporate change as a central element. Political events are an important independent variable in determining the saliency of cultural conflict at any moment in time. At one moment, ethnic conflict may appear to eclipse all other factors in the political equation; a few years later, the same cleavage may appear entirely muted, and quite irrelevant to explication of the political process.

Before allowing the policeman to retire into the obscurity he will surely by now desire, let us suggest one other sense in which he has contributed to this volume. Our brief acquaintance—and many comparable experiences—compelled taking his question into account in my effort to impose at least analytical order to the turbulent initial years of Zaire independence.[5] In collaboration with Charles Anderson and Fred von der Mehden, the tentative explanatory framework developed in the Zaire study was then utilized on a comparative basis for the developing world generally.[6] A year in Uganda offered the occasion to explore the interaction of ethnicity and politics in a second polity where cultural conflict was salient. Since that time, I have sought to enlarge the comparative base of the inquiry and reformulate the theory in the light of subsequent events and a rapidly growing literature on various aspects of the subject.

5. The result was a chapter on "The Politics of Ethnicity," in Crawford Young, *Politics in the Congo* (Princeton: Princeton University Press, 1965), pp. 232-72.

6. Charles W. Anderson, Fred R. von der Mehden, and Crawford Young, *Issues of Political Development* (Englewood Cliffs, N.J.: Prentice-Hall, 1967), pp. 15-83.

VITALITY OF CULTURAL CLEAVAGES

The flow of history in recent years lends indisputable confirmation of the enduring importance of the subject. Two of the most traumatic crises in Afro-Asia in the intervening period were the civil war in Nigeria and the successful lunge to independence of Bangladesh, both of which we will explore. In the Nigerian instance, we find at the vortex of conflict the crystallization of Ibohood, an identity pattern which became salient only in the twentieth century. Social competition in Lagos and other cities, first for place and preferment, political competition in the Nigerian arena subsequently, placed ethnicity in the center of public cognition of political struggle. Finally, circumstances which appeared to threaten the very survival of the Ibo as a group—in particular the pogroms in the North— led to the desperate adventure of secession. In the Bangladesh case, we find an instance where a historically well-established nationality, the Bengali, were internally divided by religious affiliation and caste-related stratification. In the context of the Indian independence struggle, the dialectic of conflict placed the religious identity in the dominant role; Bengali Muslims accepted alignment with the new Islamic state of Pakistan, albeit with some misgivings. The radical transformation of the political arena served to pit Bengalis against Punjabi-dominated West Pakistan. The linguistic referent supplanted religion as the operative solidarity principle. Gradual polarization became massive mobilization when the Pakistani army launched a sanguinary repression of the Bengali movement; as with Biafra, circumstances then mandated revolt as the only means to group survival. The principle of national sovereignty set no boundaries to the violence with which domestic conflict can be conducted. When polarization occurs along communal cleavages, the conflict situation describes entire collectivities as enemies. Such confrontation is intense in its mobilization effect and swiftly escalates fears to a level where the very physical survival of a collectivity may appear to be at stake.

In the face of such holocausts, few indeed would be disposed to debate the power of the ethnic factor in African and Asian politics. No African leader would be found today to endorse the view put forward by Sekou Toure of Guinea, who at the time of independence declared: "In three or four years, no one will remember the tribal, ethnic or religious rivalries which, in the recent past, caused so much damage to our country and its population."[7] Nor is any Asian leader likely to follow the secular faith of a Jawaharlal Nehru in the integrative effect of nationalism and modernization; although a profound student of history, he was taken wholly by surprise by the magnitude of the communal violence which accompanied Indian partition in

---

7. Sekou Toure, *Toward Full Reafricanisation* (Paris: Présence Africaine, 1959), p. 28.

1947.[8] A year later, he made the equally saddening discovery of the force of linguistic solidarity, when he listened to the evidence submitted to the Linguistic Provinces Committee in 1948: "The work of sixty years of the Indian National Congress was standing before us, face to face with centuries-old India of narrow loyalties, petty jealousies and ignorant prejudices engaged in mortal conflict and we were simply horrified to see how thin was the ice upon which we were skating. Some of the ablest men in the country came before us and confidently and emphatically stated that language in the country stood for and represented culture, race, history, individuality, and finally a sub-nation."[9]

The widespread conviction that triumphant anticolonial nationalism would eclipse cultural pluralism derived powerful reinforcement from the dominant paradigm of assimilation in the industrial world. Theories of political development and modernization which appeared in the 1950s virtually all rested on the premises, if only implicit, that the universe of industrial nation-states was a model of the future of the underdeveloped world. At that moment, observable reality in the northern hemisphere seemed to validate the integrative hypothesis. In the United States, the "melting pot" theory was almost unchallenged. The big city machines, last redoubt of ethnic patronage politics, were breaking apart. The Supreme Court and the civil rights movement could be relied upon to complete the integrative process by extending the incorporative framework to the Black population. The viability of the assimilationist paradigm then came under growing attack in the 1960s, as evidence began to accumulate that ethnicity was far more persistent than the melting pot model would permit; major challenges to assimilationist orthodoxy came from Glazer and Moynihan, Fishman, Parenti, and Novak, among many others.[10]

8. For Nehru's interpretation of India's history, written in 1944, see *The Discovery of India* (London: Meridian Books, 1946).

9. Quoted in S. Harrison, "The Challenge to Indian Nationalism," *Foreign Affairs,* XXXIV, no. 4 (July 1956), 621.

10. Nathan Glazer and Daniel P. Moynihan, *Beyond the Melting Pot* (Cambridge: M.I.T. Press and Harvard University Press, 1963); Joshua A. Fishman (ed.), *Language Loyalty in the United States* (The Hague: Mouton & Co., 1966); Michael Parenti, "Ethnic Politics and the Persistence of Ethnic Identification," *American Political Science Review,* LXI, no. 3 (September 1967), 717-26; Michael Novak, *The Rise of the Unmeltable Ethnics* (New York: Macmillan, 1971); Robert P. Swierenge, "Ethnocultural Political Analysis: A New Approach to Ethnic Studies in America," *Journal of American Studies,* V, no. 1 (April 1971), 59-79; Andrew M. Greeley, "An Alternative Perspective for Studying American Ethnicity," mimeo, Center for the Study of American Pluralism, National Opinion Research Center, University of Chicago (1972); A. H. Miller, "Ethnicity and Political Behavior: A Review of Theories and an Attempt at Reformulation," *Western Political Quarterly,* XXIV, no. 3, (September 1971), 483-500.

It is not without significance that nearly all the writers who have challenged the melting pot are themselves identifiably "ethnic," whereas the artisans of the assimilationist premise were largely from the modal Anglo-Saxon Protestant culture.

Glazer and Moynihan set the tone for the new analytical mode, in claiming: "The notion that the intense and unprecedented mixture of ethnic and religious groups in American life was soon to blend into a homogeneous end product has outlived its usefulness, and also its credibility."[11] Parenti points out the contradiction arising when mainstream assimilationists found their own data belied their premises. Robert Dahl noted in his influential New Haven study that "in spite of growing assimilation, ethnic factors continued to make themselves felt with astonishing tenacity," yet reverts to the conclusion that "the strength of ethnic ties as a factor in local politics surely must recede."[12] Parenti observes that the melting pot theory may lead to irrelevant conclusions grounded upon false questions: "If, in fact, it can be demonstrated that assimilation is not taking place, then . . . the question, why do ethnics continue to vote as ethnics despite increasing assimilation, becomes the wrong one to ask."[13] The wave of Black urban riots, 1966-68, and the rise of aggressive, anti-integrationist Black nationalism as a significant force punctuated the new interpretations of ethnicity.

Other evidence confirmed that the integration of the modern state could not be an article of faith. Quebec separatism in Canada emerged from the long slumber of the Duplessis years. By the late 1960s, a pro-independence party had become a significant force; the possibility that it might obtain a majority in the Quebec legislature was a chilling prospect to those committed to Canadian unity. The 1970 kidnapping of a British diplomat and the abduction and murder of a provincial minister by the small terrorist wing of the separatist movement gave further indication of the seriousness of the challenge to Canadian unity. Galvanized by these events, the Liberal government of Pierre Trudeau from 1968 to 1972 sought to remove francophonic grievances by extensive measures to symbolize the equality of English and French in the Canadian confederation. The poignancy of Canada's dilemma was then starkly illustrated by the 1972 elections, which saw the Liberal Party largely confined to French-speaking districts, as many English-speaking voters apparently reacted against what they perceived as an excessively pro-French orientation of the Trudeau government.

Long-stable Belgium also presented a quite different visage in the 1960s. The linguistic frontier between Fleming and French-speaking Walloon has been stable for 2000 years; the new dimension came from the sharp rise in linguistic mobilization. Belgium as a state was founded upon francophonic cultural domination, a pattern which persisted throughout the nineteenth century despite the beginnings of Flemish cultural nationalism. World War I saw a marked rise in Flemish self-awareness,

11. Glazer and Moynihan, *Melting Pot*, p. v.
12. Robert Dahl, *Who Governs?* (New Haven: Yale University Press, 1961), pp. 59, 62.
13. Parenti, "Ethnic Politics," p. 718.

which required a number of political concessions in the postwar years. Flemish communal political parties made their first entry into Parliament in the interwar period. In the first postwar decade, further advances were made by Flemings toward making good their claim to full linguistic equality. However, the dissolution of the old stratified relationship between Flemish and French speakers meant that the Walloons for the first time began to feel threatened as a community. Differential birthrates were producing a relentlessly growing Flemish numerical majority. Postwar industrial and economic growth was far more vigorous in Flanders; Wallony was saddled with inefficient coal mines and declining industries. The ability of the Belgian state framework to provide prosperity and security to francophones came into question for the first time. The 1960s witnessed a dialectic of aggressive linguistic nationalism in both camps. From 1945 to 1961, linguistic parties never had more than 1 of the 212 seats in the lower house of Belgian Parliament. This number increased to 6 in 1961, 17 in 1965, 22 in 1968, and 47 in 1971. In addition, the three traditional parties—Social Christians, Liberals, and Socialists—by 1968 had all split into linguistic fragments. The formation of governments became increasingly difficult, and their survival perilous. Linguistic demands were often irreconcilable. The intense mobilization of the mass public on linguistic criteria was such that political leaders were confronted with an impossible dilemma: compromise, as a good broker should, and immediately risk denunciation and disavowal by one's following; maintain intransigence, and create a paralyzing impasse of the political institutions. In 1955, a prudent observer could well have forecast that the abiding sense of Flemish grievance was well on the way toward elimination through the steady expansion of the zone of linguistic equality and cultural autonomy and that Belgium was a living tribute to the capacity of representative democracy to cope with its most difficult challenges. In 1973, the conclusion seems unavoidable that only consummate statesmanship abetted by good fortune can see Belgium through the twentieth century as a single unit; in the words of one recent analyst, "The future of Belgium is very much in doubt, and the strongest factor inhibiting its separation is the lack of a reasonable alternative."[14]

Perhaps the unkindest cut of all to the assimilationist premise dealt by remorseless history is the spread of violent cultural conflict to everyman's

14. George Armstrong Kelly, "Belgium: New Nationalism in an Old World," *Comparative Politics*, I, no. 3 (April 1969), 365. For other useful recent accounts of linguistic politics in Belgium, see Val R. Lorwin, "Belgium: Religion, Class, and Language in National Politics," in Robert A. Dahl (ed.), *Political Opposition in Western Democracies* (New Haven: Yale University Press, 1966), pp. 147-87; Alvin Rabushke and Kenneth A. Shepsle, *Politics in Plural Societies: A Theory of Democratic Instability* (Columbus, Ohio: Charles E. Merrill Publishing Co., 1972), pp. 105-20; Cynthia H. Enloe, *Ethnic Conflict and Political Development* (Boston: Little, Brown and Co., 1973), pp. 118-21.

model polity, the United Kingdom. Postwar Britain seemed to have resolved in its unwritten constitution the age-old political problems of reconciling liberty with authority, progress with order, stability with change. Social science models of the modern polity, more often than not, employed Britain as the inarticulate major paradigm; through the fog of abstractions, the towers of Westminster loomed, dim but unmistakable. When Ulster visibly entered its dreary downward spiral into the maelstrom of communal terrorism and murder in 1969, and massive violence seems averted only by military occupation, the creed of inevitable integration surely lies shattered—utterly, beyond repair.

Yet perhaps we despair prematurely; let us concede that the argument can no longer be made that inexorable historical forces such as urbanization, industrialization, secularization—in short, mass society—will automatically pulverize communal identities below those attaching to the national state. But conceivably, in a multinational society, if the total authority and coercive means available to the modern state were linked to a coherent strategy of assimilation, then the integrative goal might after all be achieved; history might require only a midwife.

In fact, the Soviet Union answers reasonably faithfully to this description. The Soviet regime has maintained a consistent policy which departs from the Leninist premise that nationality is a bourgeois concept created within the specific historical context of capitalism. The necessary goal is a universal socialist commonwealth, with one language, one culture. In the Soviet context, the incorporative language and culture could only be Russian. In its five decades, the Soviet state has denied itself no means in the pursuit of this goal. And, once Communist power had been consolidated, the means were considerable. Tactics have run the spectrum from encouraging limited autonomous cultural life in nonpolitical spheres, to virtual extermination of some Caucausus groups accused of collaboration with Hitler's armies. Large-scale population resettlement has been utilized. Russians have been dispatched in large numbers to dilute the Central Asian and Baltic nationalities. Ukrainians and Byelorussians have been relocated elsewhere in the Soviet Union where they can be more readily assimilated.

And yet, when the Soviet Union as multinational federation celebrated its fiftieth anniversary in 1972, all the signs were that many non-Russian nationalities were very restive. A. Amalrik languished in prison for raising the impertinent question as to whether the Soviet Union could last till 1984 or whether it would be engulfed in a sea of troubles, with non-Russian nationalism a leading source of turbulence. The nationalities problem had been changed, but far from obliterated; the universal socialist commonwealth with its Russian linguistic vehicle kept receding disconcertingly over the horizon. When we add to this the parlous state in which Yugoslavia contemplates the post-Tito period, we see further confirmation of the perennity of pluralism.

OBJECTS AND PURPOSES

Neither post-independence Afro-Asian politics nor contemporary political processes in the industrial world permit any other conclusion than a candid recognition that subnational solidarity is of enduring importance as a political determinant. In this study, we wish to inquire into the causes and processes of cultural pluralism in third world politics. Our central thesis is that processes of integration and disintegration, and crystallization of identity are dynamic; that the definition and boundaries of cultural groups are fluid rather than static; that the secular trend is toward broader patterns of incorporation, both at the national and subnational level. Because change and process are central, we need pay particular heed to the social vectors which alter identity patterns and to the political arenas which define their saliency. Africa and Asia will serve as the major geographical focus of our inquiry; here the newness of public recognition of the phenomenon, the diversity of circumstance, the fluidity of groups, and the pace of change offer a view of the entire range of human experience of cultural pluralism. We need to also examine the apparently quite different Latin American pattern, to see whether the same theoretical framework can explain the seeming disparity. Since subnational cleavage will endure, it must be endured; we will examine the formulas advanced for the preservation of intercultural harmony.

We will first seek to establish a comparative framework through examination of differing patterns of collective cultural identity and their political role, the political arenas within which they may (or may not) become activated, the prime factors in identity change, enlargement, and catalyzation. We will then explore, from a comparative perspective, the operation of cultural pluralism in the political processes of a number of specific cases. Zaire and Uganda we include as representative African examples, where cultural pluralism has been of obvious importance—yet in both cases the nature of its operation has altered under different types of regimes, illustrating the significance of the character of the political arena as independent variable. We should also confess a quite arbitrary consideration in their selection; they are both polities we have had the opportunity to study at first hand. Tanzania bears close scrutiny because of its remarkable success in molding from its diversity an integrative national culture. Nigeria and India represent the apogee of pluralism; the magnitude of their populations, compounded by the scope of their diversity and intensity of cultural solidarities, makes mandatory consideration of their experience. There is an interesting historical parallel between them: in each case, a phase of communal polarization on a bipolar or tripolar basis raised the level of conflict to an unbearable level. Pakistan was severed from India, and Nigeria fought a bitter civil war to reorganize itself on new criteria. Since, both have found some integrative virtue in the sheer complexity of their cultural divisions. Indonesia and the Philippines are two archipelago republics, political entities which were artifacts of colonialism but have developed interesting patterns of integration. The Arab world commands our attention not only for its vast dimensions, but for the important force of a supranational idea—pan-Arabism—which challenges the ultimate legitimacy of the present state system and the assimilative capacity of Arab identity in some but not all of its frontier zones. In Latin America, we wish to explore the intriguing case of the Amerindian. Why has cultural pluralism not been a significant factor in the Latin republics, in particular those with large present (or historically large) Indian populations? Finally, the ultimate failure of the culturally plural polity comes when one of its cultural segments takes arms to fight for separation. We examine three of the most dramatic recent separatist movements—Biafra, Bangladesh, and the southern Sudan—to inquire into the dynamics of crisis and breakdown.

As a generic label for the whole aspect of politics we are describing, cultural pluralism has the advantage of reasonably common currency in roughly the sense we wish to convey. Definitions, of course, are not subject to falsification, but are only guides to usage. The meaning we intend has three basic components: (1) Plurality is with relationship to an authoritative arena, the sovereign territorial state (polity, political system), which provides sharply demarcated boundaries within which groups define themselves and each other, and their interaction occurs; (2) Two or more socially and politically significant aggregates, differentiated by cultural criteria, may be identified by both analyst and actors, whose competition, interaction, and conflict constitute one important ingredient in the overall pattern of political transactions in the polity; (3) The basis for these solidarity groupings are commonalities or affinities of ethnicity, language, race, caste, assumed blood tie, custom, and/or territory. No unique merit other than clarification of our own usage is claimed for this definition. Throughout, we use the term "communal" as the functional equivalent of "cultural" as a modifier.

At the same time, we would like to state three fundamental propositions concerning cultural pluralism to which we will constantly return: (1) The set of groupings which constitute plurality are not necessarily permanent, frozen collectivities, but in a state of flux in response to long-run forces of social change, shorter-run alterations in political context, and continuous processes of interaction with other groups; (2) The individual actor is not necessarily assigned by birth to a single cultural aggregate; the possibility exists of two or more simultaneous cultural affiliations or more than one layer of meaningful identity or cultural migration from one identity to another when social circumstance alters; (3) Each cultural aggregate may vary widely in the degree to which its identity pattern is given ideological formulation, ranging from highly developed theories of a group's collective history, cultural heritage, and common destiny to amorphous, ill-formed, and only barely manifest self-awareness. In the next three chapters, we will further elaborate on these propositions. At this juncture, we turn to an inventory of the several intellectual traditions which bear upon our subject.

SCHOOLS OF ANALYSIS

In the existing literature a number of distinctive approaches may be distinguished. The most venerable of the schools of analysis is the study of nationalism. Two early writers, Carleton Hayes and Hans Kohn, exerted an immense influence on the field.[15] Both were drawn to the study of nationalism by its impact on reordering the map of central Europe with the demise of the multinational Austro-Hungarian empire and the role of the Wilsonian principle of national self-determination as applied at the Versailles peace conference. The emergence of malignant, pathological forms of nationalism in Germany and Italy also had a strong impact on this school of writing. The approach is historical and philosophical; nationalism is seen as a form of political thought, and its evolution traced in good part through those who have contributed to its intellectual elaboration. Subsequent scholars in this tradition, among whom Rupert Emerson stands out, have extended the analysis to the rise of self-assertion among non-Western peoples.[16] Among their conclusions, three are of central im-

15. See especially Carleton Hayes, *The Historical Evolution of Modern Nationalism* (New York: Richard R. Smith, 1931); Hans Kohn, *The Idea of Nationalism* (New York: Macmillan, 1943).

16. Rupert Emerson, *From Empire to Nation* (Cambridge: Harvard University Press, 1960). Among other noteworthy contributions we may cite Boyd C. Shafer, *Nationalism: Myth and Reality* (New York: Harcourt, Brace & World, 1955), and *Faces of Nationalism: New Realities and Old Myths* (New York: Harcourt, Brace & World, 1972); Anthony D. Smith, *Theories of Nationalism* (New York: Harper & Row, 1971); Elie Kedourie, *Nationalism* (London: Hutchison, 1960); Florian Znaniecki, *Modern Nationalities* (Urbana: University of Illinois Press, 1952); K. Minogue, *Nationalism* (New York: Basic Books, 1967); David C. Gordon, *Self-Determination and History in the Third World* (Princeton: Princeton University Press, 1971).

portance for our study. Nationalism is a modern phenomenon: although its roots can be traced to antiquity, in the sense now understood it does not extend much back beyond the nineteenth century. Secondly, nationalism arises as part of an array of changes in the pattern of human organization commonly associated with modernization. Thirdly, the idea of popular sovereignty alters the conceptualization of the political community. The state is an embodiment of the collective will of the populace and not an emanation of the ruler; it therefore reflects their common heritage.

The focus upon nationalism places nationality, and through it the territorial state, actual or potential, as the object of inquiry; thus, its concern with cultural subnationalism is only indirect. Its contribution to our concerns is further limited by the stress on nationalism as an idea, or even ideology. Much of what will concern us in the analysis of cultural pluralism must deal with observed solidarities and visible collective behavior patterns.

A second major cluster of studies have developed the theme of national integration. Two categories of political phenomena have generated the bulk of these studies: the process of building new supranational political communities, particularly in Europe, and conditions under which they might succeed; and the "nation-building" issue among the new states of Africa and Asia. Insights relevant to our inquiry were generated by the quest to identify effective mechanisms leading to creating attachments to the idea of a European community and the institutions designed to achieve it; the work of Ernest Haas and Leon Lindberg is especially noteworthy.[17] Related to this group is the seminal contribution of Karl Deutsch, who identified the social communication process as defining the boundaries of communities and the level of transactions as defining the intensity of identification.[18] Careful qualification is required in any direct application of the Deutsch approach, and there are striking contradictions in his own writings over the years on the central issue as to whether social

17. Ernest B. Haas, *The Uniting of Europe* (London: Stevens & Sons, 1958); Leon Lindberg, *The Political Dynamics of European Economic Integration* (Stanford: Stanford University Press, 1963); Leon Lindberg and Stuart Scheingold, *Europe's Would-Be Polity* (Englewood Cliffs, N.J.: Prentice-Hall, 1970), and *Regional Integration: Theory and Research* (Cambridge: Harvard University Press, 1971).

A useful summary of the accomplishments of the national and supranational integration is provided in the latter volume.

18. The most important of the Deutsch works, for our purposes are *Nationalism and Social Communication* (Cambridge: M.I.T. Press, 1953); *Political Community and the North Atlantic Area* (Princeton: Princeton University Press, 1957); *Nation-Building,* with William J. Foltz (New York: Atherton Press, 1963); *Nationalism and Its Alternatives* (New York: Knopf, distributed by Random House, 1969); "Social Mobilization and Political Development," *American Political Science Review,* LV, no. 3 (September 1961), 493-514.

mobilization in the developing world is inexorably integrative.[19] The "nation-building" literature peaked in the early 1960s, then fell into the doldrums when some of its major premises and prescriptions were contradicted by events, in particular the viability of the comprehensive nationalist parties which fought the battle for independence as primary vehicles for integration.[20] Just now on the horizon are a second generation of studies, much more closely tied to careful, empirical data; many of these have grown out of the Northwestern University "national unity" project.[21] Fred Hayward has shown in an interesting seven-village survey in Ghana that levels of political information concerning national institutions are surprisingly high and that many rural Ghanaians have a strikingly benign attitude toward the national entity.[22] The vast majority of contributors to the national integration school are political scientists; Cynthia Enloe suggests that the predisposition of the discipline to use the polity as the unit of analysis generates a subtle bias toward underestimating subnational solidarity patterns.[23] Certainly this caveat is pertinent with respect to the national integration literature.

A pair of related approaches, in which sociologists have been predominant, may be grouped under the themes of assimilation and race relations. Studies of assimilative processes have primarily focussed upon the American and Israeli experiences, the two most conspicuous "melting pots" in recent history. In both instances, large bodies of immigrants appeared to be successfully incorporated into a new political culture. The central concerns of the assimilation school are suggested by an early, influential definition of the process by sociologists Robert Park and Ernest Burgess: "Assimilation is a process of interpenetration and fusion in which persons and groups acquire the memories, sentiments, and attitudes of other

19. These are given searching scrutiny in an excellent article by Walker Connor, "Nation-Building or Nation-Destroying," *World Politics,* XXIV, no. 3 (April 1972), 319-55.

20. Representative of this era of analysis is James S. Coleman and Carl G. Rosberg (eds.), *Political Parties and Political Integration in Tropical Africa* (Berkeley: University of California Press, 1964). Other national integration studies which deserve mention are Claude Ake, *A Theory of Political Integration* (Homewood, Ill.: Dorsey Press, 1967); Philip E. Jacob and James V. Toscano (eds.), *The Integration of Political Communities* (Philadelphia: J. P. Lippincott Co., 1964); "Political Integration in Multinational States," *Journal of International Affairs,* XXVII, no. 1 (1973), special issue.

21. The papers presented at the Workshop on National Integration, Northwestern University, 4-6 February 1972, are reflective of the important contributions which may be expected from this set of studies. Already completed is a superb compendium of data on ethnicity in sub-Saharan Africa, Donald G. Morrison et al., *Black Africa: A Comparative Handbook* (New York: Free Press, 1972).

22. Fred M. Hayward, "Political Expectations in Rural Ghana," *Rural Africana* (Fall 1972), pp. 40-59.

23. Enloe, *Ethnic Conflict,* pp. 7-8. Connor makes a similar point in more pungent form, "Nation-Building," pp. 319-55.

persons and groups and, by sharing their experience and history, are incorporated by them in a common cultural life.[24] Although both the United States and Israel are quite exceptional polities in foundation and composition, nonetheless the evidence amassed in the quest for comprehension of the assimilative process is of considerable value in the study of the dynamics of ethnic interaction in Afro-Asian polities. It is noteworthy that a particularly thoughtful recent study by Milton Gordon carefully delineates the limits of assimilation in American life: "In actual fact, the American experience approximates some elements of this model and falls short of others. The most salient fact . . . is the maintenance of the structurally separate subsocieties as the three major religious and the racial and quasi-racial groups, and even vestiges of the nationality groupings, along with a massive trend toward acculturation of all groups."[25] The assimilation school generated the first use of the term "cultural pluralism," by way of early challenges to the normative validity of the "melting pot" by immigrant scholars; the first such usage appears to have been Horace M. Kallen, in his *Culture and Democracy in the United States.*[26] Kallen called for a confederation of cultures rather than assimilation as a societal goal. In Israel, the remarkable achievement of absorbing the huge postwar influx of Jewish immigrants and establishing the once-dormant Hebrew language as a national medium attracted sociological attention, both because of the scale of absorption and the vital necessity of success in incorporation to secure the survival of the young state.[27] Anthropologists until recently used "acculturation" as a somewhat kindred concept; it was a major theme in the works of Bronislaw Malinowski, Ralph Linton, and Melville Herskovits. The dominant concern was the unequal interaction between colonizing Western culture and the subjugated, non-Western culture; in this context, attention tended to gravitate toward transmission of traits from the Western to the non-Western. The end of the colonial era and the sensitivities of the postindependence role of anthropology have muted the acculturation theme.[28]

Race relations as a distinctive school of inquiry emerged from the situations where the assimilation approach clearly failed to operate. In the United States, in particular powerful institutions served to enforce sep-

24. Quoted in Milton M. Gordon, *Assimilation in American Life* (New York: Oxford University Press, 1964), p. 62.

25. Ibid., p. 159.

26. Ibid., pp. 142-44. Kallen first set forth his arguments for cultural pluralism in the *Nation* in 1915.

27. Two particularly important studies are S. N. Eisenstadt, Rivkah Bar Yosef, and Chaim Adler, *Integration and Development in Israel* (New York: Praeger, 1970); and Judith T. Shuval, *Immigrants on the Threshold* (New York: Macmillan, 1968).

28. For a useful resume, see Edward H. Spicer, "Acculturation," *International Encyclopedia of the Social Sciences* (New York: Crowell, Collier and Macmillan, Inc. 1968), I, 21-25.

aration, differential treatment, and segmented relationships, despite linguistic assimilation and a wide range of shared American political culture traits. This pattern of subnational differentiation directed attention to mechanisms of discrimination, persistence of structural separation, the barriers between the groups, and the nature of prejudice. South Africa, where the preservation of racial stratification has been since 1948 an overtly avowed government policy, has also been a stimulus to race relations studies. The brief period in the 1950s during which a naive and fundamentally unequal multiracialism was put forward as an end goal of British colonial policy in East and Central Africa also stimulated a flurry of inquiries in this mode.[29]

A particularly influential school of analysis of cultural pluralism was founded by the economist J. S. Furnivall, working in prewar Indonesia and Burma. Furnivall was struck by the total segmentation of the colonial society; though for generations of colonial rule the European residents, intermediate immigrant groups such as Chinese or Indians, and indigenous populations had shared habitation of the same land, been part of the same economy, interacted with each other, yet in the most important domains of social life they remained wholly separate. "Each group holds by its own religion, its own culture and language, its own ideas and ways. As individuals, they meet, but only in the market place, in buying and selling."[30]

The Furnivall thesis was enlarged and transformed into a general theory of cultural pluralism by M. G. Smith.[31] In Smith's concept, the plural society is composed of socially or culturally defined collectivities demarcated by wholly separate and autonomous institutional structures. The collectivities are closed corporations; they are bound within a state framework through the domination of one group, for whom the state becomes the agency of subjugation. Thus, pluralism has as its natural corollary inequality and stratification. "In the plural society, a politically autonomous unit ruled by a culturally distinct and politically privileged minority,

29. Among the vast literature under this heading, Brewton Berry, *Race and Ethnic Relatives* (3rd ed.; Boston: Houghton-Mifflin, 1965); and George E. Simpson and J. Milton Yinger, *Racial and Cultural Minorities* (rev. ed.; New York: Harper & Bros., 1958) are useful overviews. On South African racial stratification, see inter alia Pierre L. van den Berghe, *South Africa: A Study in Conflict* (Middletown: Wesleyan University Press, 1965).

30. J. S. Furnivall, *Colonial Policy and Practice* (London: Cambridge University Press, 1948), p. 304.

31. The most important statements of M. G. Smith's theory of cultural pluralism are "Social and Cultural Pluralism," in Vera Rubin (ed.), *Social and Cultural Pluralism in the Caribbean*, Annals of the New York Academy of Sciences no. 83 (January 1960), pp. 763-77; Leo Kuper and M. G. Smith (eds.), *Pluralism in Africa* (Berkeley: University of California Press, 1969).

the sole institutional framework that incorporates the aggregate is government, which normally has the form of a state."[32]

The Furnivall-Smith approach has had an important impact on the study of culturally plural societies. One excellent recent study, departing from the Smith framework, is the Leo Despres inquiry into racial politics in former British Guiana.[33] It is noteworthy that this approach has primarily been used for the study of racially stratified Caribbean polities and South Africa; here the very rigorous conditions of cultural pluralism stipulated by Smith can be approximated. The limitation to his theory lies in the large numbers of culturally diverse polities where the subnational groups are far from possessing the attributes of institutional exclusiveness. In his most recent essay, Smith excludes India from his domain; yet the intricate interplay of caste, language, and religion are central to political outcomes. Definitions, of course, are stipulative, and in offering a different definition to cultural pluralism we do not mean to imply that Smith is wrong. His theory, indeed, is brilliantly elaborated, but we feel it to be too limited in application.

Several recent studies within the framework of ethnic conflict have adopted a view closer to our own. Robert Melson and Howard Wolpe situate the crescendo of ethnic conflict in Nigeria leading to civil war in 1967 within the context of competitive modernization.[34] Cynthia Enloe argues that ethnicity (which she defines to include tribal, nationality, and racial differentiation) and political development are not necessarily inversely related; she seeks a reformulation of "mainstream" political development theory to make way for this revised view of the future of ethnicity.[35] Alvin Rabushka and Kenneth Shepsle develop an intriguing application of theories of the logic of coalition formation to conditions of salient ethnicity; their analysis suggests the rationality of ethnic strategies for both political entrepreneurs and broader publics in a risk-laden environment of politicized communal identities.[36] A Nigerian scholar, Victor Olorunsola, persuaded of the depth and significance of ethnic factors in African politics from his own research on Nigeria, brought together case studies showing similar patterns in Uganda, Sierra Leone, Zaire, and Kenya.[37]

Meanwhile, anthropologists have engaged in a searching re-examination of the intellectual legacy bequeathed by the discipline, in particular raising troubling questions about the very meaning of the term "tribe" which

32. Kuper and Smith, *Africa,* p. 36.

33. Leo Despres, *Cultural Pluralism and Nationalist Politics in British Guiana* (Chicago: Rand McNally, 1967).

34. Robert Melson and Howard Wolpe, *Nigeria: Modernization and the Politics of Communalism* (East Lansing: Michigan State University Press, 1971).

35. Enloe, *Ethnic Conflict,* pp. 1-14.

36. Rabushke and Shepsle, *Plural Societies,* pp. 2-61.

37. Victor A. Olorunsola (ed.), *The Politics of Cultural Sub-Nationalism in Africa* (Garden City, N.Y.: Doubleday, 1972).

had been the traditional unit of analysis. The importance of change and incorporative processes which had created substantially new entities is argued by several of the contributors to the volume edited by Ronald Cohen and John Middleton, *From Tribe to Nation in Africa*.[38] The 1967 annual spring meeting of the American Ethnological Society was devoted to the elusive search for the meaning of "tribe," and the dominant view held that its expurgation from professional vocabulary was long overdue.[39] Aidan Southall has developed a telling argument that in much of Africa, highland South Asia, and Oceania, "tribe" was a reification of the anthropologist, who presumed the unit, sought to identify its traits by detailed participant-observation of a small segment at what was assumed to be the central core of the cultural zone to assure representivity, then generalized his findings to the presumptive boundaries of the cultural entity.[40]

The emergent field of socio-linguistics has begun to make a major contribution to our understanding of cultural pluralism. Language, of course, has long been recognized as a central aspect of identity. What has been less well appreciated is the importance of bilingualism, diglossia (existence within speech communities of distinctive dialects particular to social strata), code-switching (circumstances in which speaker chooses alternative languages), and emergence of creolized or pidgin versions of languages. Joshua Fishman's meticulous explorations of language loyalties in the United States are rich in insights; his subsequent shift of focus to the developing areas have produced some highly suggestive insights and explanations, upon which we shall subsequently draw.[41] Other contributors of especial note include Charles Ferguson, Joseph Gumperz, and Einar Haugen.[42]

38. Ronald Cohen and John Middleton, *From Tribe to Nation in Africa* (Scranton: Chandler Publishing Co., 1970).

39. These provocative essays were published under the editorship of June Helm, *Essays on the Problem of Tribe* (Seattle: University of Washington Press, 1968). Other important contributions in a similar vein include Fredrik Barth, *Ethnic Groups and Boundaries: The Social Organization of Cultural Difference* (Boston: Little, Brown and Co., 1969), and P. D. Biebuyck, "On the Concept of Tribe," *Civilizations,* XVI, no. 4 (1966), 500-511.

40. See his excellent contribution, "The Illusion of Tribe," to the valuable collection, *The Passing of Tribal Man in Africa,* in the special issue of the *Journal of Asian and African Studies,* V, nos. 1-2 (January-April 1970), pp. 28-50. See also his contribution, "Stateless Society," *International Encyclopedia of the Social Sciences,* XV, 157-67.

41. Fishman, *Language Loyalty;* Joshua A. Fishman, Charles A. Ferguson and Jyotirindra Das Gupta (eds.), *Language Problems of Developing Areas* (New York: John Wiley & Sons, 1968).

42. Charles A. Ferguson, *Language Structure and Language Use* (Stanford: Stanford University Press, 1971) Charles A. Ferguson and John L. Gumpers, "Linguistic Diversity in South Asia," *International Journal of American Linguistics,* XXVI, no. 3 (July 1960); Einar Haugen, *The Ecology of Language* (Stanford: Stanford University Press, 1972).

In the final analysis, identity is a subjective, individual phenomenon; it is shaped through the constantly recurrent question to ego, "Who am I?" with its inevitable corollary, "Who is he?" Generalized to the collectivity, these become, "Who are we?" and "Who are they?" These questions involve the basic processes of cognition, perception, and symbolformation which lie within the domain of the social psychologist, and allied social scientists who have relied particularly heavily upon social psychology. The very term "identity" instantly evokes the name of Erik Erikson. Although much of Erikson's concern is with identity as an individual phenomenon, he also found it necessary to place it within the setting of social groupings to which the individual belongs. Indeed, identity, wrote Erikson, "is a process 'located' *in the core of the individual* and yet also *in the core of his communal culture* [italics in original], a process which establishes, in fact, the identity of these two identities."[43] The quest for belonging and self-esteem is pursued through communal group affiliations. Fear, anxiety, and insecurity at the individual level can be reduced within the womb of the ethnic collectivity; at the same time, threats to the security of the group provide a mobilizing imperative for its members. Especially valuable in offering a link between cultural pluralism and social psychology are Murray Edelman and Harold Isaacs.[44]

Religion and caste are two important bases of communal identification which have developed separate analytical traditions. On the religion theme, setting aside the massive literature concerned with theology as exegesis of sacred texts and history of philosophy, a growing body of studies have explored the themes of concern here: religion as a basis of social identity and cultural conflict. The greater part of this deals with Asia, where the political role of religious communities has been most obvious. Donald Smith has been the most copious contributor with specific focus upon the interaction of religion and politics.[45] The determinant role of religion in the dismantling of the British empire in India has meant that attention to the religious factor is unavoidable for all students of Indian or Pakistani politics. The institutionalization of religious segmentation in Lebanon also compels close inquiry into the religious basis of identity

43. Erik Erikson, *Identity, Youth and Crisis* (New York: W. W. Norton, 1968), p. 22. See also his *Childhood and Society,* (rev. ed.; New York: W. W. Norton, 1963).

44. See in particular Murray Edelman, *Politics as Symbolic Action: Mass Arousal and Quiescence* (Chicago: Markham Publishing Co., 1971); and Harold R. Isaacs, "Group Identity and Political Change: The House of Mumbi" (Paper presented to the 1971 meetings of the American Political Science Association, Chicago).

45. Donald C. Smith, *India as a Secular State* (Princeton: Princeton University Press, 1963); *Religion and Politics in Burma* (Princeton: Princeton University Press, 1965), and his excellent edited volume, *South Asian Politics and Religion* (Princeton: Princeton University Press, 1966). See also Fred R. von der Mehden, *Religion and Nationalism in Southeast Asia* (Madison: University of Wisconsin Press, 1963).

groups.[46] In Africa, Islam and its brotherhoods have been the primary basis of politically relevant collective identity, although Catholic-Protestant competition did generate some enduring cleavages here and there, with Uganda the most important example.[47] Messianic and prophetic syncretic movements derived from the Christian tradition have also received some attention.

Caste as a basis for social alignment is most intimately identified with India, although it is also of significance in Ceylon, Pakistan, and, in quite different and limited form, in West Africa. The real nature of caste as a system of social action was for many years misunderstood, because it was studied through the normative prescriptions of certain Hindu sacred texts, rather than empirically. However, the now decades-old operation of electoral politics at various levels of the Indian polity, as well as the focus on processes of development and social change, have yielded a wealth of observed data on the dynamics of caste identities. In the last two decades, a wholly reformulated interpretation of the social and political role of caste has emerged, particularly associated with the brilliant work of M. N. Srinivas.[48] Lloyd and Susanne Rudolph also elaborate on the changing political role of caste.[49]

Thus the array of material which confronts the student of cultural pluralism is vast—indeed, intimidating in its range and depth. In this survey of some of the major approaches which bear upon the topic, we have intended to suggest the many different trails which may be followed to seek our elusive quarry. To these there need to be added the political and social history of the numerous polities which fall within the bounds of this comparative essay. It is all too obvious that a lifetime's investigation by teams of students would not exhaust all possible material, which is being daily augmented by the flow of human events. We have deliberately sought to cast our net broadly, with the recognition that our coverage

46. See especially Michael C. Hudson, *The Precarious Republic: Political Modernization in Lebanon* (New York: Random House, 1968); Leonard Binder (ed.), *Politics in Lebanon* (New York: John Wiley, 1966); Kathleen Goodman Lockard, "Religion and Political Development in Uganda, 1962-1972" (Ph.D. diss., University of Wisconsin-Madison, 1974).

47. On the political role of Islam in Africa, useful contributions include James Kritzeck and William H. Lewis, *Islam in Africa* (New York: Van Nostrand-Reinhold, 1969); Lucy C. Behrman, *Muslim Brotherhoods and Politics in Senegal* (Cambridge: Harvard University Press, 1970); Vincent Monteil, *Islam Noir* (Paris: Editions du Seuil, 1964); and the several contributions of J. S. Trimingham, *Islam in West Africa* (Oxford: Clarendon Press, 1959), *Islam in East Africa* (Oxford: Clarendon Press, 1964), *Islam in the Sudan* (London and New York: Oxford University Press, 1949), and *Islam in Ethiopia* (London and New York: Oxford University Press, 1952).

48. See especially M. N. Srinivas, *Caste in Modern India and Other Essays* (Bombay: Asia Publishing House, 1962).

49. Lloyd and Susanne Rudolph, *The Modernity of Tradition* (Chicago: University of Chicago Press, 1967).

will inevitably be somewhat uneven. However, we hope to discover, at least in broad outline, the range of variation in the politics of cultural pluralism.

Our own approach has no doubt been shaped by the intellectual history of this enterprise. We were preoccupied with the impact of ethnicity upon political behavior within the setting of an African state. Here, we have sought to reverse the investigatory priorities of the national integration studies; our primary focus is pluralism. However, the polity remains the arena. We cannot wholly escape our own disciplinary identity; a political scientist without a state is a man adrift. The subtle bias decried by Enloe may after all have crept in unbidden here and there. Nonetheless, the choice of the cultural pluralism prism does dictate a different set of questions. In pursuing them, we employ an essentially inductive method, both at the level of theory and example.

Some distortion may arise from this very choice of focus. Any given topic will exert a kind of autonomous sovereignty over the range and nature of the inquiry. In the particular choice we have made, we would utterly disavow any intent to rule out as insignificant social and political determinants which do not fall within our purview. Such a rudimentary view of political study would be so obviously without merit that this disclaimer seems almost superfluous. Yet perhaps it should be stated; to cite but one example, emergent patterns of social stratification are intimately related to the distribution of political power and thus to the allocation of resources and values within the polity. At times, social stratification may overlap with cultural cleavage, with each reinforcing the other; in such circumstances, it becomes analytically difficult to demonstrate which factor is primary, which variable independent. Happily, there seems no imminent danger that stratification will be ignored by students of political change. Global understanding, of course, requires many other sectoral prisms: power, micropolitics, specific institutions (military, bureaucracy, parties), to name but a few. We claim only that the politics of cultural pluralism does have reasonable claim for inclusion among the sectors of analysis.

2 The Varieties of Cultural Pluralism

A Liberian participant among the outstanding assortment of scholars, statesmen, and cultural custodians assembled in the 1972 Conference on Manding Studies organized by the School of Oriental and African Studies in London offered the following remarkable account of his belated, adult discovery of his own identity:

> Up to the time I was sent to school, I knew nothing about my Vai background. This is why when I was in the United States in School I wrote a short biographical sketch entitled GOLA BOY IN AMERICA. The only reference in GOLA BOY to show my Vai connection is a line stating that my father came from Vai country.
>
> When I returned home from America in the forties, after an absence of eleven years, the first problem that confronted me was, to establish my tribal identity. . . . My childhood associates, especially those who were initiated into Poro with me, were all Gola, in Jene Sese.
>
> Fortunately for me I had living at Dimei, my father's adopted home in the Dei country, older brothers and sisters who knew all about our paternal background. One of the brothers, Fahn Taweh, made it clear to me that we were Vai, because a child belongs to his father.
>
> In the effort to establish my identity I soon realized the advantage to me to speak Vai fluently. And so I brushed up on my Vai. . . .
>
> In conclusion I may state that my identity as a Vai keseng is based on these criteria, patrilineal descent, language and name.[1]

Writ large, this intriguing autobiography of identity search can be said to recapitulate the experience of mankind over the last two centuries. In the face of accelerating change human groupings redefine their social identities in ways which appeal to new imperatives of security and status. Political events and social conflict enmesh ever-widening circles of people in their ebb and flow. Contexts alter; with them, identities are set in flux. Gola boy becomes a Vai; broader contacts, the new setting of adult life lead to a cultural migration.

RISE OF NATIONALISM

Cultural pluralism is a quintessentially modern phenomenon. As a global pattern, it is really a creature of the present century. It is part and

---

1. Bai T. Moore, "Problems of Vai Identity in Terms of My Own Experience," in *Conference on Manding Studies* (London: School of Oriental and African Studies, 1972), p. 5.

parcel of the process by which, in post-Renaissance Europe, kingdoms gradually became nations, with England and France the most important precursors. The personal, patrimonial institutions of monarchy became bureaucratized into an impersonal state. The royal writ became gradually transformed into a uniform legal code. Latin was displaced as the language of elite discourse by the national vernaculars; these in turn became regularized and homogenized, with standardization departing from the dialect used in the central core of the kingdom. Parliaments changed from assemblages of feudal estates to representative legislatures. With the French Revolution providing the most dramatic crystallization of the transformation of the ideology of the state, the territorial collectivity came to be defined by popular sovereignty, rather than as a royal domain pieced together by patterns of conquest by a king's legions, or legacy by monarchical matrimony. The kingdom became the state; the state became the nation. The nation-state provided the ideological model for the sweeping reconstruction of the political map of Europe. It was in terms of this new normative prescription of the modern political community that Germany and Italy emerged as unified nation-states, that the multinational Ottoman and Austro-Hungarian empires began to crumble, beginning with the Greek revolt in 1821-29. The historical processes which shattered the Austro-Hungarian empire, leading to its final demise after World War I, well illustrate the political force of cultural pluralism as social transformation, in dialectic with the new ideological model of the nation-state, destroyed one of Europe's major landmarks. This was the first major historic instance where political mobilization along lines of cultural cleavage reached such proportions that a polity centuries old could no longer survive. World War I was the executioner, but modernization was the scaffold. So portentous was the chain of events leading to dismemberment that a recapitulation of its demise serves well to introduce the themes of this chapter.[2]

Austria-Hungary was a dynastic entity stitched together by the House of Hapsburg. Although its central core can be traced back to about A.D. 1000, it became a multinational entity with the extension of Hapsburg rule over non-Germanic Bohemia, Croatia, and Hungary in 1526-27. In the course of dynastic struggle against the Protestant Reformation and the "infidel" Turk, over the next three centuries the empire came to rule over Germans, Croats, Czechs, Italians, Hungarians, Poles, Rumanians, Ukrainians, Serbs, Slovaks, and Slovenes, not to mention a widely dispersed Jewish grouping. As a dynastic conglomerate, the Hapsburg kingdom exhibited many of the same trends toward transformation of

2. This account is derived primarily from the excellent inquest into the inability of Austria-Hungary to solve its nationality problem by Robert A. Kann, *The Multi-National Empire*, 2 vols. (New York: Columbia University Press, 1950).

monarchy into state as were to be observed in England and France in the eighteenth century. An imperial bureaucracy and army grew, and German replaced Latin as the language of imperial administration. But in the nineteenth century, an exceedingly complex dialectic of competitive spread of self-awareness gathered speed. The process was first visible among the nationalities which had some historic identity related to previous kingdoms (Czechs, Hungarians, Poles, Croats), and spread subsequently to those Robert Kann has labelled "nationalities without history," the Ukrainians, Slovaks, Slovenes, and Serbs. The rise of professional and commercial middle classes to challenge the dominance of the landed nobility in the outlying lands of the Hapsburg domain, whose feudal ties to the monarchy had been the initial basis of its overrule, was a critical development. From this group emerged the cultural leaders who unified the languages, provided them with grammars, dictionaries, and literature and invested the cultural heritage with a historical sanction. Nationality armed with ideology then acquired the potential to slowly percolate into the submerged rural peasantry.

By mid-century, a leading spokesman for the pacesetter nationality, Count Stephen Szechenyi, could express himself in the following terms:

> I for one knew of no real Magyar who, though his hair may have grayed and worldly wisdom may have furrowed his brow, would not, as a lunatic whose idée fixe has been touched, disregard doctrines of fairness and even of justice when the affairs of our language and nationality are touched upon. On such occasions the most cool-headed becomes ecstatic, the most perspicacious, stricken with blindness, and the fairest and most just, ready to forget the first of the unalterable rules of eternal truth.[3]

Growing Magyar militance compelled a major recasting of the imperial constitution in 1867, which granted substantial autonomy to Hungary. And when it came to treatment meted out to emergent nationalities under the Hungarian wing, in particular Croats, Rumanians, and Slovaks, the Magyars did indeed "disregard doctrines of fairness and even of justice"; in 1910, the Hungarian parliament included only eight non-Magyars, though Hungarians were only 45 percent of the population. Some 96 percent of government employes were Magyars.[4]

German, Italian, and Polish unification movements all posed a grave threat to the multinational empire in the latter half of the nineteenth century. The Russian sponsored pan-Slav movement was a constant preoccupation. Meanwhile, Slovak acquired a written language and self-conscious identity separate from the almost identical Czech. The Serbs, whose language differed from Croat only in having a Cyrillic rather than Latin

3. Quoted in ibid., I, 109.
4. Ibid., p. 110.

script and who were Orthodox rather than Roman Catholics in religion, asserted their own distinctiveness and eventually assumed the leadership of the southern Slav movement which ultimately led to Yugoslavia.

Finally, even the most downtrodden nationality of all, the Ukrainians, divided between Austria-Hungary, Poland, and Russia, achieved self-awareness. As a submerged, rural peasantry, Ukrainians had only a latent identity—and it was frequently claimed by Poles and Russians that there was no such thing as a separate Ukrainian identity. In the late nineteenth century a Ukrainian movement finally arose, with ideological leadership from the clergy and a very small intelligentsia.[5] An interesting reflection of the lateness of the diffusion of Ukrainian nationalism lies in the near-total absence of strongly asserted ethnic community among the early waves of Ukrainian immigrants to the United States, drawn almost wholly from peasant milieux. The emergence of active Ukrainian associations was largely the work of post-World War II Ukrainian refugees, who were much better educated and keenly aware of their national identity.[6]

There are several themes to note in the tale of the demise of the Hapsburg multinational conglomerate. The idea of the nation-state, rather than the dynastic domain, was deeply subversive. The rise of a middle class both produced the cultural entrepreneurs who elaborated the ideology of nationality and provided them with an initial constituency, while the slower processes of mobilizing the peasantry and nascent working class went forward. Standardization and codification of languages was a critical step; the accelerating growth of an educational system and other media provided the vehicles for its consolidation.

DIMENSIONS OF SOCIAL CHANGE

These patterns find their close parallel in the social transformations which gave rise to the crystallization of cultural pluralism in the developing world. So familiar are they that they are often taken for granted; we need to pause to remind ourselves of the sheer magnitude of change processes. Urbanization has been a very powerful factor in the activation of cultural pluralism. In 1800 there were only a handful of towns of any size in Latin America, Africa, or Asia: Mexico City, Lima, and a few other administrative seats in Latin America; Cairo, Alexandria, the seats of a few traditional kingdoms in Africa; in Asia, Calcutta, a group of villages before the British arrived, numbered only 140,000. In 1973, there were ninety-two cities in

5. For an excellent account of Ukrainian nationalism, see John A. Armstrong, *Ukrainian Nationalism* (New York: Columbia University Press, 1955).

6. Vladimir C. Nahirny and Joshua Fishman, in Fishman (ed.), *Language Loyalty*, pp. 320-28.

these regions with over 500,000 inhabitants (not including China or Japan).[7] The trend toward urbanization has accelerated sharply in the postwar period and shows no signs of abating. Kinshasa has grown from 40,000 in 1940 to 1.5 million in 1970; in the same period, Dakar has grown from 100,000 to 580,000 and Teheran from 500,000 to 2.7 million. The list could be indefinitely extended. The polyglot urban center throws cultural groupings in much more intensive interaction with each other; as we shall argue later, the city often spawns new or significantly transformed identity groups. Although residential segregation of ethnic groups frequently develops, they still remain in contact with each other. In the countryside, the smallholder lives on what he can grow by his efforts in the soil. In the city, the individual must survive on what he can earn from employment or trade, in direct and often desperate competition with others. Collectively perceived, social competition is much more intense and direct. Further, the workplace will frequently be an enterprise employing substantial numbers of persons of culturally heterogeneous background. The exigencies of survival thus impose more or less intimate association for forty hours weekly of individuals and groups with each other.

Communications have greatly affected the process of spreading communal awareness. In the traditional rural world, the effective horizons for most were bounded by a day's travel in any direction by foot. With the development of river and rail systems, then with the advent of motor travel the penetration of road networks almost everywhere enormously multiplied physical mobility and communication. The slow spread of the printed word was a major development, though limited by the extent of literacy. In the last few decades, the emergence of media which do not require literacy—radio and, to some extent, television—have further revolutionized communication. Most recently, the development of inexpensive mass production processes via the transistor has accelerated the spread of the radio throughout the rural world. One should note, however, that the printed word remains much more important in the ideological articulation of cultural pluralism. Radio broadcasting is almost invariably a state function or under close state regulation. The use of standardized versions of local languages in itself may make some contribution to consolidation of cultural identities. But the printed media offer more opportunities for active spokesmen for cultural communities to overtly propound communal concerns and demands.[8]

7. According to population figures in the 1973 *World Almanac and Book of Facts.*

8. The central role of communication is given seminal treatment in the classic study of Deutsch, *Nationalism and Social Communication.* Other innovative studies of the role of communications include Daniel Lerner, *The Passing of Traditional Society* (Glencoe: Free Press, 1958); Everett M. Rogers, *Diffusion of Innovations* (New York: Free Press, 1962), and *Modernization Among Peasants* (New York: Holt Rinehart and Winston, 1969).

The spread of literacy, primarily via the education system, is another important change in the social parameters affecting cultural pluralism. Almost everywhere, colonial powers based the educational system on the metropolitan language; for the most part, educational development was at only a modest pace until independence or shortly before. However, everywhere since World War II the educational system has been very rapidly expanded, as the demand for it has been strong; the intimate linkage between education and social mobility is now almost universally perceived. Simultaneously, educational opportunity has been understood to be a group asset as well as an individual advantage; the sociological weight of a cultural group will depend in part on the size of its educated elite, which in turn will have the capacity to defend the interests of the collectivity in competitive allocations of the political system.[9]

A natural corollary of the processes of urbanization and economic change and the spread of education was the emergence of a middle-class intelligentsia from whose ranks came the cultural entrepreneurs who gave ideological form to subnational communities. In India, it was the Bengalis who were first prominent in this role, followed soon after by Marathi and Tamil intellectuals.[10] In Nigeria, as James Coleman ably describes, a spate of local histories by Nigerian authors began to appear in the 1930s and 1940s.[11] In many cases, the task of language codification and standardization was carried on at an earlier stage by missionaries, who needed to equip themselves with a vehicle for translation of the Bible and evangelical pursuits.

All of these processes of change profoundly altered the environment within which cultural pluralism occurred. On the one hand, the saliency of the national political arena was greatly enhanced and potent instruments were available to the political and administrative elites, who directed the institutions of the state to inculcate positive orientations toward it and a sense of active identification with it—in short, national integration as usually understood. At the same time, the social capacity for solidarity patterns and networks at subnational levels was similarly enlarged.

9. This process is particularly ably analyzed by David B. Abernethy in *The Political Dilemma of Popular Education* (Stanford: Stanford University Press, 1969). See also Philip Foster, *Education and Social Change in Ghana* (London: Routledge and Kegan Paul, 1965), and James S. Coleman (ed.), *Education and Political Development* (Princeton: Princeton University Press, 1965).

10. See J. H. Broomfield, *Elite Conflict in a Plural Society: Twentieth Century Bengal* (Berkeley: University of California Press, 1968); Anil Seal, *The Emergence of Indian Nationalism* (London: Cambridge University Press, 1971).

11. James S. Coleman, *Nigeria: Background to Nationalism* (Berkeley: University of California Press, 1958), pp. 332-33.

PLURALISM IN THE BEGINNING

Informed by these transformations, let us return to what might be considered the historical base point for the development of cultural pluralism to consider what patterns of identity might be observed. There is, needless to say, a substantial conjectural element in such an exercise. We must partly infer, through tracing backwards, the crystallization of cultural pluralism as a modern phenomenon. In part, we draw upon historical accounts, which themselves may rest in good measure upon the classifications made by foreign visitors. An explorer had a natural predisposition toward applying collective labels to the human groupings he visited. The vast confusions which subsequently arose, particularly in Africa, over the applicability and real content of these appellations are ample demonstration of the cursory basis upon which they were often constructed.

Fascinating evidence of the imprecision of early categories is offered by Philip Curtin in his seminal exploration of the composition of the Atlantic slave trade.[12] He drew upon slave listings established by ship operators and the categorizations of slave origins utilized by plantation operators. Various stereotypes grew up as to the docility and labor value of different groups, which had some effect on their market value. Slavers were also conscious of the servile insurrection threat and anxious to avoid large concentrations of what they believed to be a single group. The classifications used fell into three categories:

1. The shipping point on the African coast where the slave cargo was purchased, such as "Calabari," "Congo," or "Angola"
2. The name of the political entity which provided the slaves, such as "Oyo" or "Fon"
3. A generalized linguistic term, which referred not only to those speaking the language, but anyone coming from that general area, such as "Bambara" or "Susu"

The name Calabari derives from the Nigerian trading port of Calabar.[13] Although this label as ethnic designation is still occasionally encountered, there is no such cultural group. The contemporary population is primarily composed of two elements: (1) the descendants of the various African trading houses which developed as slave-trade intermediaries (in present-day categories, these are of Ibibio origin) and (2) what are today known as Ibo, whose human hinterland provided most of the slaves shipped from Calabar. Oyo was, at the height of the slave trade, the most powerful of the states now collectively labelled Yoruba, while the Fon state is in

12. Philip D. Curtin, *The Atlantic Slave Trade* (Madison: University of Wisconsin Press, 1969.)

13. For an excellent discussion of identity formation in Calabar, see the chapter by Richard W. Henderson in Melson and Wolpe, *Politics of Communalism,* pp. 215-21.

contemporary Dahomey. The slaves were more likely to be persons acquired by these kingdoms in surrounding areas than actual subjects of these principalities. The present cultural-linguistic group bearing the name Bambara is centered in contemporary Mali, but the slave-trade usage referred generically to persons brought from the far interior and shipped through one of the Senegambian ports.[14] The confusion in the externally applied labels was compounded by the underlying fact that actual social identity was a very diffuse matter.

In the overwhelmingly rural world on which European rule was fastened, most meaningful social aggregates were extremely localized. For the sedentary community, it was the grouping which shared a common jural order, participated together in ritual observance, often had at least metaphorical kinship bonds, and recognized the needs for mutual solidarity for purposes of defense and security. In transhumant and nomadic communities, it was the band which travelled together in tight interdependence. Within such an order, the need to define identity on a broader scale simply did not arise; the human needs of social existence and material survival were met within the frame of "the little community."[15] The local community was not, of course, wholly isolated; it had relations of conflict and exchange—war, trade, and marriage—with neighboring groups or trading communities. But these were "others," for whom, depending on the distance and frequency of contact, increasingly diffuse labels would serve.

Expansion of scale could come about in three primary ways: state formation, long-distance trade networks, and incorporation in a universal religious community. The formation of large-scale states superimposed a supplementary pattern of relationships, which in the case of the most centralized and highly articulated empires, such as China or Persia, provided a powerful basis for subsequent nationalism through the emergence of a well-developed central bureaucracy and common symbols. In China, cultural unification was greatly extended through the construction of a widely recruited imperial mandarinate, with a common language of administration which, through the ideographic script, could provide written unity for the wide variety of mutually unintelligible dialects of the kingdom.

The centralized state generally departed from a common cultural core, but as it expanded it frequently extended its hegemony over different groups. At the core of the kingdom, there was an obvious need for a court language, a shared set of legitimizing symbols which bound the key set of officials through whom rule was exercised to the throne, which invariably lay at the center of empire. However, rule over the periphery was often intermittent and sporadic, limited to extraction of some resources

14. Curtin, *Atlantic Slave Trade*, pp. 182-90.

15. To borrow the term of Robert Redfield, *The Little Community and Peasant Society and Culture* (Chicago: University of Chicago Press, 1960).

in tribute and perhaps manpower, and pre-emption of control from rival kingdoms. The Ottoman empire, for example, though Turkish at its core, never sought to enforce cultural assimilation on its dominions; it was Ottoman, not Turkish, in self-concept. In the summation of Kemal Karpat, whose important work on rethinking of Ottoman studies has had a major impact on this neglected field:

> It is a well known fact that the Ottoman state, despite some incipient symptoms in the 14-15 centuries, did not develop a politically oriented sense of national identity. The idea of ethnic identity based on language, religion or modes of life were considered objective factors useful for achieving communal cohesion, and treated as such for administrative purposes. . . . Ethnicity had no political meaning, though awareness of ethnic differences existed. . . . One may mention the fact that the Ottoman high society referred, and occasionally pejoratively, to Turks as one of the many groups in the state and felt no identification with them. Thus, the Ottoman ruling class was deprived of a sense of ethnic identification with the Turkish speaking groups despite the fact that Turkish was the language of the administration and played a role as a means of assimilation.[16]

Moroccan dynasties, whether of Arab or Berber origin, sought to impose recognition of the sultanate, but not the central culture, on a fluctuating periphery.[17] The Mughal empire from the sixteenth to eighteenth centuries in India, with a Muslim ruling class, did not until its final phases try to implement a policy of cultural imposition. Nehru attributes the birth of political Hindu subnationalism to the bitter reaction to these policies. Similarly, the first manifestation of linguistic community came in the revolt of the Marathas, about whom Warren Hastings wrote in 1784:

> The Marathas possess, alone of all the people of Hindustan and Deccan, a principle of national attachment, which is strongly impressed on the minds of all individuals of the nation, and would probably unite their chiefs, as in one common cause, if any great danger were to threaten the general state.[18]

The Inca empire went farther than most historical states in imposing linguistic unity. After Quechua became the royal language in 1438, it was used by all officials and was spread to some previously non-Quechua speaking areas. However, Aymara remained as a major separate language in highland Bolivia, despite subjugation to the Inca empire. And the

16. Kemal H. Karpat, "Ethnicity and Community and the Rise of Modern Nations in the Ottoman State," unpublished paper.

17. The best discussion of the relations between the institutions of the Sultanate and its outlying domains is found in several of the contributions of Ernest Gellner and Charles Micaud (eds.), *Arabs and Berbers: From Tribe to Nation in North Africa* (Lexington, Mass.: D.C. Heath, 1972).

18. Quoted in Nehru, *Discovery of India*, p. 269.

central symbols of the kingdom were associated with Inca, not Quechua, language or culture per se.[19] In Africa, the greatest of precolonial states, the Mali empire, was built from a Mande cultural core, but extended its sway over a large number of other groups. The mercantile, religious, military, and administrative nets which bound together the Mali kingdom were all emanations of the Mande core and influenced, but did not supplant, other languages. The later series of Fulani states, established through a series of jihads in the eighteenth and nineteenth centuries, sought to impose a purified form of Islam, but were not rationalized in terms of Fulani ethnic objectives. After the establishment of Fulani rule over the older Hausa city-states of northern Nigeria, a self-concept of Fulani superiority emerged, although at the same time Fulani and Hausa ruling lineages began to interpenetrate and a continuing process of linguistic assimilation of the Fulani began.[20]

The development of trading networks are another significant mechanism of the expansion of scale in social identity patterns. A frequently repeated pattern is the emergence of a trading diaspora group. A specialized group is required which can overcome the serious problems of long-distance trade across cultural and political zones. Transportation of goods through hostile territory must be negotiated. There must be a communications system which can supply adequate market information at a distance. The trader must have an agent in whose reliability he can trust at distant locations. Problems of payment, exchange, and credit must be resolved without the aid of a banking system or the backing of a legal structure to enforce contract and protect property. Curtin demonstrates that the origin of the present identity of certain groups in the Senegambian hinterland can be directly traced to the trade diaspora.[21] In Iboland in eastern Nigeria, the Aro Chuku arose as a trading community which, given security of movement by possession of a powerful and terrifying oracle (the "long juju"), formed the first communication system which presaged the later development of Ibo subnationalism.[22] The Dyula and Hausa in West Africa, Swahili in East Africa, Arabs, Malays, and Chinese in Asia erected comparable diaspora networks.

The universal religions, which became separated from hearth and locality, also provided a significant social identity where they penetrated. In

19. Victor W. von Hagen, *Realm of the Incas* (New York: Mentor Books, 1957), p. 48.

20. For the debate on the ethnic basis of the Fulani states in Hausaland, see Marilyn Robinson Waldman, "A Note on the Ethnic Interpretation of the Fulani Jihad," *Africa,* XXXVI, no. 3 (July 1966), 286-90.

21. Philip D. Curtin, "The Watern Juule in the 18th Century," in *Conference on Manding Studies.*"

22. Argued by Robert F. Stephenson to be a veritable protostate, in *Population and Political Systems in Tropical Africa* (New York: Columbia University Press, 1968), pp. 190-210.

precolonial Africa and Asia, this was especially true of Islam, which frequently operated in the guise of an intensely political religion. Islam is equipped with especially powerful identity-reinforcing mechanisms by the nature of its ritual, its socialization mechanisms, and its special religious obligations. The routine of prayer, the collective observance of the Friday prayer in the mosque, the Islamic calendar and annual obligations, such as the fast of Ramadan, unite the faithful in communal rite. The pattern of the Koranic school, even if it does no more than enforce rote memorization of the Arabic verses of the Koran by those who cannot comprehend the tongue, nonetheless maintains a formal apparatus of inculcation of habits of piety and sense of membership in the community of Islam. For the exceptionally pious, the powerful, and the wealthy, the injunction of the hajj to Mecca maintains a constantly self-renewing flow through the inspirational communion with Muslims from all corners of Dar-ul-Islam. The pilgrimage sustained among the political and religious elites an active sense of membership in a universal community, a flow of religious ideas from the centers of piety and religious learning to the outermost periphery of the Islamic world. Buddhism through its pervasive network of monasteries, particularly in Burma and Thailand, also could be argued as an enlarged identity system, though historically it was unlikely that the diffuse sense of shared religious value would carry political obligation.

Thus, at the point where the third world stood poised on the brink of subjugation to European empires, cultural identities had, with some exceptions, not become strongly affirmed. For the great majority of the rural population, only the local community commanded active membership and loyalty. In each of the three continents, traditional organization ran the gamut from the acephalous societies of the Dayak in Bornea, the "hill tribes" of India and southeast Asia, the Mongo cultural area of the Zaire basin, and the Tupi cluster of the Brazilian coast and the Amazon valley, through principalities and kingdoms of varying complexity to the bureaucratic empires of the Mughals, Bantams (Java), Ottomans, some of the Fulani and Mande states, Incas, and Aztecs. At the central core of the centralized states, there was certainly a political identity. But nationalism as the handmaiden of empire had not emerged. Where policies of cultural integration were pursued, as in the Inca kingdom, they were designed as mechanisms of perfecting sociopolitical control.[23] In some times and places, Islam in particular had been an active political identity—in the wars against the Crusaders, in the initial Arab burst of conquest, in the Ottoman destruction of Byzantium. The formidable mobilization potential of Islamic movements in precolonial society was well

23. For an excellent, broadly comparative perspective on historical kingdoms, see S. N. Eisenstadt, *The Political Systems of Empires* (New York: Free Press, 1963).

reflected in the remarkable rise of the Mahdist state in Sudan in response to the first Turko-Egyptian-British penetration of the area.[24] The politicization of Hinduism and Buddhism, however, was yet to become really visible.

THE ILLUSION OF "TRIBE"

This does not, of course, add up to a cultural tabula rasa. But it is an identity map radically different from the mobilized cultural cleavages which have become politically salient in postindependence politics. We would suggest, as a point of departure, that contemporary cultural pluralism is not usefully viewed as a resurgence of "primordial" sentiments, as argued in a penetrating and very influential article by Clifford Geertz.[25] Historical parameters defined the bounds of subsequent crystallization of social identities. But the basic units of contemporary cultural conflict, themselves fluid and shifting, are often entirely novel entities, in other instances substantially altered and transformed, in most cases redefined versions of cultural groups. The massive alterations in the social and political environment which followed in the wake of colonialism and the eventual nationalist response to it were crucial determinants of the ultimate pattern. The imposition of a whole new state system, which almost nowhere matched the pre-existing political divisions, even where centralized institutions had emerged, and which became vested with a vastly expanded set of functions; the mobilization of the populace in the nationalist struggle to assume control over the colonial states; the accelerating urbanization; the manifold increase in the scope and intensity of the communications system; the spread of formal education and extension of literacy far beyond the narrow confines of priests and mandarins who monopolized it, where a written language existed at all; and the rise of an intelligentsia who provided political leadership both for the nationalist movement and for the mobilization of cultural segments—these change processes were the crucibles of contemporary cultural pluralism.

The "primordial" theme is worth some further elaboration, for it suggests one of the major sources of confusion over the precise nature of cultural pluralism. Many of the problems have been well illuminated in the

24. L. Carl Brown, "The Sudanese Mahdiya," in Robert I. Rotberg and Ali A. Mazrui (eds), *Protest and Power in Black Africa* (New York: Oxford University Press, 1970), pp. 145-68; Peter M. Holt, *The Mahdist State in the Sudan 1881-1898* (Oxford: Clarendon Press, 1958).

25. Clifford M. Geertz, "The Integrative Revolution: Primordial Sentiments and Civil Politics in the New States," in Clifford M. Geertz (ed.), *Old Societies and New States* (New York: Free Press, 1963).

active debate on the concept of "tribe," which has been carried on by anthropologists in particular and to which brief allusion was made in the preceding chapter.[26] The beginning of the difficulties lay in the very term "tribe," which came into general use in the colonial period to describe cultural units in the hill country of southeast Asia, Oceania, and virtually all of tropical Africa, and for Indians in the North America. (It was of considerable import that the metaphor of "tribe" was absent from Spanish conceptualization of Indian communities.) In the African case, the rise of "tribe" to common currency was closely associated with the advent of a pejorative stereotype of peoples of African origin. For evolutionist anthropologists, "tribal" society was a relatively early stage of human development, characterized by a lack of state organization, class structures, literacy, and other features of "civilized" societies.[27] For most, the idea of "tribe" conveyed the image of a world neatly dissected into a series of tribal compartments; a tribal map could be drawn, with firm black lines demarcating boundaries. The standard anthropological investigation for many years was a monograph devoted to one such entity. Many of these studies unwittingly conveyed an exaggerated image of the consistency of the social patterns and presumptive identity of the group through choosing an area near what was assumed the cultural core of the group, to ensure that the ethnographic data were representative, then inferring similar patterns extending outwards to what the maps indicated were the boundaries. Particularly under British administration, an effort was made to build the subdivisions upon this image of tribal blocks. In the process, Raymond Apthorpe argues, "certainly in Anglophone Africa, what happened was that the colonial regimes administratively *created* tribes as we think of them today."[28] Elizabeth Colson echoes, "At least in Africa, tribes and tribalism as we know them today are recent creations reflecting the influences of the Colonial era when large-scale political and economic organization set the scene for the mobilization of ethnic groups based upon

---

26. The most important contributions are the special issue on *The Passing of Tribal Man in Africa*, of the *Journal of Asian and African Studies*, V, nos. 1-2 (January-April 1970); the proceedings of the 1967 spring meeting of the American Ethnological Society devoted to this topic, edited by June Helm, *Essays on the Problem of Tribe* (Seattle: University of Washington Press, 1968); Cohen and Middleton, *Tribe to Nation;* P.H. Gulliver (ed.), *Tradition and Transition in East Africa* (Berkeley: University of California Press, 1969). See also the excellent discussion in Nelson M. Kasfir, "Controlling Ethnicity in Uganda Politics: Departicipation as a Strategy for Political Development in Africa" (Ph.D. diss., Harvard University, 1972).

27. Julian Steward, *Theory of Culture Change: The Methodology of Multilinear Evolution* (Urbana: University of Illinois Press, 1955), p. 44.

28. Raymond Apthorpe, "Does Tribalism Really Matter?" *Transition*, VII, no. 6 (October 1968), 18.

linguistic and cultural similarities which formerly had been irrelevant in effecting alliances.''[29]

In fact, traditional reality was far more complex, as we argued earlier. Identities beyond the most local were not clearly developed. Cultural zones were not sharply demarcated, but often blurred; in the many areas where communities of somewhat different linguistic origin interacted, complex patterns of borrowing, assimilation, and interpenetration occurred—abetted by the very fact that identity lacked a sharply ideological content. Migrations were constant; rare is the group which cannot recite a legend of origin which located their first beginnings somewhere else. Movements of groups did not necessarily entail dislodging of those found to occupy the new area; a whole range of relationships, from clientage through interstitial coexistence to conquest and perhaps amalgamation or assimilation were possible. The revisionist testimonials accumulate. Morton Fried quotes the Douglas Oliver study of the Siuai in the Solomon Islands:

> Precisely on these grounds Douglas Oliver refuses to classify the Siuai as a tribe. They do possess a common language, but, notes Oliver . . ., "They do not all together cooperate...in any kind of common enterprise, nor are they united in any sort of separate hierarchy." The Siuai do not act together in land use, are fuzzy about boundaries, intermarry with people speaking another language and, as a matter of fact are bilingual. All Siuai do not comprise a potentially exclusive interactive network; what is more, some Siuai interact more frequently and regularly with some adjacent non-Siuai than they do with Siuai.[30]

Or, in the words of Edmond Leach:

> . . . it has usually been accepted as dogma that those who speak a particular language form a unique definable unit, and that this unit group of people has always had a particular culture and a particular history. . . . It is groups of this sort which are meant when we find reference to the "races" and "tribes" of Burma.
>
> This convenient academic doctrine does not relate to the facts on the ground. It can easily be established that most of these supposedly distinct "races" and "tribes" intermarry with one another. Moreover it is evident that substantial bodies of population have transferred themselves from one language group to another even within the last century. Language groups are not therefore hereditarily established, nor are they stable through time. . . . since race and culture and language are supposed to coincide, one should expect the Palaung (of Austro-Asiatic linguistic classification) to be culturally very different from their (Tai-speaking) Shan neighbors. But in fact Shans and Palaungs intermarry, and

---

29. In Helm, *Problem of Tribe*, pp. 201-2.

30. Douglas Oliver, *A Solomon Island Society* (Cambridge: Harvard University Press, 1955), p. 103, quoted in Morton H. Fried, "On the Concepts of 'Tribe' and 'Tribal Society'," in Helm, *Problem of Tribe*, p. 5.

in general culture the tea-raising Palaungs are far closer to the Shans than any of the other hill peoples of the area.[31]

Or, Southall, citing a study of a group in Luzon:

The larger ethno-linguistic units recognized by the ethnologist are useful for descriptive and administrative purposes but have little basis in native society.[32]

From these examples, we may share Southall's conclusion:

To hammer home the importance of interlocking, overlapping, multiple collective identities is one of the most important messages of social and cultural anthropology.[33]

A natural outgrowth of the traditional view of "tribe" was the concept of "detribalization." If "tribe" referred to the self-sufficient rural unit, it stood to reason that those who migrated from the homeland to a new, polyglot city ipso facto removed themselves from the "tribal" system, and became by this fact "detribalized." Indeed, this view was held not only by anthropologists and colonial officials, but also by nationalist elites in the terminal colonial period; the unifying experience of the independence struggle and the ideological commitment to a united nation were frequently believed to eclipse mere parochial ties. Yet nothing could be further from the truth. Identities alter in urban circumstance, in function of the markedly different social requirements. At bottom, the "detribalization" metaphor confuses structure with identity. The individual is subtracted from the total pattern of social relationships of the countryside, at least partially. However, identity is quite another matter. Ethnic self-definition requires reconceptualization to meet the needs of urban life—a process facilitated by the "interlocking, overlapping, multiple" nature of the identity phenomenon suggested by Southall above.[34]

31. E. R. Leach, *Political Systems of Highland Burma* (Boston: Beacon Press, 1965), p. 49.

32. Quoting Fred Eggan, "The Sagada Igorots of North Luzon," in George Murdock (ed.), *Social Structure in Southeast Asia*, cited in Southall, "The Illusion of Tribe," *Journal of Asian and African Studies*, V, nos. 1-2 (January-April 1970), p. 36.

33. Ibid., p. 44.

34. Among the most useful analyses of urban identity change, see Immanuel Wallerstein, "Ethnicity and National Integration," *Cahiers d'Etudes Africaines,* 1 (July 1960), 129-39; Paul Mercier, "Remarques sur la signification du 'tribalisme' actuel in Afrique noire," *Cahiers Internationaux de Sociologie,* XXI (1961), 61-80; J. Clyde Mitchell, *The Kalela Dance* (Manchester: Manchester University Press, 1958); Max Gluckman, "Tribalism in Modern British Central Africa," *Cahiers d'Etudes Africaines,* 1 (July 1960), 55-70; Abner Cohen, *Custom and Politics in Urban Africa* (Berkeley: University of California Press, 1969); G. William Skinner, (ed.), *Social Ethnic and National Loyalties in Village Indonesia* (Yale University Cultural Report Series, 1959); Melson and Wolpe, *Politics of Communalism.*

IDENTITY AS SOCIAL ROLE

Identity, in the final analysis, is a subjective phenomenon. Cultural pluralism exists because individual actors include among their repertory of social roles one or more culturally defined identities. The conscious sense on the part of an individual that he belongs to a given collectivity is the basic building block. The linkage between individual awareness of membership and collective social response by the group derives from the common set of symbols and cognitions shared by the group. The social stimulus of a given political event comes from the capacity of the cultural aggregate, through its common symbol system, to arrange the perception of the event into a distinctive message, conveying special meaning to the group.

Each individual has a varying number of social roles, through which he may relate himself to unfolding events in the course of daily life. Not all of these, by any means, are culturally defined. Occupation, social stratification, sex, family relationship, associational membership—all of these provide alternative social roles. The role selected in response to any given situation depends upon the definition and perception of the particular events, the context in which the messages are received, and anticipation of the possible consequences which the events may have. These points can perhaps be made more clearly through the vehicle of a sustained illustration.

Let us take a hypothetical Indian, for example a rural tenant. In the marvelously complex society in which he dwells, we may list at least the following identity roles:

Occupational, as a cultivator

Social strata, as a tenant

Family, as a household head and member of a more extended kin network

Subcaste, as a member of the particular ritualized grouping which regulates and sanctions much of his daily social behavior

Caste grouping, in terms of the set of closely related subcastes who have tended to join forces for social and political action in the broader arena

Language, as a member of one of the linguistic groupings

Region, especially in the arena of state political competition

Faction, in the frame of the political party he may support

Client, as a dependent upon landowner or influential notable who may serve as patron-broker in gaining access to certain resources, such as credit, or some government service

Religion, in relation to other communities, such as Muslims or Sikhs

Rural person, in the occasional situation where the urban society, with its different needs, may compete for the same resources

Indian, in the infrequent occasion when some international event may impinge upon his existence.

If land reform became a salient issue, the identification as tenant would tend to be activated, although it might well conflict with his role as client. In the observance of one of the many rituals of village life, his role would be dictated by subcaste membership. If the state or national arena spawned a dispute over language policy, as at the time of the establishment of linguistic states in the mid-fifties or the crisis in Punjab between Sikh Punjabi-speakers and Hindu Hindi-speakers which led to the partition of that province in the mid-sixties, then linguistic loyalty would dictate response. In the context of an electoral campaign, caste grouping, region, and faction would all be likely to come into play. When China invaded India in 1962 or during the brief Indo-Pakistani wars of 1965 and 1972, the Indian role (reinforced in the latter instance by Hindu religious identity) became relevant.

CULTURAL PLURALISM AND SOCIAL CLASS

The linkage, as well as the contrast, between cultural pluralism and social class becomes clear through this perspective. In many instances, social strata and cultural segment may offer simultaneously relevant role definition. This is particularly apt to occur when a group comes to feel itself relatively deprived in relation to other significant reference groups.[35] If we pursue our Indian example, during the twentieth century Muslims came to feel that as a community they suffered a major social disadvantage in relation to the educated Hindu elite. Our rural tenant will be sensitive to his poverty and dependency both as tenant and caste member. In Assam state, Assamese-speakers feel disadvantaged in relation to Bengali-speakers in the province. Such examples could be multiplied a hundredfold: Malays in relation to Chinese in Malaysia, Afro-Guyanese vis-à-vis East Indians in Guyana, Hutu in relation to Tutsi in Rwanda and Burundi, and innumerable others. It is this pattern of overlap or oven fusion of roles which has led some scholars to conclude that ethnicity is only an artificial adjunct of social class.

35. The sociological concept of "relative deprivation," which dates back to Samuel Stouffer's study of the American soldier in World War II, is given useful statement in Robert Merton, *Social Theory and Social Structure* (New York: Free Press, 1968), pp. 281-90. See also David Aberle, "A Note on Relative Deprivation Theory as Applied to Millenarian and Other Cult Movements," in Sylvia L. Thrupp (ed.), *Millenial Dreams in Action* (The Hague: Mouton, 1962).

This argument deserves brief examination. It is made with particular force, from a Marxist perspective, by Archie Mafeje:

This is not to deny the existence of tribal ideology and sentiment in Africa. The argument is that they have to be understood—and conceptualized—differently under modern conditions. There is a real difference between the man who, on behalf of his tribe, strives to maintain its traditional integrity and autonomy, and the man who invokes tribal ideology in order to maintain a power position, not in the tribal area, but in the modern capital city, and whose ultimate aim is to undermine and exploit the supposed tribesmen. The fact that it works, as is often pointed out by tribal ideologists, is no proof that "tribes" or "tribalism" exist in any objective sense. If anything, it is a mark of *false consciousness* on the part of the supposed tribesmen, who subscribe to an ideology that is inconsistent with their material base and therefore unwittingly respond to the call for their own exploitation. On the part of the new African elite, it is a ploy or distortion they use to conceal their exploitative role.[36]

In other words, although traditional rural communities may exist, ethnicity is nothing but an erroneous comprehension of social deprivation which should be understood in class terms.

We would argue that it is not necessary to deny cultural pluralism in order to assert class. Perhaps the simplest illustration may be drawn from the American racial situation. Poverty and being Black closely correlate; Black anger derives in part from the myriad social obstacles which have kept the bulk of the Black population at the bottom end of the economic ladder. Yet it is surely untenable to argue that the Black community should simply be viewed as a social class and that Black self-awareness, in all its cultural dimensions, is therefore merely false consciousness. The persistent failure of Blacks and poor Whites to form durable alliances is eloquent testimony to the analytic necessity of conceptualizing the problem both in terms of cultural pluralism and social stratification. One needs only to imagine General Yahya Khan telling Sheikh Mujibur Rahman in 1971 that Bengalis were deluded by "false consciousness" to appreciate the inadequacy of this formulation.

In arguing the objective reality of cultural mobilization in certain times and places, we do not wish to adopt the converse position and imply that class solidarity is only false cultural consciousness. Certainly the Vietnamese revolution can only be understood in terms of a fusion of a class ideology of the deprived with Vietnamese nationalism. Workers in Nigeria, in a culturally traumatized atmosphere, did participate in 1964, at least in the southern regions, in a general strike conceived in class

36. Archie Mafeje, "The Ideology of 'Tribalism'," *Journal of Modern African Studies,* IX, no. 2 (August 1971), 258-59. For other similar arguments, see Richard Sklar, *Nigerian Political Parties* (Princeton: Princeton University Press, 1963); Robert I. Rotberg, "Tribalism and Politics in Zambia," *Africa Report,* XII, no. 9 (December 1967), 29-35.

terms. The most powerful ideologies of protest in the third world are usually constructed in a class metaphor; in the case of Latin America, we will argue in some detail in chapter 11 that the dominant ideologies in effect pre-empt ethnic responses by defining Andean Indians as peasants. At the same time, even Marxist-Leninist ideologies in Africa and Asia, where solidarity founded on class is an absolute philosophical imperative, have difficulty avoiding the sponge of cultural pluralism. The once-powerful Indonesian Communist Party had a Javanese flavor; the splintered Communist movement in India finds itself, on close examination, communally encapsulated, as we shall see in chapter 8.

SELF AND OTHER: RELATIVITY OF IDENTITY

Identity, then, is a subjective self-concept; cultural self-definitions are among the social roles individuals may assume in a given situation. As stated thus far, these role definitions would appear to exist in a vacuum—yet nothing could be farther from the truth. Ego is conceived in relation to alter; identity is relational and is shaped by the nature of the "relevant others" in the social arena. The matter is succinctly stated by Theodore R. Sarbin:

It is axiomatic that in order to survive as a member of a society, a person must be able to locate himself accurately in the role structure. The simplest way to accomplish this is by seeking and finding answers to the question "Who am I?" Since roles are structured in reciprocal fashion, the answers can also be achieved through locating the position of the other by implicitly asking the question "Who are You?"[37]

A sense of membership in a given cultural community involves recognition of certain features of the group which render it distinctive; implicitly, these attributes are contrastive. Appreciation of uniqueness requires perception of what differentiates the group from others—speech code, symbols, values, religion, ritual, or physical appearance. Michael Moerman makes this point well in an influential article on the ambiguities of being Lue in northern Thailand:

Lue ethnicity consists largely of the fact that persons in Chiengkham and neighboring districts often use ethnic labels when they talk about the people and the activities of Ban Ping and certain other villages. . . . Further, in order to call themselves by an ethnic label, villagers are semantically required to use or imply a contrastive ethnic label for others. To phrase the issue somewhat more generally

37. Theodore R. Sarbin, "Role: Psychological Aspects" in *International Encyclopedia of the Social Sciences*, XIII, 547.

and accurately, using one member of a set of identifications provides the context which makes other members of that set appropriate.[38]

The importance of the "relevant other" in the definition of cultural roles helps make clear the frequent fluidity of identities, and in particular the changes which often occur in an urban environment. Urban residence places persons in juxtaposition and social interaction with culturally differentiated individuals, perceived as groups from far more diverse provenience than would be characteristic in the countryside. For both self and other, it is inconvenient to interpret social reality through too complex a mapping system. A reductionist process occurs, whereby roughly similar groups in language or even general area of origin are grouped in ordinary social discourse. Reductionism is most pronounced in the perception of others. For a Muslim in British India, those who were not fellow Muslims could be conveniently grouped as Hindus; their caste or other subdivisions were of only subsidiary interest. For a Ganda in Kampala, those who had come from northern Uganda and spoke one of the Luo languages (Alur, Lango, Acholi, or some other) were for most purposes simply "northerners," or "Nilotic" or simply "Bacholi." In terms of stereotypic perceptions of the groups, formulating some generalized attitudes toward them and fixing expectations as to behavior, no more precise identification was necessary. One of the first to establish this point was J. Clyde Mitchell, in relation to the Zambian copperbelt towns:

> For Africans in the Copperbelt "tribe" is the primary category of social interaction, i.e., the first significant characteristic to which any African reacts to another. Frequently relationships never penetrate beyond this and tribes appear to one another to be undifferentiated wholes . . . their own ethnic distinctiveness which they took for granted in the rural areas is immediately thrown into relief by the multiplicity of tribes with whom they are cast into association. Its importance to them is thus exaggerated and it becomes the basis on which they interact with all strangers.
>
> . . . The more distant a group of peoples is from another, both socially and geographically, the greater the tendency to regard them as an undifferentiated category and to place them under a general rubric such as "Bemba," "Ngoni," "Lozi," etc. In this way, from the point of view of the African on the Copperbelt, all tribes other than those from his particular home area tend to be reduced into three or four categories bearing the label of those tribes who, at the coming of the European, were the most powerful and dominant in the region.[39]

38. Michael Moerman, "Being Lue: Uses and Abuses of Ethnic Identification," in Helm, *Problem of Tribe*, p. 161. For a similar argument, see F.K. Lehamn, "Ethnic Categories in Burma and the Theory of Social Systems," Peter Kunstadter, *Southeast Asian Tribes, Minorities, and Nations* (Princeton: Princeton University Press, 1967), I, 93-124.

39. Mitchell, *The Kalela Dance*, pp. 28-29, 32.

Subjective identity itself is affected by the labels applied by others. Through a feedback process, when a designation achieves general currency, it may be gradually internalized by the group itself. Southall cites the interesting case of the Sukuma and Nyamwezi, two of the largest groups in Tanzania. Although at the time of colonial penetration, there was no evidence of any comprehensive identity linking the area, their designation as two different groups, today accepted by both, is purely arbitrary. Further, each label has its origin in a term applied by strangers. "Nyamwezi" in etymology meant simply "people of the west," while Sukuma conveyed vaguely the notion of "north." West and north, of course, were with reference to the caravan trading routes by which Arab and Swahili traders and subsequently European travellers entered the area.[40] During the colonial period, the two groups were placed in different administrative jurisdictions, which tended to crystallize the modest sense of difference and fix the labels. The "Bangala" grouping in Kinshasa, now important both within the urban social field and in the national politics of Zaire, had its origins in the label applied by Europeans and by other Africans to all those arriving in town from upstream; ultimately, it has acquired subjective value within the urban context for many of those to whom the appellation is applied.[41]

Jean Rouch found that a large number of the labels used by immigrants into Ghana were not the same as their original identities, but readily accepted as a subjective term, even when they were pejorative in origin. Thus in southern Ghana, migrants from southern Upper Volta and some of Northern Ghana will accept the term "Gurunsi," even though there is no rural group bearing such a label, and the name is a Dagomba word for bushmen.[42] Terms such as Negro and Black had their genesis in collective labels applied by persons of European ancestry to those of African antecedents, but they have long had subjective application.[43] And it scarcely needs stating that no western hemisphere Indian would have dreamt of applying the term "Indian" to himself before the coming of the Europeans.

Although identity is subjective, multiple, and situationally fluid, it is not infinitely elastic. Cultural properties of the individual do constrain the possible range of choice of social identities. Physical appearance is the most indelible attribute; where skin pigmentation serves to segment com-

40. Southall, "The Illusion of Tribe," pp. 37-38.

41. For a detailed discussion of "Bangala" origins, see Young, *Politics in the Congo,* pp. 242-50.

42. Jean Rouch, *Migrations au Ghana* (Paris: Société des Africanistes, 1956), pp. 35-40.

43. For the intellectual history of White perceptions of Africans, see Philip D. Curtin, *The Image of Africa* (Madison: University of Wisconsin Press, 1964); Winthrop D. Jordan, *White Over Black: American Attitudes Toward the Negro 1550-1817* (Chapel Hill: University of North Carolina Press, 1968).

munities, only a handful of persons at the color margins may be permitted any choice of identity on racial lines. Caste, where it exists, tends toward the ascriptive and sharply constrains role choice. Language is important in delimiting cultural fields, but not necessarily permanent; it is well within human capabilities to master more than one language and even to change the primary language of communication about the hearth. Probably the extreme case of bilingualism on a mass level is Paraguay, where 52 percent of the population can speak both Spanish and Guarani.[44] Religion is a relatively durable identity, which encloses its members within a framework of constantly renewed ritual affirmation of affiliation which is not easily shed, particularly in the case of the universal religions. However, even in this instance noteworthy examples of contemporary change can be cited: one spectacular case was the mass conversion of a large number of low-caste Hindus to Buddhism in the 1950s in Maharashtra state (a process now continuing in north central India) in order to reject the disabilities imposed upon them by Hindu views of caste hierarchy. Indeed, historically a large fraction of the conversions to Islam and Christianity in India have come from low-caste persons, for whom change of religious identity offers an escape from religiously ascribed servile status.

VARIATION IN INTENSITY

A crucial characteristic of cultural identities is their variation in intensity. Not all cultural segments have the same degree of collective solidarity. Some are particularly susceptible to erosion under changing circumstances; others are held with extraordinary fervor. Some seem to come into play, perhaps defensively, at moments of exceptional cultural polarization; others seem constantly visible. In Indonesia, Javanese and perhaps some Sumatran groups like the Minangkabau and Toba Bataks have far more clearly articulated identities than the Borneo (Kalimantan) groups generally labelled Dayaks. In the Philippines, Ilocano identity seems the most clearly affirmed. In Uganda, Ganda identity is far more salient than that of groups like the Lugbara, Kiga, or Gisu. In Zaire, the ethnic self-image of the Kongo is far more sharply delineated than those of groups in the central basin of the Zaire (Congo) River. In the United States, the identity of Blacks, Italian-Americans, or Jews is much more salient than that of Swedes or, contemporaneously but not historically, German-Americans.[45]

Intensity, then, represents degree of cultural mobilization. The Deutsch approach of measuring the phenomenon in terms of the growth of effective,

44. Joan Rubin, *National Bilingualism in Paraguay* (The Hague: Mouton, 1968), p. 14.

45. Novak in his recent appeal for a recognized role for ethnics as ethnics excludes Germans as irremediably Anglicized, *Unmeltable Ethnics*, p. 46.

dense communications channels within a group taps one important aspect.[46] We also find particularly valuable the perspective developed by Joshua Fishman, who differentiates ethnicity from what he terms nationalism in function of the degree to which identity has been ideologically formulated. This distinction was first stated in his studies on ethnicity and language loyalties in the United States.

> An ethnic group becomes a nationality when it has an image of its collective past and when its members are aware of and responsive to that image. Such a development most certainly presupposes a specialized group of persons exclusively concerned with creating and propagating general symbols and values, at once expressing and expressive of this collective past. We know next to nothing about the conditions under which these plural and parochial values become transformed into or replaced by a singular set of national ones.[47]

Subsequently, in his efforts to summarize the state of socio-linguistics in understanding change processes in the third world, he further elaborated on his views:

> At the socio-cultural level it is the transition between ethnic group and nationality that is initially crucial to our immediate purposes (although prior transitions occurred along the band-to-clan stages). As a result of symbolic elaboration the daily rounds of life that constitute traditional ethnicity (including ways of speaking, dressing, harvesting, cooking, celebrating, worshipping, etc.) come to be viewed not as minimally ideologized (which is not to say unrationalized), localized, and particularized "innocent" acts but, rather, as expressions of common history, common values, common missions, longings, goals.[48]

Taken together, the density of communications within a cultural segment and the degree to which it has acquired an ideological statement of its uniqueness, historical virtues, and future destiny account for a large part of the variation in intensity. The ideologization of identity depends upon the emergence of cultural entrepreneurs, almost always associated with the rise of a professional middle class and intelligentsia; although the basis for historical mystique may exist in rich measure in the reservoir of folk tradition and myths of origin, the move from the oral repository of the traditional elders to the written page multiplies the potential mobilization of identity. This cultural educated class has many tasks to absorb its energies: the language must be standardized and a literature of verse and prose accumulated; history must be recorded and a vision of the future defined.

46. Deutsch, *Nationalism and Social Communication*, passim.
47. Fishman, *Language Loyalty*, p. 329.
48. Fishman et al, *Language Problems of Developing Nations*, pp. 40-41.

A distinction is worth making between the cultural entrepreneur, who devotes himself to enlarging the solidarity resources of a community, and the political broker, who mobilizes ethnicity in a given situation, crystallizing collective aspiration in the social and political realm. The latter archetype, the cultural politician, applies his skills to the optimum combination of the existing stock of factors of cultural mobilization; he plays an important part in our analysis, and we will return to him many times. The actor we are seeking to introduce, the cultural entrepreneur, commits his energies to multiplying the capital. Language is a crucial expression of identity and will command much of his attention. The prestige of the language is affirmed by making it uniform so that it can serve as an effective written medium and intensify the solidarity of the entire potential speech community through ending the discontinuities of mutually unintelligible dialects. The language is at once modernized and classicalized; it must be equipped with a vocabulary which describes the artifacts and conveys the ideas of a technological world and at the same time is bound to its origins by the resurrection of classical usage (if any can be found). Literature is of prime importance to an ideological culture; it provides a powerful medium of socialization, where the symbols of commonality are made familiar and intimate, where history is conveyed through poetry, fable, and saga, where a catechism of identity is elaborated. The history of the group must be unravelled and rewoven as epic poetry. The founding fathers, the great kings, the triumphant generals, the high priests must be rescued from obscurity and accorded their place of veneration in the cultural hagiography.

A passionate challenge thus awaits the cultural entrepreneur. Where many respond to this exalted calling and an unmistakably ideologized identity is fashioned, the consequences are important for the multicultural state. An ideologized culture is highly institutionalized. The matrix of language, literature, and socialization vehicles entrenches it more solidly than ethnicity. The policy options of the state in coping with it are correspondingly reduced; for example, the Tanzanian nation-building strategy of employing a modal national culture in Swahili could not possibly work with a group whose identity was as highly ideologized as, say, the Bengali. Not all, it should be added, have the same initial resources. The task is greatly facilitated by a linguistic community of large scale, awaiting unification, or a past rich in great events, realized by historical political units of a scope and centralization to have carved out a large domain. The clay in the hands, say, of Arab, Vietnamese, Burman, or Persian cultural entrepreneurs was malleable and rich.

It was precisely this process of metamorphosis of latent ethnicity into manifest nationalism, gathering force in the nineteenth century, which we argued earlier made the Austro-Hungarian empire unsustainable.

Early Soviet nationality policy spawned a generation of cultural entre- preneurs, who enthusiastically attended to the unification of their languages; in Central Asia a number of languages were reduced to writing for the first time. Encouragement was given to purely cultural expression in non-Russian languages, which gave some leeway for the development of literatures. The intent of the policy for the managers of the Soviet state was, by giving nonpolitical ventilation of cultural expression, to remove in- securities and fears of forcible assimilation and thereby to promote inte- gration. In the Muslim areas of Central Asia in particular, pre-Soviet identity was largely in terms of the distinction between nomadic and sed- entary (Sart) groups rather than in linguistic terms. The Soviets have nurtured into life and provided cultural equipment for what have become, in Fishman's definitions, nationalities where only ethnicity was visible previously. Their high resistance to Russification and integration consti- tutes a major long-run problem for the Soviet Union.[49]

Herein, we would argue, lies a central distinguishing feature between differing forms of cultural pluralism. Speaking generally, the most highly ideologized cultural segments are to be found in Asia—with groups such as Burmans, Vietnamese, Bengalis, and Persians having thoroughly ideologized identities. However, the hill country groups, outer island collectivities in Indonesia, and many of the partly nomadic groupings of Afghanistan and Iran have only minimally articulated identities. In Africa, apart from the Arab tier, there is far greater diffuseness of most ethnic groups. Only a relatively small number, like the Ganda in Uganda or the Amhara in Ethiopia, are significantly ideologized. For this reason, the present pattern of cultural pluralism is very different in Africa than in Asia. In Latin America, as we will suggest in greater detail, the pattern is again remarkably distinctive. Here Indian identities are almost com- pletely lacking in ideological formulation; potential cultural entrepreneurs as well as ethnic politicians are continuously absorbed into the Spanish- speaking mestizo communities.

TYPES OF CULTURAL DIFFERENTIATION

Ethnicity

Finally, a few words are in order on the major categories of cultural differentiation; these may be grouped as ethnic, race, religion, caste, and

49. Erich Goldhagen (ed.), *Ethnic Minorities in the Soviet Union* (New York: Praeger, 1968) pp. 229-70; Brian D. Silver, "Ethnic Identity Change Among Soviet Nationalities: A Statistical Analysis" (Ph.D. diss., University of Wisconsin, 1972); Conquest, *Soviet Nationalities Policy in Practice;* Theresa Harmstone, *Russia and Nationalism in Central Asia* (Baltimore: Johns-Hopkins Press, 1970).

region. Ethnicity we have already considered in some detail during the course of this chapter. By way of résumé, it can be stated that the defining attributes of ethnic commonality may include language, territory, political unit, or common cultural values or symbols. In any given case, these factors may be important defining characteristics to differing degrees, or one or more may even be absent. A shared language is usually present; a speech community is an obvious candidate for common identification. The shared language creates a communication system which tends to exclude those not sharing this code. Language can be identified—at least in terms of intelligibility or non-intelligibility—with the first word uttered. However, important limitations to the linguistic criteria should be noted. Some groups, such as the Amba in western Uganda, consider themselves a group but live in interspersed villages in which either Bwezi or Bulibuli, wholly distinctive languages and not just dialects, are spoken.[50] Even at a moment when they believed themselves to be struggling for ethnic survival, language was insignificant in the Ibo self-image in Nigeria. The Ibo language has not been effectively standardized and many of its dialects are mutually unintelligible. In the Punjab, in India, language became caught up in the dispute between Sikh and Hindu religious groups. The Hindu group renounced Punjabi as their mother tongue and claimed attachment to Hindi (which is closely related); Sikhs, on the other hand, clung to Punjabi, but only in the Gurumakhi script.[51] In the United States, attachment to language has been of relatively small import in the maintenance of Italian-American identity; standardized Italian derives from the Tuscan dialect, while most Italian immigrants came from southern Italy. In Byelorussia, where the indigenous language remains mainly a peasant dialect, and in Scotland, where Gaelic is entirely extinct, the survival of ethnicity is clearly separate from the maintenance of the language per se.[52]

Territory and political unit also are frequent correlates, but not universally valid criteria. In most instances, the ethnic group will have some territorial homeland which aids in the delineation of the identity. Again, there are important exceptions. However, primarily urban ethnic groups, such as the Ngala in Kinshasa, have no precise rural territorial referent—though all arrived in the city from the same general direction. In Israel, where ethnicity derives mainly from time of immigrations and general area of provenience, the "Oriental" Jew is territorially identified only in the very general sense of originating somewhere between Morocco and Yemen. What John Armstrong has identified as "mobilized diaspora"

50. Kasfir, "Ethnicity in Uganda Politics," p. 30.
51. Gerald A. Heeger, "The Politics of Integration: Community, Party, and Integration in Punjab" (Ph.D. diss., University of Chicago, 1971), pp. 152-53.
52. Fishman, *Language Loyalty*, p. 136.

groups in the Soviet Union (Jews, Armenians, Germans) have their equivalents in groups such as the Dioula in West Africa, where identity is related far more to function than to territory.[53]

Political unit also runs into difficulties, given the wide distribution of acephalous traditional societies on the one hand and multi-ethnic kingdoms on the other. Groups such as the Kachin and Karen in Burma were partly incorporated into the Shan state system, while retaining separate identities. Groups such as the Ibo in Nigeria and Kikuyu in Kenya, with quite strong contemporary identities, had no historic political structure incorporating the whole cultural area. As with territorial criteria, political unit as defining attribute runs amuck of the phenomenon of urban ethnicity.

Finally, shared values and common symbol systems have greater generality, but become so vague as to run the risk of tautology. This really brings us back to the beginning; ethnicity is in its essence a subjective phenomenon. Students, such as Raoul Naroll, who attempt to develop a rigorous set of objective criteria to distinguish what he terms a "cultunit," to permit quantitative comparison, build upon sand.[54] In any given instance, only a portion of the criteria apply. All of this serves to reinforce the Southall injunction to visualize ethnic identities as "interlocking, overlapping, and multiple".[55]

Race

Race enters the list of cultural differentiators as a stepchild of prejudice, above all a legacy of stereotypes developed by Europeans in the age of expansion of Europe to world dominion. It is based above all on conspicuous physical differentiation, especially skin pigmentation and facial characteristics, which facilitate the stereotyping process which is so valuable in the maintenance of prejudice. Once established, it hardens into a systematic misperception of facts and a propensity to see all members of another racial category as looking alike.[56]

The first use of the term "race" is quite recent in human history; one student found the first reference in Italian to date from the fourteenth century, the first English use in 1570, and the first French reference as late as 1685.[57] The first two racial categories grew out of the South Atlantic triangle of Europe, Africa, and the New World. Western hemisphere inhabitants became racially designated as "Indians," and Afri-

53. Goldhagen, *Soviet Union,* pp. 8-14.

54. For a recent statement, see Raoul Naroll, "Who the Lue Are," in Helm, *Problem of Tribe,* pp. 72-82.

55. See also the excellent discussion in Kasfir, "Ethnicity in Uganda Politics," pp. 23-95.

56. Simpson and Yinger, *Racial and Cultural Minorities,* pp. 14-15.

57. Berry, *Race and Ethnic Relations,* pp. 35-36.

cans came to be viewed as a comprehensive category. The inveterate taxono-
mist Linnaeus, though best known for his botanical and zoological classifications, also sought to arrange the human species by racial families;
in a 1738 publication, he offered the following categories and accompanying stereotypes:

Europaeus albus: "lively, light, inventive, and ruled by rites"
Americanus regesceus: "tenacious, contented, free, and ruled by custom"
Asiaticus luridus: "stern, haughty, stingy, ruled by opinion"
Afer niger: "cunning, slow, negligent, and ruled by caprice"[58]

Although the slave trade came quickly to dominate European-African
relations and exploitative relationships were fashioned with alacrity in
administering the subjugated Indians, it was only in the nineteenth
century that racialism became an elaborated cultural ideology. The
theory of evolution—highlighted by the 1859 publication of Darwin's
Origin of Species—was a major turning point; the rationale for a hierarchical view of racial accomplishment and civilization was stated. Europeans represented the highest point of evolution, diverse Asians and Indians
fell in somewhere well behind, and Africans brought up the rear.[59]

Gradually, racial differentiation became incorporated in a set of institutional forms which gave rigid expression to race as a prime basis for
social segmentation. Slavery was the most conspicuous of these, but
mechanisms such as the encomienda in Hispanic America—and subsequently the hacienda and Brazilian fazenda—served comparable
purposes. A whole set of taboos developed which sustained the differentiation and limited social intercourse—most jealously maintained in
the sexual domain. So well were these fortifications constructed that, even
after the abolition of slavery per se in the western world, other devices of
racial segregation took their place. In different cultural traditions, contrasting treatment was accorded to the growing numbers of racially mixed
persons; within the Anglo-Saxon tradition, these were classified as Black,
while in Latin contexts the mestizo and mulatto tended to be at least partly
incorporated in the socially dominant White community. Further complexity was added to racially stratified communities in the Caribbean when,
after the end of slavery, plantation operators sought another source of
cheap labor in the import of indentured workers, mainly from the Indian
subcontinent. In time, these too became a racial community in Guyana,
Trinidad—and in the African context, South Africa and East Africa.

With the rise of pan-Africanism, beginning at the turn of the century,
racial identity came to be asserted as a basis of solidarity by the subor-

58. Quoted in ibid., p. 37.
59. Philip D. Curtin, *The Image of Africa* (Madison: University of Wisconsin Press,
1964), provides a cogent analysis of this intellectual history.

dinated groups. Characteristic of the emerging pattern of thought were the prolific writings of W. E. B. Dubois:

> There is slowly arising not only a curiously strong brotherhood of Negro blood throughout the world, but the common cause of the darker races against the intolerable assumption and insults of Europeans has already found expression. Most men in this world are coloured. A belief in humanity means a belief in coloured men. The future world will in all reasonable possibility, be what coloured men make of it.[60]

More than four decades later, Julius Nyerere of Tanzania expressed comparable sentiments:

> Africans all over the continent, without a word being spoken either from one individual to another, or from one African country to another, looked at the European, looked at one another, and knew that in relation to the European they were one.[61]

In short, Black racial solidarity in America, the West Indies, and Africa itself had become a powerful ideology. As it became elaborated as a conscious ideology by a succession of spokesmen—from Dubois through Marcus Garvey, George Padmore, Aimé Cesaire, and Leopold Senghor, to name but a few—the idea of negritude took form, asserting a common cultural tradition and unique virtues associated with Black identity. But the essential origins of African racial self-awareness lie in the factors stated by Dubois and Nyerere: a common subjugation, collective incorporation by Europeans into institutionalized subordination, linked to an ideology of racial superiority. Blacks were united in the first instance by "the intolerable assumptions and insults of Europeans"; from this came the recognition that "in relation to the European they were one."

Race as a scientific basis for the classification of mankind has long since fallen into utter discredit. But race as a subjective basis for social differentiation and collective consciousness remains a potent factor. Notwithstanding the philosophical subtleties of a Senghor, race is perhaps the least "primordial" of all the bases of cultural differentiation. However, in settings where racism has become a deeply rooted pattern of social separation, as in South Africa, the Caribbean, and the United States, it creates a particularly intractable and bitter form of cultural pluralism.

Religion

Religion offers not only a comprehensive world view, but also an all-embracing social identity. Indeed, the very term "communalism" entered

60. Quoted in Victor Bakpetu Thompson, *Africa and Unity: The Evolution of Pan-Africanism* (London: Longmans, 1969), p. 36.
61. Lecture at Wellesley College, Massachusetts, April 1961, from my notes.

Framingham State College
Framingham, Ma

common discourse as describing the politicized competition between Hindu and Muslim on the Indian subcontinent. There are several important reasons for the high political mobilization potential of religious identities. The highly developed ritual and ceremonial practices associated with religious observance serve as a constant reaffirmation of identity; they both reinforce the sense of membership in a community and also visibly demarcate the faithful from other religious groups. The world religions have highly developed symbol systems, which provide a basis for common perceptions and shared emotional reactions to real or imagined threats from other groups. In India, hundreds of communal riots between Hindu and Muslim have been triggered by such banal events as the killing of a cow or a boisterous Hindu procession passing by a mosque.[62] In many cases, distinctive dress will be associated with a given religious community, facilitating instant recognition—the uncut hair bound in a turban for the Sikh, the flowing white *kanzu* for the Muslim in eastern Africa. The obligations to rally for the defense of the faith when it is presumed to be in danger carry the divine sanction of the angry gods. Although the major religions vary in the extent to which a specialized, institutionalized clergy exists, there are invariably religious leaders whose claims as spokesmen command general assent, whether it be derived from unusual piety, theological learning, or ritual function. The combination of divinely ordained solidarity imperatives and the structural and communications capability to transmit the message in times of crisis gives a formidable political mobilization potential to communal attachment. One needs only to recollect the extraordinary orgy of violence in the Indonesian countryside in late 1965, directed in part by Muslims against the secular challengers to religious community, the Communists, or the massive popular Muslim reaction in Sudan in summer 1971 to the belief that a Communist coup had been attempted, for testimony to the continuing force of religious identity in contemporary politics. Finally, the rich theological texture of the world religions provides a thoroughly elaborated ideology of identity.

Religion as an element in cultural pluralism is limited to the great world religions—Islam, Buddhism, Hinduism, Judaism, and Christianity. The older folk religions, although aspects of them are incorporated in the universal religions which have supplanted them in most parts of the world, lack the minimum requirements for becoming meaningful cultural segments in modern politics. They are entirely rural and localized, an indistinguishable part of the unmobilized little community. Because they are inseparably linked to the hearth, they are not readily translated into more generalized identity systems conceived on a scale which can be meaningful in contemporary social and political arenas. Further, they are incapable of generating the cultural entrepreneurs to provide

62. Smith, *South Asian Religion and Politics*, p. 22.

ideological content to folk cults. The intellectual leadership which might fill this role passes through the educational system. In much of the colonized world, formal education was dominated by Christian missions in areas where a world religion was not already established. Evangelization was a major objective and was pursued with fair success. Elsewhere, educational systems are either suffused with the values of the dominant universal religion or are resolutely secular. Although this socialization process does not necessarily extinguish all beliefs and values embedded in the womb of folk religion, it makes it highly improbable that the products of the school system will become either cultural entrepreneurs or political brokers for it.

Christianity has been an operative political identity almost wholly through its subgroups—Catholics, Russian and Greek Orthodox, diverse Protestant sects, the Coptic church. Often, its political role has been in symbiosis with the affirmation of a nationality. For the Poles, Roman Catholicism became one aspect of the affirmation of Polish solidarity, which differentiated them from the Lutheran Germans on the west and the Orthodox Russians on the east. Serbs and Croats became separate communities, despite the extremely close cultural and linguistic similarities, partly by virtue of Roman Catholic (Croats) versus Orthodox (Serbs), which brought with it a Latin script for the former, a Cyrillic for the latter. Slovaks became differentiated in identity from the Czechs with Jesuits as the cultural entrepreneurs, rejecting the Czech literary language and developing Slovak as a distinctive tongue.[63] In the United States, one of the determinants of the persistence of ethnicity is the availability of an ethnic church, particularly if it maintains a parochial school network as well as a focal point for the ethnic community.[64] We will argue in a subsequent chapter that one of the major factors in the failure of ethnic subnationalism to emerge among Latin American Indian communities was the effectiveness of the Spanish in swiftly and decisively imposing Christianity upon the newly conquered population—in Mexico, the razing of temples and construction of churches on their sites was the ultimate symbol of religious imposition. In Africa, politicized religious identity has been most conspicuous in Uganda, where party competition in the early 1960s was in good part built around a Protestant-Catholic rivalry.[65] In Asia, Christian missions had only very modest success, except for the Philippines. However, Christian communities have coalesced into political formations in Kerala state in India (where they are 23 percent of the population), in Indonesia (where major pockets of conversion are

63. Kann, *Multi-National Empire*, p. 274.
64. Heinz Kloss, in Fishman, *Language Loyalty*, p. 206.
65. F. B. Welbourn, *Religion and Politics in Uganda* (Nairobi: East African Publishing House, 1965).

found among the Sumatran Toba Bataks and Sulawesi (Celebes) Mena-donese, and the Ambonese of the eastern islands. In Burma, Christians were numerous among the Karen elite, and Christianity formed a significant basis of differentiation from the Buddhist Burmans.

Islam is a political religion par excellence; from its seventh-century beginnings, it has periodically contributed to state formation, beginning with the first caliphate and continuing in subsequent political creations such as the Ottoman empire, the Mughal empire in India, the Fulani states growing out of the wave of jihads in the eighteenth and nineteenth centuries in West Africa, the Mahdist state in Sudan from 1883 to 1898, and, most recently, the creation of Pakistan as the political homeland for Muslims on the Indian subcontinent. As a religion of revelation, Islam readily becomes an expansive missionary faith—and by that fact may often be interpreted by other religious communities as a threat, thus contributing toward a dialectic of communal conflict. In many periods and places, Islamic states may grant cultural autonomy to other faiths, especially Christians and Jews, recognized in some Koranic passages as also being "people of the book"; the price of toleration and cultural encapsulation was the payment of tribute. In practice, de facto toleration was also afforded to other groups in certain circumstances. In Africa, Islam was frequently diffused by trading diasporas, who would have endangered their commercial operations by aggressive imposition of religion. For those nineteenth-century trading groups such as the Khartoum- or Zanzibar-based merchants, who were deeply involved in slave commerce, conversion to Islam of the African populations among whom they operated would have had the serious economic disadvantage of prohibiting enslavement.

Islam was an important basis for nationalist response to colonial rule in Asia and the Arab world. In Indonesia, the Sarekat Islam was the first major political movement articulating nationalist demands and grievances.[66] In Algeria, the Association des Ulemas in the 1920s was among the first modern organizations to contribute toward the elaboration of nationalist thought. At the same time, colonial rulers often found ways in which Muslim religious notables could lend powerful sanction for a doctrine of quiescence, provided only that Christian evangelization was curbed and no threat to religious identity was provoked by colonial policies. Both British and French found very efficacious support in West Africa from such sources. In India, the growing awareness of a new Muslim elite in the late nineteenth century of the social and economic advance of upper-caste Hindus and fears of Hindu domination in a

66. von der Mehden, *Religion and Nationalism in Southeast Asia*, pp. 26-53 and passim.

decolonized India frequently made bedfellows of the British raj and Muslim leaders in the early part of the twentieth century.[67]

Islam is far from a united cultural grouping, providing a single framework for political action. As with Christianity, its internal subdivisions frequently come to overlap with other patterns of cultural identity. The major cleavage between Shi'ite and Sunni interpretations, dating back to an early dispute over succession to the Prophet, is one important example. The largest center of Shi'ite Islam emerged in Persia, where it took on the attributes of a national church. Abner Cohen has given a fascinating account of the process in Ibadan, Nigeria, by which the Muslim Hausa trading community became differentiated from the native Yoruba, among whom Islam has spread very rapidly in this century. The separateness of Hausa linguistic-cultural identity found reaffirmation in rallying to the Tijaniyya tariq (brotherhood), which provided a religious vessel for the practice of ethnic segmentation. In the course of only two years, in 1951 and 1952, the overwhelming majority of Ibadan Hausa joined Tijaniyya.

The Hausa adopted the order in the 1950s, because the Tijaniyya provided solutions to some of the political problems they faced as a result of the coming of party politics. The process was of course neither rational nor intended by individuals. It was "vehicled" in a series of countless small dramas in the lives of man. . . .

Thus on the one hand intensive social interaction which the Tijaniyya brought, creates strong moral obligations between members of the same community and between them and members from other communities in the Hausa diaspora, while on the other hand it inhibits the development of similar moral obligations between Hausa and Yoruba. The political consequences of such a situation are far-reaching. . . . with the rise of the Tijaniyya, Hause identity and exclusiveness, which were imperilled by the coming of party politics, are now cast in a new form and validated in terms of new myths.[68]

Thus, the ethnic parish in Catholic America has its analogue in the ethnic mosque in Islam.

Islam is also fractured by its relationship with both folk religion and contemporary secular ideologies. In Java, while almost everybody is a Muslim, there is a sharp distinction between those whose membership in the community of Islam is only nominal, who blithely disregard ritual prescription and pious duty and continue to adhere to pre-Islamic beliefs (*Abangan*) and those who devoutly pursue Orthodox Islam and are active

67. The strategy of the British-Muslim alliance was notably argued, on the Muslim side by the first great Muslim modernizer, Sir Syed Ahmad Khan (1817-98), and on the British by Sir William Hunter in an important and influential book, *The Indian Mussalmans*, in 1871. Khalid B. Sayeed, *The Political System of Pakistan* (Boston: Houghton Mifflin, 1967), p. 12.

68. Cohen, *Custom and Politics in Urban Africa*, pp. 152, 159.

in their faith (*Santri*). Add to this a secular impulse, identified with contemporary doctrines of nationalism and Communism, and the Procrustean bed upon which political cleavages have formed takes clear shape.[69] In the Arab world, the unresolved task of reconciling Islam with secular ideologies has likewise been rich in political fragmentation.[70]

The absence of a formally invested and recognized religious hierarchy has often been cited as a prime cause of its disunity and shortcoming in serving as an enduring basis of political community—as most recently evidenced by the failure of Islam to serve as the foundation of unity in Pakistan. It is nonetheless well equipped with religious specialists who serve as foci of identity—ulema, or wise and learned interpreters of theology and Islamic law; variously designated saints of exceptional piety and presumed extraordinary powers of divine intervention; leaders of brotherhoods; mosque officials and prayer leaders; imams and sheikhs who are religiopolitical leaders. In the first and central pillar of Islam, the confession of faith ("there is no god but Allah, and Muhammad is his Prophet"), a doorway to identity is provided which makes entry to the community almost effortless. The other four pillars of faith—the five daily prayers, the month of fast at Ramadan, the pilgrimage to Mecca, and the obligation of alms—are also singularly efficacious buttresses of identity.[71]

Judaism, although a religion of revelation and universal principle, is not a proselytizing faith. Over the years, it has often become difficult to distinguish between religious community and ethnic identity as the essential bond linking Jews. For a long time, in many parts of the diaspora, a special language, Yiddish, also reinforced distinctiveness. It is interesting to note that both religion and language seem to be giving way as elements of identity among the two largest Jewish communities outside Israel, the United States and the Soviet Union. In the United States, growing secularism had diluted religious observance, and the command of Yiddish is in sharp decline. A comparable trend is found in the Soviet Union, where Jews have been earmarked for a particularly forceful assimilation program. In 1897, Yiddish was the language of 97 percent of the Russian Jewish community. Since 1930, the Soviet regime has placed

69. The *santri-abangan* distinction was made familiar by Clifford Geertz, *The Religion of Java* (Glencoe, Ill.: Free Press, 1960).

70. Kemal H. Karpat (ed.), *Political and Social Thought in the Contemporary Middle East* (New York: Frederick A. Praeger, 1968); Nadav Safran, *Egypt in Search of Political Community* (Cambridge: Harvard University Press, 1958).

71. The classic general treatments of Islam are H. A. R. Gibb, *Mohammedanism: An Historical Survey* (New York: New American Library, 1955), and Wilfred Cantwell Smith, *Islam in Modern History* (Princeton: Princeton University Press, 1957). For a cogent assessment in briefer compass, see Charles F. Gallagher, "Islam," *International Encyclopedia of the Social Sciences*, VII, 202-16.

severe restrictions on Yiddish publications, has outlawed Yiddish-medium schools. In the 1926 census, 70 percent listed Yiddish as mother tongue, while in 1959 the figure had fallen to 18 percent. Religious training has also been virtually suppressed; at last report, the Soviet rabbinate had only sixty survivors, whose average age was seventy.[72] And yet, in both the Soviet Union and the United States Jewish identity persists as a significant cultural and political phenomenon.

Judaism as a part of the cultural mosaic which concerns us entered the scene with the rise of Zionism in the latter half of the nineteenth century. This political expression of religious identity had as its conscious model European nationalism of the societies which englobed the diaspora, and it asserted a comparable program—a revival of national language and culture (politization of Jewish identity in secular form) and a politically autonomous nation-state. These aspirations became centered upon Palestine as the biblical homeland. Beginning about 1882, waves of Jewish migration to Palestine built upon a tiny core of Jews—numbering an estimated five thousand in 1800—to create a semi-autonomous quasi-state during the interwar years of British Palestine mandate. Hebrew—a virtually dead classical language—was resurrected to become the linguistic vehicle of identity, rather than Yiddish. In 1948, when Britain abandoned its mandate without having been able to find a political formula acceptable to the contending Jewish and Arab communities in Palestine, the Jewish community was of sufficient strength and organizational capacity to assure the establishment of the independent state of Israel and defend it from the immediate attacks by Arab armies. Since that time, Israel has served as the political focus of Judaism.

Judaism too has important internal cleavages, however united Israelis may be in the defense of the survival of their state. So thorny has been the issue rendering a legal definition of the religious basis of the state that no constitution has ever been adopted. A whole spectrum of perceptions of the essential basis of the Jewish community exists, ranging from the wholly secular to the strenuously Orthodox. The historical difference between Sephardic and Ashkenazim Jewry played some role. Most important, however, has been the deepening cleavage between Jewish immigrants from Europe and the Americas, and the postindependence, massive immigrations from Arab lands and elsewhere outside Europe. The latter group, "Oriental" Jews, has become a numerical majority, but is heavily concentrated at the bottom of the social scale.[73]

Buddhism is, in the first instance, a Western term for an immensely diverse system of beliefs and practices, all of which depart from the

---

72. Joseph Blumberg and Abraham Blumberg in Goldhagen, *Soviet Union*, pp. 274-332.
73. Eisenstadt et al., *Integration and Development in Israel*.

teachings of Buddha two millennia ago. There are three main variants: Theravada (Sri Lanka, Burma, Thailand, Laos, Cambodia), Mahayana (Nepal, Sikkim, China, Korea, Vietnam, Japan), and Tantrayana (Tibet, Mongolia). The Theravada stream, of primary interest to us here, is characterized by a relatively unified orthodox teaching, a highly developed monastic network, and a long history as the established church. Mahayana is diffuse, syncretic—a complex combination of many sects and schools—and has been generally less significant as a political identity, with the exception of Vietnam. The Tantrayana form gave rise to the theocratic states of Tibet and Mongolia.[74]

In Burma, Sri Lanka, and Vietnam, political Buddhism played an important role in recent years. The extensive network of monasteries—through which, in Thailand and Burma, most young men pass at least for a brief period—provides a ready-made framework for the activation of Buddhist sentiment. The politically oriented among the permanent monks constitute a natural leadership, which can clothe its program in the garb of religious identity; the very large number of young men novitiates is a reservoir of active support; in Burma, the number of monks is estimated at between 80,000 and 120,000. The high prestige of the monasteries and the popular reverence for the monks make their influence substantial if they do actively exercise it. In Burma, the emergence of Buddhism as a court religion was coterminous with the rise of the Burman kingdom and ultimate crystallization of Burman identity. In the words of one recent student, Burmese Buddhism "is a loose church with little treasure, much honor, and a great capacity to sanction power, but not to hold, lead, or capture it."[75]

As a political identity, Buddhism was a major factor in Burmese nationalism; it was around the symbols and structure of Buddhism that the first nationalist organizations emerged. During the years U Nu was in office after independence, the monks were a vocal pressure group, and Buddhism was elevated to the status of an official state religion.[76] In Vietnam, Buddhism as a political force was primarily centered in the Hue region and emerged for a time in the last days of the Diem regime as an identity group of some significance. Political Buddhism in Sri Lanka was fuelled by more abiding fears and resentments; it represented a response of hill and countryside to the social hegemony of the coastal,

74. Peter A. Pardue, "Buddhism," *International Encyclopedia of the Social Sciences,* II, 165-84; Richard H. Robinson, *The Buddhist Religion* (Belmont, Calif.: Dickenson Publishing Co., 1970); Thieh Nhat Hanh, *Vietnam: The Lotus in the Sea of Fire* (London: SCM Press, 1967).

75. Manning Nash, in Robert F. Spencer (ed.), *Religion and Change in Contemporary Asia* (Minneapolis: University of Minnesota Press, 1971), p. 108.

76. von der Mehden, *Religion and Politics in Southeast Asia;* Smith, *Religion and Politics in Burma.*

partly Christian elite, as well as the reinforcement of Singhalese cultural demands in relation to the non-Buddhist Tamils.[77] In Thailand, the common value framework provided by Buddhism has been one of the factors favoring the relatively high degree of incorporation of the immigrant Chinese. Divisions in Buddhism may also overlay other cultural cleavage. In Sri Lanka, there are three different sects of Buddhism, which closely relate to three main castes. In Burma, Buddhism as state religion fails to unite even those who share its identification. A Buddhist monk has helped lead the Arakanese separatist movement; minority groups like the Shans, even though Buddhist, strongly opposed the state religion act as Burman-inspired.

Hinduism, found in Nepal, among Tamils in Sri Lanka, and indigenized on Bali in Indonesia, in addition to India, is the most diffuse of all as a religious framework, yet through the mechanism of caste and the behavioral codes associated with it provides extremely detailed regulation of social life. Its sacred texts are many and scattered; its doctrines are rich in contradictions. Although by historic tradition the Brahman castes served priestly functions, this has long since ceased to be the case. The assorted temple priests, gurus, and astrologers who perform specialized religious functions have neither the intellectual resources nor the social prestige to provide political and cultural leadership. Historically, Hinduism was neither proselytizing nor the basis for a broader identity; religious observance for the overwhelming majority was confined to the village temple and the local subcaste.

The rise of Hinduism as a political identity system can probably first be dated with the efforts of Mughal King Aurungzeb (1658-1707) to Islamicize his administration and domains. In the nineteenth century, in reaction to a growing sense that the outside world looked down upon Hinduism as hidebound and retrograde, a Hindu renaissance movement took root, which revisited the sacred texts to find responses to derogatory appreciations. Beginning with the founding of the Arya Samaj in 1875 and continuing through the Hindu Mahasabha in the last decades of colonialism and the Jana Sangh Party since independence, a series of militant Hindu communal movements arose. The agitation to replace Urdu, associated with the Mughals and hence Muslims, with Hindi in Devnagri script began in 1867. Hindu enthusiasts in the years following sustained a continuing campaign to "purify" Hindi, to purge it of Persian and Arabic words and restore long extinct Sanskrit vocabulary and structure. Gandhi's political vocabulary was rich in Hindu connotations, although he himself was certainly not a communalist.[78]

77. Smith, *South Asian Politics and Religion*, pp. 453-546.

78. Chaudri Muhammed Ali, *The Emergence of Pakistan* (New York: Columbia University Press, 1967), pp. 9-30; Khalid Bin Sayeed, *Pakistan: The Formative Phase* (Karachi: Pakistan Publishing House, 1960), pp. 79-103; Smith, *India as a Secular State*, pp. 87-94.

All of these trends gave rise to quite new forms of Hindu identity. Hinduism came to be associated in part with India and Indian nationalism. Many of the specific communal organizations operated at a regional or provincial level; this pattern of political mobilization of Hindu sentiment also involved horizons far broader than the village and subcaste. The intensifying communal conflict with the Muslims likewise contributed to vast enlargement of scale of Hinduism as social identity.

Caste

Caste as a cultural differentiator is primarily a South Asian phenomenon, although castelike stratification is to be found in a number of West African societies, stretching from Senegal to Nigeria.

It may be defined as a rigid, ranked system of social strata, endogamous and ascriptive. The ranked categories are often occupationally specialized. Rank is constantly expressed and validated in interaction among the castes. In Wolof society, in Senegal, where the caste pattern is particularly clear, there is a separation into royal and noble higher castes, and artisanal, praisesinger (griot), and slave lower castes. Normatively, these castes are endogamous. A clear correlation is discernible between upper-caste origin and representation in the modern elite. However, caste is by no means as thorough a regulator of social life as in India nor are the barriers to social interactions between castes remotely comparable. As one moves from Senegal to the east and south, traces of castelike social organization become more diffuse and infrequent, in many cases merely being distinctive customs and ascriptive status for smiths. Although the African variant appears to us as analytically comparable to the Indian version, it has not experienced the same transformation and expansion as has Indian caste nor has it played a significant role as an arena of cultural pluralism.[79]

Indian caste, however, has been a prime feature of political conflict. At first view, one is tempted to conclude that the intrusion of caste in politics is yet one more dismaying strand in the web of primordial attachment which binds India to a static past. Such an impression is utterly false; the patterns of caste alignment through which the political impact occurs are radically different from the timeless ascription of rural India. Caste, indeed, ranks with "tribe" as one of the most misunderstood and misrepresented phenomena of the developing world. The sociology of confused knowledge is similar in the two cases. Students of caste, like investigators of "tribes," began with a mistaken image and failed to look in the right places and processes. Empirical focus on the process of change began to offer greater congruence between observable reality and received knowledge.

79. James Vaughan, in Arthur Tuden and Leonard Plotnikov (eds.), *Social Stratification in Africa* (New York: Free Press, 1970), pp. 90-91.

Here the intellectual history begins to diverge. In the Indian case, misperceptions have their origin in the sacred sociology of the Vedic texts. Until the postwar generation of anthropologists began the intensive study of village structure, both English and Indian scholars relied heavily on the normative and literary interpretation of caste contained in the classic Hindu scriptures. In these, stress is placed on comprehensive categories, labelled varna, which are not the actual units of social membership. The varna, in ranked order, are the Brahmans (priests), Kshatriya (warriors), Vaishya (merchants), and Sudras (artisans and servants). Below these are the polluted and defiled—the untouchables. Roughly speaking one-fifth of the Hindu population falls within the top three categories, considered to be "twice-born" castes. About three-fifths are in the Sudra class, and the remaining one-fifth is in the untouchable category.

The base point for understanding the caste system, postwar empirical inquiry suggests, is the jati. It is a localized unit, centered in a group of villages. The jati has jurisdiction over the greater part of the individual's social behavior; through the jati council (panchayat), a scale of sanctions may be imposed extending to the extreme deprivation of outcasting, a measure which removes from the individual his social status and in effect banishes him from the community. Rank and hierarchy of jatis have their meaning within the local community; individual behavior in relation to other rank groups is very closely regulated, embedded in the customary value system, and sustained by the strong sanction armory available to the jati. Segmentation, hierarchy, and boundaries are maintained through the concept of pollution; depending upon the relative position of the jatis on the ranked scale, an increasingly comprehensive array of taboos are defined, in relation to the distance between the jatis of any two interacting individuals. At a minimum, cohabitation, marriage, and commensality are confined to the jati. The interdependency of the different jatis in the local community is expressed through different ritual function, as well as economic and social division of labor.

Between subcaste and varna, an intermediate classification exists which has become the common vocabulary of political caste. Within the frame of the small, self-sufficient community, little reason existed for any caste identity beyond the jati. But social change and modern politics produced new identity needs. The gradual introduction of electoral politics and progressive enlargement of the franchise created a dramatically new arena of competition and interaction. Here social power was ultimately defined by numbers, and not the local ascriptive hierarchy—although this is not to suggest that the injection of electoral politics immediately obliterated existing relationships. Education, urbanization, and economic change opened a wide range of new roles and sharpened social competition for these resources. The jati was not a commodious group for pursuit of collective welfare and mobility; related jatis had to organize themselves through affirmation of broader, common caste identities for efficacious pursuit of social goals.

Thus groups such as Jats and Rajputs, Nairs and Ezvayas, Reddis and Kammas became socially mobilized identities. Caste associations were formed, which functioned as social interest groups for the set of allied subcastes. These groups could pursue the collective welfare of their following in several ways:

1. By seeking to alter upwards the hierarchical standing of the group within the caste framework, by a process which M. N. Srinivas has labelled "Sanskritization"—i.e., progressively adopting ritual practices associated with the twice-born castes, for example, in becoming vegetarian—in order to lay claim to a higher varna ranking
2. By bargaining the electoral support of the group in return for patronage and other social advantages
3. By acting as a pressure group in pursuit of specific allocations, through a range of tactics running from informal influence to agitational politics
4. By providing services to caste members—one particularly widespread activity being the construction of caste hostels in towns so that secondary and university students could live and eat with their caste-mates

In addition to the process of political mobilization of castes over a widened social universe, Srinivas, who has probably contributed more than any other social scientist to modernizing the conceptualization of caste, has argued that a three-fold process of change is occurring at different levels of the caste scale. At the top, Brahmans and others who had earliest access to the Western educational system introduced in the nineteenth century have tended to become secularized. Representative was the late Premier Nehru; although of Brahman antecedents, his condemnation of the caste system was unequivocal:

> The conception and practice of caste embodied the aristocratic ideal and was obviously opposed to democratic conceptions. . . . But the ultimate weakness and failing of the caste system and the Indian social structure were that they degraded a mass of human beings and gave them no opportunities to get out of that con-dition—educationally, culturally, or economically. . . . In the context of society today, the caste system and much that goes with it are wholly incompatible, reactionary, restrictive, and barriers to progress.[80]

A second trend has been the gradual upward mobility of caste groups through the Sanskritization process. The Rudolphs estimate that a significant segment of those now classified as Sudra, as well as some of the

80. Nehru, *Discovery of India*, p. 253.

present untouchable castes, will move to twice-born status in the next few generations. For the untouchables, Sanskritization is difficult. An alternative escape from the ascription of defiled status is through conversion; in 1956, at least 3,000,000, and perhaps as many as 20,000,000, untouchables, mainly in Maharashtra, became Buddhists.[81]

The third trend, at the bottom of the scale, is the gradual Hinduization of peripheral populations who remained hitherto outside the organized framework of Hindu society. These are the groups described in Indian administrative vocabulary as the "tribal" population, dwelling in sparsely inhabited forest and hill areas. As their interactions with the settled Hindu population increase, they are incorporated at the nether end of the hierarchy as a new caste.[82]

The broadened caste categories which tend to be the units of political solidarity, with few exceptions, are coterminous with linguistic frontiers; thus caste primarily enters the political equation at the state and district level, rather than in national politics. The central importance of electoral politics since independence has tended to shift the balance of political power further down the caste hierarchy. Although Brahmans are very strongly represented in the professional elite, their numbers are too small for effective competition in an electoral frame. Relatively numerous and rurally dominant landowning castes have particularly benefited; even untouchables carry strong political weight in some states, such as the Marathas in Maharasthra or the Ezhavas in Kerala.

Thus, caste, like ethnicity, has both shaped politics and been shaped by it. The dynamics of change have transformed its boundaries and altered its content. At the same time, politically mobilized caste identities have an impact in the political arena which came as a great shock to India's leadership in the second general elections in 1957, when its full force became unmistakably apparent.[83] The lament of two Indian social scientists at a symposium on state politics in 1967 may serve as epitaph:

> The interdependence of castes, facade of cooperation between them, face-to-face group character, hereditary leadership, ritualistic and social functions which they performed, small village area in which their community life operated and character of their cohesion—all these changed with the development of new channels of communications. Instead, there has emerged fierce competition between castes which are organized into district/regional-wide associations, with elected leadership, with greater degree of openness, with service-orientation towards its membership. . . . Organization of caste over long distances also in-

81. Rudolph and Rudolph, *Modernity of Tradition*, pp. 119-20, 137-38. Conversion, of course, does not instantly transform status; the escape is only partial, and in practice law and behavior continue to reflect the untouchable past.

82. Srinivas, *Caste in Modern India*.

83. Ibid., p. 2.

volved a change in the pattern of recruitment of caste-leadership which can neither be restricted to a locale nor can it be hereditary, but has to be elective. . . . A second effect is, therefore, the emergence of fierce competition between the castes for political power and capture of scarce developmental resources, replacing the old spirit of harmony and uneasy cooperation characteristic of the small village, imposed by primitive means of communications.[84]

In the pre-independence days, Indian leaders were concerned about the influence of caste in politics and tried to minimize its influence in public life. After independence, however, caste seems to have found wider scope to operate and has operated more effectively than before, and seems to be gaining a tighter grip on the body politic.[85]

Regionalism

A final basis of identity is regionalism. This is, in part, a residual category, and we need to give it only brief attention. However, for the sake of completeness, regionalism is sufficiently widespread and salient to merit mention. In many states, subnational loyalties adhere to portions of the country with a special history, a particular ecological configuration, or an established tradition as an administrative entity. Regionalism is especially pronounced in Latin America, where a number of factors particular to the nineteenth-century development of the newly independent states embedded localized cleavages in the political pattern. The importance of the hacienda as the operative social unit in many parts of the countryside; the strong tradition of autonomy and inward focus of civic life in the municipality, or *cabildo*; the political role carved out by the *caudillo*, or flamboyant patron, of an area; the extreme poverty of communications in many states, which left important zones isolated from the political capital; sharp contrasts in economy, needs, interests, and even racial composition between coastal plain and highland plateau—all of these contributed to strongly entrenched regional loyalties.

Elsewhere, administrative history at times left a legacy of identity configurations with a lingering political impact. In a number of Indian states, zones which under the British raj had been indirectly ruled "princely states" are poorly integrated into the reorganized linguistic states, even when they form part of the dominant language community. Thus Maharashtra and Andhra Pradesh have faced secessionist pressures, despite their linguistic homogeneity. In Nigeria, distinctive administrative traditions in the Northern Region left in its wake an incipient "northerner" identity, vigorously promoted by the dominant Hausa-Fulani elite in the early years of independence. The reshaping of Nigeria into twelve

84. N. G. Kini, in I. Narain (ed.), *State Politics in India* (Meerut: Meenakshi Prekeshan, 1967).
85. K. S. Mune Gowda, in ibid., p. 588.

states in 1967, with the North broken into six parts, plus the advent of military rule diluted the structural basis for northern solidarity and diminished the socio-political influence of the most dedicated artisans of northernism.

Thus we can place in its broader context the metamorphosis of Gola boy into Vai spokesman at a conference on Mande culture. By way of recapitulation, it may be useful to summarize some of the main points of this chapter in terms of ten propositions. (1) Cultural pluralism as a political phenomenon is emerging from such social change processes as urbanization, the revolution in communications, and spread of modern education. (2) At the historical basepoint, when the pace of social change was about to accelerate, social identities in the third world were for the most part localized and of small scale, although some broader patterns linked to historical kingdoms, long-distance trade networks, and universal religions did exist. (3) Cultural identities are not usefully described as primordial, but are for the most part relatively new, and vastly expanded in scale. (4) Although identities are frequently politicized and mobilized by the competitive pursuit of wealth, status, or power, they constitute distinct social roles, and not simply surrogates of nascent social classes; cultural pluralism is more than simply "false consciousness." (5) Identity, at bottom is a subjective self-concept or social role; it is often variable, overlapping, and situational. (6) "We" is defined in part by "they"; the relevant other in a social setting is central in shaping role selection. (7) Although fluid, identity is not infinitely elastic; it is shaped by the initial cultural resources which the individual acquires by birth—language, religion, perhaps caste—although new identities can be acquired by learning new languages and by marriage, migration, or conversion. (8) Cultural segments vary widely in degree of politization and extent to which an elaborated cultural ideology exists. (9) A pivotal role is played by the cultural entrepreneur, who adds to the cultural resources of language development, literature, or history, and the political broker, who relates identity to conflict. (10) Cultural solidarity units are founded upon any of several commonalities—ethnic-linguistic, racial, religious, or regional.

3 The Arena: State, Nation, and Nationalism

Perhaps the most remarkable aspect of the successful secession of Bangladesh in 1971, which we will explore in greater detail later in this study, is its uniqueness. In the face of the ubiquity of cultural pluralism in the 107 independent states (in 1972) of the third world, it is truly stupendous that this instance stands almost alone as the breakdown of an existing post-independence state, in the three decades since World War II. Its only companions are the Syrian withdrawal from the short-lived fusion with Egypt in 1961, the Singapore divorce from Malaysia after two years of partnership in 1965, and the separation of Senegal from Mali after two months of independence. Bifurcated Pakistan was created in defiance of geopolitical, and even cultural, logic; its sole bond was the common fear of politically mobilized Muslims of submergence in a Hindu-dominated India. Yet it survived for twenty-five years. Despite the overwhelming support for separation when it came in 1971, its realization could be assured only through the decisive armed intervention of India. How many times have we been reminded of the historical artificiality of most states in the developing world. All the more extraordinary, then, is the durability, the persistence of the state system.

MODERN STATE AS NORMATIVE CONCEPT

We need, then, to examine more closely this cast-iron grid superimposed upon the culturally diverse populace of the third world. So much is the state system a part of our routinized perceptions of the world that its existence seems utterly banal and ordinary—yet we would suggest that it exercises a transcendent despotism over reality. Its reality-shaping power is exercised in multiple ways: fixation of boundaries, orientation of the communication system, patterning of economic activity, containment of population movement, parameter-setting for political conflict. Powerful inertial forces appear to sustain the persistence of the system. What is, will continue to be, except only when there is large-scale disruption of the international framework which loosely contains—and reinforces—the state system. Perdurable, but not static; a slowly cumulating momentum seems visible, by which power aggregates, and the institutions of the state exercise a more pervasive hegemony over the populace. The state, in short, is the authoritative arena which defines the framework for cultural pluralism.

The idea of the modern state assumed shape and form beginning with Machiavelli in the sixteenth century. As empirical reality, the political forms which provide the normative model of the contemporary state were the European polities which took form in the seventeenth, eighteenth, and nineteenth centuries. The modern state, of course, has its precursors extending back to the Greek polis and beyond. The term "state" is frequently applied to any form of human government exhibiting at least some rudimentary signs of centralization and continuity. But for our present purposes, the concept of state which operates as prescriptive formula for contemporary polities must be our focus.

The major universal properties are territoriality and sovereignty. The territorial attribute, in the developing world, was fixed by the imperial partition. Historical states had far more diffuse boundaries, demarcated by zones of intermittent influence; these peripheral zones were useful to the central core only for occasional extraction of resources through tribute or seizure of men for war or labor or women for procreation. The competitive dialectic of colonial conquest not only superseded the historic states, but required far more precise boundary demarcation. The consolidation of empire depended upon the "effective occupation" of territory to which claim had been staked. Traditional states which resisted colonial conquest—Iran, Afghanistan, Thailand, and Ethiopia—found their previously vague borders given sharp definition by the neighboring imperial systems. Particularly in the twentieth century, as colonial rule became more thoroughly organized, an administrative system backed by the coercive power of the colonial state extended its regulatory apparatus to the outlying perimeter of the territory. First taxation and colonial order, subsequently a ramifying array of state activities enlarged the presence of the state throughout its territory: labor recruitment, agriculture, health, schools, public works. Territoriality was defined by the accidents of administrative division of the Spanish empire in Latin America and the flow of colonial rivalry in Africa and Asia. While territories were enclosed within the colonial frame, transfers within the same colonial system could readily be made. Thus Upper Volta was abolished in 1930 and recreated only in 1947. Burma and Sri Lanka for a time were administered as part of British India. Nigeria and Zaire were ruled as single entities, rather than divided into separate ones. The administrative federations of Afrique Occidentale Française and Afrique Equatoriale Française were transformed for decolonization purposes into twelve states. But once territoriality became linked with sovereignty, with independence, the frame congealed into an apparently permanent grid.

Sovereignty, then, is the second critical property of the modern state. As international precept, sovereignty is the untrammelled prerogative of the state to the exercise of authority within its territory and over the population contained within its frontiers. It may apply any sanctions to its subjects in the enforcement of its regulations. It may compel its populace to fight, and if need be to die, in its defense. It may impose sweeping disabilities upon whole categories of the population, such as apartheid in South Africa, deportation of recalcitrant minorities in the Soviet Union to remote areas, or even extermination, as in Hitler's "final solution" for Jews trapped in the Nazi net.

Absolute sovereignty, of course, exists only in theory. In practice, its exercise is constrained by the interdependency of states in the international system. Even the most powerful of states, such as the Soviet Union and the United States, are not totally exempt. Crop failure in the U.S.S.R. in 1972 forced Soviet leaders to solicit access to American agricultural commodities. The U. S., at the same time, was made vulnerable by the weakness of the dollar in Western Europe and Japan. Far more dependent are most of the new nations of Africa and Asia—for aid, for technical personnel, for currency backing, for capital and technology. Former colonial powers retain, especially in the early years of precarious independence, extensive capacity for influence in their ex-dependencies. The major powers in the pursuit of their global competition have exhibited a persistent propensity to participate in the internal affairs of smaller states, to bring or maintain in power political leaders or groups who are ideologically congenial or politically friendly.

In some instances, a group of states will see an overriding moral imperative which should supersede the sovereignty principle. Thus African states call for international intervention to eliminate apartheid in South Africa. Arab states do not accept the legitimacy of Israeli sovereignty within the 1973 boundaries. Even viewed internally, the capacity of a state to make effective use of its theoretically absolute prerogative is limited in practice. The constitution may contain self-denying ordinances which circumscribe the authority of central institutions. Those exercising the authority of the state "cannot apply its force to every issue and trouble spot but must husband it, defending strategic regions or institutions."[1]

However, despite these derogations from the theoretical absoluteness of sovereignty, it remains in most states of sufficient scope to make of the

1. Morton H. Fried, "State: The Institution," in *International Encyclopedia of the Social Sciences,* XV, 143-50.

territorial polity an unambiguously authoritative arena—and in nearly all it is becoming more so with the progressive accumulation of power resources by the central institutions. The well-nigh universal acceptance of the norm of sovereignty legitimizes the trend we will discuss below toward greater approximation of unrestricted state authority.

A subsidiary but important aspect of sovereignty, which relates it to the idea of nationalism, is the normative derivation of its legitimacy from its constituent population. In its etymology, sovereignty was a concept bound to the dynastic state—"L'Etat, c'est moi," in the lapidary formulation of Louis XIV. The sovereign was the king, and the state apparatus his household creature. The very success of the dynastic European states in globalizing their domains from the fifteenth century on gave rise to ramifying bureaucracies of growing power. Parliamentary institutions, also, challenged the personal suzerainty of the monarch; they laid claim to a superior legitimacy as spokesmen for the people. Political parties emerged to structure the linkage between parliament and populace. Through these multiple processes, the European state became depersonalized. Sovereignty attached, no longer to a dynasty, but to a matrix of institutions through which the growing authority of the state was exercised. The dominant paradigm justifying the state presumed that its institutions were the embodiment of the will of the people; no longer was the legitimacy of state authority bound to the pedigree of its king. This transformation of the idea of sovereignty is, of course, quite distinct from the empirical question as to how much actual influence the "people" had in the formulation of public policy; what concerns us here is the process by which "state" and "nation" as normative concepts flowed together.[2]

THE STATE AS NATION

The remaking of Europe's political map on the basis of national self-determination through the German and Italian unification movements and political settlements after the First and Second World Wars extended the process. Finally, the anticolonial revolt in Latin America, Africa, and Asia, which asserted the higher authority of the populace over the colonial territory, completed the task of investing the contemporary state system with a legitimacy founded upon the mandate of its people.

Rupert Emerson has offered a cogent definition of the nation:

> The nation is a community of people who feel that they belong together in the double sense that they share deeply significant elements of a common heritage and

2. For a stimulating treatment of these processes, see George Modelski, *Principles of World Politics* (New York: Free Press, 1972), pp. 9-108.

that they have a common destiny for the future. In the contemporary world the nation is for great portions of mankind the community with which men most intensely and most unconditionally identify themselves, even to the extent of being prepared to lay down their lives for it, however deeply they may differ among themselves on other issues. . . .

The nation is today the largest community which, when the chips are down, effectively commands men's loyalty, overriding the claims both of the lesser communities within it and those which cut across it or potentially enfold it within a still greater society, reaching ultimately to mankind as a whole. In this sense the nation can be called a "terminal community."[3]

The normative model of the contemporary polity calls for the coincidence of nation and state. The state, in order to possess the legitimacy necessary for the successful achievement of its ultimate end of a life more prosperous, just, and equitable for its inhabitants, must command as a matter of course the affective attachment of its citizenry. Purely coerced compliance is not enough; the basic survival of the state will always appear in doubt if large numbers of subjects, particularly if they are cultural collectivities, reject the state as a legitimate framework. Thus, the first pattern was that of the state-nation, with the loyalty to nation growing up around the pre-existing state. With the rise of mass politics and the emergence of self-conscious linguistic-cultural collectivities in nineteenth-century Europe, a series of nations succeeded in acquiring statehood through unification movements in Germany and Italy, out of the wreckage of Austria-Hungary, the Ottoman empire, and some domains recovered from Russia and Germany. Nation preceded state in these instances, through struggle, the good fortune of the defeat of Austria-Hungary, Turkey, Russia, and Germany in World War I, and a peace settlement governed by the Wilsonian principle of self-determination in Europe (but not elsewhere). Then came the anticolonial revolt in Africa and Asia (earlier in Latin America). In practice, this could only be effectively carried out within the territorial framework established by imperial partition. Its legitimacy depended upon securing a united front with demonstrable mass support, to force decolonization upon colonizers for whom, normally, the dissolution of empire did not come naturally. In certain cases—most of Latin America, Algeria, Vietnam, Indonesia—this was achieved through armed struggle. In most instances, mass agitational strategies or at times mere peaceful electoral organization were sufficient—which gave a sense of historical inevitability to decolonization. But whatever the process, the requirement was the same: the anticolonial nationalist leadership had to make convincing demonstration that their claims to inherit the authority of the territorial state carried the sanction of the populace at large, that

3. Emerson, *From Empire to Nation*, pp. 95-96.

they had the ultimate capacity to organize the subject peoples in conflict so costly that colonialism was no longer worth the price. In seeking the mandate, the anticolonial leadership began the process of transforming the often-arbitrary colonial state into a nation.

The task, however, was far from complete at the time of independence. The state now became itself the main vehicle in the hands of the nationalist elite for fulfillment of the mission, rather than the foil against which unity was forged. In struggle, the nationalist movement was the nation in formation; the state was an alien apparatus, owned and operated by the foreign ruler. Yet even as antithesis to nationalism, the colonial state necessarily defined the spatial framework of the embryonic nation. In triumph, the nationalist elite acquired title to the state—and in turn was absorbed by it. Nationalism as anticolonial struggle had laid the basis for the nation; now the state had to complete the task. That state must be nation is indisputable; rare indeed is the political elite whose statecraft is not informed by this premise.[4]

THE IDEA OF NATIONALISM

From nation comes the idea of nationalism; here we may call upon the definition of its most distinguished analyst, Hans Kohn:

> Nationalism is a political creed that underlies the cohesion of modern societies, and legitimizes their claim to authority. Nationalism centers the supreme loyalty of the overwhelming majority of the people upon the nation-state, either existing or desired. The nation-state is regarded not only as the ideal, "natural," or "normal" form of political organization but also as the indispensable framework for all social, cultural, and economic activities.[5]

Nationalism, then, is an ideological formulation of identity. By stipulating the nation as terminal community, to whom ultimate loyalty is owed, it invests the nation with transcendent moral sanction and authority. It is a profoundly political theory; implicit within it is active obligation to the national community and not merely passive acceptance of subject status. Through postulating a given aggregate of human beings as a natural collectivity, it must necessarily seek to make them so; there is thus a compulsive duty of mobilization, of extending awareness horizontally and vertically to the farthest periphery and lowest strata. Critical to the concept is the premise of independence; the terminal community can

4. For an interesting treatment of the nation-state versus state-nation sequence, see Philip D. Curtin, "Varieties of Nationalism in Modern Africa," *Review of Politics*, XXVIII, no. 2 (April 1966), 129-53.

5. Hans Kohn, "Nationalism," *International Encyclopedia of the Social Sciences*, XI, 63-70.

only be independent if it frees itself of all constraints upon its autonomy. Subjugation is an intolerable constraint upon the fulfillment of destiny. Societal organization can be suffused with the cultural values of the nation only if the shackles of colonial rule or subordination to a dominant grouping which controls the state and is viewed as a "significant other" are sundered. Nationalism can be successfully expressed only through the modern state.

This is not to suggest that nationalism was always strongly developed at the moment of independence. It was certainly weak in most of the states of Latin America. In Africa, territories such as Chad, Upper Volta, the Central African Republic, and Swaziland were in the backwaters of the independence movement and acquired sovereignty almost by default. However, the state must be nation; the new political elites inherited from the normative environment an inescapable prescription, whose dictates they were bound to follow.

Nationalism, therefore, is one dimension of cultural pluralism, but not all manifestations of cultural pluralism are equivalent to nationalism. Ethnicity in the great majority of instances in the developing world differs from nationalism in its lack of ideological elaboration and in the absence of any serious aspiration to the total autonomy required by nationalism. In certain instances, cultural identities may become politicized, mobilized, and ideologized to the point where they cross the ill-defined threshold of nationalism; certainly Ibo and Bengali were operating as nationalities in their respective secession movements. But in most instances conflict arises over distribution of resource and advantage within the given state context. We will restrict our own use of the term "nationalism" to instances where the definitional conditions are met. We will make occasional use of the term "subnationalism," to designate identities who meet some of the criteria of politization and mobilization but are not firmly committed to separate statehood.

The idea of nationalism has strong unitarian undertones: "la Republique une et indivisible" of French liturgy, "one nation, indivisible," of the American pledge of allegiance. "Concern for homogeneity," notes George Modelski, "thus led to nationalism and homogeneity in turn became a test of loyalty, the underlying supposition being that a society is strong or rich or fruitful only if it is homogeneous."[6] The nation must be one, a promise which commands the quest for homogeneity. This inner impulse toward oneness latent in nationalism brings it into frequent relations of tension with cultural pluralism. The unitarian impulse sires policies aimed at producing greater homogeneity; these measures are a threat to subnational solidarities and mobilize pluralism. The ensuing conflict

6. Modelski, *Principles of World Politics*, p. 100.

may reach a level where the unity of the polity is indeed impaired, at which point the dissident groups are either coerced into silence or the homogenizing pressures are slackened. But so powerful is the paradigm of oneness that there is every possibility that a new generation of comparable policies may re-emerge some years later.

The trinity of state, nation, and nationalism define the political field of cultural pluralism. They constitute an epistomology of political reality. In the Kantian sense, the nation-state system has become a model of the world firmly implanted in the political cognitions of mankind, and in particular political elites. It provides the categories through which the chaotic flow of events is given structure and meaning.[7] Or, in Kuhn's terms, we may suggest that the modern state system and related nationalist ideologies constitute a contemporary paradigm of political organization so pervasive in its impact that conscious political thought is shaped and molded by a model so thoroughly assimilated as to be largely unconscious. It becomes difficult to conceptualize identity and conflict apart from the authoritative arena of the state system.[8] We do not, of course, intend to suggest that the state system has no empirical reality; rather, beyond existential fact, there is a potent supplementary impact through the effect of this paradigm in the categories of perception through which human groups understand themselves, define the collectivities through which they interact, and relate each self-conscious group to its significant others.

The centrality of the state system as authoritative arena has, moreover, steadily increased during the period of its ascendancy as dominant paradigm. This secular trend had gained momentum during the present century, as third world states have extended the coverage of the system to global dimensions. Three major clusters of factors may be identified which have intensified the normative power of the nation-state system: (1) the progressive expansion in generalized expectations as to the role of the state; (2) continuing accretion of the power capabilities of the state, which increase its penetration of the human periphery, and, in most instances, sharpen the disparity between the state arena and subordinate socio-political zones; and (3) the force of the international system in enforcing the maintenance of the existing state system, through a flow of resources primarily directed to the reinforcement and support of existing units. Each of these dimensions deserves our careful attention.

7. Smith, *Theories of Nationalism*, p. 31. The Smith study offers a perceptive discussion and critique of extant theories of the antecedents and nature of nationalism.
8. Thomas Kuhn, *The Structure of Scientific Revolutions* (2nd ed.; Chicago: University of Chicago Press, 1970.) See also the debate on epistomology in political knowledge triggered by Eugene F. Miller, "Positivism, Historicism, and Political Inquiry and its Rebuttals," *American Political Science Review*, LXVI, no. 3 (September 1972), 796-873.

EXPANSION IN SCOPE OF THE STATE

When the modern state system began to assume its present basic form in the sixteenth to eighteenth centuries in Europe, the scope of the dynastic state was initially modest. As the repository of sovereignty, the state regulated its territory to preserve domestic peace and assure the supremacy of its writ. As international actor, the state manned its barricades against external assault and, when opportunity and resources permitted, frequently sought enlargement of its domain through policies of aggrandizement, which reached their apotheosis in the colonization of the western hemisphere, and subsequent imperial partition of Africa and Asia. As defender of the national wealth, the state promoted the trade interests of its commercial groups through mercantilism. With the rise of industrialism and capitalism, the legal frame of the state provided security to property, sanctions for the enforcement of contract, and protection for capital. But the philosophical flowering of liberalism in the nineteenth century, while not devoid of concerns for justice and equity in the arbitration of social conflict, nonetheless advocated a limited role for the state.

The idea of progress entered the philosophical field with the eighteenth-century Enlightenment. Only by a circuitous path, however, did progress become development. The perfectability of man was initially to be accomplished through the rationalization of social institutions so that impediments to improvement could be removed. When the theory of evolution joined the idea of progress, the doctrine of social Darwinism emerged to argue that the state, through restricting its intervention, should ensure that the free play of social competition should improve mankind by selective survival of the fittest. The state could play a role in economic change through subsidizing infrastructure (American railways) or directly constructing it (resurrection and extension of India's irrigation canal system beginning in the nineteenth century). Colonial powers sought the *mise en valeur* of their overseas domains. But the idea of development, as a clearly identified central mission of the state, is primarily a phenomenon of the postwar world. Third world nationalism played a major role in elevating development to its present place as a central purpose of the state. Nationalism could not be a mere rejection of foreign rule; the positive goals of cultural regeneration and escape from poverty were an inseparable component. Earlier variants of nationalism were not centrally concerned with economic backwardness, but with cultural deprivation. Anticolonial nationalism identified spoliation and exploitation as a critical deprivation; from this followed, necessarily, the ideological commitment of the life more abundant—in short, development—as a corollary of independence.

From the premise of nation-state as primary vehicle for development flow many important consequences. The accomplishment of this goal requires a comprehensive role for the state. It must actively seek to mobilize resources, internally and abroad. It must seek rationality in their allocation through the mechanism of planning. Even if development is not accompanied by at least a diffuse commitment to socialism, the state must assume responsibility for filling all the socioeconomic infrastructural points which private initiative does not supply. One need only scan any five-year plan or examine the roster of public corporations in any developing state to be persuaded of the comprehensive role dictated for the state by the concept of economic development.

Development also has a political component. Since the 1950s, the theme of political development has become a major topic in the study of comparative politics. Particularly relevant to our present discussion are some of the prime conclusions reached by an able team of political scientists invited by the Social Science Research Council, who over more than a decade were engaged in a collegial search for understanding of the process of political development. In the concluding volume of a series of studies generated by their work, political development is seen as the successive resolution of a series of crises:

1. Identity: the extension of an active sense of membership in the national community to the entire populace; in essence, this is the issue of making state equivalent to nation
2. Legitimacy: securing a generalized acceptance of the rightness of the exercise and structure of authority by the state, so that its routine regulations and acts obtain voluntary and willing compliance
3. Participation: the enlargement of the numbers of persons actively involved in the political arena, through such devices as voting, party of other group activity, extending eventually and ideally to the entire polity
4. Distribution: ensuring that valued resources in society, such as material well-being and status are available on equal terms to all persons and that redistributive policies inhibit heavy concentrations of wealth in a few hands
5. Penetration: extending the effective operation of the state to the farthest periphery of the system[9]

Taken together, this development syndrome is a far-reaching normative statement of the role of the nation-state. The analysis focusses upon the crises, and not the nation-state unit which is to master them—yet, im-

9. Leonard Binder et al., *Crises and Sequences in Political Development* (Princeton: Princeton University Press, 1971).

plicitly, there is no entity but the polity which can carry out these functions. And the state cannot resolve these crises without in the process becoming greatly enlarged in scope and function. This is not to gainsay the analysis of the SSRC committee, but merely to note its implications. Its importance lies in the virtual consensus among scholars it represents. Nor is this merely an ivory tower view; although statesmen use a different dialect, the normative theory of the requirements of political development is closely comparable.

Along with the idea of development came the ideology of socialism. The first modern state to deliberately marshall the total resources of the polity to the goal of rapid development was the Soviet Union, beginning especially with the first Five Year Plan in 1929, thus creating a first linkage between development and socialism—which in its earlier forms was entirely an ideology of redistribution. Socialism in its third world forms has become a widespread philosophy of development, although differing in specific content; the gap between specific development policies of, say, China and Kenya could hardly be wider. Yet the fact that an essentially liberal economy such as Kenya chooses to garb itself in socialist rhetoric is in itself significant. Various factors may be identified to explain the attractiveness of socialism to third world political elites: reaction to the intimate link between capitalism and colonialism, domination of the private sector by foreign nationals or interests, the prestige of socialism as an ideology of the oppressed, the influence of the European left on nationalist elites. Development socialism is not universal as regime commitment; a recent survey showed that it had important impact on the political life of nearly two-thirds of Latin American, African, and Asian states—but as an explicit ideological commitment, governed policy choice on only one-third.[10] Yet the importance of socialism in a number of major pace-setter states, with a strong regional or even international influence gives it a significance beyond what these numbers would suggest; as models of the developing state, China, India, Egypt, Tanzania, and Allende's Chile are far more potent than Paraguay, Liberia, and the Philippines, or for that matter the Ivory Coast and Japan, despite the extraordinary growth rates achieved by the latter two. For our present purposes, the relevance of the diffusion of a socialist perspective, however defined, is the further ideological load placed upon the state. Socialism prescribes not only the guiding, direction, and stimulating role for the state—which is common to all development theory—but also direct command and management by the state of a significant segment of the economy.

Not only is the state enjoined to an ever-growing role by the dictates of development and socialism, but its actual capacity to fulfill its prescribed functions steadily increases. The state bureaucracy slowly expands and

10. Charles W. Anderson, Fred R. von der Mehden and Crawford Young, *Issues of Political Development* (2nd ed.; Englewood Cliffs, N.J.; Prentice-Hall, 1974).

ramifies. The technical quality of its personnel improves, as each generation is somewhat better trained that its predecessor. Increments of technocratic capability become available first to the central bureaucracy. Central public services usually offer better terms of service than provincial or local ones, not to mention superior status and prestige. If development does occur at all, great fiscal resources will immediately result, which permit expansion of the bureaucratic apparatus. The trend line is not without its oscillation and, in some instances, its backward dips. Neither should one overlook the instances where subordinate units of government also increase their political resources, either in tandem with the central institutions or, at some times and places, at the expense of the center. There is no reason to posit a zero-sum relationship between power available to central and regional units of government within a nation-state; India is a clear case in point. During the 1960s, regional and district polities acquired important new resources through legislation vesting new functions in local governments. There may also be moments of contraction of the power of polity over society. Although precise measurement is of course impossible, there seems some reason to believe that in Burma there has been actual deterioration of administrative capabilities over the past decade. Temporary dislocations or political crises which provoke an exodus of experienced cadres may produce setbacks; evidence suggests that such may have been the case in Uganda in 1972-73 following upon General Idi Amin's brusque transformation of Uganda society; or during Duvalier's reign in Haiti. Some polities are so devoid of material or human resources that it is quite ridiculous to speak of centralized administrative capabilities; Equatorial Guinea is a case in point. But in polities such as Brazil, Nigeria, Algeria, Zaire, Saudi-Arabia, Iran, Kenya, and Indonesia, the increment in centralization over the past decade is palpable, and the mastery of the central bureaucracy over the periphery of the system indisputable. The preponderant vectors of development and change favor the enlarging power of the bureaucracy; short of decomposition of a given polity, despite frequent invocation of the virtues of decentralization, there seems no reason why the trend should not continue.

INCREASING POWER OF THE STATE

The pattern is even more unmistakable with respect to the instruments of coercion. The increase in scale and scope of armed forces in the developing world in recent years has been formidable. Consider the case of Nigeria, although the example may be extreme. In 1967, armed forces numbered only 11,500, and heavy equipment was limited to a small number of armored cars. Today, Nigeria has 250,000 men under arms, has acquired armor, artillery, and combat aviation to go with its infantry battalions. Or take the example of Zaire, which entered independence with an army of 24,000 organized as light infantry and constabulary units. A mutiny of the army against the wholly European officer corps rendered its reliability and capacity very low for some years following. However, by 1972, the size had increased to approximately 50,000, led by an increasingly self-confident Zairian officer corps. The acquisition of C-130s and helicopters had provided a wholly new airlift capability, a fact of no small importance in a polity as far-flung as Zaire.

The dialectic of expansion of armed forces, despite their absurd profligacy, seems beyond human agency to arrest. In Latin America, the long tradition of military involvement in politics has strongly entrenched armed services as an avaricious interest group. Local rivalries—Peru versus Ecuador and Chile, Brazil versus Argentina—produced an interlocking tendency toward competitive expansion. The availability of American military aid after World War II, purportedly to develop collective security against the Communist powers but also to enhance the internal security capabilities of the existing regimes, gave a powerful stimulus to expansion. The ubiquitous, buccaneering arms salesmen of various European and North American weapons merchants haunted the anterooms of the defense ministries. Military expenditures, in real terms, increased by 4 1/2 times in 1970 as compared with 1940 in the six leading South American nations—Argentina, Brazil, Chile, Colombia, Peru, and Venezuela.[11] India and Pakistan have sustained a steady arms spiral since independence. The cold war assured a huge flow of weapons and training support to the arc of states along the Sino-Soviet perimeter, from Turkey to Korea. The permanent Arab-Israeli tensions in the Middle East have inflated all military establishments, abetted by the súb-theme of Soviet-American rivalry in arming states each deems friendly. Even in the least militarized zone in the world, sub-Saharan Africa, the trend is clear. States close to the White redoubts of southern Africa feel constrained to arm against the threat of being held hostage to Portugal or South Africa. Elsewhere, the widespread entry of the military into politics guarantees that their claims on the treasury will be heard with respect—and usually effect.[12]

We may digress momentarily to situate our emphasis upon the growing power capabilities of the state system in relation to the influential theses

11. Gertrude E. Heare, *Trends in Latin American Military Expenditures 1940-1970.* Department of State Publications 8618 (Washington D.C.: Government Printing Office, December 1971), p. 1.

12. The extraordinary pace of military expansion in the third world is thoroughly documented in Stockholm International Peace Research Institute, *World Armaments and Disarmament: SIPRI Yearbook 1972* (New York: Humanities Press, 1972).

of Samuel Huntington, who argues the likelihood—indeed, actuality—of political decay in many third world states, as participative opportunities and attendant political mobilization outstrip national integration and political capacity.[13] Due note should be taken of the difference in focus. Huntington argues that mobilization cannot be permitted to outpace the institutionalization of such legitimacy-building structures as political parties and sees "a shortage of political community and of effective, authoritative, legitimate government."[14] We are arguing that a clear trend exists toward the cumulation of power resources in the central institutions of the polity; further, particularly in Africa and Asia, the most important of these institutions have been the bureaucracy and military. This, of course, is far more likely to achieve "effective and authoritative" government than legitimacy and political community. In the immediate aftermath of colonialism, some shrinkage of effectiveness no doubt occurred, with the swift localization of the bureaucracy and officer corps and the transitional difficulties of coping with mass followings which nationalist movements had mobilized in the anticolonial struggle. In a few cases, such as India and Tanzania, effective mechanisms were developed to sustain participation, but not at the cost of diluted effectiveness and authority. In a very few, such as Uruguay, Haiti, and Burma, long-run decay processes diminishing the effectiveness of central institutions do appear salient. But in the preponderance of instances, diverse variations on the authoritarian theme have enhanced the role of the nation-state as authoritative arena.

STATE AS MOLD FOR SOCIETY

To this must be added the powerful forces of autarchy in economy and communications. The state insulates its economy with various frictional disabilities to transactions crossing frontiers. The fine-meshed net of the customs barrier must be traversed. A national currency is a mark of sovereignty, and a spectrum of difficulties are associated with currency exchange, ranging from the virtually unscalable barrier of a nonconvertible money such as the Guinea franc (now Sili), to only minor impediments within an international currency zone, such as the franc or sterling areas. Normally, within the boundaries of the state interregional trade flows are not inhibited by legal restrictions, despite such curious anachronisms as the existence of customs barriers between mainland and Zanzibar in Tanzania. Development planning is a conceptualiza-

13. Samuel P. Huntington, *Political Order in Changing Societies* (New Haven: Yale University Press, 1968).
14. Ibid., p. 2.

tion of economic change within the state; the systemic theory which underlies it is based upon promoting the linkages, relationships, and interdependencies within the national economy. This is not to belittle the significance of the international economy or the extreme dependency of many third world states upon the industrial world. But once again they are linked to this network as state units. In exceptional cases, domestic economic regulation may create profits so great through illicit trade across borders as to promote clandestine interstate linkages which can evade the boundary-maintaining machinery. But smuggling, in the total scheme of things, is an enterprise of very modest proportions and less social significance.

One needs only to examine any road or rail map at random to be persuaded of the extraordinary impact of state boundaries in shaping their contours. As economic infrastructure, transport networks fall within the same autarchic frame of development reference as the rest of the economy. As facilities which will guide and shape the flow of persons, goods, and services, national elites are acutely aware of the import of the communications system in the overall strategy of national integration. Transnational communication nets become an affair of state, arranged at the level of polity, and conceived in terms of polity-oriented benefits and disabilities. Postal services normally surcharge mail which will cross a frontier. Newspapers serve a primarily national market. Radio and television are mainly state monopolies and are consciously used as instruments of national policy—although radio waves do readily cross frontiers, and broadcasting is utilized internationally by major powers or by those, such as Egypt, with a self-image of regional leadership. International movement of persons is subject to severe regulation, which has become more comprehensive in the postindependence period. Colonial powers were often willing to tolerate or even encourage migration of traders and labor. Since independence, immigration is permitted in very few cases on any scale, with the special exception of refugees.[15] Burma expelled Indian traders and moneylenders; Uganda drove out her Asians in 1972 and has made life difficult for Kenyan laborers; Zaire expelled West African traders shortly before that; Ghana deported foreign Africans in large numbers in 1969-70, to cite but a few examples.

15. Refugees admittedly are no small exception. No less than 15 million persons crossed the border in the massive unscrambling of a population that accompanied the partition of India and Pakistan. Arab refugees who left former Palestine after the independence of Israel number over one million. Zaire accommodates 250,000 Angolans, 25,000 Rwandans, and until the Sudanese settlement in 1972, 40,000 southern Sudanese. Burundi received 78,000 Rwandans, Uganda 25,000 Zairians, 70,000 Rwandans, and 45,000 southern Sudanese (1966 estimates). All told, there are at least one million refugees in Africa. Louise W. Holborn, "Refugees: World Problems," *International Encyclopedia of the Social Sciences*, XIII, 361-73.

STATE-PRESERVING ROLE OF INTERNATIONAL SYSTEM

Finally, the global system of states exercises a pervasive influence in maintaining its component units. Relationships are organized and structured through the states. International bodies, such as the United Nations or the International Coffee Agreement secretariat, are based upon states. Transactions are regulated, power is exercised predominantly through states. Even neocolonialism is carried out through the structural frame of the state system, at both the superordinate and subordinate ends. No doubt such transnational bodies as multinational corporations are of significant scale and import—but the fundamental cellular composition of the international system remains tied to the nation-state.

One may discern a marked inertial propensity for system maintenance at the international level. Resources are funnelled from the major actors to the lesser ones through the states. Aid, whether or not it is effective in promoting growth and development for the receiving society as a whole, is beyond doubt efficacious in augmenting the resources available to the central institutions of the state, through whose machinery it necessarily passes. The cold war epoch channelled huge increments of state-building resources to the national units through the competitive recruitment of dependents and reinforced their military capabilities through aid, weapon sales, and training programs.

Not only are the state units maintained by unconscious processes, but also through deliberate choice. With few exceptions, the international arena has been resolutely hostile to the fragmentation of its components. Secessionists in the postwar epoch have elicited an icy response in their search for external support. Indonesia was able to suppress outer island insurrection in the Moluccas and subsequently in Sumatra, although both insurgent groups appealed for Western assistance. Both received some aid through unofficial or clandestine channels, but it was limited and ineffectual. Katanga envoys crisscrossed the globe in quest of even one state that would grant recognition, even offering Costa Rica a cash payment of $2.5 million.[16] To no avail; despite some initial Belgian assistance and warm sympathies in some conservative milieux and corporate boardrooms, the Katanga secession was doomed from the outset. Katanga was perhaps handicapped by unsavory associations with neocolonialism and mining interests; the same could not be said about the equally unsuccessful secessionist uprisings in Biafra and southern Sudan. Each had a strong claim upon the moral sympathies of the world at large and overwhelming communal support from the groups involved. Biafra progressed as far as four recognitions and did receive some aid from diverse sources, running

16. Jules Gérard-Libois, *Katanga Secession* (Madison: University of Wisconsin Press, 1966), p. 175.

the gamut from Portugal through France to China. But Nigeria had a decisive advantage in diplomatic support, some arms aid, and, more important, creditworthy standing as a state to purchase large quantities of armaments. Southern Sudan had even less success; Israel and Ethiopia provided sporadic sub rosa assistance, but diplomatic support was nil. The Kurdish rebellion in Iraq faced the same crippling difficulty.

In recent times, Bangladesh stands alone in having successfully separated by force of arms against the resistance of the national institutions. Here India provided all of the advantages normally denied to secessionists.

Partly because separatism is one latent political option for cultural segments in every plural state, there is an instinctive reaction against fragmentation. The potential for splintering is highest in Africa, and here official diplomatic doctrine is most firmly set against secession. The Organization of African Unity, legatee of the aspirations of the Pan-African movement, has transformed its bequest from an ideology of Black unity to a coalition of territorial states, whose maintenance is a charter principle, a paradoxical benediction of the colonial partition.

Embedded within the congealing and hardening matrix of the state system is a core elite with a profound commitment both by intellectual conviction and personal interest in the state. The elite mans the crucial institutional structures of the state—the bureaucracy, the military, the top political positions. Its members speak the administrative language of the state. They are attuned to a set of reference standards partly drawn from the international arena—in ideological currents, in development models, in aspirations, and even life styles. By profession and career, they are firmly tied to the state. They are susceptible to assignment throughout the country, in many cases as a matter of policy. They are a nationalizing elite; through their commitment to state as nation, their articulation of this commitment, and the calculated use of the institutional resources of the state to promote this concept, they are the human incarnation of the state-consolidation process we have argued.

Thus, despite the frequently arbitrary and artificial manner in which it came into being, the state system is firmly anchored in contemporary reality, and the central trend appears to be its aggrandizement and reinforcement. If we look backward over the last century, the era of its global diffusion and complete ascendency, we find that the elements of persistence are overcome only during periods of calamitous disruption of the international system itself. Major reshufflings of the state frame have occurred only during the two world wars and their aftermath. Whether it is viewed as the ultimate framework for human fulfillment or a constricting straitjacket of discord and division, that the state system in approximately its present form is here to stay seems one of the most durable axioms of modern politics.

If it is granted that the state-becoming-nation is of fundamental importance as the political field within which cultural pluralism is confined and operative, then it becomes pertinent to inquire more closely into the precise nature of the state as arena. In this respect, several relevant issues emerge: the origin of the state, the particular patterns of cultural identification borne in the state itself, and the varying types of cultural segmentation within the state.

ORIGIN OF THIRD WORLD STATES

The first states within our analytical universe to enter independent existence were the Latin American republics; to these we turn first. The point of departure for Spanish conquest of the New World was the Antilles foothold established by Christopher Columbus. The lure of riches led the conquistadores to the two major centers of Indian organization—the Aztec empire of Mexico and the Inca kingdom centered in Peru. Here were situated not only immediately recoverable wealth in the form of gold and silver, but also organized systems of control of large human populations by which it could be multiplied. The extraordinary success of Cortes in 1517 and Pizarro in 1537 in decapitating these empires and, with only a handful of men, utilizing their structures to fasten Spanish rule upon very large populations seems more like heroic mythology than actual history. Upon these imperial underpinnings were established the two mainland viceroyalties of Mexico City and Lima. From these primary centers of diffusion, Spanish settlement slowly spread through along the west coast of South America, up from the La Plata delta, inland into the Andean highlands of Columbia and Venezuela, and through Central America. New viceroyalties of La Plata (Argentina, Uruguay, Paraguay, and Bolivia) and New Granada (Panama, Colombia, Venezuela, and Ecuador) were created in the eighteenth century. In addition, semi-autonomous captaincies general were established in the final century of Spanish rule for Cuba (the Antilles), Guatemala (Central America), Venezuela, and Chile. Brazil, by virtue of the exploration of its coast in 1500 by one of Prince Henry's navigators, became Portuguese territory. These boundaries, augmented by some smaller subdivisions into which the primary administrative units were demarcated, provided the basic structures of statehood for most of Latin America. As a basic juridical principle, it was generally accepted that the boundaries of 1810— at the start of the independence—were the point of departure, with some negotiated adjustments.

In a confused, interlocking yet discrete series of uprisings from 1810 to 1826, all of the continental Spanish and Portuguese dependencies became independent. Three centuries of Spanish rule had produced a populace whose main sociocultural cleavages were between peninsulares (mainland Spaniards), creoles (pure Europeans born overseas), mestizos (European-Indian mixtures), mulattos (European-African mixtures), zambos (Indian-African mixtures), Indians, and Africans. Imperial security was deemed to require reservation of virtually all of the ranking positions in the royal bureaucracy to peninsulares. Although some uprisings of the subjugated Indian and enslaved African populations had occurred, the independence revolutions were in most cases of, by and for the creoles; only in Mexico were Indians and Mestizos significantly involved. Nor were all creoles in the independence armies; a goodly number joined loyalist forces.

There were three main focal points for uprisings: Mexico, La Plata, and the northern Andes zone. Although the independence movements fought a common enemy and each was influenced by the existence of the others, yet they never integrated their forces nor sought a common political destiny. Regional military heroes such as Simon Bolivar and San Martin participated in the liberation of several countries each (Ecuador, New Granada, Bolivia and Venezuela for Bolivar; Argentina, Paraguay, Chile, and Peru for San Martin); they were not able to unite them in triumph.

The only colonial institution in which creoles had been able to assert leadership and enjoy participation was the *cabildo*, or municipality. When New Spain was founded, the Iberian municipality still enjoyed many medieval privileges and immunities and had not yet succumbed to centralizing royal absolutism. It was this sixteenth-century model of the *cabildo* which was transplanted and subsequently remained in a conflicted relation of tension and partial subordination to the superstructure of royal administration managed by the peninsulares. It was thus logical that the *cabildos*, in loose confederacy, would provide the initial political vessel for the independence movements. The military campaigns themselves offered a supplementary and alternative institutional framework; the military leaders swiftly emerged as complements and competitors to the *cabildo* juntas. The periodic spectacular military successes had as their contrapuntal accompaniment sustained factionalism and dissension.

The independence wars never came to a clear-cut end. A measure of international recognition for the self-constituted new states and the eventual abandonment of the struggle by Spain—without formally ratifying the independence of its former dominions—marked the inconclusive end of the independence campaigns. At the beginning of their existence, there was only the barest beginning of a state framework and even fainter traces of the future nationalism; sovereignty had come to a settler aristocracy, resentful of the frictions and constraints of centralized imperial administration and its peninsulare agents. The insurrections were anticolonial, but not founded upon an ideology of nationalism. The evaporation of royal administration left an institutional vacuum uneasily filled by constitutions which tried to conjure into existence representative modes of government. But the initial formless void at the center and the legacy of regional armed forces bequeathed by the independence struggle left the new states vulnerable to intervention by caudillos and dictators, who sought to erect personalist regimes. The absence of national identities, weakness of central institutions, exceedingly poor communications, and the *cabildo* tradition gave free rein to regionalism, reflected in the federal constitutional experiments in Mexico, Venezuela, Argentina, and Brazil.

The early years of independence saw some further fragmentation before the state structure became stabilized and national identities began to crystallize. Simon Bolivar's dream of uniting Venezuela, Colombia (then including Panama), and Ecuador in Gran Colombia lasted only from 1821 to 1830. In 1839, the Central American federation which had been the lineal descendent of the captaincy general of Guatemala broke apart into Nicaragua, Honduras, Costa Rica, El Salvador, and Guatemala. The Dominican Republic, which came under Haitian rule from 1821 to 1844, went its separate way. Uruguay was severed from Argentina in 1828. With American connivance, Panama was split off from Colombia in 1903. The first century of independent life saw the gradual transformation of what began primarily as the territorial heirs to colonial administrative divisions into nation-states.

Latin American creoles already had a cultural tradition by the time of independence, although it was not particularly associated with the territorial frame which formed the basis for statehood. During the unstable and tumultuous years of the nineteenth century, the creole elite indelibly stamped its cultural imprint on the new states. The key culture-forming groups—lawyer, *caudillo*, intellectual, or priest—were firmly Hispanic. The nodal points of urban culture—the towns and cities—were a generalized model of the Iberian community, remarkably uniform in spatial configuration and cultural pattern from the Rio Grande to the Straits of Magellan.[17] Even in states like Peru and Bolivia, where Indians were a large majority at the time of independence, national identity crystallized around the creole culture which dominated the authoritative institutions. Through the mestization process, to which we will return, the Hispanic cultural pattern continuously incorporated broader elements of the population. Thus, the enlargement of the political arena and entry of new strata of the populace into conscious participation did not threaten the cultural basis of the nation-state—rather the contrary. The only politically significant form of cultural pluralism in Latin America has been regionalism.[18]

17. This point is well developed by George M. Foster, *Culture and Conquest* (Chicago: Quadrangle Books, 1967).

18. For a useful summary of the state-forming period, see William W. Pierson and Federico G. Gil, *Governments of Latin America* (New York: McGraw-Hill, 1957), pp. 34-159.

Antilles society under British and French rule developed along quite different lines. The early emergence of sugar as a high-value plantation crop and early demise of the sparse Indian population quickly led to the creation of slave societies, with huge African majorities. In Haiti, the White planter minority was eliminated in the Black revolution from 1794-1804, and an explicitly Black state formed. Elsewhere, slavery was abolished before the greatly feared servile insurrections overwhelmed the plantation colonies. In Trinidad and Guyana, a further dimension of pluralism was added through the importation of indentured East Indian labor to replace the freed Africans, who in many cases preferred to eke out peasant subsistence on poor, unused land rather than to remain in the low-wage plantation economy. In contrast to the incorporative processes at work on the Latin American mainland, the changes ensuing from the end of the slave plantation system led in the West Indies to the reinforcement of racial segmentation, with Whites, Blacks—and where they were present, East Indians—becoming closed communities.[19] The maintenance of a loose colonial overrule for more than a century after the abolition of slavery permitted the consolidation of the racial stratification which had its roots in the initial plantation system. Under British tutelage, the state institutions were oriented to the colonial-settler culture. The transition to independence in the Antilles came less on the basis of irresistible nationalist demands than through an overall postwar commitment to decolonization forced by events elsewhere. Representative institutions had a long history (indeed, Barbados has the oldest assembly in the Western hemisphere), but, needless to say, these assemblies were based upon very limited franchise and were dominated by the White segment. After World War II, the British tried to regroup all the Caribbean possessions into a West Indian Federation. However, despite the constitutional ingenuity which went into this creation, the habits and associations which had developed during the centuries of separate colonial administration of the various units which were regrouped in the federation were too strong. Decolonization on the basis of universal suffrage necessarily resulted in accession to power of the numerically preponderant racial segment, inheriting the institutional structures of the divisions of colonial administration.

The contours of colonialism in Asia were shaped more closely by the existence of historic states. Burma, Cambodia, and Vietnam had well-established political identities, although the colonial territories incorporated fringe areas such as Upper Burma or mountain areas of Vietnam where the historic states had exercised only loose suzerainty at best.

19. Philip D. Curtin gives thorough treatment to the pattern of closure of racial communities which occurred at the critical moment of abolition of slavery in Jamaica, in *Two Jamaicas* (Cambridge: Harvard University Press, 1955.)

Laos was a series of principalities, which in the nineteenth century was coming under growing control of the expanding Thai and Vietnamese kingdoms; had a modern state system emerged without Western colonial intervention, it is quite likely that Laos would not exist. As it is, the majority of ethnic Lao live in northeastern Thailand and constitute less than half the population in Laos itself.[20] But French expansion from its Vietnamese and Cambodia base pre-empted the Thai and loosely incorporated Laos in the Indochinese framework. Although some efforts were made by the French to promote an Indochinese state, the divergent traditions of the historic entities of Vietnam and Cambodia were too strong—and Laos, as a residual category, was also launched on its own. Thailand and Persia, although not superpowers, had sufficient integrity and capacity as historic states to inhibit the kind of cost-free conquest which was the favorite mode of imperial expansion. Afghanistan, although lacking the history of centralized rule of Thailand or Persia, was sufficiently remote and turbulent to escape occupation by either Russia or Britain. After some costly fiascoes, the British abandoned desultory attempts in the mid-nineteenth century to expand the northwest frontier of India into Kabul, and Afghanistan was abandoned as a frontier buffer zone. Thus insulated, it gradually became a state. Polities like Persia, Thailand, Japan, and China that escaped direct colonial rule were faced with the defensive necessity of transforming themselves from historic kingdoms into modern states.

India, Indonesia, and the Philippines were somewhat different cases. India was not conquered as a single state; rather British expansion occurred piecemeal from the three footholds of Calcutta, Bombay, and Madras, initially under the mercantile auspices of the East India Company. By the eighteenth century, Portuguese and French competitors had been confined to small coastal enclaves. The Mughal empire was in decomposition when British mercantile-political forces expanded inland, although until 1835 East India Company agents operated in the shadow of the imperial symbol; but the British raj was not a lineal descendent of the Mughal ruler. The strongest Indian kingdoms as British penetration gained momentum at the end of the eighteenth century were Maharasthra and Mysore; by 1818, both of these had been defeated. By stages, the mercantile dynasty of the East India Company became officially the imperial domain of the British raj, with the final transfer in 1858. But its patchwork expansion over the Indian subcontinent involved very differential degrees of incorporation; one of the first pressing problems of independent India was the incorporation of 552 princely states, which covered one-third of the land area. But although no historic kingdoms

20. Nina S. Adams and Alfred W. McCoy, *Laos: War and Revolution* (New York: Harper & Row, 1970), pp. 3-66.

ever spread their domain over the entire area of contemporary India, the Indian past contained a rich lode of cultural commonalities which could form the basis of an intensely felt identification with Bharat Mata (Mother India), given eloquent expression by Nehru:

> It is fascinating to find how the Bengalis, the Marathas, the Gujuratis, the Tamils, the Andhras, the Oriyas, the Assamese, the Canarese, the Malayalis, the Sindhis, the Punjabis, the Pathans, the Kashmiris, the Rajputs, and the great central block compromising the Hindustani-speaking people, have retained their peculiar characteristics for hundreds of years, have still more or less the same virtues and failings of which old tradition or record tells us, and yet have been throughout these ages distinctively Indian, with the same national heritage and the same set of moral and mental qualities. . . . Ancient India, like ancient China, was a world in itself, a culture and a civilization which gave shape to all things. Foreign influences poured in and often influenced that culture and were absorbed . . . Some kind of a dream of unity has occupied the mind of India since the dawn of civilization.[21]

The framework of India was not, however, strong enough to contain Pakistan, compromising the Muslim-majority areas of northern British India. Sri Lanka, for some time administered as part of British India, was severed well before independence. Although for much of its history it contained several kingdoms and two main cultures, the island itself defined the state. Malaya, another outpost of empire which sprang from British dominion in India, was established through a series of treaties with autonomous sultanates. The common language and Muslim religion facilitated the ultimate coalescence of the Malay states into a territorial unit; pan-Malay nationalism also arose in part from the growing competition and sense of threat from the large Chinese immigrant community which developed in the nineteenth century.

Indonesia and the Philippines were both archipelagos united by common colonial conquest. The Dutch East India Company did bring under their control some important historical kingdoms, especially in Java. However, the political entity which became the object of nationalist identification was defined explicitly and exclusively by the boundaries eventually set by Dutch colonial rule. Reflecting this fact, on the one hand, was the single-minded determination of Indonesia to incorporate West Irian, pursued at the cost of an expensive rupture with the Dutch in 1957 and huge arms outlays. West Irian lay totally outside of the historical zone of the central core of Indonesia, and the vast majority of its population was of sharply different cultural and linguistic heritage. Yet the completion of Indonesia by the absorption of West Irian was an imperative for all shades of Indonesian political opinion. On the other hand, no claim has ever been advanced for the inclusion of the Portuguese territory of

21. Nehru, *Discovery of India*, p. 49.

Timor, despite its curious position as a colonial enclave in the archipelago. This contrasts with India's territorial self-concept: she insisted to a reluctant France that Pondicherry be evacuated, and finally dealt with intransigent Portugal by seizing Goa by force of arms; India was the subcontinent, not only British-ruled territory.

Prehispanic Philippines had the beginnings of centralized systems only in the southern reaches of the archipelago, which experienced initial contacts with Islamic and associated ideas of kingship. In the remainder of the islands, the Spanish encountered only village communities, with a number of major languages. However, the unusually extensive cultural influence of the colonizer, through the vehicle of Christian conversion and Hispanization of the elite, provided the basis for a distinctive Filipino identity, expressed in nationalist terms by the late nineteenth century.[22] The secondary layer of American colonial imprint was of particular import in the institutional legacy of competitive, if nearly identical, national parties, a largely Filipinized bureaucracy, and a high saliency of national electoral politics.

The state system in the Middle East is a product of the decomposition of the Ottoman empire, World War I diplomacy, and imperial whim. Morocco alone was beyond the Ottoman impact and has been a dynastic center since the eighteenth century; it and Egypt are the clear lineal descendants of virtually continuous historic states. Algeria, Tunisia, and Libya were provinces of the Ottoman empire, whose Turkish governors severed their ties with Istanbul. French occupation of Algeria greatly enlarged the scope of the territory and is largely responsible for the country's present identity. Tunisia has a rich history as a political center, extending back to Carthage—although its continuity as a state is less clear-cut. The identity of what is now Libya has gone through several permutations: as pirate lair, under the descendants of the Turkish beys; as colony; as precarious and impoverished UN-ward state, turned over in effect to the Senussiya Islamic order which had been a focus of anticolonial resistance; and as fervently religious, pan-Arabist military regime, heir to enormous wealth.

Sudan, in a curious way, owes its separate existence to one of the most successful primary resistance movements, the Mahdiya, which defeated General Gordon at Khartoum in 1885. When the British assumed political control over Egypt in 1882-83, Sudan was a part of it. However, in Sudan almost at once they were pushed out by the Mahdists. When an Anglo-Egyptian expeditionary force defeated and dismantled the Mahdist state in 1898, Sudan was established as a juridically separate territory, with

22. This process is well described in John L. Phelan, *The Hispanization of the Philippines: Spanish Aims and Filipino Resources, 1565-1700* (Madison: University of Wisconsin Press, 1959).

British rule exercised under the cloak of Anglo-Egyptian condominium. When Egypt recovered nominal independence in 1922, Sudan was not included. In the 1950s, when decolonization neared in Sudan, the British cast their lot with the anti-Egyptian wing of the nationalist movement; Sudan became independent as a wholly separate state.

In the Levant, the British government—or, more precisely, different representatives of the Crown—made wholly contradictory promises during World War I to the French, the Arab nationalists, and the Zionists. In the impossible effort to reconcile them, Syria and Lebanon were created as French mandates and Palestine, Jordan, and Iraq as British mandates—with Palestine given an ambiguous designation as Jewish homeland. In the Arabian peninsula, the Saud family, as the leaders of the Wahabi Islamic purification movement, succeeded in unifying most of the area as the Saudi-Arabian state. The Yemen Arab Republic ranks with Egypt and Morocco as a historical state of great antiquity, at times loosely tied to the Ottoman state. South Yemen, successor state to the Aden Protectorate, by contrast is an arbitrary amalgamation of the former entrepot and British naval base of Aden, highly politicized and a hinterland of nomadic tribes, wholly traditional.

Finally, along the Persian Gulf and Arabian Sea rimland of the Arabian peninsula are a series of microstates which, beginning in the nineteenth century, had accepted loose British "protection." As utterly traditional societies facing independence and development with unlimited resources, they are a wholly novel form of state. The independent states of Kuwait, Qatar, Bahrein, and Oman are principalities whose traditional institutions are likely to be drowned in a tidal wave of oil revenues. Seven other sheikhdoms were painfully stitched together under British patronage and became independent as the United Arab Emirates in 1971; as a federation of Sheikhs rather than states, this precarious polity is an exotic experiment.

Sub-Saharan Africa is the home of the artificial state. Arbitrary artifacts of the colonial partition, most African states have both the handicap of small size and the lack of any historical or cultural criteria for their boundaries. We may note that the pattern of colonial expansion was quite different from Asia. Until the last quarter of the nineteenth century, European interests in Africa were for the most part adequately served by the maintenance of coastal trading ports. Certainly the conduct of the slave trade required no occupation of the hinterland; African intermediaries served admirably. After the end of the slave commerce, most of Africa lacked the visible, immediately exploitable wealth which could excite mercantile appetites and was much too poor to be a significant market. But in the final two decades of the century, a veritable paroxysm of competitive expansion took place. France, after the humiliation of the Franco-Prussian war, sought restoration of national self-respect in empire-building. Germany, Italy, and Leopold II of Belgium appeared as aggressive new competitors for colonial territory; Britain and Portugal were not disposed to rest on their laurels. The machine gun and limited access to firearms of most African kingdoms gave a decisive advantage even to small European military expeditions. Adventurers on the spot, such as Cecil Rhodes or Carl Peters, were prone to initiate campaigns on their own authority, on the normally correct assumption that if they succeeded they would secure retroactive approval. Once well underway, the dialectic of partition generated its own momentum and halted only when, in 1911, every square inch of African territory, save Liberia and Ethiopia, had been placed under a European flag. With only minor adjustments afterwards, in particular the redistribution of German territories after World War I, the territorial divisions created by the partition became the basis for the present state system. Cameroon recovered a portion of the former German territory which had been attached to Nigeria. Somali nationalism was of sufficient force to bring about amalgamation of the British and Italian portions of its territory. Zanzibar became loosely stitched to Tanzania after the 1964 revolution. Rwanda and Burundi became independent separately, roughly within the bounds of the historic kingdoms, rather than united as they had been under Belgian mandate. France chose to devolve power upon the smaller territorial subdivisions, rather than the large administrative groups of A.O.F. and A.E.F. Otherwise the colonial grid was indissoluble.

Only a few African states deviate from the norm of purely capricious origin; these merit brief mention. South Africa was established in 1910 as a consolidation of four settler-dominated territories: Natal and Cape Colony, dominated by English immigrants, and Transvaal and Orange Free State, which were Afrikaner republics. Britain acquired sovereign title to three southern African enclaves—Lesotho, Swaziland, and Botswana—which were either emergent kingdoms (Lesotho and Swaziland) or culturally homogeneous areas (Botswana). They were slated for incorporation into South Africa until after World War II, when it became clear that the increasingly rigid racial policies practiced by Pretoria made this unfeasible. As lack of contiguity made amalgamation impractical, they became independent more or less in their historic form. Ethiopia had the good fortune to be in an ascendant phase of growth under King Menelik II during the crucial period of colonial partition. Aided by its relative remoteness and the disastrous defeat inflicted on an unusually large Italian expeditionary force in 1896, the kingdom was able to greatly expand its own boundaries and secure recognition as an independent state. Liberia and Sierra Leone were founded as coastal homes for freed slaves and places of deposit for illicit slave cargoes intercepted on the high seas after the traffic was banned. In each case, a hinterland was attached which had no relationship to the returned slaves, partly acculturated by their residence beyond seas.

TYPOLOGY OF CULTURAL BASES FOR STATES

To draw together what has been thus far outlined, we would propose an eight-fold classification of the state system in the developing world, which relates the historic origin and cultural basis for the state. These distinctions, we feel, are important in fixing the parameters of the state as political field for cultural pluralism. With this taxonomy sketched, we may then turn to the main patterns of cultural segmentation which may be encountered within the state.

A first set of states are distinguished by their historically arbitrary boundaries, the influx of a substantial body of immigrants from the colonial homeland or other European countries, and the transfer of sovereignty to the settler population. The national culture of the state is identified with the dominant immigrant group, which of course derives its identity and culture from the homeland but modifies it in response to the new environment of transplantation. Examples of the pattern are most Latin American states and South Africa. The latter case is distinguished from the former group by its denial of access to the participative institutions of the polity to the indigenous population, as well as non-European immigrants. Parenthetically, New Zealand, Australia, Canada, and the United States are also in this category, although not a primary focus of this study.

A second type is composed of states created by colonization but where power was transferred to numerically dominant immigrant groups of African or Asian provenience. The state has thus no historic derivation or cultural connections; in most such states the original population had either become extinct or dwindled to a very small minority. The institutions of the state are thus overwhelmingly identified by their colonial ancestry, though independence has reduced the political influence of the colonial settler community to very little. The social configuration is divided along racial lines; the cultural units of political conflict have tended to be Africans, East Indians, Amerindians, or Whites. Examples include Guyana, Jamaica, Barbados, Trinidad and Tobago, and Singapore.

A third, very special type, might be labelled homeland states. These are territories designated through the initial agency of external force to serve as homelands for diasporas. The diaspora group lacked the force and, above all, the status of a state actor to secure immigration rights for sufficient of their numbers to acquire political control over the homeland unit. However, they were able to secure and hold political power with the transfer of sovereignty. The state is strongly associated with the identity of the diaspora group which inherited its central institutions. Only two specimens now exist, Israel and Liberia. Sierra Leone as a colonial territory would have qualified, but the political formula for power transfer was founded on numbers, and the mechanism of universal suffrage elections decisively shifted power from the diaspora group—in this case, returned African slaves—to the indigenous elites. Israel, of course, is distinguished by the aggressive and active role played by the diaspora representatives, the Zionist movement, in the recruitment of immigrants and the seizure of power at the moment of British withdrawal.

A fourth set of states are entirely arbitrary colonial creations, without historic antecedents or sanction but where new territorial elites representing the populace within its boundaries have inherited power. These are the states which face the greatest challenge today in giving national content to the territorial institutions. Their shared historic memory is limited to the common experience of a single colonial ruler and the collective struggle to secure independence. Nation-building involves a dual imperative: to define a new cultural identity linked to the dimensions of the polity and related to commonalities among the polity's populace, while eschewing identification of the state with any one of the cultural segments within it, which would immediately threaten the identity of other collectivities. This is a very large category, especially in Africa. Among the many examples we may cite Nigeria, Zaire, Tanzania, Cameroon, Indonesia, the Philippines and Jordan.

Fifth comes a group of states created by colonialism but with a clearly defined cultural identity. A dominant pattern of communal solidarity suffuses the polity, even though it had not been previously expressed in the form of a state. The legitimation of the contemporary state therefore rests not simply on the fact of its existence as a colonial territory, but upon a will to nationhood which could be founded upon a cultural basis for community. At the same time, the territorial framework developed under colonial tutelage remains an important aspect of the state as political arena. Representative of this set are such states as Algeria, Syria, Iraq, India, and Sri Lanka. The existence of a dominant common culture at one level of identity does not, of course, imply there was no pluralism at other levels; such is present in all of the cases cited. But in, for example, India, an overarching layer of common culture composed of the richly diverse symbols of Hindu cosmology and history has had to adjust as best it can to the linguistic, caste, and religious cleavage.

A sixth category consists of historical states which predated colonial overrule but survived as polities through being utilized as units of colonial administration. In all cases, the traditional state was a monarchy. The colonial experience had the uniform result of diminishing the legitimacy of kingship. Where the monarchical institutions were nurtured and utilized to transmit colonial directives, kingship was relegated to the periphery of government, a position which only unusually skilled dependent princes could turn to their advantage. The colonial institutions of administration and justice provided structural alternatives to the king's servants. The eventual nationalist response also developed outside the monarchical frame, although not always in opposition to it. In some instances, the colonizer himself eliminated the ruling house: Libya, Madagascar, and Burma are examples. In many others, the monarchy was destroyed by the nationalist movement, either before or not long after independence: cases in point are Tunisia, Rwanda, Burundi, Egypt, and Vietnam. In a few places, the monarchy succeeded in relating itself to nationalism and political change—or colonial overrule had been so slight in its impact that royal prestige had been little eroded. In this category fall Morocco, Swaziland, Kuwait, Oman, Qatar, and Nepal.

Seventh comes a small group of historic states who escaped formally organized colonialism. Most had their share of near escapes and even, in cases like Ethiopia and Iran, brief military occupations. But they never became sufficiently incorporated in the colonial orbit for their historic continuity to be ruptured by external force or their institutions to be dismantled by outside agency. In these states, the links between past and present are strongest—certainly in cultural identity, usually in institutional form. The kingly form of rule in the polity has not always survived; China has utterly transformed her historic state structures in two revolutionary stages. Absolute sovereignty of the monarchy was overthrown in Thailand in 1932; in Japan, the emperor's role has dwindled to well-delimited symbolic functions. In Iran, Afghanistan, and Ethiopia, the monarchy has played a far more central role and is closely linked to a core cultural tradition, which thus becomes inseparable from the state.

Finally, an eighth category is composed of states which were established out of the wreckage of colonialism by cultural self-definition. This is the sole group which is a true parallel to the polities which came into being in central and eastern Europe after World War I on the basis of the doctrine of a national self-determination. State-forming nationalities have been exceedingly rare in the third world—and indeed qualifications are required for each of the three cases we would cite. Pakistan was created through the successful assertion of the premise that Muslims in India constituted, not a religious minority, but a nation. The Muslim nation, of course, was in contrapuntal distinction to the preponderant Hindu culture in British

India, and its boundaries were defined by Muslim-majority zones in the colonial domain. Somalia was the fusion of two colonial territories, both of which were almost exclusively populated by Somalis. But only the powerful sanction of the sense of common nationality could have brought these two separately administered territories together. The force of Somalihood as a state-forming idea is also reflected in the remarkable fact that, despite the historical artificiality of most state units in the third world, Somalia is the base for virtually the only culturally based irredentist movement. Active demand for incorporation of Somali-inhabited areas of eastern Ethiopia, northeast Kenya, and the French-ruled Territory of the Afars and Issa (renamed from French Somaliland as an explicit rebuff to Somali nationalism) became dormant in the late 1960s but revived in early 1973. Saudi-Arabia was built around the common core of desert Arab nomadic culture and the Wahabite Islamic purification movement. Monarchy, represented by the Saud family, was the secular arm of the Wahabites as agency of polity.

CATEGORIES OF CULTURAL DIVERSITY

To complete the taxonomic matrix suggestive of the range of diversity in the developing world, we need to add to the typology of bases for the state a second set of categories which derive from the underlying cultural plurality of the society defined by the state boundaries. To accomplish this, a six-fold division will serve:

1. Homogenous societies
2. Single clearly dominant groups, numerically and socially with minorities
3. Core culture, linked to central institutions, with differentiated groups in the peripheral zones
4. Dominant bipolar pattern
5. Multipolar pattern, with no dominant groups
6. Multiplicity of cultures, with more than one basis of differentiation (ethnic, religious, caste and race)

Let us give brief elaboration to each of these categories.

The truly homogeneous polity in Asia, Africa and Latin America is a deviant case. Even in some polities where a highly developed sense of nationality exists, an important element of cultural pluralism may subsist. Thus in China, despite the intensity of feeling and the powerful historical traditions on which Chinese nationalism rests, outlying non-Han minorities are numerically, if not politically, significant (such as Tibetans, Mongols, Turkic peoples of the western frontier regions, Thai-related groups of the southern mountains). In Taiwan, a sharp distinction exists between the Chinese of the postwar flight from the mainland and the Chinese of migrations in earlier centuries. In Somalia, powerful as Somali nationalism was in state-forming and irredentism, Somali politics flowed around the vivacity of cultural identities from the two major eponymous ancestries of Sab and Samale and the great clanic divisions of Digil, Rahanwin, Dir, Isaq, Hawiye, and Darod.[23] Examples of polities which may be considered as culturally homogeneous include Uruguay, Costa Rica, Botswana, Tunisia, Bahrein, Qatar, Barbados, Lesotho, Japan and the two Koreas.

In the second category, we include societies where one cultural group is present in sufficient numerical preponderance and sociological weight to clearly dominate the territory. However, other groups are also present, whose relationship with the dominant group situates them in the distinctive role status as minorities. Cases of this type include Jamaica, Cuba, Algeria, Morocco, Iraq, Rwanda (since the 1959 revolution), Sri Lanka, and Mauritania.

A third group, closely related to the second, is composed of polities containing cultural groups lying at the central core of the system, with outlying differentiated identities. The distinction from the second category lies in the linkage of the core culture with the historic institutional frame of the state, which is suffused with the symbols and attachments of this politically dominant identity. In many instances, the core culture is not numerically preponderant; its hegemony is based upon its centrality and not its sheer numerical weight. Other groups lie on the periphery, not only geographically, but generally socially and politically. In this set are found Latin American states such as Peru, Bolivia, Ecuador, and Guatemala, where Hispanic culture is the basis of the nation but where substantial unincorporated Indian populations remain, Sudan, Ethiopia, Iran, Thailand, Burma, Cambodia, Laos, and both Vietnams.

A fourth group of states may be defined by a single, bipolar cultural division. The very simplicity of conflict in such contexts renders it peculiarly difficult to manage; latent within the bipolar structure is the constant risk of total polarization of conflict. Cyprus is perhaps the extreme prototype—a polity frozen between disintegration and communal civil war only by the continuing intervention of the international system, in the form of a United Nations buffer force. Malaysia, Burundi, and Guyana are other clear examples.

23. The importance of clans in postindependence Somalia has been extensively documented in the abundant writings of I. M. Lewis; see inter alia Arthur Hazelwood (ed.), *African Integration and Disintegration* (London: Oxford University Press, 1967), pp. 256-75; I. M. Lewis, "The Politics of the 1969 Somali Coup," *Journal of Modern African Studies*, X, no. 3 (October 1972), 383-408.

A fifth set, particularly characteristic of the African scene, contains states with a single type of cultural cleavage, normally ethnic but with at least three, and often many, identity groups in the political arena. Multiplicity of cultures almost necessarily means removing the state itself from the cultural arena and preserving its institutions in a status of neutrality, distinct from any of the component cultures. Most sub-Saharan African states fall into this category; so also, on the basis of religious diversity, would Lebanon, Syria, and (North) Yemen.

Finally, we have a small array of states where cultural diversity is determined along more than one axis of differentiation. India is the model entry: religion, caste, and language provide interlocking, interacting, but distinctively separate bases for politically relevant identity groups. Here the sheer complexity of divisions creates a situation akin to that argued by group theorists and conflict analysis of the Simmel school where cross-cutting affiliations and cleavage may facilitate integration.[24] Examples include, in addition to India, Indonesia, Nigeria, and Uganda.

Let us again offer, by way of summary, a propositional inventory of our main concerns in this chapter. (1) The nation-state system into which the globe is divided is an extremely powerful normative concept, which profoundly affects the self-image and orientations of political elites throughout the world. (2) The nation-state with its territorial imperative and theoretically absolute sovereignty defines the arena in which cultural pluralism operates. (3) The paradigm of the nation-state prescribes as norm the vocation of unity for the populace contained in its frontiers. (4) Dominant concepts of the role of the third world nation-state, such as "development" and "socialism," greatly increase the scope of its activity. (5) Greater material, technological, communications, and military capabilities are sharply increasing the power of the state. (6) The postwar international system operates to maintain the existing territorial pattern of state organization. (7) The successful revolt of a cultural segment within an independent state to achieve political sovereignty is extremely rare in the contemporary world. (8) The third world state system is largely the outcome of the imperial partition of the globe during the age of European expansion. We have then suggested a taxonomic recapitulation of types of nation-states and patterns of pluralism within them. State and society, as culturally defined, form the two ends of our analytical field. In the interaction between the cultural basis of the state and the pattern of cultural pluralism in the society may be discerned the shape and nature of communal conflict.

24. George Simmel, *Conflict* (Glencoe: The Free Press, 1955).

4 Patterns of Identity Change and Cultural Mobilization

The Vanniya Kula Kshatriyas who till now were proverbially considered to be backward in education have made long strides in a short space of time and have come almost on a level with other communities . . . , [but] the community has not realized its deserving status in society . . . A cursory view of the book will show every reader how many a desirable fruit of the community was veiled by the leaves . . . , will stimulate the younger generation to greater deeds and will fill the hearts of the older with just pride in the achievements of the community."

—Graduates and Diploma Holders among
the Vanniya Kula Kshatriya, 1952[1]

Cultural identity, the very element of analysis in this study, is itself subject to constant flux and change. In this chapter, we will examine some of the more important patterns of change in more detail. With the greater net of interaction at both individual and group levels which accompanies the modernization process overall, an intensifying process of social competition ensues. Actors as individuals and members of identity groups seek to improve their material well-being. At the same time, newly acquired economic and political resources are utilized to raise social status. Changes of scale occur through the increased salience of the nation-state entity, in its varying cultural definitions, and visibility of a wider range of reference groups against which the adequacy of one's level of prosperity and status may be measured. Many of the roles through which this competitive dialectic occurs are, of course, not related to cultural pluralism. However, in important respects collective cultural identities, constantly redefined, are role resources through which actors relate to and participate in the social fray.

HOPE RISING: GROUP SOLIDARITY IN SOCIAL PROMOTION

In 1942, a group of young men—aspirant, mobility conscious—in Idoma division of Northern Nigeria founded an association to advance

1. Quoted in Rudolph, *The Modernity of Tradition*, p. 53

their collective ambitions. Its goals included the unity of the Idoma people, an effective representation of their needs, and a halt to the influx of Ibo settlers on Idoma lands. The name they chose for their association gave perfect expression to its role and context—the Idoma Hope Rising Union.[2] Hope Rising is rich in connotations: hitherto unperceived opportunities, expectations which have new points of social reference. The colloquial vocabulary of social change offers many synonyms. In Iboland, local communities viewed their goal as "getting up."[3] Many African ethnic associations entitled themselves "improvement unions." In India, the keyword was "uplift." Whatever the label, the theme was the same: through group effort and solidarity, a life more abundant and status befitting.

Neither mobility nor status is evenly distributed in a society. Collective labels for conceptualizing inequality are in many contexts devoid of cultural referents—nobility, aristocracy, bourgeoisie, upper class. But in plural societies, uneven distribution of social, economic or political resources is frequently defined, both in objective reality and subjective perception, in terms of the communal segments. In extreme cases, such as the Indian caste system or the South African racial oligarchy, cultural hierarchy is extensively ritualized and invested with religious sanction or comprehensively formulated in law and institutions. More often, the relative well-being of one group serves as a reference point and aspiration level for another.

Status is not defined only by economic criteria. Control of ritual or symbols of high standing may create its own hierarchy. The historical preeminence of the Brahman varna in the Indian caste system was associated with their priestly function and monopoly of the most sacred domains. In many traditional settings in Africa, a given group attained cultural hegemony through validating as social premise superior control over the incorporeal universe—be it rain-making, powerful charms, or other forms of *baraka*. Arabic culture attained a unique standing through its association with the liturgy and scripture of Islam. The Catholic religion played a comparable role in sanctioning the superordinate place of Hispanic culture with relations to Indian groups in colonial Latin America.

In the contemporary world, the enlargement of social horizons, intensification of interactions through urbanization, widening communications networks, and political competition have increased the number and salience of reference groups. Hope Rising, but how? through what roles? by what means? In the efforts of individuals and groups to

2. Alvin Magid describes the rise and fall of the IHRU in Melson and Wolpe, *Nigeria: Modernization and the Politics of Communalism*, pp. 345-59.

3. The idea of "getting up" is well described by Victor C. Uchendu, in *The Igbo of Southeast Nigeria* (New York: Holt, Rinehart and Winston, 1965), pp. 34-36.

answer these questions we touch one of the most sensitive nerves of the cultural pluralism system.

Many individuals seek their response entirely outside the framework of whatever set of cultural segments they may identify with; we need to keep constantly in mind the fundamentally multifaceted nature of social mobility and competition. However, within our analytical field falls the very important set of responses which come through culturally defined roles. In this sphere, we may note both individual and collective pathways. The individual may alter his status, in certain circumstances, by shifting his identification from a low status cultural segment to one enjoying a higher rank. The ambitious Mayan in Guatemala, by donning Western dress and adopting Spanish as his means of communication, may become a Ladino (mestizo of Hispanic culture). At the small group level, Islamicized clans on the fringes of the Arab cultural sphere could rework their genealogical mythology to adduce an ancestral link to Arabia, and in so doing become Arabs. Oral traditions of many groups give unmistakable evidence of identity changes made necessary by migration or conquest.

Where incorporation is not possible, individuals and groups may seek to raise their status by emulation of traits identified with higher status communities. Within the colonial context, persons adopted the dress and language of the colonizer. In extreme form, exemplified by the Straits Chinese of Singapore, this extended to the total adoption of English language, dress, and Victorian mores. More often, the emulation was selective and partial.

The challenge of perceived cultural stratification could also be met through competitive devices. Certainly this was the choice of the Idoma Hope Rising Union. The critical resources required for mobility could be identified: education, preservation of land rights, access to government service, entry to trade. Awareness of group identity could be enlarged and mobilized; a sense of relative disadvantage could be generalized to galvanize the social energies of the collectivity in response.

These, then, are some of the patterns we wish to explore in the pages that follow. Through examination of the diversity of process, we hope to delineate some of the determinants of cultural strategies of uplift and change. Overall, we may discern two very general situation-response sets. On the one hand, where a rigidly established pattern of cultural hierarchy exists, improvement may be possible only within its frame. This implies either redefinition of the group in terms of the values governing the hierarchy, so that the group may alter its relative rank within it, or incorporation into a group of higher standing. If, on the other hand, no strong societal consensus on cultural hierarchy exists, then group uplift may be efficaciously pursued by mobilization of communal identity, reinforcement of differentiation, and cumulation of economic, social, and political resources to alter the distribution of advantage. These points are best argued through a series of sustained illustrations, drawn both from hierarchical and competitive contexts.

GROUP MOBILITY WITH CULTURAL STRATIFICATION

We turn first to situations characterized by cultural stratification. The Indian caste system is an irresistible example. Uplift here may be sought through the process of Sanskritization, to which reference was made in chapter 2. As Srinivas has argued, there has always been some movement within the caste structure; a subcaste which acquires a level of economic well-being incongruent with its social standing can ultimately alter its status ranking; over a period of time resources in one domain can be translated into others.[4] In practice, the effective reference benchmark indicating the trail to upward caste mobility is the locally dominant caste.[5]

In order to make the process clear, two well-documented cases may be recounted in brief synopsis, the Nadars of Tamilnad (former Madras) in south India and the Konds in Orissa state in the northeast. The Nadars, formerly known as Shanans, were at the onset of colonial rule toddy tappers, an occupation deemed to pollute its practitioners. They extracted the sap from palmyra palms, converting it into raw sugar or distilling it into sweet or fermented toddy. Defiled by their function, they were situated by varna theory below the Sudra category, though above some even more polluted castes.[6] Among the ritual disabilities prescribed by this low rank were exclusion from temples to deities associated with Brahmans, denial of use of wells of higher castes, maintenance of a prescribed physical distance from Brahmans, and appearing bare-breasted before higher castes.

Changes associated with the colonial regime offered new social resources to the Nadars. Christian conversion, chosen by many, offered a partial escape from low status, although not easily enforceable in everyday social relationships in the rural community—but it could affect self-concept. No ritual inhibitions restricted entry into extending trade networks, and Nadars became an important commercial group. One of the first overt challenges to their status ranking in the nineteenth century came when Nadar women adopted clothing associated with higher castes. High caste

4. T. S. Epstein, though she feels Srinivas has oversold Sanskritization, offers some detailed evidence on the process at the local level in *Economic Development and Social Change in South India* (Manchester: Manchester University Press, 1962), pp. 128-32, 158-65.

5. Srinivas, *Caste in Modern India*, pp. 9-10.

6. See the discussion of caste in chapter 2 for a description of the varna system.

hostility to this impertinent violation of hierarchy norms led to a major riot in 1858 and a government-imposed compromise permitting breast-cloths provided they were different from those worn by higher castes.

By the latter part of the nineteenth century, Nadar jatis (subcastes) were becoming mobilized over wider areas and asserting their claims to higher status on a broad front. They sought to force entry to temples from which they were excluded. Marriage ceremonies copied aspects of higher caste ritual. They asserted the right to wear the sacred thread symbolic of the three twice-born varnas and recruited less prosperous Brahman priests to tend to their ritual needs. Pamphlets began to appear setting forth historical claims to Kshatriya status; for the 1901 census, in which a thorough effort was made to establish an official register of caste hierarchies, a special volume was prepared claiming that Nadars were the first settlers and former rulers of southern India.

It should be stressed that Sanskritization was not the only strategy available to the Nadars. Especially in the twentieth century, Westernization and the political arena offered supplementary channels for communal uplift, both of which were effectively used. A first effort to found a Nadar caste association failed in 1895, but in 1910 the Nadar Mahajana Sangam was successfully launched. Its official statement of associational goals clearly reveals its recognition of group advantage through westernization:

...to promote the social, material, and general welfare of the Nadars; to protect and promote the interests and rights of the community; to take practical measures for the social, moral, and intellectual advancement of the Nadars, to start schools and colleges for imparting western education to Nadar children and to help poor but deserving pupils belonging to the community with scholarships, books, fees, etc.; to encourage and promote commercial and industrial enterprise among the members of the community; the raising of funds by subscription, donation or other means for the above objects, and the doing of all such things as are incidental and conducive to the attainment of the above objects or any of them.[7]

The rise of modern political competition offered another mobility resource for the Nadars. They were active participants in the non-Brahman movement which became increasingly important in Madras after World War I; the ideology of this movement directly challenged the legitimacy of the stratification pattern imposed by Hindu culture. The expansion of suffrage was the death knell of Brahman social and political hegemony in Madras. In 1940, formerly Brahman-dominated Tamilnad Congress gave recognition of this shift of political gravity in the choice of a Nadar, Kamaraj Nadar, as provincial president. Participation in electoral politics as a relatively cohesive and numerically significant bloc yielded signif-

---

7. *Rules and Regulations of the Nadar Mahajana Sabha, Madurai,* quoted in Rudolph and Rudolph, *Modernity of Tradition,* p. 45.

icant advantages. Today, the Nadars are recognized as an "advanced" community—a status reversal accomplished over the past century through horizontal mobilization of group solidarity, challenge to servile traditional ascription through ritual transformation, effective utilization of modern opportunity through education and commerce, and skillful communal exploitation of the political arena. In the judgment of the Rudolphs, "Nadars . . . have breached the pollution barrier, changed their rank within traditional society, and occupy an important place in the modern society of Madras and India."[8]

The Kond are a hill people in Orissa state, whose Kui language is related to the south Indian Dravidian group. For centuries they lived in uneasy and conflicted symbiosis with various Oriya states of the plains, whose rulers tried with indifferent success to extend their authority over the hill Konds. The Oriyas did establish some military colonies in the hills and a loose political hegemony. These relationships were defined in caste terms, with the Konds being partially absorbed into the Hindu cultural sphere as a distinctive caste ranked below the warrior caste of Oriyas, who were socially dominant among the settlers. Although Konds generally respected the outward ritualized norms of deference toward the Oriya warriors, they never fully accepted their subordination—claiming privately they had once been warriors but had been tricked into submission by treacherous Oriya.

By about 1855, colonial administration had been firmly established in the Kond hill area. With regularized administrative control came more continuous relationships between Konds and Oriyas; the Konds became more firmly linked as subordinates to Oriya institutions. At the same time, the government undertook some measures to protect Konds from Oriya exploitation, through opening the area by road and the introduction of schools. Since independence, special consideration has been given the Konds through such "uplift" facilities as scholarship quotas and job reservation. Throughout, Konds and Oriya have been treated administratively as clearly separate categories. In some respects, the economic distinctiveness of the Konds—and thus the particularity of their communal interests—has increased. Konds shunned trade and have remained cultivators; commerce was monopolized by Oriyas and a low caste group within the Kond community. Thus Konds are united as producers against the Oriya traders.

To compete effectively in the changing sociopolitical arena, Konds have had to simultaneously assert their own cultural identity and yet transform it to conform to the dominant Oriya model operative within the Orissa state political arena. Universal suffrage has been a distinct

8. Ibid., p. 47. The account of Nadar mobility is based upon the Rudolph data, pp. 36-49; and Robert L. Hardgrave, *The Nadars of Tamilnad* (Berkeley: University of California Press, 1969).

asset for the Konds. By maximizing horizontal solidarity the numerical weight of the Kond influence is optimized, compelling political parties to cultivate Konds by responding to their interests as a community. A Kond association, the Kui Samaj, has been active in recent years; it has been preoccupied with regulation of caste ritual and its upgrading by emulation of the dominant Oriya castes. At the same time, it has been valuable as a communal spokesman in state politics. F. G. Bailey gives cogent summation to the process:

> . . . organizations like the Kui Samaj, which start with the object of improving group status with their neighbors and in their own locality, continue and even intensify these cultural activities when they move into the larger political scene. In order to compete effectively and to command respect the Konds, being very much in a minority in the new arena, must take on Oriya culture and try to become the cultural equals of the Oriyas. Just as they have to learn the Oriya language, so also they have to learn Oriya etiquette.[9]

Another example of this process, although in this instance met with frustration, is provided by the Coloured population in South Africa. This racial category had its genesis in the sexual gratification sought by European settlers clustering around the Cape station of the Dutch East India Company, beginning in 1652, from women of the African groupings then inhabiting the Cape area, who were given the collective labels of "Hottentots" and "Bushmen" by the immigrants. To this was added a slave population recruited in West Africa. Madagascar, East Africa, Ceylon, India, and Malaya; again there were frequent irregular unions of European men and slave women. To these were added an additional influx of mainly Javanese immigrants, some indentured, many political deportees. Over the three centuries following foundation of the Cape station, Hottentots and Bushmen disappeared as organized societies, fusion of these disparate groups proceeded, Afrikaans became the mother tongue of most (and English for the remainder), and the group became a distinctive racial category as Coloureds. The category's group characteristics and identity solidified, and it became largely endogamous. As a crystallized racial community, until recently the dominant White society served as its cultural reference point; Coloureds sought status through emulative self-improvement, which was designed to bring about equality with Whites.

However, unlike the Nadars and Konds, the Coloureds found themselves progressively removed from the political arena. Before the foundation of the Union of South Africa, Coloured males in Cape Colony had equal voting rights with Whites, although franchise restrictions were

9. F. G. Bailey, *Tribe, Caste, and Nation* (Manchester: Manchester University Press, 1960), p. 190. Material for this description of Kond transformation is drawn from the Bailey study, pp. 157-92.

weighted in favor of Europeans. Since the independence of South Africa in 1910, Coloured political rights deteriorated, with a particularly steep decline after the accession of the Nationalist Party regime in 1948. Even as late as 1956, when the Nationalist government implemented its pledge to remove Coloured voters from the common roll, the Coloured vote was influential in nearly half the Cape constituencies and decisive in seven of the fifty-five. Coloured leaders vigorously fought the series of measures to legally entrench a status distinct from Europeans.

Even in the conflict-ridden, rigid racial-caste structure which has taken form in twentieth-century South Africa, both on the White and Coloured side arguments are on occasion advanced for a cultural strategy of amalgamation. The 1.5 million Coloureds are approximately 10 percent of the population. The argument runs that Coloureds as a cultural amalgam have fundamentally adopted European language and culture. Whites could thus partly redress the numerical imbalance by adding the Coloured 10 percent to the European 20 percent. For the politically dominant Afrikaners, an additonal benefit follows from the use of Afrikaans by nearly 90 percent of the Coloureds. However, the racial ideology of the Nationalist Party has never permitted such a tactic but has rather hedged Coloured status with increasing disabilities. The only meaningful cultural strategy under these circumstances for the Coloured community is to move toward political solidarity with other nonwhite groups, especially the African majority. This relationship too has its ambiguities; from the "Hope Rising" era of Coloured identity, when upward movement seemed possible, they had been keen to maintain the distinctions which separated them from the African majority and to stress their purportedly more "advanced" standing. In a culturally stratified system, status is affirmed not only by emulative advance up the rungs of the ladder but also by emphasis on traits which separate the group from those lying below.[10]

GROUP MOBILITY THROUGH INCORPORATION

An alternative to collective promotion through some form of Sanskritization is the incorporation of subordinate groups, either as individuals or as collectivities. An interesting example lies in the disappearance in the Arab world of the very large number of African slaves who have been absorbed into Arab societies. Leon Carl Brown advances the estimate that during the Middle Ages some 20,000 African slaves a year were transported across the Sahara and sold in the Mahgreb. However, they

10. Leonard M. Thompson, *The Republic of South Africa* (Boston:Little, Brown and Co. 1966), pp. 30-36; Leo Marquard, *The Peoples and Policies of South Africa* (3rd ed.; London: Oxford University Press, 1962), pp. 74-85.

were not placed in a plantation style economy, where as in the Western hemisphere their initial ethnic attachments would undergo metamorphosis into racial identity. Rather, they were attached to households and thus were atomized individuals. Although they had in common their place at the bottom of the social scale, they were unable to gain cohesion as a community or gain recognition as a collectivity. The integrative mechanisms of Arabization and Islam ultimately completed the task. Progeny were raised as Arabs and Muslims, and color consciousness, though not totally absent, never objectified the group as a racial collectivity.[11]

In a folk society, individuals cannot exist apart from a community. Incorporative mechanisms are invariably available to cope with a certain number of individuals who may attach themselves to a new local community. Sometimes persons were added to the community through warfare and enslavement; others in rebellion against their group of origin might accept voluntary dependency. Within the kinship frame of most little communities, secure incorporation was achieved through integration, fictive or real, into one of the constituent lineages.

Aidan Southall has carefully documented the process by which the Alur community in a traditional, rural setting in Uganda and northeast Zaire steadily enlarged itself through incorporating a number of groups over which it assumed overrule.[12] Alur rule was established through a series of chiefly patrilineages, bearing the title of Lwoo, who moved gradually from a southern Sudan point of dispersion. Although not a highly centralized system, Alur chiefs were nonetheless able to obtain a largely peaceful recognition of suzerainty through services of governance they were able to provide. Alur rulers established the useful reputation of having influence with rainfall, a life-giving power which was no small asset for any agricultural community. Their charisma extended to power over another deeply threatening part of the supernatural domain, the witches and evil spirits who are responsible for illness, misfortune, and death. In Southall's words, "a chief's superiority over and immunity to witchcraft was the supreme demonstration of his personal and supernatural qualification to rule."[13] The dominant Alur lineages greatly augmented their numbers by a unidirectional intermarriage pattern; Alur men married large numbers of women from dependent groups, whereas Alur women were denied to subordinate communities. A gradual process of cultural Alurization transpired over a few generations, as incorporation became

11. Leon Carl Brown, "Color in Northern Africa," *Daedulus*, XCVI, no. 2 (special issue on *Color and Race*), 463-88.

12. For the full detail, see Aidan Southall, *Alur Society* (Cambridge: Heffers and Sons, 1956). A brief summary of this aspect is given in his contribution to Cohen and Middleton, *From Tribe to Nation in Africa*, pp. 71-92.

13. Ibid., p. 84.

institutionalized. Languages of dependent communities first absorbed many Alur words and then tended to disappear entirely. Some distinctions were preserved; a sense of superiority on the part of the noble Alur patrilineage, as well as a preservation in oral legend of separate origin even among groups which appeared entirely Alurized. Colonial administration arrested the gradual extension of Alur domains, and in the Belgian case a number of groups were assiduously dissociated from the Alur by the removal of Alur chiefs. But where incorporation was sufficiently advanced to pre-empt unscrambling, Alur identity has become consolidated. Particularly in the context of interactions in a social or political arena with other groups, incorporation was effectively accomplished.

The Kanuri state of Bornu in northeastern Nigeria reflects the somewhat different context of a relatively centralized traditional kingdom. The Kanuri constituted the cultural core of the kingdom and the ruling nobility; however, the rule of Bornu state extended over many non-Bornu groups. Politically subordinated groups were placed under the fiefdom of a Bornu Kanuri noble, who used one of his clients to directly supervise the headman. The Kanuri overseer participated in the designation of local leaders and arbitration of local disputes. Through this clientage system, groups were first brought within the Kanuri political order. Over a period of time, sedentary groups tended gradually to enter the Kanuri cultural orbit as well, even while retaining some sense of distinctiveness. As in the Alur case, the saliency of cultural stratification was in no way comparable to the Indian caste system or South African racial cleavage. But Kanuri culture was associated with a powerful kingdom. It was related to a broader religious community through Islam and to a world of trade through its commercial caravans. Power naturally transmutes into cultural prestige. Becoming Kanuri was, for dependent ethnic groups, a means of moving closer to the sources of power. The two groups within the Bornu state who steadfastly maintained their own identity were the Fulani and Shuwa Arabs; they were politically, but never culturally, incorporated. In part, this may be attributed to the greater difficulty of incorporating pastoral nomads and the tightly knit solidarity of migrant transhumant communities. But the Fulani and Shuwa Arabs had in common a prior conversion to Islam and a strong conviction of cultural superiority. Identity change is attractive only for the social advantages presumed to accrue; it is an implicit acknowledgment of a higher prestige inhering in the assimilating culture.[14]

Another interesting incorporative pattern may be observed among the Fur, of western Sudan. The Fur are found mainly in a mountain area; nomadic Arabs dominate the plains of Darfur province. The Fur are in

14. Ronald Cohen, in ibid., pp. 150-74.

contact with Arabic culture along several axes. For many decades, they have been in relation, sometimes hostile, with the nomadic Arab groups who move back and forth along the southern fringe of the desert. From them, the Fur acquired Islam, a religion whose prestige is associated with the Arabs. Secondly, in the small trading and administrative towns of Darfur, Arab culture tends to predominate; here one encounters administrators, teachers, and traders carrying an urban Arab culture, as well as Arab townsmen recruited from the nearby nomadic groups. Thirdly, the main alternative to rural life is migration either to the tri-city conurbation at the junction of the White and Blue Nile (Khartoum, Khartoum North, and Omdurman), or the Gezira cotton scheme. In either case, the migrant enters an overwhelmingly Arab cultural zone. Finally, in dealings with the state—through the school system or the local administration—the Fur encounter a structure whose medium is Arabic. Fur culture, thus, is local, rural, parochial, poor, culturally impoverished. Fur language has at least six major dialects and has not enjoyed loving nurture at the hands of missionaries or administrators—nor has it been valued by its own intellectuals. Arabic is associated with superior force, a religion of great prestige, social and economic modernization opportunities through school or urban migration, and the majesty and power of the modern state. Thus, there should be little surprise in noting a striking pattern of linguistic incorporation. Arabic is accepted without question as the language of communication with any outsider. Arabic is the language of the town; it is the language of any dealing with government. Arabic is known in all the mountain fastnesses of Furland, but more in the foothills than in more remote areas. Command of Arabic is a fair measure of the internal distribution of social mobility opportunity among the Fur; men are far more likely than women to speak it, and young people more than older.[15]

The remarkable propensity of the Fur to Arabize is reflected in the 1956 census data, which indicated that of 96,775 Fur tabulated in greater Khartoum, only 240 listed themselves as Fur-speaking.[16] Peter McLoughlin, who made imaginative use of this census to study linguistic incorporation, well summarizes the forces reinforcing incorporation in the Khartoum context:

The non-Arabic speaker . . . must learn Arabic to retain his job, or perhaps to be employed in the first place. He might also need to learn Arabic to purchase commodities in the shops and markets, read legal notices that affect him, and so on. Social pressures are equally strong and take many forms, such as being snubbed or scorned for use of poor Arabic, for inability to converse about events

15. Bjorn Jernudd in Fishman, Ferguson, and Das Gupta, *Language Problems of Developing Nations*, pp. 167-81.

16. Peter F. M. McLoughlin, *Language-Switching as an Index of Socialization in the Republic of the Sudan* (Berkeley: University of California Press, 1964), p. 54.

and people, or to read newspapers or communicate with neighbors. If the language barrier is combined with other factors that denote lower status, such as very dark complexion, heavier facial features, nonobservance of Moslem dress or customs. . . .working at menial wage labor, and so on, then there is a nexus of interrelated pressures to conform, and learning Arabic is perhaps the fastest and easiest start on the road to social and economic acceptance.[17]

Thus the likelihood of incorporation is increased when a given culture enjoys pre-eminence on several axes of prestige. It occurs when the disparity between two cultures in power and social resources is so great that a competitive response is unlikely to be of avail. It is facilitated when upward mobility of the young and ambitious is advanced through incorporation and when there are few barriers to identity change. The aspirant young Fur can achieve identity as an Arab for most social purposes by fluent command of the language, careful observance of Islam, and appropriate dress. An Indian caste or the South African races are closed cultural communities, with no room for newcomers. It is the very Fur who is most readily incorporated who, if frustrated, might be most disposed to organize the cultural mobilization of the ethnic group.

In support of these points, we may briefly note two more examples. In Senegal, Wolof has become a modal, pacesetter culture in its urbanized, Dakar-centered version. As the predominant culture of the central place of power, modernity, and prestige, it takes on some of the reflected glamor of the capital. Although the Wolof are only 37 percent of the population, approximately 60 percent can speak the language, and this number is swiftly growing.[18] In Dakar, although only 49 percent of preschool children are from families with both parents Wolof-speaking, yet 70 percent of the children use Wolof as a first language.[19] In Northern Nigeria, Hausa begins with the prestige of its association with the seven city-states, loosely united under the suzerainty of Sokoto after the Fulani jihad of the early nineteenth century. The ruling Fulani elite accepted Hausa as a language of administration and have now been in good measure linguistically assimilated (although not in cultural identity). Unlike southern Nigeria, where English was the sole language of administration, Hausa was entrenched as an administrative language for all of Northern Nigeria, where only about half speak Hausa as their native language. This was the highest status accorded any African language in sub-Saharan Africa by any colonizer. When this is added to the unusual deference accorded by the colonizer to the Hausa-Fulani emirate rulers, one can readily understand that Hausa was far less eclipsed

17. Ibid., p. 42.

18. Morrison et al., *Black Africa*, p. 325.

19. A. Tabouret-Keller, in Fishman, Ferguson, and Das Gupta, *Language Problems*, pp. 114-15.

by the colonial language than was normally the case. To these factors must be attributed the assimilative vitality of Hausa, which is spoken by roughly half the Nigerian population, although only a quarter are native speakers. A number of small groups on the cultural fringes of the Hausa zone are visibly undergoing incorporation.[20]

CULTURAL MOBILIZATION: THE SIKHS

In the cultural situation where there is no recognized hierarchy of communal prestige, a quite different response to the anxieties and perceived inequities of competitive social change is often found: cultural mobilization. As this phenomenon covers a wide range of situations and is absolutely central to the politics of cultural pluralism, we will delve into several examples of the extension of awareness process. The one overriding regularity which runs through all cases, which was argued in chapter 2, is the role of contemporary conditions of competitive change in triggering cultural mobilization.

The politization of the Sikh community in the Punjab region of India well illustrates several important facets. The Sikh religious community has its origins in the ferment of the fifteenth century. The impact of some central ideas from Islam may be noted, in particular the unity of God and the equality of man. At the same time, Sikhism can be seen as one of the many historic movements of Hindu reform. Some identify the Sikh movement as an offshoot of Islam; commentators in the Hindu tradition tend to view it as a Hindu reform movement. Sikh sacred doctrine was laid down by an apostolic succession of ten Gurus. It became a church militant in reaction to persecution by the Muslim successors to Akbar as Mughal rulers. The tenth and last Guru, Gobind Singh, transformed the Sikhs from a pietist to a paramilitary community in the seventeenth century. He decreed the five symbols of identity for all male Sikhs—unshorn hair, short drawers, an iron bangle, a distinctive comb, and a dagger.

A series of politico-religious wars with the Mughals ensued, resulting in a series of Sikh principalities, briefly united as a single Sikh state in the early nineteenth century, before succumbing to the British raj in 1849. The effective end of the Muslim threat to the Sikh religious community had softened its contours. The difference between Sikh and Hindu communities was not sharply drawn; they shared use of a number of religious shrines. However, by the end of the nineteenth century, the mobilization of Sikh identity in interaction with modern forms of social competition was in process. The first Sikh association, the Singh Saba, was founded, and called for de-Hinduizing Sikhdom, to enhance the distinctiveness of the community. Its emergence was in dialectic response to the first associational manifestations of political Hinduism in the Punjab, the Arya Samaj, an organization promoted by upwardly mobile urban commercial Hindu castes.

British policy was then in a phase of stressing communal differentiation in administrative procedures. The 1901 census sharpened the distinctions. Sikh settlers were used to open new lands made arable by the extension of irrigation in the western Punjab, the "canal colonies." They were also favored recruits for the army; although only 2 percent of the population, at times they were as much as 33 percent of the Indian army.[21] The army contained special Sikh battalions and regiments, and itself made use of the Sikh baptismal ceremony and used the military disciplinary apparatus to enforce the five symbols. Despite such marks of favored status, the Sikhs developed a sense of enduring discrimination.

After World War I, the Akali Dal, political expression of militant Sikhdom, appeared on the scene as a middle-class reform movement. Its first major campaign, which made it a mass movement, was built around an issue of high symbolic content, which sharpened the identity boundaries between Sikh and Hindu. The Akali Dal demanded the reform of a set of religious shrines and replacement of their priests; Hindus, who also used these shrines, bitterly opposed. In the final decades of colonial rule, an intensely political Sikh ideology was shaped. The Sikh must, it was asserted, be a political community if the religion itself was to be preserved. Otherwise, it would be slowly reabsorbed by Hinduism. The Panth (Sikh community) was, in the most militant expression, a nation. Master Tara Singh, who for three critical decades (until 1962) was unchallenged leader of political Sikhdom, described himself as "a Sikh first and last"; Indian nationalism, he conceded, "has a place but in a corner."[22]

In the 1930s and 1940s, the greatest threat to the Sikh community appeared to come from the Muslim League; in prepartition Punjab, Muslims had a small majority. The growing specter of partition intensified fears of submergence in a Muslim-dominated political arena and subdued for a time Sikh-Hindu rivalry. The trauma of partition brought the flight of Sikhs from Pakistani Punjab and led to a regrouping of the Sikh community to achieve a narrow majority in a compact, well-defined area; Sikh political identity now enjoyed a territorial base. The elimination by

21. Baldev Raj Nayar, *Minority Politics in the Punjab* (Princeton: Princeton University Press, 1966), p. 64. See also, on the martial race policy, Stephen P. Cohen, *The Indian Army* (Berkeley: University of California Press, 1971).

22. Nayar, *Minority Politics in the Punjab*, p. 70.

exodus of the Muslim factor in the Indian Punjab left the Sikh-Hindu polarity as the most politicized cultural cleavage.

The Akali Dal swiftly fixed upon the demand for a Sikh state as its central goal. In the process, an intriguing metamorphosis of the claimed basis for solidarity and identity occurred. The searing experience of partition and the long struggle of the Congress Party for Indian unity made the premise of religious self-determination totally unacceptable to India's national leadership. However, linguistic claims could be entertained; Congress itself had been reorganized on a linguistic basis after World War I. Although all Punjabis spoke a language closely related to Hindi, with gradual dialectical change as one moves from east to west, the remarkable proposition was advanced that a Sikh state should be created on the grounds of a separate language. In 1949, the Akali Dal demanded that Punjabi in the Gurumukhi script be recognized as the official language for all Punjab and used as the medium of instruction.

Communal politization in north India had led to linguistic differentiation. Muslims who were literate used Urdu—a somewhat Persianized form of the north Indian, Hindi-related language cluster. Hindu-oriented cultural leaders pushed the Sanskritization of the language and used the Devnagari script; vigorous cleansing of the Persian influences associated with Muslim rule was pursued. The Punjabi variant of the Hindi cluster—often classified as "western Hindi" by Hindu scholars—could also be written in the Devnagari script, but literate Punjabi Hindus normally used the standard Hindi. The Gurumukhi script was, for Punjabi Hindus, a Sikh religious script and thus politically unacceptable.[23] Thus, when the 1951 census was taken, the Punjabi Hindu community collectively renounced their mother tongue and listed themselves as Hindi-speakers. The language arena, in the words of one student of Punjab politics, "quickly emerged as the basic framework for the integrative crisis" in Punjab.[24]

Over the first two decades of independence, Punjab drifted to ultimate linguistic-religious partition in 1966, marked by episodic moments of intense Sikh mobilization, with the whole array of quasi-violent mass-action techniques perfected in the Indian nationalist movement brought into play. In mid-1960, some 50,000 young volunteers came forward to court mass arrest. In late 1961, Master Tara Singh undertook a forty-eight day fast unto death to force recognition of a Punjabi-speaking state. Although these particular campaigns did not lead to immediate

23. On the implausible complexity of north Indian linguistic politics, see Jyotirindra Das Gupta, *Language Conflict and National Development* (Berkeley: University of California Press, 1970); Charles A. Ferguson and John L. Gumperz, "Linguistic Diversity in South Asia," *International Journal of American Linguistics,* XXVI, no. 3 (July 1960), 1-100.

24. Heeger, "The Politics of Integration," p. 152.

surrender by the government of India, they did sustain Sikh political mobilization at a level which maintained an atmosphere of polarization and eventually an institutional impasse in undivided Punjab.

Several points deserve emphasis in the interpretation of Sikh subnationalism. Although the theological doctrines of the ten Gurus provided a religious base point and a powerful set of symbols for Sikh identity, the Akali Dal is a modern movement, which has reinterpreted Sikh identity in the framework of the competitive sociopolitical arena of contemporary India. Issues which lean heavily upon religious symbols, such as control of shrines, have occasionally been used, and with potent mobilizing effects. Even here, it is worthy of note that administration of shrines by Akali Dal-oriented priests has been a lucrative revenue source for the secular pursuit of Sikh political goals.[25] But Akali Dal programs have primarily incorporated such demands as use of Punjabi in schools and administration, job reservation for Sikhs, and communal representation both at the state and national levels. The Sikh movement has constantly invoked the claim of anti-Sikh discrimination to rally its faithful. In concrete detail, discrimination refers particularly to areas such as education and employment, of special concern to upwardly mobile middle strata Sikhs. Curiously, the conviction of discrimination seems quite at variance with the facts. In the early 1960s, 9 of 17 department heads, 40-50 percent of cabinet members, 8 of 18 district heads, and 60 percent of the police were Sikhs. The head of Punjab Congress was a Sikh from 1947-63.[26] The Sikhs constituted just over one-third of undivided Punjab state population. Political Sikhdom leaders are recruited, not from the most traditional milieu, but from mobility-conscious middle sectors. Its political entrepreneurs are educated men, not shrine priests. An interesting survey of Sikh candidates in the 1962 elections showed that there were no significant differences in education or occupation between Congress Sikhs (presumably nationally oriented) and Akali Dal Sikhs (with a paramount subnational commitment).[27] Indeed, 94 percent of the Akali Dal candidates had at least a high school education. The most potent ancillary organization of Akali Dal is the All-India Sikh Student Federation—militant in propagandizing the ideal of Sikh political community, a vast reserve of cadres and manpower for mass actions.

Although political Sikhdom is a basic cultural fact in the Indian and Punjabi political arena, yet we must carefully note that not all Sikhs are faithful followers. Salient communal cleavage structures and constrains social role choice by individuals, but it is not necessarily determinant. At one level, the 20 percent of Sikhs who belong to untouchable

25. Nayar, *Minority Politics in the Punjab*, pp. 174-188.
26. Ibid., pp. 113-15.
27. Ibid., pp. 121-22.

castes have been quite hostile to the political goals of Akali Dal. Although Sikh theology rejects caste, Sikh social reality sustains it; in rural areas, Jat castes dominate the ranks of the landed and prosperous. Sikh Harijan spokesmen bitterly objected that a Punjab (Sikh) state would deliver them up to the unrestrained social oppression of the Jats. At the upper end of the social scale, there have always been a large contingent of Sikhs in the Congress ranks. Over time, there has tended to be a continuing process of defection from the leadership ranks of Akali Dal to Congress. Until the Sikh state was created, communal arithmetic condemned the Akali Dal to a permanent minority position. Thus, political mobility—actual accession to office—was possible only through apostasy. Without necessarily accepting a complete ambition theory of politics[28] or denying the ideological attractions of all-India nationalism as represented by Congress, we may still observe the corrosive effects over time on the middle and upper leadership levels of Akali Dal of permanent minoritization. The individual mobility aspirations of these cadres and the collective goals of political Sikhdom were in contradiction. Pungent illustration of this process is found in the career of Hukam Singh, whose weekly *The Spokesman* was long belligerently anti-Congress. In 1953, Singh wrote:

> . . . there is always an element in every society, which is immature, egocentric, paranoic and destructive. . . . They suffer from a serious mental disease underneath. Some of them . . . grow up as dacoits, sexual perverts, maniacs, political traitors and war saboteurs. . . . These political perverts are so egocentric, selfish and morally debased that they would sell their country to the highest bidder. . . . The nationalist [i.e., Congress] Sikhs amongst us, is the latest version of this unscrupulous, immoral and shamefaced gang which is out to sell, undermine, and malign their own community for personal gains or out of sheer malice for their own brothers.[29]

Singh subsequently qualified himself for his own eloquent epithets by joining the apostates, and in 1962 he became Speaker of the Lok Sabha (lower house of Indian parliament) with the backing of Nehru.

POLITICAL ARENA AS IDENTITY MOLD: THE TAMILS

Finally, it is important to note that the saliency and intensity of communal integration waxed and waned with the shifting definition of political conflict. Cultural identity is a political factor. At the same time, its ac-

28. Joseph Schlesinger, *Ambition and Politics: Political Careers in the United States* (Chicago: Rand McNally, 1961).

29. *The Spokesman*, 18 February 1953, quoted in Nayar, *Minority Politics in the Punjab*, p. 136.

tual mobilization at any point in time is a function of political variables from the overall field of politics within which the cultural community operates. Gerald Heeger, in a careful analysis of the complex factionalism of Punjabi politics, argues persuasively that cultural segments should not be viewed as constants but that the "definition of a particular group's interests as well as the definition of a group's social constituency can change radically as integrative coalitions within the political system shift."[30]

The political arena itself imposed constant tensions between the cultural politicians who led the Akali Dal and their mobilized following. In practice, achievement of even the collective goals of the cultural community required bargaining, compromise, and coalition with both non-Akali Dal Sikhs and Hindu groups. Cultural mobilization is thus a two-edged sword; the force it brings to bear upon political allocations is the basic resource which the elites bring to the bargaining table. At the same time, it is a massive constraint on settlements which fall short of cultural victory. Above all, goal-pursuit through coalition with Congress—tried by Akali Dal several times—imposed grave tensions on the mass-leader nexus within the movement; coalition inevitably rouses the apostasy suspicion—that elites have sacrificed community goals to achieve their own ambitions for political status. Thus, consociational politics of the model developed by Arend Lijphart are both indispensable and extraordinarily difficult.[31]

Another Indian case of identity transformation which merits close scrutiny is the triangular relationship between political non-Brahmanism, Dravidian culture, and Tamil subnationalism in Tamilnad (former Madras). Here caste, culture, and language offered an intricate lattice of interlocking solidarities around which modern ideologies of cultural mobilization could form. The caste distribution in southern India, especially Tamil areas, is somewhat unusual in the sharpness of the gap between the Brahmans at the very top, who constituted roughly 3 percent of the populace, and the next-ranked castes. In terms of the varna hierarchy, Kshatriya and Vaishya castes were absent, and the bulk of the population was grouped in agricultural and service castes labelled by Brahmans as Sundra. About 20 percent fell in the untouchable category.

Tamilnad was a part of the old Madras presidency, which covered most of southern India (excepting the princely states). The new opportunities which became available through Western education and government em-

30. Heeger, "Politics of Integration," pp. 334-35.

31. Lijphart, *The Politics of Accommodation: Pluralism and Democracy in the Netherlands* (Berkeley: University of California Press, 1968). This section on Sikh politics has drawn heavily upon the excellent studies of Nayar, *Minority Politics in the Punjab*, and Heeger, "Politics of Integration." Briefer analyses of Punjab politics may be found in Myron Weiner (ed.), *State Politics in India* (Princeton: Princeton University Press, 1968), and Narain (ed.), *State Politics in India*.

ployment in Madras were monopolized to an extraordinary degree well into the twentieth century by Brahmans. Of the 8,821 graduates of the University of Madras through 1913, 72 percent were Brahmans. Tables 4.1 and 4.2 further document this social hegemony.

Table 4.1—Distribution of Selected Government Jobs in Madras, 1912

	% of total male population	% of appointments
Deputy Collectors		
Brahmans	3.2	55
Non-Brahman Hindus	85.6	21.5
Muslims	6.6	10.5
Indian Christians	2.7	5
Europeans and Eurasians	.1	8
Sub-judges		
Brahmans		83.3
Non-Brahman Hindus		16.7
All Others		nil
District Munsifs		
Brahmans		72.6
Non-Brahman Hindus		19.5
Muslims		1.6
Indian Christians		3.9
Europeans and Eurasians		2.4

Source: Great Britain, Parliamentary Papers, vol. XXI (Reports from Commissioners, etc:, vol. XI), "Royal Commission on the Public Services, Appendix vol. II." Minutes of Evidence relating to the Indian and Provincial Services taken in Madras from the 8th to the 17th of January, 1913, Cd. 7293, 1914, pp. 103-4, cited in Eugene F. Irschick, Politics and Social Conflict in South India (Berkeley: University of California Press, 1969), p. 14.

Table 4.2—Male Literacy of Selected Tamil Castes, 1901-21

Caste	1901	1911	1921
Brahman	73.6	71.9	71.5
Chetti	32.0	39.1	39.5
Indian Christian	16.2	20.4	21.9
Nadar	15.4	18.1	20.0
Balija Naidu, Kavarai	14.3	20.9	22.3
Vellala	6.9	24.6	24.2

Source: India, Census Commissioner, Census of India: Madras, 1921, XIII, pt. 1, 128–29, cited in Irschick, Politics and Social Conflict in South India, p. 16.

The initial groundwork for the non-Brahman Dravidian Tamil response was to a large extent the work of British missionaries, scholars, and to some extent administrators. An interest in Tamil culture goes back to Jesuit missionaries in the sixteenth century; at an early date, Tamil grammars and dictionaries were compiled. Particularly important cultural ammunition was provided in the labors of a Scottish missionary, the Reverend Robert Caldwell, who learned all four of the major Dravidian languages (Tamil, Telugu, Kannada, and Malayalam), showed the close relationships they bore with comparative grammars and offered theories of their origin, which identified Tamil as the purest and most ancient Dravidian language. Missionaries also pioneered the historical interpretation that the Brahmans were Aryan invaders, who then made use of the Hindu metaphor of hierarchy through varna to give sacred sanction to their subjugation of Dravidians. The power of this historical ideology as an explication of social deprivation to newly self-conscious non-Brahman Tamils needs no elaboration.

In the early crystallization of cultural self-awareness, non-Brahmans also received encouragement from British administrators, which derived from several motivations. From the mid-nineteenth century, the British became aware of the magnitude of Brahman domination of those public service posts open to Indians. They feared both uncontrolled Brahman nepotism and a dilution of British influence through collusion of Brahman subalterns. Subsequently, after the 1885 establishment of Congress and first stirrings of intellectual Indian nationalism, the heavy Brahman role among the first generation of leaders was duly noted and Brahmans came to be viewed as arrogant malcontents, who had the self-serving aim of undermining the British raj so they could exploit the lower castes. For a time, the non-Brahman political movement was resolutely pro-British and anti-Congress; such fidelity deserved its rewards. To this must be added a diffuse grievance of British functionaries serving in Madras presidency that they were isolated, ignored, and excluded from the promotional ladder in the central government; the Madras neglect syndrome was bequeathed to the Tamil movement as well. A striking public statement of views which enjoyed currency in British milieu came in an address to graduates of the University of Madras by then Governor Mountstuart Elphinstone Grant-Duff in 1886: "The constant putting forward of Sanskrit literature as if it were pre-eminently Indian, should stir the national pride of some of you Tamil, Telugu, Cannarese. You have less to do with Sanskrit than we English have. Ruffianly Europeans have sometimes been known to speak of natives of India as 'Niggers,' but they did not, like the proud speakers or writers of Sanskrit, speak of the people of the South as legions of monkeys."[32]

32. Eugene F. Irschick, *Politics and Social Conflict in South India* (Berkeley: University of California Press, 1969), p. 281.

By the end of the nineteenth century, Tamil scholars were beginning to join in the task of cultural renaissance. Professor P. Sundaram Pillai set forth one of the first Tamil cultural manifestoes in 1897, arguing in an essay in the *Madras Standard*, "The Basic Element in Hindu Civilization," the antiquity of Tamil civilization, and cultural self-sufficiency of Dravidians. V. K. Pillai published in 1904 *The Tamils 1800 Years Ago*, arguing that Tamil civilization was fully developed two millennia ago. S. S. Bharati, in *Tamil Classics and Tamilakam*, situated the origins of Dravidian civilization in the sixth or seventh century B.C. and maintained that the Aryans had contributed absolutely nothing to it. The great Tamil poet, C. S. Bharati, gave lyrical expression to Tamil patriotism; the Tamil language, he wrote, "has a LIVING philosophical and poetical literature that is far grander, to my mind, than that of the 'vernacular' of England."[33]

The first non-Brahman groups to be politically mobilized were those closest to the Brahmans in status. It was the emergence of new elites among these groups, who came up against the Brahman domination of white collar employment and the professions, who first felt the frustrations of initially uneven social competition. Particularly in the urban context, Brahman use of the "Sudra" label for those who felt themselves equipped with the same skills and educational standing was sharply resented. The first political vehicle for the non-Brahmans was the Justice Party, founded in 1916. Through this movement, the ideology of the Dravidian heritage was given explicit political content, and Brahmans labelled as destructive alien intruders of a different race in the terminology of the times.

Thus a wholly new solidarity group was shaped; prior to this time, "non-Brahman" was a category devoid of social or political meaning; as Marguerite Barnett has argued in a perceptive study of Tamil cultural sub-nationalism, "the very idea of a non-Brahman movement represents a significant reorientation of perception about castes and communities."[34] Initially, however, the non-Brahman concept was more restrictive than the name implies; Barnett carefully shows that the Justice Party was, in fact, an organ of what she terms "forward non-Brahman castes"—that is, those closest to Brahmans in ritual status and modern standing. However, the political category of non-Brahman was well established; even non-Brahmans in Congress were obliged to organize around this radically restructured perception of social reality.

The Justice Party won the first limited franchise elections in Madras in 1920 and largely succeeded in its initial goal of forcing open the public employment arena preferentially to non-Brahmans—indeed, in all but blocking recruitment of Brahmans. In the late 1920's, a more radical

33. Ibid., p. 287.
34. Marguerite R. Barnett, "The Politics of Cultural Nationalism: The D.M.K. in Tamil Nadu, South India" (Ph.D. diss. University of Chicago, 1972).

movement was founded, drawing upon the same cultural stimuli, the Self-Respect League. It called for a more far-reaching levelling of caste hierarchies and even, in some cases, for utterly repudiating the religious basis of caste.

As Independence neared, political awareness extended to less-favored non-Brahman castes, who organized themselves as the Madras Province Backward Classes League. The welcome address to the 1943 convention of this group illuminates its objectives and identity:

> The first and foremost thing that is required at present is the unification of the different Backward Classes of this province and setting out organization on a proper footing and strong basis through sustained and coordinated effort. The educational advancement . . . should constitute the main plank. . . . No effort should be spared in this direction, as it is education that gives consciousness of power and rights and claims. The next thing . . . is the representation of *Backward Classes* in public services . . . The fact that *out of about 2100 gazetted appointments in the Madras* government only 2 percent are occupied by the Backward Classes [who constituted about 50 percent of the population] will speak volumes.[35]

There was thus an undercurrent of tension between "forward" and "backward" non-Brahmans. The latter also were preoccupied with boundary maintenance between themselves and the untouchables just below; tales were recounted with indignation of harijan impudence in refusing to remove their shoes and upper clothes in the presence of "backward" non-Brahmans.[36]

With the approach of independence, a new set of political issues emerged: the relationship of Madras to the rest of India, the national language policy. In this issue context, the Dravidian and Tamil identities came more to the fore. Symptomatic was the supplanting of the Justice Party by the Dravida Kazagam in 1944; in 1949, a split gave birth to the Dravida Mumnetra Kazagam (DMK), which in 1967 became the dominant party in Tamilnad. In 1938, the demand for a separate Dravidian nation was first publicly made. However, after independence, tensions between Tamils and Telugu in north Madras were a prime cause for the Telugu demand for the linguistic state of Andhra Pradesh. Kerala and Mysore, the other Dravidian language states, had quite distinctive problems and never really shared the enthusiasm for Dravidian separatism. By degrees, Dravidian and Tamil subnationalism became all but synonymous.

By the time of independence, the enthusiasm for Tamil culture had gone far beyond its intellectual progenitors. Vernacular media had swiftly developed. Particularly important was the flourishing Tamil

35. Ibid., p. 88.
36. Ibid., p. 94.

film industry, enormously popular in rural areas and a potent medium for Tamil patriotism. The DMK, under the leadership of C. N. Annadurai, was overtly separatist. It drew together the anti-Brahman, Dravidian heritage and the Tamil cultural themes in a belligerent challenge to the Indian government. The tone of DMK cultural self-assertion is captured in the following quotation from Annadurai's key book, *The Aryan Illusion:*

> It is an indisputable fact that in the ancient times, the Tamilians excelled in intelligence, efficiency, business and cottage industries. . . . But the Aryans, who came in the middle ages polluted the Tamilian culture and resorted to many devices to perpetrate their own glory and their own supremacy, pushing to the background the Tamilian civilization.
>
> In the course of time the false propaganda resorted to by the Aryans—that the Aryans conquered the Tamilians in battle, . . . that it was only after the advent of the Aryans, that civilization and culture began to spread in India—gradually gained prominence. . . . The Aryans show the Vedas, their own creation as an evidence to substantiate this point. . . .
>
> By the irony of fate, the people who came here with their cattle, badly in search of a place for living, have today become our rulers and masters; the Aryans by intoxicating us with their stories of imagination, have perverted us and have plunged us into desolation and the gloom of Brahmanism.[37]

We may note that in the post-independence context the references to Aryans and Brahmans touch upon not only Madras Brahmans, but on the whole relation of Tamilnad to the "Aryan," Sanskritic civilization of northern India.

The DMK entered electoral politics only in the 1957 elections, in which they did very badly—partly because of poor use of caste balancing in candidate selection, a cultural error which seems surprising for a movement founded upon communal mobilization. However, the DMK was having a powerful effect in the diffusion of the Dravidian self-concept of Tamilhood. In the 1962 elections, they won fifty seats and frightened Delhi sufficiently with their advance to provoke hasty adoption of a constitutional amendment forbidding advocacy of secession by political parties or candidates. The fear of dissolution plus the popular reaction to the Chinese invasion led the DMK to drop its separatist demands—but not the assertion of Tamil rights. The magnitude of popular mobilization was given tragic demonstration when the fatal day fixed by the 1950 Constitution for Hindi to become national official language came, on 27 January 1965. The DMK marked the occasion by initiating a mass agitation campaign against the imposition of (Aryan) Hindi and in so doing sowed the dragon's teeth which reaped a harvest of massive violence. The DMK was outflanked in militance by its student wing. Five students immolated

37. Ibid., p. 136.

themselves in the fortnight following Hindi day. Then on 10-12 February, massive rioting occurred; police stations, factories, and public buildings were attacked. Police opened fire on mobs in twenty-one different towns, killing 60 and arresting 10,000. The central government was taken by surprise by the scope of the rioting; it had failed to appreciate, in Barnett's words, "the effectiveness with which D.M.K. and Dravidian movement cultural and political ideas had been widely spread and internalized in Madras State . . . specific D.M.K. identification often lagged behind the spread of Tamil as a focal point of cultural national-ism."[38]

DMK swept to power in 1967, winning 138 seats to 47 for Congress, and was re-elected in 1971. Cultural reality in Tamilnad has been reshaped in the last century. The sense of an overarching Indian culture cut to the dimensions of the subcontinent, of which Nehru and Gandhi dreamed, cannot be rooted in Tamil soil. The Dravidian myth is too deeply implanted and a literate Tamil culture which effectively reaches the rural mass is now founded upon it. Many hands have helped shape the new iden-tity, from Scottish missionaries to Tamil poets. Particular political issues have powerfully affected the course of its development—most recently, the Hindi language question. The silent processes of change, of course, continue; but mobilized identities alter less readily than do unmobilized ones—all the more as they become reinforced by a growing written cultural tradition of history and literary expression, widely diffused ver-nacular media of press, radio and film, and formally established social-ization mechanisms through a school system operating in Tamil and committed to its nurture.[39]

DEFENSIVE NATIONALISM: THE MALAYS

Malay nationalism has developed in a primarily bipolar setting, with the very large Chinese immigrant community serving as both foil and threat. As a meaningful political identity, it is clearly a product of the present century. It rests upon the twin pillars of language and religion. Also present is some continuing affiliative tie to the nine historic sul-tanates which form the core for contemporary Malaysia.

British rule was extended by degrees beginning in 1874 over the sul-tanates; the six southern states were federated in 1895. The four northern

38. Ibid., p. 218.
39. This section is primarily based upon Irschick, *Politics and Social Conflict in South India*; Barnett, "The Politics of Cultural Nationalism"; and Robert Hardgrave, "The DMK and the Politics of Tamil Nationalism," *Pacific Affairs*, XXXVII, no. 4 (Winter, 1964-65), 396-411.

states came under British protection only in the early twentieth century. By the end of the century, three of the southern federated states already had Chinese and Indian majorities. British colonialism in its early Malay stages was unusual in the degree that an expatriate administrative and economic superstructure was built upon a largely untouched rural Malay society. The economy was already oriented to Chinese initiative; some sultans had begun inviting Chinese immigration in the early nineteenth century, and by mid-century they were developing tin mines. With the opening of plantation rubber at the beginning of the twentieth century, new waves of Chinese peasant immigrants manned the enterprise. Chinese quickly became the dominant population group in the entrepot port of Singapore, which had contained only a few Malay villages when leased by Britain in the early nineteenth century. An implausibly large European bureaucracy swarmed over the federated states; for one-fifth the population of Ceylon, there were twice as many British functionaries. Of the three towns over 10,000 in 1901, Malay population accounted for less then 10 percent.[40]

Initially, the salient aspect of identity beyond the most local attachments lay in Islam. A number of the ulema and imams had made the haj and established links with the broader world of Islam. Itinerant Malay holy men and traders operated throughout Malaysia and coastal Indonesia, constituting the embryo of a cultural communications net; indeed, from their trading language Indonesian as well as Malay have developed. The British were very careful not to threaten Islam, however; Islam remained an important identity component but was never thrust into a position of aggressive reaction to policies which appeared to challenge its sway over Malays. Still, traditional religious elites from Arab-Malay and even Arab milieu provided the first generation of spokesmen for Malay rights in the early twentieth century.

The desire to leave Islam untouched and the ready availability of Chinese and Indian subalterns, in addition to the abundant supply of European cadres, meant there was little urgency to educating Malays. Of the thirty English boys' schools in the Federated Malay States in 1921, there were less than 700 Malay pupils of a total enrollment of 10,000. Malay College was established in 1905 to train a modest number of Malay elites for service with the sultanates; until the 1930s, enrollment stayed at about 140, mainly drawn from the ruling families.[41] The main training ground for a more radical Malay intelligentsia came from Malay vernacular schools which began to grow.

By the 1930s, self-awareness began to crystallize more swiftly, as the full dimensions of the Chinese challenge became clear. The Chinese

40. William R. Roff, *The Origins of Malay Nationalism* (New Haven: Yale University Press, 1967).

41. Ibid., pp. 104-12.

were for long assumed to be a transient population, and indeed many did return to China; between 1911 and 1921, 1.5 million Chinese immigrated, and 1 million returned. But what these figures concealed was the speed with which a permanent Chinese population was building; by 1931, 29 percent of the Chinese populace had been born in Malaya, in contrast to only 8 percent in 1911. In the 1931 census, the Chinese proportion of the population reached its peak of 39 percent as compared to 44.7 percent Malay.[42] By this time, the Chinese community itself was becoming politicized, demanding an end to limitations to their access to public employment, and a political voice.

Pan-Malay anticolonial nationalism received a sharp stimulus from these Chinese demands. Malays began to appreciate their social lag across the board and the need for cultural self-assertion lest Malay society be simply submerged in rural stagnation. A congress of state Malay associations was convened on the eve of World War II, but these were linked to the various ruling houses and too divided by loyalties to the component states to form a united Malay association.

After World War II, communal cleavage was sharpened by the Communist uprising in 1948, which drew its support almost wholly from poorer segments of the Chinese community. Electoral politics were first introduced in 1952, and the first national elections held in 1955. Certainly the absence of elections in prewar Malaya had delayed the activation of communal political movements; equally inevitably, despite some early efforts to build a national movement, parties were swiftly drawn within the cultural mold. Intercommunal collaboration developed, at the summit, as a coalition of political organizations representing Malays, Chinese and Indians.

Running through Malay nationalism is a note of fear and frustration regarding their relationship with the immigrant communities, above all the industrious and frugal Chinese. Before Malays became politically self-conscious, the level of immigration had made them strangers in their own land, with only 44 percent of the population. Colonial educational policy, while undeniably tranquilizing with respect to Islam, left the Malays far behind the Chinese and Indians. Unlike the situation in many African territories, no administrative pressure was placed on Malays to draw them into the labor market—which left the urban economy and commerce entirely in immigrant hands. Characteristic of the shaken self-confidence the Malays felt was a very influential postwar nationalist work by a Malay physician, Dr. Mahathir bin Mohammad, *The Malay Dilemma*. Mahathir argues that inbreeding had made Malays inferior to the Chinese in a number of characteristics. The only salvation for Malays was to cling tightly to political power to assure their own self-protection. A recent study of Malay and Chinese schoolchildren's attitudes in Singapore reports that expressions of

42. Ibid., pp. 110, 208.

low self-esteem came up repeatedly in interviews with Malay pupils.[43] Table 4.3 shows the dramatic contrast in self-image between Chinese and Malay children.

Table 4.3—Relative Self-Image of Malay and Chinese Schoolchildren, Singapore

Race	% feeling own group superior	% feeling own group equal	% feeling own group inferior
Malay	36.2	46.2	18.6
Chinese	80.2	19.8	1.2

Source: Peter A. Busch, "Political Unity and Ethnic Diversity: A Case Study of Singapore" (Ph.D. diss., Yale University, 1972), p. 209.

In order to symbolize the security of political power, Malays insisted on entrenching special constitutional status for their two most important pillars of identity. Islam was given recognition as the state religion, and Malay was installed as the official language. The Chinese found these symbolic concessions easy to make because neither really threatened Chinese identity or communal interests. The United Malay National Organization, dominant Malay political movement, was eminently secular and had no interest in a theocratic state, proseletyzing other communities, or installing a regime of ulemas and imams. On the linguistic front, English remained as administrative language. Chinese and Indians never had been brought into top civil service ranks in any numbers; unlike the Tamilnad Brahmans, they had little to lose in a public employment policy heavily oriented toward Malay interests or in use of government resources to promote Malay development. Their interest lies in a relatively unrestricted private sector; communal peace is their best protection.

Electoral politics, the civil war, and the tensions of defining a stable postindependence polity have completed the process of political mobilization of the three main cultural communities. The Lijphart model of the consociational polity has applied to Malaysia during most of its postindependence life. The communal segments are relatively closed at the base; Lucian Pye found among the surrendered Chinese prisoners he interviewed in the early 1950s that over 40 percent had never had personal relationships with any Malay and only 15 percent had close associations with individual Malays.[44] The leaders of the communal parties act as cultural brokers, share a desire for negotiation and compromise; however, especially in the Chinese case, they had difficulty in retaining their fol-

43. Peter A. Busch, "Political Unity and Ethnic Diversity: A Case Study of Singapore" (Ph.D. diss, Yale University, 1972), p. 177.

44. Lucian W. Pye, *Guerilla Communism in Malaya* (Princeton: Princeton University Press, 1956), p. 207.

lowing. The United Malay National Organization faces a significant challenge from the Pan-Malayan Nationalist Party, which calls for a more rigorous application of the Islamic vocation of Malaysia. At bottom, however, PMNP is less a religious party per se than a more aggressive Malay communal party. The dangers inherent in a consociational polity with politically mobilized cultural communities were underlined by the very serious communal rioting in 1969. However, the formula which trades deference to Malay identity symbols and Malay domination of governmental institutions and policies for Chinese and Indian leeway in the economic sphere has yielded sufficient mutual benefits to survive at least the early tests of independent existence.[45]

CHANGING IDENTITY REFERENCE POINTS: THE KIKUYU

The Kikuyu have emerged since independence as the dominant cultural grouping in Kenya; their self-awareness took shape in the context of intense deprivation and has been consolidated in circumstances of unprecedented opportunities for collective advance made possible by the configuration of ethnic politics since independence. In terms of the historic basepoint, the Kikuyu case would seem to fall in an intermediate position on an identity continuum running from the large number of segmentary societies where there is no evidence of any self-awareness going beyond the most local level[46]—such as the Ibo in Nigeria, Kru in Liberia, Mongo in Zaire, or Tonga in Zambia—to well-established kingdoms with crystallized, although not mobilized, identities, such as Buganda or the Kongo kingdom. Kikuyuland in the nineteenth century had no centralized political structures, although the myth of origin of Kikuyu-speakers tells of an eponymous king-ancestor Gikuyu, by whose name his fictive descendants are identified. However, in addition to the common tradition of genesis, there were some identity-maintaining institutions which linked together the politically autonomous ridge settlements and kinship groups. The most important of these was an age-set system, binding those who experienced certain rites of passage at the same time. Approximately every thirty years, a major ceremony was performed throughout Kikuyuland which marked the promotion of a generation of mature men from the sta-

45. On Malay nationalism and politics, in addition to works cited, see also K. J. Ratnam, "Religion and Politics in Malaya," in Robert O. Tilman (ed.), *Man, State, and Society in Southeast Asia* (New York: Praeger, 1969), pp. 351-61, and *Communalism and the Political Process* (Boston: Houghton Mifflin Co., 1967); James C. Scott, *Political Ideology in Malaysia* (New Haven: Yale University Press, 1968); Gayl D. Ness, *Bureaucracy and Rural Development in Malaya* (Berkeley: University of California Press, 1967).

46. For details on several cases falling in this category in Africa, see Anderson, von der Mehden and Young, *Issues of Political Development*, pp. 31-39.

tus of warriors to the role of elders and leaders.[47] This ceremony was last performed between 1890 and 1898; the ritual was begun in 1925 but was promptly halted by the colonial administration. Another identity-integrating institution was the clan system; Kikuyu society was divided into nine clans, which were widely dispersed geographically. Although their social functions were not great, they were nonetheless linkages which spanned Kikuyuland. While there was no recognized institution of kingship, there were "big men," who acquired their reputation through military prowess or trading success.

Before European penetration, the primary cultural reference point for the Kikuyu were the neighboring Masai, whose military strength had a decisive impact on the political geography of the area, keeping the Zanzibar trade routes well to the south. Although the Kikuyu were relatively secure from the pastoral Masai in their fertile, forested hills, accumulation and prestige came primarily from successful trade with them. The high status enjoyed by Masai in Kikuyu eyes is suggested by the oral testimony of a Kikuyu elder:

> Who can ask who had the better life? In Masailand there was meat and milk, but here there was only soil. So why would anyone want to live here? We lived on sweet potatoes and arrowroot then—and we live on sweet potatoes and arrowroot still.
>
> In Mahiga only a few rich men owned any cattle at all, but in Masailand even a poor man owned many. Here we counted a man's wealth by his sheep and goats, but there they counted his cattle.[48]

Thus Kikuyu precolonial identity was sustained not only by its internal institutions, but by reference to the neighboring group whose action most impinged upon them.

The establishment of colonial rule replaced the Masai with Europeans as the focus of social reference for Kikuyu. It also placed the central institutions of the new colonial territory of Kenya in Nairobi, on the edge of Kikuyuland. And, through the alienation of large blocs of fertile land in Kikuyu and Masai country to European farmers, a framework of economic deprivation was fixed for the subsequent mobilization of Kikuyu cultural self-assertion. Kikuyu land was already under some pressure; the establishment of a White reserve in their midst, as growing population sharpened land hunger, soon threatened the most elemental needs of the collectivity.

During the interwar apogee of colonialism, some portentous trends may be discerned. The first organizational vehicles for articulation of

47. This ceremony, Itwika, is described by Jomo Kenyatta, *Facing Mount Kenya* (New York: Vintage Books, 1962), pp. 182-93.

48. Peter Marris and Anthony Somerset, *African Businessmen* (London: Routledge and Kegan Paul, 1971), p. 31.

Kikuyu interests took form, in the shape of the Kikuyu Association (1920) and the Kikuyu Central Association (1924). Although these two bodies had different geographical zones of influence within Kikuyuland and represented somewhat different responses to the challenge posed by colonialism, they were joined in the task of cultural mobilization. In the 1920s, both associations—motivated by a sense that unified, dignified representation could better press their claims and influenced by the considerable deference accorded by the British to the royal institutions of Buganda not far away—asked that a paramount chief be invested to represent all Kikuyu.[49]

Christian missions found propitious terrain in Kikuyuland and made a deep impact. For restless, aspirant Kikuyu, the missions offered a pathway to emulation of those European traits which seemed to confer high cultural status. Also, the Christian schools were the doorway to social promotion. However, both in the religious and educational spheres important Kikuyu initiatives took place, aimed at bringing these mobility resources in more congruent relationship with Kikuyu culture. On the religious side, a bitter dispute occurred, peaking in 1928-31, over the issue of female circumcision. For the missionaries, the practice was barbaric and medically dangerous and required suppression. For the Kikuyu, female circumcision was an important affirmation of identity, linking the present with the past. The Kikuyu Central Association, in upholding the custom, "stood as a champion of Kikuyu cultural nationalism; its members did not seek the rejection of Christianity, but the preservation of selected aspects of Kikuyu culture."[50] The school controversy grew out of the female circumcision problem; a remarkable net of Kikuyu-organized primary schools were created on local initiative, to offer a cultural alternative to the mission monopoly of this key institution. In 1934, to provide a united voice for the independent school movement, the Kikuyu Independent School Association was founded "to further the interests of the Kikuyus and its members and to safeguard the homogeneity of such interests in matters relating to their spiritual, economic, social and educational upliftment."[51]

A very significant step in setting forth the claims of Kikuyu for cultural recognition came with the 1938 publication of Jomo Kenyatta's anthropological study, *Facing Mount Kenya*. While resident in London, Kenyatta equipped himself with a diploma in anthropology at the London School of Economics in order to master the analytical categories through which Kikuyu culture could be communicated in a form which commanded respect. The data for his study, as he states, had been "verbally handed

49. For details on these associations, see Carl G. Rosberg, Jr. and John Nottingham, *The Myth of Mau Mau: Nationalism in Kenya* (New York: Praeger, 1966), pp. 71-104.
50. Ibid., p. 113.
51. Ibid., p. 127.

down from generation to generation," and like other Kikuyu he "carried them in my head for many years."[52] His book is intended as a riposte to what he viewed as the pejorative portrayal of various aspects of Kikuyu culture, such as the circumcision issue, by European writers.

At the same time, I am well aware that I could not do justice to the subject without offending those "professional friends of the African" who are prepared to maintain their friendship for eternity as a sacred duty, provided only that the African will continue to play the part of an ignorant savage so that they can monopolize the office of interpreting his mind and speaking for him. To such people, an African who writes a study of this kind is encroaching on their preserves. He is a rabbit turned poacher.[53]

Kenyatta met the female circumcision issue head on; clitoridectomy, he argued, "is still regarded as the very essence of an institution which had enormous educational, social, moral and religious implications, quite apart from the operation itself." The purpose of anthropological analysis, he continued, "is to show that clitoridectomy, like Jewish circumcision, is a mere bodily mutilation which, however, is regarded as the *conditio sine qua non* of the whole teaching of tribal law, religion, and morality."[54]

Rapidly transforming Kikuyu society clashed directly with the entrenching pattern of European domination. The settler community sought to assure the permanence of its privilege through devolution of political power from the colonial administration; land hunger in Kikuyuland intensified and agrarian discontent swelled as the conspicuous prosperity of the white farms contrasted with African poverty. Nairobi grew into a sizable town, with a very wealthy core; Kikuyu flocked to the city, but found their mobility blocked in the civil service ranks by Europeans and commerce solidly in the hands of the Asian community. Colonialism and modernization bore far more heavily upon Kikuyuland than any other part of Kenya. Modernity at once brazenly displayed its wares but kept them just beyond Kikuyu reach. The barriers to mobility blocked every trail to progress: modern commercial farming, trading, public service. From here to Mau Mau—nationalist revolution and cultural self-affirmation—was but a short step.

The Mau Mau movement, a loosely structured insurrection whose "forest fighter" required the deployment of a large-scale repressive apparatus, exploded in 1952 and had petered out by 1956. Its complex symbiotic interaction of Kenyan nationalism, Kikuyu cultural mobilization, and internal strife within the Kikuyu community foreshadowed postindepen-

52. Kenyatta, *Facing Mount Kenya*, p. xvi.
53. Ibid., p. xviii.
54. Ibid., p. 128.

dence issues, as the Kenya territorial arena per se loomed larger in the calculations of the political elite. The movement had indisputably nationalist objectives—independence for Kenya, with power to its African majority. Kenya was the natural, necessary territorial frame; no other possibility was ever considered. Political objectives, insofar as they were programmatically defined, never were asserted in Kikuyu terms, although some of the specific grievances, in particular the land question, affected the Kikuyu above all. African rights, not Kikuyu rights, were the rallying cry; "General China," one of the major military leaders, explains in his autobiography that he and his fellow young men "had the formidable job of uniting a nation and peeling off the top coats of slavery and discrimination to the common undercoat of blackness that was all we had underneath."[55] By axiom, African rights could only be assured within a Kenyan frame.

Mau Mau (a term of uncertain origin, not used by Kikuyu themselves), on closer examination, had important consciousness-raising effects for the Kikuyu community itself. The contrast with Akali Dal in Punjab or the DMK in Tamilnad is striking in the absence of an explicit assertion of the cultural heritage and rights of the ethnic community. But aspects of the organizational tactics and *modus operandi* restricted its effective orbit to Kikuyuland.

In 1944, the Kenyan African Union was founded, with a leadership representing most areas of Kenya, as an organizational vehicle for African nationalism. However, only in Kikuyuland had politization proceeded very far; inevitably, the central core of the KAU support came from Kikuyu. Neither the European settler community nor the colonial administration were prepared to respond to the civic, constitutional style of the KAU initial leadership. When in 1949, settler milieu published a "Kenya Plan," which Africans interpreted as the South Africanization of Kenya, pressures built for more militant, direct action. For this to occur, mechanisms to achieve a level of unity and discipline of a wholly new order of magnitude were indispensable. For these purposes, the institution of the oath was developed and utilized on a very large scale.

The political oath of unity was a powerful instrument of solidarity. Although there were local variations and different levels of oaths, the vow as described by former Mau Mau fighter Josiah Kariuki illustrates its main themes:

> I speak the truth and vow before God
> And before this movement,
> The movement of Unity,
> The Unity which is put to the test,

55. Waruhia Itote, *'Mau Mau' General* (Nairobi: East African Publishing House, 1967). p. 40.

The Unity that is mocked with the name of "Mau Mau,"
That I shall go forward to fight for the land,
The lands of Kirinyaga that we cultivated,
The lands which were taken by the Europeans.
  And if I fail to do this
  May this oath kill me,
  May this seven kill me,
  May this meat kill me.

The oath was administered, before witnesses, in a secluded place; the novice bit into goat flesh, which the oath administrator had circled seven times over the head of the oathers.[56]

The awe-inspiring solemnity of the oathing ritual sacralized political commitment. At the same time, it raised the level of political consciousness, through its social aspects. Although the oathing was usually individual, there were always other persons present. The social functions are well summarized by Carl Rosberg and John Nottingham: ". . . [oaths] probably combine with a positive allegiance to the group to produce a high level of conformity. This is important in situations of political conflict, where ordinary people may be called upon to defy laws and to face violence or imprisonment. In such situations, oaths may reassure individuals that they are not alone, that many others are committed to the same values and behavior. The sacred and social nature of oaths may help to clarify individual duties and obligations in situations of social conflict or confusion."[57] The oath also established clearcut solidarity boundaries, separating the ritualized community from those beyond its pale.

The oath derived its supernatural sanctity not only from the majesty of its present purpose of Kikuyu unity in the freedom struggle, but also from the familiarity of its ritual and symbols. Kenyatta in his 1938 book describes similar oathing rituals in traditional society; however, they were utilized as ordeals for ferreting out guilty persons and malignant spirits in the community.[58] Oaths were then adopted for a modern political purpose, beginning about 1925 in the Kikuyu Central Association; these oaths were used mainly at the elite level as vows of loyalty to the KCA and Kikuyuland, with the Bible replacing goat meat as the sanctioning element. After World War II, the oath was de-Westernized and began to be used on a much wider scale; it ceased to be a selectively applied device to ritualize elite commitment, but became a mass weapon. From 1950, it spread rapidly from its Kiambu base to Nairobi and the

56. Josiah Mwangi Kariuki, 'Mau Mau' Detainee (London: Oxford University Press, 1963), p. 26.
57. Rosberg and Nottingham, The Myth of Mau Mau, p. 245.
58. Kenyatta, Facing Mount Kenya, pp. 214-16.

Fort Hall and Nyeri districts. The forest insurgents in the violent phase, 1952-56, made frequent use of oathing ceremonies to sustain the commitment, morale and self-confidence of their following.

Thus the ritual dimension of what was intended as nationalist revolution served to sharpen the distinctions between Kikuyu and other ethnic communities in Kenya. There was some participation in the culturally closely akin groups of Embu and Meru—indeed, Kenyatta includes these groups within his definition of Kikuyuland.[59] Some oathing also occurred among the Kamba, neighbors to the east. But the symbols invoked in the oathing rituals were Kikuyu; via the oath, African nationalism passed through Kikuyu unity. Thus political leaders from other ethnic areas were profoundly ambivalent toward Mau Mau. There was widespread admiration for the militant nationalist aspects of the challenge to European domination. At the same time, they could not wholly identify with the movement because of its cultural specificity—and they were troubled by some of the more violent aspects.[60] At the same time, the intensity of colonial grievance was far less in other parts of Kenya, and the political elites were not under the strong pressures for direct action from a politicized mass that prevailed in Kikuyuland. Thus insurrection was confined to Kikuyuland; African troops recruited in non-Kikuyu areas could be joined to British security forces for the repression of the forest insurgents. The dialectic of differentiation left a profound imprint on subsequent Kenyan politics: non-Kikuyu felt excluded when militant nationalism was enshrouded in a penumbra of Kikuyu ritual and symbols; Kikuyu felt they were left to shoulder the entire burdern of anticolonial struggle alone. There can be no doubt that the searing experience of Mau Mau and the costs of its military repression ruptured the premises upon which earlier British official thought on the future of Kenya had rested. Although it was not till 1960 that the critical commitment was made to transfer power to an African government, Mau Mau had subverted the assumptions of ultimate viability of a state where the power of the small settler minority was entrenched. In a framework of cultural self-awareness, it is only natural that the communal capital of suffering and sacrifice in the nationalist cause should command a return in recognition and reward when independence came.

59. See the map in ibid., p. 2.

60. Rosberg and Nottingham, *The Myth of Mau Mau*, offer an especially insightful interpretation of oathing, as well as the cultural and nationalist aspects of "Mau Mau." Their study was an important rectification of a generally negative European interpretation of "Mau Mau" as atavistic and backward-looking, an argument put forward in such influential works as L. S. B. Leakey, *Defeating 'Mau Mau'* (London: Methuen, 1954) and the British government official inquiry, *Historical Survey of the Origins and Growth of Mau Mau* (Corfield Report), Comnd. 1030 (London: H.M.S.O., 1960).

In the process of building Kikuyu unity, the Mau Mau movement also escalated some divisions within the group. The construction of unified commitment to militant action implied also the application of sanctions against those who failed to respond to the summons. These include, primarily, the elements in Kikuyu society who had achieved the greatest social mobility within the colonial framework and were most committed to European values: some major chiefs, whose standing derived from colonial investiture; some administrative cadres; Kikuyu Christian clergy, who had committed themselves on the European side in the female circumcision controversy; some teachers and prosperous traders. The trigger for launching the all-out repressive campaign against Mau Mau was the assassination in October 1952 of Senior Chief Waruhiu, leading Kikuyu spokesman for government policy. From a Mau Mau perspective, Kariuki explains the severe sanctions imposed by the movement on those who failed to join:

> There is no question that at times the oath was forced upon people who did not wish to take it, though these were nothing like so many as the Government spokesmen would have had us believe. . . . It is also true that by 1953 and 1954 severe punishment sometimes including death was meted out by the courts of the Movement to those whom it considered traitors or spies. This was not the first political organization, nor will it be the last, which had been driven to set up its own judicial system parallel to that of the state. We had rejected the authority of the Kenya Government. We had organized in its place another Government, accepted by the large majority of our people, which was compelled to undertake in its infancy a desperate battle for survival. . . . It is not surprising that the leaders insisted on military discipline or that failure to join and obey were considered most serious crimes against our Government. Nothing but absolute unity, implicit obedience and a sublime faith in our cause could bring victory.[61]

The 1960 British commitment to African self-rule in Kenya fundamentally altered the cultural structure of the political arena. The immigrant Asian and European communities simply ceased to figure prominently. The barriers to African mobility were suddenly removed. The Kikuyu found themselves in a peculiarly advantageous position in the social competition which ensued. Although they were only 19 percent of the population, they were situated at the geographical heartland of Kenya; they were the dominant component of the Nairobi population. Their vanguard role in winning independence sanctioned a claim to political leadership and bestowed an aura of charisma on their paramount leader, Kenyatta. They had developed a very large political elite, as well as a numerous class of educated young men well qualified to take advantage of the opportunities offered by Africanization of the public service. The huge schemes under-

61. Kariuki, 'Mau Mau' Detainee, p. 32.

taken to transfer ownership of the bulk of White farms to Africans primarily interested the Kikuyu.[62] The land title acquired gave access to credit for expansion. The new African business class, vigorously fostered by the state Industrial and Commercial Development Corporation, was heavily Kikuyu; Marris and Somerset found that, up to 1966, 64 percent of the industrial loans and 44 percent of the commercial loans had gone to Kikuyu. Even though the senior staff of the ICDC was Kikuyu, they found no evidence that these figures were distorted by favoritism. Kikuyu were the only African businessmen operating outside their ethnic area.[63] Thus, in the years immediately following independence a spectacular social promotion of Kikuyu occurred across the board. Other groups, of course, shared the benefits of independence, but not in the same numbers—nor were they as well situated to exploit the new opportunities in business, commercial farming, or political and administrative leadership.

The political party organized in 1960 to lead the final, now constitutional phase of decolonization, the Kenya African National Union (KANU), was led by Kenyatta but was able to enlist the support of important areas of the country behind its comprehensive nationalist platform. The main competitor, the Kenya African Democratic Union (KADU), embodied and politicized the fears of smaller groups of domination by both Kikuyu and the second largest group, the Luo (14 percent). KADU, however, merged with KANU in 1964; by 1966, the main opposition came from a new party, the Kenya People's Union (KPU), whose cultural center of gravity was Luo; this, in effect, marked the demise of Luo-Kikuyu coalition in Kanu. By this time, perception of the political situation was increasingly in terms of "Kikuyu domination." A 1966 survey by Donald Rothchild showed a strong sense among smaller groups that they were failing to receive their share of government services and mobility opportunities.[64] Expression of this grievance became more public, and began to be heard in Parliamentary debates; in a 1968 session, a KPU member charged:

> Today, when we look at the top jobs in the government, we find that in most of the ministries, including certain cooperatives, practically all these have been taken over by people from the Central Province (i.e., Kikuyu). . . . If one tribe alone can take over about 72 percent of the Kenya jobs, and they are less [than] two million people, how can you expect 25 percent of the jobs to go to more than eight million people who belong to other tribes?[65]

62. For detail on this process, see John W. Harbeson, *Nation-Building in Kenya* (Evanston: Northwestern University Press, 1973).

63. Marris and Somerset, *African Businessmen*, pp. 70-71.

64. Olorunsola, *The Politics of Cultural Sub-Nationalism in Africa*, pp. 298-99.

65. G. F. Oduya, *National Assembly Debates*, XIV, sixth session, February 27, 1968, quoted in Olorunsola, *Cultural Sub-Nationalism in Africa*, p. 302.

In mid-1969, a period of intense polarization occurred, coincident with the assassination of probably the ablest and most influential non-Kikuyu minister, Tom Mboya. Many Luo were unwilling to accept the official solution of the crime as the mad act of a demented individual. The resumption of mass oathing, with truckloads of urban Kikuyu being trundled off to a rural retreat for performance of this ceremony, redoubled fears—as did the political slogan, first widely heard about that time, that "the flag must not leave Kikuyuland," a reference to the imminence of a political succession, in view of President Kenyatta's advanced age.

There is clearly a deep-seated ambivalence regarding the interlocking relationship between Kikuyu self-awareness and their dominant role in the political institutions. Kikuyuhood was diffusely present in the precolonial context, with the Masai as the primary point of competitive reference. The imposition of European domination transferred the relevant other for Kikuyu, offered a new set of pathways to progress, while simultaneously erecting barriers along them. In reaction to European rule, an extremely thorough and far-reaching political and cultural mobilization occurred in Kikuyuland—at once nationalist and ethnic. During the colonial period, the Kikuyu acquired the skills, aspirations, and resources to assume a dominant role socially, economically and politically; this was swiftly realized after 1960. Their pre-eminent role in liquidating colonialism offered an obvious rationale for their de facto situation. Kikuyu hegemony, since it exists, may be viewed as a natural state of affairs, worthy of preservation.

Yet the ideological traditions of African nationalism prohibit open advocacy of this type of cultural objective. In contrast to the Malays, who can claim that the Malaysia state is and of right ought to be symbolically identified with their cultural identity, or the Sikh, who avow their religio-linguistic community to be a "nation," Kikuyu spokesmen could not possibly adopt such a position. As we argued in chapter 3, such is the force of the idea of the state and nation in shaping reality, it would not even occur to them to do so. Territorial Kenya cannot be asserted to be a Kikuyu polity; this banal but elemental fact sets important limits on the character of Kikuyu subnationalism itself. Kikuyu unity was indispensable as an organizational weapon in the broader African nationalist purpose of smashing European domination; thus mobilization relied upon Kikuyu cultural symbols and rituals as well as anticolonial grievances. The Kikuyu hegemony which followed independence could be enjoyed and even defended but not ideologically articulated.

Nor should the importance of sub-Kikuyu units of identification be overlooked. The inner council of Kenya leadership comes from Kiambu district, a pattern which emerged clearly with the development of the

Kenya African Union. Kiambu is adjacent to Nairobi, and thus urban-rural interchange is most intense. Nationalism drew its manpower and resources most heavily from Kiambu. The internal hegemony of the Kiambu group became a part of the everyday vocabulary of politics in the latter 1960s, in relation to less advantaged Nyeri and Fort Hall Kikuyu. There was also a significant social division between the new middle sectors of prosperous Kikuyu and those who remained land-hungry, or unemployed in Nairobi. Forest fighters had been heavily recruited among these last two categories; whispers were heard that those who had endured the greatest personal risks had not been proportionately rewarded.[66]

DIOULA TRANSFORMED

One other example of identity transformation, illustrating a rather different pattern, is the case of the forest Dioula of the Ivory Coast. The Mande cultural-linguistic zone covers a vast arc of West Africa from Niger to Senegal. The Mandinka (Manding, Mandingo, Malinke) were rulers and warriors; the Bambara, sedentary, non-Muslim cultivators; and the Dioula, long-distance traders and clerics. In the shadow of French colonial rule, a trading community soon established itself in southern Ivory Coast, with the administrative capital of Abidjan as its focal point. The complexities of ethnic identities are well reflected in the Dioula question; there is an area of northeast Ivory Coast settled by a group also often called Dioula in the early ethnic catalogues, although this was not a trading diaspora group, but rather the whole Mande array of Mandinka, Bambara, and Dioula. But the forest Dioula were at first recruited from the trading community.[67]

Quickly, however, "Dioula" acquired a somewhat different connotation in Ivory Coast. The label was applied to all those who were strangers, traders, Muslims and who spoke one of the Mande languages. In time, the social functions filled by Dioula extended beyond trade; however, the distinctiveness as Muslim strangers, sharing a lingua franca, provided an integrative frame for this somewhat diverse community. There were

66. On Kenya politics, in addition to works already cited, see Cherry Gertzel, *The Politics of Independent Kenya* (Evanston: Northwestern University Press, 1970); George Bennett, *Kenya: A Political History* (London: Oxford University Press, 1963); Susan Wood, *Kenya: The Tensions of Progress* (London: Oxford University Press, 1960); George Bennett and Carl Rosberg, *The Kenyatta Election: Kenya 1960-1961* (London: Oxford University Press, 1961); Oginga Odinga, *Not Yet Uhuru* (London: Heinemann, 1967).

67. Yves Person, "The Dyula and the Manding World," and Peter Gingiss, "Dyula: A Sociolinguistic Perspective," in *Conference on Manding Studies*.

for the colonial period important links with the classical Dioula trading communities in Mali, through the kola nut trade, a crop grown in the forest, purchased by Dioula, and marketed in the savanna. However, independence in 1960 of Ivory Coast and Mali and the rigorous socialism practiced in the first postindependence years in Mali, ruptured this trading network. Dioula reoriented their commerce to sea-borne trade and truck transport in southern Ivory Coast. These trade patterns were fundamentally different in that the operations could no longer be contained within a single ethnic framework; in particular, the Dioula did not control shipping. Other radical changes in the definition and nature of the community seem imminent. Islamic identity and the satisfying socioeconomic role available through the Dioula trading system had led earlier generations to shun Western school. The vertiginous social ascent of those with formal educational credentials after independence was not lost upon the Dioula community; a recent inquiry found that the present generation is being pushed through the school system—Catholic schools if need be. Nor did parents particularly desire their children to follow their occupational roles; rather, they were anxious for their offspring to seize opportunity where it might be found.[68]

The structure of the political arena in Ivory Coast offered fewer inducements for intensive political mobilization of ethnicity than in Kenya. At an early point, the dominant party, the Parti Démocratique de la Côte d'Ivoire, had found it expedient to organize its subsections in greater Abidjan on an ethnic basis.[69] Because of the efficacy of their communications network, a number of Dioula were to be found as party branch functionaries elsewhere in the southern Ivory Coast. But the territorialization of nationalism threatened their position, as many had their original family connections outside the Ivory Coast. With independence, some representatives of the Dioula community were strategically placed in the upper reaches of the political structure; interests of the ethnic collectivity could best be advanced by using these individuals as ethnic patrons, rather than by mobilizing the community as a communal pressure group. President Felix Houphouet-Boigny was prepared to accept ethnic clientelism as a basis of operation, while treating it as a formally illegitimate basis of political demands.[70]

Thus Dioula identity has been in a constant process of redefinition in the present century. Its initial core came from the classical trading diaspora. In the colonial context, it became an incorporative, "super-

68. Barbara Lewis, "The Dioula Disapora in the Ivory Coast South," in conference on Manding Studies.

69. Aristide Zolberg, *One-Party Government in the Ivory Coast* (Princeton: Princeton University Press, 1964), p. 116.

70. Lewis, "The Dioula Diaspora in the Ivory Coast South," pp. 15-16.

tribal" framework which absorbed Mande-speaking Muslim migrants to the southern Ivory Coast. Most recently, it has been cut off, in socio-commercial linkages, from its original hinterland base. The quest for social mobility is now pursued within a framework similar to that for other southern Ivory Coast groups. The definition of the political arena made aggressive cultural mobilization dysfunctional; the risk of illuminating the non-Ivory Coast origins of many and the lack of numerical strength in relation to groups such as the Bete and Baoule were obvious cultural disincentives.[71]

We have by no means exhausted the possible range of variation in patterns of cultural identity change. One very important category is the null mobilization case. In several important cultural pluralism situations, congeries of closely related groups, which appear to have the potential for expansion of communal scale in terms of cultural commonalities, simply fail to coalesce. Major examples of this phenomenon are Latin American Indians, the Berbers of North Africa, especially Morocco, and the Galla populations of Ethiopia. In subsequent chapters, we shall explore this theme further.

Through the cases we have examined here, we hope to have illustrated the dynamics of identity change; from them, a number of propositions may be distilled. (1) Cultural responses are shaped by the structure of the field of pluralism, perceived collective inequalities, the range of feasible communal options, and the cultural attributes of the polity within which cultural competition occurs. (2) Where identities are firmly hierarchical in dominant paradigms of society, mobility must be achieved by improving the ranking of the group within the order of stratification or through incorporation into a more highly ranked collectivity. (3) Where no entrenched social consensus exists on cultural hierarchy, uplift goals may be pursued through cultural mobilization and competition. (4) In caste or racially stratified systems, barriers to individual mobility of rank endogamy and social taboo may make incorporation strategies impossible and force groups to seek mobility through collective emulation of higher ranks. (5) Mobilization of cultural strata in a hierarchical system may facilitate the emulative process, through enforcement of new traits, and the suppression of practices associated with

71. Other useful studies on Ivory Coast politics include Philip Foster and Aristide Zolberg (eds.), *Ghana and the Ivory Coast* (Chicago: University of Chicago Press, 1971); Ruth Schacter Morgenthau, *Political Parties in French-Speaking West Africa* (Oxford: Clarendon Press, 1964), pp. 166-218; Richard E. Stryker in Michael F. Lofchie (ed.), *The State of the Nations* (Berkeley: University of California Press, 1971), pp. 119-40; Martin Staniland, in Colin Leys (ed.), *Politics and Change in Developing Countries* (Cambridge: Cambridge University Press, 1969), pp. 135-76. On the general theme of this chapter, see also the excellent article by Donald L. Horowitz, "Three Dimensions of Ethnic Politics," *World Politics*, XXIII, no. 2 (January 1971), 232-44.

lower strata. (6) Democratic, electoral politics, even though hierarchy is not eliminated, can provide important resources for groups seeking uplift within a stratified system. (7) In cultural hierarchies, rank-ladder climbing requires not only emulation of groups above, but reinforcement of differentiation with those below. (8) Where no institutional barriers exist and identities are not highly politicized or intensely held, uplift through incorporation into higher ranked groups may be feasible through language change, fictive or real kinship ties, or other means. (9) Where power and prestige, and mobility institutions are monopolized by a given cultural entity, aspirant individuals seeking high status roles may be forced to accept incorporation. (10) In stratified cultural settings where differentiation is highly visible and salient, as in racial hierarchies, incorporation strategies may be impossible. (11) In culturally competitive situations, groups may find attractive strategies aimed at securing control of territorial subunits, in order that resource allocation within a delimited field may be culturally determined in their favor. (12) Cultural mobilization requires sharpened boundary definition; thus quite small differences become reinforced, as in the linguistic expression of the Sikh-Hindu cleavage in Punjab. (13) Cultural mobilization may be a powerful group phenomenon, without necessarily affecting the behavior of all individuals; cultural polarization is a constraint upon individual role choice but does not necessarily eclipse all of the other complex motivations which enter into human behavioral calculations. (14) Cultural mobilization may set some limits on political mobility; as with the Akali Dal elites, top leadership roles either at the provincial or national level required reorientation toward the national identity or majority culture within the province. (15) The use of cultural mobilization as a political weapon is a two-edged sword; cultural politicians must compromise and bargain with the national elite and other groups to obtain material advantage, yet in so doing must not appear to betray their following. (16) In competitive situations, very wide inequalities in access to modernity often develop between cultural segments. (17) Cultural mobilization is likely to occur when these disparities become salient, and a threat of permanent disadvantage looms, as illustrated by the Malay case. (18) When elections are introduced in a climate of communal mobilization and perceived disparities, political organization is likely to reflect the cultural cleavages. (19) The dominant paradigm of the nation-state, in cultural terms, constrains the form of expression of cultural solidarity; while Tamils and Malays strongly asserted their identity in relation to the state, Kikuyuhood in Kenya could not be articulated in these terms. (20) The relevant others of cultural self-definition are prone to change over time; for the Kikuyu, Masai once played this role but were replaced by Europeans in the colonial period and by Luo after independence.

5 Symbols, Threats, and Identity

In the late eighteenth century, a Muslim scholar, Shah Waliullah, wrote from north India to an Afghan leader imploring his military intervention:

> In short, the Muslim community is in a pitiable condition. All control of the machinery of government is in the hands of Hindus because they are the only people who are capable and industrious. . . . Certainly it is incumbent upon you to march to India, destroy Maratha domination and rescue weak and old Muslims from the clutches of non-Muslims. If, God forbid, domination by infidels continues, Muslims will forget Islam and within a short time become such a nation there will be nothing left to distinguish them from non-Muslims.[1]

This text is cited as perhaps the first statement of protonationalism among Indian Muslims, the precursor of Pakistan. Its theme is interesting and important: community in danger. A perilous hour was at hand, when the very survival of the cultural collectivity was in question. To Shah Waliullah, cultural extinction loomed. At the time of his letter, only external military intervention could salvage the situation; cultural mobilization and self-defense apparently was not feasible—"weak and old Muslims" seemingly could not be relied upon. His prophecy, of course, was false; Muslim political identity eventually became mobilized as never before under His Christian Majesty, the British raj. But its message is no less important; the threat to communal identity is the ultimate categorical imperative of cultural pluralism.

Two centuries later, in Nigeria in 1966, the ranking civil servant of the short-lived secessionist state of Biafra offers a moving description of a powerfully mobilizing event: the arrival of a train in the Biafran capital of Enugu from northern Nigeria, bearing a tragic cargo of Ibo refugees from the massacres in the Hausa cities of September-October 1966. The sight of the battered, broken, and terrified fellow Ibo dismounting brought the crowd to a frenzy. The most grisly spectacle of all was the appearance from the train of a naked woman, holding aloft the severed head of her child.[2] The emotionality of the scene, reports Akpan, was simply indescribable. A moment's reflection on the meaning of that macabre spectacle will serve to introduce further the themes to be considered in this chapter.

1. Sayeed, *Pakistan: The Formative Phase*, p. 2.
2. N. V. Akpan, *The Struggle for Secession 1966-1970* (London: Frank Cass, 1971), p. xii.

Within the highly polarized context of that moment, there could have been hardly a soul who failed to invest the child's death with the same social meaning. No one would perceive it as the tragic and brutal loss of a single child's life. For it was not a mere child, but an impersonalized symbol standing for the Ibo community. The symbolic chain of cognition immediately identified the assassin; it could only be a Hausa. What individual it was did not matter; within the symbolic logic of the moment, the felon was not an individual at all, but an archetypal Hausa. The assassin was visualized in the mind's eye by the stereotypes of the modal Hausa—the characteristic dress, physical appearance, demeanor, lightly retouched by the pejorative perspective. The death of the child was a grim summons to the cultural choices: resistance or genocide. The child's fate, within the cognitive processes of the Ibo crowd, was the destiny of the entire collectivity unless it took arms. The Hausa—fanatic Muslims, backward in education, consumed with hatred for the Ibo— had now unveiled their true intentions. Little matter that the atrocities had been the work of a relatively small segment of the Hausa-Fulani— that a major part of the massacres were the work of leaderless, undisciplined troops, many not Hausa, themselves disoriented by the earlier slaying of a number of their leading officers by Ibo conspirators. Nor would anyone have believed, at that moment, that many northerners, prominent and humble, had risked their own lives to conceal Ibo acquaintances until the storm abated. Human perception, social psychologists instruct us, always tends to selectivity; polarized perception selects absolutely. The Ibo community was subjected to transcendent threat; all of the threats and insecurities were condensed into a single response of intense emotion, rage blended with fear, to the bestial symbol before the crowd.

Cultural pluralism, we have argued, is at root a subjective phenomenon. Its identity units are a set of categories in which the individual orders the social universe and relates himself to it. For this reason, the social psychology of cultural pluralism deserves consideration. The two examples suggest the themes we wish to explore. Group categorizations are perceived through characterization in symbolic form; the role of symbols and stereotypes in conveying cultural differentiation bears scrutiny. Detection of threats to the collectivity is a potent factor of cultural mobilization; anxieties and insecurities dictate solidary responses. Moments of crisis engender acute anxieties and highly polarized perceptions; the part played in cultural mobilization by the social psychology of crisis we will examine through several sustained illustrations.

SYMBOLS AND IDENTITY

Cultural identities, then, contain a set of symbolic representations of reality. The sense of collective self and the relevant others within the social perceptual field are mapped with cognitive guideposts which invest the particular events and facts of daily life with communal meanings. The activation of cultural perceptions of social conflict unleashes a spiral of hostility-building and fear-evoking responses, which require the most consummate statesmanship to manage. Murray Edelman, in a brilliant study of the symbolic aspects of political behavior, notes the potency of cultural issues in this arena:

> In a secular age in which class divisions are vague it is doubtful that racism and nationalism can be surpassed as potent symbolic issues. Religion has often served the same symbolic function at other times. . .
> Divisions based upon race, nationality, religion, and clearly demarked class or caste evoke the most sensitive and cherished anxieties regarding self-definition and survival.[3]

Man as a social being is unique in his symbolizing ability. It is the capacity to relate past, present, and future through a set of reconstructed images which generalize individual experiences, formulate them in group and collective terms, and invest them with social meaning. Man thus relates himself to his social universe through abstracted constructs of it, which then become the reality through which the messages of the sensory apparatus are received. In different ways, Karl Mannheim and Kenneth Burke have both stated the problem well:

> Only in a quite limited sense does the single individual create out of himself the mode of speech and of thought we attribute to him. He speaks the language of his group; he thinks in the manner in which his group thinks. He finds at his disposal only certain words and their meanings. These not only determine to a large extent the avenues of approach to the surrounding world, but they also show at the same time from which angle and in which context of activity objects have hitherto been perceptible and accessible to the group or the individual.[4]

And however important to us is the tiny sliver of reality each of us has experienced firsthand, the whole overall 'picture' is but a construct of our symbolic systems. To meditate on this fact until one sees its full implications is much like peering over the edge of things into an ultimate abyss. And doubtless that's one reason why, though man is typically the symbol-using animal, he clings to a kind of

3. Murray Edelman, *Politics as Symbolic Action*, pp. 100-101.
4. Karl Mannheim, *Ideology and Utopia* (New York: Harcourt, Brace and Co., 1936), p. 3.

naive verbal realism that refuses to realize the full extent of the role played by symbolicity in his notions of reality.[5]

The cognitive map shaped by cultural identity symbols is but one page of a mental atlas. Other social codes, related to other roles held by the actor, provide alternative charts of reality. We need to recollect here our argument in chapter 2 concerning the underlying fluidity of cultural pluralism as behavioral determinant. Evocation of the cultural map of reality depends upon the reception of social cues which prompt this response. Such cues are numerous in culturally plural environments; they are encountered in everyday life through hearing a different language, the sight of persons whose physical appearance or dress betrays communal difference, transactions and interactions involving others whose cultural distinctness is mutually perceived. Probably more often, the cues are supplied by messages—communication face-to-face or through the impersonal media—which have already processed reality through a cultural symbol system and transmit information in a communal structure: Whites assault a Black; Palestinians kidnap a diplomat; Muslims attack a Philippine police post.

At moments of complete polarization—the scene at Enugu station—the intensity of culturally cued messages may be such as to exclude all others. However, most of the time they will compete for cognitive attention with sensory perceptions and information flows which evoke alternative social images. Thus the saliency of cultural identity may ebb and flow; a careful charting of the flow of perception during a single day would doubtless reveal a series of minor fluctuations. Over longer periods, one would also note periods where the confluence of events generated a heavy flow of culturally laden messages, evoking a high degree of mobilization of communal solidarity sentiments, alternating with interludes where other patterns of socially structured information dominate the scene and cultural identity is quite quiescent.

Some further elements of complexity require consideration. Not all cultural maps are drawn with equal clarity; furthermore, as we argued

5. Kenneth Burke, *Language as Symbolic Action* (Berkeley: University of California Press, 1966), p. 5, quoted in Edelman, *Politics as Symbolic Action*, p. 2. Marshall Singer, in a particularly useful article, develops the argument that identity groups are formed by individuals who perceive the external world in more or less similar ways, and communicate to each other this perception. The ease of communication provides constant increments of perception similarities, through its own feedback processes, which in turn reinforce group identity. The set of commonalities, and shared symbol sets—verbal (language) and nonverbal—which define cultural groupings, render them particularly potent in the hierarchy of solidarities of each individual. "Group Perception and Social Change in Ceylon", *International Journal of Comparative Sociology*, VII, nos. 1-2 (March 1966), 209-26.

in chapter 4, they are subject to constant rectification and reordering, through the processes of assimilation, incorporation, differentiation, and rearrangement of cultural hierarchies. At one extreme, we have instances such as the racial cleavages in South Africa, Guyana, or the United States, or caste in rural India, where the identities are salient, intense, and symmetrical. There is social consensus on the nature of White and Black as racial categories in the United States, with ambiguity only in a small number of cases where the skin coloration so closely approaches the White category that physical distinctiveness disappears. Similarly, in South Africa, Whites, Africans, Coloureds, and Indians are absolutely clear categories, with uncertainty only in a small number of cases of Coloureds where physical appearance may closely approximate the White category; here administrative reinforcement of racial castes intervenes to maintain the sharpness of the boundaries. In village India, where all of the ritual and behavioral aspects of subcaste differentiation may be fully operative, jatis as identity systems are constantly reaffirmed in the symbolic recognition accorded differentiation, with the detailed prescriptions for marks of deference of lower subcastes to higher ones and the strongly sanctioned norms for avoidance of polluting interactions on the part of higher groups. At the other end of the spectrum, in Lima or Guatemala City the difference between mestizo and Indian, where the latter speaks Spanish and drops distinctive costume, is not readily distinguishable in casual interactions. In many African cities, where multilingualism is widespread, no obvious visible marks of ethnicity fix the boundaries, and identities are fluid, overlapping, and situational, cultural ambiguity stands out.

Arousal-quiescence and saliency-diffuseness constitute two key axes defining the operation of symbols of cultural identity. A third dimension lies in the clarity or ambiguity of the social cues. The refugee train at Enugu station was of pristine clarity to the waiting Ibo crowd; there were no two ways of interpreting that experience. But the very extreme nature of that example has led us to repeated reference to it; the ordinary social messages which daily bombard the individual may be far less clear. In the Nigerian army coup in January 1966, the first public reaction was one of general rejoicing at the overthrow of a corrupt and discredited regime, as the first messages communicating the event laid stress on the cleansing and nationalist objectives of the coup-makers. Subsequently, supplementary messages contained a differently structured social interpretation; the high ethnic homogeneity of the central figures in the coup (Ibo), and an equally high ethnic selectivity in those assassinated in the execution of the coup (nearly all non-Ibo) introduced a large measure of ambiguity in public orientations.

The first battery of messages was highly gratifying and free of cultural cues; the second set carried deeply unsettling ethnic connotations. In the 1964 Kwilu rebellion in Zaire, to which reference was made in our opening pages, the cues received in the national political arena and in arenas removed from the immediate Kwilu context related to symbols of radical nationalist revolution invoked as the justification for revolt. Within Kwilu itself, the rebellion swiftly acquired symbolic identification with the two ethnic groups which gave it its main support, the Pende and Mbundu—through the ethnic identification of the leaders most closely associated and the localization of its activities. In distant regions, the ethnic symbols were not familiar, and it was much easier to understand as an antigovernment movement. Thus, in other zones of rebellion, the name of its paramount leader, Pierre Mulele, was invoked as a ritual incantation by insurgent troops on the attack; this usage, symbolizing the force of successful rebellion, was totally devoid of ethnic connotations. Thus the same political message may, in different areas or milieux, be perceived through completely different cognitive structures. Social messages may vary across a whole spectrum of cultural loadings, from the uniformly perceived, stark cultural threat, through zones of ambiguity where cultural connotations are perceived only by the unusually self-conscious communal cognescenti, to meanings utterly devoid of culturally plural implications.

In many, probably most situations, cultural symbol systems are not symmetrical. Each individual has his own perceptual field; the configuration of cultural units within it is not necessarily identical to that of his neighbor. Even in cultural self-identification, we have argued the ample possibility for multiplicity of attachments and ambiguity of self-placement. The range of variation is much greater in the perception of significant others. To Guyanese of African derivation, East Indians may be perceived as a single social conglomerate; within the East Indian community, distinctions of original language, religion, and even caste may be of critical social significance. However, the Afro-Guyanese devote no mental energy to distinguishing the internal subdivisions of the East Indian community. In Kinshasa, for Kongo, in most circumstances, no cognitive purpose is served by perceiving migrants from up-river who use Lingala as an urban language as other than "Ngala." Among the up-river groups, cultural symbol recognition to distinguish area and ethnic group of origin is much more precisely developed. In contexts where the array of cultural symbol cognitions available for recognition of different groups varies from one individual or group to another, the likelihood that social messages will be subject to differential interpretation is enhanced.

THE FORCE OF SYMBOLS: THE PROPHET'S HAIR

The place of symbols in mapping cultural pluralism should be clear enough. Edelman cogently observes that "It is through their power to merge diverse perceptions and beliefs into a new and unified perspective that symbols affect what men want, what they do, and the identity they create for themselves."[6] In this perspective, we may appreciate the peculiarly galvanizing force of some issues which appear quite devoid of material significance. A case in point is the implausible crisis over the Prophet's hair in the Indian-administered portion of Kashmir, an area still contested by India and Pakistan. The saliency of religious symbols was sustained in part by the continuing state of tension at the interstate level over the future of the area. Kashmir had been a princely state under British India; its ruling house was Hindu, but the majority of the populace was Muslim. Its status was not yet settled at the moment of independence in August 1947; shortly thereafter the maharaja announced his accession to India. Irregular Muslim forces invaded in October 1947, followed shortly after by the Pakistan fledgling army. Although a segment came under Pakistan rule by terms of the cease-fire finally arranged to halt the war, the greater and more populous portion remained under Indian administration. The province of Jammu and Kashmir is a culturally quite divided entity; Muslims were dominant in the prosperous vale of Kashmir, while there was a Hindu majority in Jammu. Moreover, the large landowners in the valley of Kashmir proper were Hindu. Jammu and Kashmir were also linguistically different. The province also contained a third area, Ladakh, which was Buddhist and Tibetan in its cultural linkages. A large fraction of Muslim sentiment initially favored accession to Pakistan, although the declining prestige of Karachi in the 1950s led to a shift toward simple secession and independence. With Indo-Pakistan border wars in 1947, 1965, and 1972, a continuing undercurrent of uncertainty as to the ultimate future status and the complex cultural cleavages, Jammu and Kashmir had a charged atmosphere. The most serious disorders generated within Kashmir came over a question which catalyzed the conflicting symbol system.

On the outskirts of the Kashmir capital, Srinigar, is found a Muslim shrine dedicated to the preservation and worhsip of a sacred relic, a hair of the Prophet Mohammed. At the beginning of 1964, the hair was suddenly found to be missing; within hours of the discovery, massive hysterical mobs were on the rampage up and down the valley of Kashmir.

6. Edelman, *Politics as Symbolic Action*, pp. 6-7. This section owes a heavy debt to this work, as well as to Edelman's earlier study, *The Symbolic Uses of Politics* (Urbana: University of Illinois Press, 1967).

The culprits were never discovered but were readily identified symbolically. Who indeed would have borne such animus to the Muslim community as to destroy its most revered artifact? The question needed no answer;
a moment of extremely grave cultural confrontation was at hand, with
communal holocaust inches away. Within a few days, the government
lowered the symbolic tension somewhat by announcing that the relic
had been found. However, for the following month disorders continued,
with scores of deaths and many more injuries. The government then
permitted Muslim divines to examine the hair to judge its authenticity.
Through what channel of revelation the verdict was reached is uncertain; however, the hair was adjudged genuine, and the crisis subsided.
In a climate of uncertainty and suspicion as to Hindu aims, both in
provincial politics and at the hands of the government of India, one hair
was a condensatory symbol drawing all of the inchoate fears into the
focus of a highly emotive sense of threat to their religious identity. A
single hair had more mobilizing force than two decades of political change
which saw quite significant measures in the field of land reform and
employment, which much more directly affected the material interests
of the Muslim and Hindu communities.[7] Many comparable examples
can be found; the Sepoy mutiny in 1857 in India was triggered in
part by the discovery by Muslim troops that pork grease was being used
to pack their cartridges. In Zaire, the 1944 Kananga (Luluabourg) mutiny
had as one immediate precipitant the appearance in mess halls of corned
beef cans whose trade label bore the face of a smiling African, erro-
neously assumed to be a self-portrait of the contents. Symbol sets are
the ultimate cultural reality.

SYMBOLS AND STEREOTYPING

To perform their labor of ordering the social universe, symbols rely
heavily on stereotyping. A set of imputed traits, physical and behavioral,
are attributed to a given communal group. Usually the stereotype has
at least mildly pejorative connotations. Once well established, it acquires
reasonable consistency across the stereotype-holding group. To some extent, one might argue that the degree of homogenization of stereotypes
was an indicator of the saliency of cultural pluralism. Two separate
studies in India showed a quite remarkable consistency of stereotypes
held concerning other regional groups.[8] Once firmly implanted, stereo-

7. Balraj Puri chapter on Jammu and Kashmir, in Weiner, *State Politics in India,* pp. 215-
42.

8. Selig S. Harrison, *India: The Most Dangerous Decades* (Princeton: Princeton
University Press, 1960), pp. 103-10.

types can orient cognitions to a powerful degree; an everyday example is the frequent claim by American Whites with few interracial contacts that they are unable to distinguish one Black from another. The stereotype overwhelms the sensory organs; there are, for such persons, no individual Negroes, but a single merged archetype so potent that it simply overrides visual perception.

Stereotypes have been most thoroughly explored in the study of "national character" perceptions, which enjoyed a certain vogue in the 1950s. [9] An earlier generation of anthropologists and sociologists in the field of race stereotypes, made important if unwitting contributions. One early (1898) sociological treatise described the Black population of Boston in the following terms: "Some have the instincts of gentlemen. . . . The majority, however, exhibit the usual characteristics of the Negro race: loud and coarse, revealing much more of the animal qualities than of the spiritual. Yet even they are good-natured and obliging people, and are often, of course, very religious in their crude way."[10] Physical anthropologists developed theories of modal head shapes ("long heads," "round heads"), cranial capacities, and other physical typing which contributed as much to stereotypes as it did to science. One noted anthropologist, Franz Boas, undertook an interesting class experiment to introduce his students to stereotyping. Each freshman was asked to stand in turn, and the class were to record their views as to his ethnic derivation. Some 40 percent of the Italians were classified as Jews, and vice versa.[11]

Jews have a particularly ubiquitous and relative consistent stereotype. A 1932 study of college students extracted the following set of stereotypic traits: shrewd, mercenary, industrious, grasping, intelligent, ambitious, sly.[12] Interestingly, the stereotype is sufficiently coherent that it has been borrowed as self-image by two particularly mobile African groups, the Ibo of Nigeria and Luba-Kasai of Zaire. The harsh edges may be modified; "grasping and mercenary" becomes "enterprising and commercially skilled." These attributes are an explanation—and by stereotypic condensation a confirmation by external reference group—of the self-concept of success and dynamism. To be the Jew of Nigeria or Zaire is also to recognize the hostilities and resentments engendered in others by too-conspicuous mobility; by implication, it further suggests these animosities are undeserved prejudice.

9. Perhaps the best such exploration of stereotypes at the national level was W. Buchanan and H. Cantril, *How Nations See Each Other* (Urbana: University of Illinois Press, 1953).

10. Quoted in Gordon W. Allport, *The Nature of Prejudice* (Garden City, N.Y.: Doubleday Anchor, 1958), p. 84.

11. George Eaton Simpson and J. Milton Yinger, *Racial and Cultural Minorities* (rev. ed.; New York: Harper & Bros., 1958), pp. 37-68.

12. The 1932 study by D. Katz and K. W. Braly is summarized in Allport, *The Nature of Prejudice*, p. 188.

Fear is a common denominator of arousal of cultural symbol sets. Perceptions which create anxieties are a call to arms. The summons of insecurity is imperative: collective solidarity reinforces group awareness and raises the cost to the individual of failure to align himself with the perception of crisis. Cultural symbols come to dominate the flow of information. When a crisis threshold is reached, message flows intensify through the circuits of cultural plural alignments. Like cancer cells, heavily distorted information in the form of rumor multiplies, a process often unwittingly abetted by authorities whose first impulsive reaction is to impose an information blackout. Such a policy leaves a clear field to the pathology of rumor. With high cultural polarization, information flows will be largely internal to communities, with a strong distorting effect. The climate of intense anxiety lends plausibility to the most lurid reports of what hostile communities have done. Rumor is often varnished with elaborate detail, which in itself lends an aura of reality to the tale (rather than "greens are killing reds," the rumor becomes "at five o'clock a gang of ten greens massacred three reds on 13th Street by the bridge"). Attribution of the rumor to a source of high social standing or purported witnesses also enhances credibility ("the doctor saw 250 green bodies in the hospital morgue"). A veritable fantasy world develops, which bears little relationship to the empirical facts; this process is one of the explanations for the frequent revelation after the event that initial reports of casualty levels have been vastly inflated.

CULTURAL THREATS: THE 1966 UGANDA CRISIS

The significance of threat and crisis in cultural cleavage may be profitably explored through some specific instances, the Uganda crisis of 1966 and the circumstances surrounding independence in Guyana and Zaire. In the Uganda case, the confrontation of May 1966 was the culmination of a slow decomposition of the political compromise through which power was transferred in 1962. The most difficult problem in defining political arrangements for an independent Uganda was the status of the kingdom of Buganda in relation to the remainder of the country. The kingdom had always enjoyed a special relationship with the colonial administration; its numerous elite held a commanding position in the modern sector, and its countryside enjoyed a relative prosperity. However, Buganda accounted for only 25 percent of the total population of Uganda, or 16 percent of ethnic Ganda, if immigrant rural labor is excluded. Thus the arithmetic of universal suffrage, necessary basis for power transfer, inexorably altered the balance of influence within the country. At various points in the negotiations leading to independence, Buganda threatened separation. Shortly before power transfer, a tenuous compromise was reached, whereby the king of Buganda, Kabaka Edward Mutesa II, became chief of state, while the prime minister was A. Milton Obote, from the once-neglected north.

By early 1966, polarization was growing; a conspiracy was mounted, supported by Kabaka Mutesa in alliance with anti-Obote elements from the southern part of Uganda within his own political party to unseat him through parliamentary action. This move came close to succeeding, but Obote outmaneuvered his opponents by suddenly arresting the ministers who had backed the anti-Obote scheme and suspending the constitution. A new constitution was then promulgated, which removed Kabaka Mutesa from his functions as chief of state, and centralized power in Obote's hands. The Kabaka and Buganda legislature rejected the new constitution; rhetoric gradually escalated, reaching an apex with a resolution on 20 May 1966 demanding in belligerent tones that the Obote government remove its offices from Buganda soil (where Uganda's capital happens to be situated) within ten days, on the grounds that it was illegal and unconstitutional. The air was heavy with ethnic tension and the foreboding that decisive events were at hand.

From a Ganda perspective, the sense of threat was very vivid and was focussed on the institution of monarchy and person of the Kabaka. The British had always accorded formal deference to the Ganda ruler, and it was widely believed throughout East Africa that the Ganda received privileged treatment from the colonizer because they had a spokesman who could treat on more nearly equal terms than they. At a critical moment in the emergence of modern politics, the British unwittingly reinforced the prestige of the Kabaka by deporting him in 1953; the monarchy was able to subtract itself from the now-cumbersome embrace of colonialism and align itself, as a symbol, with the growing forces of rural populism and cultural sub-nationalism in Buganda. In 1961, a political movement took form in Buganda founded on the symbol of monarchy as the embodiment of ethnic unity; this party, Kabaka Yekka (the Kabaka alone) completely swept the electoral boards in Buganda. As the 1966 crisis took form, the Kabaka was at the symbolic heart of the confrontation.[13] In a seminar session, a Ugandan student (non-Ganda)

13. On the transformation of the monarchy, see Crawford Young, "Kingship in Buganda," paper delivered to the 1971 Annual Meetings of the African Studies Association, Denver, November 1971, to be published in Rene Lemarchand, *The Politics of Kingship in Africa*, forthcoming, 1974. Among the numerous sources on Buganda, see especially Lloyd A. Fallers (ed.), *The King's Men* (London: Oxford University Press, 1964); David Apter, *The Political Kingdom in Uganda* (Princeton: Princeton University Press, 1961); D. Anthony Low and R. Cranford Pratt, *Buganda and British Overrule* (London: Oxford University

summed up the centrality of the royal symbol in Buganda by saying, "You just can't talk political science about it."

The view from other regions of Uganda was quite different. In many areas, Ganda chiefs had initially been used to establish colonial rule. Everywhere, the special status of Buganda was a source of envy and irritation. Political awakening had increased consciousness of Buganda's commanding position in the modern sector. Many had been unhappy about the choice of the Kabaka as chief of state. Although some political factions were prepared to combine with Buganda to oust the Obote government, the premise of Ganda pre-eminence drew little support, and the threats of secession being made would deliver a truncated country unto an uncertain future. Elites from districts such as Acholi and Lango, where Obote had particularly strong support, found themselves increasingly insecure in the Ganda-dominated capital; the Buganda ultimatum to remove government offices in ten days made their anxieties more precise and carried the possibility of mob actions directed against northerners. Such was the social psychology of imminent confrontation; all parties to the crisis were scanning the horizon for the dark clouds of cultural threat.

Kabaka Mutesa describes the beginning of the armed confrontation in his autobiography:

> It was not yet dawn—about 5:30 in the morning—when I was awakened suddenly by the sound of gunfire: quite near, I reckoned, certainly inside the wall that surrounds my palace and grounds. . . .
>
> Troops from the Uganda Army were attacking my palace on the orders of the Prime Minister, Dr. Obote. So much was clear. Nor should it have been in the least surprising. We had been suspecting such a move for weeks, and I myself had been surprised when nothing happened the previous evening. Yet I was filled with a sense of outrage now that it was happening. . . .
>
> Many people from the city, Kampala, and the villages had come up and waited round the palace the previous day, not from knowledge of imminent disaster, but instinctively, uncertain whether they were giving or receiving protection. . . .
>
> There seemed to be an endless follow-up supply of enemy soldiers, many of whom were occupied with destroying my rooms. I think they believed their own stories about hidden supplies of arms, and even indulged in fanciful ideas that a king must have hoards of treasure buried beneath his palace. . . . Once I was overwhelmed with emotion, and foolishly returned to the palace garden alone. There I selected a looter and shot him out of honest rage. I felt calmer and somewhat uplifted as I made my way back.[14]

It was, indeed, no surprise that the attack came at the symbolic core of the kingdom. The palace was desecrated; the ultimate material symbol of

---

Press, 1960); Low, *Buganda in Modern History* (Berkeley: University of California Press, 1971).

14. Sir Edward Mutesa, *The Desecration of My Kingdom* (London: Constable, 1967), pp. 1-3.

the crown, the royal drums, were reported destroyed.[15] During the period immediately before the strike, men had appeared on the Kampala streets in aging World War II uniforms; these were Ganda ex-servicemen, manifesting their readiness to come to the defense of the Kabaka. Not only the evening before, as the Kabaka reports, but for a number of nights preceding many of the ex-servicemen had slept on the palace grounds, to be ready.

With the atmosphere thus saturated with cultural threat, communal mobilization was almost impossible to resist, even for many Ganda who were, intellectually, unwilling conscripts. So central was monarchy to Ganda identity that few spoke against kingship as such, though a number would have downgraded it. More numerous were voices raised concerning the political sagacity of the incumbent Kabaka. In ideological terms, many Ganda elites were committed to a united Uganda, rather than a Buganda-centered political focus. The orthodox dictates of African nationalism certainly commanded such a view; Buganda offered only a very narrow stage—and on its own would likely fall under greater domination of the monarchy and the "king's men." Further, a substantial segment of the Ganda elite were employed in central government ministries or parastatal bodies; in August 1965, a careful survey showed that 37 percent of the 233 top public service positions were held by Ganda, although they were only 15 percent of the population.[16] But in the intense emotionality of a culturally polarized situation, a prudent, career self-interest perspective is not easy to maintain in the face of intense cross-pressures from kinsmen, neighbors, and friends. Indeed, the very polarization was bound to give rise to uneasiness about career prospects themselves, if the incumbent regime were to take an anti-Ganda stance (or, put another way, conclude the Ganda loyalty to the state could not be relied upon). The purge of a number of Ganda officers from the armed forces prior to the armed confrontation was an ominous sign.

Particularly illuminating is the pattern of message diffusion which accompanied the crisis. There was no information given initially on the government radio; for an entire day, informal channels of dissemination had the field to themselves. Every morning, about six o'clock, "taxis" (aging vehicles bulging with passengers, held together by baling wire, prayer, and the ingenuity of their drivers) and busses depart from a central location in Kampala bound for different parts of the country, with a particularly dense traffic covering the well-developed road network of

15. For detail on the battery of royal drums, see Allen J. Lush, "Kiganda Drums," *Uganda Journal*, III, no. 1 (July 1935), 7-25. Although it was universally believed at the time that the drums were destroyed, subsequently it became less clear whether this had happened.

16. Kasfir, "Controlling Ethnicity in Ugandan Politics", p. 255.

Buganda. Within a couple of hours, these vehicles would reach the outer extremities of the kingdom. In each trading center, reports were diffused as to the dramatic events in Kampala. More important towns, especially administrative centers, would also have telephone links. The critical fact is that, in the absence of national information, the entire volume of communication passes through the perceptual screening of cultural networks. Within the passionate context of the moment, the symbolic frame of Ganda identity established a formidable screening apparatus, which eliminated elements dissonant with cognitive anticipations.[17]

The elements of information which immediately diffused were those most consonant with the generalized perception of cultural threat: king and palace under unprovoked assault by the northern-dominated security forces; the three county chiefs closest to the king under arrest; the leading Ganda politician of the king's entourage, Amos Sempa, seized by police (this last piece of information was false at the moment of diffusion, although the anticipation was subsequently confirmed by events). The nature of rural perceptions and reactions is well captured in a diary kept by a Ganda university student, at that moment in the countryside on a research mission:

> The reaction of the people in the villages was that of relief. . . . One man told me that young people in Buganda feared fighting but old people were ready. They have no alternative and Dr. Obote's moves have gone beyond human tolerance. Probably the point to make here is that Kabaka is sacred to Baganda, is part of their lives, and the way Dr. Obote was addressing his name whenever he made a public speech or press conference could not be accommodated by even educated Baganda. This is true even of the students at Makerere:
> Drums (traditional ones) were beaten and all people came from all corners of the sub-county armed to the teeth and all had this to say:
> "Today we want to finish Obote. We are tired of his deliberate attempt to belittle our Kabaka. A man whom we helped to form a government has turned against us. Let him lead his army and the Kabaka will command us."
> . . . While there in dilemma, information came that soldiers were almost entering the palace. It was astonishing and unfortunate news which was followed with a decision by the mob to catch any kind of vehicle which could carry them with their pangas, spears and homemade guns to the palace. . . .
> I was not to be left alone. Some people approached me and told me to be armed like others; otherwise, I was to be branded a detective. . . . What interested me was the determination people had, not even prepared to listen to their chiefs or any suggestion which was not to their thinking. They were all convinced that the Kabaka would get help, say, from Ethiopia. Secondly, he was finishing up the Special Force (an elite commando unit). It was rumored that Kabaka himself was

17. A useful conceptualization of what transpired is offered in Leon Festinger, *A Theory of Cognitive Dissonance* (Stanford: Stanford University Press, 1957).

doing the shooting and that a great many soldiers had been shot. This made people exceedingly happy and the more they heard so, the more they decided to fight. . . . At almost 1 p.m., information came through that Kabaka had escaped after doing a good work of shooting the Special Force. Rumors said that Kabaka had sent instructions that all people should stay in their homes and that he did not want them to go to the palace, that he would fight alone. Secondly, rumors spread that fighting had broken out at the borders between Uganda and Congo in the west, and that help was to come in at 3 p.m. . . .

[The next day] was crowded with fear. People started to leave their homes but were convinced that Kabaka had escaped. Soldiers . . . robbed everything . . . raping, looting and shooting anyone found. It is said that when they found someone and discovered him to be a Muganda—if not killed he would suffer all sorts of things . . . the general aim of soldiers was to kill as many Baganda as they could possibly kill.[18]

Several themes emerge from this document. Perceptions were attuned to key events symbolizing the anticipated confrontation: the arrest of the chiefs, the attack on the palace. Even a false report, on the arrest of Sempa, attains instant credibility, because it is so consonant with expectations. The spontaneous reaction was directed toward the core symbol of identity, the Kabaka. The first instinct of the mob was to get to the palace, to defend the Kabaka; they defend themselves by preserving the symbolic representation of the community. This suicidal disposition is deflated only by a doubtless false report that the symbolic fount had itself spoken against such a reaction; Mutesa's autobiography makes no mention of any instructions to the countryside, but rather stressed his preoccupation with the battle on the palace grounds and personal escape once the conflict was hopeless. In a calamitous situation, reassurance was sought in the nurturing royal symbol; the power of the Kabaka was so great that he could overcome the Special Force. Even if not, his standing in the world was such that he could count upon the intervention of a fellow monarch in Ethiopia—or Britain.[19] Rumors continued to flow in the weeks that followed that "King Freddie's friends," in Britain (some Tory aristocratic milieu where the Kabaka had close ties during his earlier period of residence in Britain), or Haile Selassie were about to make a decisive intervention. The rich symbolic connotations of the widely believed tale of the Kabaka at the palace gates, mowing down hordes of assailants, require no elaboration.

18. This document was composed immediately after the events and captures the passions of the moment well. The author was a cautious, prudent young man, who in more normal times was not given to extravagant prose.

19. Earlier, as Mutesa concedes in his autobiography, he had approached the British high commissioner and "some African ambassadors" concerning possible external support—*The Desecration of My Kingdom*, p. 186. This became a central element in Obote's argument that the Kabaka had abused his powers as chief of state.

The reactions to crisis were remarkably uniform throughout Buganda, as attested by eyewitness accounts from different parts of the kingdom. The relative coherence of the information distortion caused by the selective cultural screen through which all messages passed is suggestive of the commonality of the symbol system throughout Buganda. After the initial reaction of the march on Kampala, crowds throughout the kingdom attacked the main symbolic artifacts of central government available in the countryside—police stations and courthouses. As realization spread that the national army was going to fan out into the countryside, trenches were dug across roads, trees felled, and plans for resistance made. The spontaneous element was paramount; chiefs, although they were the official local representatives of royal authority, were not in control of the situation; they realized better than the mob the suicidal nature of the crowd reactions, but were powerless to halt them. The demand for solidarity was overwhelming; the student himself, sympathetic to the crowd but well aware of the likely consequences of their action, was given no choice but to join forces, or be considered a "detective." When the crowds were dispersed by the army, with considerable loss of life, selective perception operated to capture the brutalities and atrocities of the process. From a non-Ganda perspective, the army was engaged in the thankless task of pacifying a hostile countryside which had embarked on open rebellion; for Ganda, northern soldiers were on a rampage, doing precisely what cultural fears anticipated— killing "as many Baganda as they could possibly kill."

In northern Uganda, the first news of the events was wholly different. The first point of diffusion was through telephonic communication; local government officials and political notables made contact with trusted acquaintances in the capital—likely to be of the same ethnic community— and received news refracted through a quite different prism. Here the threat came from the arms believed stored in the Kabaka's palace and imminent rebellion in Buganda which would endanger the survival of the country. Ganda mobs were claimed to have assaulted certain key northern figures—in particular, Akeno Adoko, a close confidante of Prime Minister Obote and head of the special security agency; this detail was never heard in Ganda versions of the crisis. Obote himself was in potential personal danger from Ganda mobs. The palace assault, therefore, had almost a defensive character; it was at the very least an indispensable step for national survival. Spontaneous popular reactions in the north were also rumored; one report suggested that an irregular army of Lango was going to march into Buganda.[20]

20. This analysis draws primarily on my own observation of the crisis. I was interviewing in northern Uganda the day of the palace attack, and returned to Kampala (by a circuitous route) late on that same day. One study undertaken by a sociologist—but unfortunately never pursued to completion—was a systematic canvass of the rumors then circulating in vast numbers.

By the end of the first day, official communiques began to be issued, and press and radio supplemented the welter of rumor with a modest compliment of more standardized data. The effectiveness of official information in overcoming the tension-creating effects of ethnically shaped rumor was limited by the antiseptic nature of what was released. Government information was sparse and obviously selective in its own right; thus the conviction was universal that the full story was not being told.[21] Of course, even the overwhelming volume of media information available during urban ghetto riots in the United States in the late sixties did not remove the potent effect of rumor oriented to the contours of the racial cleavage. Pervasive fears in the alchemy of crisis became grotesque misinformation; American urban riots were frequently accompanied by rumors in White communities that Black mobs were enroute with guns and torches, while in the Black ghetto White-dominated police were seen to be engaged in brutal repression. Depending on your identity, the bullet overhead came from a sniper or a policeman.

ELECTIONS AND CULTURAL ANXIETY

Competitive elections, if the contest is structured along communal lines, can have comparable effects of catalyzing fears and insecurities and mobilizing cultural identities, a process we will illustrate through the Guyana case. The very ritualized aspects of elections, which are highly dramatized social enactment of competition, are vectors of tension if alignments are through cultural pluralism. We may speculate that this tension-breeding attribute is most strongly present in new polities where the electoral process is not yet institutionalized and routinized. In theory, a national election in a democratic society places the entire system "up for grabs." Were that really to be the case, unbearable tension levels would surround the electoral process in Western societies as well— as witness late Weimar Germany balloting or the reconstruction South in the United States or, for that matter, the implausible fears generated in Berkeley by the election of a radical-led coalition. In practice, party systems over the years become so well institutionalized that changes can occur only within well-understood and circumscribed limits. In a situation such as that of Guyana, elections at the moment of power transfer carry the possibility of cultural calamity. After repeated verifications in social interactions of the reality of racially based allocations,

21. On the 1966 crisis, in addition to literature cited, see G. F. Engholm and Ali A. Mazrui, "Violent Constitutionalism in Uganda," *Government and Opposition*, II, no. 4 (July-October 1967); M. Crawford Young, "The Obote Revolution," *Africa Report*, XI, no. 6 (June 1966).

an electoral system permits a communally perceived political party to avail itself of the winner-take-all traditions of the Westminster model at the expense of another cultural party, which then becomes a total loser. There appears a very real possibility that a parliamentary majority ensuing from such an election may invest a regime which becomes an engine of discrimination, if not domination.[22] To recognize that this is no chimera, we need look no farther than Ulster, where the structure of British electoral organization subjected the Catholics to permanent, entrenched minoritization, a condition from which many disabilities derived. The very novelty of the process and the wide range of uncertainty concerning the outcomes are very unsettling. Thus the communal anxieties attending elections were not simple primordial prejudices but well-founded, rationally calculated apprehensions.

In Guyana, the two major communities are Africans (33.5 percent), and East Indians (48.2 percent). Africans were brought as slaves and used on coastal sugar plantations. The abolition of slavery in 1833 led to the swift collapse of much of the plantation economy. Many bankrupt plantations were taken over by Africans, but their operation as sugar estates required maintenance of an intricate and costly system of sea dikes, which the freed slaves had neither the capital nor the capacity to do. Their land reverted to meager subsistence utilization; subsequent African mobility came through entering, via the educational system, into white collar employment or prospecting in the interior, not through farming. East Indians began coming as indentured labor in the 1830s, with influx halted in 1917. The conditions of indentured service, however, did not pulverize social organization, as had slavery; the Indians, mainly Hindus from Uttar Pradesh province drawn from agricultural and artisanal castes, preserved many aspects of their rural society, went into rice cultivation, and became a viable peasantry. The two communities, functionally and socially, evolved as wholly distinct entities. The sense of differentiation is sustained by sharply drawn stereotypes; according to Leo Despres: "Generally, village Africans tend to think of East Indians as a miserly people who devote all of their time and energy to work and who are so bent upon accumulating land and money that they are not able to enjoy the fruits of their labor. East Indians, on the other hand, view Africans as a people without ambition, lazy, wasteful, and so preoccupied with sporting that they are unable to put anything aside to improve themselves."[23]

Until World War II, Guyana was a somnolent colonial backwater; political activity on a territorial level was virtually nil, and influence

22. This argument, in more pungent and graceful style, was forcefully put by W. Arthur Lewis, *Politics in West Africa* (Toronto: Oxford University Press, 1965).

23. Despres, *Cultural Pluralism and Nationalist Politics in British Guiana*, pp. 74-95.

largely in the hands of the tiny European minority (2.3 percent). The first elections were held only in 1953, at which point it was proposed that representative institutions be developed in a very telescoped sequencing. The first generation of parties were not racially based and had a significant ideological component; the winning party, the Peoples Progressive Party, campaigned on nationalist goals and early independence. Within its leadership, there was a significant Marxist-Communist core, although the PPP also included other tendencies. The British, alarmed by the ideological coloration of the PPP, slowed down the power transfer process. Three more elections were held, in 1957, 1961, and 1964, which saw a progressive communal alignment of the party structure and electorate. By the third elections, in 1961, racial polarization was extreme; every campaign meeting ran the risk of igniting a race riot. The PPP became an East Indian party, and the Peoples National Congress, led by L.F.S. Burnham, emerged as an African racial party. Cultural pluralism displaced ideology as an aligning principle; elections became a catalyst of insecurity for the racial contenders. As one of the PNC leaders told Despres, "Burnham's outlook is too radical for me on most issues; but man, this fight is now for survival and the Afro-Guianese must stick together or lose the country to the Indians and the communists."[24] Cultural pluralism is now deeply embedded as the organizing principle for politics, and elections are crisis catalysts. It would be quite misleading to dwell solely upon the hazards and risks of elections in a culturally plural seting. Even where mobilized communalism affects electoral behavior, one can also point in certain circumstances to an element of reassurance that cultural interests may be effectively represented in the national arena; such an argument could certainly be supported from Indian, Pakistani, and American data. Nor do we argue an automatic triggering of pluralism by the electoral process; we examine in chapter 9 the intriguing Filipino example, where electoral competition inhibited cultural mobilization. But we do suggest that an atmosphere laden with fear and uncertainty about the status and security of cultural segments imposes special hazards in an electoral setting.

INSECURITY AND ABRUPT TRANSFORMATIONS

A sudden transformation of the nature of the political arena also is likely to generate insecurity. For some polities, abrupt decolonization created such anxieties; Zaire is a case in point. A mere four

24. Ibid., p. 251.

years before independence, the suggestion by a Belgian professor that a thirty-year plan should be devised for decolonization was greeted with incredulous derision. In mid-1958, I was told by an African university student that independence was yet fifty years away; Belgian officials still counted on fifteen years. Massive riots in Kinshasa in January 1959 shattered the complacency of the colonial regime and accelerated the pace of events; in January 1960, the demoralized colonizer agreed to transfer power on 30 June 1960.

To place the psychology of power transfer in context, it must be recalled that the colonial apparatus was far more pervasive and rested more heavily upon African society than was the case in, say, Nigeria, India, or Uganda. Thus the magnitude of transformation of the social system implied by independence was much greater. The colonial colossus would be no more; but what would take its place? No one, at the moment independence was promised, could have the faintest idea. The elections out of which an African government was to come were set only for May 1960; a multiplicity of parties, daily increasing, were to compete. Most were built upon an ethnic or regional base, but not even the leaders knew what the orbit of their appeal would be. Anxious politicians flocked to the Lovanium University anthropology department to ask how many votes could be expected on the basis of a given ethnic alignment. But the very fluidity and ambiguity of ethnic identities made such questions impossible to answer.

A situation beyond the scope of the imagination to anticipate is a guaranteed source of anxieties; in a context of cultural mobilization, fears are quite likely to focus upon what hostile actions other groups may be expected to take. The social competitor becomes predator. For the contending African political parties, the stakes were enormous, and there was almost no time to organize. Rural masses could be organized most readily through ethnic linkages; appeals for cultural unity rested both upon the promise of extraordinary benefits which solidarity might bring— and also the perils of disunity. The unfathomable nature of the new era ahead led, for many Africans, to ambivalent anticipations. On the one hand, the millenium just might be within reach and the miraculous goods pledged by politicians around the corner. But foreboding was also in the air. The evidence offered by Alan Merriam, who spent the year preceding independence in a Songye village in east central Zaire, provides interesting insight. The vexatious aspects of colonial rule were certainly resented, and there was a warm response to the anticolonial appeal. The hopes generated were embodied in the comments of two villagers. "After independence there will be no taxes. Everyone will have plenty to eat, lots of clothes, cars to drive. Everything will be wonderful." And,

"When independence comes, I'll go on cultivating. Probably things will be better, but it is hard to know what will happen. There won't be anyone to tell me what to do. I can do what I want."[25] The nether side of ambivalence was the fear of attack by the neighboring Luba. At the moment of independence, the villagers, with three neighboring communities, were busy constructing a new fortified village for better security against the anticipated Luba assault. Two months before independence, Merriam was visited by a delegation of seventy-five men who wanted to discuss the problems of self-government. They had three questions to pose: (1) Why was the White doctor at the nearby hospital leaving? (2) What were they to do after independence, with the Luba arming themselves for war, and no Whites to help them? (3) What kind of help did they really need?[26]

For the European community, the situation was less ambivalent; only a small number identified with Zairian nationalism. More were resigned to the inevitability of independence but relatively few thought any possible good could come. Those accustomed to the warm nurturance of the womb of colonial privilege, of course, were quite right. The climate of opinion is well expressed in a memorandum sent by the European civil service unions to the king on 8 May 1960:

> On the eve of Congolese independence, the European population of the Congo asks itself anxiously about the nature of the protection that Belgium is prepared to give to its nationals.
> The fear expressed by our compatriots is far from being vain and unjustified.
> Many Congolese publications contain virulent appeals to racial hatred, and even encouragements to massacre of the Belgians, and rape of our wives and daughters.
> Large sections of the native population identify independence with our expulsion, even by bloody means.[27]

The dike that gave way five days after Zaire independence, inundating the sprawling new state with disorder was the army, at that time racially segmented—all the officer corps was European, while the enlisted ranks (excepting a few senior Belgian NCO's) were Zairian. An excellent description of the psychology of the mutiny which triggered the "Congo crisis" is provided by Jules Gérard-Libois and Benoit Verhaegen:

> 1. Reciprocal panic fed by false news, by the declarations carried by the radio, and by rumors spread, systematically or otherwise, among the two populations

25. Alan P. Merriam, *Congo: Background of Conflict* (Evanston: Northwestern University Press, 1961), p. 178.
26. Ibid., pp. 173-94.
27. J. Gérard-Libois and Benoit Verhaegen, *Congo 1960*, II (Brussels: Centre de Recherche et d'Informations Socio-Politiques, 1961), 523-24.

2. Amongst the white population: preventative constitution of self-defense groups; action of armed Volunteer Corps; parallel to this action: efforts made to remove or neutralize the arms of the soldiers of the Force Publique, with or without the complicity of the officers

3. On the part of the soldiers, the fear of being killed by the Whites, civilian or military, led to the desire to seize, by attack if necessary, the arsenals and arm depots, and then, the hunt for Europeans to disarm them, with search of house and vehicle. Sometimes the soldiers oppose the departure of the civilians and imprison their officers to hold some Whites as hostages and thus avoid being attacked by airplanes or parachutists

4. Once the metropolitan forces have intervened, virtually all the White population leaves when the Belgian troops can no longer guarantee their security. The White officers of the Force Publique must abandon their men.[28]

This is another classic illustration of the way in which, in circumstances where fear and uncertainty suffuse perception, culturally distinct communication systems carry radically different—and distorted—messages. To the normal military caste distinctions between officers and other ranks was added the racial one; in crisis, the communication links between these two were so charged with distrust that message flow networks became virtually completely dissociated. As in Uganda, in such conditions the distortion of information is magnified by the absence of any corrective interaction between divergent versions.

Also comparable to Uganda was the remarkable similarity in behavioral responses which were undertaken independently and spontaneously; in army garrisons across the country, almost identical scenarios were enacted, although it may be regarded as conclusively established that there was no central direction or plan among either Europeans or Africans. The orders were dictated by fear, signed by distrust, and executed by emotion. Each group had a generalized perception of the other, clothed in insecurity and hostility, which swiftly imputed aggressive and threatening intent in the response of the other to each stage of the unfolding crisis.

From the foregoing, a number of tentative propositions may be culled. (1) At the group level, cultural identities are sustained by shared symbol systems which tend to create their own paradigm of social reality. (2) Social cues carrying cultural symbols are likely to be perceived in communal terms at moments of cultural threat and insecurity. (3) When cultural communities collectively perceive serious threats to communal status in the political environment, group solidarity tends to increase. (4) In a culturally sensitized and threat-laden environment, selective perception of information serves to differentiate sharply communal cog-

28. Ibid., I, 425.

nitions of social and political events. (5) The symbolic representation of the social universe is simplified by stereotyping of significant other groups; the greater the saliency of cultural pluralism, the more likely these stereotypes are to be homogenized. (6) Where clearly defined cultural stereotypes exist, other groups tend to perceive the stereotyped group to be behaving politically as a single actor. (7) Heightened cultural anxieties renders incoming message flows more susceptible to communal interpretations. (8) A period of intense cultural threat intensifies rumor flow and tends to distort information to render it congruent with the pattern of fear. (9) Although intensity of identity of individuals with cultural segments varies widely in moments of communal threat the group pressures escalate and strongly constrain individuals to align their overt behavior with the interests of the cultural collectivity. (10) Historical moments when basic power relationships within a polity are to be fundamentally altered in unpredictable ways engender deep anxieties.

We have by no means exhausted the subject of the social psychology of cultural pluralism; indeed, we feel this is a crucial area for further inquiry. Edelman, in his signal contribution to the role of anxieties and attitude ambivalence in determining mass arousal and quiescence, although his concern is with societal conflict on a far broader scale than simply its cultural plural aspects, provides an invaluable conceptual framework within which further exploration could be undertaken.

6 Ethnic Politics in Zaire

*Leopoldville, Brazzaville, Kwango, Angola and Pointe Noire
formed in times past, for centuries, the united state of the
Ancient Kingdom of the Congo. This state [was] divided in 1885
between France, Belgium and Portugal.
. . . Let us submit for your meditation the following words of
the eminent sociologist Georges Balandier: "Bakongo society was
one of the best prepared of this part of Central Africa to absorb
the multiple changes implied by colonization. They early
displayed networks of social relations which encouraged the
diffusion of the Kikongo language, which gave them an
assimilative capacity utilized in certain cases to 'digest' Bateke
entities swallowed by their progress."*

—1957 press release of the Alliance des Bakongo[1]

*It is time that Congolese of the towns and countryside let the
world know that they are in no way divided, that they are united
for a single just cause.*

—Patrice Lumumba speech, 1959[2]

*. . . the cultures of the Congo resemble each other strongly
when one compares them to other African cultures, and even
more if they are compared to other cultures in the world . . .
The thoroughgoing unity of Congolese cultures is the most
important conclusion of our study. It will permit, we hope, the
achievement of a general Congolese culture.*

—Jan Vansina[3]

The paradoxes and dilemmas of political development in Zaire are embedded in the contrasts between these statements. The formidable suc-

1. Quoted in *A.B.A.K.O. 1950-1960* (Brussels: Centre de Recherche et d'Information
Socio-Politiques, 1962), pp. 104-5.
2. Jean van Lierde (ed.), *La Pensée politique de Patrice Lumumba* (Brussels: Livre
Africain, 1963,) pp. 16-17.
3. Jan Vansina, *Introduction à l'Ethnographie du Congo* (Kinshasa: Editions
Universitaires du Congo, 1966), p. 10.

163

cess of Leopold II in parlaying quite modest resources into the lion's share of Central Africa as a personal fiefdom left as its legacy tropical Africa's largest state, over 900,000 square miles. Under Belgian rule, the vast claims staked by Leopold II became a highly centralized, authoritarian bureaucratic colossus. A defective decolonization strategy shattered the despotic shell of the colonial state and provided in 1960 the first empirical example of the political force of unbridled ethnicity in Africa. In large measure due to international intervention, the territorial frame of the colonial state was preserved during its most difficult days in 1960-61 and institutional authority partly restored. After a debilitating wave of rebellions in 1964-65, a military coup in November 1965 swept away the fragile political superstructure erected in 1960.

A series of centralizing steps within a frame of personalist authoritarian rule radically altered the structure of power and established a veritable leviathan state. Over the first decade of independence, from a starting point when the state itself appeared to be disappearing into the quicksands of ethnicity, Zaire has transformed into a polity whose central institutions seem to eclipse cultural pluralism. This remarkable metamorphosis merits our close attention.

The Zaire case will serve to introduce the second part of this study, where we will turn from general comparative theoretical discussion to the detailed examination of a number of particular political systems. In so doing, we will draw upon the body of middle-range theory set forth in the early chapters and hope to demonstrate its utility in specific settings. Zaire merits our attention for several reasons. The dramatic contrasts in the perception of ethnic conflict in the various historical phases through which it has passed even in the brief period since independence well demonstrate the force of the political arena in structuring conceptions of cultural pluralism. The fluid and situational character of ethnicity in Africa is illustrated through its complex permutations in the last two decades of Zaire history. The interaction between ideologies of national integration, oriented to a Zaire-wide loyalty, and mobilized ethnic solidarities stands out. The sheer scale and significance of Zaire within the African firmament, of course, provides a subsidiary reason. We will enter farther into the minutia of ethnic politics in this example than in those which follow; although this may at times strain the patience of the reader, we believe it is important to show that any level of generalization will obscure some of the richness of diversity. Even here we stop very far short of encyclopedic analysis; anyone who wants to explore cultural pluralism further will discover even more startling and fascinating possibilities to follow up.

ZAIRE: IDENTITY AT THE BASELINE

At the point of colonial penetration, the social landscape of Zaire was dominated by small-scale, localized political groupings. A series of kingdoms had developed along the southern savanna fringe of the equatorial forest, often incorporating several linguistic groups (Kuba, Lunda). In the west, the Christian kingdom of the Kongo, of sixteenth-century fame, had broken apart, although its historical core remained intact in Angola, and its memory persisted. Along the eastern lakes, favorable environment had permitted population concentrations and political centralization in the Shi and related states. In the northeast, the conquest states of the Zande and Mangbetu were known by the identity of the rulers. But in the vast forest zone of the central basin, although broad linguistic and cultural uniformities could be discerned, these were not reflected in subjective identities.

Upon this base was erected the superstructure of the colonial state. The diluted Belgian version of indirect rule did not found administrative divisions on presumed "tribal" divisions; indeed, many culturally similar groups are separated by provincial lines, with identity differentiation today apparently primarily attributable to this fact. Rural local administration was founded upon political units, adapted to an appropriate scale. If they were too small, they were regrouped; if too large, peripheral zones were detached. However, "tribe" was an important unit of classification. Ethnic maps were drawn; "tribe" became a blank on administrative forms, and identity cards. Perceptions of what the operative units were changed over time. Nonetheless, the "tribal" paradigm which governed European perceptions of African society had important consequences in altering pre-colonial identity patterns. The baseline pattern was too complex and fragmented; cartesian logic cried out for a simplification, regrouping, reduction—to bring order out of cultural chaos. By the time that subjugation of Africa occurred, it was natural to conceive of any society as composed of cultural collectivities—a metaphor which was not dominant, as we shall argue subsequently, at the time of Spanish conquest of Latin America and the Philippines, with very important consequences. Early explorers and state agents in Africa, in their memoirs and chronicles, found irresistible the inclination to apply ethnic labels to whole areas which went far beyond any manifest identities. Although the limited orbit of authority of many rulers was appreciated, the corollary segmentation of identity was not inferred. The "tribal" conceptualization of tropical Africa was general, although colonizers varied in the policy conclusions derived; the French were most prone to disregard the ethnic paradigm as present but undesirable, destined in the long run to give way to broader identifications, fidelity to the empire it was hoped. For the British, "tribal" units were natural bases for administrative organization; the Belgians fell somewhere between. In time, the administrative model of ethnic reality has a feedback effect—through its use in the schools, through its application to the individual on his identity card.

Cultural patterns were of more moment to the missionary arm of European penetration than to the administrators, in the early years. The spiritual conquest of Zaire, an exalting challenge, had to be undertaken with painfully limited resources. Language was an indispensable weapon; evangelization could not wait until a generation of Africans had been instructed in European tongues. Thus one had to discover the orbit of different languages, the linkages between apparently dissimilar dialects. Religious personnel had to acquire African languages; for the Protestants, it was a matter of priority to translate the Bible. Economies of scale were obvious and compelling; a language which gave access to a large population was vastly preferable to one covering but a tiny area. Language had to be transcribed, dictionaries and grammars developed. Thus enbalmed, the mission version of the language became a standard form, to be used in schools, diffused through the written word. All of this represented, in the context of the times, a very considerable investment; it was only natural to amortize it by maximizing the diffusion of the standardized language forms to neighboring groups, where possible. This process had the unintended, but no less important, consequence of extending identities and broadening ethnic communities.

The colonial epoch, then, was a phase of extending cultural self-awareness, important modification of groups, and, in some cases, creation of entirely novel identities. It was only on the eve of independence, with the introduction of political parties and electoral competition, that ethnicity became actively politicized. The phase of cultural mobilization, at its peak from 1959 to 1965, saw not only the activation of ethnic solidarity, but important further changes in the cultural arena. Politics posed the "who am I" question in a more blunt and possibly threatening way than did the census-taker; neither politicians nor actors could be certain what the answer might be until it had been posed in several competitive contexts.

Against this background of overall historical trend, we may sketch in three of the more important factors which have shaped the process of identity change. The pattern of development of the modern socioeconomic system, around its urban nodal points, shaped group definitions through the social interactions it stimulated. Secondly, differential modernization left visible disparities between groups and relative deprivation as a result. Thirdly, the partial ideologization of some identities deserves exploration.

URBANIZATION AND IDENTITY CHANGE

In many African polities, the scale of the state is so modest that the capital and major port are the only focal points of social communication. Zaire, however, had a far more complex pattern. Kinshasa and the Copperbelt towns of Lubumbashi, Likasi, and Kolwezi constituted two poles of large-scale urbanization at opposite ends of the country.[4] Kisangani and Kananga were vital regional nodal points; to a lesser extent, the smaller provincial capitals of Mbandaka and Bukavu also played this role. The smaller towns, mining centers, and plantations recruited their population within a circumscribed ambit. Map 6.1 illustrates the process; it will be noted that the migration pathways constitute two-way communication channels. The movement is not only to the urban nodal points, but back and forth in both directions. Townsmen do not, at least in the short run, rupture their linkages with their area of rural origin. Relatively frequent visits occur, depending on the distance. A number of the urban migrants do not succeed in finding an economic niche and return to take up land in the rural area. Thus what is of significance is not only the constitution of urban ethnic communities, but the urban-rural networks which come into being, which ultimately serve as the basis for diffusion of political consciousness.

The urban central places enlarge the scope of meaningful solidarities of the migrants. They become aware of the linguistic and cultural factors which they share with groups to which they are closely related. At the same time, the urban arena places them in competitive interaction with "relevant others," with whom, often, they had no historical contact. Ethnic associations were founded to provide mutual support, promote the cultural values of the group, and build solidarity. It was in the cities that the relative size of elite groups became visible, through perceived preponderance of particular groups in the most advantageous occupational roles.

In Kinshasa, the primary polarization was between Kongo, and migrants from up-river collectively labelled "Ngala" by Kongo and Europeans. Although Kinshasa lay on the fringe of their cultural zone, Kongo believed that the city lay in "their" territory and that they had a natural

4. Under the Mobutu regime, place-names of European origin have been rebaptized. Thus Congo became Zaire in 1971. Other name changes of cities to which we will refer are as follows: Leopoldville to Kinshasa; Elisabethville to Lubumbashi; Stanleyville to Kisangani; Luluabourg to Kananga; Jadotville to Likasi; Coquilhatville to Mbandaka.

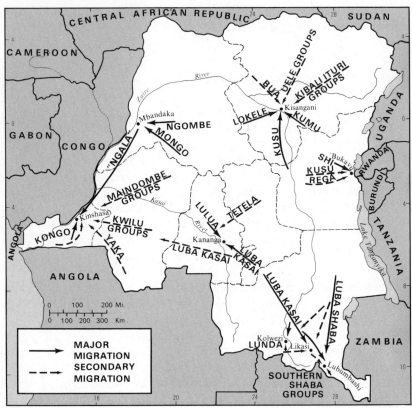

Map 6.1   Migration Patterns in Zaire

Cartographic Laboratory UW-Madison

prerogative of social leadership. From the earliest days, they had always been numerous in the city's population; by the 1950s, they were convinced that Kongo represented the overwhelming majority—the figure of 82 percent was often cited.[5]   Both Catholic and Protestant missions had established a dense network in the Kongo zone, and the Kongo were well equipped with an educated elite.   However, after World War II, they felt their position increasingly threatened by the Ngala. Lingala, the up-river lingua franca which served as urban medium for the Ngala, was standardized, whereas there were at least four major variants of Kikongo, plus a debased form of "state Kikongo" used by the administration in other parts of western Zaire.   Kongo elites were visible in the

5. *A.B.A.K.O. 1950-1960*, pp. 30, 103-6. The figure of 82%—a substantial exaggeration—was reached by inclusion of the numerous Angolans, mainly Kikongo-speakers, in the calculations. The 1957 census showed 40.7% Kongo, with Angolans an additional 20.8%.

first timid expressions of anticolonial sentiments after the war; also, memories persisted of the force of the Kimbanguist religious movement in 1921 and in sundry reincarnations thereafter, with strong protest overtones. The Kongo port city of Matadi had been the scene of major riots in 1945. Thus the Kongo were the objects of colonial suspicion, while the Ngala elites enjoyed the reputation of fidelity to the Belgian connection. The powerful Scheutist Catholic mission order was committed to the promotion of Lingala. Thus Lingala was increasingly used as a language of primary school instruction in Kinshasa, and Kongo perceived the language policy as part of a generalized menace to their social role.

Accordingly, in 1950 the Association (later Alliance) des Bakongo was founded in Kinshasa, with the initial goal of the unification of Kikongo and promotion of Kongo culture, to restore the place of Kikongo in the capital. Its first section outside Kinshasa was established in 1953; however, it was not really until 1959 that ABAKO extended its organization to rural areas. It was an urban-centered organ, whose preoccupations reflected the concerns of the new elite. However, its emergence and growth may be seen as an organic expression of crystallizing cultural solidarity felt by Kongo at the urban vortex of social change.

The ABAKO established itself as the spearhead of nationalism by demanding immediate self-government in 1956. Significantly, the demand came in the context of rebutting a manifesto discussing a thirty-year plan for independence, which was seen by Kongo leaders as emanating from a Catholic-"Ngala" milieu. The aggressiveness of the political rhetoric from Kongo circles led the colonial administration to align more explicitly with the "moderate" Ngala. All of these developments, in an environment of rapid politization, of social cleavage and anticolonial grievances, fixed in the layman's map of the Kinshasa social field a firm conviction of its Kongo-Ngala polarity.

The reductionism in this paradigm of ethnic reality was important. Within the Kongo group, there were four major subdivisions, Yombe, Manianga, Ntandu, and Ndibu. However, these labels in turn appear of quite recent origin, and are not synonymous with subdivisions of the ancient kingdom.[6] The terms Ndibu and Ntandu appear to have originated during the construction of the railway in the 1890s. Further, a recent study of the Yombe indicates that a number did not consider themselves Kongo until shortly before independence. With the cultural mobilization of the period of party organization, the label became readily accepted. Further, according to Doutreloux, "the inhab-

6. Laurent Monnier, *Ethnie et intégration régionale au Congo* (Paris: Editions Classiques d'Expression Francaise, [1970]), pp. 370-71.

itants of Mayombe rarely called themselves Yombe . . . Villagers designated themselves by the name of their administrative subdivision, or
their clan, or a segment of a clan."[7]   In 1954, the ABAKO committee
encountered criticism in Kinshasa that it was dominated by Ntandu; to
counter this charge, Joseph Kasavubu, a Yombe, subsequently first
president of the republic, was coopted as president. Within the competitive context of the Kinshasa social field, these divisions were not
very visible, especially outside the Kongo sphere; to their relevant others, Kongo appeared a cultural monolith.

The process by which cultural mobilization of the rural hinterland
occurred is illuminating. A meticulous study by Laurent Monnier
demonstrated that the politization was not accomplished through the
labors of urban elite organizers dispersing into the countryside to fashion
a party. Rather, after the mystique of omnipotence of the colonial
behemoth was shattered by the 1959 Kinshasa riots, the manifold resentment toward the Belgian administration was expressed in radical
protest. The ABAKO "did not, in fact, organize itself in the interior,
but it was rather the rural populace that expressed themselves spontaneously through ABAKO, and organized themselves under its em-
blem."[8] Thus, the hinterland coopted the symbols of the Kinshasa social
field; ABAKO leader Kasavubu, unknown in the hinterland until 1959,
suddenly became the personalization of Kongo political awakening.
Further, the urban polarity between Kongo and Ngala was incorporated
into the protest paradigm. This can only be interpreted as a reflection of
the reality-creating force of the social communications net extending from
the urban community to its human hinterland. The Ngala were manifestly
not a problem for rural Kongo; there were very few up-river immigrants in
the Kongo port city of Matadi or in the smaller regional centers of Boma,
Tshela, or Mbanza-Ngungu (formerly Thysville). The only symbolic
presence of Ngala was through the army unit. The military was not
particularly Ngala in composition, but it did use Lingala as a command
language and was not viewed as a Kongo institution. Thus, the
mobilization of cultural identity rested upon the symbols and paradigm
generated by urban competition.

The boundaries of the Kongo grouping within the urban field were long
ambiguous. Basic Kikongo was utilized by the state and missions as a
lingua franca in Kwango and Kwilu districts to the southeast. Kongo
leaders hoped to align these groups behind the ABAKO banners; they
cited not only the common vehicular language, but the historical
interpretation of a highly influential missionary-scholar, Father Van
Wing, which placed the origin of the founders of the ancient kingdom of

7. A. Doutreloux, *L'Ombre des fetiches* (Louvain: Nauwelaerts, 1967), p. 30.
8. Monnier, *Ethnie et intégration régionale au Congo*, 351.

the Kongo in the Kwango-Kwilu area and postulated deep-seated cultural affinities.[9] A number of persons of Kwango-Kwilu origins served on ABAKO committees in its early years; in the words of one ABAKO leader: "An amalgam of peoples have chosen the simplified Kikongo as a language of communication. This option has as its immediate çonsequence a conscious or unconscious participation of these peoples in Kongo culture."[10] It was only through trial by political combat that the operative cultural boundaries in the urban setting were clarified. After 1959, regional political movements claiming the loyalties of Kwango-Kwilu immigrants were formed and dissipated the illusion of the greater Kongo community.

The other end of the polarity, the Ngala, were an urban identity group which took form during the colonial period. We have recounted elsewhere the fascinating process by which Ngalahood as a meaningful reference group emerged;[11] a brief recapitulation will suffice. The label entered the written record with the passage of Henry Morton Stanley down the Zaire River in 1876. In an area of the river not far upstream from Mbandaka, "Ngala" was the answer he received to the explorer's inevitable query, "Who are you?" In contrast to the hostile treatment which the Stanley flotilla received in a number of places during its descent, here the reception was cordial. Stanley's abundant writings fixed in initial European perceptions not only the "Ngala" label for riverain groups in that zone, but also an unusually favorable stereotype: "the Ashanti of the Congo," said Stanley, "unquestionably a very superior tribe."[12]

The initial favorable image had far-reaching consequences. The river was the sole means of reaching the interior; therefore the establishment of both state and mission bases were essential to political and spiritual conquest. With resources very limited, the choice of the first stations was critical, and there was little to go on besides Stanley's reports. Thus "Ngala" country became the beachhead for penetration of the upper river; the label swiftly became a generic term utilized by Europeans to describe the Africans who were recruited from this area for the service of the state and who clustered around the mission

9. The Van Wing thesis is persuasively challenged by Jan Vansina, *Les Anciens royaumes de la savane* (Kinshasa: Institut de Recherches Economiques et Sociales, 1965), pp. 32-33.

10. Quoted in Monnier, *Ethnie et intégration régionale au Congo,* p. 55.

11. Young, *Politics in the Congo,* pp. 242-46; Anderson, von der Mehden and Young, *Issues of Political Development,* pp. 31-33. See also the fascinating exchange, Mumbanza mwa Bawele, "Y a-t-il des Bangala?—Origine et extension du terme," *Zaïre-Afrique,* XIII, no. 78 (October 1973), 471-84; and G. Hulstaert, "A propos des Bangala," *Zaïre-Afrique,* XIV, no. 83 (March 1974), 173-86.

12. Henry M. Stanley, *Through the Dark Continent* (New York: Harper & Bros., 1878), II, 301-2.

and state outposts. With the foundation of a state base camp at Stanley Pool, which eventually became Kinshasa, an embryonic Ngala community took form. Riverain traders from upriver had come this far to exchange with Teke and Kongo even in pre-colonial times. Their numbers increased, while employees of the state and soldiers were joined to them.

The great river had been a natural artery of African trade, although its precolonial dimensions were limited by the lack of political unity and at times by insecurity. However, a river trading vernacular was already in existence, to which Lobobangi was the biggest single contributor. This language was simplified and standardized as Lingala and used by both state and missions for communication with Africans; it very quickly became the medium of urban communication for the community of up-river immigrants in Kinshasa. It also became the command language for the colonial army. The process by which the river lingua franca became identified as a linguistic basis for the nascent Ngala community was described by a Protestant missionary in 1903: ". . . already thousands have been born to the State forces to whom 'Bangala' [Lingala] is the only mother tongue they knew; and that thousands of the workers, drawn from the different tribes of the Congo basin, are forgetting their parent speech."[13]

The social duality of Kinshasa served to consolidate Ngala identity as a reference group in the capital. Whatever their origin, up-river immigrants found themselves within a social field where their cultural commonalities were more enhanced by their competitive contrast with the Kongo. Above all, they were united by the use of Lingala as an urban medium. Rural ethnic groups on the upper river were small and individually could carry no social weight; the 1957 census showed that no up-river group numbered more than 2.9 percent of the Kinshasa population.

Significantly, the term "Ngala" evaporated over time in their presumed home areas. As the administrative and mission infrastructure became relatively dense, Europeans became aware that this designation was not used as subjective self-definition in the presumptive home area. Early ethnic maps showed a vast area, up to 40,000 square miles, as falling in an Ngala zone.[14] By the end of the colonial period, Belgians had become aware that there was no real Ngala group;

13. Walter H. Stapleton, *Suggestions for a Grammar of 'Bangala'* (Bolobo: Baptist Missionary Society, 1914), quoted in Thomas Turner, "Congo-Kinshasa," in Olorunsola, *The Politics of Cultural Sub-Nationalism in Africa*, p. 207.

14. Cyr. Van Overbergh, *Les Bangala* (Brussels: Institut International de Bibliographie, 1907); this work appeared in the first ethnographic survey of Zaire and played no small role in entrenching the myth of the Ngala.

an ethnographic survey of the upper river published on the eve of independence, concluded that, although "we believed for a long time in the
existence of a people called the Bangala . . . we know today with
certainty that, in all the Belgian Congo, there exists no ethnic
group bearing this name."[15] Nor did it survive as an urban label
in the towns along the upper river; in Mbandaka, the ethnic polarity
was described in terms of Ngombe-Mongo. Even in the 1957 Kinshasa
census, the Ngala category was dropped by the administration. However, it remained as a meaningful identity in everyday sociopolitical
vocabulary.

With the politization of ethnicity in the 1950s, the question of the precise urban boundaries of Ngalahood was sharply posed, as it had been for
the Kongo. With the rapid urban expansion after World War II and
improved communications, significant clusters of immigrants began to
arrive from new hinterland areas. Some, like Kwango and Kwilu groups,
had never fit the Ngala category. Others, like Luba-Kasai, Tetela,
and Mongo, came to explicitly reject it; as one Mongo intellectual
wrote in 1956, "We are astonished to bear a name which is not ours
and has no significance . . . [and] are discontent when people try
to degrade us."[16] Leaders who sought to give political expression
to the Ngala identity ran into immediate difficulties. In the early 1950s,
an effort was made to launch a pan-Ngala cultural association based
upon an extended definition of the group, the Liboke-lya-Bangala; in
1958, this was transformed into the Fédération des Bangala and in 1959
into the Intérféderal. Within the Kinshasa social field, Ngala took on
a more restricted definition, including primarily riverain groups like
the Ngombe, Bobangi, and Budja.

Comparable processes were at work in other urban centers. Redef-
initions of identity in ways relevant to urban social needs occurred;
these new self-definitions over time altered the model of ethnic reality
in zones linked to the urban social fields through large migrant communities. When political organization came, it departed from the urban
nodal points and was decisively affected by the particular structure of
ethnic polarization which obtained in a given town. The intensity of
polarization was not everywhere the same. Kananga was the most
conflictual, with one major contender, the Luba-Kasai, physically
expelled after independence. Of the major centers, Kisangani was the
least divided. In the latter instance, the largest single group, the Lokele,

15. H. Burssens, *Les peuplades le l'entre Congo-Ubangi* (Tervuren, Belgium: Musée
Royal du Congo Belge, 1958), pp. 14, 37.

16. Quoted by Bolamba, in "Vie, coutumes et moeurs des Mongo de l'Equateur," *La
Voix du Congolais* (April 1958), p. 373. In recent years, a trend toward acceptance of the
Ngala label was observable among Mongo in Kinshasa.

were only 15 percent of the population. There were perceptible prestige and stratification differences; Lokele were generally conceded to rank at the top, while Topoke and Kumu were at the bottom. The intimacy of the rural-urban social communications networks differed considerably in function of the proximity of the ethnic hinterland, ease of journey to it, and continuing economic transactions. The Lokele, a riverain group extending 100 miles downriver from Kisangani, sustained very close linkages. Their access to easily transportable food supplies for the urban markets gave their women traders an important competitive advantage, and the Lokele early became a relatively prosperous community. The Bua, by contrast, were over 200 miles from their home area and had only weakly maintained rural connections. Although ethnicity was certainly a factor in social relationships in Kisangani, the absence of a sharp polarization diffused its impact. Patrice Lumumba emerged as a local charismatic hero who readily aligned virtually all of Kisangani; thus political organization did not immediately stimulate competitive cultural mobilization.[17] In a spectrum of intensity where Kananga and Kisangani constitute extremes, the Copperbelt cities of Lubumbashi, Likasi, and Kolwezi (Luba-Kasai v. others), Bukavu (Kusu v. Shi), and Mbandaka (Ngombe v. Mongo) fall between, but closer to the polarization model. Matadi was overwhelmingly Kongo.[18]

One might speculate that, in the repressive context of colonial Zaire, the oppressed were constrained to ventilate their hostilities through ethnic channels. The White-dominated colonial system, source of the frustration, was until nearly the end too apparently powerful to permit the overt expression of hostility by Africans. Psychologists have suggested that sentiments of aggression, when inhibited from acting directly upon their source, may be deflected upon substitute objects or groups. When ethnic categories provide the labels for channeling displaced aggression, a potential for violent confrontation is created.[19]

17. The relative impact of ethnicity, stratification, and neighborhood in patterns of urban incorporation is given careful treatment in Valdo Pons, *Stanleyville* (London: Oxford University Press, 1969).

18. The concept of the urban social field is used to excellent effect in Turner's essay on the cultural subnationalism in Zaire, in Olorunsola, *The Politics of Cultural Sub-Nationalism*, pp. 195-283. Other useful studies of urban social change include Jacques Denis, *Le Phénomène urbain en Afrique centrale* (Brussels: Académie Royal des Sciences Coloniales, 1958); P. Caprasse, *Leaders Africains en milieu urbain* (Lumbumbashi: Centre d'Etudes des Problèmes Sociaux Indigenes, 1959); André Lux, "Luluabourg: Migrations, Accroissement et Urbanisation de sa population congolaise," *Zaire*, XII, nos. 7-8 (1958); Franz de Thier, *Le Centre extra-coutumier de Coquilhatville* (Brussels: Institut de Sociologie Solvay, 1956); J. S. LaFontaine, *City Politics: A Study of Leopoldville 1962-63* (Cambridge: Cambridge University Press, 1970); Bruce Fetter, "Elisabethville and Lubumbashi: The Segmented Growth of a Colonial City" (Ph.D. diss., University of Wisconsin, 1968).

19. I am indebted to Okello Oculi for this observation.

DIFFERENTIAL MODERNIZATION

A second process variable of critical import was the differential rate of access and entry to modern social roles. In this way, ethnicity as a political determinant becomes entwined with social class formation. The perception of relative deprivation enters social cognitions through ethnic categories; the politization of competition within such a perceptual framework is particularly bitter. Even in polarized social fields, stratified perceptions are not inevitable. In Kinshasa, neither Kongo nor Ngala perceived the other as possessing a commanding lead; the genuinely disadvantaged groups, such as the Yaka, lacked the numbers and leaderhsip to give political expression to their deprivation. But in Kananga and the Copperbelt, animosities founded on perceived difference of opportunity were crucial; we may illustrate the process through examination of these cases.

The Luba-Kasai were the pace-setting group in both instances. In Kananga, the conflict reached a point by late 1959 where arson, murder, and terrorism between Lulua and Luba were daily currency. Yet, remarkably, the two groups are culturally identical, speak the same language, and have only developed a sense of differentiation since the foundation of the Congo Free State. Examination of the genesis of the differentiation leads down some illuminating pathways.

The Luba cultural-linguistic zone actually covers a very broad area of Shaba and Kasai. The emergence of a far-flung Luba empire in the sixteenth and seventeenth centuries covering much of this area offers a saga of common history. Recent events, however, have reinforced differences within this area. At the time of colonial penetration, the Luba groups of Kasai (Lulua and Luba) encountered sharply different circumstances. Shortly before conquest, the groups now known as Lulua entered into a profitable slave-and-ivory trading relationship with Angola-based traders; the new resources entering the system permitted Mukenge Kalamba to acquire a number of firearms and establish his authority over the group. At nearly the same moment, the Luba-Kasai who today bear that label were also linked into a slave-and-ivory trading network, but as victims rather than participants. The African auxiliaries of Tippo Tip and other Zanzibar-based Afro-Arabs carried out a number of extremely destructive raids in Luba-Kasai country, leaving in their wake a dislocated and demoralized populace. Belgian authority in the area was first established in alliance with Kalamba. However, by 1891 conflict developed, and Kalamba's followers were seen as hostile and refractory.

The lack of a clear distinction between the groups in identity terms is demonstrated in the works of one of the first explorers to visit the area,

Von Wissmann. In his first book, *Im Innern Afrika*, he pays glowing tribute to the "Luba," "more than any other people in Africa" a fit target for evangelization. However, in his second work, *Through Equatorial Africa*, he reports that this was an error, that his praises were intended for the Lulua. The followers of Kalamba were identified by the administration as Lulua, and came to accept the designation; other Tshiluba-speakers in Kasai were labelled as Luba.[20]

But events soon confirmed the stereotype he had unintentionally given to the Luba. Uprooted, many sought protection around the new European outposts; others came as ransomed slaves. Still others sought and received land in Kalamba's domains and settled among the Lulua. When the first schools were opened in the 1890s, Luba were the first to enter. Over time, these footholds in the new socioeconomic structures became major beachheads. The construction of a rail line from Ilebo (Port Francqui) to the Copperbelt opened up important opportunities, which the Luba were first to exploit. The train provided ready access to the swiftly growing Copperbelt towns in Shaba. It also opened an extremely profitable market for maize and other staples readily produced in Kasai. Luba farmers and traders acquired land all along the railway path in Kasai, in Lulua and Kuba country as well as their own.[21] By the 1950s, Luba were 56 percent of the population of Kananga; they were conspicuously dominant among the white-collar ranks.

From 1891 to 1925, sporadic resistance was encountered in Lulua areas. Secure in a stable social order, rural Lulua did not have the same incentives to seek out the European posts or the mission stations. In the course of time, Lulua did move into the modern sector in some numbers, especially after World War II. Land was becoming scarcer and the presence of large and prosperous rural Luba communities in Lulua areas was a major irritant. And in Kananga, Lulua found themselves immediately up against Luba schoolmasters and personnel officers.

Thus, although the conscious differentiation between Lulua and Luba-Kasai dates from approximately 1885, a sense of hostile confrontation developed only after World War II and became acute only in 1958. Until World War II, Luba agricultural immigrants were readily given land and women in marriage by Lulua.[22] Symptomatic of growing militance on the part of Lulua was the foundation of the ethnic association, Lulua-Frères, in 1952. It swiftly became the best disciplined of Zairian

20. Turner, in Olorunsola, *The Politics of Cultural Sub-Nationalism*, p. 217.

21. A fascinating account of the impact of the rail line is found in J. Nicolai and J. Jacques, *La Transformation des paysages congolais par le chemin de fer*. L'example du B.C.K. (Brussels: Académie Royale des Sciences d'Outre-Mer, 1954).

22. Mabika Kalanda, *Baluba et Lulua. Une ethnie à la recherche d'un nouvel equilibre* (Brussels: Editions de Remarques Congolaises, 1959), p. 40.

ethnic organizations; within a year, it had forty sections, not only in Kasai, but other provinces, and even in neighboring countries.

Luba intellectuals, like Kongo, were conspicuous in the ranks of the critics of colonialism. Luba upward mobility was blocked by Europeans, while Lulua frustrations were in large part directed against Luba. In this three-person game, it requires no ingenuity to foresee the likely coalition. A series of acts by the colonial administration, partly unwitting, served to exacerbate the tensions between Lulua and Luba; at the critical moment when ethnic cleavages were becoming politicized and cultural fears were escalating in 1959, the proclivity of colonial officials to seek "moderate" allies rather than promoting inter-ethnic unity and collaboration played an important part in the sequence of events leading to violent rupture and holocaust. Lulua-Frères benefitted from the informal support of the colonial administration. In August 1959, with the logistics support of the administration, a Congress of Lulua chiefs and notables was organized. On the colonial question, the congress was suitably moderate, asking only internal autonomy, not independence. However, the posture toward the Luba was more aggressive; all Luba were to be expelled from Lulua rural milieu, while those in Kananga could stay if they pledged to stay out of politics. In the event, Lulua attacks against Luba began in October 1959 in Kananga; shortly after, an exodus of the approximately 50,000 Kananga Luba back to their homeland was in full swing. But this was only the beginning; the congress resolution was thoroughly implemented, and indeed the example was followed by other groups, such as the Kuba, who resented the Luba immigrants. From 1958 to 1963, the population of the Luba homeland of South Kasai increased from 332,620 to 1,348,030.[23]

Thus, within a populace culturally and linguistically indistinguishable, came first a distinction, then through unequal rates of social mobility, a difference. The distinction (ethnicity) fused with the difference (class); the resulting conflagration illumined the Kasai landscape. In its heat and incandescence, it was easy to forget that all of Kasai was not heard from. The Lulua could be seen as socially disadvantaged only with reference to the Luba; by any other yardstick, they were favorably placed. But it was precisely the Luba who occupied the Lulua cognitive field as relevant others; no solace was to be found in contemplation of the forlorn state of the Kete, Kuba, Shilele, or the fragmented groups in the isolated forests of north Kasai.

In the Copperbelt, it was also the Luba-Kasai who represented the pole of social privilege. Manpower needs in the mines and related industries grew rapidly after the founding of Lubumbashi in 1911. The im-

23. Turner, in Olorunsola, *The Politics of Cultural Sub-Nationalism,* p. 223.

mediate hinterland was sparsely populated and could not supply the voracious labor requirements of the mineral centers; company recruiters cast their eyes toward the more populous areas to the north. Kasai-Luba readily migrated to the new centers. Further, even by the time the mines started, Luba with some education were entering the labor market, long before potential white-collar employees could be found in Shaba in any numbers. In the interwar years, the postive stereotype of Luba-Kasai as "intelligent," "hard-working," and pro-European was confirmed. Over half the clerks and school teachers in the Union Miniere Lubumbashi camp were Luba; they were station masters and telegraphers on the BCK railway, and clerks in the banks.[24]

The social role of the Luba-Kasai was well elucidated in a little-known episode during World War II. The oppresive features of the colonial regime affected differing strata of the African population in contrasting ways. For the upper segment of the nascent African elite, mainly Luba-Kasai, Europeans had become a meaningful reference group, and the pervasive racism and discriminatory regulation of Africans became a deepening source of grievance.[25] Elite discussion groups had been organized under European auspices in the 1930s. In the war years, one such group, which came to be a Luba-Kasai entity, met on a clandestine basis with the European editor of the *Echo du Katanga,* A. Dekoster. He encouraged them to consider a general strike, taking advantage of the disorganization in the colony which accompanied the Nazi occupation of the mother country. For the Luba-Kasai elite, the strike would be a means of enforcing their demands for equal status; for Dekoster, the opportunity to emerge as the leader of a powerful African movement seemed to hold the promise of improving his controversial status in the European community. However, the scheme ran away from Dekoster. The Luba-Kasai elite made contact with noncommissioned Zairians in the local army garrison, only to discover that plans were afoot for a more revolutionary mutiny of the Kananga garrison. A high proportion of these noncoms were Luba-Kasai, and discontent within the army ranks was running high. It was agreed to merge the two schemes, and with Luba-Kasai army personnel as the main communications network, contacts were established with the army bases at Kamina and Likasi, as well as Kananga and Lubumbashi.

However, the conspiracy backfired badly. The Luba-Kasai elite tried to build support from their less educated fellows; they were tepid about the scheme, and non-Luba elements of the populace, as rumors spread,

24. Fetter, "Elisabethville and Lubumbashi", provides an exceedingly detailed social history of then Elisabethville from 1911 to 1940.

25. The discriminatory features of Belgian colonial administration are detailed in Young, *Politics in the Congo*, pp. 59-105.

were thoroughly hostile. The Lubumbashi phase of the plot was nipped by the Belgians, who had by now obtained complete information on the plans. The Luba railway telegrapher who was to have relayed the signal for action to Kananga was arrested prematurely. Tension grew unbearably at the Kananga camp, when no message came. A banal incident then sparked a mutiny, but not the one planned by the Luba-Kasai. Neither the Luba-Kasai elite in Kananga, nor anyone else in the civil population supported the actual uprising, which was led by a Songe sergeant; the isolated mutineers were easily hunted down, imprisoned or executed.[26]

The conspiracy, intended as a nationalist revolutionary coup, failed not only because its organizers lacked the capacity to carry it out. For the Luba-Kasai, as the most educated elements in the African populace, it was natural to look upon themselves as trustees for their less fortunate compatriots. Such a concept of representation was not shared, however, by the rest of the population. Humbler strata of Luba-Kasai, not at that moment mobilized behind issues of cultural solidarity, were not confident that their interests were being served in this adventure. For non-Luba, among whom was found a negative stereotype of Luba as haughty, arrogant, and nepotistic, the monopoly of leadership by Luba-Kasai elicited the hostile conviction that this was not "their" movement; a scheme suspected of concealed motives of ethnic and elite self-interest was likely to provoke a bloody and indiscriminate repression, directed at all Africans. The prudent response in these circumstances was to inform the administration, which is precisely what happened. At this time, although the Luba-Kasai were a substantial majority of the top African elite, they were only 22 percent of the African population as a whole.

After the Luba-Kasai, the next largest group in Lubumbashi in the late 1950s were Luba-Shankadi, with 18.1 percent. This category too, was more complex than it first appeared. There was an important distinction in identity between Luba from northwest Shaba, the center of the historic Luba empires, and those farther east. In northeast Shaba, one encounters a zone of cultural transition, where Luba linguistic influences have been strong; these groups are sometimes described as Hemba, or Luba-Hemba. Within the urban social field, they were likely to be called Luba-Shaba, or Luba-Shankadi, however, many stress their distinctiveness, and reject the Luba label. During the 1950s, efforts were made to form a pan-Luba association, uniting those from Kasai and Shaba, built upon the common language and shared historical myths of the glorious epoch of the Luba empire. But the pan-Luba concept lacked

26. This is based upon Bruce Fetter, "The Luluabourg Revolt at Elisabethville" (Typescript).

mobilizing force, and the resentment of Luba-Kasai as a socially privileged category was not shared by Luba-Shaba. Equally unsuccessful were initiatives for a Luba-Shaba association.[27] The failure of Luba-Shaba to structure identity for all of its presumptive clientele was again demonstrated in 1960, when a political movement sought to build upon this base.

The next largest group in Lubumbashi were the Lunda, with 6.3 percent, with all others less than 5 percent. In the late 1950s, social antagonisms coalesced around the concept of "authentic Shabans," a term which excluded Luba-Kasai but was ambiguous towards Luba-Shankadi. The "authentic Shaban" category had the advantage not only of differentiating the less favored from the Luba-Kasai, but also of connoting the illegitimacy of their presence, as "strangers" from another province. The coalition assembled under the "authentic Shaban" banner were mainly Lunda and small groups from southern Shaba.

The salience of the ethnic correlation of social stratification was sharpened in 1957 by both political and economic developments. Politically, the first Lubumbashi local elections found Luba-Kasai candidates conspicuously successful; the new municipal office-holders were believed to be extravagant in their nepotism, and generated real fears among "authentic Shabans." Hard times economically reinforced their insecurity when in 1957 the copper market broke. Those who became unemployed were compelled to return to their impoverished rural areas. Thus the authority of the new Luba-Kasai officeholders to influence the grant of urban residence permits became a highly politicized issue. In 1958, the "authentic Shabans" organized a political movement, the Confédération des Associations Tribales du Katanga (Conakat). (Katanga is the former name for Shaba.) The objects of this multiethnic alliance and the fears which stimulated its birth are expressed by two of its founders:

To combat the policy of the companies who have recruited a large part of their labor force from outside the province. This policy had handicapped Katanga tribes in their material and intellectual development, owing to the fact that most good schools are found only in the industrial centers. . . .
To avoid any repetition of the results of the municipal elections of 1957. (Evariste Kimba)

The Katangans of birth wonder with good reason whether the authorities are not deliberately granting permanent residential permission to the people from Kasai in our towns so that the natives of that province can, thanks to their ever-growing number, crush those from Katanga. This fact could well cause violence in the near future between the inhabitants of the two provinces. We would respectfully point

27. Caprasse, *Leaders Africains en milieu urbain*, pp. 24-25, 36-37.

out to you that very numerous are the native sons of Katanga who would like to work in the great cities of their province; mercilessly, they are told that there is a decree forbidding access to the towns. And yet they are the ones who should have priority. (Godefroid Munongo)[28]

As in Kananga, the interplay of stratification and identity led to a European-Conakat alliance. Luba-Kasai elites since World War II and the mutiny episode were suspected of nationalist predispositions by Belgians. The Conakat shared the fears of all Africans that the policy of massive European settlement loudly advocated by the settlers might be adopted, and were not more enamored of European rule than anyone else. But the fears of Luba-Kasai hegemony were keen; in the shared hostility to the "strangers" from Kasai, the basis was found for an uneasy alliance with European interests. This development in turn posed a profound threat to the Luba-Kasai, whose ranks were closed by the implied menace that they might be deported from the province— a fear which was realized in 1962, during the period of Shaba secession, when the United Nations was forced to repatriate Luba-Kasai temporarily to their home area.

A similar pattern of stratified ethnicity dominated social conflict in Bukavu. Until independence came into view, differences within the African community were of little saliency, as the White settler community was strong and the atmosphere heavy with racism. When independence was in sight and it became clear that Zaire was to be an African state (and not a Eurafrican "partnership," as the settlers had dreamed), cleavages within the African population became perceptible and swiftly politicized. The elite group were Kusu immigrants from the western part of the province; their numbers were not large, but their migration had been very selective and markedly white collar. The lower social ranks were dominated by the Shi, migrants from the immediate environs. This conflict also reached a point after independence where many of the Kusu were forced to flee the city in 1962.

IDEOLOGIZATION OF ETHNICITY

The third process variable we will consider is the degree of ideological affirmation of ethnicity. It was argued in chapter 2 that ethnicity becomes akin to nationalism when the commonalities which underlie the shared identity become articulated by intellectuals and woven into

28. Crawford Young, "The Politics of Separatism: Katanga, 1960-1963," in Gwendolen M. Carter (ed.), *Politics in Africa* (New York: Harcourt, Brace & World, 1966), pp. 173-74.

a theory of solidarity. This was the process through which peasant ethnicity in Eastern and Central Europe became nationalism. History is rewoven as cultural saga. The language is unified, equipped with grammars and dictionaries. The affective dimensions of cultural solidarity are given lyrical expression through song, poetry, and literature. An ideology is a relatively coherent set of propositions defining social and political reality, which suggest the imperatives of social behavior for those who share it. Thus identity clothed in ideology imposes more comprehensive solidarity requirements, creates a more immutable solidarity community. Ethnicity in Zaire was indisputably highly politicized at the time of independence. To what extent was it also ideologized?

We will argue that the degree of ideological development of ethnicity was in most instances very weak. The two cases which appear to most closely approximate the model of ideologized identity are the Kongo and Luba-Kasai; however, the intellectual bases of identity are quite different in these two cases. These two instances of partial ideologization bear examination, and some speculative explanations for its absence in most instances may be put forward.

The foundation of the proto-ideology of Kongo identity is the mythology surrounding the ancient kingdom of the Kongo; the intellectual history of the prevalent concepts of its heroic period is illuminating. The Kongo state took form in the fourteenth century from an initial embryo in the vicinity of San Salvador, now in Angola. By the time of the arrival of the first Portuguese explorer in 1482, there was a kingdom stretching from the Zaire (Congo) River from the Atlantic to present Kinshasa, down into what is now northern Angola. The cultural core of the kingdom was Kongo, although not all the peoples incorporated within the state belonged to this linguistic community. The royal house of Kongo, in an expansive, state-building phase, was attracted by the potential resources which could be extracted from a controlled association with the visitors. Kongo emissaries visited the Portuguese court in Lisbon; the king asked for Portuguese missionaries, carpenters, and masons. It must be recalled that at this juncture, Portuguese had not yet evolved an ideology of imperial conquest, nor had the slave-hungry fazendas of the Brazilian coast yet come into being. Lisbon and the Vatican were attracted by the opportunities for spiritual expansion the kingdom offered. In 1491, the royal family and many nobles were baptized. The apogee of the Christian kingdom was during the reign of Affonso I from 1506 to about 1545. Affonso won his throne after a bitter combat, in which Christianity was an important political resource. His triumph was attributed to the intervention of St. James, who was said to have appeared miraculously at the side of Affonso, with an army of celestial knights.[29] Historically, this may best be understood, not as Christian revelation, but the injection into Kongo politics of a new idiom of power. In the words of an important recent anthropological study: "Affonso achieved a new *luyaalu* [government], a regime peculiar to himself, with a new tradition (*kinkuku*) of its own, Christianity, and a new *mpeve* (spirit), the Holy Spirit. Validating his candidacy, he overcame his opponents in battle by the aid of supernatural forces marshaled under a white cross by St. James the Apostle."[30]

In the years immediately following, Affonso undertook to convert his entire kingdom. Intensive commercial and diplomatic exchange with Portugal flourished for a time, and many young Kongo were sent to Portugal for education. Affonso embarked on a remarkable program of deliberate acculturation. But the Christian kingdom was overcome by various calamities. Portuguese interest in exploitation soon outweighed the evangelical impulse; the slave trade began in earnest. Portugal began its colonial foothold to the south, in Angola, and lost interest in relations as diplomatic equals with an African kingdom. A disastrous invasion in 1568 by marauders from the east, the Jaga, shook the monarchy. The kingdom had lost its authority by the eighteenth century; although the idea of kingship as a Kongo cultural symbol remained important at the San Salvador core, the king was remote and powerless. The generalization of a set of symbols of identity by the eighteenth century is evidenced by the intriguing episode of the Kongo Joan of Arc, the prophetess Beatrice, who emerged about 1704. She, too, had heard voices; her body was entered by the spirit of St. Antoine, through whose intermediary power she was the bearer of divine appeal for the resurrection of San Salvador and the reunification of the kingdom. The use of Christian symbols was incorporated within a Kongo self-affirmation frame; Beatrice maintained that Christ was Black, and had been born at San Salvador. She was burned at the stake in 1706, for heresy.[31]

By the time of the nineteenth-century colonial partition, centralized structures had completely evaporated, and the Christian identification had almost vanished. However, the exceptional features of Kongo history had two critical legacies: a reservoir of cultural symbols was available, even if many had fallen into disuse; and the Christian con-

29. Vansina, *Les Anciens royaumes de la savane,* p. 37. Vansina's reinterpretation of Kongo history is the basis for this account; it alters on many important points the earlier missionary versions.

30. Wyatt MacGaffey, *Custom and Government in the Lower Congo* (Berkeley: University of California Press, 1970).

31. Louis Jadin, "Le Congo et la secte des Antoniens," in *Bulletin de l'Institut Historique Belge de Rome,* XXXIII (1961), 411-601. Current historical research calls into question the standard interpretation of the "Jaga" invaders coming from the east; they may have been recruited from the Kongo peasantry—Jan Vansina, personal communication.

nections attracted the passionate interest of a generation of missionary scholars, who played a central role as cultural entrepreneurs. In influencing the course of cultural ideology, the two most important were J. Cuvelier and above all J. Van Wing.[32] Although important contributions were also made by Protestant missionaries, they wrote in English, making their works inaccessible to the new Kongo elite. From the Catholic perspective, the ancient kingdom was a miraculous achievement, the Christian kings crusaders of faith. Kongo history had a special place, was on a higher plane than the history of its neighbors. This unusual recognition was readily converted into intense cultural pride by the new elite.

It was the missionary version of Kongo history, rather than legends passed down by elders around the village hearth, which was the basis for contemporary Kongo cultural ideology. The epoch accounts of the heroic period of Christian rule became the basis for the school texts, through which literate Kongo learned about themselves. Father Van Wing taught a whole generation of Kongo seminarians at Kisantu; the founder of the ABAKO, Edmond Nzeza-Landu, has described the critical influence of Van Wing in his own appreciation of the Kongo cultural heritage.[33] It is remarkable to note the extent that ABAKO documents in the 1950s cite Cuvelier, Van Wing, Balandier, and others as scriptural authority for assertions about the cultural achievements of the group. Over time, the impact of the rediffusion of this European version of Kongo history was pervasive; MacGaffey found that most "tradition" relating to broader aspects of Kongo culture, as opposed to purely local matters of land and lineage, was that bequeathed by the Catholic missionary scholars.[34] The Belgian administration operated under its images as well; "native administration" was founded upon a royalist model of Kongo society which had long ceased to be an empirical description.

Kongo cultural ideology wove together the myth of the ancient kingdom with a sense of special endowment for modernization; the testimonial by the French sociologist Balandier quoted at the opening of this chapter, is representative of this self-concept. These themes run through the Kongo press and party documents and manifestos. "Of all the nations inhabiting western and even eastern Ethiopia (i.e., Africa), the Kongo stand out for their intellectual and moral qualities, and were from the beginning more polite in their customs, less barbarous, and

32. J. Cuvelier, *L'ancien royaume de Congo* (Bruges: Desclee de Brouwer, 1946); J. Van Wing, *Etudes Bakongo* (2nd ed.; Brussels: Desclee de Brouwer, 1959).

33. Rene Lemarchand, "The Bases of Nationalism among the Bakongo," *Africa*, XXXI, no. 4 (1961), 344-54.

34. MacGaffey, *Custom and Government in the Lower Congo*, p. 29 and passim.

more governed by reason"; thus spoke the ABAKO weekly, *Notre Kongo*.[35] In more subtle vein, the political thought of ABAKO leader Joseph Kasavubu captured the Kongo present as the prolongation of the past, "expressed with particular clarity the diffuse aspirations of the Kongo (of Kinshasa) in the urban and colonial context."[36] He called for cultural authenticity and denounced the destructive impact of colonialism on African (and Kongo) culture.

Language development and unification was advanced as a plank in the ABAKO platform, largely to counter the threat of Lingala in Kinshasa. The initial ABAKO charter in 1950 set forth the grievance: "Our numerous children attending schools in the city are educated in an artificial African language [i.e., Lingala] and are ignorant of the beauty and the infinite richness of their own literature. Some of them, after a few years of school, feel a certain shame in expressing themselves in Kikongo. This attitude diminishes us considerably and has a tendency to lessen the influence of our beautiful language.

"Experience demonstrates that our children thus trained in this artificial language increasingly lose the delicacy, the dignity and warmth characteristic of the Kongo people."[37] The language unification and modernization campaign was overtaken by more immediate political challenges, and little was accomplished. Lingala has continued to expand in Kinshasa, at the expense of Kikongo.

The cultural myth of the Kongo, in its most expansive moments, went far beyond the actual historical bounds of the kingdom. The six historical provinces were all south of the Zaire River; thus Mayombe is a modern addition to the orbit of Kongo territory, as is most of the area in Congo-Brazzaville which identifies itself with Kongo culture. In late 1959, the ABAKO journal staked a claim, on behalf of the ancient kingdom, to all the territory as far north as Cameroon and the Central African Republic and as far west in Zaire as the Kasai River.[38] In their extreme forms, these territorial claims were ludicrous and obviously found no support from those not identifying with Kongo culture. However, in the decolonization period, the establishment of a Kongo state, uniting portions of Congo-Brazzaville, Zaire, and northern Angola was seriously contemplated. The first president of Congo-Brazzaville, Abbé Fulbert Youlou, a Kongo, launched his often-quoted epigram, "Tous ceux qui se ressemblent, se rassemblent." Holden Roberto, head of the UPA, whose strength was concentrated in the Kongo zone of northern Angola, approached Kwame Nkrumah in 1958

35. *Notre Kongo*, 19 November 1959.
36. Monnier, *Ethnie et intégration régionale au Congo*, p. 63.
37. *A.B.A.K.O. 1950-1960*, p. 11.
38. *Notre Kongo*, 8 November 1959.

for support for a Kongo state (and received a frosty reception since Nkrumah felt an ethnic state was an improper goal for Angolan nationalism, a "tribal anachronism").[39] After the early 1960s, the possibility of an independent Kongo state receded. Youlou was overthrown in Brazzaville in 1963, and Kongo were no longer politically dominant. The UPA, at one point the most dynamic of Angolan liberation movements, lost ground to the MPLA and UNITA. After the Mobutu coup in Zaire, Kongo autonomy was abruptly ended. The conviction of a possible territorial fulfillment of Kongo cultural ideology was an important sustaining factor. Its virtual elimination as a conceivable scenario has contributed to the demoralization of Kongo subnationalism.

In the late 1950s, Kongo identity seemed on the verge of acquiring an institutionalized ideology; a decade later, the trend toward affirmation of identity seemed arrested. The ABAKO was dissolved; ethnic associations were forbidden. Modern politics were carried on within the central institutions of the state and extended outwards by a tightly controlled national movement, the MPR, carefully constructed to avoid incorporating ethnic grievances. Journals crusading for ethnic objectives were suppressed; intellectuals were absorbed in the national institutions, and the Kongo middle class could not safely express itself through a cultural medium. This is not in the least to imply the imminent extinction of Kongohood as ethnic identity; we are merely arguing that the process of ideologization of Kongo culture has been arrested, at least for the moment. It probably remains the most intensely held cultural identity in Zaire. There is, nonetheless, a critical distinction between Kongohood and a fully articulated cultural ideology, such as that of the Tamils or Bengalis.

The second most significant ethnic group, in terms of saliency of identity and socio-political impact, is the Luba-Kasai. Though the 1970 census did not include an ethnic breakdown, one may estimate their numbers at approximately 1.5 million. In 1960, when they were driven out of many areas to which they had migrated during the colonial period, they briefly established an independent state and maintained an ethnic province until 1966. This searing experience of exodus and momentary fears of genocide led to a quest for Lubahood, efforts at defining an ethnic ideology for their state. Symbolic resources available for this task were strikingly different than those used by the Kongo.

History, to begin with, was an ambiguous tool. Luba-Kasai trace their ancestry to the glorious days of the sixteenth-century Luba empire of Ilunga Mbidi. More recently, Luba historians attribute their derivation

39. John Marcum, *The Angolan Revolution*, 1 (Cambridge: M.I.T. Press, 1969), 67.

to the largest of the successor states to Ilunga Mbidi's kingdom, Kasongo Nyembo. However, they had apparently emigrated to Kasai during the two centuries preceding colonial rule to remove themselves from the authority of Kasongo Nyembo.[40] Although Luba-Kasai and Luba-Shaba shared a language and common historic myths, they had sharply different social roles and operated from quite separate political fields. Although there was some advantage in drawing upon the luminescence of the Luba empire, one could not claim continuity with it nor found the cultural legitimacy of Luba-Kasai as a group upon it. More recent history had been calamitous; Luba-Kasai were victims of Afro-Arab and Songe slave raids, dislocated and uprooted, fugitives settled for protection around the European posts.

Language has played some role, although not a large one. Unlike Kikongo, Tshiluba faced no immediate threat; it was used as a vehicular language in former Kasai Province, and extensively employed in the Copperbelt cities. One of the most important Luba-Kasai intellectuals, Mabika Kalanda, chose to write an important text of cultural self-affirmation in Tshiluba, and one Luba history was published in the vernacular.[41] But the key social resource of the Luba-Kasai elite was their capacity to compete in the modern sector, for which the linguistic tool was French.

The linchpin of Luba-Kasai identity is the remarkable success in exploitation of the new opportunities accompanying social change. The perception of Luba-Kasai as socially mobile in large numbers was shared by other ethnic groups—with resentment and hostility, by Europeans—with approbation until the new elites began to speak the language of nationalism, and by Luba-Kasai themselves. The assessment of Mabika Kalanda of the saga of Luba-Kasai adaptation may be taken as representative: "... the Muluba, brutally thrown back upon himself by the slave wars ... created ... a personal insecurity which he did not hesitate to cure by the force of individual adaptation to change, and by the sense of self-confidence conferred upon him by his personal experiences in travelling. The Muluba thus became the man who counts above all on himself, and established authority."[42] Mobility required emigration. There was no complete secondary school in the Luba homeland; the pathways to prosperity led to Kananga, the Copperbelt, or the Kinshasa. Luba success thus was tied to the broader arena; a territorialization of ethnic self-concept came only under the cultural shock of the enforced exodus.

40. Theodore Kanyinda-Lusanga, "Pouvoir traditionel et institutions politiques modernes chez les Baluba du Sud-Kasai" (Mémoire de Licence, Université Lovanium de Kinshasa, 1968), p. 3.

41. Mabika Kalanda, *Tabalayi* (Kinshasa: Imprimerie Concorida, 1963); L. M. Mpoya, *Histoire wa Baluba* (Mbujimayi, 1966).

42. Kalanda, *Baluba et Lulua*, pp. 95-96.

The proclamation of South Kasai independence was based, not upon declarations of historic fulfillment of cultural self-determination comparable to autonomist manifestos from ABAKO, but as a matter of survival; "Given the profound hatred and irreducible spirit of vengeance, irremedial consequence of eleven months of arson, pillaging, massacres, mutilations, hatred and vengeance . . . in consequence . . . the division of Kasai . . . is necessary at any cost."[43] Politically, the Luba-Kasai leader, Albert Kalonji, attempted to create a metaphor of unity in royalist idiom, through proclaiming himself "Mulopwe," or emperor. An assembly of chiefs was gathered for this purpose. According to Kalonji, the chiefs would have nothing less than his investiture and beatification: "At the moment each of [the chiefs] is presenting me to the populations over whom he exercises power, and ordering them to recognize me as the sole chief. . . . Simultaneously, secret ceremonies are going forward which will result in my becoming divine. . . . The final ceremony . . . is beyond imagination. The chiefs will dress me as a native, and for certain circumstances, I will not be able to dress otherwise. I will have an entire leopard skin. All the chiefs will be there. It is really the return of our most ancient traditions."[44] In fact, the Luba-Kasai had no tradition of unity, nor was their customary warrant for the office Kalonji assumed. One leading chief who had participated in this travesty of tradition explained. "This child had such extraordinary thirst for power that we consented to give it to him."[45]

The royalist metaphor as a vehicle for cultural unity satisfied neither chiefs nor intellectuals; the latter were swiftly alienated by the capricious authoritarian rule of the new emperor and took refuge in Kinshasa to plot his overthrow. This division between "intellectuals" and "royalists" came to be described in regional terms as "Bena Tshibanda" (those from down-river, or northern South Kasai), and "Bena Mutu wa Mukuna" (those from up-river, or the southern part of the province). Like the royalist metaphor, this characterization of cleavage is largely new and is little noted in the classic ethnographies. The end of provincial autonomy eclipsed this duality; as Kanyinda-Lusanga observes laconically: "Since then, things have changed: other divisions and subdivisions have emerged."[46]

The restoration of personal security throughout Zaire under the Mobutu regime has permitted Luba elites to return to more attractive social arenas. Although the Luba self-concept of success remains firmly anchored, there are manifest social risks in the aggressive articulation

43. *Courrier d'Afrique,* 9 August 1960, reprinted in *Congo 1960,* II, 799-800.
44. Interview in *Dernière Heure* (Brussels), 2 April 1961.
45. Kanyinda-Lusanga, *Pouvoir traditionnel et institutions politiques modernes,* p. 97.
46. Ibid., p. 31.

of Lubahood. Luba-Kasai have a sense that, as a group, they are some-what distrusted by the Mobutu regime. Although Luba-Kasai hold high positions in the central institutions, the impression is general that care is taken to avoid the concentration of Luba-Kasai around any institutional nodal points. Yet their self-concept depends upon the Zaire national arena and their success within it; Luba-Kasai cultural identity is thus mortgaged to territorial integrity and national integration. The keys to their kingdom are to be found in a self-denying ordinance with regard to overt cultural ideology.

AMBIGUITIES OF IDENTITY: THE TETELA-KUSU

Explanatory factors in the crystallization of contemporary forms of identity are far from exhausted by these three process variables, although they seem of sufficient importance to deserve particular attention. Taken together, they help explain why particular cultural labels became the basis for politization of identity in the last two decades, and also some of the reasons for the variation in intensity of ethnic self-awareness. To further illustrate the complexities of ethnic labelling and the ambiguities of identity in a context where cultural ideology is much less developed we may take advantage of the excellent documentation available on the Tetela-Kusu group, of Sankuru and Maniema districts of east central Zaire.

At the time of the nearly simultaneously Belgian and Zanzibari Afro-Arab penetration of this region, the zone was populated by peoples sharing a common language, closely related cultural institutions, and very decentralized political structures. The most common self-identification appears to have been Nkutshu a Membele, after an eponymous ancestor, Onkutshu, son of Membele. However, the evidence suggests the legend of common ancestry and the label derived from it were not of prime significance in social life.

The arrival of Afro-Arabs and Belgians opened a new era in identity; group labels were an indispensable conceptual accoutrement of domination. The earliest visitor to leave a written account, the Afro-Arab trader-cum-empire builder Tippo Tip, used the term "Tetela" to refer to the entire cultural zone, and elsewhere applied the label "Kusu" in apparently synonymous meaning.[47] However, the area in which Tippo Tip operated was in contemporary Maniema, where the label Kusu (and not

47. Tippu Tib, *Maisha ya Hamed ibn Muhammed ec Mujerbi yaani Tippu Tib*, supplement to the *East African Swahili Committee Journal*, 28 (1958), 2, and 29 (1959), 1, paragraph 97.

Tetela) is used. "Kusu" is probably a corruption of Nkutshu; the etymology of Tetela is unclear. Turner, who carefully explored this question, elicited nearly a dozen overlapping and conflicting explanations from contemporary informants.[48]

The scorecard of subjugation was complicated by new entries arising from the era of colonial incorporation. Tippo Tip extended his political control through bands of African auxiliaries, the most famous of whom was Ngongo Lutete. Ngongo, probably of Songe origin, raised his bands primarily from zones now bearing the Kusu label. However, the Belgians, who succeeded in inducing Ngongo to change sides, referred to his men as Tetela. In 1895, 1897, and 1900, major mutinies in the Belgian colonial army occurred; these were primarily men absorbed into the forces with Ngongo's defection, and related ex-auxiliaries of the Afro-Arabs. In fact, in contemporary terms, most were probably Kusu and Songe, as well as from other southern Maniema groups.

During this time, the occupation and pacification of Sankuru district, home of the modern Tetela, was carried out. The same pool of auxiliaries was used for this purpose, and initially placed in political charge of the areas they subjugated for the Belgians. For those filling this role, the label Sambala, another term without historical antecedent, came into use. After 1908, the political jurisdiction of the Sambala chiefs was ended, but communities of Sambala remained interspersed among the populace, often clustered near the European posts. Their established pattern of collaboration with the Europeans tended to give them first option on the available subaltern employs as menials and messengers. This first step on the social escalator led to early school entry for their children and, over a generation or two, a privileged standing within the local arena. As the Tetela label came to be territorially fixed in Sankuru, it was applied to both Sambala and those they had dominated; however, Sambala remained an important identity for both the group itself, and its relevant others.

Meanwhile, in Maniema the idea of Kusuhood developed in complex fashion, in symbiosis with some overlapping and complementary labels. Persons who clustered around the prosperous Afro-Arab trading towns were quick to emulate certain cultural traits of the invaders: the East African coastal dress, rice diet, Swahili language, and, for some, Islam. As Afro-Arab political outposts were extended down the Zaire River as far as contemporary Kisangani, Kusu auxiliaries accompanied the Zanzibarites. Those who became Muslims were adorned with the designation of "Wangwana" by the Afro-Arabs (free men and Muslims). The Belgians, on their side, labelled those exhibiting the external traits of

---

48. Thomas Turner, "A Century of Conflict in Sankuru" (Ph.D. diss., University of Wisconsin, 1973). This account is drawn primarily from Turner.

East African coastal culture as "Arabisés." The ambiguity of the largely overlapping "Arabisé" and "Kusu" labels is illustrated in the most comprehensive monograph devoted to this city, by Valdo Pons and associates. In a 1956 version, Arabisés are not listed as a separate category, but rather listed in terms of their ethnic labels, mainly Kusu; thus the Kusu are the second largest group, with 10 percent. In a 1969 reworking of the same data, the Kusu are dropped and the Arabisé category utilized instead, totalling 11.8 percent of the population.[49]

As colonial administration became established and routinized, the Tetela-Kusu area was divided by the Kasai-Kivu provincial boundary, which seems to have been decisive in creating a pattern of separate identity development. The cultural domain was also partitioned evangelically; different mission orders, both Catholic and Protestant, operated on either side of the provincial frontier. The educational ladder leaned in different directions; primary schools in Maniema led to post-primary establishments in Kindu, while pupils in Sankuru aimed for Kasai secondary schools. Communication routes in Maniema were oriented toward the provincial capital of Bukavu, or the regional center of Kisangani; Lodja, Lusambo, and Kananga were the nodal points in Kasai. Thus, Tetela referred to Sankuru, while Kusu was identified with Maniema.

In the Bukavu social field, the term Kusu came to have an enlarged sense, describing all immigrants from Maniema district who belonged to the social and professional elite. Thus, Kusu became virtually a class and prestige term. As Verhaegen points out, "Prestige was attached to the 'Kusu' appellation, which greatly contributed to a generalization of its usage. One called oneself 'Kusu' solely in order to benefit from the esteem attached to this origin."[50]

In Sankuru, a further important distinction linked to the ecological difference between the forest and savanna zones must be noted. The savanna Tetela were often called Eswe, while those of the forest were termed Ekonda. The savanna was somewhat more prosperous and had a denser infrastructure of modern amenities; the bulk of the Tetela elite were either Eswe or Sambala. The forest Tetela were also frequently called Hamba at an earlier date; in some usages, the Tetela term was reserved to the Eswe.

The Ekonda-Eswe cleavage became intensively politicized during the 1960-64 period and by 1963 had reached a level of tension where the dismal spiral of arson, assaults, assassinations, and terrorism set in. What is remarkable is that the potential impact of this cleavage

49. V. Pons et al., "Social Effects of Urbanization in Stanleyville, Belgian Congo," in *Social Implications of Industrialization and Urbanization in Africa South of the Sahara* (Paris: UNESCO, 1956), p. 265; Pons, *Stanleyville,* p. 63. This interesting alteration is pointed out by Turner, in Olorunsola, *The Politics of Cultural Sub-Nationalism,* p. 236.

50. Verhaegen, *Rebellions au Congo,* II, 37.

was entirely ignored until the eve of independence. Sankuru's favorite son was Patrice Lumumba, a savanna Tetela, charismatic hero, and political organizer of exceptional skill. In the 1950s, Lumumba had acquired wide experience in building organizations, learned the importance of balancing tendencies and representing visible groupings. In his political organization in Sankuru, he was very careful to balance Protestants and Catholics, a division which had played some conflict role in the Tetela elite association in Kinshasa. However, he appeared totally unaware of the Ekonda-Eswe problem; in overrepresenting savanna Tetela, he lit the fuse of a conflict which exploded after his death in January 1961. Students of Tetela society were aware of the distinction, but did not lay great stress upon it. It was only in 1960 that "Eswe" and "Ekonda" appeared as political-ethnic labels.[51]

Migration to the city was very selective for both Tetela and Kusu. Kusu elite communities were found in the Copperbelt, Bukavu, and Kisangani—although in the latter case, as mentioned above, Kusu and Arabisé labels overlapped. Tetela communities were found in the Copperbelt, Kisangani, Kananga, and Kinshasa. Where both Tetela and Kusu were present, as in the Copperbelt or Kisangani, they formed separate ethnic associations. In Kananga, although Tetela were only 2.7 percent of the population in the late 1950s, they had the highest average educational level of any group, including the Luba-Kasai, and were concentrated at the top of the African social scale.[52] In all cities, both Tetela and Kusu numbers were very small; there was no incentive to promote ethnic interests through intensive cultural mobilization in the urban context.

The final aspect of Tetela and Kusu ethnic options was the incorporative concept of Mongohood.[53] Linguistic and cultural uniformities over a vast area of the central basin of Zaire, stretching from Mbandaka to Maniema, led several Flemish administrators and missionaries to postulate the ethnic unity of all Mongo. The Mongo idea is of very recent vintage; the first published appearance of the term as an incorporative label was only in 1938.[54] The most powerful scriptural testament for Mongo cultural unity was the massive, two-volume work of Georges Vanderkerken, a provincial governor who urged regrouping all Mongo within a single province; this work, *L'Ethnie Mongo*, was published in

51. The origins of the Eswe-Ekonda conflict are carefully documented in Turner "A Century of Conflict in Sankuru."

52. Lux, "Luluabourg," pp. 12, 71.

53. The origins of Mongo identity are discussed in Young, *Politics in the Congo*, pp. 247-50.

54. E. Boelaert, "De Nkundo-Mongo, een volk; een taal," *Aequatoria*, I, no 8 (1938), 3-25.

1944.[55] Vanderkerken included the Tetela-Kusu as the eastern frontier of his Mongo grouping. The Flemish spokesmen for Mongo unity called for the unification of Lomongo and its elevation to status as a major vehicular language. Stress was laid on the mythical first ancestor Mongo, as the proof of common origin and warrant for shared destiny. Turner, however, shows that the idea of the eponymous ancestor was by no means universally accepted among Tetela-Kusu—nor, for that matter, in other parts of the greater Mongo area. The fact that elders were more likely to reject the "children of Mongo" concept than young persons who had been to school suggests that the missions and school texts had played an important role in generalizing if not creating this tradition.

What is established beyond dispute is that, whatever standing the eponymous ancestory legend had, the idea of Mongohood as a meaningful identity as a logical inference from the myths of origin is very recent. Vanderkerken himself notes that "the conviction that all Mongo belong to one ethnic group" was limited to Mongo notables and those who had widely travelled through the area. According to a Lovanium thesis by a Tetela student, the idea of Mongo unity began to be taken up by Kinshasa intellectuals about 1950.[56] Lumumba sought to make use of the pan-Mongo concept as a means for broadening his regional base in 1960 and organized an Anamongo (children of Mongo) congress in the Sankuru town of Lodja in March 1960, bringing together both urban elites and rural chiefs and notables from the Sankuru-Maniema area (but not representatives from Mongo areas farther to the west). Interestingly, the most divisive issue before the congress was the name to be adopted; notables and chiefs from Maniema rejected the Anamongo label and insisted that the designation Ankutsu be chosen. In Solomonic compromise, the group labelled itself Ankutshu-Anamongo.[57] Since 1960, however, the dynamics of cultural politics have diminished the utility, and hence the interest, in the Mongo appellation among Tetela and Kusu; a Mongo province existed between 1962 and 1966, but Tetela-Kusu were not a part of it and evinced no interest in it. The province was organized around the Mbandaka social field, in which the Tetela-Kusu had no involvement.

We have been able to penetrate this far into the tangled forest of identity in the Sankuru-Maniema area because the winding pathways have

55. Georges Vanderkerken, *L'Ethnie Mongo* (2 vols.; Brussels: Académie Royale des Sciences Coloniales, 1944).

56. Jules Mbolandinga-Katako, "Conflict Ekonda-Eswe au Sankuru de 1960 à 1964" (Unpublished mémoire de licence, Lovanium University, 1970), quoted in Turner, "Conflict in Sankuru."

57. The resolutions of the Ankutshu-Anamongo Congress are reproduced in *Congo 1960*, III, 7-18.

been unusually well mapped. The lush and exhuberant growth of cultural labels—and even here we have not been exhaustive—is a veritable forest of symbols. As we wander, now one species is dominant, and later another. Many, if not most, have only recently been discovered and labelled. No clearcut, transcendant cultural self-concepts have emerged. Situation and circumstances have determined the saliency of any set of labels at a given political moment. The bewildering complexity is instructive, the pattern revealed in Sankuru-Maniema is representative in its confusion of large parts of Zaire. Kongo and even Luba-Kasai identity stand out by comparison in their relative clarity; the Kongo in particular, at least in the decade straddling independence, appeared close to the articulation of a cultural ideology akin to nationalism. Tetela-Kusu are a long ways from it, even though their identity is still some distance from the end of a spectrum running between the poles of specificity and diffuseness of cultural identity.

AMBIGUITIES OF ETHNICITY: WHO IS MOBUTU?

The contrast in intensity is well illustrated in the striking difference in cultural attachments of the two heads of state since independence, Joseph Kasavubu and Joseph Mobutu (now Mobutu Sese Seko). Kasavubu was deeply attached to Kongo culture and strongly identified with it. The very salience of the Kongo group, through their ethnic self-affirmation, size, and importance in the Zaire political arena made Kasavubu's ethnicity very visible, his Kongo identification universally known.

The confusion surrounding Mobutu's ethnicity is remarkable. His parents were both from the Banzyville region, on the frontier with the Central African Republic. His biographer, Francis Monheim, refers to him as "Bangwandi"; a more precise term is Ngbandi.[58] The Ngbandi are culturally linked to groups of the northern savanna of Zaire, such as the Banda, Ngbaka, and Zande.[59] Indeed, Mobutu is related to Colonel (now Marshall) Jean Bokassa, president of the Central African Republic. Mobutu himself was born in Lisala, in the Ngombe region, and achieved political visibility as a journalist in Kinshasa in the late 1950s; in Kinshasa, Ngombe generally accept the label of Ngala. Two generally reliable dictionaries of political biography published shortly after independence offer different—and erroneous—identifications. Pierre Artigue cites

58. Francis Monheim, *Mobutu, l'homme seul* (Brussels: Editions Actuelles, 1962), p. 19.
59. Vansina, *Introduction a l'ethnographie du Congo*, pp. 27-37.

Mongo ethnicity;[60] CRISP identifies him as a Ngala, perhaps because of his Lisala birthplace.[61]

The Ngbandi are very isolated and distant from all major urban centers. In the provincial capital of Mbandaka, they were only 2 percent in the 1950s. Education came late to this area, and its economic development is slight. Thus, they simply are not a part of the social field for urban Zairians, nor do they constitute an elite community that is generally recognized by an ethnic label. In my own research in the early 1960s, when Mobutu was very visible but not yet president, I found very few persons who could identify his ethnic origin. No doubt there are now more, but the label itself is devoid of real meaning for most Zairians; it is simply not a part of the social vocabulary. Like any unfamiliar word, even if it is heard occasionally, one is prone to forget it. More would have been able to say that he came from a "Sudanic" language group, a label once in currency but now in disuse among linguists which differentiated the populations of the northern fringe from those speaking "Bantu" languages. But "Sudanic" is wholly devoid of subjective meaning for those who might be thus classified by others. This is not to suggest that the public holds no perceptions of Mobutu's cultural antecedents and draws no inferences from them. Mobutu uses Lingala as his primary African language and generally employs this medium at public gatherings. Many observers believe that the Mobutu regime hopes gradually to establish Lingala as a national language. There is a widespread conviction that key levers of power are in the hands of those from Mobutu's home province of Equateur. He may be seen, in a vague way, as an Ngala or, regionally, as an Equateurian or, linguistically, as a Lingalaphone. These images involve generally recognized symbols and may offer meaningful cues in interpreting the president and his regime. But these are all new categories; what stands out is the diffuseness and fluidity of ethnicity as it relates to President Mobutu.

Cultural pluralism in Zaire, then, is built upon complex, fluid, shifting units, which vary greatly in their degree of clarity and specificity. The broader significance of cultural pluralism as a dimension of Zaire politics overall has undergone dramatic transformation in the last two decades. In each successive political phase, the lines have been differently drawn, and the relevance of ethnic roles is quite variable. By way of drawing together the analytical threads of this chapter, we must now turn to the impact of the political arena, viewed through time, on the process of cultural competition. Five distinct phases may be distinguished: (1) the first overt political competition with African parti-

60. Pierre Artigue, *Qui sont les leaders congolais?* (Brussels: Editions Europe-Afrique, 1961), p. 217.
61. *Congo 1960*, III, 112.

cipation, in the urban elections of 1957-58; (2) the formation of political parties and competition for national power, 1959-60; (3) political fragmentation, through the restructuring of the polity in new provinces in 1962-63; (4) the wave of rebellions in 1964-65; (5) the Mobutu era of recentralization beginning in November 1965.

URBAN POLITICS AS A CONFLICT ARENA

Sequences are of considerable significance in political development; in Zaire, it is of no small importance that the colonizer chose to situate the first open electoral competition at the urban level. At that juncture, the colonizer was in full control of the polity and could dictate the terms of its transformation. The metaphor which guided Belgian calculations at this juncture was political construction "from the ground up." Zairians were first to acquire political experience in the administration of local problems before being entrusted with the broader responsibilities of territorial direction. Thus, elections were held in 1957 in Kinshasa, Likasi, and Lubumbashi, followed by balloting in 1958 in Mbandaka, Kisangani, Bukavu, and Kananga. Although the consequences of this choice seem obvious enough in retrospect, one must realize that neither Africans nor Europeans clearly foresaw the social psychology of electoral choice.

We have argued at some length the centrality of the urban social field in shaping ethnic perceptions. It was here that social competition was most intense, that groups defined both themselves and their relevant others in the daily interactions of urban life. It was also important to recall the Madisonian views held by the colonial administration in the conduct of these elections. Political parties were dangerous and thus evil; elections should permit the emergence of meritorious individuals, who earned the confidence of their constituents because of their particular leadership qualities. It was not desirable that parties be formed to compete on a group basis. Fear of nationalism and ideology, not ethnicity, shaped this perspective.

The ethnic polarization which resulted from these elections was not simply a function of the electoral campaign itself, but came about through the perception of the results and fears generated among the losers by the conduct in office of the victors. The ABAKO, at that time officially an ethnic association and not a political party, did put forward lists of candidates. Of the 170 councillors elected, 133 were Kongo, which at first view suggested an overwhelming Kongo triumph. However, the successful Kongo candidates were in many instances not those nominated by ABAKO. Kongo candidates received a total of 46 percent of the total vote as a group, which is not much more than the total fraction of Kongo in the Kinshasa population in 1957 (40.7 percent, although this figure is total population and not registered voters, for which no ethnic breakdown is available). We have earlier described the polarization of perceptions of the Kinshasa social field as Kongo-Ngala; Ngala identity did not, in fact, draw together all those who migrated to Kinshasa from the east. It would appear that many voters supported the candidate most familiar to them. At the same time, Kongo candidates (though not necessarily the ABAKO nominees) derived some benefit from the clear lead of the ABAKO in audacious challenge to the legitimacy of the colonial system.

To non-Kongo, the results came as a galvanizing shock. The outcome was attributed to ethnic solidarity of the Kongo behind the ABAKO, and the indispensable response was felt to be countermobilization. Some leaders, such as Jean Bolikango, believed that the Ngala self-concept could serve as the cultural rallying point. Others sought to strengthen their own ethnic associations.

In Lubumbashi, there was no real equivalent to the ABAKO, and one protoparty, the Union Congolaise, was organized by a European lawyer with the support of some Zairian elites. In this instance, the electoral results simply reflected the social leadership of immigrants from outside Shaba, especially Luba-Kasai. Of the five African communes in Lubumbashi and the neighboring city of Likasi, the burgomasters nominated by the newly elected councillors were all from outside the province (three Luba-Kasai). Those from Shaba, who believed they had voted for the best-qualified candidates while Luba-Kasai voted ethnicity, were further irritated by the conviction of generalized nepotism. In one commune, a student inquest discovered that 280 of 300 urban plots allocated had gone to Luba-Kasai.[62]

In Kananga and Mbandaka, it was ethnic insurgents, rather than the socially dominant groups, who won. The Lulua triumphed in Kananga, despite the fact that Luba-Kasai had 56 percent of the population, to 25 percent Lulua. In Mbandaka, Ngombe (19 percent) won the burgomastership over the Mongo (41 percent), who considered themselves the original settlers in the town. The result, however, was the same; the losers were convinced that lack of ethnic solidarity in the face of their adversaries had cost them their fair share of power and influence. In riposte, the Mouvement Solidaire Muluba was organized in Kananga, and Mongo elites founded the Union des Mongo (Unimo). In Bukavu

62. Young, *Politics in the Congo*, p. 127. Social polarization and the impact of ethnicity were less clear in Likasi than in Lubumbashi.

and Kisangani, the voting did not have an immediately polarizing effect. Within the urban context, the Shi were a large majority in Bukavu and were not threatened by the campaign or balloting. In Kisangani, as argued earlier, ethnic perceptions of the social field were not in simple polarities.

As a social learning process, these elections communicated the message that ethnic solidarity was likely to play a large part in voting alignments. To the communal competition within the urban social fields was added an alarming new dimension: the risk of ethnic hegemony through control of the political institutions. The anxieties aroused by this realization were compounded by the sudden worsening of the economic situation. The tensions of social competition were partly absorbed by the continuous expansion after World War II. Real wages rose for the first time since the 1920s, and the urban economy was expanding swiftly enough to absorb most who wished to enter it. But recession set in simultaneous with the first elections; unemployment appeared; the administration rigorously limited access to town and expelled the unemployed from the cities. Thus social mobility was suddenly blocked, and the stakes were raised in allocation of resources.

Thus the impact of the first urban elections was to instill an ethnic perception of political competition, oriented to the cultural polarities of the urban social field. Mobilization or urban ethnic communities was seen to be an indispensable means of social self-defense. The magnitude of the polarization was a major constraint facing political organizers oriented toward the territorial arena in the next stage. At this juncture, the politization of ethnicity was almost wholly an urban phenomenon; the institutional competition was limited to the cities, and there was no inducement to build urban-rural political linkages.

POLITICAL PARTIES AND ETHNICITY

After the January 1959 Kinshasa riots, the tempo of decolonization suddenly quickened. In the phase of political party organization, the arena was redefined. Urban institutions virtually dropped out of the picture; the important spheres of political power were at the provincial and above all national level. However, the urban social fields continued of paramount importance. Political organization departed from the major urban centers, particularly the provincial capitals. The colonial period had not produced an elite operating on a territorial scale. Within the African population, each urban social field was wholly autonomous and was not linked at the top by an elite network who moved between the centers. Thus, political party construction had as its starting the various patterns of communal polarization; rural areas were linked to politics through the major regional central place. Aspirant politicians, for the most part based in the cities, had to develop an electoral base in the countryside, which could normally be done only in their region of origin.

The whole process occurred in the atmosphere of mingled exaltation and anxiety described in the preceding chapter, especially after the January 1960 agreement that independence would come on 30 June 1960. For the most part, rural extension of parties occurred only after the independence date was set and the crucial elections to determine the heirs to power scheduled for May 1960. There was thus a world to win—but also to lose—and but three months to do it in.

There were two major efforts to construct national movements, the Lumumba wing of the Mouvement National Congolais (MNC/L), and the Belgion-sponsored Parti National du Progrès (PNP). Lumumba had two points of diffusion: Kisangani and his Sankuru homeland. Kisangani had not been polarized by the urban elections, and Lumumba's stature as nationalist here won a nearly universal following. MNC/L was thus able to dominate easily the hinterland whose urban communications node was Kisangani. Through use of the Anamongo extension of savanna Tetela identity, he hoped to incorporate Maniema and Sankuru and expand eastward through the Mongo cultural zone: probably 30 of the 33 seats (out of 137) he won in the elections can be explained by one or the other of these patterns. The provincial elections, held at the same time, showed a comparable result. Of the total of 420 seats up for elections, MNC/L won 92, of which 80 were in Orientale Province and Sankuru and Maniema districts. Elsewhere, despite the fact that Lumumba achieved general recognition by 1960 as the most articulate spokesman for radical nationalism, and based his appeal on a united Zaire, he was unable in the time available to superimpose his vision of a unitary, centralized nation upon the existing patterns of polarization. In Kinshasa, the ABAKO was hostile to the Lumumbist vision; the Kongo self-image of primacy both in nationalism and cultural self-affirmation prohibited affiliation to the Lumumba movement. With one pole of conflict fixed by the ABAKO, other elements in the Kinshasa population reacted in function of the Kongo. The Kinshasa political field was altered in an important way by the impending significance of provincial politics. The Ngala core had immigrated from Equateur Province and thus had no relevant ethnic hinterland within the province to organize. Thus Ngala faded from the scene, with the groups of Kwango and Kwilu districts coming into the forefront.

In Kananga, the Lulua-Luba hostility was incandescent. Winning both sides to his alliance was inconceivable; Lumumba had to pick an ally, which meant also choosing an enemy. Lumumba opted for the Lulua alliance, at the price of bitter hostility from Luba-Kasai. In Mbandaka, Mongo and Ngombe were preoccupied with their own competition, and neither was available for alliance. In the three-cornered contest on the Copperbelt, the social space was all occupied by the time Lumumba arrived. In ideological terms, the Luba-Kasai elites would have been natural partners, but the Lumumba alliance with the Lulua in Kananga inhibited this combination. The southern Shaba groups who had organized the Conakat in reaction to Luba-Kasai had absorbed the attitude common to the Shaba European community that the wealth of the province was drained off to sustain Kinshasa; they thus argued decentralization and federalism, anathema to Lumumba. The close Conakat connections with European interests were another ground for Lumumba's suspicion. The third movement, the Balubakat, organizing primarily the Shaba Luba, had emerged in reaction to Conakat and was too concerned with this rivalry to dissolve itself into the broader framework of the MNC/L. Finally, in Bukavu, the terrain was occupied by an older, local movement, although not at that moment communally polarized.

The PNP does not require extended analysis; it was an effort, with the unofficial blessing of the colonial administration, to create a "moderate" national movement, disposed toward close cooperation with Belgium after independence. The party was a loose confederation of local groups, whose primary national structure was the theoretically invisible administration. The PNP assumed a rural strategy, based on the illusion that universal suffrage would permit the administration to mobilize influence through its appointed chiefs in the interest of its designated candidates. The cities would no doubt be lost, but the moderate countryside would swamp the cities with its numbers. In the event, the communication networks that were built outwards from the urban social fields, joining anticolonialism with cultural mobilization, were far more effective; the PNP won only 15 seats.

Although the polarized patterns of the urban social fields left by the 1957-58 elections fixed the initial contours of conflict, it soon became vastly more complex. A communal perception of conflict provided an abstracted symbolic image of the forces in contention within a ritualized confrontation such as an election. After the election, however, parliament and the provincial assemblies became the arenas for power and profit to be allocated. An intense scramble for place and preferment ensued, fought on an individual basis for personal advancement. The nature of this process is well captured in the paradox of Lumumba's investiture as prime minister; although the parties represented in his cabinet which sought the parliamentary vote of confidence equalled

120 of the 137 seats, yet the government received only 74 votes, or only five more than the bare minimum. Roughly a third of the favorable votes came from those designated as ministers. In the months following independence, parties fragmented into different wings and factions; dissidents within a movement broke away to form another, competing for the same clientele. A handlist of parties published in 1964 listed 205.[63]

In sum, then, the second phase saw a reorientation of political perspective toward the provincial and national institutions. In a climate of uncertainty and often fear, political parties were swiftly organized, departing from the major urban centers and incorporating in their own competition the dominant polarities these contained. The requirements of universal suffrage meant building urban-rural linkages, with cultural mobilization the simplest path. From the perspective of the rural mass, many were asked to relate themselves to an unfamiliar political process through a choice of identities which may have been ambiguous or had no relevance to the rural arena. The invitation to the ballot box posed for many the question Who am I? Whom should I fear? In a number of areas, the answer was clear enough, and the categories of the urban social field could be made to fit. In others, when the response was ambiguous, the questions themselves were disturbing and unsettling.

FRAGMENTATION: NEW PROVINCIAL ARENAS

Following the calamitous breakdown across a broad institutional front after independence, a fragile compromise was reached by August 1961, which included a commitment to reconsider the provincial structure of the state. Phase three, then, saw the splintering of the six colonial provinces into twenty-one new ones, based upon regional and ethnic self-determination. The changing political arena thereby offered a new challenge to self-definition. At the same time, the stakes appeared to be substantial, as a large measure of decentralization had occurred, partly by default, since the central institutions were in no position to use their full powers and significant prerogatives had been legally delegated to the provinces. Further, the provinces had sizable budgetary resources and also were major employers. Patronage opportunities related to the provincial institutions were thus extensive.

The dialectic of fragmentation which produced the new provinces represented, in a number of cases, the ultimate denouement of conflicts which crystallized during phase one. The three most urgent cases came in former Leopoldville Province, Kasai, and Shaba. In

63. Monnier, *Ethnie et intégration régionale au Congo*, pp. 406-10.

the first instance, the 1960 elections had produced a demographic shock for the Kongo; they were convinced that they had a cultural majority in the original Leopoldville Province, but discovered that ABAKO was only a minority provincial party, despite the unanimous backing it received within the Kongo ethnic area. They were wholly unwilling to accept a subordinate status within the provincial frame, and the erection of an autonomous Kongo province was an imperative demand; at this juncture, the central leadership, confronted with the Shaba secession, dissidence in the Lumumbist strongholds, and autonomous pretentions from the Luba-Kasai as well, could not afford to resist Kongo desires. The Kasai case, the calvary of the Luba driven back into their impoverished homeland, made it clear to all that there could be no possibility of meaningful cooperation of Luba and other Kasai groups within the existing provincial framework. *De facto* recognition of their claims to separate provincial status was the *sine qua non* of recuperating the temporarily secessionist Luba state of South Kasai. In Shaba, the government was anxious to reward the Luba-Shaba zones which had revolted againt the secessionist regime by granting them a separate province.

In the provinces thus severed, the truncated remainder faced a wholly new distribution of power and influence among politically relevant groups. This compelled communities to recalculate their interests, in terms of opportunities for a political role balanced by the risks of an unfavorable distribution of resources. This process involved an identification of the likely contenders, reconceptualization of ethnicity in function of this prospective field of interaction, and assessment of probable relationships with these groups. In more individualistic terms, political elites were concerned with defining provinces in a way which enhanced leadership opportunities. Once the door was open to fragmentation, in fact the probability was high that at least some group would find separation in its interest.

This process had the effect of keeping ethnicity at a high level of saliency; at the same time, the roster of ethnic conflict began to change in function of the new parameters of the political arena. Communal calculations triggered by the provincial breakdown now went beyond the classic urban cases. Substantial areas were in dispute between two provinces, often because of the ethnic complexity of the zone and the lack of clearcut consensus on which province had closest affinities. These contested areas were the scene of bitter disputes, rapid politization of a new set of cleavages, and extensive violence; the police forces of the competing provinces on occasion joined in the fray, producing a series of small-scale, yet very unsettling, border skirmishes. These disputes involved rural areas or small towns, which had not previously been the focus for major ethnic conflict.

A major premise of the provincial reform was that smaller, more homogeneous units would be able to function harmoniously and avoid the paralyzing conflicts which impaired the operation of the former provinces. Within a year, it was clear that this premise was false. The new provinces themselves constituted novel fields of political interaction. Wholly new lines of conflict began to emerge; some were simply factional, involving alignments of clients and allies of rival political leaders. Others developed new or little-used communal vocabularly to describe the contenders. It would be tedious to list all of these; representative examples were the Eswe-Eskonda rivalry in Sankuru and the Bena Tshibanda-Bena Mutu wa Mukuna struggle in South Kasai, to which we have already alluded.

The new provinces, accordingly, transformed but did not diminish the role of ethnicity. Some of the bitter social conflicts of an earlier day—Kongo v. Ngala, Luba v. Lulua—did lose their venom; Luba-Kasai could begin to return to some areas from which they had been driven in 1960, with prudence but with tolerable security. A whole new range of disputes were activated over contested areas and distribution of roles and resources within the new institutions. New provinces failed to have the tranquilizing, stabilizing effects many had hoped; the virtual incapacitation of several of them created an institutional vacuum which helped lay the groundwork for the 1964-65 rebellions.[64]

REBELLION AS POLITICAL FIELD

The fourth phase was marked by a series of overlapping uprisings, which shared the goal of overthrowing the Kinshasa regime. Different insurgents employed similar symbols of resistance, above all the martyred memory of Lumumba, common rituals of revolt, and recurrent themes of protest (pre-emption of the material benefits of independence by a class of politicians, functionaries, and soldiers, complaisance toward imperialism, especially Belgian and American). At its peak, the rebellions eliminated central authority in the northeast quadrant of the country, as well as in an important segment of Kwilu district. However, the rebellions never had a single leadership nor an integrated overall structure. The insurgents were racked by internal feuds. The Zaire national army, after a period of near collapse, was reinforced with

64. On the new provinces, see Young, *Politics in the Congo*, pp. 533-71; Benoit Verhaegen, "Présentation morphologique des nouvelles provinces," *Etudes Congolaises*, IV, no. 24 (April 1963); and especially the series of monographs by J. C. Willame, *Les Provinces du Congo*, Cahiers Economiques et Sociaux, Collection d'Etudes Politiques, nos. 1-5 (Kinshasa: Université Lovanium, 1964-65).

Map 6.2   Rebellions in Zaire

Cartographic Laboratory UW-Madison

several hundred White mercenaries and some additional Belgian and American logistical support. Rebels fell back before the mercenary-led columns. A Belgian-American paratroop intervention at Kisangani and Isiro, partly motivated by a desire to rescue White hostages held by the rebels, marked the collapse of a short-lived "People's Republic" centered in Kisangani. Resistance continued in several pockets of insurgent control for most of 1965. Our purpose here, however, is not to recount the chronicle of insurrection in any detail, but rather to relate the wave of rebellion, as a redefinition of the arena of political conflict, to patterns of cultural pluralism.[65]

65. Of the abundant literature spawned by the rebellions, see especially Verhaegen, *Rébellions au Congo*; Crawford Young, "Rebellion and the Congo," in Rotberg and Mazrui (eds.), *Protest and Power in Black Africa,* pp. 968-1011; Renée Fox et al., "La Deuxième Indépendance-étude d'un cas: La rébellion au Kwilu," *Etudes Congolaises,* VIII (January-February 1965), pp. 1-35.

For less favored strata of Zaire society, independence had failed to bring the anticipated rewards. Indeed, unemployment had shot up in urban areas, aggravated by a large influx of new migrants. In the countryside, rural marketing networks had shrivelled, and terms of trade of commercialized produce against the range of goods normally purchased by villagers had sharply deteriorated. These grievances were quite general, although the poles of relative prosperity in Kinshasa, the Copperbelt, and their immediate hinterland were less affected than other parts of the interior. Yet the response to the appeal to insurrection was selective and can be understood only in the framework of identity patterns and the way in which the option of rebellion was perceived by specific populations.

With the wave of rebellion the dominant challenge, the structure of choice was different than in the earlier phases. When the possibility of rebellion as a remedy for present discontents came within the purview of a given group, it was called upon to evaluate the balance of advantage and risk, congruence or threat represented by the rebels. This required scanning the symbols and leaders which were visible, to relate the generalized concept of insurrection to more familiar aspects of the social code held by the group and its members.

The most important centers of dispersion for rebellion were Kwilu and Maniema. In the Kwilu case, the principal organizer, Pierre Mulele, inspired by the Chinese model of peasant revolution, sought to develop an insurgent force of rural partisans. Before assaults on government installations began, several months were devoted to intensive ideological and military training of his village recruits. Despite the sophistication of his blueprint for rebellion, Mulele swiftly ran up against the dilemmas of horizontal mobilization in a fragmented polity.

To initiate anything so adventurous as formation of partisan bands, he had to operate in a milieu which he knew well and where he was known. He thus began in his own Mbunda zone and built intensive support. From there, he had excellent success in extending his network into neighboring Pende country. There had been a measure of collaboration in the late nineteenth century between Pende and Mbunda, when Cokwe bands began to move into the area. Although the groups were quite distinct linguistically, there was a high degree of bilingualism in the area and extensive intermarriage. Both Pende and Mbunda participated in what was generally known as the "Pende revolt" of 1931 and its aftermath. More recently, Mulele, and the most prominent Pende politician, Antoine Gizenga, were on the same factional side in the internal politics of the regionally dominant political movement, the Parti Solidaire Africain (PSA). Gizenga at that time was confined by the Kinshasa authorities, a source of grievance for Pende.

Thus the Pende were ready allies. Some chiefs were reluctant; these were assassinated. For most, the symbols of rebellion were familiar, in terms of its leadership and Mbunda associations. Kinshasa as well as the provincial government were felt to be in the hands of other groups; opposition was a natural choice. And Mulele offered both natural and supernatural reasons why his movement could succeed.

After establishing his initial base, Mulele sought to enlarge his network of allies among neighboring groups. But, by virtue of its initial base and leadership, the Mulelist movement took on a cultural hue. Calculations by groups such as the Ding, Cokwe, and Yanzi were different from those of the Pende. Although the "second independence" slogan was attractive, one had to reckon with the fact that it was a Mbunda-Pende dominated movement that proposed to bring it. Although none of these groups viewed the Kwilu provincial government with enthusiasm, and all were politically marginal, the balance of risk and advantage was different. Some Ding clans did join the Mulele movement; others remained on the sidelines.

The Mbala and Ngongo, however, were less able to maintain even an ambiguous attitude. Although a handful of intellectuals had been attracted by Mulelist ideology, these groups were particularly well represented in the provincial government. Thus the insurrection contained overtones of threat. The objective social situation of the average Mbala or Ngongo was not dramatically different from that facing the Mbunda, Pende, or Ding. However, Gizenga and Mulele were negative symbols. Although the Mulelist ideology was not formally defined in ethnic vocabulary, yet the perception of what the movement really represented invoked cultural images.

In the neighboring new province of Kwango, the Suku and Yaka were contacted by Mulelist emissaries. Traditional leadership, especially influential among the Yaka, was hostile to a movement led by young men. Further, the area had just achieved provincial status; rallying to Mulelism implied accepting the leadership—and, by extension, domination—of Kwilu groups. No obvious advantage outweighed the risks of an anti-government uprising.

Evaluation of the balance of force was an important aspect of choice. Had the Mulelist partisans been able to sustain their initial military successes, the attitudes of a number of groups—particularly those who were ambivalent rather than hostile—might well have changed. The risks of government retaliation would be reduced, and the possible cost of reprisals by Mulelists in the event of their eventual triumph would have been increased. Had additional groups joined, the cultural arithmetic would have been altered, and configuration to which yet other groups, drawn into the orbit of rebellion by its expansion, were forced to react could have been quite different. As it was, after some humiliating encounters in which poorly armed guerrillas routed regular army units and killed the chief of staff, the national army rallied and confined the insurrection to the forests of Mbunda and Pende country. At this point, the encapsulation of the Kwilu rebellion was complete, and it no longer had any real prospect of success. Under the pressure of the repressive campaign of the national army, Pende groups began to break away, and severe tensions between Pende and Mbunda within the Mulelist structure began to appear.

In eastern Zaire, rebellion coalesced and diffused from a more broadly defined symbolic base. The legend of Lumumba and political symbols of the MNC/L party were the two pillars. The martyrdom of Lumumba and accession of his enemies to power in Kinshasa provided a natural linkage between the bitter disappointments of independence and the hagiology of the region. The writ of Lumumba's charisma ran through a vast area of northeastern Zaire and offered to rebel organizers a quite different scale of operation.

The strategy of rebellion stood in sharp contrast to Mulelism as well. There was never a period of careful ideological and military training of partisans. Rather, in its phase of expansion, the wave of rebellion spread swiftly from its point of diffusion in southern Maniema, altering its cultural contours as it developed. The first significant center under insurgent control in the east was Uvira; most of the rebel partisans at that point were Fulero, and the dynamics of revolt turned largely around an internal conflict over chieftaincy and Fulero relationships with provincial authorities in Bukavu. Neither Fulero insurgent leaders nor troops played much role outside their own region. However, the next town to fall, Fizi, became a diffusion base. The dominant Bembe group, like the Fulero, had been internally divided in response to shifting definitions of the political arena. One Bembe clan parlayed a nineteenth-century alliance with Afro-Arab traders and subsequent coalition with the European administration into a socially advantageous position. In consequence, radical nationalist parties in 1960, and insurgents in 1964 recruited their following particularly among other Bembe clans newly awakened to their relatively disfavored position. The rule of numbers made their party, Unebafi, an MNC/L ally, dominant in 1960. During the formation of new provinces, Fizi was bitterly torn between three possible provincial affiliations: North Katanga, South Kivu, and Maniema. Many chiefs and some educated Bembe elites, generally from the dominant clan, preferred South Kivu; Bembe who had migrated along the lakeshore to Kalemie called for joining North Katanga; while MNC/L followers, including many young men attracted by the radical nationalist style of Lumumba, urged Maniema. A loosely knit insurgent force, composed largely of Bembe from disadvantaged clans, moved out in two directions, one southward towards Kalemie and a second eastward toward Kasongo. Although the southern column initially had the greater success and overran virtually without resistance a large part of northern Shaba, they failed to gain the active support of the local population; this was a zone of ambiguous receptivity to the symbols of rebellion and had not been an area of MNC/L dominance. But neither was the rebellion initially a cultural threat; when government authority simply vanished, there was no local resistance. But neither was there support for the insurgents when government forces regrouped and moved back into this zone.

The column which moved west across southern Maniema engendered a strikingly different response. They moved into an area where Lumumba and MNC/L offered an integrative symbolic frame, within which a continuous adjustment of the ethnic composition of insurgency could occur. At each town, new recruits were absorbed in large number. Important local leaders had already established links with the rebellion, and thus the encapsulation phenomenon of Kwilu was avoided. Across this area, a shared sentiment of exclusion from the distribution of power and influence within the incumbent provincial regime in Maniema created an immediate contingency of opposition, related to the continuing efficacy of the Lumumbist symbols. Groups such as the Bangobango of Kabambare and the Zimba and others of the Kasongo region readily identified with the rebel column, and the initial Bembe preponderance was diluted. This process was not without friction, especially in Kasongo there were visible tensions between Bembe rebels and those locally recruited. But the most prominent rebel leader at this juncture, Gaston Soumialot, was of mixed Kusu-Songe origin, which along with the central role of Lumumbist symbols and the antitribal ideology of the movement, made integration readily acceptable.

From Kasongo, rebel columns, now greatly enlarged by new recruitment, turned north along the Zaire (Lualaba) River and headed for the Maniema provincial capital of Kindu. The conquest of the provincial capital absorbed into the matrix of rebellion important new bases of support but also a pattern of conflict which had become politicized during the 1960-64 period within the provincial institutions, pitting Kusu against Rega. Kindu became the political capital of the rebellion in the east for a brief period. Recruitment at Kindu again altered the composition of the insurgent army, now known as the Armée Populaire de Libération (APL). It also permitted the affirmation of control over the army by a Tetela officer, Nicolas Olenga. The Tetela-Kusu element in the APL now became significant, especially within the officer corps.

The army itself became a more important institution within the rebel complex, under Olenga's leadership.

Massacres of persons assumed to be enemies of the rebellion occurred on a large scale, and Rega were particularly numerous among the victims. Rega had also believed themselves the object of exactions and assassinations at the hands of Bembe in Fizi; the rebellion thus became a clear cultural threat to the group. The politization of Rega identity had occurred primarily in response to Kivu and Maniema provincial politics since 1960. With a sense of ethnicity heightened by competitive interaction, especially with Kusu, Rega were galvanized into active resistance by fears of ethnic massacre at the hands of the rebellion, whose Bembe and Kusu participants dominated their perceptions. The only defeats inflicted on rebel forces at this expanding stage were by Rega irregulars.

From Kindu, rebel columns were sent west into Sankuru, north to Kisangani, and, with some delay, east toward Bukavu. The Kisangani column reached its objective with little resistance, and again a large transfusion of new recruits affected the composition of the rebel forces. Kisangani, as capital of Lumumbism, was highly receptive to the political symbols of the insurrection. Ethnic perceptions were quite different. The original Bembe predominance had evaporated. Further, the Bembe, as a distant group unrepresented in the capital of Lumumbism, were not within the cognitive field of Kisangani. The ethnic labels which came to be attached to the rebel army, and particularly its officer corps, were Tetela-Kusu. Many of the key officers were of this origin; General Olenga relied on ethnic colleagues to help maintain his personal control of the army. The initial political spokesman for the rebellion in Kisangani, Soumialot, was viewed as a Kusu. However, in Kisangani the integrative power of the Lumumbist symbols was so potent that ethnic tensions within the rebel structure did not seriously threaten it.

The further dispersion of the rebellion following the communication routes radiating outward from Kisangani followed closely the limits of the Lumumbist and MNC/L success in 1960; its points of farthest expansion went somewhat beyond the Lumumbist radius, but at this juncture receptivity fell away. This moment coincided with the reinforcement of demoralized national army troops with White mercenaries, which no longer left groups with the choice between collaboration or resistance on their own resources. In late August, the rebel assault on Bukavu failed, a critical turning point. On the outskirts of the city, rebel columns had to pass through the lands of the Kabare chieftaincy of Shi. Their hostility to a Maniema invading force was sufficient to align them at the sides of the beleaguered national army garrison. The army itself, cut off from retreat, was compelled to fight. Between the Shi irregulars and the national army, the attack was repelled with heavy rebel losses.[66]

The column which entered Sankuru overran the district without much resistance. Here the difference in ethnic perceptions between 1960 and 1964 was dramatically clear. Although in 1960, Lumumba, in his home district, had completely swept the field, a movement marching in his memory had more ambiguous support in 1964. In particular, the politization of the Eswe-Ekonda division interfered with the diffusion of the rebellion. Many Ekonda viewed the rebellion, not as a movement in which Tetela-Kusu symbols were prominent, but as an Eswe threat. Rebel occupation of the Ekonda-Tetela forest zone was precarious and ephemeral, whereas the rebels hung on longer and with much greater support in the savanna zones.

Rebellion thus mobilized ethnicity on a quite different basis than earlier political moments. The risks were high as violence stalked the land. Particularly in the eastern zone, disorder was frequent during the 1960-64 period, and fears of communal massacres were by no means chimerical. Although the eastern rebel symbols were integrative and ideology explicitly anti-ethnic, this did not exempt the rebellion from close scrutiny by those in its path, to ascertain its composition. In the nature of things, this could only be done in very generalized terms, likely to exaggerate the actual patterns; no one was publishing figures on the ethnic distribution of rebel forces. The visible leadership was important in projecting an image of ethnic identification onto the body at large. In speaking of the cultural distribution within the ranks, the speculative element was necessarily very large—and thus the likelihood of finding what one looked for, of anxieties serving as self-fulfilling prophecies. Fears had many roots: rebels, if they really did come from hostile groups, might use the opportunity of conquest to exact a blood tribute. If one resisted and lost, the likelihood of retribution was increased; if one collaborated and the national army returned, equally sanguinary reprisals could be anticipated. With such intense anxieties for those who did not find identity with the symbols of rebellion, the insurrection committed to a pan-ethnic, radical nationalist vision of Zaire had the paradoxical effect of heightening fear-bred communalism.

---

66. For details on the Bukavu battle, see P. Masson, *La Bataille pour Bukavu* (Brussels: Charles Dessart, 1965).

THE RETURN OF THE CENTRALIZED STATE

A fifth political phase was ushered in by the Mobutu coup of November 1965. The lessons of the first half-decade of independence were not lost on the new regime; although the potential role of cultural pluralism had been little understood by the 1960 generation of politicians, even as they mobilized ethnic sentiments, the complex impasse reached in the aftermath of the rebellions appeared to dictate a strategy of cultural demobilization. This has been consistently pursued by the Mobutu regime, through the recentralization of power and the withdrawal of political resources from regional arenas. The number of provinces was reduced in two steps from twenty-one to eight. Provincial assemblies were abolished; the province became, as it had been during the colonial era, simply an administrative echelon. Provincial governors were no longer responsible to a political majority in an assembly, no longer chosen from the local party leaders; they were named by President Mobutu, were responsible only to him, and were posted outside their region of origin. The police, initially under provincial jurisdiction, were nationalized and subsequently merged with the army. The principle of central nomination and posting outside one's own area was extended in due course to the lower echelons of the administration, down to the urban communes. Political parties were dissolved, replaced in 1967 by a single national party organized from the center, the Mouvement Populaire de la Révolution. The party as well was constructed on a very carefully integrated basis, with provincial committees leavened with persons assigned from other areas. Party and administration were fused, with the local administrative officials—by definition from outside—serving ex officio as local party heads. The first national elections organized under the new party system were held in 1970; there was a single nominee for each constituency, screened by local party branches but approved by the national political bureau. Members of the political bureau had to run in constituencies outside their own area. In 1968, ethnic associations were outlawed, thus eliminating all organizational structures through which ethnic mobilization could occur.

Few who had followed Zaire politics in the early independence years would have dreamed that such a thoroughgoing centralization was feasible. However, the unitary legal framework of the colonial system provided a commodious vessel for the Mobutist philisophy of political organization. The utter discrediting of the first generation of political institutions, a general lassitude toward the pattern of largely ethnic competition, and the yearning for peace and security which grew out of the harrowing experiences of conflict and rebellion were all facilitating factors. The overriding fact of military genesis as the ultimate backing for the currency of power shaped the perspectives of all actors.

Politics were accordingly radically restructured. Mobutu over his initial years in power gradually isolated and eventually disgraced politicians who had autonomous power bases. The personal patronage of the president was the *sine qua non* of ranking position, held at the pleasure of the presidency. Nothing was more risky than even the appearance of constituting a political network which did not emanate from the top. Organizations such as trade unions were unified and brought under the aegis of the party. Spheres of autonomy, such as the universities and churches, were likewise brought to heel.

By the end of his first seven years in power, Mobutu had effectively eliminated any group basis for social organization apart from the party. By dispersing groups through which pressures on behalf of social collectivities, ethnic or other, could flow, Mobutu made it possible to deal with elites on an individual basis. The relative prosperity made possible by the return of stability and order provided resources adequate to provide attractive incentives for those who were prepared to cooperate within the Mobutist frame.

A product of the new era was a national mandarinate, integrated into the primary agencies of the state, administration, parastatal enterprises, and the party. Application of the principle of ethnic scrambling meant that in each provincial capital, or lower administrative echelons, an elite network not linked with the local populace took shape. Their mobility depended upon the political center; their most intensive interactions were with each other. Frequent transfers kept a steady circulation within the national mandarinate, who developed no locality ties. The fortunes of the mandarinate were bound with those of the state; they had no personal stakes in the local cultural configuration and thus remained relatively impartial with respect to it.[67]

Personalist authoritarian rule does not, of course, obliterate cultural pluralism. Critics of the regime pointed out that key posts, particularly in the security apparatus of the regime, were held by persons from Mobutu's region, bound by close ties of ethnic affinity and personal dependence. The two groups with large elites and relatively well-developed cultural awareness, the Kongo and Luba-Kasai, felt themselves held at arm's length by the regime. The very scale of the elite networks of these groups and concentration of quality secondary schools in areas to which they had access—especially Kinshasa and the Copperbelt—continued to strengthen their standing in the elite ranks, as sug-

67. On the Mobutu period, see Jean-Claude Willame, *Patrimonialism and Political Change in the Congo* (Stanford: Stanford University Press, 1972); "Le régime presidentiel au Zaire." *Etudes Africaines du C.R.I.S.P.,* Travaux Africains 144 (20 December 1972).

gested by Table 6.1. In interpreting these data, it is important to note that Kongo not only represented all of the enrollment in Bas Zaire province, but also an important fraction of that in Kinshasa. The Luba-Kasai were numerous not only in Kasai Oriental schools, but also those of Shaba, concentrated in the Copperbelt, and to a lesser extent in Kinshasa. Although these figures are from only one secondary sector, there is no reason to believe they are not representative of overall secondary distribution.

What may we conclude from this excursion through ethnic politics in Zaire? We have seen that, in the beginning, ethnicity as a political phenomenon took form in the rapidly growing urban sectors after World War II. This was where social competition for prestige, material goods, and security was most direct and intense, where identity groups structured by labels appropriate to the urban social field acquired a degree of self-consciousness and constructed ethnic maps to situate relevant others, where the resentments born of perceived socioeconomic disparities between ethnic collectivities coalesced. The struggle for place and preferment was most intense at the elite level; ethnic inequalities were measured by degree of access into high status roles, not the lowest ranking occupations and activities. The introduction of the electoral process at the urban level first provided a specific incentive for mobilization of ethnic constituencies by aspirant elites. When the electoral focus then shifted almost immediately to the national and provincial level, political parties formed to build urban-rural political linkages were shaped by the paradigm of ethnic conflict which had emerged in the urban centers. The multiplication of provinces created new conflict arenas relatively well endowed in patronage resources, which in turn created from the lush foliage of available ethnic symbols quite new patterns of conceptualization of conflict. The institutional atrophy of the first independence years produced an array of deprivations for humbler strata of Zaire society and bred a wave of rebellion. Cultural pluralism had nothing whatsoever to do with the general causes of insurrection; however, once insurrection occurred, ethnicity did enter the picture as one prism through which individuals and groups sought to understand the social composition of the insurgents and the balance of threat and advantage which the movements offered. Dominant modes of ethnicity underwent a further transformation under the Mobutu regime, where centralization and elimination of autonomous conflict arenas greatly reduced the visibility of cultural pluralism.

These striking changes suggest that ethnicity has not congealed into a firmly fixed pattern. Individuals have a choice of a wide range of potential ethnic roles. Solidarity patterns are not translated into permanent institutional structures. Ethnicity has not become ideologized,

Table 6.1—Secondary Enrollment by Province, Humanitiés Pédagogiques Section, 1968-69

Province	Population (1970 census)		Secondary enrollment					
	No. (millions)	% of total	3rd yr.	4th yr.	5th yr.	6th yr.	Total	% of total
Kinshasa	1.3	6	1,710	1,610	1,176	637	5,133	20
Bas Zaire	1.5	7	1,829	1,114	517	303	3,763	14
Bandundu	2.6	12	1,606	809	405	300	3,120	12
Equateur	2.4	11	659	496	240	145	1,540	6
Haut-Zaire	3.4	16	926	523	218	130	1,797	7
Kivu	3.4	16	913	598	331	174	2,016	8
Shaba	2.8	13	1,259	845	491	211	2,806	11
Kasai Occidental	2.4	11	899	622	274	153	1,948	7
Kasai Oriental	1.9	09	1,736	1,118	703	413	3,970	15
Total	21.6	101[a]	11,537	7,735	4,355	2,466	26,093	100

[a]Total percentage does not equal 100 because of rounding.

Source: Ministère de l'Education Nationale, "Projet d'investissement dans le domaine de l'éducation," October 1970 (enrollment); "Les resultats du recensement de la population 1970 au Zaire," Etudes Africaines du C.R.I.S.P.. Travaux Africaines, no. 140 (15 June 1972).

although in the 1950s this process seemed in course for the Kongo. However, it became arrested after independence, and the labors of enlarging the cultural capital of literature and history are not being energetically pursued. The Flemish missionary-scholars who played such a key role as cultural entrepreneurs in the past are passing from the scene. Who will take their place is uncertain, although of course one cannot exclude the possibility that the interrupted labors will one day be resumed.

Perhaps most important of all is the validation of the Southall proposition cited in chapter 2, stressing "the importance of interlocking, overlapping, multiple collective identities." To this we may add the crucial significance of the political variable in defining identity choice. Because identities are interlocking, overlapping, and multiple, we have observed in the last two decades startling shifts in the identities which achieve social visibility and the saliency of ethnicity generally as a political determinant. Ethnicity in this sense becomes the dependent variable in the political equation, with the independent variables deriving from changing contexts of political process and conflict.

The triumph of the territorial polity over the cultural segments within it is not an end in and of itself. Centralization does not automatically produce a better life for the mass of the Zairian populace. Most, however, welcome the diminished level of ethnic tension. A political arena which is not structured to induce cultural conflict may create the circumstances for the realization of the Lumumba prophecy, and the fulfillment of the underlying cultural unity found by Vansina.

7 Tanzania and Uganda:
Integration or Impasse

A century ago, as the colonial grid was about to descend on East Africa, there was little to differentiate the areas which later came to bear the territorial labels of Tanganyika (since 1964, Tanzania) and Uganda. True, in Buganda and Bunyoro, Uganda had states that were somewhat more centralized than their counterparts in Tanzania; however, in the interlacustrine area, there were also kingdoms in Tanzania, among the Haya, Ha, and other groups. Uganda, on the other hand, did not share in the coastal culture which had emerged over the centuries in contact and commerce with Arabs, Persians, Indians, and even Chinese. Although these contrasts are not without significance, they would not have seemed very important as one surveyed the nineteenth-century landscape. Indeed, the many visitors who recorded their impressions of the hinterland, drawn by the race to "discover" the sources of the Nile or to follow the caravan routes developed by Zanzibar-based Afro-Arab traders (and slavers) into the heart of central Africa, do not draw any sharp distinctions. Cultural patterns were broadly similar; histories were interwoven.

As contemporary polities, however, these neighboring states are a study in contrasts. Tanzania had made remarkable strides toward national integration, without recourse to the authoritarian formulas which have been used to reduce cultural tensions in neighboring Zaire. Even if appropriate discount for what Ali Mazrui has termed the academic malady of Tanzaphilia, we cannot fail to be impressed by the high order of affective attachment to the Tanzanian polity. A modal national culture, with Swahili as its linguistic base, is taking rapid shape. Ethnicity and religion are audible, but muted themes in the political process; the racial cleavage between European, Asian, and African, which once bade fair to dominate conflict patterns, has quietly faded into the background.

In Uganda, however, ethnic and religious conflict have both been severe. The most economically developed and socially favored segment of the system, Buganda, threatened secession in 1960, on the eve of independence, and again in 1966. Militarily humiliated, the Ganda countryside broods in a sullen hostility towards the central institutions. Its Asian community was dramatically expelled in 1972. Its security forces have been torn by debilitating animosities, which have led on several occasions to serious armed encounters within the military, split on ethnic and religious lines. If Tanzania exhibited noteworthy progress toward national integration in its first decade of independence, Uganda seemed more characterized by cultural impasse.

In this chapter, we will seek out the factors which may explain the divergent patterns in these two neighboring and fundamentally similar societies. After comparing the initial creation of the colonial territory, we will inventory the nature of cultural diversity, examine the impact of social change processes on the transformation of identities, and inquire into successive definitions of the political arena. Finally, we

Map 7.1   Ethnic Groups in Tanzania

Cartographic Laboratory UW-Madison

will look at the integrative mechanisms available to political leaders in the two countries. The relatively harmonious integration of Tanzania has more parsimonious explanations than does the complex pluralism of Uganda; we must therefore engage in more detailed examination of the latter case.

BASIC PATTERNS OF CULTURAL PLURALISM

The foundation of German East Africa, later to become Tanganyika, may be dated from 1884, with the signing of a string of bogus treaties, for the German East Africa Company, by the intrepid explorer-adventurer Carl Peters, who far exceeded his instructions. In 1890, Germany officially assumed sovereignty over the territory, as the sharpening imperial competition overcame whatever initial reticence was felt in Berlin. Resources for the consolidation of German rule over the 370,000 square miles the Germans claimed were initially very slim; in 1896, there were only 163 Germans in the administrative service, with territorial revenues of a mere £ 310,000.[1] Extensive resistance to colonial conquest made the early years very precarious. Intermediaries were indispensable, and there was only one source: coastal Swahili speakers, who had earlier served as auxiliaries for the trading outposts established by Afro-Arab merchants plying the caravan routes. Thus the Germans were the unwitting agents of an important diffusion into the hinterland of Swahili culture, placed in a position of authority and prestige by the political rank afforded the Swahili auxiliaries.

After surviving a wave of rebellion in the first decade of this century, German rule was just becoming thoroughly consolidated when World War I intervened. German East Africa was partitioned, with Rwanda and Burundi awarded to Belgium; the British assumed control over Tanganyika. However, some years went by before a clearcut strategy of administration emerged. Beginning in 1926, local administration was thoroughly reorganized, based upon British precepts of indirect rule. The Swahili intermediaries were gone, but the effects in terms of the impact of coastal culture, above all the Swahili language, were of lasting importance.

In Uganda, the sequence of colonial penetration was crucial in setting the cultural contours of the colonial system. From the mid-nineteenth century, Zanzibari traders were at the court of the Buganda monarch. Beginning in 1877, Anglican missionaries were present in the kingdom, and they were joined by French Catholic competitors in 1879. Although

---

1. Roland Oliver and Gervase Mathew (eds.), *History of East Africa*, I (Oxford: Clarendon Press, 1963), 448-49.

the initial hopes of converting the kingdom through its monarch were not realized, the missions and Muslim traders did compete for the commitment of a singularly critical group: the several hundred boys attached to the royal court as pages. It was from this group that the chiefs and royal officials were chosen; thus, in gaining access to them, the missions and Muslims were engaged in a competitive recruitment of the future political elite.

In the 1880s, Anglican, Catholic, and Muslim clusters took shape among Ganda elite. To the fluid factionalism of court politics was added a radical new dimension—ideology. The traditional formulas for royal management of conflict and control through constantly shifting alliances no longer could function, as factions became institutionalized around

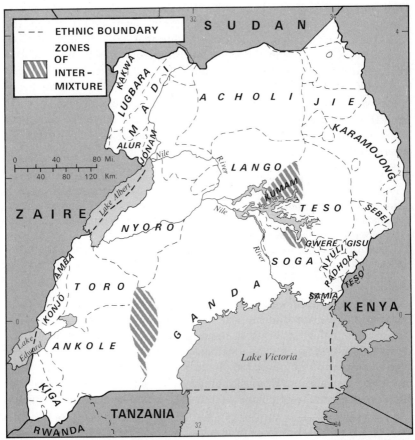

Map 7.2—Ethnic Groups in Uganda

the religious division. When a new king, Mwanga, ascended the throne in 1884, he was never able to master the new factional pattern—all the more because each party had a foreign patron. We need not enter into the complex and fascinating detail of the struggle for power in Buganda during this period;[2] suffice it to note that in 1888 Kabaka Mwanga was first overthrown by a Muslim faction, that a civil war ensued which was ultimately won by the Protestant faction with decisive British intervention on their side, that the British flag was raised in 1893, and that in 1897 Mwanga was permanently removed and power placed in the hands of a Christian revolutionary elite. The kingdom was internally restructured with a division of religious spheres of influence, massive conversion occurred, and large-scale movements of persons took place to relocate in a part of the kingdom where their religion was dominant. The form, ritual, and symbols of monarchy were maintained, but with an infant Kabaka on the throne, actual authority was exercised by the Christian revolutionary elite, with Protestants holding the key posts. The capstone of this edifice was a treaty negotiated between the British and the Christian revolutionary elite in 1900, which regularized the status of Buganda in the Ugandan protectorate. Not only did this treaty confirm in power the Christian revolutionary elite, but it was seen by Ganda as a treaty between two equal nations. The Ganda negotiators were literate men, who bargained with some skill; this was far from the characteristic "treaty" imposed upon an unlettered chief who had no understanding of its contents. The last Kabaka, Mutesa II, describes the treaty thus in his autobiography:

[The British] had conquered all opposition, though not, of course, the Baganda, who had invited them into the country and shared their victories and reverses. It cannot be too strongly emphasized that this was a treaty between victorious allies, not conqueror and conquered. The British supported one faction against another. They never fought the Baganda as a people.

[The treaty's] influence would be hard to exaggerate; it became a charter of rights, almost a constitution, reference to which could justify or condemn an action. The text gradually became dogma.[3]

One other powerful kingdom existed in Uganda at the time of colonial penetration, Bunyoro; at its peak, prior to the nineteenth century, its domains were far vaster than those of Buganda. After a period of decay in the first half of the nineteenth century, Bunyoro was in a new phase of expansion in the latter decades of the century under the leadership of a vigorous king, Kabarega. The accidents of history cast Bunyoro in the role of enemy of colonial penetration, while Buganda

2. For a brilliant analysis, see John A. Rowe, "Revolution in Buganda 1856-1900. Part One." (Ph.D. diss., University of Wisconsin, 1966); also especially valuable is Low, *Buganda in Modern History.* A fuller list of Buganda references is given in chapter 5.

3. Mutesa, *Desecration of My Kingdom,* 61-62.

was Britain's ally. The two kingdoms had long skirmished at their frontiers; the British alliance decisively altered the balance of force and permitted Buganda to expand dramatically, mainly at the expense of Bunyoro; the size of Buganda nearly doubled in the process of consolidation of British overrule.[4] The cost to Bunyoro was devastating. Kabarega was hunted down and exiled. Ganda chiefs were imposed upon the kingdom, which received none of the deference accorded to Buganda. Many Nyoro were expelled from territories awarded to Buganda. Devastating outbreaks of smallpox ravaged the human population, and rinderpest decimated their cattle herds. It was not until 1924 that a more benign relationship began to develop, and Ganda chiefs were not finally withdrawn until 1933. There was no Nyoro equivalent of the Ganda Christian revolutionary elite; not only did Buganda as a kingdom enjoy a wholly different status, but Ganda built up an enormous lead in entry into privileged social strata, through education and economic change.

Although the eventual boundaries of Uganda were determined by the dialectic of imperial partition, the effective occupation of a large part of the territory was achieved through Ganda intermediaries. In all but the northernmost strip of Uganda, Ganda played a critical role in the initial articulation of colonial institutions. In many areas, initial conquest was by Ganda armies. A local administration based on the Ganda model of chieftaincy was organized and in large measure staffed by Ganda chiefs in the first decades of colonial rule. Ganda were equally important in spiritual conquest; the thinly manned Christian missions made extensive use of Ganda catechists to establish their presence outside of Buganda. Buganda itself was thoroughly evangelized in the 1890s, before Christianity was significantly established anywhere else; this produced a very large pool of Ganda religious personnel to augment mission capacities.[5]

Thus the colonial state in Uganda was built around the kingdom of Buganda, which enjoyed an extraordinary status within it. The internal revolution which coincided with colonial penetration brought to power within Buganda an elite particularly adapted to reap the advantages of their new situation. The context was epitomized in the name given the colonial domain; "Uganda" is simply a Swahili form of "Buganda." Until the final years of colonial rule, the entrenched hegemony in all domains of Buganda was appropriately summarized in the territorial label.

Thus the parameters set by the definition of the colonial state stand out by their contrasts. We need now to examine the patterns of cul-

4. A. D. Roberts, "The Sub-Imperialism of the Baganda," *Journal of African History*, III, no. 3 (1962), 435-50; A. H. Cox, "The Growth and Expansion of Buganda," *Uganda Journal*, XIV, no. 2 (September 1950), 153-59.

5. John V. Taylor, *The Growth of the Church in Buganda* (London: SCM Press, 1958).

tural distributions within these two polities, before turning to an examination of processes of identity crystallization and change. Three bases of differentiation may be noted which have had some political impact: ethnic, religious, and racial—although the importance of the last factor is fading fast.

In Tanzania, classification by ethnic unit played a far less central role in the process of colonial control or subsequent political organization. It is frequently asserted that the secret to integrative success in Tanzania is the large number of small identity groups which compose the population. In fact, the difference between Tanzania and Uganda on this criterion is less clear than might be imagined. The largest identity group in Tanzania are the Sukuma, who are approximately 12 percent of the population. We referred in an earlier chapter to the process of emergence of Sukuma identity and the lack of clear demarcation with the Nyamwezi group; both labels date from the colonial period and were applied by others to these linguistically related peoples. In the course of time, the labels have acquired subjective meaning. However, it is sheer accident that Sukuma and Nyamwezi are now considered to be separate groups; they might well have acquired a common label. Had this occurred, the two together would number 17 percent, as against only 16 percent for Ganda.[6]

Thus the distinction lies not in the historical diversity, but rather in the fashion whereby identities became crystallized and labelled and the process by which they became politicized and mobilized. The Sukuma-Nyamwezi cluster lies in the center of the country, relatively distant from the political capital, and was not a focal point for social and economic development; the Ganda, by contrast, were in the crucial heartland of Uganda. One should also recall the doubling of the size of Buganda at the beginning of the colonial period; much, though not all, of this newly incorporated territory was culturally Gandanized during the colonial era. Further, the fertility of Buganda and early development of successful cash agriculture attracted a substantial immigrant rural labor force, mainly from Rwanda. This group, which is 40 percent of the Buganda population, is absorbed into complex relations of patronage and dependency. In sociopolitical conflict pitting Buganda against other areas, the Rwanda will align with the Ganda, as was clearly shown in the 1966 crisis. Indeed, given their total dependency

6. A Tanzanian linguistics scholar, M. H. Abdulaziz, notes, "The Wasukuma themselves did not have one single tribal name for the clans inhabiting the districts of Shinyanga, Maswa, Kwinba, Mwanza, and Geita before the arrival of the European colonists and missionaries. . . . Furthermore, among the large groups of clans who today are divided into the Wasukuma and Wanyamezi, group names were often directional. . . . " Wilfred Whiteley (ed.), *Language Use and Social Change* (London: Oxford University Press, 1971), p. 162.

for land and livelihood and the tendency of many to settle permanently, it would be extraordinarily imprudent of them to do otherwise. With this group included, the Ganda become approximately 25 percent of the national total.[7]

In terms of labels in common currency, no other group in Tanzania exceeds 5 percent. There is an unusual distribution pattern, with the fertile zones of the country that contain relatively dense concentrations being strung out along the northern, western, and southern boundaries; an infertile scrub savanna with unreliable rainfall covers much of the central area. Tanzania is a rimland state par excellence; two-thirds of the population is located in 10 percent of the area.[8]

Within this context of fragmentation and rimland dispersion, the swift diffusion of Swahili in the last 150 years is of central importance. Zanzibar and the coastal areas contained the initial nucleus of a Swahili cluster. The language emerged as a coastal lingua franca, with a Bantu base and a large number of Arabic (and more recently, English and Portuguese) loanwords. In a complex way, it has also become an identity group, although the label is used quite differently on Zanzibar, the coast, and up-country. No one is a Swahili and nothing else; however, Morrison et al. classify 5 percent of the population as "Swahili,"[9] while Whitely cites the figure of 1,000,000 as the number who speak Swahili as a first language,[10] or 7.5 percent. But language is not the only criteria; Swahili identity is often linked to being Muslim. Until recently it was used by those who labelled themselves Arabs as an expression of cultural stratification, demarcating one's social inferiors or, in Zanzibar, any African. Since independence and the 1964 Zanzibar revolution, which decimated the Arab elite, "Arab" as a self-concept has been devalued and the cultural standing of Swahili identity raised. Up-country, persons of coastal origins who used Swahili as a primary language would be labelled by self and others as Swahili.[11]

From its coastal foothold, Swahili as a lingua franca followed first the Afro-Arab trading routes inland, then the network of colonial administrative outposts. A standard version of Swahili was adopted only in 1930, which then began to be used in the schools. Although a 1942 estimate calculated that only 52 percent of the population could speak Swahili,

7. The absorption of immigrants in Buganda is described in A. I. Richards (ed.), *Economic Development and Tribal Change* (Cambridge: W. Hefner and Son, 1954).

8. Margaret Bates, "Tanganyika," in Gwendolen M. Carter (ed.), *African One-Party States* (Ithaca, N.Y.: Cornell University Press, 1962), p. 396.

9. Morrison et al., *Black Africa*, p. 354.

10. Wilfred Whiteley, *Swahili: The Rise of a National Language* (London: Methuen, 1969), p. 3.

11. For a careful dissection of the ambiguities in this identity, see Carol M. Eastman, "Who Are the Waswahili?" *Africa*, XLI, no. 5 (July 1971), 228-36.

recent estimates hover around 90 percent, an astonishing rate of diffusion.[12] President Nyerere, who always uses Swahili as a political language, maintains that in all his travels through the country he has only had to use an interpreter twice.[13] Remarkably, there is no sign of any resistance to the active promotion of Swahili.

Religion is of modest significance as a differentiator. Muslims, who number 30.9 percent of the populace, are the largest group. There are, according to the 1957 census, 17.1 percent Catholic, and 7.8 percent Protestant. Muslims are strongest along the coast, while Christian missions were most active along the northern and western fringes of the country.

Race, a vanishing vector, did play a significant role in the sequencing of cultural competition in the 1950s. At their peak in the late 1950s, Europeans numbered about 21,000 and Asians 96,000. Within the colonial context, their social and economic importance was overwhelming, as Europeans dominated the government and Asians the economy. During much of the important transitional period, it was assumed that the long-run importance of these immigrant communities would be considerable, and hence defining a political role for them was a central issue in decolonization. However, only a small number of Europeans really considered themselves permanent residents. They, too, were rimland dwellers, concentrated in the fertile and temperate mountain zones of the north and southwest. As it has become clear to the Asian community that in the long run they cannot maintain their economic niche, their numbers are melting fast.

In Uganda, the Ganda cultural subnation model played a decisive role in structuring the colonial administration. Thus units were created on the basis of presumed ethnic community, and given political structures inspired by the Ganda model of administration, modified to meet the needs of the colonial framework. The ethnic district, in the long run, had a clear feedback effect in helping establish a coherent focus for identity which in many instances was not present at the time of colonial penetration. Because Ganda identity and status provided the emulative model for the rest of the country, we need to turn first to the nature of Ganda subnationalism.

Ganda identity was well developed at the time of colonial penetration. It was grounded upon, not only language, but above all a highly centralized state with powerfully integrative symbols of kingship. All roads led to the royal court; social mobility for young men passed through the

12. Morrison et al., *Black Africa*, p. 355; Abdulaziz, in Whiteley, *Language Use and Social Change*, pp. 168-69.
13. Whiteley, *Swahili*, p. 102.

palace page corps. The frequent wars against Bunyoro probably stimulated identity, as did the experience of participation in the military campaigns for the large numbers of young men conscripted for this purpose.

Early European visitors established a very favorable stereotype of Buganda. The first such traveller, J. H. Speke, records in his chronicle his surprise at the broad, straight roads, the neat gardens, the people well-clad in bark cloth, and the imposing palace grounds. "I cut a poor figure in the comparison with the display of the dressy Waganda," he wrote. "They wore neat bark cloth cloaks resembling the best yellow corduroy cloth, crimp well set, as if stiffened with starch, and over that as upper-cloaks, a patch work of small antelope skins which I observed sewn together as well as any English glovers could have pieced them."[14] Henry Stanley, who rarely let slip an occasion for an ethnic stereotype, reinforced the laudatory image:

[The Baganda were] . . . an extraordinary people, as different from the barbarous pirates of Uvuma, and the wild, mop-headed men of Eastern Usukama, as the British in India are from their Afridi fellow-subjects, or the white Americans of Arkansas from the semi-civilized Choctaws. . . .

Mutesa impressed me as being an intelligent and distinguished prince, who, if aided in time by virtuous philanthropists, will do more for Central Africa than fifty years of Gospel teaching unaided by such authority, can do.[15]

This positive image quickly was absorbed into the Ganda self-concept, which was then reinforced by the special status of the 1900 agreement. While other areas had provincial and district commissioners to give orders, Buganda had a resident at the Kabaka's court to proffer advice. Although at flood tide of colonialism the difference was not very great, the self-image of unchallenged status remained. Characteristic of these sentiments was the sharp rejoinder composed by Kabaka Daudi Chwa in 1929 to contest a proposal for making Swahili an official African language in Uganda:

I feel, however, that it is my duty to add here in conclusion, that it is quite unnecessary to adopt the Ki-Swahili language as the Official Native Language in Buganda, and I am entirely opposed to any arrangement which would in any way

14. Quoted in Peter M. Gukiina, *Uganda: A Case Study in African Political Development* (Notre Dame, Ind.: University of Notre Dame Press, 1972), pp. 45-46.

15. Stanley, *Through the Dark Continent*, 187-93. Another characteristic quote, reflecting the strong admiration for Ganda among early European visitors, comes from one of the first governors, Sir Harry Johnston. Addressing an elite London audience, he commented: "In politeness, quickness of intelligence and appreciation of beauty, they are the Japanese of Africa."—quoted in Michael Twaddle, "The Bakungu Chiefs of Buganda under British Colonial Rule, 1900-1930," *Journal of African History*, X, 2 (1969), pp. 309-22.

facilitate the ultimate adoption of this language as the Official Native Language of the Baganda in place of, or at the expense of, their own language, since I feel convinced that such a course will assuredly bring about the loss of our tribal status and nationality among the Native tribes of Africa.[16]

Some four decades later, the then-deposed Kabaka Mutesa II wrote:

Perhaps another reason for the calm of the Baganda is that, unlike many Africans, they have not lost their identity. . . .

We are invariably accused by our detractors of being tribalist in a sense of the word that it is a wicked retrogressive thing to be. But I have never been able to pin down precisely the difference between a tribe and a nation and see why one is thought so despicable and the other is so admired. Whichever we are, the Baganda have a common language, tradition, history and cast of mind. While we stood alone, we were accepted as the most civilized and powerful of the kingdoms. Does this justify our being totally dominated by our neighbors, unnaturally yoked to us as they were by Britain? It was through the qualities of Baganda that Europeans were attracted to the country, hurrying through Kenya and Tanzania to reach the "pearl of Africa," as Stanley called Buganda.[17]

Cultural self-assurance was also reinforced by the role of leadership which came quite naturally to Buganda. In the early days the mantle of primacy was born by the Ganda conquistadores, catechists, and chiefs who organized the rest of the state. When this role passed, a new one began to open, as Ganda heavily dominated the modern elite ranks and were the first African professionals and civil servants. The Kabaka was careful to equip himself with a Rolls-Royce of slightly larger dimensions than that of the governor. The first political movements to emerge were Ganda-led and centered. Nothing could be more natural than the dispatch of Ganda notable Ham Mukasa and Prime Minister Apolo Kagwa to attend the coronation of King Edward VII in 1902.[18] Kabaka Mutesa I had proposed marriage to Queen Victoria; a young Ganda scholar recollects that during the forced exile in Britain of Mutesa II 1953-55 "it was common gossip in my home and school area that while in exile the Kabaka was hosted in Buckingham Palace, where he was seduced by Queen Elizabeth II but had refused her."[19] This scurrilous rumor is of interest for its symbolic content; the personification of Buganda is clearly cast in the superior role, dramatized by the intrusion of the sexual motif.

16. Whiteley, *Swahili*, p. 11.
17. Mutesa, *Desecration of My Kingdom*, pp. 78-79.
18. Ham Mukasa wrote an interesting account of this journey, *Uganda's Katikiro in England* (London: Hutchison and Co., 1904).
19. Gukiina, *Uganda*, p. 99.

The task of building a cultural ideology was taken up immediately by the Christian revolutionary elite. The most important contributor was the great Protestant Katikiro prime minister, Sir Apolo Kagwa, with several historical chronicles (*Basekabaka be Buganda,* 1901; *Ekitabo kye Mpisa za Buganda,* 1905; *Ekitabo kye Bika bya Buganda,* 1908). Ham Mukasa and, later, Serwano Kulubya were other major figures. These testaments chronicled the saga of Buganda, from the descent of the mystical god-ancestor Kintu through the rise of the kingdom to its nineteenth-century greatness. The symbol of kingship received particular stress; Mukasa produced an interesting collection of proverbs which revolve around the themes of his strength, invincibility, omnipotence; his majesty, his terrifying power.[20] Kulubya maintained that the suggestion that the Kabaka might eat or sleep was a grave act of *lèse-majesté:*

To convey the idea that the Kabaka is always guarding his country and, hence, cannot fall asleep like the other people who have no responsibility; he merely takes a rest, meanwhile thinking out what he is going to do next. From the above it will be seen that the Kabaka was not looked upon as an ordinary human being. He was regarded as a kind of superman without the weaknesses of common folk. Theoretically, he required neither food nor sleep, he was above such things.[21]

In the interpretation of these statements, kingship must be viewed, in the context of cultural ideology, as the personification of the people. The invincibility of the Kabaka was the omnipotence of his people. His power was the measure of the cultural status of the collectivity. In their cultural myth, Ganda were able to interpret even colonialism, so humiliating to most subject peoples, as a relationship between equals. Through elaborate metaphors of equality, re-enacted at each opportunity, the Ganda viewed themselves as above colonial status. Subjugation was the crude lot of less-favored folk; within the confines of the Uganda Protectorate, the Ganda were prepared to work with the British to bring good government to others. As a subsequent parameter of cultural politics, this self-concept was of paramount import. Although the map showed that Buganda was a mere sub-division of the pink-shaded area labelled Uganda, in their own eyes they held a coordinate status with the British Crown and were clearly distinct from the rest of the country. This self-image locked Buganda onto a collision course with the remainder of the state, once independence came on the horizon; to this point we will return presently.

20. Ham Mukasa, "The Rule of the Kings of Buganda," *Uganda Journal,* X, no. 2 (September 1946), 136-43.

21. Owekitibwo S. W. Kulubya, "Some Aspects of Buganda Customs," *Uganda Journal,* IX, no. 2 (May 1942), 53.

In the continuum between ethnicity and nationalism, measured by degree of cultural ideology, Gandahood stands well along toward the latter pole: not as far as Tamils, Sikhs, or Bengalis, but farther than the Kongo or any other East African group. Their language was unified even before its reduction to writing in the late nineteenth century. Through the agency of the missionaries, very quickly aided by Ganda drawn from the new Christian revolutionary elite, Luganda was swiftly equipped with grammars and dictionaries and was taught in standardized form in schools which reached a large number of young Ganda. Ganda history and society were well chronicled by both Ganda and European researchers, tailored to the heroic dimensions of their self-image. Although there was not a strong literary tradition, a vernacular press emerged at an early date. And, above all, there was the peculiar force and vitality of the symbols of kingship.

Within the colonial frame, the Ganda model was a powerful model for identity-building. It was apparent to all that Buganda enjoyed a status and relative deference from Britain that was denied to other groups. At a time when the colonial order was unassailable, the only possible response was, as with caste groups in India, emulation of the high status group. To command the value of esteem, controlled by the colonizer, cold logic dictated acquiring the special attributes that seemed to explain the privileged status accorded to Buganda. The 1900 treaty seemed one key to the status kingdom; Bunyoro and Toro demanded comparable treaties incessantly—and were just as frequently turned down by the British, who came to regret the scope of privilege that had been bargained away to Buganda. Another apparent secret to Ganda standing was the kabakaship; one after another, districts began to demand the designation of a single paramount ruler, including the many groups where neither history nor legend provided warrant for such an office. Emulation of these traits, of course, is not to be confused with admiration of Buganda; indeed, in seeking the secret to equal treatment, groups were partly expressing their resentment of the demeaning disrespect accorded them by both British and Ganda. Interesting insight on this point is provided by A. G. G. Gingyera-Pinycwa, a Ugandan scholar, who argues the influence of the European contribution toward investing kingly institutions with special dignity. Anthropologists developed the distinction between centralized and stateless societies as a critical axis of differentiation of African traditional systems.[22] Many studies in this school, "barely hid their

22. The seminal study in this respect was the extremely influential work by M. Fortes and E. E. Evans-Pritchard (eds.), *African Political Systems* (London: Oxford University Press, 1940).

assumption that those societies which had the machinery for the administration of a state, like monarchical institutions, resembled the 'civilized' states of Europe and, hence, had a higher level of cultural development, while the other societies were regarded as still, in the main, savages at a lower level of cultural development." As a consequence, Ugandans from kingdom areas "tended to regard themselves as being in a way superior to the rest of Ugandans."[23]

Another dimension of emulation lay simply in the affirmation of identity; the Ganda were powerful because they appeared to be a large, self-assured group. The high intensity of Ganda self-awareness was a normative model for groups such as the Kiga and Gisu who had no collective identity at all at the pre-colonial baseline.[24] In Tanzania, there was no comparable model of status and modernity.

The Ganda impact on the shape of ethnicity may be seen in another direction; Michael Twaddle has offered some interesting evidence as to the role of ethnic classifications undertaken in the eastern region by Ganda agents as creating the categories which then became enshrined in the district and county administrative structure. The Ganda *weltanschauung* assumed the ethnic group, as did colonial officials in many other contexts; they used linguistic and cultural commonalities to infer the units, as in noncentralized societies political units could not provide the typology.[25] But some alternative lists drawn up by British officials in the same area show that, even departing from the ethnic unit metaphor, quite different classifications were possible.

The premise of ethnic-based districts encouraged incorporative processes within the administrative frame set. A number of closely related principalities were administratively fused as Busoga. A kingdom of modest dimensions was enlarged by attaching several smaller chiefdoms, under the designation of Ankole. Perhaps fifty warfare units of varying size, whose leaders exercised leadership primarily in military operations, were grouped, on the basis of linguistic and structural similarities, under the Acholi label (first as East and West Acholi, then amalgamated). A secessionist segment of the old Bunyoro kingdom, culturally and linguistically identical with the Nyoro, was con-

23. A. G. G. Gingyera-Pinycwa, "Some Dimensions of the Pre-Independence Politics in Uganda, 1952-62: A Case Study Based on the Catholic Church and Politics in Northern Uganda in the Decade 1952-62" (Ph.D. diss., University of Chicago, 1972), p. 11.

24. Ali A. Mazrui makes an interesting argument that competitive emulation of Buganda had an integrative effect on other parts of Uganda, in "Privilege and Protest as Integrative Factors: The Case of Buganda's Status in Uganda," in Rotberg and Mazrui, *Protest and Power in Black Africa,* pp. 1072-87.

25. Michael Twaddle, "'Tribalism' in Eastern Uganda," in Gulliver (ed.), *Tradition and Transition in East Africa,* pp. 193-208.

firmed in its independence and consolidated as a separate identity as Toro. In southwestern Uganda, Kigezi district became the focus for the birth of Kiga identity; a century ago, this group was culturally indistinguishable from the non-Tutsi populace of neighboring Rwanda, today known as Hutu.[26] The process of identity formation among the second largest group by contemporary categories, the Teso, is cogently described by Joan Vincent:

> It was clear that a Teso awareness, as opposed to ongoing social interactions between culturally related groups, came about only with the establishment of British overrule, and so one may profitably inquire into how this awareness was created. There were many centralizing procedures. During the first twenty years, boundaries were constantly changed until linguistic homogeneity was achieved and the Ngoratok dialect recognized as that of the District, this vernacular being used in schools. Statutory distinctions were made between the "natives of the district" and "settlers": the unification of the land tenure system was attempted; exchange of cattle bridewealth was required of all natives of the district apart from Muslims; cotton growing was made compulsory regardless of primary occupations of different ethnic groups; District by-laws were molded upon Teso tribal customs relating to Clan elders, witchcraft accusations, the adoption of children. . . . The culmination came with an effort to provide Teso with a symbolic figurehead like that of the western kingdom.[27]

This is not to say that the pliability of cultural frontiers was of infinite elasticity. Even without political organization, language and ritual provided on the one hand identity-orienting unifirmities and on the other some clear discontinuities, especially between quite distinctive language families, such as the Bantu zone of southern Uganda and the Luo diaspora family, now classified as Alur, Acholi, Lango and Padhola. Existence of regularized patterns of conflict resolution, common customs, and shared myths of origin and migration may also have provided a basis for recognition of commonality, at least in some circumstances. Thus, on Mount Elgon, on the eastern frontier, the boundary on the northwest side of the mountion between Gisu and Sebei is clearcut; the languages are unrelated, and Sebei practice female circumcision. However, the difference on the south side where the Kenya frontier intersects are very slight; on the Uganda side the accepted label is Gisu, while in Kenya the term Vugusu is used. Yet, today, the Gisu and Vugusu claim to be different cultural entities; the Gisu, through administrative structure, shared hostility to the Ganda agents, and a similar curcumcision ritual, have developed a pronounced sense of unity. Educated Gisu formed an association for the unification of Gisu dialects, so that Luganda could be displaced as a local

26. M. Edel, "African Tribalism: Some Reflections on Uganda," *Political Science Quarterly*, vol. LXXX (1965).

27. Joan Vincent, *African Elite: The Big Men of a Small Town* (New York: Columbia University Press, 1971), p. 259.

administrative language. The circumcision ceremony, which retains its vitality, has become more explicitly a ritual affirmation of Gisu identity.[28]

Cultural divisions in Uganda are often summarized in terms of traditional anthropological-linguistic families—of "Bantu" (Ganda, Nyoro, Nkole, Kiga, Soga, Gisu and others), "Nilotic" (the Luo group listed above), "Nilo-Hamitic" (Teso, Karamojong, and others), "Sudanic" (Lugbara, Kakwa, and Madi), and "Hamitic" (Sebei). Bantu and Nilotic did come into brief currency as political labels in 1965-66; however, it is important to stress that these are not salient actor's maps of the ethnic landscape. The Luo groups do share clear traditions of their dispersal but have not acted or identified as a collectivity; indeed, Acholi-Lango hostility is a recurrent theme during the colonial period and beyond. Cultural exchange between Acholi and Nyoro has been extensive, while Bunyoro and Buganda, as independent kingdoms, were in constant struggle, which continued over the questions of Ganda agents and recuperation of some of the Bunyoro lands annexed by Buganda during the colonial penetration phase. The important restructuring of linguistic theory by Joseph Greenberg has cast grave doubt on the validity of the classification of the non-Bantu languages, which he has incorporated within a broader Eastern Sudanic category.[29]

Thus a grid of ethnicity, with Ganda subnationalism as a normative model and the administrative subdivisions as a structural expression was laid upon the territory. Crosscutting this pattern was an unusually intense and politicized religious division, founded upon the competitive proselytizing of Protestant and Catholic missions and the slower diffusion of Islam. Here again events in Buganda were pattern-setting. We have already suggested that the competition of English Protestants, French Catholics, and Zanzibari Muslims in the royal court for the evangelization of the pages gave ideological structure to factionalism and led to sporadic civil war following the death of Kabaka Mutesa I in 1884. The linkage of religious ideology with an epochal power struggle for control of Buganda left in its wake a high degree of mobilization around symbols of religious difference, rendered the more acute by the external powers allied with each theological faction. The restructuring of the kingdom which accompanied the Christian revolution and the treaty with Britain included a territorial partition of religious influence; of the twenty counties in enlarged Buganda, ten were to have Protestant chiefs, eight Catholic, and two Muslim. A large-scale shuffling of population accom-

28. J. S. La Fontaine, "Tribalism among the Gisu," in Gulliver, *Tradition and Transition in East Africa*, pp. 177-92.

29. Joseph H. Greenberg, *The Languages of Africa* (Bloomington, Ind.: Indiana University Press, 1966), pp. 85-129.

panied this settlement, with many converts locating themselves in a jurisdiction where authority was to be exercised by a coreligionist. The quest for converts in Buganda was more than a spiritual exercise; it was a struggle for power. It is significant that the Christian factions were known by Ganda as "Bafalansa" (French) and "Bangereza" (English).[30]

The initial extension of Christianity relied heavily upon Ganda catechists in the early years; to the natural competition between the missionaries was added the acute sectarian orientations of the catechists. In due course, the key auxiliary roles in the evangelical structure—catechists and primary school teachers—were localized. Internalized within the district churches was a powerful socializing mechanism for instilling a keen sense of religious identity as a conflict role. For the Catholics, this was sharpened by the perception that the British administrators exhibited an unmistakable preference for Protestant chiefs and local government employees. The battle for conversion spread across the land in an intricate matrix of conflict; establishment of a post by one church was a challenge to the other to create one nearby, so no souls would fall by default. The primary schools, long operated by the missions, were efficacious agencies of sectarian indoctrination. They were also communications channels, through the pupils, to their families and communities. There is important variation in the intensity of religious differentiation, which seems to have been especially sharp where the Catholic missions were mainly foreign, such as the French White Fathers or Italian Verona Fathers. At its peak of intensity, in Kigezi, the Protestant-Catholic rivalry succeeded in cutting across kinship lines and imposing a higher order of obligation and solidarity than that of family and lineage.[31] Religious division was most attenuated in the east, sharpest in Kigezi, Ankole, Acholi, and West Nile.

Though the Muslims were a strong Buganda faction at the time of the civil wars, they lacked effective external backing and came out a poor third in the British settlement. Thereafter, Islam diffused slowly based upon two focal points: the Ganda Muslim faction and scattered settlements of Sudanese soldiers. They lacked the backing of the colonial system, an organized evangelical apparatus, and above all the mobility resources represented by the Christian schools. Muslims were found in such functions as trade, taxi driving, and soldiering, which did not require access to the educational system; they were very scarce in the civil service or professional elites. Within the colonial cultural stratification, Muslims were a low status group. At the time of independence, they were 5.2 percent of the population.

30. For a careful study, see F. B. Welbourn, *Religion and Politics in Uganda* (Nairobi: East Africa Publishing House, 1965).

31. Fred G. Burke, *Local Government and Politics in Uganda* (Syracuse: Syracuse University Press, 1964), p. 16.

The Ganda Muslim community did have a link to the monarchy through its titular head, Prince Badru Kakungulu, uncle of the late Kabaka Mutesa II. Muslims were 13 percent of the Ganda population; from Buganda, a modest Muslim community developed in neighboring Busoga. The Sudanese settlements were mainly in the northern part of the country. Originally, these soldiers had been recruited in the 1870s, under European and Egyptian officers, as a part of Khedive Ismael's effort to expand the Egyptian domain to the source of the Nile. With the establishment of the Mahdist regime from 1884 to 1898, the southernmost Egyptian garrisons, in what is now northern Uganda, were cut off but not overrun by the Mahdists. They were used for a time as auxiliaries by the British in establishing their rule over Uganda, but they mutinied in 1897 and were demobilized. The remnants of these bands were then dispersed into small settlements. Originally, they were a miscellaneous assortment of fugitives, slaves, and other unfortunate young men who came within reach of the man-catchers conscripting soldiers for the Egyptian garrisons in the upper Nile; they were mainly from southwestern Sudan and the Nuba mountains. A new identity emerged from their shared role as an expeditionary force operating in zones where they were all strangers. The Egyptian encadrement of this polyglot force established Islam and Arabic as the cultural norms; although the bulk of these men could not have been Muslims at the time of their conscription, they adopted Islam as soldiers and referred to themselves as "Nubians."[32] Subsequently, as dispersed communities, they established links through marriage with those amongst whom they found themselves. The "Nubian" identity has remained; Islam diffused from these nuclei, and on conversion many also called themselves Nubians. In Madi district, Muslims reached 37 percent of the total; in West Nile, they were 10 percent, but were particularly numerous among the Kakwa, who dominated a county in the northwest tip of Uganda.[33]

Unlike Tanzania, Uganda as a colony was always assumed to be an African state, despite such quaint episodes as the short-lived discussions between the British and the Zionists on Uganda as Jewish homeland. At its peak, the European population was no more than 10,000, almost all transient. The Asian community, which dominated trade and commerce, totalled 72,000 at the 1959 census. As colonial influence groups, both were powerful; once decolonization became a serious prospect, both these racial communities lost their political importance.

32. Sir Harry Johnston, *The Uganda Protectorate*, (2 vols.; London: Hutchison & Co., 1904), I, 233.

33. Martin Lowenkopf on Islam in Uganda, in James Kritzeck and William H. Lewis, *Islam in Africa*, pp. 214-26. On patterns of Islamic diffusion, see especially Trimingham, *Islam in East Africa*.

Thus Tanzania and Uganda, despite the importance of their cultural similarities, differed in important respects in their communal makeup. Tanzania lacked a polar subnationality whose intensity of ethnicity would serve as a foil for the emulative mobilization of communal solidarity. Neither did it have a politicized religious cleavage, although there was a degree of competition in the diffusion of Islam, Catholicism and Protestantism. During the colonial phase, conceptualization of Tanzania as a polity, when it occurred, was guided by the metaphor of the multiracial society, although the proportions of immigrants were not very different. Within this image of society, Africans were a single category, which they never really were in Uganda.

SOCIAL CHANGE AND COMMUNAL CLEAVAGE

We have thus far described the basic patterns of cultural pluralism; our next task is to consider processes of change and their impact on the definition of communal differentiation. A decent respect for brevity commands selectivity in this effort. Two particularly important dimensions of change which have been argued as critical to identity development and transformation will be considered: competitive modernization and the nature of urban social fields.

For the record, the obvious may be briefly stated: during the colonial period, social privilege accrued above all to Europeans, followed by Asians. All things are relative, and the actual wealth of Europeans and Asians needs to be seen in the context of the society. European government officials and missionaries were not, by Western standards, hugely affluent; indeed, it is worthy of note that salaries of colonial officials were far less than those of the new generation of technical assistance experts, international functionaries, and American academics who flowed in after independence. But relative to most Africans, they were infinitely rich, and their standard of life established the point of reference as to what affluence was. Asians had been present on Zanzibar in small numbers for generations as traders. The establishment of security for commerce and protection of property in the hinterland brought an influx of Indian and Pakistani petty traders and clerks, who became the shopkeepers, crop-buyers, ginnery operators, and, in the second generation, lawyers, doctors, and owners of light industries. Although Asian communities were internally fragmented along religious, linguistic, and to some extent caste lines, the various segments had a high degree of solidarity, and were capable of raising much of their own capital, constructing efficacious commercial nets, and financing their own social mobility through their own school systems.[34]

More central to our purpose is the differential rate of entry to modern roles among the overwhelming African majority. We have already noted that in both countries one cultural group from the first days of establishment of a colonial administration had an elite literate in at least an African language, the Ganda Christian revolutionary elite, and the Swahili. These groups, however, were radically different; the Ganda a veritable subnationality, the Swahili a diffuse grouping defined by language, religion, and culture, but not conceiving of themselves as a political entity. Tanzania overall was far behind Uganda in the size of its modern elite; German administration was never well enough established for much of the infrastructure of socioeconomic change to develop. World War I was a harsh experience, with continuing military campaigns waged on Tanzanian territory; some years went by after the war before British administration took hold. Figures calculated in 1953 showed that Uganda had a rate of 21 per 100,000 enter Makerere College in Kampala, which then served all East Africa; the Tanzanian rate was only 2.8.[35]

Within Tanzania, the most conspicuously successful are the Chagga, of Mount Kilimanjaro. This group, which appears to have developed a salient collective identity only in the twentieth century, enjoyed an especially favorable ecological setting. The mountain provides both rich volcanic soil and relief rainfall to water it. Arabica coffee produced marvelously and was a very remunerative cash crop. Missions—Lutheran and Catholic—were early established on the mountain and provided educational opportunities. The local government coffers were well filled and could provide generous support to educational expansion. Chagga also were attracted into trade and the civil service; Chagga were to be found in both roles all over Tanzania.

In precolonial times, Chaggaland was organized by mountain valley; the dialects were related but quite different—and even at the peak of Chagga self-assertiveness in the 1950s, an effort by Chagga elites to produce an effectively unified Chagga language failed.[36] There was one period in the nineteenth century when a given ruler achieved pre-eminence on the mountain, but no institutionalized Chagga polity or identity resulted. Affirmation of identity and social unity came first through the

34. On Asians in East Africa, see H. S. Morris, *The Indians in Uganda* (Chicago: University of Chicago Press, 1968); Dharam P. Ghai, *Portrait of a Minority* (Nairobi, London: Oxford University Press, 1965).

35. J. E. Goldthorpe, *An African Elite* (London: Oxford University Press, 1965), pp. 28-30.

36. Whiteley, *Swahili*, p. 12.

very successful Kilimanjaro Native Cooperative Union, formed in 1931 to market Chagga coffee. Political expression of the concept of Chaggahood was found through the creation of the office of paramount chief, and designation of a popular figure to fill it. The Chagga ratio of Makerere entrants was more than four times the territorial average.

Chaggahood evolved under the image of success. At the apex, with coffee prices at £591 per ton in 1953 (compared to less than £30 in the late 1930s, and £308 in 1965), Chaggaland was at a peak of prosperity. Political awareness was directed mainly toward Chagga interests; it was only belatedly, in 1960, that TANU became solidly implanted in Kilimanjaro. Chagga did not subsequently play a leading role in national politics. Their relationship with TANU was ambiguous; several aspects of TANU policy brought the party into conflict with Chagga interests. Chagga traders and prosperous farmers were tepid about the socialist ideology of the Nyerere regime. Further, the egalitarian premises of TANU called for concentrating resources in sectors like education for the less developed regions. In practice, however, the regime was not able to halt the rapid expansion of educational facilities in Chaggaland; the drive for mobility was too strongly enrooted, and local communities simply founded schools whether or not the government wanted them.[37]

If ratios of university entrants be considered a valid indicator of mobility success, what stands out is the concentration of the achievers along the northern fringe. The Haya, on the west shores of Lake Victoria, the Pare, just to the east of the Chagga, and the Zigua, on the northeast coast, shared this ranking with the Nyakusu, the only group from a different area, who occupied an ecologically comparable fertile highland zone in the southwest.[38] None of these identity groups developed a strongly articulated communalism. To take the example of the Haya, most important of those listed, their political culture belonged to the interlacustrine kingdom area; their region contained a fluctuating number of principalities, which formed the basis of the administrative subdivisions. Those in the westernmost county, Karagwe, tend to refer to themselves as Nyambo, rather than Haya. There was a sharp vertical cleavage between the top-ranking Hima pastoralists and Iru cultivators, a replica of the situation in neighboring Ankole district, in Uganda. Catholic White Father missions got an early start in Buhaya. The lakeshore

37. On the Chagga, see inter alia Kathleen M. Stahl, in Gulliver, *Tradition and Transition in East Africa*, pp. 209-22; Joel Samoff, *Tanzania: Local Politics and the Structure of Power* (Madison, Wis.: University of Wisconsin Press, 1974); Basil P. Mramba, "Kilimanjaro: Socialism and Nationalism," in Lionel Cliffe (ed.), *One Party Democracy* (Nairobi: East African Publishing House, 1967), pp. 105-27.

38. Goldthorpe, *African Elite*, p. 30.

areas were well suited for coffee cultivation, and a relative prosperity was achieved, although less striking than that of Chaggaland.[39]

What stands out in the Tanzanian pattern is the self-contained nature of the group mobility patterns. Groups were not locked in direct competition for scarce mobility resources. Chagga and Haya did not interact directly; there was no arena in which direct social struggle occurred. Although the Chagga success image was well enough known, change was not a zero-sum game between ethnic contenders. Chagga prosperity was largely generated from within their well-endowed area; these were resources that other groups would have no expectation of directly sharing. True, after independence, there was some moderate tension between Chagga and the priorities of the national political system; however, this was not expressed in terms of a direct rivalry between Chagga and other ethnic entities. Chagga were only 3 percent of the total population; even those among them who ventured outside their area, such as entrepreneurs, bureaucrats, or professionals, were not present in such numbers as to constitute an ethnic threat in the towns where they settled. Their sociological weight was not comparable to the Kikuyu, Ganda, Ibo, or Luba-Kasai. We may also note that the relatively advantaged groups were, on the whole, in the ecologically favored areas of higher agricultural potential. Naturally enough, these were the same zones where European settlers clustered; the reference group, and object of hostility, became in part the settler community.

The other side of the coin is that groups which were far behind the pacesetters did not become aware of their relative deprivation in terms of Chagga and Haya. The Sukuma, at the time of the Goldthorpe study, had a rate of university entry not much more than 10 percent of the Chagga or Haya, yet this fact did not come to pattern their perceptions of disadvantage. The strong national orientation of TANU, in this context, can be argued as both cause and effect; its ideological formulation of deprivation as an African, and not an ethnic, phenomenon helped direct aspirations and ambitions toward the territorial framework. At the same time, this national vocation was powerfully abetted by the relative absence of ethnic perceptions of deprivation, structurally embodied in culturally based political movements. The relative absence of ethnic struggle for mobility resources had a further implication; there was no group which served as a model for competitive emulation. "Becoming more modern" did not have an ethnic reference point, as it did in Uganda.

39. For a valuable survey of Haya politics, see Goran Hyden, *Tanu Yajenga Nchi* (Lund: Berlingska Boktrycheriet, 1968).

The Ganda succeeded in the early years of the protectorate in building up simply an overwhelming lead across a very broad front. We have already stressed the high status accorded the symbols of Ganda identity. In the social realm, this had its counterpart in a massive advantage in education, in entry to the professions, in the civil service. Even rural Ganda were made aware of their advantageous position by the presence of a large number of agricultural laborers from other areas; very modest farmers hired a porter or two. Audrey Richards, in her study of the migrant labor phenomenon, quotes a revealing schoolroom exchange during a debate:

14-year-old girl: "If we are all equal we ought to give our porters food on plates with us, and not on banana leaves at the back door."

Answer, from another student: "But we are not equal. The Europeans and Ganda are clean and the others are dirty."[40]

The 1900 settlement with the British had allocated freehold title, among other things, to some 4,000 chiefs and dignitaries. Over the years, these holdings tended to fragment; by 1956, it was estimated that there were 20,000 Ganda landowners with estates of ten acres or more.[41] Virtually all of these farmers would hire immigrant labor and could attain a relative prosperity.

Trade was a field of difficult entry for Africans, with competition from the well-organized Asian sector. In 1953, of the 11,600 registered African traders, 6,700 were in Buganda.[42] Religion had been another important sphere of Ganda leadership; the initial catechists were Ganda, and at the time of independence, both in the Catholic and Anglican hierarchies, a large majority of the priests were Ganda. During the 1920s, 78.7 percent of the Ugandan entrants to Makerere were Ganda; this fraction fell slowly, but by the early 1950s, was still over 50 percent. The rate of Ganda matriculations per 100,000 was 80, as compared with a territorial average of 21 (the comparable figure for the Chagga was only 12).[43] Table 7.1 reflects the Ganda domination of the higher civil service. The only major occupational category which was not dominated by Ganda, the security forces, was of low prestige during the colonial period; these functions were positively shunned by the Ganda, with grave consequences after independence when control over the instruments of coercion played a crucial role in the regional

40. Richards, *Economic Development and Tribal Change*, p. 161.
41. Fallers, *The King's Men*, p. 114.
42. Ibid., p. 145.
43. Goldthorpe, *African Elite*, p. 28.

Table 7.1.— Ethnic Distribution in the Uganda Higher Public Service

Ethnic unit	% of total 1959 population	In higher public service					
		September 1959		July 1963		March 1967	
		%	No.	%	No.	%	No.
Ganda	16.3	40.7	11	38.1	51	35.6	105
Teso	8.1	3.7	1	5.2	7	8.1	24
Nkole	8.1	0.0	0	7.5	10	6.8	20
Soga	7.8	7.4	2	9.0	12	3.4	10
Kiga/Hororo	7.1	3.7	1	6.0	8	4.7	14
Rwanda	5.9	11.1	3	3.7	5	4.4	13
Langi	5.6	3.7	1	1.5	2	4.1	12
Gisu	5.1	0.0	0	4.5	6	2.7	8
Acholi	4.4	7.4	2	6.7	9	4.4	13
Lugbara	3.7	0.0	0	1.5	2	1.4	4
Toro	3.2	7.4	2	3.0	4	7.1	21
Nyoro	2.9	7.4	2	5.2	7	5.1	15
Karamojong	2.0	0.0	0	0.7	1	0.7	2
Alur	1.9	0.0	0	0.7	1	0.7	2
Gwere	1.7	0.0	0	0.0	0	0.3	1
Konjo	1.7	0.0	0	0.0	0	0.3	1
Padhola	1.4	0.0	0	2.2	3	4.1	12
Nyole	1.4	3.7	1	0.7	1	1.4	4
Madi	1.2	3.7	1	1.5	2	0.3	1
Kumam	1.0	0.0	0	0.0	0	0.7	2
Samia	0.7	0.0	0	0.7	1	2.4	6
Kakwa	0.6	0.0	0	0.7	1	1.4	4
Sebei	0.6	0.0	0	0.0	0	0.3	1
Jonam	0.4	0.0	0	0.7	1	0.0	0
Other	7.0	0.0	0	0.0	0	0.0	0
			27		134		295

Source: Nelson Kasfir, "Controlling Ethnicity in Ugandan Politics: Departicipation as a Strategy for Political Development," (Ph.D. diss., Harvard University, 1972), pp. 225-26.

distribution of power. In 1961, Ganda were only 3.8 percent of the police force.[44]

Competitive modernization in Uganda was dominated by the polarity between Ganda and all others. There was also a more diffuse differentiation between the Bantu language zones of southern Uganda overall and the north, but this difference was less spectacular. Within some districts, there were also palpable disparities; the most important such instance was in Toro, where the dominant Toro group enjoyed a marked advantage over the Konjo and Amba, who joined in a secessionist re-

44. Kasfir, "Controlling Ethnicity in Uganda Politics," p. 124.

volt after independence. There was also some differential development along the religious axis. Moslems were the most disfavored community; there were, in 1955, 539 Christian schools but only 46 Muslim schools.[45] Catholics also believed themselves restricted in access to the large pool of central and local administration posts under the colonial regime, a sentiment largely responsible for the political mobilization of religious ties in the 1950s. But towering over other social divisions was the house of prosperity in Buganda. The ambivalent response was, on the one hand, the resentment and animosity of group-related inequality; on the other, envy, admiration, and emulation of the social achievements of the Ganda.[46] The Uganda pattern, although not the Tanzanian, did follow the mold argued by Melson and Wolpe in their hypotheses on competitive communalism: that competition engendered by social mobilization will tend to be defined in communal terms and that differential rates of mobilization among communal groups exacerbate communal conflict by multiplying coincident social cleavages.[47]

URBANIZATION: ITS ABSENT IMPACT

The second dimension of change to be examined is the nature of urban social fields. In both countries, the growth of towns has been relatively slow, and the capital city remains the only community over 100,000. In nearly all cases, the towns have their origins as administrative centers. The central institutions of government and the host of ancillary activities surrounding them made the capital cities the dominant central places—in both cases, three to four times the next largest town. Small consumer industries then tend to cluster around this major population center. Transport functions, as rail hub or port, have played some part. Through most of the colonial period, urban functions were dominated by the immigrant communities—Europeans and Asians. The towns were very small—until 1950, Kampala had only 38,000 persons. There were almost no large-scale enterprises employing a substantial labor force; until recently, in many towns in both countries, Africans were an actual minority.

The three largest towns in Tanzania—Dar es Salaam, Zanzibar town, and Tanga—all face the sea and are part of the heartland of Swahili

45. Fallers, *The King's Men,* p. 139.
46. This point is well argued by Mazrui, in Rotberg and Mazrui, *Protest and Power in Black Africa,* pp. 1072-86.
47. Robert Melson and Howard Wolpe, "Modernization and the Politics of Communalism, A Theoretical Perspective," *American Political Science Review,* LXIV, no. 4 December 1970), 1112-30.

culture. Zanzibar had known a sharp cultural stratification between Arabs (a label of superior cultural status, rather than linguistic identification) and Asians, and Africans; this hierarchy was destroyed in the 1964 revolution, with the Arab category effectively removed.[48] However, its conflict patterns were unique to the island and did not carry over to the mainland. The immediate ethnic hinterland of Tanga and Dar es Salaam is constituted by Digo and Zaramo respectively; neither group had been politically centralized or had developed a clear cultural ideology. Both had been strongly influenced by the integrative Swahili culture.

In the Dar es Salaam case, Zaramo were 36 percent of the population in 1957 but have probably somewhat declined in percentage since. There was no Zaramo ethnic association in town, nor did one hear the argument advanced that the capital was in any exclusive sense "Zaramo territory." Asians were the second largest group, with 21 percent of the urban total; they were the main reference point of hostility because they dominated commerce. The next largest group, the Rufiji, were no more than 7 percent. A careful study of Dar es Salaam, undertaken in the late 1950s, came to the conclusion that ethnicity was fast diluting as a basis for social organization. It tended to exist at two levels: route of migration to town created several incorporative categories, which overlay more particularized identities.[49] This conclusion was confirmed by patterns of political mobilization; Dar es Salaam rallied massively and virtually unanimously to TANU. The four largest African groups, taken together, numbered about 50 percent of the population; they were all coastal ethnic communities, almost completely Islamicized and strongly integrated into Swahili culture. For many, "Swahili" and "Zaramo" or "Rufiji" would be alternative identities and Swahili had become a mother tongue.[50] A self-conscious, social pacesetting group such as the Chagga might have made a difference; however, they numbered very few and were not conspicuous enough to serve as an orienting factor in perceptions of the urban field.

Up-country towns were generally small communities dominated by the group in whose territory they were founded. Dodoma was a Gogo town; Tabora was dominated by Nyamwezi and the Swahilized descendants of those associated with its initial function as a station on the nineteenth-century caravan routes. Moshi was a Chagga community, Mwanza overwhelmingly Sukuma, and Bukoba a Haya community. One of the

48. This does some violence to the complexity of identities; for a full account, see Michael Lofchie, *Zanzibar, Background to Revolution* (Princeton: Princeton University Press, 1966).
49. J. A. K. Leslie, *A Survey of Dar es Salaam* (London: Oxford University Press, 1963).
50. Dar es Salaam politics are summarized by Dandi Mwakawago, in Cliffe, *One Party Democracy*, pp. 208-26.

few exceptions was Arusha town, at the foot of 14,000-foot Mount Meru, which adjoins Mount Kilimanjaro. The mountain was shared by Meru and Arusha groups, who lived in a complex symbiosis of conflict, inter-penetration, and amalgamation. The Meru seem to have the same general origin as the Chagga. The Arusha are an identity group which crystallized in the nineteenth century from a diverse set of populations who took refuge on the mountain from the pastoral Masai, who served as an external point of cultural orientation and linguistic influence. The Arusha were better structured militarily and dominated the mountain for a time, absorbing some Meru lineages and exercising a profound influence over all Meru. Superposition of colonial control and an influx of European and Asian settlers to the fertile mountain lands ended Arusha domination and gave rise to an embittered triangular conflict pattern. In the midst of this, Arusha town was founded, initially as a European administrative post harboring Asian traders; the African influx that followed was heavily recruited from outside Mount Meru, with Chagga and "Swahili" the dominant elements. The Meru were merely the tenth largest African group in the town, and the Arusha only third, with less than 10 percent of the population, in 1957. Thus both urban and rural Arusha became a zone of multiple conflict, pitting immigrants against Africans, rural Arusha against rural Meru, urban Chagga and Swahili Africans against rural Meru and Arusha, Chagga against Swahili in town. It is thus not surprising that ethnicity was unusually salient, by Tanzanian standards, in TANU politics in Arusha. At the same time, the impact of this urban-rural social field was limited to the narrow confines of Arusha town and Mount Meru and did not have broader repercussions. It stands out as the exception to the norm of low ethnic temperature to socio-political competition in Tanzania.[51]

In Uganda, delineation of ethnic social fields in the new towns is somewhat more salient than in Tanzania but has not been of comparable intensity to Zaire or Nigeria. The small scale of the towns has been a major factor in confining the influence of urban-defined communal competition. Also, some unusual aspects of the social composition of the two largest communities, Kampala and Jinja, have diluted the impact of this factor.

Kampala, estimated at 331,000 in 1970,[52] had a dual origin. The initial nucleus, Mengo, was the site of the main royal compound at the moment of British occupation. Kampala was an adjoining hill on which

51. P. H. Gulliver, *Social control in an African Society:A Study of the Arusha* (Boston: Boston University Press, 1963); Lionel Cliffe and Paul Puritt, "Arusha," in Cliffe, *One Party Democracy,* pp. 155-85.

52. Morrison et al., *Black Africa,* p. 367.

Lord Lugard, in 1890, built a fortified position where his guns could command Mengo hill. Other hills became identified with the three religious factions, and three hills became the embryon of a European-Asian commercial center. Kampala-Mengo was thus a twin city, administratively joined only after the Obote coup of 1966. Kampala was an immigrant enclave which gradually attracted an African population serving the labor needs of European and Asian dominated enterprises. Mengo was the royal capital of Buganda, under Ganda administrative control, with land title generally reserved to Ganda. The colonial administrative capital, Entebbe, was located 20 miles distant, to be somewhat removed from the Buganda institutions; only after independence did Kampala become the capital.

Until after World War II, Mengo was an exclusive cultural preserve of the Ganda. Kampala probably had an African majority but was regarded as a township catering to the needs and activities of Europeans and Asians; the African population was of low status and regarded as transient. Indeed, a study published on the eve of independence found that less than 20 percent of the African workers in Kampala had been there as long as five years; this inquiry served as the basis for a more general theory that urban Africans were essentially transitory migrants without lasting commitment to town residence, and thus did not crystallize into a proletarian subculture.[53] The essential contours of cultural politics in Kampala were suggested by a study of a tobacco factory by the same author; the stable element in the work force was overwhelmingly Ganda and Luo (from Kenya), as revealed in Table 7.2. Taking Kampala-Mengo as a whole, Ganda, in 1959, were 48.8 percent, Luo 7.2 (with an additional 3.7 percent of other western Kenyans), and Toro 7.6 percent; all others were less than 4 percent.[54]

With independence, some important transformations occurred. A national political and administrative elite, not tied to Buganda institutions, became prominent. Non-Ganda did not really become politically important until 1960; within the territorial civil service, the Ganda pre-eminence had been pronounced. Further, as late as 1959, there were only 27 Africans in the higher grades, as Table 7.1 showed. The European and Asian hegemony in Kampala rapidly eroded and wholly vanished in 1972 with the expulsion of the Asians and concurrent withdrawal of the majority of the Europeans. With the fusion of Mengo into

53. Walter Elkan, *Migrants and Proletarians* (London: Oxford University Press, 1960), pp. 1-3 and passim.

54. David John Parkin, "Social Structure and Social Change in a Tribally Heterogeneous East African City Ward" (Ph.D. diss., University of London, 1965), p. 22. This study has since been published as *Neighbors and Nationals in an African City Ward* (Berkeley: University of California Press, 1969).

Kampala, the institutional dominance of the Ganda among the African population came to an end.

Table 7.2.—Ethnic Composition of East African Tobacco Company Kampala Factory, 1956

Ethnic group	% of all employees	% of workers with over 3 yrs. service	% of workers with over 5 yrs. service
Ganda	26	54	53
Nkole	21	4	2
Rwanda	12	7	3
Kiga	4	3	2
Luo	10	25	35
Other	27	7	5

Source: W. Elkan, *An African Labour Force,* East African Studies no. 7 (Kampala: East African Institute of Social Research, 1956) p. 8.

Until this point, however, the supremacy of the Ganda was an unchallengeable premise. So secure was their primacy that Ganda identity was not much shaped by the urban context; there was no Ganda association, for example. Parkin develops from the sharp contrast between diffuseness of Ganda urban structures and solidarity and the specificity and high organization of Luo groups, the interesting hypothesis that segmental rural systems give rise to more intense levels of urban social organization. His argument bears quotation:

Solidarity does of course obtain between members of the centralized Bantu tribes, but, in the absence of an agnatic principle strong enough to delineate and specify groups clearly, it is not internally differentiated and is generally less intense. A certain diffuse solidarity exists among the Ganda in Kampala concerning help in getting jobs. It reflects a reaction on their part to the large numbers of "foreigners" employed in Kampala for whose clerical and skilled positions larger numbers of Ganda are competing. Again, it appears that there is a Buganda-wide solidarity with respect to the position of the Kabaka. Since, however, this does not give rise to the common binding interests of smaller groups of kin and clan within the collectivity and so lacks the pyramidically constituted solidarity of the segmentary lineage societies, it is unlikely to affect much the behavior of the ordinary urban migrant.[55]

The fact that the second socially influential group in Kampala, and main competitors within the urban social field, were Luo—and thus foreign Africans—decisively affected perceptions, especially as territorial politics became salient. The Luo were in an exceedingly precarious position, and the avenue of political mobilization of ethnicity was foreclosed. They

55. Parkin, "Social Structure and Social Change," pp. 141-42.

did find an outlet in active participation in the trade union movement—indeed, dominated its leadership for years—but this, too, was a vulnerable role. It was not tolerable to independent Ugandan governments that a sensitive organizational resource such as the unions could be in the hands of outsiders; the unions were compelled to merge under the tutelage of the Ministry of Labor.[56]

Within the frame of these general ethnic categories, one must always keep in mind the fluidity of behavior and import of situational selection of reference groups. Parkin extracts from his field notes an intriguing illustration from two successive dyadic interactions, which exhibit no less than eleven reference categories:

A Kisii [Kenya Bantu] commiserated with a semi-skilled Luo in Swahili about the discrimination in employment against Kenyans in Kampala. Together they blamed members of the local tribe, the Ganda, for this discrimination. Next day the Kisii went to the house of an influential Soga, who had a temporary Ganda wife, to ask him in Luganda if he could get him a job as a messenger in the Post Office where he [the Soga] worked as a clerk. The Kisii stressed the fact that he was a Muntu [singular of Bantu] and urged the Soga to regard this as being more important than his not being a Ugandan.[57]

In each case, identity was important to the interaction; again we find illustrated the importance of multiplicity of ethnic roles.

The second largest city in Uganda, Jinja, has grown very swiftly to an estimated 1970 population of 100,000.[58] As recently as 1948, Jinja was a sleepy administrative headquarters for Busoga district, with 8,400 inhabitants. Its social parameters were transformed by the construction beginning in 1949 of the Owen Falls dam, where the Nile emerges from Lake Victoria. The abundant power produced by this project made of Jinja a major center for industrial development, and swiftly attracted a labor force which greatly diversified its populace. In 1948, when the rapid growth began, the population was 61 percent Asian and 12 percent European. Today it is overwhelmingly African.

In 1951, when the last major monograph on Jinja was completed, Soga were 30.5 percent of the African populace, with Ganda coming next with 16.3 percent. Kenyans, mainly Luo, were 19.1 percent; all other groups were less than 6 percent. The Soga dominated the local institutions and continued to do so in 1966, when I visited Jinja. Soga and Ganda tended

56. Roger Scott, *The Development of Trade Unions in Uganda* (Nairobi: East African Publishing House, 1966).

57. Parkin, "Social Structure and Social Change," p. 61. On Kampala, see also A. W. Southall and P. C. W. Gutkind, *Townsmen in the Making*, East African Studies no. 9 (Kampala: East African Institute of Social Research, 1957); on Mengo, see Gutkind, *The Royal Capital of Buganda* (The Hague: Mouton, 1963).

58. Morrison et al., *Black Africa*, p. 367.

to coalesce against "foreigners"; Buganda began just across the Nile bridge from Jinja. As in Kampala, the Ganda, Soga, and Luo were the most stable groupings, with Luo limited in the political resources accessible for collective pursuit of social objectives.[59]

The third largest town, Mbale, had a 1969 population of only 23,539; in 1959, this had been only 8,433. It happened to be situated at the ethnic frontier of the Gisu and Gwere, both of whom laid claim to it. The town served both Bukedi and Budisu districts as an administrative seat, a source of great tension between them. However, the dispute was conducted by political elites at the district level and reflected rivalries between them; the town was the object of conflict rather than the generator of it. At the time this dispute was at its peak, in the late 1950s, the Gisu were only 26 percent of the population, and the Gwere 6 percent; roughly half were Europeans and Asians. Within the urban social system itself, an inquiry in the mid-1960s found that, although social relations were communally segmented at the mass level, among the elites leisure networks were founded mainly on shared occupational role and social status.[60] Other towns were, almost without exception, not only small but relatively homogeneous in their African population.

Urbanization in Uganda, to all intents and purposes, refers to Kampala and Jinja. The sociological weight of the immigrant communities and anamolous role of Kenyan Luos as the most significant socially competitive group with the local population failed to offer ethnic entrepreneurs any incentive for cultural mobilization. In the Kampala case, the urban field did not shape the concept of Ganda identity; rather the urban role of the Ganda was oriented toward the Kabaka-centered cultural ideology which preceded urban development. Probably the most important confrontation pits Ganda against the national elite (which includes a number of Ganda) whose orbit is defined by the central institutions of the state; this was made overt by the Buganda ultimatum in May 1966 to the Obote government to vacate its territory. Certainly elite persons from outside Buganda are quite conscious of their vulnerability in an atmosphere of polarization and crisis. Although the nature of the urban field was not positively integrative, as was the Tanzanian case, it did not define communal conflict.

59. Cyril and Rhona Sofer, *Jinja Transformed* (Kampala: East African Institute of Social Research 1955).

60. David Jacobsen, "Stratification and Nationalism in Uganda," *Journal of Asian and African Studies*, VI, nos. 3-4 (July-October 1971), 217-25. On the dispute over Mbale, see Uganda Protectorate, *Report of the Commission Appointed to Review the Boundary between the Districts of Bugisu and Bukedi* (Entebbe: Government Printer, 1962).

POLITICAL SEQUENCES IN DECOLONIZATION

We now turn to sequences of politics and to the impact of the political arena upon the parameters of pluralism. Three political phases may be distinguished, which cumulatively are a serviceable résumé of modern politics. The first political moment lay in the devising of a decolonization strategy by the colonizer at a time when the initiative still lay in metropolitan hands; the second phase is the political formula negotiated between nationalist elites and the withdrawing power; and the third conjuncture lies in the post-independence transformation of political structures and the distribution of power.

The decolonization strategy nurtured by the British was strikingly different in the two instances; the blueprint for Tanzania was a multiracial partnership, while Uganda was to be a united African state. Paradoxically, the promotion of multiracialism facilitated the consolidation of integrated African nationalism, while the moral engagement for African unity in Uganda inadvertently fostered disunity.

In 1953, only eight years before independence but at a time when it was still assumed to be decades away, the idea of racial parity as the cornerstone for the eventual Tanzanian polity became official doctrine. Despite their enormous numerical disparities, the three races—European, Asian, and African—were conceptualized as pillars of equal socioeconomic solidity upon which the territorial community might rest. The following year, African political opinion acquired a structural base—through the foundation of TANU—and a leader, in Julius Nyerere. The TANU riposte to multiracialism was African nationalism and official nonracialism. However inevitable the triumph of the TANU formula seems in retrospect, it is important to recollect that the currents of "multiracialism" were in flood tide at that point and the outcome by no means appeared foreordained to the participants at that moment. The colonial government sponsored the launching of the United Tanganyika Party in 1956, as an organ for the imposition of multiracialism. An ingenious electoral system was devised for the first elections in 1958; a restricted franchise limited the number of African voters but enfranchised most Asians and all Europeans. Each racial group was allocated an equal number of seats, but each candidate had to seek votes among all races.

After some agonizing, TANU decided to participate in the elections and solicited European and Asian candidates to stand under its banners, although at that point TANU membership was restricted to Africans. The result was a striking TANU victory, even within the limitations of the parity premise. TANU's political supremacy was thus assured in a context where the competitive reference points for Africans were the Asian and European communities. On the one hand, the constraint imposed on TANU to recruit European and Asian allies lent credibility to its nonracial theses. On the other, African unity became an absolute imperative to avert entrenchment of racial privilege and permanent minoritization of Africans on the pretext they were only one race of three. This unity was facilitated by the predisposing factors in the contours of communalism discussed earlier. During 1959, the colonial government officially abandoned its multiracialism theses, and universal suffrage common roll elections were slated for 1960 to define the successors to the political kingdom. TANU hegemony was so well established in its triumph over racial parity that in 58 of the 71 seats its candidates were unopposed. Although the effortless triumph thus achieved left in its wake a degree of sloth and lethargy in the party structures, it did avert the mobilization of cultural solidarities which attended competitive elections so frequently in Africa and Asia.

In Uganda, the points of departure were the foundation of the first nationalist party, the Uganda National Congress (UNC), and arrival of Sir Andrew Cohen as governor with a decolonization mandate, both in 1952. The UNC, which grew out of the Uganda Federation of African Farmers, was led by Ganda but did not seek to build upon the nuclei established in Busoga, Bukedi, Teso, and Lango by the UFAF. Its most prominent leaders, I. K. Musazi and J. W. Kiwanuka, were at that time thinking in territorial terms and certainly were not instruments of the royalist group in Buganda; in the very different context of 1962, both did rally to the party of Ganda subnationalism. Governor Cohen arrived with the assumption that Uganda was the most "advanced" of the East African territories and closest to the political maturity which would merit transfer of power. A commission of inquiry was at once appointed, which argued that the logic of the district-based structure of African political involvement—wherein African councils were encouraged at the kingdom or district level, but the central institutions were viewed as an entirely British frame—implied an unworkable "federation of native states." The commission echoed Governor Cohen's desire for steps toward converting the territorial administration into an executive responsive to African opinion reflected by elected representatives to a national legislature.[61]

Before the Cohen master plan could gain momentum, a crisis arose which brought him into direct conflict with Buganda. A Nairobi speech by the colonial secretary in July 1953 referred to the desirability of an East African Federation, anathema to Buganda for decades as a device

61. C. A. G. Wallis, *Report of an Inquiry into African Local Government in the Protectorate of Uganda* (Wallis Report), (Entebbe: Government Printer, 1953).

to subordinate the kingdom, as well as the rest of the country, to the domination of Kenya's clamorous White settlers. Although the East African Federation proposal was quickly repudiated, Buganda remained equally suspicious of Governor Cohen's schemes for a unified Uganda; to the Buganda leadership, creation of African central institutions superior to Buganda represented a demotion for the kingdom and violated the spirit of the 1900 agreement. The Kabaka and the Buganda legislative council refused to name representatives for a central legislative council, as first urged, then directed, by Governor Cohen, and the impasse was complete. The governor, encouraged by some evidence of hostility to the young Kabaka Mutesa II—felt by many to be overly fond of Mediterranean beaches, hunting trips, and fast automobiles—tried to slice through impasse by deposing and deporting the Kabaka.

The consequences of this confrontation were incalculable. The Kabaka, in his autobiography, maintains that his sister Alice died of the shock of the news, and thousands attended her funeral. "The most educated of the young." he wrote, "who thought they had left behind their tribal life, found themselves obscurely unhappy and at a loss. Friendship with the most sympathetic Europeans had to be suspended."[62] A perhaps more objective observer, Audrey Richards, gives vivid description of the trauma of this event:

> It is difficult for an onlooker to describe the sense of shock in the capital of Buganda. Work was at an end; people stood in knots at road junctions, mostly silent and staring; women sat at their house doors weeping. Girl interviewers employed by the East African Institute of Social Research spoilt their questionnaires by the tears that fell on them and they had to be let off work. Educated men were angry, and even previous critics of the Kabaka were violent in their denunciation of Protectorate Government.[63]

The result of this operation was the massive cultural mobilization of Buganda around the symbols of monarchy, the refurbishing of the tarnished credentials of Mutesa II, and an even more complex impasse. In 1955, after prolonged negotiations the Kabaka was permitted to return, with enhanced autonomy for Buganda. Following his return, a purge of the Buganda government ensued, with "disloyal" chiefs replaced by "king's men." Political construction could not really proceed at the center until the Buganda problem was resolved; neither could it be held up in other districts while awaiting this day. Thus during this period, "native administrations" were converted into elected district councils.

The UNC was placed in a grave dilemma by the Ganda content of this crisis. If the party ignored the dispute, it placed itself beyond

62. Mutesa, *Desecration of My Kingdom*, p. 123.
63. Fallers, *The King's Men*, p. 322.

the pale in Buganda. But if it made the royal deportation its main issue, it subordinated the national orientations of the movement to what was essentially a Buganda issue. No satisfactory resolution was found, and the initial momentum was simply lost during this period. Among the consequences of this sequence was the separate emergence in each district arena of a new political elite; in several cases, these leaders were associated with the UNC, but the party was simply unable to surmount the dilemmas of the crisis and provide central direction. As a result, the frame of reference of the district politicians was the ethnic district. A less obvious implication of the sequence was the politization of complex cleavages within the district—emergence as political spokesman for a district did not occur without an intense struggle, which in one district after another gave rise to regional, clan, ethnic, and religious conflicts, which for the most part had not previously been of high saliency.

In a complex dialectic, cultural division became institutionalized at the national level. In 1956, with the patronage and support of the Catholic hierarchy, the Democratic Party was launched, conceived in the mold of European and Latin American Christian Democratic parties. Despite the de facto support which Protestant evangelical effort had received over the years, Catholics were somewhat more numerous than Protestants; they were 34.5 percent of the population, as opposed to 28.2 percent Protestant. The pervasive sense that Catholics were unfairly treated in the distribution of government posts provided a ready rallying point.

A bewildering series of parties had followed each other into ephemeral flowering in the 1950s, with a common theme of Ganda leadership. In 1960, the non-Ganda—and non-Catholic—political elite which had emerged through district-based politics coalesced to form the Uganda Peoples Congress (UPC), a party which tapped the deep-rooted resentment of Ganda hegemony, explicitly invoked the political language of territorial African nationalism, and implicitly conveyed Protestant associations. In 1961, the picture was completed by the emergence of a political movement expressing Ganda cultural subnationalism, the Kabaka Yekka (the Kabaka alone).

The first territorial elections, held in 1958, well reflected the multiple dilemmas of decolonization. Although in 1955 Ganda representatives had asked that their representatives to a legislative council be elected, in 1957, when it was proposed to extend this principle to the entire country, Buganda changed its mind and boycotted the balloting. The Ganda leaders were becoming increasingly apprehensive of subordination to central institutions which it was clear they could not dominate; the 1900 treaty was dusted off as buttress for the claim that the Kabaka dealt directly with Her Majesty's Government and not through intermediaries. Local conflicts in two other districts—Ankole and Bugisu—prevented voting there, and one—Karamoja—was felt to be too undeveloped for meaningful elections. Thus the voting was for only ten seats, in nine districts.

The election boycott in the very heart of the country limited their visibility and impact. The only effective national party was the DP, whose mobilization of Catholic grievance politicized the religious line of conflict. But the campaign as a whole lacked a central focus; the district races were totally compartmentalized. Although the theme of religious division was common, it was separately enacted on each district stage; in four of the ten races, religion was paramount, and in three others important.[64]

Elected Africans were still a minority in the new legislative council; the protectorate government was committed to a fully elected parliament in 1961. A constitutional commission was established without Ganda participation, and it proposed that a unitary state should issue from the 1961 elections. The impasse was again complete. Buganda returned to its barricades; in the Kabaka's words, the proposals "returned us to the familiar position of joining a body that could control us."[65] Buganda demands were very far-reaching: a separate army and right to make its own military alliances, control over all police operating in Buganda, a separate judiciary from which no appeal to any other Uganda court was permitted, exclusive licensing of all commerce and industry in Buganda, and control over all educational institutions in Buganda except Mekerere University College.[66] When both British and Africans from other parts of Uganda refused to countenance this dismemberment of the territory, the Buganda legislature resolved, on 30 December 1960, that its secession would take effect the following day. When this unilateral declaration was studiously ignored by all and sundry, Buganda announced that it would boycott the 1961 elections.

The 1961 elections, which at the time were assumed to be, quite possibly, a direct prelude to independence, contained two distinct yet interactive bases of division: Catholic (DP) versus non-Catholic (UPC), and Ganda versus non-Ganda. Outside of Buganda, perception of the structure of political competition was dominated by the religious factor seemingly subsumed in the DP-UPC contest. The importance of religious identity in circumscribing party affiliation is well described by a Ugandan scholar from West Nile district, where the religious cleavage was espec-

64. Martin Lowenkopf, "The 1958 Elections in Uganda," typescript.
65. Mutesa, *Desecration of My Kingdom,* p. 158.
66. Gukiina, *Uganda,* p. 104.

ially deep; as a Catholic who backed the UPC, he found himself regarded as a political deviant:

> I constituted a kind of constant irritation to argumentation; and much time was usually spent especially during home vacations in friendly political argumentation and mutual denunciations of their political party, the Democratic Party, and of my party. In this way I came to see, perhaps better than many people, certainly better than my own party colleagues who, when the pace of political contest quickened, usually did not consort with them (Catholics), not only the depth and breadth of the political feelings of these friends, but also the crucial role of the Church they adhered to in arousing and promoting these feelings.[67]

At the same time, examined constituency by constituency, a complex mosaic of local factions appears. Although nearly all DP candidates were Catholic, not all aspirant Catholic politicos enlisted under the DP banners. In Madi and West Nile, important Catholic figures ran for the UPC. In Bugisu and Sebei, where religion as an orienting principle of politics was more diffuse, the DP and UPC labels became badges of opportunity readily exchangeable as circumstance dictated.[68]

In Buganda, the axes of conflict intersected; retrospectively, outcomes always seem predetermined, but they were by no means viewed as certain by contemporary observers. The UPC, as an anti-Ganda coalition, could hardly hope to challenge the Buganda royalists on their home turf; however, this inhibition did not extend to the DP, whose national leader, Benedicto Kiwanuka, was a Ganda. With 50 percent of Buganda Catholic, and many resentful of Protestant domination of the royal establishment, the DP appeared to have some prospects. In the event, however, the moral suasion—and perhaps social intimidation—of the cultural subnationalism appeal, linked to the powerful symbols of the throne, triumphed. The boycott order, transmitted through the chiefly hierarchy, totally eclipsed the contrasting messages diffused through Catholic channels; less than 2 percent of eligible Buganda voters went to the polls. However, the tiny fraction that did vote were moved by the contrary cultural imperative; they backed the DP candidates, with the result that, on an infinitesimal vote, the DP was credited with 20 of 21 Buganda seats. Elsewhere, with the Catholic and Protestant fractions of the population over sixteen almost evenly divided (27.7 to 28.5 percent), the UPC com-

---

67. Gingyera-Pinycwa, "Some Dimensions of the Pre-Independence Politics in Uganda," p. 11.

68. The most useful summary of political dynamics at the district level is contained in a series of district government and politics monographs edited by Nelson Kasfir, Michael Davies, and Emory Bundy, scheduled for publication by Oxford University Press.

manded 50.1 percent of the vote and 30 seats, while the DP finished with 41.5 percent and 24 seats.[69]

The consequences of these elections restructured political reality for all major actors. Overall, the DP paradoxically had a parliamentary majority, even though their Buganda seats had come by the boycott fluke, and they ran behind the UPC elsewhere. This brought to power the first African prime minister, the Ganda DP leader Benedicto Kiwanuka. To many Ganda, the Kiwanuka government was an intolerable affront; the Ganda Kiwanuka placed himself above the Kabaka, making himself a cultural apostate. According to the Kabaka, Kiwanuka as prime minister "was puffed up with pride and success. . . . it was our vision of life under such a government as the worst of all possible futures that led us astray."[70] The parameters of political choice for Buganda were now fixed by some narrow constraints: there was no sympathy, either among the British or the other Ugandans, for the separatist position. Buganda could not expect to dominate territorial politics; Buganda's interests could only be protected by alliance with forces outside the kingdom. On the positive side, from a Buganda perspective the effectiveness of the boycott had demonstrated both to Ganda and others the potency of the neotraditional political communications network emanating from the throne, and the mobilizing force of cultural subnationalism.

To other major participants, options were also severely limited. The political mobilization of religious cleavage, with proportions closely divided, made it extremely improbable that either DP or UPC could sweep the boards. The DP was too closely linked with its Catholic sponsors to extend its appeal beyond that base; yet it was sufficiently well-endowed with efficacious communications channels, a solid cadre of militant organizers in the Catholic school teachers, and a reservoir of relative deprivation sentiment to preempt large-scale UPC penetration of its cultural clientele. With the British still in control of the administration outside Buganda, the walls of cultural solidarity could not be breached through patronage or coercion; in Buganda, however, the 1955 agreement had involved important devolution of power to the Kabaka's government, which could now be turned to the tasks of electoral organization. Independence was blocked by the Buganda impasse; the 1961 elections

69. Welbourn, *Religion and Politics in Uganda*, p. 22. Other valuable summaries of politics in this phase are found in D.A. Low, "Political Parties in Uganda 1949-1962," reprinted in his *Buganda in Modern History*, pp. 167-226; Donald Rothchild and Michael Rogin, "Uganda," in Gwendolen M. Carter (ed.), *National Unity and Regionalism in Eight African States*, pp. 337-440.

70. Mutesa, *Desecration of My Kingdom,* p. 160.

made clear that neither the UPC nor the DP could lift the Buganda mortgage by electorally defeating the linked forces of Ganda cultural subnationalism bound to its royal symbols, and the patronage-disposing, social coercion-wielding structures of the largely autonomous kingdom government.

Thus, the politics of decolonization reduced to a three-person game conducted in a communally defined arena. Whereas the political arena in Tanzania had facilitated an integrative, nationally oriented movement of African solidarity, political leaders in Uganda were forced by the implacable logic of cultural arithmetic into coalition-building. The three-actor model was not wholly symmetrical; the DP had been locked in direct electoral combat, with a high degree of communal partisanship, with both other actors. Buganda and the UPC, however, had not directly confronted each other. The solution, then, was an alliance between these two uneasy partners. Buganda was granted a federal status with a significant measure of autonomy, and agreed for its part to participate in a final set of elections in 1962 designed to lead directly to independence.

The 1962 elections confirmed the cultural contours which had emerged in 1961. Outside of Buganda, the UPC polled 52.4 percent, and won 33 seats; the DP, with 45.5 percent, took 22 seats. The near-stability of the aggregates concealed some local shifts which occurred because of particular circumstances, but the changes tended to cancel each other out. Moreover, most of the constituencies had bitterly contested elections, with the religious theme cross-cutting sectional, subethnic, and other factional patterns. In Buganda, on the other hand, the elections were a massive expression of cultural solidarity. Buganda had won the right to have its parliamentary elections chosen by indirect election, so the actual balloting was for the Buganda legislature. KY took 63 of 66 seats, with the votes of 80.5 percent of those registered; 9.6 percent voted for the DP, and 9.7 percent stayed home from the polls. The three seats which were lost were in areas annexed from Bunyoro at the time of colonial penetration, where the majority of the population were Nyoro, not Ganda. Electoral choice was clearly structured in terms of cultural subnationalism in Buganda; "Do you love the Kabaka?" the chiefs asked the voters they registered.[71] The KY electoral symbol was a chair—transparent to all as a representation of the throne. To "love the Kabaka," within the constellation of Ganda symbols of identity, was an act of cultural self-affirmation. The observations of Buganda's leading young Muslim intellectual, a radical nationalist in his undergraduate days, Abu Mayanja, are instructive:

71. Welbourn, *Religion and Politics in Uganda*, p. 26.

One of the brightest features of the Kabaka Yekka victory is that it dealt what I should like to think was a fatal blow at the ugly head of religion in politics. Until the Kabaka Yekka victory, even a person as normally reasonable as myself used to regard every Roman Catholic as a member of the Democratic Party or a DP sympathizer until he proved the contrary. The Roman Catholic church entered the Lukiko election with a zeal and a relish and a determination which left most of us really aghast. But as the poll showed, most Roman Catholics, including, by the way, a few nuns and priests, voted Kabaka Yekka and not for the Democratic party.[72]

In appreciating the pattern of cultural mobilization produced by the electoral process and party competition in the terminal colonial years, it is of fundamental import to note the radically different structure of communal perceptions within and without Buganda. For Buganda, the dominant paradigm was cultural threat. The innermost symbols of identity, above all the Kabaka, were under attack. The superiority of status which Buganda had come to assume as a matter of right now tottered under the impact of the new principles of universal suffrage and majority rule. It had always sufficed in the past to rely upon the 1900 agreement and the social preeminence of Ganda elites; these were now to be swept aside by an African government whose sources of power and legitimacy came from a demographic, not a sociological, majority. Threat is a compelling mobilizer of identity; Buganda faced an imperative of unity and had, through its autonomy, through its purged chiefly hierarchy, and through the cultural force of its identity symbols, the means of achieving it.

Elsewhere, for the most part, no immediate threat was posed to the district-based ethnic identities; the structure of the situation did not call for the mobilization of all Teso, all Langi, all Acholi. Rather, the competition—bitter and partisan—took place within the districts, both for control of district councils and for parliamentary seats. The logic of internal district competition politicized, not the incorporative district identities which had been the building blocks of colonial administration, but lines of division either cross-cutting—like religion— or internal to them—like subdistrict levels of ethnicity. Here we again see at work the situational basis of identity, the multilayered and fluid character of ethnicity in most of Uganda, which did not compare with Buganda in the high degree of ideologization of cultural solidarity or the stability and clarity of its identity symbols.

The importance of the district arena was underlined by secession movements by groups fearful of minority status. In Sebei, the approach

72. C. J. Gertzel, "New Government in Uganda," *Africa Report* (May 1962), p. 8, quoted in Gukiina, *Uganda*, p. 84.

of independence created apprehensions that, within the district frame, the Sebei would be locked into a permanent minority role in Bugisu district, where they were a mere 35,000 against 275,000 Gisu. Near-complete cultural solidarity was generated behind Y. K. Chemonges, who proposed the solution of local secession, to form a homogeneous Sebei district. Although initially elected on the UPC slate, he readily crossed the carpet under the brief Kiwanuka regime in return for recognition of his district. He was then re-elected by an equally large majority on the DP ticket in 1962, only to cross the carpet again when the UPC/KY coalition came to power; Sebei cultural interests could best be defended by aligning with the winning team nationally.[73] In Toro district, imminent independence posed a comparable threat to Konjo and Amba on the Ruwenzori mountains, who could cite convincing evidence of discrimination by the Toro local government. In this instance, the central government would not accede to the separate district demand, which led to the proclamation of a secessionist Rwenzururu state. The remoteness of the mountain strongholds of the Konjo, in particular, made it impossible for the Uganda army to wholly dismantle this challenge to its exercise of territorial sovereignty, although central authority was restored over the more accessible zones.[74]

Thus, in Tanzania and Uganda we find quite different formulas for independence. Self-rule came to Tanzania with nonracial African nationalism in unchallenged ascendancy. The allocation of not only parliamentary constituencies, but important ministries to Europeans and Asians by TANU permitted the tensions of the "multiracialism" phase of decolonization to slip quietly away. Although the long-run role of both immigrant communities is peripheral at best and their numbers are dwindling, the symbolic reassurance provided by their symbolic incorporation into the TANU fold allayed immediate fears and anxieties. At the same time, the integrative legacy of the linked struggle against colonialism and "multiracialism" remained.

TANU, it is true, was a less muscular organism than its overwhelming success suggested, and Nyerere resigned as prime minister immediately after independence to devote himself wholly for a number of months to invigorating this flabby mechanism. However, the sanctity of its doctrines of national integration were not open to real challenge; although

73. On Sebei politics, see my chapter in the forthcoming Kasfir-Davies-Bundy volume on district politics in Uganda.

74. Detailed accounts of the Rwenzururu movement may be found in Kasfir, "Controlling Ethnicity in Ugandan Politics," pp. 151-61, and also in his Uganda chapter in Olorunsola, *The Politics of Cultural Sub-Nationalism in Africa*, pp. 97-103; see also Martin Doornbos, "Kumanyana and Rwenzururu: Two Responses to Ethnic Inequality," in Rotberg and Mazrui, *Protest and Power in Black Africa*, 1088-136; Tom Stacey, *Summons to Ruwenzori* (London: Secker and Warburg, 1965).

in the process of mobilization of support it had made occasional use of ethnic or religious organizations, by 1961 it was in a position to denounce such associations and threaten to ban them if they sought to act as communal pressure groups.[75] Although members of Parliament had to be attentive to questions of regional allocations and delivering tangible development benefits to their followings, they were not beholden to mobilized ethnicity per se. The central leadership of the party was even less so; cultural pluralism was not a constant reference point in policy formulation and conflict resolution among the national political elite.

Partly because there was no delicate cultural equilibrium to protect, it was possible to incorporate the offshore islands of Zanzibar following the revolution which destroyed the Arab oligarchy in January 1964. The shared commitment to Swahili culture was an important facilitating factor. At the same time, Nyerere was able to accord Zanzibar one-quarter of the parliamentary seats, far in excess of its demographic entitlement, and distribute several key ministerial portfolios without compromising TANU's effectiveness—despite the fact that the Zanzibaris were insistent on preserving the separate identity of their own political movement, the Afro-Shirazi party, and an extraordinary degree of internal autonomy on the islands. Had the structure of national politics in mainland Tanzania been founded upon culturally based factions and coalitions, the infusion of a substantial block of Zanzibaris into the interplay of cultural segments would almost certainly have been profoundly destabilizing and difficult to absorb.

POST-INDEPENDENCE POLITICAL FORMULAS

In Uganda, the independence political formula required an uneasy marriage between incompatible partners. The UPC and KY formed the government which brought the ritual lowering of the Union Jack in October 1962; Milton Obote, UPC leader, became prime minister and in 1963 forced upon a disgruntled party investiture of the Kabaka as chief of state—conveying the important symbolism, to Buganda, that there was no man higher than the Kabaka. The tensions which this coalition was slated to experience were immediately forecast, when the five KY members of Obote's fifteen-member cabinet went straight upon their designation to the Kabaka to undergo a ritual of fealty. Uganda newspapers carried the photographs of this extraordinary scene, where the five ministers (including one Englishman) were prostrate on the floor

75. Henry Bienen, *Tanzania: Party Transformation and Economic Development* (Princeton: Princeton University Press, 1967), pp. 68-70.

before the Kabaka; this, of course, was prior to Mutesa II's designation as chief of state.[76]

In the 1962-66 period, Uganda politics were characterized by an important dispersal of political resources into several arenas of allocation. At the central level, ultimate legitimacy, by Westminster precepts, resided in the national parliament, with its triangular pattern of competition(UPC-KY-DP). The cabinet which issued from the UPC-KY alliance ruled over a central bureaucracy—still primarily expatriate at the moment of the lowering of the flag but rapidly Africanized—which extended its reach into the hinterland through provincial and district administrative services. Outputs meaningful to the population at large—schools, dispensaries, roads—were filtered through this structure and shaped to an important extent by it. The central administration had no competitors at the provincial level (except for Buganda, of provincial rather than district scale), but at the district level its capillaries intertwined and competed with the substantial powers exercised by local government. It will be recalled that the first steps in political development had been taken through establishment of elected district councils to gradually assume these responsibilities, which include such important prerogatives as primary education, water supplies, markets, and local licensing. The districts had, as a legacy of the emulate-Buganda era of status-assertion, acquired ceremonial heads and also political secretaries-general, responsible to a majority in the district council. At the height of the phase of devolution of prerogatives to the districts, the councils had acquired the right to appoint the microbureaucracy of chiefs who were the farthest ramifications of the political system in its penetration of the rural periphery, charged with collection of taxes, maintenance of law and order, and the key, face-to-face level of administrative linkage with the rural mass of the population.[77] There was no central government presence, except for police forces, in Buganda.

The vocabulary of political analysis usually took into account only the central parliamentary arena of politics. In fact, because political resources in the districts were at that point significant, the national images were very incomplete and even misleading. The interactions between levels and arenas were complex and afforded ample room for maneuver between competing factions. Members of parliament and district secretaries-general were both partner spokesmen for the same ethnic-regional interest and competitors for the same

76. Gukiina, *Uganda*, p. 113.

77. A particularly valuable summary of local governance may be found in S. Griffith, "Local Politicians and National Policies: The Secretaries-General of Uganda" (B. Phil. diss., Christ Church, Oxford, 1969).

support base. Obote and his opponents could seek access points to local supports both through the MP and through the secretaries-general.

Only once during these first four years of independence did a near-crisis arise, when a final resolution was found to the "lost counties" issue in 1964. This involved part of the area annexed by Buganda from Bunyoro at the beginning of the colonial period, where the bulk of the populace had remained culturally Nyoro. The claim for restitution dominated all other issues in Bunyoro, a district which defected to the DP in 1962 in protest over Obote's alliance with Buganda. With consummate skill, Obote arranged for a referendum to determine the future of the two disputed counties. Ethnic arithmetic left no doubt as to the outcome, but Buganda, and particularly the neotraditional faction of "king's men," committed its prestige heavily to the issue. Obote had induced a sufficient number of DP and KY MPs to cross the carpet by this time so that the UPC could rule alone, and its alliance with KY was dissolved. Buganda miscalculations on this issue made of the results another stinging humiliation for the kingdom and forced the resignation of the Kabaka's chief minister.

Around the two poles personified by Obote and the Kabaka, shadowy coalitions formed and dissolved. Within Buganda, free of the crisis atmosphere of immediate cultural threat, ongoing patterns of internal conflict reasserted themselves, with divisions of interest and orientation between "king's men," who wanted to control Buganda tightly from the palace through the chiefly network, and "progressives," who wanted a wider distribution of power and privilege within Buganda—but would rally in time of crisis about the cultural symbols. The rapidly growing number of Ganda holding top positions in central ministries and parastatals had a career interest as well as intellectual commitment to a united Uganda. At the lower end of the social scale, the undercurrents of resentment at the entrenched privileges of the chiefly hierarchy continued, as did Catholic and Muslim dissatisfaction over the hegemony of the Protestant establishment. Obote and the UPC tried hard to find in this labyrinth of diffuse conflict a pathway into Buganda—but the trails always doubled back on themselves and led to a dead end.

In late 1965, a group began to take shape with links to the palace, which wove together several ministries and a somewhat larger number of MPs and began extending into the factional beds of district politics. This phantomal coalition acquired the appellation of the "Bantu," as its key operatives were from southern Uganda's Bantu language zone. This was in contradistinction to the growing perception, at the central level, of a "Nilotic" inner council which Obote placed special reliance on. These labels are intriguing; they are not meaningful terms to mass publics, but rather terms developed by linguists and anthropologists to connote analytically perceived commonalities. We would suggest that such abstracted labels could gain currency only in the context of a phase of vague maneuvering when no structured, overt competition—as through elections—is present. The categories filtered through veils of secrecy and rumor; for the political elites, amongst whom interest in the shifting currents was high, these labels brought some apparent order out of great confusion. Ideological and cold war codes were also essayed but obviously failed to capture the meaning of conflict. The main protagonists in these tortuous maneuvers did not signal their moves; only a very few persons had any real idea of precisely what was afoot. Even the derivative, speculative analysis available to the attentive and interested is tongue-tied without vocabulary. In a culturally sensitized environment, there is a high probability that communal taxonomies will be borrowed. There was a very real cultural conflict, pitting Buganda and the central authorities against one another, which underlay the complicated events of late 1965 and early 1966. Interlaced with this conflict was a more immediate cabal, to which Buganda was linked, seeking to oust Obote. However, we would argue that the "Bantu"-"Nilotic" perceptions of the latter were symbolic extrapolations which became social myth. They had too little subjective meaning to mass publics to serve as the basis for ethnic mobilization.

To illustrate the difference as well as linkages between central and local arenas of politics, during this phase when districts remained important foci with a meaningful political resource base, we may use Kigezi District as an example. Kigezi lies in the far southwest of Uganda, snuggled between Rwanda and Zaire. The largest group in the district are the Kiga, who, according to an anthropologist who did field work in the area in the 1930s, had no real sense of collective identity as recently as four decades ago.[78] The two smaller groups are Rwanda and Horohoro, both internally stratified between pastoral overlords (Tutsi and Hima) and sedentary cultivators (Hutu and Iru). Religious conversion was massive in the 1930s; it began to find political expression in 1947—interestingly, at a football game between a Catholic and Protestant secondary school. The highly ritualized conflict of an athletic contest apparently made manifest the latent cleavage. In the 1950s, as competitive politics were introduced in the district, religion and relative representation of the three groups—and strata within them—governed the cognitive codes by which politics was verbalized and perceived. The entry of political parties powerfully mobilized the religious dimension; at the same

78. Mary Edelman, "African Tribalism: Some Reflections on Uganda," *Political Science Quarterly*, LXXX, no. 3 (September 1965), 368-69.

time, the numerical preponderance of the Kiga meant that only Kiga candidates could aspire to district-wide offices. By 1965, factions had come to be aligned around two leading Kiga personalities: J. Lwamafa, who had been first UPC local chairman, then a successful MP candidate, and later minister of regional administration in the Obote government; and J. Bikangaga, who succeeded Lwamafa as UPC district chairman, and had become constitutional head of Kigezi District. The post of secretary-general was up for contest; the two candidates were Bitwari, of the same clan as Lwamafa and regarded as his political associate; and S. Mpambara, who had left a post in the prime minister's office to return to district politics. Mpambara was regarded as both Bikangaga's candidate and a representative of the prime minister.

In the midst of the conflict, Bitwari's supporters held a feast in his honor, at which a cow said to be stolen from Bikangaga was slaughtered. On the basis of this audacious insult to the ceremonial district head, Bikangaga, the feasters were labelled "Banyama," or meat-eaters; swiftly, by extension, the label came to be applied to all Bitwari (and Lwamafa) supporters. The Bikangaga-Mpambara faction came to be known as "Baboga," or vegetarians. Later in 1965, as the "Bantu" clique began to enter informal discourse at the central level, Lwamafa and the Banyama were linked to it. Through their opposition to the Banyama and through Mpambara's links with the prime minister, the Baboga came to be seen as the pro-Obote faction. The Banyama-Baboga division did not correlate with religious cleavage; the DP had faded into the background in district politics.

Thus we can see that the district political arena had its own distinctive patterns of conflict, yet these shifted quite swiftly over time. The structure of conflict in the central arena was important in the overall parameters it set; at the moment when national conflict, outside of Buganda, was dominated by the DP-UPC conflict, local clusters founded upon these labels locked in a bitter struggle, involving an intense level of religious mobilization. When the DP subsided into relative impotence nationally and UPC factionalism interwoven with the Obote-Buganda power contest became the national paradigm, the basis of factionalism within the district shifted. The cultural parameters of the district were, on the one hand, constraints within which external linkages had to operate; on the other, they were of sufficient complexity to permit a number of different alignments. The "Bantu-Nilotic" stereotyping of national conflict had no meaning in the local Kigezi context; all actors were "Bantu," and the "Nilotic" concept was devoid of local reference points.[79]

79. This is based upon the Kigezi chapter in the Kasfir-Davies-Bundy volume and my own research in Kigezi in 1966.

We turn next, then, to the contemporary patterns of interaction of cultural pluralism and national politics. We have described the 1966 confrontation in chapter 5; this marked the end of the independence political formula in Uganda. In Tanzania, there has been no sharp discontinuity, and we may briefly deal with the affirmation of certain trends carrying forward the logic of TANU's integrative commitment.

Tanzania has developed an original formula for optimizing both participation and integration. An institutional frame was devised, which provides a one-party system, but instills a competitive process within the party. Mainland Tanzania is divided into over a hundred single-member constituencies. In the parliamentary elections held each five years, two candidates from within the party—which is open to virtually all—compete. The process of screening candidates to bring the figure down to two is carried on primarily by local party committees and is relatively open. The most eloquent testimonial as to the effectiveness of the electoral device is the remarkable turnover it produced on the first occasion it was employed, in 1965. Of the 81 members of the independence parliament, 31 did not run—in a number of cases in anticipation of the likely outcome. Twelve more failed to secure nomination, including 3 junior ministers. Seventeen incumbents were defeated, including 2 ministers and 6 junior ministers. Only 21 were re-elected, 6 of whom were unopposed.[80] The turnover was less spectacular in the 1970 elections, but the process was again significant in providing a meaningful ritual of politics which involved large numbers in many different roles.

For our purposes, what is noteworthy in this formula is the skill with which legitimacy-building participation is made possible but so structured as not to mobilize cultural pluralism. The election does not offer incentives or provide opportunities for aggregative communal coalitions, as did the balloting in Zaire or Nigeria. Each constituency was a separate universe; neither the structure of the party nor the nature of the campaign induced the stitching together of factional coalitions across constituencies. Within the constituency, localized identities frequently played some part in the outcome; however, this encapsulated segmentation was of little moment at the national level.

Ideology has been given an unusually salient place in the Tanzanian pantheon of values. The major turning point was the adoption of the "Arusha Declaration" in 1967, committing the regime to a strongly egalitarian, rural-oriented socialism.[81] The groups most threatened by Tanzanian socialism are probably the immigrant communities, especially

80. Cliffe, *One Party Democracy*, provides a thorough coverage of this important election.

81. Tanzanian socialism is summarized in Julius K. Nyerere, *Ujamaa: Essays on Socialism* (London: Oxford University Press, 1968).

the Asians. The rigorous egalitarianism of the distinctive Tanzanian version of socialism has certainly had the indirect impact of Africanization of the economy, but without the costs associated with the abrupt expulsion resorted to by President Amin in Uganda. It has encountered a frosty reception from groups such as the Chagga, who had become prosperous in commercial agriculture and trade. A fraction of the Tanzanian elite, who had begun to taste the ambrosia of urban land speculation and rental properties, grumbles ever so softly. But an egalitarian rhetoric with sufficient bite to maintain reasonable credibility can claim credit on its balance sheet for attenuating the sharp social inequalities which are so readily perceived in ethnic terms.

SWAHILI AS INTEGRATIVE VEHICLE

Language has been a crucial agency of integration. Swahili has been an official language from the moment of independence, but the regime commitment goes far beyond passive recognition. In 1967, a National Swahili Council was established to continue the work of promoting the language, developing Swahili literature and enlarging its vocabulary. At the same time, a directive was issued requiring that Swahili be used for all government business and that "unnecessary use" of English was to cease forthwith.[82] Symbolizing this commitment was the translation made by President Nyerere himself of Shakespeare's *Julius Caesar* into Swahili. Mazrui makes the interesting point that socialism ceases to be a European abstraction through invocation of the Swahili term "Ujamaa":

> But say *Ujamaa*, and a whole new world of subtle associations and connotations is suddenly revealed. Nothing could have given Nyerere's socialism a more strikingly African ring than that simple Swahili label which he gave it. Nyerere was using an old Swahili word in a new context. All the subtle associations of bonds of kinship, tribal hospitality, and welfare obligations of the extended family were compressed within that single Swahili expression. . . . No English word could possibly have achieved the same result.[83]

Swahili is at once an instrument of cultural and social integration. Not only does it provide a culturally neutral vehicle of communication, but it permits the conduct of government to be vastly more visible and proximate to the mass of the population. Most African states labor under the enormous burden of carrying on public affairs in a medium

82. Ali A. Mazrui, *Cultural Engineering and Nation-Building in East Africa* (Evanston: Northwestern University Press, 1972), p. 87.
83. Ibid., p. 93.

which to many citizens is arcane and remote. This makes of the elite a quite literal mandarinate, whose monopoly of an esoteric medium symbolizes their social distance from the common citizen.[84] Through the rapid development of a literature, Swahili becomes more than a simple linguistic expedient; it acquires the status of cultural ideology functioning on a national level.

CONFRONTATION WITH BUGANDA

In contrast to the tides of integration within a stable framework in Tanzania, the structure of politics have been transformed beyond recognition in Uganda—without, however, altering the grave strains of cultural pluralism. Following the 1966 coup, Obote sought to centralize the polity and withdraw resources from arenas where cultural conflict had been salient. As in Zaire, district-based political competition was the first target. Elections at this level were halted, the patronage at the disposal of the district council and secretary-general reduced, and the tutelary powers of the district commissioner refurbished. After Amin came to power in 1971, the district councils were abolished altogether, and regional administration became a hierarchical extension of central authority to the periphery. A further step was taken in 1972, when the districts themselves were scrambled, presumably in part to dilute the linkage between administrative entities and the ethnic identity which had grown up around them.

Buganda was the prime target for Obote. The Kabaka, who fled to England after the 1966 confrontation, was not only deposed as president, but also removed as Kabaka. The kingdom was divided into four districts and no longer recognized as a single entity. The "King's men" were removed from office, and the local offices staffed by appointees of the central government. The handsome new building which housed the Buganda Assembly and government offices was made into the headquarters for the ministry of defense. The paraphernalia of monarchy was relegated to the National Museum. Buganda was humiliated—its most precious symbols in exile, under military occupation, or on exhibit as museum trophies. And one should not overlook the sudden unemployment of large numbers of stalwarts formerly on the kingdom payroll.

Many Ganda intellectuals were prepared to surrender any notion of special status. However, although an earlier generation of Ganda elites had once been prime custodians of Ganda identity and through their

84. Ibid., pp. 87-110.

writings breathed life into cultural ideology, Ganda subnationalism was no longer a special preserve of the political class. Cultural mobilization was pervasive and closely bound to populist sentiments in the countryside. Buganda lay sullen and brooding, a reservoir of discontent awaiting the day of deliverance. There was no organized resistance, but a series of isolated attacks, the most serious of these being an assassination attempt on Obote in 1969, in which he survived miraculously a bullet through the jaw. Obote felt unable to travel publicly through Buganda. The silent hostility of the Ganda countryside hung oppressively over the presidential palace.

That Ganda subnationalism remained entire was dramatically confirmed on three occasions during 1971. In January 1971, when General Amin overthrew Obote, Buganda was delirious. In a catharsis of rejoicing, crowds destroyed images of Obote and relics of the former regime. A second scene occurred that summer, when Prince Ronald Mutebi returned from England for a visit. Kabaka Mutesa II had died the lonely death of exile in a drab east end flat in London in 1969. The coroner's judgment was alcoholic poisoning, a verdict which failed to allay all suspicions. A group of Ganda exiles in London invested Mutebi as Kabaka; although the succession was unlikely to be contested, yet the crucial rituals of ascension could only be performed in Buganda. When Mutebi returned, the crowd began to gather along the twenty-mile route between the airport and Kampala twenty-four hours in advance. The actual scene was indescribable; a million people were gathered along the route, transported by a collective rapture, an orgiastic moment of recaptured identity which is poorly conveyed by words, and a close replication of the 1955 scene when Mutesa II returned from exile. A few weeks later, General Amin invited several hundred "leaders of thought"—notables of diverse provenience—to engage in a day-long dialogue with him on their concerns and aspirations, an exercise carried out in a number of areas in the country. The proceedings were carried over the national radio. The message was simple, reiterated by one speaker after another: Buganda was empty inside and must be made whole. This could be accomplished by two far-reaching steps: restore the kabakaship, and reunify the kingdom. Ordinary Ganda often expressed the intimate tie between kingship and identity: Without our Kabaka, we do not know who we are. Amin, on reflection, was not interested in assisting the recovery of lost identity; neither king nor kingdom was restored, although the late Kabaka was permitted a state burial with full honors.

The abolition of kingship by Obote was extended in 1967 to the three other kingdoms of Bunyoro, Toro, and Ankole. But here the reaction

was quite different, reflecting the lower intensity of cultural mobilization in these districts, a different political situation, and more marginal
attachment to the idea of kingship. The Ankole kingdom was a partly
artificial British creation, little cherished by most of Ankole. The ruling
group was drawn from the Hima pastoral aristocracy, whose domination
was much resented by the Iru cultivators and whose deposition was warm-
ly welcomed. Toro had just invested a young prince, well enough accepted, but not bound up personally or through his office in the innermost affective attachments of his subjects. In Bunyoro, the incumbent
monarch was seventy-six years old when deposed by Obote. Although
revered as an elder statesman, he had lost his real powers in 1955, when
provision was made for an elected district council. At that time he
was "so convinced of the impracticality of local democracy he is in-
clined to think that when the system breaks down, 'as it inevitably will,'
the country will regain its senses and revert to the old system."[85] It
did indeed break down, but not in the sense anticipated; both district
council and monarchy were dismantled from the center. The king had
his last hurrah in 1955 and was too old to resist—nor was there anyone
to step forward on his behalf. Also, Toro and Bunyoro had special reasons for gratitude to Obote: Toro for his refusal to accede to Amba-Konjo
demands for secession from the kingdom, and Bunyoro for his skill in
managing the return of the "Lost Counties," or Bunyoro territory given
to Buganda by the British. The contrasting relationship between identity and monarchy in Buganda and in the three western kingdoms stands
out. The measures taken against Buganda struck at the very core of
Ganda identity and were an overriding threat to Gandahood. All
participants recognized this—the Ganda with deep foreboding about their
future, most other parts of Uganda with active approbation or at least
benign acquiescence. In Bunyoro, Toro, or Ankole districts, the blow
against kingship, set against the more favorable views toward the Obote
regime, hardly constituted a cultural threat—and in Ankole was a positive delight to most.

THE ROAD TO MILITARY RULE

Obote labored with an energy and ingenuity that deserved a better
reward to find an integrative political formula for Uganda which rested
on more secure bases than personal authoritarian rule. He was anxious
to find a formula for electoral legitimacy; yet the constraints were
severe. There could be no illusion about the hostility in Buganda. The

85. Burke, *Local Government and Politics in Uganda*, p. 97.

high turnover of incumbents even in Tanzania and the enthusiasm which had greeted coups in West Africa were sobering facts; Obote was not anxious to provide an electoral pathway for his enemies to take power (or, more uncharitably, for him to lose it). In an open contest, the DP might well revive to knit together Catholic solidarity and diverse discontents to secure a majority, especially if Buganda were in their camp. Further, central control over the district party branches was so weak that grave difficulties could be foreseen in the nomination process. If independent candidates or dissident UPC contenders were permitted, such was the state of the UPC that it could well defeat itself, even without the DP. The parliamentary profession remained attractive, not only because of the wellsprings of ambition which propel political man, but also because of a favorable hourly return on labor and sundry opportunities in diverse domains which a parliamentary role might make available. Thus in most districts there was a restive pool of candidates, most of them battle-hardened in district frays and in many cases closer to the constituencies than the incumbent MPs. Add to this the risks of religious and ethnic mobilization, and one can well recognize that Obote found elections at once indispensable and yet a very intimidating prospect.

The formula devised was ingenious. Within the framework of a one-party state—DP and KY were removed from the arena—elections were to require each candidate to compete in three areas outside of his home region in addition to his basic constituency—in popular parlance, the "1 + 3" scheme. Up to three candidates in a given constituency could be nominated by the constituency party committee, under central tutelage. Each candidate was then assigned by lot one "national constituency" in each region, for a total of four: his basic constituency and three national constituencies. Elections were won by "electoral votes," consisting of the percentage obtained in each of the four constituencies. The obvious objective was to force candidates to seek support outside their home base, to reward nationally oriented campaigns and punish politization of communalism. Whether this goal was attainable will never be known, as the Amin coup intervened. There is some reason to believe the complexity of the mechanism would have favored incumbents; shadowy syndicates of candidates were taking shape, who apparently were finding ways to pool their efforts.[86] Obote clearly stated the considerations which led to this formula:

86. D. L. Cohen and J. Parson, " 'The Last Oyee': The Uganda Peoples Congress Branch and Constituency Elections of 1970," *Journal of Commonwealth Political Studies*, XI, no. 1 (March 1973), 46-66.

If the pull of the tribal force is allowed to develop, the unity of the country will be endangered. To reduce it to its crudest form, the pull of the tribal force does not accept Uganda as one country, does not accept the people of Uganda as belonging to one country, does not accept the National Assembly as a national institution but as an assembly of peace conference delegates and tribal diplomatic and legislative functionaries, and looks at the Government of Uganda as a body of umpires or referees in some curious game of "Tribal Development Monopoly."[87]

Although the depth of Obote's commitment to One Uganda is not open to doubt, the cold facts of the insecurity of new power led to security measures which carried clear ethnic connotations. In the middle 1960s, a secret police-cum-intelligence network took shape operating out of the president's office, bearing the dissimulating label of "General Service Unit." Head of the General Service Unit was Akeno Adoko, a fellow Lango and relative of Obote. The clandestine nature of this gumshoe outfit permitted a widespread, but apparently false, public conviction that they were largely Lango. Secret police agencies are efficacious in spreading fear and intimidation but less successful in nation-building or winning popularity. The projected 1971 elections were to include a plebiscite for Obote himself as president; the name of a successor, drawn from high court judges, was to be placed in a sealed envelope. It was widely believed that Akeno Adoko would be placed on the high court and that his name was to be in the envelope.[88]

The necessity of using the army as arbiter in the 1966 crisis also had profound effects. Traditionally, army and police recruitment was heavily concentrated in the north, both because service in the disciplined forces was relatively attractive to northerners, whose other options were fewer, and because of the metaphorical power of the "martial races" concept developed in India. In the colonial era, northerners were believed to be strong of body and apolitical of mind. The mutual antagonism between the armed forces and Buganda was intense and was greatly increased by the repression of the Ganda uprising, plus the army's continued presence as profane intruders in the precious sites of palace grounds and Buganda assembly. Further, the Obote coup had been preceded by a subterranean contest for the backing of the army between the "Bantu group" and Obote himself. Obote's triumph was accompanied by a purge of many southerners and nearly all the few Ganda in the officer ranks. The army was not loathe to remind Obote that its backing had turned the match in his favor; further, the fissures within it which opened up in 1965-66 were not healed. A continuing undercurrent of bitter factionalism—partly ethnic—plagued the army,

87. Quoted in Kasfir, "Controlling Ethnicity in Ugandan Politics," pp. 252-53.
88. Gukiina, *Uganda*, p. 173.

only occasionally breaking surface, as for example in the murder of a senior Acholi officer at his Gulu home. It was almost certainly an effort by Obote to resolve the factionalism in his favor which was the immediate precipitant of the Amin coup in 1971.

Amin has completed the process of depolitization and centralization but without a clear political strategy. Although the coup was initially popular, the army itself was divided, and Amin's control has never been complete. A serious armed clash occurred in Mbarara barracks in mid-1971, with Lango and Acholi the apparent losers. An ill-organized invasion in September 1972 by a small force from Tanzania, seeking to restore Obote, was accompanied by disturbances in Jinja barracks. Despite the enormous popularity of the Asian expulsion in the fall of 1972, Amin's insecurity has been transparent. He has frequently given public expression to the ethnic categories which people his perceptions of the web of conspiracy surrounding him. In October 1971, he reported that the people undergoing training in Tanzania were mainly Alur, Acholi, and Gisu. At other moments, Lango, Jonam, and Lugbara were cited as ringleaders in treasonous plots.[89] In 1972, he decried the involvement of Kiga, renewed his warnings to Lango, and Acholi not to follow evil councillors, and attributed the presence of Madi among his enemies to excessive drinking in that district.[90] Members of these groups were urged not to follow their errant brethren, and the public was called upon not to blame the entire group for the misdeeds of some among them. The use of ethnic labels to describe adversaries, however, is a step which Obote had always carefully avoided. Fears and anxieties are inevitably introduced among designated groups. These are not chimerical; ill-disciplined army elements may well interpret such communal earmarking as license for various depradations, whose net effect is heightened insecurity. Ethnic factionalism within the security forces has placed Amin on the same forked stick which impaled Obote: in an environment of insecurity, where power is precarious, how can trustworthy lieutenants be found? When the culturally neutral obligations of hierarchy can no longer be relied upon, the leader must then seek personalized bases of fidelity and trust among his immediate collaborators. Amin's own group, the Kakwa, is very small (0.6 percent), although it has the advantage, in national terms, of its very low saliency and visibility. Islam has given a second solidarity resource, upon which he has drawn in the delicate maneuvering for control of the armed forces. He has also incorporated an undisclosed but significant number of southern Sudanese, as outsiders whose fortunes are presumably

89. Kasfir, "Controlling Ethnicity in Ugandan Politics," pp. 265-66.
90. *Uganda Argus (Voice of Uganda)*, 16 April 1971, 20 September 1972, 3 January 1973, 21 February 1973.

linked with those of Amin and who are outside of the immediate matrix of ethnic conflict within the armed forces. Communal calculus is, of course, only one of Amin's devices for coping with the armed forces. Large outlays have been made in improving their equipment. Army officers were major beneficiaries in the distribution of Asian property. Amin's innate shrewdness, physical courage, and easy camaraderie with men in the ranks contribute importantly to his survival capacities.

The shift of the central stage of conflict to the security forces is reflected in the vocabulary of ethnicity in the Amin era. Groups such as the Madi, Lugbara, Jonam, and Alur had played almost no role in national politics, when the major actors were recruited from an elite defined by educational attainment. By 1953, the largest of these groups, the Lugbara (3.7 percent of the population) had never had a student enter Makerere University.[91] All five, taken together, had 7.8 percent of the population, but only 2.9 percent of the Ugandan student body at Makerere.[92] Ganda had become disenchanted with Amin when the demands for reunification and restoration were rejected, but neither were they enthused about an Obote second coming. As they were almost completely unrepresented in the security forces, they simply stood outside the currents of conflict.

INTEGRATION VERSUS IMPASSE

What, then, can be learned from the comparative inquest into a decade of independence in two closely related polities and a further exploration into the antecedents of the contrasting development patterns? Why does Tanzania appear to have resolved its integration crisis, while Uganda faces a host of unresolved issues of identity and pluralism? Is Tanzania the future of Uganda, or is Uganda the future of Tanzania?

Tanzania, although dealt an unusually poor hand in natural resource endowment, was blessed with important advantages in the ecology of cultural diversity and in the communal impact of the historical sequences leading up to its emergence as an independent polity. Once in command of their destinies, Tanzania's leaders skillfully exploited the integrative potential of their legacy. The distribution of population around the rimland; the absence of direct competition for social resources by modernizing groups; the location distant from the locus of political power, with a base of prosperity which did not require aggressive outward expansion for groups such as the Chagga who were social pacesetters; the situation of strategic urban fields in zones of diffuse ethnicity—all these ecological

91. Goldthorpe, *African Elite*, p. 28.
92. Kasfir, "Controlling Ethnicity in Ugandan Politics," pp. 124-25.

variables, attributable to no conscious human agency, were important facilitating factors. The initial structure of the political arena, which induced African solidarity against the twin challenges of colonialism and multiracialism, falls in the category of beneficent miscalculation; the colonizer, who charted the first structural blueprints, had quite different purposes in mind. From the point at which Tanzanian political elites came to command arena and structure of politics, however, integrative ends and statesmanly means were brought into direct relationship. Here, at the risk of Tanzaphilia, one must accord high marks to the extraordinary skill used in developing TANU as an instrument of national integration and cultural engineering through promotion of Swahili as an agency of national culture. We need harbor no illusions about the magnitude of the problems remaining. Integration does not include the islands of Zanzibar, which remain only loosely stitched to the mainland fabric and where the level of civility in politics falls far below the standards on the mainland. The country remains very poor; the capacity to simultaneously raise rural productivity and apply the rigorous dictates of Tanzanian socialism remains unproved. The exceptional personal qualities of Tanzania's first president, Nyerere, leave open nagging questions as to whether the integrative accomplishments are institutionalized regime achievements or the individual legacy of a talented leader. Careful studies have shown that TANU operating at the local level is very far from the ideological instrument which its central image would suggest.[93] But, when set against the magnitude of the cultural pluralism challenge, none of these caveats can diminish the luster of the Tanzanian performance.

Ugandan politics have changed beyond recognition during this same period, but it is less certain that the polity is any closer to a permanent formula for coping with cultural pluralism. At the very outset of colonial rule, two patterns were fixed which had far-reaching consequences: an institutionalized pattern of intensely competitive religious proselytization and the special status accorded to Buganda, which quickly equipped itself with a cultural ideology befitting its special place. The incorporation of the religious motif into party organization and the entrenchment of ethnicity through a district-centered pattern of political organization fixed a communal orientation of political conflict which could not be overcome within the independence formula.

The significance of the changes since independence cannot be overemphasized. On the religious front, the government has assumed control of the school systems, which had been powerful vehicles for soc-

---

93. On this point, see especially Bienen, *Tanzania;* and Samoff, *Tanzania: Local Politics and the Structure of Power.*

ializing the new generation into religious identities. Within both the Protestant and Muslim communities, Ganda domination of religious leadership roles has been ended.[94] The premise of Ganda preeminence, so deeply entrenched in colonial folkways, has been shattered, although the political cost of the cultural humiliation of Buganda is not yet clear. The illusion of the separatist alternative has probably been laid to rest, but no formula beyond coercion has been found to marry status self-respect for Ganda to purposes of national integration. The cultural abasement of Buganda has many ramifications; in the domain of language policies, Luganda has lost ground and Swahili—command language of the armed forces—has gained. Low status communities such as the Muslims have been consciously promoted under the Amin regime. The liquidation of arenas of competitive politics has removed political resources of power and patronage from the hands of both district and national political elites. Power for the foreseeable future rests with the military—the only perceived alternative to the Amin regime is another military group. The regional selectivity of army and police recruitment fundamentally alter the parameters of communal conflict; for the moment, the only ethnicity that counts is that which obtains in the security forces. Finally, the rapid development of educational infrastructure in parts of the country once poorly served in this regard and the profound economic changes flowing from the expulsion of the Asian commercial community have greatly enlarged the mobility channels. A new Uganda is being born in the process. But the political void leaves unanswered the question as to what issues of pluralism have been resolved. Assuredly different, probably transformed; but the balance of integration and cultural pluralism remains obscured rather than resolved in the uncertain politics of survival of Amin's regime.

Finally, let us return to the more general themes set forth in the initial chapters. The striking differences in structure and function of cultural pluralism today in the two polities underline the importance of politics as an independent variable shaping ethnicity. From colonial structure through nationalist movement to postindependence state, political contours in Uganda have constrained actors to ethnic responses far more intensively than in Tanzania. Buganda, with its special status, to a significant degree gave a core culture definition to the state in Uganda, which had no parallel in Tanzania. Such a definition of the state was quite unacceptable to other groups in Uganda, once representation based on numbers began to measure political influence; the Ganda,

94. Fascinating documentation of this process is found in Akiiki B. Mujaja, "The Fusion of the Spiritual and the Temporal: The Crisis of Church Institutions in Uganda," (Seminar paper, Department of Political Science and Public Administration, Makerere University, Kampala, 1972), and Lockard, "Religion and Political Development in Uganda."

on the other hand, were unwilling to relinquish their pre-eminence, voluntarily. Much of politics was about a wrenching redefinition of the state to purge it of its Ganda attachments in the first years of independence.

The contrasting nature of competitive interaction among groups also stands out. To one degree or another, so salient were the Ganda and so visible their privileged status that most other groups were forced to identify themselves, in part, in relation to the kingdom. In Tanzania, the particularities of political geography tended to separate groups; the pursuit of scarce ends did not directly and immediately pit ethnic entities against one another or offer to ethnic entrepreneurs high incentives for the cultural mobilization of their groups.

Lastly, the significance of an ideologically articulated cultural identity in a plural environment is illustrated. Although Ganda cultural ideology is not comparable in intensity or scope to, say, Bengali or Tamil, it went substantially beyond most identity systems in tropical Africa. The deference accorded by the colonizer, the image of successful modernization, and the powerful set of myths and symbols associated with the kingdom gave to the Ganda a potent sense of self-awareness and a self-concept of primacy which was difficult to reconcile with the norms of the territorial state. Tanzania faced no comparable challenge. Gandahood has experienced a decade of intensive bombardment by a chain reaction of cultural misfortune; the consequences, at this juncture, cannot be fully assayed. At other times and places, a sense of collective status withdrawal has led to intensified self-awareness. But it is not certain that such will be the outcome in Buganda; the Ganda elite, in particular, has a strong interest in the maintenance of the institutions of the territorial state. In the answer which the future will provide to this riddle lies a vital clue to the larger puzzle of whether Uganda will find a path to rejoin Tanzania on a higher plateau of integration.

8 Nigeria and India: The Integrative Role of Cultural Complexity

Nigeria is not a nation. It is a mere geographic expression.

—Chief Obafemi Awolowo, 1947[1]

Is it supposed that the different castes and creeds living in India belong to one nation or can become one nation, and their aims and aspirations be one and the same? I think it is quite impossible.

—Sir Saiyid Ahmad Khan, 1888[2]

If the nation-state is to prove a durable shelter for mankind in Africa and Asia, wherein sustenance may be taken and shared and social harmony discovered, then the survival of Nigeria and India lies close to the heart of the drama. Outposts of diversity, pitched in the winds of communal conflicts, destined by their scale and human densities to be testing places where the hopes and fears of many more than their own populations are at stake, these two political communities are the abode of pluralism. Contained within their boundaries is every form of cultural challenge to civil politics which has come within human ken.

At moments of discouragement and disaffection, leaders in both polities have decried the artificiality of the collectivity, the doubtful possibility of civil collaboration among its solidary groupings. Chief Awolowo, quondam ethnic federalist, national coalition builder, sometime radical socialist rebel, was not alone at moments of political adversity in calling into question the legitimacy of the territorial frame of politics. Northern Nigerian leaders frequently expressed similar sentiments; Ibo notables, at a time when the higher moral mandate of a separatist Ibo state was claimed, also pointed to the British paternity of the idea of Nigeria. In India, Sir Saiyid, an eloquent exponent for the view that modernity was sanctified, not prohibited, by Islam, gave voice to a per-

1. Quoted in Arthur A. Nwankwo and Samuel V. Ifejika, *The Making of a New Nation: Biafra* (London: C. Hurst & Co., 1969), p. 31.

2. Quoted in P. Hardy, *The Muslims of British India* (Cambridge: Cambridge University Press, 1972), pp. 127-28.

ception of India which has recurred many times. A smug demurrer to nationalist claims by the British raj, a battle cry for diverse cultural segments for whom separatism has at one point or another seemed attractive, a theory ultimately spun by Sir Saiyid's lineal descendants into the premise for Pakistan—the impossibility of India is a hardy perennial.

One African in six is Nigerian; one human being in seven is an Indian. Nigerian unity only barely survived the decolonization negotiations; its steel was tempered in the fires of civil war. The dialectic of independence struggle in India thrust forward the idea of the Muslim nation as well as the Indian, a contradiction resolved by a bitter partition. In both lands, the voice of Jeremiah has often been heard lamenting the curse of division and the doom which must surely ensue. Yet the world awakens each morning to find them still there, now many ordeals away from independence day. As the 1970s began, both were in a buoyant mood: Nigeria, unified and afloat on a petroleum boom; India ebulliant after its crisply executed campaign to aid Bangladesh, some early successes in the Green Revolution, and the resurrection of the Congress Party under Indira Gandhi.

In contemplating Nigeria and India in tandem, a parallel pattern is visible. Both polities went through a phase when the manifold lines of conflict became structured about a single code of confrontation. British India could not survive the superposition of its cleavages into the single Hindu-Muslim division. Reduction of Nigeria's diversity to the lapidary formula of Ibo-Yoruba-Hausa created a three-person game whose stakes of cultural anxiety were far too high. The political arena was then redefined—by partition in India, by the creation of twelve states in the place of the original three regions in Nigeria. Cultural politics are thereby transformed and diffused. Not, of course, eradicated; but the segmentation of conflict tends to encapsulate it, to contain its tensions at the periphery of the system. This suggests the applicability of a theory put forward by Dahrendorf in connection with class conflict: "The proposition seems plausible that there is a close positive correlation between the degree of superimposition of conflicts and their intensity. When conflict groups encounter each other in several associations and in several clashes, the energies expended in all of them will be combined and one overriding conflict of interests will emerge."[3] We have argued earlier the proposition that the nature of cultural pluralism itself is, to some extent, a dependent variable, which alters in function of the structure of the political arena. Nigeria and India offer the opportunity for a comparative exploration of the hypothesis that cultural

3. Ralf Dahrendorf, *Class and Class Conflict in Industrial Society* (Stanford: Stanford University Press, 1959), p. 215. This argument is ably defended by Baldev Nayar, *Minority Politics in the Punjab*, pp. 333-35.

complexity may play a positive role in national integration if the polity is so structured as to draw advantage from it.

CULTURAL DIVERSITY: NIGERIA

To pursue this argument, we first offer a portrait of the cultural diversity of these two systems. Breakdown under circumstances of communal polarization may then be contrasted with the relative stability of structured complexity. Admittedly, the Nigerian case rests upon a more compressed time frame; the twelve states were created only in 1967 and have yet to be tested within the context of overtly competitive politics. Nonetheless, enough of the parameters are visible to permit a tentative inventory of implications.

Ethnicity, language, region, and religion interactively form Nigeria's matrix of cultural pluralism. In chapter 12, we will examine the gene-

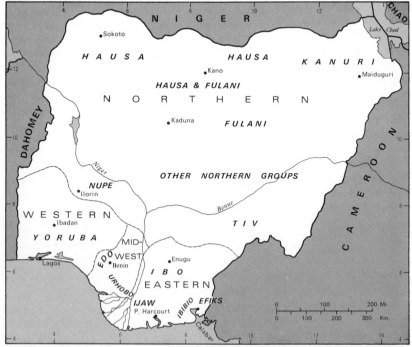

Map. 8.1—Nigeria: Ethnic Groups and Four Regions

Cartographic Laboratory UW-Madison

sis and ambiguities in Ibo subnationalism. We need not repeat here what is treated elsewhere. Some consideration is appropriate of the nature of the other two major identity groups whose rivalry dominated perceptions of politics until the civil war.

The largest ethnic category, the Hausa-Fulani, constitute 29 percent of Nigeria's population. Language and religion were the main defining characteristics of this cultural amalgam. Hausa were organized in a series of city-states; at the beginning of the nineteenth century, these were conquered in the name of Islamic purification by Fulani warrior-clerics, who then established themselves as a ruling aristocracy. Extensive intermarriage occurred between the Fulani rulers and Hausa noble lineages, and most Fulani have come to use Hausa as a first language; the leading Fulani political figure in Nigerian politics, the late Sir Ahmadu Bello, intensely proud though he was of his ancestral affiliation with the conquerers, spoke no Fulani.

As political identity, Hausa-Fulani defined themselves by opposition to the cultural threat posed by southern Nigeria. The British had carefully crafted their administrative system in northern Nigeria to allay any identity-related anxieties. The incumbent political hierarchy was defeated but not humiliated; peace with not only honor but advantage within the British framework was provided to the Fulani elite. Mesmerized by the mobilizing force of Islam and conscious of the thinness of the red line of British forces, the colonizer gave careful deference to hierarchy, language, and religion. The Fulani rulers were confirmed in their functions; Hausa was used as a language of administration; and Christian missions were excluded from Islamic areas.

It was only after World War II that the need for a political expression of Hausa-Fulani culture became clear, as it became evident central power was to be allocated by new principles which strongly favored southern Nigeria. The vehicle for identity mobilization was Northern solidarity, a concept which nearly doubled the numerical scope, and thus electoral impact, of the Hausa-Fulani core. This concept operated reasonably well to link the Kanuri state of Bornu to the political fortunes of the Hausa-Fulani emirates; shared religion and culture and a common sense of antagonism to the political ambitions of southern politicians, civil servants, and entrepreneurs provided an ample frame for this 5 percent of Nigeria's populace. It also served to accelerate the incorporation of many small, fragmented traditional communities, who lay outside the orbit of Christian evangelization and tended to find cultural security through acquiescence in Hausa-Fulani domination, and even assimilation to Hausa language and Islamic religion. The "One North, One People" doctrine worked, with greater friction, in areas such as the Ilorin province of Yorubaland or the Nupe (1.2 percent), where

Fulani conquest had also occurred and Islam was ascendent, although cultural assimilation to the Hausa system had not occurred. Northernization required active coercion in zones such as Tiv (9 percent), Idoma, Igala, and Igbirra (collectively 2.6 percent), where neither Fulani hierarchy, Hausa language, nor Islam served as brokerage mechanisms relating these solidary communities to the concept of Northernization; a serious uprising occurred in Tiv country in 1964.[4]

Thus until the era of contemporary politics Hausahood was a linguistic classification rather than an ethnic community. Confronted with a clear threat of incorporation in subordinate status to an Africanized Nigeria, cultural mobilization around the symbols of Islam, traditional hierarchy, and speech community was organized by a political elite recruited within the traditional aristocracy.[5] In the nurturant security of colonial indirect rule, identity was related to locality, town, and emirate rather than to a still-vague Hausa community; self-awareness as Hausa was most visible amongst the migrant Hausa trading clusters in southern towns. The invocation of Northern rather than specifically Hausa-Fulani patriotism was at once optimizing electoral tactic and testimonial to the diffuseness of the Hausa-Fulani cultural self-consciousness.[6]

Yorubahood is also a singularly elusive concept. Interesting insight into the genesis of the idea of Yoruba unity may be found in the autobiography of the most prominent Yoruba leader in the independence campaign, Chief Awolowo:

> If the members of each ethnic group feel happy among themselves; if they are free, within prescribed limits, to order their own lives and advance their culture as they like; and if the solidarity and devotion exhibited within their ranks can be sublimated to the cause of the nation, the federal unity of Nigeria would have been assured. But whilst there was an Ibibio Union and an Ibo Federal Union, there was no comparable all-embracing union for the Yorubas. Since the strength of a chain is that of the weakest link, I thought it would be in the interest of the federal unity of Nigeria if one was founded.
>
> The Yorubas were a highly progressive but badly disunited group. They paid lip-service to a spiritual union and affinity in a common ancestor—Oduduwa. But in all their long history they had waged wars against one another. When the Por-

4. The Tiv rebellion and its antecedents are well described by M. M. Dent in Melson and Wolpe, *Nigeria: Modernization and the Politics of Communalism*, pp. 448-61.

5. Cohen, *Custom and Politics in Urban Africa*.

6. On Hausa-Fulani and Northern politics and identity, see especially John Paden, *Religion and Political Culture in Kano* (Berkeley: University of California Press, 1973), and his chapters in Fishman et al., *Language Problems of Developing Nations*; Cohen and Middleton, *From Tribe to Nation in Africa*, pp. 242-70; C. S. Whitaker, *The Politics of Tradition* (Princeton: Princeton University Press, 1970); B. J. Dudley, *Parties and Politics in Northern Nigeria* (London: Frank Cass & Co., 1968); M. G. Smith, *Government in Zazzau, 1800-1950* (London: Oxford University Press, 1960).

tuguese and the British had visited their coasts in the course of their slave trade, the Yoruba had shown no qualm of conscience in conducting violent and merciless slave raids on one another. These inter-tribal wars and slave raids had come to an end under the so-called *pax Britannica*. But the mutual hatred and acerbity which were attendant on them lingered. Furthermore, the propaganda of Dr. Azikiwe was already having a deleterious effect on a once dynamic group. The Yorubas now indulged in mutual recrimination and condemnation. The younger elements thought that the Yorubas were inferior to the go-ahead Ibo people, and that whatever might be their past glories they had become effete and decadent. To cap it all, it was freely bandied about that the Yorubas were no longer capable of leadership in any sphere of life. I thought that it was in the best interests of Nigeria that the Yorubas should not be reduced to a state of impotence, into which they were fast degenerating.[7]

In this illuminating statement we find contained the causes and ambiguities in the pan-Yoruba ideal.

Save in the legendary penumbra of the eponymous ancestor legend, the collectivity now bearing the name of Yoruba have never been organized in a single political unity. The appellation of Yoruba as applied in recent times is an innovation; the absence of a self-concept of ethnic community in precolonial times is unmistakably attested by the absence of any term which described the entire group. The Yoruba label did apply to the Oyo kingdom, which at its zenith in the eighteenth century did extend its influence over a wide area of Western Nigeria. The operative identity terms, at the precolonial baseline, related to the names of the major kingdoms, such as Oyo, Ijebu, Ife, Ijesha, Ekiti, and the like (some fifty-odd in all).[8]

Yoruba language and culture provided the ingredients of pan-Yorubahood. Although the dialects are widely variant, a standard Yoruba was developed in the nineteenth century. The term came into use to describe returned slaves from Western Nigeria; two of these, Samuel Crowther and Samuel Johnson, were major artisans of Christian evangelization and the establishment of British authority in Yorubaland. The first step towards a Yoruba cultural ideology was Johnson's 1897 study, *History of the Yorubas*. P. C. Lloyd suggests that the educated "have adopted a 'basic Yoruba culture' devoid of most of its local peculiarities." This process, he notes, is paralleled by comparable developments among neighboring groups, with the differences "probably more starkly defined now than at any time in the past."[9]

7. Chief Obafemi Awolowo, *Awo* (Cambridge: Cambridge University Press, 1960), pp. 165-66.

8. N. A. Fadipe, *The Sociology of the Yoruba* (Ibadan: Ibadan University Press, 1970), pp. 29-42.

9. P. C. Lloyd, "The Yoruba of Nigeria," in James L. Gibbs (ed.), *Peoples of Africa* (New York: Holt, Rinehart and Winston, 1965), p. 551.

But the effort to mobilize Yoruba identity actively came in response to the perception of cultural threat. British rule had not been a source of anxiety for the Yoruba; indeed, many welcomed it as a way to end the civil wars. There was already a pool of educated Yoruba at the moment that Nigeria was created in 1900. Yoruba pre-eminence in the new elite came effortlessly and seemed in the natural order of things until the trauma of the Ibo challenge in Lagos in the 1930s. Awolowo expressed the self-doubt arising from that shock: Could it really be that Yoruba were "inferior," "effete and decadent"? The signs of degeneration were all around; only the purifying drive of pan-Yorubahood could bring spiritual renaissance. Further, within a future Nigerian state, safety and security were to be found only in unity.

Despite the aspirations to Yoruba unity and the diverse associations founded to secure that end, at the political level this remained tenuous and incomplete. In the key urban centers of Lagos and Ibadan, well-institutionalized pattern of conflict existed between Yoruba groups indigenous to the town and those who were immigrants. In the interplay of party competition, movements whose communal center of gravity lay outside Yorubaland could always find local allies. Indeed, during the era of triangular political conflict, the proposition gained currency that Yoruba disunity was the key to Nigerian instability; three-person coalition politics failed to function, in this view, because the Yoruba were unable to act as a group.

Although the three major communal groupings accounted for only two-thirds of the Nigerian population, the administrative structure of the territory until 1967 served to nearly eclipse the remainder. Each of the three regions existing at the time of independence and serving as units of the Nigerian Federation was dominated by one of the major configurations. Edo, Urhobo, Itsekiri, and Midwestern Ibo in the Western region: Tiv, Igala, Idoma, Nupe, and others in the North; Ibibio, Efiks, Ijaws, and others in the East were placed in a very exposed and dependent position by the three-cornered communal federation of the first phase of independence.

Religion is a secondary but not insignificant basis of division. Islam was dominant in the North and spreading rapidly in the Western region. However, Yoruba Islam is influenced by different brotherhoods than in the North. Hausa and Yoruba pray at different mosques, and Islam does not function as a cross-cutting interethnic solidarity structure. Christian influences were largely Anglican in Yorubaland, with important indigenous Protestant churches breaking off. In Iboland, Islam has made no impact; Catholics, mainly Irish-staffed, outdistanced the

Protestants. Protestant-Catholic differences have been one dimension of cleavage in intra-Ibo politics.[10]

CULTURAL DIVERSITY: INDIA

In India, there are three axes of differentiation: religion, langauge, and caste. Each, however, is bound up with the other in a vast honeycomb of such complexity as to beggar the imagination. At first glance, the religious dimension appears the simplest; every schoolchild can recount the tale of Hindu-Muslim holocaust and the separation of India and Pakistan. On closer inspection, each of these communities dissolves into a multitude of segments. The 1961 Indian census listed 1,549 native "mother tongues."[11] Subcaste (jati) units number many thousands. The complexities are only moderately reduced by considering only the caste groups which operate politically at the provincial level; every state has its own unique array. When the door was opened to linguistic claims to statehood, the States Reorganization Commission appointed in 1953 received no less than 150,000 documents, petitions, and memorials from groups and individuals.[12]

In British India, Muslims were approximately 25 percent of the population, while in post-partition India they are 10.6 percent. Although the two biggest concentrations were in East Bengal and the Sind-East Punjab-Northwest Frontier area, clusters of Muslims were distributed throughout the country. In occupation, origin, and status it was a quite diverse community. In East Bengal, Muslims were mainly poor cultivators; in Punjab and Uttar Pradesh, court officials and land owners; on the western coast, traders and seafarers; in Bombay, weavers and capitalists. In present-day India, Muslims are a majority in Jammu & Kashmir state, and over 10 percent of the population in four other states (West Bengal, Kerala, Uttar Pradesh, and Bihar).

Three other religious communities, although small on an all-India scale, are of great importance in local politics because of their concentration. Sikhs are 1.8 percent nationally, but a majority in Punjab (after its partition); Christians are 2.4 percent, but 21.2 percent in Kerala. Buddhists are a mere 0.7 percent, but a factor in Maharashtra politics because of the mass conversion of A. M. Ambedkar's *harijan* followers in the late 1950s.

10. Abernethy, *The Political Dilemma of Popular Education*, p. 46.
11. Das Gupta, *Language Conflict* p. 33.
12. Marcus F. Franda, *West Bengal and the Federalizing Process in India* (Princeton: Princeton University Press, 1968).

Map 8.2 India: Twenty-one States

Cartographic Laboratory UW-Madison

   Hinduism manifests itself in many incarnations. The diversity of its scriptures, the multiplicity of its sacred figures, the many faces of its reconciliation or rejection of Western influences give it a far-reaching eclecticism as an identity system. Secularism and the Hindu tradition wrestled for the soul of Indian nationalism; the former tendency reached its highest fulfillment in Nehru, while Gandhi, despite his profound commitment to Indian unity and Muslim reconciliation, was closer to the latter, especially in his style and idiom. Movements such as the Arya Samaj and Hindu Mahasabha were quasi-political embodiments of Hindu revivalism in the nationalist period; since independence, this tradition is represented in the Jana Sangh Party. Explicitly Hindu movements have been mainly confined to the Hindustani heartland of the center and north. In the south Dravidian perspective commands a quite different orientation towards the Hindu tradition, which, in its extreme form in Tamil Nadu, takes the form of outright hostility to what is argued to be a moral sanction for Brahman domination. In these states, where communal tensions were far less pronounced along the Hindu-Muslim line, political Hinduism as a response to Muslim nationalism had far less immediate relevance.

Language has been the primary basis of regional segmentation in postpartition India. Although the Congress Party organized itself into linguistic sections as long ago as 1920, in the immediate aftermath of independence the national leadership feared that the delicate fabric of national unity could not withstand the strains of linguistic self-determination in reshaping the internal structures of India. However, it rather quickly became clear that the converse proposition was at least equally valid and politically more compelling: whatever the abstract merits of multilingual provinces, the Indian system was too fragile to withstand the agitations for linguistic states. The floodgates were opened when Potti Sriramulu fasted unto death for recognition of the Telugu state on Andhra Pradesh. Under the emotional impact of this tragedy, the Telugu state was conceded and the States Reorganization Commission established to consider other claims. Although it was denied that the principle of linguistic self-determination was accepted, in fact the new lines proposed were primarily linguistic. The one multilingual showpiece the commission insisted on retaining, Bombay state, was quickly set aflame with linguistic agitation and broken into Marathi and Gujarati states. The Sikhs, appreciating that linguistic self-determination had a legitimacy that religious separatism was denied, reformulated their demands in terms of a Punjabi-speaking state and over time forced the issue to a successful culmination.

Fourteen major languages were recognized by the Indian constitution as deserving legal recognition (Assamese, Bengali, Gujarati, Hindi, Kannada, Kashmiri, Malayalam, Marathi, Oriya, Punjabi, Sindhi, Tamil, Telugu, and Urdu); these plus English are mother tongues for 87 percent of the population (which leaves unaccounted 71 million people, or more than the total 1963 population of Africa's most populous polity, Nigeria). Fewer than 7 percent of the population, according to the 1961 census, know any Indian language other than their mother tongue. Despite the recognition of Hindi as the official language in the 1950 constitution, over a decade later the number of people who spoke English as a second language (11 million) still exceeded the equivalent figure for Hindi (9 million).[13]

The four main languages of south India—Tamil, Telugu, Kannada, and Malayalam—belong to the Dravidian family, totally unrelated to the languages of north India. These are the state languages of Tamil Nadu, Andhra Pradesh, Mysore, and Kerala, respectively. Punjabi

13. Das Gupta, *Language Conflict*, pp. 33-35.

and Urdu are very close to Hindi, differing above all in the script and symbolism attached to it. Punjabi is written in the Gurumukhi script associated with the Sikh religion; it will be recalled that, as a result of the Hindu-Sikh political conflict, Punjabi Hindus en masse reported themselves as Hindi- rather than Punjabi-speaking in the 1951 census. Urdu differs from Hindi in its Persian script and infusion of Persian loan words, deriving from its connections with the Mughal empire.

The Hindi question deserves our closer attention, for it lies close to the heart of the integration crisis in India and stands at the intersection of the currents of linguistic identity, Hindu revivalism, and the Brahmanical tradition. Its claim to official language status derives from the unacceptability and impracticality of English as a national language (which after 150 years of British rule was spoken by only 2.5 percent of the population), the numerical preponderance of Hindi, as the largest single Indian language, and its strategic location at the heartland of the country. Six of the twenty-one states (Uttar Pradesh, Bihar, Rajasthan, Madhya Pradesh, Himachal Pradesh, and Haryana) are Hindi-speaking. The 1951 census which lumped Punjabi and Urdu with Hindi, showed 42 percent in the Hindi group, a figure that was then frequently cited in misleading fashion in the polemics of the national language policy.[14] The 1961 census showed 30 percent Hindi mother tongue speakers.

The more closely one looks at Hindi, the more evanescent it becomes. It must be seen in relation to Sanskrit, Urdu, and Hindustani; to the village, bazaar, and the cloisters of the literati. Sanskrit is the classical language of the great Hindu tradition, to which Hindi bears a genetic relationship, but which is extinct as a living form of speech.[15] Through its association with many of the sacred texts of Hinduism, Sanskrit enjoyed the reverence of Hindus, and especially Hindu revivalists. The Urdu form, because of its linkage to the Mughal court and, through it, its ties to the Persian and even Arabic scholastic legacies, came to be associated with the Muslim community. Hindustani was less a language, *sensu stricto*, than a state of mind, a concept of Indian nationalism, promoted by Gandhi (though his mother tongue was Gujarati) and Nehru. Hindustani, in Gandhi's view, was the popular speech used by the masses in north India, freed of the constraining classicism which the sectarian literati in both camps kept trying to inject. The

14. Ibid., pp. 45-46. The aggregation of these languages occurred because of the intense emotions over the Punjabi and Urdu questions, not through a deliberate intent to inflate the Hindi totals.

15. Ibid., p. 47. In the 1951 census, some 555 of 356,879,394 listed themselves as Sanskrit-speakers.

question of script, he felt, could be left to solve itself; Gandhi believed that, "when there is absolutely no suspicion left between Hindus and Muslims—when all causes for distrust between the two have been removed, the script which has the greater power will be more widely used and thus become the national script."[16]

Village Hindi remains highly dialectal, with an internal diglossia reflecting the caste hierarchies. A Muslim in the village will refer to his speech as Urdu, while Hindus will claim to speak Hindi. Objectively, the difference between the speech of high caste Hindi and the untouchable in the village may be greater than between the speech of untouchable and low-status Muslim. Dialects used on the frontier marches of the Hindi speech community may be closer to neighboring language groups than they are to the Hindi of the mass media. Bazaar Hindi is a more standardized, simplified code usable as a medium for trade interactions by persons who do not speak this form of Hindi around the hearth. The dialectal forms, functionally viewed, serve as affirmations of particular roles and statuses in the microcommunity. For many rural persons, these roles are the everyday behavioral garb, and the meaning of the language issue does not penetrate beyond. The bazaar dialects exist in several subregional variants and are used by trading and service castes who cater to the rural population.[17]

Hindi as a language may be traced back perhaps a thousand years. However, its literary tradition is very sparse and, according to Selig Harrison, "cannot compare in literary development to at least three of its rivals, Bengali, Tamil, and Marathi."[18] In its cultural prestige, most non-Hindi would rate Hindi below at least one other Indian language.[19] It was in its Urdu form that it first began to acquire literary currency. However, with the decline of the Mughal court and advent of British rule, a school of Hindi turned to the Devnagari script and sought to exclude Persian influences.

The hostile symbiosis of Urdu and Hindi explains many of the peculiar features of Hindi as a national language. As conflict relationships sharpened between Hindu and Muslim, the literati who served as censorial custodians for the two languages were moved to symbolize their

16. M. K. Gandhi, *Thoughts on National Language* (Ahmedabad: Navajivan, 1956), pp. 5-6, quoted in Das Gupta, *Language Conflict*, p. 110.

17. John J. Gumperz and C. M. Naim, "Formal and Informal Standards in the Hindi Regional Language Area," in Charles A. Ferguson and Gumperz, "Linguistic Diversity in South Asia," special issue of *International Journal of American Linguistics*, XXVI, no. 3 (July 1960), 92-118.

18. Selig S. Harrison, *India: The Most Dangerous Decades* (Princeton: Princeton University Press, 1960), p. 305.

19. Paul Friedrich, "Language and Politics in India," *Daedalus*, XCI, no. 3 (Summer 1962), 552.

hostilities through strengthening the differences between the languages. Muslim ulamas feverishly pursued the Persianization of Urdu, while their Hindu counterparts assiduously Sanskritized Hindi. The amplification of initially small differences helped reinforce the linguistic manifestation of communal cleavage.

After partition, the tradition of standardization through Sanskritization of Hindi continued. Those to whom the government had to have recourse in execution of its policy of overhauling and modernizing Hindi, who held the "commanding heights" over language development, were precisely the literati whose interpretation of their mandate was to purify through classicalizing. Thus Hindi was subjected to a continuing tugging toward the esoteric, which separated it from the spoken version in common use in lingua franca form.[20]

In north India, Rajasthani and Bihari are very close to Hindi; both states have adopted Hindi as the official language at the state level. Indeed, until the congeries of dialects spoken in Bihar state were classified as a separate language by the monumental nineteen-volume linguistic survey of George Grierson (1903-28), it was not generally held to be a distinctive speech community.[21] Gujarati and Marathi are not very far removed from Hindi. Oriya, Bengali, and Assamese also form a related cluster, with Bengali and Assamese using the same script

Table 8.1— Major Languages of India, 1961

Language	% of speakers in total population
Hindi	30.37
Telugu	8.57
Bengali	7.71
Marathi	7.57
Tamil	6.95
Urdu	5.31
Gujarati	4.62
Kannada	3.96
Malayalam	3.87
Oriya	3.57
Punjabi	2.49
Assamese	1.54
Kashmiri	0.44

Source: Jyotirindra Das Gupta, *Language Conflict and National Development* (Berkeley: University of California Press, 1970), p. 46. Copyright © 1970 by The Regents of the University of California; reprinted by permission of the University of California Press.

20. Das Gupta, *Language Conflict*, pp. 159-75.
21. Baldev Raj Nayar, *National Communication and Language Policy in India* (New York: Frederick A. Praeger, 1969).

and partially mutually intelligible. Table 8.1 gives the distribution of speakers of the major Indian languages.

At the greatest linguistic and cultural distance from the Hindi core are four newly formed small states on the eastern frontier: Nagaland, Meghalaya, Manipur, and Tripura. They are Indian by default, have little cultural commitment to a system in which they are mere appendages. Dissidence has been endemic, with the most sustained uprisings in Nagaland. Cultural units are small and localized, and the process of building more incorporative identities has occurred only recently, in response to the sense of imposition of an alien administration. The Nagas, for example, have only recently developed a common name for themselves; the Mizos, another collectivity formed in dissidence, are of even more contemporary vintage.[22] These states are peripheral in every respect; they are too small, poor in resources, and sparsely populated to constitute a major challenge to India, yet they are so far removed from the cultural symbols about which the integrative impulses flow as to be difficult to bring into the Indian mainstream.

We have described the operation of caste as a social differentiator and political solidarity system in chapters 2 and 4 and need not retrace that ground here. Let us simply recollect that, in terms of caste vocabulary applied at the state political level, it was neither the subcaste (jati) which was the actual immediate frame of establishing hierarchy and regulating individual social behavior nor the broad varna categories of Brahman, Kshatriya, Vaishya, Sudra, and outcaste, but rather caste groupings incorporating a number of closely comparable subcastes under a common designation. These caste groupings, as solidarity units, operated within linguistic and therefore state lines. Because of the linguistic segmentation of caste groupings, caste was not a particularly salient determinant in coalition-building at the national political level. However, it was of critical importance in state politics.

It is unusual for any caste group to approach a numerical force where they can aspire to dominance without joining a coalition. The most noteworthy examples are the Ezhavas and related untouchable castes in Kerala, with 34 percent, and Nairs and Namboodiri Brahmans with 19 percent in that state. In Mysore, Lingayats total 20 percent and Okkaligas 15 percent; factionalism revolving around their rivalry had dominated the politics of this state. In Andhra Pradesh, Reddis

22. Philip Mason, *Patterns of Dominance* (London: Oxford University Press, 1970), p. 174. The Mason book is an important study, based upon years of study of those variants of cultural pluralism which involve domination of one racially defined community by another. Mason served as a civil servant in India, and also on the Commission of Enquiry into the Minorities question in Nigeria, to which reference has been made earlier.

with 12 percent and Kammas with somewhat fewer have dominated politics; both are landholding caste groups. In Rajasthan, Jats, with only 9 percent, are the most politically visible caste group; Jats are also important in Punjab and parts of Uttar Pradesh. Overall, caste groups belonging to the three highest, twice-born varnas are much more numerous in the north than in the south. In Bengal, the political elite was dominated less by caste groups per se, than by the "bhadralok," or "respectable people," recruited among several of the twice-born castes.[23]

The Rudolphs have cogently analyzed the caste role in state politics:

> Castes do not pose the same kind of potential threat to the nation-state that tribes, religious communities, and linguistic groups do. . . . Castes have not demanded separate political identities. As parts of a larger society, they are symbiotically related to each other, and as participants in Hindu culture, this relationship is integrated and legitimized. When castes come to mobilize themselves politically, they are concerned with the distribution of values, status, and resources within a political system, not with the realization of nationhood.[24]

Within the Hindu cultural zone, caste is a ubiquitous political factor. In eight states, mobilized caste groups play a prime role at the state-wide level (Andhra Pradesh, Bihar, Gujarat, Kerala, Maharasthra, Mysore, Orissa, Rajashtan, Tamil Nadu). However, as the Rudolphs argue, they operate as interest groups, seeking benefits for their members within the political process rather than aiming to redefine the cultural basis of the political community.

At the level of state politics, regionalism also requires mention as a politically relevant cleavage. When India became independent, roughly one-third of its area was made up of "princely states," under British indirect rule, but not integrated into the administrative system of the British raj. The incorporation of these 552 princely states, most of whom had been only lightly touched by Congress and the independence movement, was an enormous challenge at the time of power transfer. States such as Jammu & Kashmir, Rajasthan, and Mysore are largely composed of former princely states. Pronounced residual attachments to these units survives in state political alignments. Andhra Pradesh in 1973 faced the paradoxical threat of being the first linguistic state to break apart, with regional conflict pitting former Hyderabad, once the largest princely state, against the rest. A level of violence comparable to the linguistic state agitation two decades earlier was enforcing the claim to separation.

In the case of Madhya Pradesh, the state was a residual category of leftover territory, whose regional subunits command more attachment

23. Broomfield, *Elite Conflict in a Plural Society.*
24. Rudolph and Rudolph, *The Modernity of Tradition*, pp. 67-68.

than the state. In Maharashtra and Oriya, sharply demarcated regional divisions are a prime factor in lines of political cleavage. Regional patterns of factionalism are also salient in the Hindi heartland state of Uttar Pradesh, where no linguistic subnationalism confers a special sanctity to the state unit.[25] Table 8.2 offers a résumé of the characteristics of the Indian states.

Thus, Nigeria and India stand together in the richly textured diversity bound together in the web of statehood. The seeming banality of the perpetuation of the units of sovereignty in the world eclipses the miracle of national survival in these giant laboratories of cultural pluralism. We may lift the preservation and development of Nigeria and India from the realm of the mundane through recollection of their respective rendezvous with fragmentation, through the 1967-70 civil war in Nigeria and the 1947 partition in India. A brief recapitulation of the circumstances of these catastrophes will help illuminate the causes of breakdown, as well as the conditions for national survival.

BREAKDOWN OF NIGERIA AS THREE-PLAYER ETHNIC GAME

On Nigeria, a summary review will suffice. As the political pulse quickened after World War II and independence was a goal which could be a concrete aspiration rather than utopian dream, political parties took form. Ineluctably, the process began in the capital of Lagos, where the largest cluster of politically conscious elites were to be found. Nigeria's first movement to define for itself a national arena of ambition was the National Council of Nigeria and the Cameroons (later renamed National Convention of Nigeria Citizens—NCNC). Its location was in an urban social field where competition for mobility resources between Ibo and Yoruba, a process which had contributed mightily to the development of these incorporative identities, made politization of this conflict very probable.

Although the NCNC cannot be faulted for the genuineness of its national orientation and nationalist commitment, an ethnic perception of it emerged, partly catalyzed by the flamboyant and controversial personality of the NCNC leader, Nnamdi Azikiwe. Thus it was that, in 1948, the Action Group was founded, as a Yoruba response to the perceived threat of Ibo domination through the vehicle of the NCNC. The AG subsequently endeavored to carry out its struggle with NCNC at a national level, yet could never escape from its Yoruba genesis, the close association between its birth and the establishment of a pan-Yoruba cultural associa-

25. Two major studies of state politics in India have been completed, Narain (ed.), *State Politics in India,* and Weiner (ed.), *State Politics in India.*

Table 8.2—Characteristics of Some Indian States

State[a]	% of total Indian population	% Hindu	% scheduled caste[b]	% scheduled tribe[c]	Dominant language	% speaking	% literate	% urban
Andhra Pradesh	8.20	88.4	13.8	3.7	Telugu	84.8	20.8	17.4
Assam	2.71	n.a.[d]	6.2	17.4	Assamese	55.0	25.8	7.5
Bihar	10.59	84.7	14.1	9.1	Hindi	81.5	18.2	8.4
Gujarat	4.70	89.0	6.6	13.4	Gujarati	90.5	18.4	26.0
Jammu & Kashmir	0.81	28.5	7.5	n.a.	Kashmiri	54.4	10.7	16.8
Kerala	3.85	60.8	8.4	1.2	Malayalam	94.3	46.2	15.0
Madhya Pradesh	7.38	94.0	13.1	20.6	Hindi	76.7	16.9	14.3
Madras (Tamil Nadu)	7.68	89.9	18.0	0.8	Tamil	82.4	30.2	26.7
Maharashtra	9.02	82.2	5.6	6.1	Marathi	76.6	29.9	27.1
Mysore	5.38	87.3	13.2	0.8	Kannada	71.1	25.3	22.0
Orissa	4.00	97.6	15.8	24.1	Oriya	82.4	21.5	6.3
Punjab[e]	4.63	63.7	20.4	0.1	Hindi	55.6	23.7	20.1
Rajasthan	4.60	90.0	16.7	11.5	Rajasthani	56.5	14.7	16.0
Uttar Pradesh	16.81	84.7	20.9	n.a.	Hindi	89.1	17.5	12.8
West Bengal	7.96	78.7	19.9	5.9	Bengali	84.6	29.1	23.2

[a]These tables are derived by the sources cited below from the 1961 census and reflect the states as they then existed. Since that time, Nagaland, Meghalaya, and Manipur become states, and Punjab was divided into Punjab (with a small Punjabi-speaking and Sikh majority) and Haryana (Hindi language, Hindu religion). There are several small territories classified as "Union territories," which are not included (the capital of Delhi, Goa, Pondicherry, the Andoman islands, etc.)

[b]"Scheduled caste" is the official designation for *harijans*, or untouchables.

[c]Scheduled tribes are hill peoples not incorporated (or only marginally so) into the Hindu cultural system.

[d]Data not available.

[e]These figures apply to undivided Punjab.

Sources: Myron Weiner (ed.) *State Politics in India* (Princeton: Princeton University Press, 1968), pp. 26-28, 33; Baldev Raj Nayar, *National Communication and Language Policy in India* (New York: Frederick A. Praeger, 1969), p. 64; Jyotirindra Das Gupta, *Language Conflict and National Development* (Berkeley: University of California Press, 1970), p. 55.

tion, the Egbe Omo Oduduwa, and the leader who founded both, Chief Awolowo. The ruling aristocracy in the Hausa-Fulani emirates of the north slowly realized that the nourishing womb of British indirect rule might be removed and that power was to be allocated, defined, and legitimized by the electoral mechanism. Thus was born the Northern Peoples Congress, built upon a triple cultural support: the fear shared by all classes of southern (and especially Ibo) domination; the linked role of religious notables and emirs as "defenders of the faith," in joining a religious imperative to ethnic fears, abetted by a prevailing view of Islam as a "religion of obedience"; and the social discipline enforceable through the authoritative hierarchy of the emirates. Thus the dialectic of fear quickly produced a tringular pattern: Yoruba fears of Ibo domination produced the AG; northern fears of southern domination gave birth to the NPC.

The tripolar image of Nigerian politics was powerfully reinforced by the administrative division of the country into three regions, each dominated by one of the three ethnic collectivities. In a critical turning point, a 1953 constitutional conference decided upon a federal form of government, with self-government to be first devolved upon the regions. This verdict was the inexorable outcome of the tripolar pattern. The north was unwilling to see a Nigerianized central government until they were better equipped politically to compete within it. The south was unwilling to defer African access to political power until the Greek calends of northern readiness. The AG had a strong incentive to consolidate its base within the Western region. Thus, there was no choice but prolonged delay or partition to acceptance of federalization—which, of course, was no choice at all within the psychology of nationalism. Although the interplay of minority politics and rivalry among Yoruba subunits permitted the NCNC to take a majority of the seats in the Western region in the 1954 elections for a federal legislature, each regional government came under the firm control of the respective dominant party.

Entrenched in the institutions of the polity as independence neared— regional governments and political parties—was the three-actor metaphor. Although some able analysts of Nigerian politics at the time argued that this image of politics was a kind of false consciousness, that ethnicity was a surrogate for other forces, such as social class, there can be no gainsaying the pervasiveness of the perception of Nigeria as a political struggle between Ibo, Yoruba, and Hausa-Fulani.[26] The arrangement of power and the demographic facts permitted no other structure of political choice. The "minorities," that third of the population which fell

26. The most noteworthy example of a class-based analysis is Richard Sklar's monumental *Nigerian Political Parties* (Princeton: Princeton University Press, 1963).

outside the three major categories, had few options. The nature of federalism, police powers of the regional governments, and their tutelage over the local administrations provided dominant groups the structural resources for asserting their authority over the minorities within the frame of regional politics. At the national level, minorities could not readily compete outside the framework of coalition with one of the three major parties.

Nigerian politics during the 1951-66 period can be described as a three-person game, with bidding shares ultimately determined by the electoral mechanism. The three actors enter the contest with a given demographic allocation—29 percent for the Hausa-Fulani, 20 percent for the Yoruba, 17 percent for the Ibo—if they succeeded in mobilizing their full cultural community. To this total might be added the minority zones in the respective regions, where control of the regional administration gave some advantage in electoral access, especially in the 1964 election. Table 8.3 lists the population breakdown by region.

Table 8.3—Regional Population Distributions, 1953 and 1963 Censuses

Region	1953 % [a]	1963 % [a]
Northern	53.8	53.6
Eastern	25.6	22.3
Western	20.5	19.7
Midwestern [b]	n.a.	4.5

[a]Total percentage does not equal 100.0 because of rounding.

[b]The Midwestern Region was created by scission from the Western Region in 1963.

Source: Sir Rex Niven, *The War of Nigerian Unity* (London: Evans Brothers, 1970), pp. 38-39.

The three players, acting through the political parties carrying their cultural imprint, competed in the electoral game by three rules: (1) mobilizing the totality of their cultural clientele; (2) soliciting the support of minorities, whose immediate fears were governed by the culturally dominant group within the region where they were situated; (3) seeking social or cultural fissures within the other two major groups. These principles were applied in somewhat different mixtures by the three parties in the two national elections carried out within the tri-polar framework, in 1959 and 1964. The NCNC was able to command the overwhelming support of Eastern Ibo, despite strong factionalism in many Ibo communities. In the Western region, NCNC exploited resentment of Ijebu and other Yoruba immigrant groups by the Yoruba sons of the soil in Lagos and Ibadan, and some other Yoruba subgroup rivalries; they were also able to rally the Midwest Ibo and other non-

Yoruba groups. In the North, the NCNC relied upon the premise of class division in the Hausa-Fulani emirates and commoner resentment of the authoritarian rule of the emirs. While such resentment certainly exists, the vertical mobilization available against the threat of Ibo-Christian domination precluded the NCNC itself from capitalizing upon it. The alternative actually pursued, alliance with the Northern Elements Progressive Union, which endeavored to speak for radical reform from within the Northern system, failed because of the capacity for imposition of social obedience of the emirates, especially among the rural populace. The AG relied upon a minorities strategy in both east and north. In the east, 13 of the 14 AG seats in 1959 were won in the Ibibio-Ekik area; its northern successes were all in the "Middle Belt" area, south of the cultural zone of Islam and Hausa-Fulani or Kanuri preeminence. The NPC did not compete outside its region in 1959. In 1964, it did so by taking under its wing one fragment into which the AG had split (with the federal government as midwife) in 1962, and exploiting anti-Ibo sentiment in the Ijaw zone of the Niger delta in the east. The outcomes of these two contests are summarized in Table 8.4.

Following the 1959 elections, the logic of the minimum winning coalition called for an alliance between two of the three contenders. Up to that point, the hostilities born of constant conflict were more intense between the AG and NCNC than between either and the NPC. Further, an AG-NCNC coalition which excluded the NPC would have fundamentally altered the game; from the northern point of view, the distinctiveness of east and west would have dissolved into a single southern front directed against the north. The most powerful NPC leader, Sir Ahmadu Bello, warned against this contingency in his autobiography and made quite clear that under those circumstances the north would have insisted on secession.[27] At that time, the British might have reluctantly permitted it.

The 1964 election campaign was fought by a pair of electoral alliances. The eastern and northern poles anchored the competition; the splitting of the AG had removed the third actor as an autonomous participant; rather east and north locked in mortal combat for the west. However, fraud and thuggery were so widespread that the rules of the game were fundamentally altered; no longer were the hearts of the voters the trump suit, but clubs—first of party thugs, quickly thereafter of the army.[28]

27. Sir Ahmadu Bello, *My Life* (Cambridge: Cambridge University Press, 1962), pp. 135-36.

28. For an excellent study of the 1964 elections, see Kenneth Post and Michael Vickers, *Structure and Conflict in Nigeria, 1960-1966* (London: Heinemann, 1973).

Table 8.4—Nigerian Federal Election Results, 1959 and 1964

Year	Region	Seats by major party			
		NPC	AG	NCNC	Other
1959	Eastern	0	14	58	1
	Western[a]	0	34	23	8
	Northern	134	25	(8)[b]	7
1964	Eastern	0	4	64	2
	Western[a]	(38)[c]	16	7	1
	Midwestern			13	1
	Northern	157	(4)[d]	0	1

[a]Lagos seats are counted in the Western totals; in 1959, AG won 1, and NCNC 2; in 1964, they were contested in alliance, which took 3, with 1 independent winning. In this table, the 3 seats won by the alliance were divided in the 1959 proportions.

[b]Seats won by NEPU, in alliance with NCNC.

[c]Seats won by the Nigerian National Democratic Party, in alliance (clientage) with the NPC.

[d]Tiv seats won by a local party, in alliance with AG/NCNC.

Sources: K. W. J. Post, *The Nigerian Federal Election of 1959* (London: Oxford University Press, 1963), pp. 358-75; John P. Mackintosh, *Nigerian Government and Politics* (Evanston: Northwestern University Press, 1966), pp. 545-609. It should be noted that carpet-crossing begins on the morrow of elections, so these figures reflect only the election results, not a precise parliamentary total at any point in time.

In January 1966, a group of young majors overthrew the first republic— initially to general rejoicing, so far had cynicism and disgust overtaken the public over the numerous failings of the *ancien régime*. But so deeply rooted, by this time, was the communal trinitarian perception of politics that the old impasse continued in new guise. The majors, it turned out, were nearly all Ibo; victims of the coup were nearly all non-Ibo. One immediate trigger had been the belief that northern leaders were moving to insert northerners in all the sensitive command positions within the security apparatus. Although the coup partly aborted, power was assumed by the Ibo commander of the armed forces, General Aguiyi Ironsi. In May 1966 the first anti-Ibo riots occurred in northern cities, followed by a second coup within the army—this time directed against Ibo officers—followed in turn by the far more serious anti-Ibo rioting in September and October.

In short, politics as a three-player ethnic game in Nigeria brought the polity to the brink of dissolution. When, in 1963, the two players in the coalition had knocked the third player out of the game by partitioning his province (through creation of the Midwestern Region) and splitting his party, the triangular contest came very close to a bipolar confrontation. When politics, metaphorically, was a titanic struggle between Ibo and Hausa, with all others as clients or spectators, impasse became paralysis. Nigeria came very close to breaking apart in the immediate aftermath of the 1964 elections and hung even more precariously in the balance in September 1966. At this critical moment, it was the intervention of "minority" interest in defense of the federation that saved it. A radically new structure for the national arena was promulgated which—one civil war later—offered a much more promising formula for unity in diversity. To that we return shortly; we now turn to the impossibility of India as a bipolar communal arena.

THE IMPOSSIBILITY OF INDIA AS A BIPOLAR ARENA

Lord Dufferin, the British viceroy in India, described the Muslim community in India in 1888 as "a nation of 50 million, with their monotheism, their iconoclastic fanaticism, their animal sacrifices, their social equality, and their remembrance of the days when, enthroned at Delhi, they reigned supreme from the Himalayas to Cape Cormorin."[29] As an able historian of Muslims in India observes, "How, by 1947, a very large number of Muslims in British India came to have Lord Dufferin's image of them as their own, and in religion and politics to act it out, is the history of Muslims under British Rule."[30]

Muslim political identity sprang from three related propositions: (1) the Muslims are a nation; (2) in British India, Muslims are a permanent minority; (3) the Muslim community was backward and losing ground to the Hindus, favored by the British. The beginnings of the two-nation philosophy go back further than Lord Dufferin; in 1867, distressed by the first Hindu agitation to displace Urdu with Hindi in Davanagari script, Sir Saiyid Ahmad Khan made his prophetic remark: "I am convinced that the two communities will not sincerely cooperate in any work. Opposition and hatred between them, which is felt so little today, will in the future be seen to increase on account of the so-called educated classes."[31] A path with many turnings joined this

29. Hardy, *The Muslims of British India*, p. 1.
30. Ibid.
31. Ali, *The Emergence of Pakistan*, p. 9.

statement to Muslim League head M. A. Jinnah's epochal speech in 1940, when the League officially committed itself to the goal of Pakistan: the refusal of many Muslim leaders to join Congress, formation of the Muslim League in 1906, successful demand for communal reservation of elected seats for Muslims, a period of relative amity with Congress following the Lucknow Pact in 1916, the first communal riots in the 1920's. Jinnah was unambiguous:

> It has always been taken for granted mistakenly that the Musalmans are a minority. The Musalmans are not a minority. The Musalmans are a nation by any definition. . . . What the unitary government of India for 150 years has failed to achieve cannot be realized by the imposition of a central federal government. . . . The Hindus and Muslims belong . . . to two different civilizations which are based mainly on conflicting ideas and conceptions . . . To yoke together two such nations under a single State, one as a numerical minority and the other as a majority, must lead to growing discontent and final destruction of any fabric that may be so built up for the government of such a State.[32]

Intertwined with the two-nation idea was the nagging awareness of the numerical preponderance of the Hindu population, exacerbated by the conviction that Muslims were falling behind in the modernization race. The factor of numbers became an issue in 1906, when the first steps toward an electoral system were under discussion. It was this conjuncture which provided the immediate stimulus for the formation of the Muslim League. Chaudri Muhammed Ali, a former Pakistani prime minister, expresses a characteristic Muslim view:

> ". . .the fact is the Muslims were greatly outdistanced by the Hindus in practically every field of social and economic endeavor, and the Hindus had come to regard this state of inequality as their birthright, due to them by virtue of their superior education, social status, and economic strength. They were determined to maintain and, if possible to improve, their position by means of political power. Prospects of democracy thus intensified the struggle between Hindus and Muslims. Democracy is rule by majority, but if the majority is fixed and hereditary, and also enjoys the privileges of superior education, greater economic and administrative power, control over the press, and talent and money for political organization, the minority is doomed forever to a position of subordination.[33]

Binding the minority awareness to the Muslim nation theory was the argument that Muslim rights could only be safeguarded with separate communal rolls. Otherwise, only Muslims who were acceptable to the Hindu majority could stand any chance of election. Such Muslims, by

32. Ibid., p. 39.
33. Ibid., p. 12.

definition, were not free to represent the true interests of the Muslim community. From 1909 on, communal rolls were a constitutional premise in British India; while this practice gave some reassurance to Muslims, it also helped entrench communalism in the political process—and in the long run failed of its intended purpose of making Muslim participation possible within an undivided India.

The Muslim decline proposition is an interesting example of the reality-shaping power of communal myths. The conviction that this had indeed occurred was well-nigh universal; yet meticulous studies convincingly demonstrate that the truth was more complex. Only in Bengal did the Muslim community clearly lose ground—and the great majority of Bengali Muslims were impoverished peasants to begin with. Hardy shows that in 1886, when the Indian Muslim community languished at its supposed nadir of ruination, Muslims in the Northwest Provinces and Awadh had 44.8 percent of the executive and 45.9 percent of the judicial appointments open to Indians, with 13.4 percent of the population; in Punjab, they held 41.8 percent and 33.6 percent of the same positions respectively, with 51.3 percent of the population; in Madras 5.4 percent and 1.6 percent, against 6.2 percent of the population; in Central Provinces, Muslims held 18.1 percent of the two types of positions combined, with 2.4 percent of the population. Only in Bengal, Bombay, and Sind were these ratios heavily unfavorable to Muslims.[34] The social legend received quasi-official benediction in an important book by an administrative official, Sir William Hunter, on *The Mussalmans of India* in 1871. The Hunter thesis was that Muslims had been unfairly blamed as a community for the 1857 Sepoy Mutiny, that their needs should receive sympathetic attention, and that special efforts should be made to help them overcome their lag. As the first stirrings of nationalism were heard, mainly from Bengali Hindu intellectuals, the loyal Muslim became an even more worthy object of official beneficence. As Hardy remarks, although the British disclaimed the intent to foment divisions, they "nevertheless accepted the fact of such divisions with the air of a man struggling joyfully in the grip of a benevolent fate."[35]

The nature of Hindu political identity was fundamentally shaped by the converse sense of its numerical preponderance. Indian nationalism was its ostensible vehicle, and Congress was the movement to which most Hindus pledged heart and hand. Explicitly Hindu communalism, reflected in such issues as the advocacy of Devnagari script Hindi in

34. Hardy, *The Muslims of British India*, p. 123. Seal, *The Emergence of Indian Nationalism*, provides comparable data.

35. Hardy, *The Muslims of British India*, p. 134.

place of Urdu or anti-cow slaughter legislation was one of the strands in Hindu political thought, but far from the only or even the most important one. One India united all Hindus; divergence came in the formulation of the cultural content of this concept. Secularism was certainly the dominant motif, but Hindu communalist movements were of sufficient influence as a pressure group within Congress to place the secular leadership on the defensive at times. In a culturally polarized setting, Muslims were often prone to identify the most communally oriented Hindus, whose claims to a thoroughgoing Sanskritization and Hinduization of the national symbols of India generated very real fears, with the position of the Hindu community as a whole. Denial only confirmed the suspicions; to Muslims, a patina of duplicity was being used by the Hindu secularists to cover over their real intentions, disarmingly revealed to the world by the Hindu communal organizations. To the two-nation *Weltanschauung* of the Muslim League, Congress opposed the ideal of one nation; characteristic of the symbolic issues in which these cosmologies clashed would be the inclusion of Muslims in Congress delegations or provincial governments. For the League, this was an impertinent provocation, implying the right of Congress to speak for Muslims as well as Hindus. For Congress, such communal ticket-balancing was equally crucial in upholding the opposite principle, that Congress was an Indian nationalist and not a Hindu communal organization.

After World War I, politics moved out of the drawing rooms of the elite into the streets. The era of the mass campaign was at hand, and the tactical armories of the political organizers began to fill with the extraordinary array of agitational weapons which are one of India's unique features: mass civil disobedience, satyagrahas, hartels, gheraos, fasts unto death, not to mention more conventional and even old-fashioned techniques such as boycotts and burning of government buildings. The mobilization process required the translation of the political ideas and demands formulated by the leadership into a set of symbols and metaphors which facilitated their transmission to mass audiences. Gandhi, particularly, was a master in many parts of India (though not in Madras and Bengal). Gandhi's appeal, in style and content, involved extensive use of India's rich legacy of cultural symbols, many of which have specific Hindu connotations, particularly for Muslims. The *Bande Matram* anthem used by Congress, containing allusions to past glorious deeds by (Hindu) Indian heroes in resisting foreign (Muslim) conquerers, was laden with anxiety-raising symbols for politically sensitized Muslims: that Muslims were historically foreign invaders, that struggle against Muslims had been of the highest order of patriotism. The assessment of Chaudri Muhammed Ali is a representative Muslim League reaction; he argued that, "The outer aspect of Indian nationalism continued to be secular and noncommunal, but its inner spirit was informed by Hindu inspirations."[36]

Nothing, of course, was further from the intentions of Gandhi, Nehru, and most other Congress leaders. So profoundly were they motivated by a sense of Indian nationalism that they continued to believe until the very end that the future would triumph over the past, that the inner impulses of Indian unity would prevail over divisive colonialist maneuvers. "The communal organizations, whether Hindu or Moslem," wrote Nehru, "were closely associated with the feudal and conservative elements and were opposed to any revolutionary social change. The real conflict had, therefore, nothing to do with religion, though religion often masked the issue, but was essentially between those who stood for a nationalist—democratic —socially revolutionary policy and those who were concerned with preserving the relics of a feudal regime."[37] "I think this sentiment has been artificially created," he continued, "and has no roots in the Moslem mind." Though he conceded that ephemeral solidarities might temporarily affect the course of events, what he believed to be the overwhelming political and economic logic of unity and the impossible difficulties of division would surely bring all Indians to their senses, despite the bad faith of Jinnah and the League.[38] Gandhi, in drawing upon India's cultural heritage for symbols, was quite sensitive to the need to incorporate Muslims. He frequently used the Koran in prayer meetings, preferred Hindustani to the Sanskritized Hindi forms, and backed the Khilafat movement among Muslims after World War I in protest against Allied intervention against the Ottoman Caliphate.

Polarization, indeed, remained incomplete until near the end. Paradoxically, the Muslim League was weakest in the Muslim majority areas, which became Pakistan after partition. Jinnah was a Gujarati speaker from Bombay; the main strongholds of the League were in the Hindi-speaking heartland. Aligarh Muslim University, the intellectual center of the Muslim League, whose students and religious teachers were League missionaries, was located here. It is probably in this area that the direct competition for mobility resources by middle class elites was sharpest. Heavily Muslim Sind was a backwater; in the overwhelmingly Muslim Northwest Frontier Agency, Abdul Gaffar Khan allied his unruly Pathan warriors with Congress. Hindu domination was certainly not a live issue for Khan. The largest single concentration of Muslims were in Bengal, the great majority of whom, as poor peasants, were very little politicized at that juncture, although the predominance of Hindu landlords and moneylenders in the East Bengal countryside created the po-

36. Ali, *Pakistan*, p. 14.
37. Nehru, *The Discovery of India*, p. 399.   38. Ibid., p. 544.

tential for class-oriented communal mobilization. In the 1937 provincial elections, the League failed to win a majority of the Muslim seats and did not win in any of the four Muslim-majority provinces. The aftermath of the 1937 elections was a critical turning point in the hardening of suspicions into resolute and unbridgeable distrust. In the politically central zone of the United Provinces, in north India, Congress under Nehru used its majority to refuse the Muslim League any seats in the cabinet, unless they abandoned their Muslim League identity. This was seen by League backers as confirmation of the Congress intent to operate on a winner-take-all basis, and was a major milestone on the road to the 1940 Muslim League commitment to separation.

The next elections were held in 1946 and reflected a quantum leap in communal mobilization. The League won 95 percent of the Muslim seats, and Congress took a corresponding proportion of the Hindu slate. Negotiations for power transfer were begun; by this time, Britain realized that it could not long count on the reliability of the security forces, that violence was very close to the surface, and that the costs of any efforts to prolong the era of the British raj would so far exceed any imaginable benefits that, Churchillian rhetoric notwithstanding, quick independence was the sole avenue. The horrifying realization of the explosive level of communal tensions was brought home to all parties when the League called for a "direct action day" on 16 August 1946, in support of its negotiating position. Calcutta dissolved in an orgy of hatred and slaughter, in which 5,000 were killed, 15,000 were injured, and incalculable property damage done. The genie of communal violence was now out of the bottle; seven or eight thousand Muslims were killed in Bihar in November 1946, and killings rippled back and forth in the zones of communal confrontation in northern India.

The actors were forced into the apocalyptic moment of choice, as constraints crowded in upon them. The British announced in February 1947 that they were withdrawing no later than 1948, no matter what the circumstances; there was now an irreversible deadline. In September 1946, a precarious Congress-League coalition interim government was put together; relations between Congress and League members were venomous and augured ill for the prospects of jointly addressing India's overwhelming problems of poverty and development. Relations between Hindu and Muslim in the towns and cities of north India were at the flashpoint. So polarized were tensions that each event fell into the communal pattern of perception, added a new dimension of fear, a further cause for anger, a new motive for vengeance.

Time, the great healer, now compounded the dialectic of fear. For Congress, a hideous dilemma was exposed: one India might still be had, but only through conceding such near-total autonomy to the Muslim community and the states that the dreams of a planned, socialist society would be emptied of their substance. The battle for India, by being won, would be lost. The bitter relations between Muslim League and Congress ministers in the interim government suggested that suspicion and distrust would color the transactions between an emasculated central government and its Muslim provinces. Autonomist stirrings were palpable in Bengal and Madras as well. The nationalist leadership, having committed decades of its life, in and out of prisons, to the goal of a single and prosperous India, found that the wells of unity were poisoned. Given politics as a comprehensive polarity between Hindu and Muslim, India could not survive. With all the politicized sectors of India aligned on one side or the other of this communal divide, conflict reached levels of intensity which could not be mediated by the political process.[39]

Thus it was that in April 1947 Nehru publicly stated that the Muslim League could have Pakistan if they wanted. There began the trauma of partition, which cost the lives of 2,000,000 and created 12,000,000 refugees. The population exchange in the Punjab was virtually total. Virtually all Hindus left West Pakistan, and many Muslims in Uttar Pradesh, who were close enough to Pakistan to find security through flight, joined the exodus. A truncated India could now turn to the tasks of development and integration, with the cultural parameters of politics radically transformed. Many Muslims remained, but the proportion had dropped to 10 percent—even though, in India's massive human densities, this still left her as the third largest Muslim power, after Pakistan and Indonesia. In both Nigeria and India, two or three-actor, culturally-defined politics could not endure. We now turn to the restructuring of the national framework of politics and the impact of the reshaped political arena upon the patterns of cultural pluralism.

STRUCTURED DIVERSITY IN NIGERIA: THE TWELVE STATES

In Nigeria, the critical step was the transformation of the original three regions into twelve states. Spokesmen for "minorities" had begun the clamor for a political structure which removed them from the domination of the three major cultural configurations in the 1950s, as independence approached. A British Commission of Inquiry was dis-

39. Many excellent accounts of this troubled period are available; see especially V. P. Menon, *The Transfer of Power in India* (Princeton: Princeton University Press, 1957); Penderel Moon, *Divide and Quit* (London: Chatto and Windus, 1961).

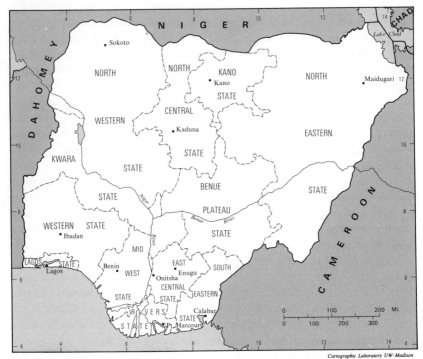

Map 8.3   Nigeria: Twelve States

Cartographic Laboratory UW-Madison

patched in late 1956, charged with inquiring into "the fears of minorities and means of allaying them"; although it found that the fears were real and pervasive, it concluded that the formation of the new states proposed would only compound Nigeria's difficulties. The commission persuaded itself that nothing united the petitioners for the new states but their mutual fears of domination, that the proposed new states would lack resources for their development, and that the strong opposition of most spokesmen for the dominant groups and existing Regions should prevail.[40] Awolowo and a few others preached the virtues of ethnic federalism, based upon a large number of ethnic states.[41] But nothing was done, and independence came with the dominant role of the three major groups firmly entrenched, reinforced by

40. *Nigeria: Report of the Commission appointed to enquire into the fears of Minorities and the means of allaying them*, Cmnd. 505 (London: H.M.S.O., 1958).

41. Awolowo, *Awo*, pp. 185-212.

the federal system which vested many important powers at the regional level. Under these circumstances, minority spokesmen could obtain returns for their areas only through establishing clientage relationships with the dominant groups. But priority access to resources went to those in the respective ethnic heartlands; as Jean Herskovits has remarked, "One can come astonishingly close to mapping the pre-1966 voting patterns just by travelling the Nigerian roads; ruling parties in each region were those of ethnic majorities, and for them there was tarmac."[42]

In May 1966, the first attempt was made to scuttle the tripolar basis of politics, when General Ironsi, who had come to power in the wake of the Majors' coup of January 1966, proclaimed the abolition of the federation and its component regions, and the establishment of a unitary republic. However, before this measure could be fully applied, Ironsi himself was assassinated.

For two months, the future of Nigeria hung in the balance. The chief of staff in the army, then Lt. Col. Yakubu Gowon, took charge of the armed forces and the nation; in his first declaration he stated, "As a result of the recent events and the other previous similar ones, I have come to strongly believe that we cannot honestly and sincerely continue in this wise, as the basis for trust and confidence in our unitary system of government has been unable to stand the test of time. Suffice it to say that putting all considerations to test, political, economic as well as social, the base for unity is not there." Apparently, this speech initially contained an announcement of secession by the north, from which Gowon was dissuaded in extremis.[43]

In September, an ad hoc constitutional conference brought together delegations from the four regions. Here the intervention of minority interests was critical, coming through two channels. The Midwest region was already in existence; under the civilian regime, it had been an NCNC ally. With parties excluded from the arena by the January 1966 coup, the Midwest now emerged as its own voice and a surrogate spokesman for other minorities as well. The other minority pressure group came from within the army, in which a very large fraction of the other ranks were recruited in the minority areas of the Northern region.[44]

The possibility of an exceedingly loose confederation of doubtful durability, or outright splintering, was precluded in September, but the simultaneous outbreak of very serious massacres of Ibo in the North brought

42. Jean Herskovits, "One Nigeria," *Foreign Affairs,* LI, 2 (January 1973), p. 403.
43. A. H. M. Kirk-Greene, *Crisis and Conflict in Nigeria* (2 vols.; London: Oxford University Press, 1971), I. 54-55.
44. Melson and Wolpe, *Politics of Communalism,* pp. 659-60.

the East to the verge of secession. Months of uneasy stalemate followed. In May 1967, Gowon took the decisive restructuring step of decreeing a reorganization of Nigeria into twelve states, which transformed the cultural parameters of Nigeria beyond recognition. Although this became the immediate pretext for the long-expected Biafran secession, which required thirty months of civil war to quell, it was the basis for a more securely united Nigeria. The secession and civil war we will consider in chapter 12; we will confine our attention here to the new twelve-state structure.

The former Eastern and Western regions each became three states, and the Northern region was divided into six. The Midwest state, already established, was confirmed, and Lagos and its hinterland became a separate state. In the east, Iboland became the East Central state, and the minority zones became Rivers state and Southeast state. The former was a zone of infinite linguistic and ethnic complexity, given the appearance of relative homogeneity by the comprehensive but only slightly ideologized label of Ijaw. The Southeast state consisted of coastal Ibibio and Efiks and a shatter zone of many small groups in the hinterland.

In the north, three of the new states—Kano, North Central, and Northwestern—had a Hausa-Fulani cultural center of gravity, although the latter contained the important Nupe group and some others. Northeastern state had the Kanuri emirate of Bornu as its most important component, but was far from homogeneous. Benue-Plateau at last provided the Tiv an administrative home freed from fears of domination, and also contained Idoma, Birom, and many small "Middle Belt," mainly non-Muslim groups. Kwara state included the Ilorin Yoruba as its cultural pivot, but also Igala, Igbira, and others.

But the entrenched domination of the three largest groups was shattered by the twelve states. The Ibo control only one state. The Yoruba are almost totally dominant in the Western state, have a heavy majority in Lagos, and probably are the predominant group in Kwara state. However, pan-Yorubaism has never been a wholly effective political ideology, and the three Yoruba-centered states have quite different circumstances. The AG never dominated Lagos politics; it could never command the loyalty either of the old Yoruba urban elite, or the urban lower strata recruited among the coastal Yoruba zones, who tended to distrust the immigrants from other Yoruba subgroups who were believed to dominate the AG. Ilorin Yoruba were conquered and converted by the Fulani, and were partly tied into the Northern political-cultural area, although the AG had captured a significant portion of the vote in 1959 and one of the four seats in a campaign which essentially pitted Northern versus Yoruba orientation against one another. Thus there is no reason to assume that these three states would form a cultural bloc in the coalition building process.

The same can be said for the three states under Hausa-Fulani leadership. The structural supports for Northern unity under Hausa-Fulani patronage have all been removed. The breakup of the old region eliminates the forcefully asserted tutelage over the "native authorities," or local administrations and chiefs. The assassination in the January 1966 coup of Sir Ahmadu Bello, Sardauna of Sokoto, a man of exceptional ability and overpowering will who dominated Northern politics, removed from the scene the only political personage who had the capacity to impose himself on the regional scale. And the dissolution of the NPC brought to an end the patronage machine which lubricated the system and gave political embodiment to the "One North, One People" slogan. Historically, the Hausa city-states were autonomous, briefly incorporated within a single political system by the Fulani jihad. Little survived of this but the loosest acknowledgement of the seniority of the Sokoto emirate (now in the Northwestern state), a concept which was of primary interest and significance to a relatively narrow circle of ruling lineages. Certainly the sense of the cultural distinctiveness of the Hausa-Fulani group, particularly with reference to the southern states, remained strong. But the structural inducements to transform cultural identity into a bid for national domination were to a large extent removed; there was no guarantee that the three Hausa-Fulani states would find a common interest in a given national issue, nor was there a political mechanism by which any one could acquire the right to speak for all.

The transformation of Bornu attitudes are an interesting reflection of the profound significance of the new formula, as well as the integrative impact of the civil war on Nigeria. Under British rule, Bornu was the farthest removed emirate from the main centers of Nigerian development. Intensely proud of the thousand-year history and continuity of their kingdom, Kanuri were only very slightly represented in the new national elite. When politics came, the traditional elite rallied to the NPC. An opposition movement, the Bornu Youth Movement, did rally the disenchanted, the small traders, the junior clerks against the indirect rule elites. The Bornu Youth Movement joined NEPU in electoral alliance with the NCNC; however, the ruling elite charged they were disloyal to Islam, and, after serious riots in 1958 which caused many deaths, the BYM was simply broken up. The Sardauna, as regional premier, was careful to accord generous status and representation to the Kanuri, symbolizing a Hausa-Fulani/Kanuri duality of leadership. There was very little real Nigerian nationalism present in Bornu during the first years of Nigerian independence; the school system glorified the Bornu past, but gave little focus to Nigeria. Although initially there was little hostility to the Ironsi regime, as time passed fears grew that an Ibo owned and operated military dictatorship was emerging. The May 1966 unification decree caused real panic and active discussion among young elites about a new country, based upon the Northern region, to be called "Hausa." It was the civil war that for the first time brought a "One Nigeria" sentiment home to Bornu. The new states remove the Kanuri from the status of junior partners in a Hausa-Fulani dominated region, to senior partners in a region in which they were the largest single group. Ronald Cohen, a student of Bornu society for a number of years, argues that a profound mutation of orientations and attitudes among Kanuri elites has occurred during this period.[45]

The Benue-Plateau state had always been the most vocal center of claims for a Middle Belt state, removed from Hausa-Fulani domination. However, through use of the ample police and administrative powers available under the first republic constitution, the NPC had brought most of this area, save Tiv country, under its effective political control. Safely secured by separate state status, there can be little doubt that this state will play a role in Nigeria quite independent of Hausa-Fulani interests. Indeed, it probably shares with Rivers state vis-à-vis the Ibo a residue of hostility towards the formerly hegemonous cultural group which would predispose it towards a coalition strategy of opposition or counterbalance to any arrangement of alliances where a single Hausa-Fulani grouping seemed to come into play.

The military interregnum which began in 1966 has also altered the structure of politics in a long-run sense. Political parties were dissolved, and elected assemblies abolished for a period which is scheduled to end in 1976. Each of the states is headed by a military governor, in most instances from the region (there have been a couple of cases in the north where governors have come from neighboring states). The governor, subject to central approval, selects a cabinet which includes some former politicians and some technocrats—but all from within the state. The military governors are, in the last analysis, part of a command hierarchy and thus stand in a different relationship to the center than did the political regional premiers under the *ancien régime*. However, the governors do have some local support, which is complemented by whatever standing the politicos among their entourage can command. The central ministry is a similar compound of politicians and technocrats, with appropriate weight given to regional balance.

45. See his chapter in ibid., pp. 559-75.

How the transition to civilian rule will occur remains an enigma. However, the first generation of parties, with their ethnic connotations, are almost certainly extinct; party-building will start anew, no doubt incorporating residual networks surviving from the first republic. If competitive elections are permitted, it will not be a simple matter to reconstitute the old patterns. No longer will it be possible to gain access to the patronage resources of a region, which can then become an ethnic redoubt to mount the assault on the center. Cultural mobilization, if it occurs, would be confined to the narrower boundaries of the smaller states. The political generation which emerged in the 1950s will be largely discredited or out of circulation. The process of political "emergence" will be complex and will probably require, in one way or another, the patronage of the military authorities.

The entire calculus of coalition formation must now assume many more players—certainly each state will represent its own configuration of interest. The former minorities are now majorities and may be independent actors, not captive clients of the three largest groups. As their role in Nigeria's darkest days demonstrates, the minorities have probably the strongest interest in the preservation of One Nigeria. Representatives of the three primary ethnic clusters could contemplate separation as a real alternative. Secession is an inconceivable option for the smaller groups, who would also be harmed by the withdrawal of any significant segment of the federation. The twelve-state system provides the minorities the structural resources to play an influential role. The polity is now constituted to make of its sheer complexity of cultures an integrative asset rather than a threat to its survival. The two groups believed capable of acquiring control over the entire federation—the Ibo and Hausa-Fulani—are wholly excluded from such an objective, which has helped to dissolve the anxieties of the early years. What appeared to others as a lunge for power by each of these groups in 1965-66 was as much a pre-emptive strike, a defensive reaction to the ethnic dictatorship fear, as a self-conscious will to dominate; Ibo and Hausa-Fulani both have reasonable security with their own states. Cultural fear is an evil councillor; the great reduction in ethnic insecurity acts as a powerful solvent of communal politics.

The new Nigerian system has not, of course, withstood the trial of electoral combat. Political demobilization under military paternalism is unlikely to endure forever, irrespective of the 1976 deadline. However, the capacity of the center to contain conflict is significantly greater than in 1966. The armed forces numbered only 10,000 at the time that civil war broke out; they now total 250,000. Although the army suffered tremendous damage in the multiple mutinies and frequent invocation of ethnic loyalty as transcending the military command structure, the cultural neutrality of army hierarchy appears to have been restored. Accordingly, recourse to separation must simply be excluded from the range of choice open to political actors.

THE INTEGRATIVE ROLE OF DIVERSITY IN INDIA

If the Nigerian renaissance is a major accomplishment in the face of its great diversity and the severity of the challenge to its survival, the accomplishment of India in sustaining over the nearly three decades of its independence a democratic and competitive political system must be judged as even more remarkable. Rabushka and Shepsle, in an interesting recent study of plural societies, conclude, on the basis of an application of the logic of collective good bidding and coalition formation in an ethnic politics framework, that "resolution of intense but conflicting preferences in the plural society" is not manageable in a democratic framework.[46] Curiously, they fail to consider the Indian case. Yet India has now held five general elections at both the state and national level and has also nurtured democratic processes in local jurisdictions. The record is not without its blemishes, but by any standard this overall probity of its electoral processes has been high. For the most part, opposition parties have been free to organize and have not been subject to disabling restrictions. Yet nowhere is cultural pluralism more pervasive; the risk of violence along any of several axes of differentiation has many times been validated since independence. Upon achievement of independence, India faced the vast communal turmoil of partition; absorption of 6,000,000 refugees; incorporation of the princely states; wars with Pakistan in 1947-48, 1965, and 1971; the dislocation of one of its principal irrigation systems through the effects of partition on the use of the Indus waters; Chinese invasion in 1962; a Communist insurrection in Hyderabad in 1948; a simmering separatist revolt in Nagaland and secession threats in Tamil Nadu; and, dominating all other preoccupations, the desperate race to provide a slightly better life for a population which has increased by 200,000,000 since independence.

In assessing India's capacity to pursue the system goals of stability, development, and democracy within a framework of extreme cultural pluralism, we need to examine salient attributes of the central political arena and then turn to the complex matrix of state politics, where most cultural conflicts occur. The first point to observe is that, once the Hindu-Muslim aggregative conflict was removed through partition, the

46. Rabushka and Shepsle, *Politics and Plural Societies: A Theory of Democratic Instability*, p. 217.

segmented nature of other pluralism was not so structured as to crystallize on a nationwide basis. Caste patterns are particular to each linguistic area and do not naturally flow together; thus caste has been a very diffuse vector at the central echelon. True, occasional whispers are heard that Prime Minister Indira Gandhi relies upon too many Brahman advisors (especially from members of middle castes hit by her socialist measures); also, the central government has assumed a tutelary role with respect to the scheduled castes and tribes, to assure them a minimum participation in public life. But politicized caste is not a serviceable resource in consociational politics at the center. Religion has not ceased to affect social interactions at the rank-and-file level, and the Muslim community does not lack grievances.[47] But whereas a Muslim applicant for a low-ranking post may face severe competition from Hindu rivals, at the upper echelons Muslims in the national elite are fully accepted partners and have neither political incentive nor ideological predisposition to advance their claims through invocation of a communal constituency. Probably the closest approximation to cultural aggregates in the national arena is in the relationship between the core areas of Hindi-speaking Sanskritic culture in north central India and the outlying provinces with distinctive, non-Hindi linguistic heritages. The issue which mobilizes conflict along this cleavage is the national language question. Early displacement of English by Hindi for an important portion of the north Indian heartland is seen as indispensable to the building of true unity, affirmation of the Indian cultural heritage, and elimination of the alienating humiliation of conducting public affairs in an imposed foreign language. For the Dravidian south, to some extent Bengal and to a lesser extent other non-Hindi states, the Hindi-only policy connotes north Indian domination, and for some a particular form of Hindu communalism. At moments when the national language question was on the national agenda, stress symptoms along the Hindi-non-Hindi axis at once appeared. These strains have been reduced through indefinite postponement of any Hindi-only policy.[48]

The nature of the party system is a second variable. Political competition and electoral campaigns are structured by an array of parties whose labels and formal symbols capture ideological difference, and not cultural pluralism. This symbolism is of very great importance; we may suggest that it represents a normative formulation of what the political system ought to be. The ideological connotations of the

47. See, for example, the 1973 controversy over the status of Aligarh Muslim University, described in *New York Times*, 24 April 1973.

48. For contrasting evaluations of the integrative potential of Hindi as a national language, see Nayar, *National Communication and Language Policy in India* (pro), and Das Gupta, *Language Conflict* (contra).

parties create a collective image of a political system whose policy choices are governed by contending social philosophies. Political debate on national issues, which relies heavily upon the array of party labels as an ideological map, can proceed without apparent overt invocation of cultural symbols; we may add that this is a crucial difference between the Indian party system and the Nigerian system of the first republic, where the regional-ethnic identifications of parties so far eclipsed any ostensible ideological difference as to render the latter wholly insignificant.

There are five major party-sets operating at the all-India level. At the right end is the Swatantra, an organ of business groups and advocate of a free enterprise economy.[49] Next, moving left, is the Jana Sangh, a party whose primary program is the affirmation of the Indian cultural heritage in all aspects of national life and policy.[50] Next, occupying a huge swath of center-left terrain, is Congress. In 1969 when Indira Gandhi engineered a split in the party, then all but eclipsed the wing dominated by the old guard in the 1971 and 1972 national and state elections, the ideological symbols of the party were nudged perceptibly to the left.[51] Overlapping the Congress left are the socialist parties, whose complex chronicle of mergers and splits need not be recounted here. In 1971, the two major socialist parties, the Praja Socialist Party and the Sanyukta Socialist Party, merged to fight the most recent elections jointly. At the left end is the Communist movement, which in 1964 split into the Communist Party of India (CPI) and the Communist Party of India (Marxist) (CPM); the scission reflected both internal factionalism and the external tensions of the Moscow-Peking struggle.[52]

Of these party sets, only the Jana Sangh is heavily invested with communal symbols. The party itself stoutly denies this, arguing that its goal is the elimination of alien Western trappings and the Indianization of national culture. However, in the eyes of all its adversaries, the Jana Sangh is a Hindu communal party. The Indian national culture which it promotes is that of the north Indian heartland—Hindi in language, Hindu in religion, Sanskritic in culture history. It is no accident that the JS is, in fact, a regional party; its 35 seats in the 1967

49. Howard Erdman, *The Swatantra Party and Indian Conservatism* (Cambridge: Cambridge University Press, 1967).

50. Angela Burger, *Opposition in a Dominant Party System; A Study of Jana Sangh, the Praja Socialist Party and the Socialist Party in Uttar Pradesh, India* (Berkeley: University of California Press, 1969).

51. Stanley A. Kochanek, *The Congress Party of India* (Princeton: Princeton University Press, 1968).

52. The best study of Indian communism is Marcus Franda, *Radical Politics in West Bengal* (Cambridge: M.I.T. Press, 1971). For an older treatment, see Gene D. Overstreet and Marshall Windmiller, *Communism in India* (Berkeley: University of California Press, 1960).

Lok Sabha (national parliament), a high-water mark, were virtually all from Hindi-speaking constituencies. Twenty-eight were won in Uttar Pradesh, Madhya Pradesh, and Delhi. In the five important non-Hindi states of Andhra Pradesh, Kerala, Mysore, Tamil Nadu, and West Bengal, Jana Sangh was able to field only 15 candidates for the 166 Lok Sabha seats in the 1971 national elections.[53]

However, all parties in their actual functioning interact with the culturally plural environment. On the right, Swatantra has as its core support mercantile and commercial leading castes outside the Hindi heartland. At its peak in 1967, it won 44 Lok Sabha seats, when its natural base was augmented by alliances made possible by a wave of anti-Congress sentiment, at which point it was a non-Communist, non-communalist alternative. However, 37 of those were in only five states (Gujarat, Rajasthan, Mysore, Orissa, and Tamil Nadu). In only the first two states was its vote over 20 percent; in Rajasthan, the mercantile base is augmented by backing of a number of princely families and Rajput landlords. On the left, Communist strength has been highly localized in West Bengal, Andhra Pradesh, and Kerala. In West Bengal, its central base lies among a *déclassé* segment of the old *bhadralok* in Calcutta, who have experienced a sharp status decline both within Bengal and on an all-India basis; Bengalis, who once dominated the Indian intellectual scheme, played a marginal role in the later stages of Indian nationalism and in postindependence all-India politics. Intellectual unemployment on a wide scale have diminished both status and resources in Calcutta. In Andhra, the cultural pillar of the Communist movement has been the Kamma caste group, a rising cultivator group locked in bitter competition with the Reddis for social leadership and status in the Telugu area. In Kerala, Communist backing has been mainly from the Ezhavas, a very numerous (34 percent) scheduled caste.

Particularly in the actual conduct of electoral campaigns, cultural arithmetic is crucial. As F. G. Bailey has shrewdly observed, candidates must, in practice, go after "vote-banks," or blocs of voters, through the alliances they form and patronage they pledge to dispense. Speaking of Orissa politics, he goes on to suggest:..."Parties have no moral appeal. The importance of caste is that this alone has the possibility of providing the politician with a ready-made *moral* element on which he can draw to form associations, without the members of those associations calculating at every step what they are getting out of it."[54] A national conference of Indian social scientists organized on the theme

53. *Asian Recorder*, April 16-22, 1971.
54. F. G. Bailey, *Politics and Social Change: Orissa in 1959* (Berkeley: University of California Press, 1963), pp. 100-101, 135.

of state politics and parties in 1967 concluded that of all the factors which might explain voting behavior, ideology was the least important, that mass publics simply did not vote ideology.[55] The 1971-72 election results suggest a partial triumph of Indira Gandhi socialism over the patronage machines of old Congress, and imply some qualification to a total discount of mass ideology. Nonetheless, we may suggest that parties and electoral competition in India function in part to diffuse the impact of cultural pluralism by acting as broker between cultural segmentation at the mass level and ideological debate among the political elite. In the Bagehot metaphor, the party system, in serving as a buckle binding populace to polity, is a transformational link converting cultural pluralism into ideology.

The Congress Party is of such prime importance in the Indian system that it requires special attention. From its birth in 1885, it has always enjoyed a primacy in Indian politics; certainly one of its enduring strengths is the rich historical tradition which it embodies. No political movement in the developing world can match the longevity of Congress or its record of accomplishment. Initially a convention of intellectuals and professionals, after World War I it became a mass movement. During the interwar period, it was an aggregative, comprehensive nationalist movement, which contained within its encompassing frame the partly distinctive movements which after independence broke out to form the pentagonal party system described above. Groups as disparate as Hindu communal organizations and Communists were for important periods within Congress in the terminal colonial era.

After independence, it has retained its position as dominant party in India through five general elections, even though it came close to losing its primacy in the 1967 balloting. Throughout this period, Congress has been in power, not only in the center, but also in most states. Congress had functioned as an aggregative, brokerage, buffering, and patronage machine which, whatever the blemishes implicit in those functions, has nonetheless been a prime agency of Indian unity and integration. At its top echelons has been a core national elite, of diverse regional provenience, whose commitment to Indian unity has provided a consociational grid for the nation. In the last analysis, it is the developmental leadership and integrative purpose in the Congress national elite which have reconciled cultural pluralism and all-Indian goals, which set India apart from, say, Switzerland and Lebanon, where cultural coexistance has as its price a self-denying ordinance in the exercise of central policy leadership.

55. Narain, *State Politics in India*, p. xxx.

The adaptive capacities of Congress were well demonstrated in the re-juvenation accomplished after the 1969 split. Indira Gandhi forced upon the party a more programmatic and ideological posture to repair the apparent damage done in the 1967 electoral debacle by the image of Congress as nothing more than a sprawling brokerage apparatus. Many of the party's elder leaders—vintage brokers all—were forced into a split, leaving the party divided between Indira Gandhi's "Reformed Congress," and what became known as Old Congress. In the 1971 national elections, the old wing of Congress formed what proved to be an ineffectual electoral alliance with Jana Sangh, Swatantra, and Sanjukta Socialists, and focussed their attack on the national leadership of Indira Gandhi. The results, however, were a sweeping triumph for the Reformed Congress, a victory then consolidated in a number of state elections in 1972. The Reformed Congress succeeded in all but eclipsing the old guard splinter and in restoring the party's hegemony within the all-India system.[56] To be complete, two other electoral categories deserve mention. In several states outside the Hindi-speaking core, local parties reflecting a specific cultural segment are important. In Tamil Nadu, the DMK, spokesman for Tamil cultural subnationalism, won the state elections in 1967 and 1972. In Punjab, the Sikh movement, Akali Dal, although not an electoral majority, is nonetheless a powerful communal interest group whose pressure forced the scission of old Punjab into a new, Sikh-majority province, with Hindu-majority zones carved out as the new state of Haryana. In Goa, conquered from the Portuguese after four centuries of Lusitanian rule, a distinctive local party persists, as was the case until the 1971-72 elections in Jammu & Kashmir, disputed between Pakistan and India. The eastern frontier states of Nagaland, Manipur, Tripura, and Meghalaya (carved out of "tribal" areas of Assam in 1971) are outside the Hindu tradition, played no part in Indian nationalist politics and have autonomy-oriented local parties. Independent candidates have also been important, expecially at the state level, winning over 20 percent of the state assembly seats in Andhra, Assam, Mysore, and Himachal Pradesh in the 1967 elections.[57] Tables 8.5-8.7 summarize electoral data in the five general elections held thus far.

The tables clearly reveal the impact of the electoral system in sustaining the hegemony of Congress. India's elections are conducted on

56. On the 1971 elections, see Stanley J. Higgenbottom, "The 1971 Revolution and Indian Voting Behavior," *Asian Survey*, XI, no. 12 (December 1971), 1133-52; and Myron Weiner, "The 1971 Elections and the Indian Party System," *Asian Survey*, XI, no. 12 (December 1971), 1153-66.

57. Narain, *State Politics in India*, p. 658. On the question of separatism among the small states on the eastern frontier, see Arthur J. Dommen, "Separatist Tendencies in Eastern India", *Asian Survey*, VII, no. 10 (October 1967), 726-38.

Table 8.5—Congress Status, Lok Sabha Elections, 1952-71

Year	% seats	% votes
1952	74.40	45.00
1957	75.10	47.78
1962	73.07	44.72
1967	54.60	40.92
1971[a]	71.07	53.48

[a]Both the reformed wing of Congress of Indira Gandhi and the old wing are included in this total. Reformed Congress alone won 67.96% of the seats and 43.00% of the vote.

Sources: Stanley A. Kochanek, *The Congress Party of India* (Princeton: Princeton University Press, 1968, p. 408; *Asian Recorder,* 16-22 April 1971.

single-member constituency plurality basis; however, Maurice Duverger's famed hypothesis on the tendency produced by the system toward a two-party politics has failed to be validated.[58] Few seats have a straight two-cornered race; in the 1971 national elections, for example, there were 2754 candidates for the 515 seats. This situation is a considerable advantage to the leading party; Congress, nationally, has never won an absolute majority (except by counting its two wings together in 1971). Reform Congress won 68 percent of the seats in 1971 with 43 percent of the votes. In Uttar Pradesh in 1952, Congress took 90.6 percent of the seats with 47.9 percent of the votes; in West Bengal in 1972, Reform Congress won a smashing 77.9 percent of the seats with a mere 50.6 percent of the vote. Although these are extreme examples, a glance at Table 8.6 reveals the potency of the multiplier which converts a plurality of votes into a large majority of seats; in only a few instances did Congress fall low enough for this mechanism to operate against it. The introduction of a proportional representation system would undoubtedly provide such inducements for fragmentation that cultural representation would be far greater.

Lijphart's theory of consociational democracy has application to the Indian pattern of integration.[59] The underlying cultural pluralism at the base becomes linked to ideological choice through the party system. The electoral system in turn serves to convert a still-fragmented expression of political will into a constitutional majority. At the summit is a national political elite who are committed to reconciling difference through bargaining amongst themselves. Although objective measures of skilled leadership are hard to come by, few would dispute the propo-

58. Maurice Duverger, *Political Parties, Their Organization and Activity in the Modern State* (London: Methuen, 1967), pp. 216-28.

59 Lijphart, *The Politics of Accommodation.*

Table 8.6— Congress in State Assemblies, 1952-72

State	1952		1957		1962		1967		1972[a]	
	% seats	% vote	% seats	% vote	% seats	% vote	% seats	% vote	% seats	% vote
Andhra Pradesh	28.1	29.7	62.1	41.3	59.0	47.4	57.5	44.7	76.3	51.6
Assam	72.3	43.8	72.3	52.4	75.2	48.3	58.1	43.5	82.5	53.2
Bihar	72.7	41.4	66.0	41.9	58.1	41.3	40.3	32.8	61.9	48.0
Gujarat	86.3	54.9	73.4	48.7	73.3	50.7	55.4	45.9	92.8	74.0
Haryana[b]					57.4	40.4	59.3	41.4	82.7	57.7
Himachal Pradesh[c]					79.6	51.5	56.7	42.6	78.5	53.5
Jammu & Kashmir[d]							82.2	52.6	77.0	55.9
Kerala	32.8	34.3	34.1	37.8	50.0	34.1[e]	6.8	35.4	f	
Madhya Pradesh	77.4	48.1	80.5	49.8	49.3	38.6	56.4	40.7	74.3	48.4
Maharashtra	82.1	45.2	51.8	48.7	81.4	51.2	75.2	47.9	82.2	57.4
Manipur[g]	19.1		36.7		51.7	28.9	55.2	32.6	30.0	32.6
Meghalaya[h]									15.0	10.1
Mysore	84.2	51.5	72.5	52.1	66.3	49.8	58.3	49.7	87.5	79.3
Nagaland[i]									f	
Orissa	47.8	38.8	40.0	38.2	58.5	43.3	22.1	30.7	63.5	
Punjab[j]	65.0	34.8	77.9	47.5	57.5	45.6	46.2	37.4	79.3	43.0
Rajasthan	50.0	39.7	68.7	45.2	57.9	36.1	48.4	41.4	f	53.2
Tamil Nadu	50.4	40.0	73.6	45.3	67.4	46.1	21.4	41.5	f	
Uttar Pradesh	90.6	47.9	66.5	42.4	57.9	36.1	46.8	32.1	f	
West Bengal	63.2	38.9	60.3	46.1	62.3	47.3	45.4	41.0	77.9	50.6

(See footnotes on next page.)

Table 8.6 *(continued)*

aThe 1972 totals lump together returns for both wings of Congress; only in Bihar (13.9%), Gujarat (23.7%), Haryana (10.8%), and Mysore (25.7%) was the old Congress vote more than 3%.

bThe 1952 and 1957 Haryana vote is included in old Punjab, of which it was then a part.

cThe 1952 and 1957 tallies for Himachal Pradesh are included in old Punjab, of which it was then a part.

dTotals are not available for the first elections in Jammu & Kashmir; Congress as such had no foothold until the 1967 elections.

eThis figure is for by-elections held in 1960.

fNo state elections were held in 1972.

gManipur was a Union territory in the early years, and no figures are available. State elections were held in 1972, but returns are not available.

hMeghalaya was created out of Assam in 1972; its earlier totals are included in the Assam figures.

iNagaland was in a disturbed state during much of this period; no elections were held in 1972. In 1964 state elections, the first after statehood, Congress won none of the 46 seats; the largest party was the Naga Nationalist Party, which won 33.

jPunjab figures for 1952 and 1957 include Haryana and Himachal Pradesh.

Sources: Figures for 1952, 1957, and 1962 are taken from Myron Weiner (ed.), *State Politics in India* (Princeton: Princeton University Press, 1968), p. 46. The 1967 figures are drawn from Stanley I. Kochanel, *The Congress Party of India* (Princeton: Princeton University Press, 1968), p. 409. The 1972 returns are found in Marcus F. Franda, "India's 1972 State Elections," *Fieldstaff Reports,* American Universities Field Staff, South Asia Series, vol. XVI, no. 1 (1972).

Table 8.7 Distribution of State Assembly Seats, 1967-72

State	Year	Congress [a]		Swatantra		Jana Sangh		Communists [b]		Socialists [c]		Other parties	
		% votes	No. seats	% votes	No. seats	% votes	No. seats	% votes	No. seats	% votes	No. seats	% votes	No. seats
Andhra Pradesh	1967	45.3	165	9.8	29	2.1	3	15.4	19	0.6	1	26.8	68
	1972	51.8	219	2.3	2	1.8	0	9.2	8	0.4	0	34.5	58
Assam	1967	43.6	72	1.5	2	1.8	0	7.2	7	10.2	9	35.7	34
	1972	53.7	94	0.6	1	0.3	0	8.2	3	5.7	4	31.5	12
Bihar	1967	33.1	128	2.3	3	10.4	26	8.2	28	20.9	86	25.1	47
	1972	48.0	197	0.8	2	12.0	26	8.6	35	16.1	33	14.5	25
Gujarat	1967	45.7	92	38.2	65	1.9	1	0	0	3.7	3	10.5	7
	1972	74.0	155	1.9	0	9.1	3	0.9	1	1.0	0	13.1	8
Haryana	1967	41.3	48	3.2	3	14.4	12	1.4	0	3.8	0	35.8	18
	1972	57.7	64	0	0	6.6	2	2.4	0	0.3	0	33.0	15
Himachal Pradesh	1967	42.2	33	1.9	1	13.9	7	3.4	2	1.3	0	37.4	13
	1972	53.5	51	0	0	8.1	5	3.2	1	0.1	0	35.1	8
Jammu & Kashmir	1967	53.0	59	0	0	16.5	3	0.5	0	1.0	0	29.0	10
	1972	55.9	57	0.1	0	10.5	3	0.4	0	0.1	0	33.0	14
Kerala	1967	35.4	9	0.2	0	0.9	0	31.0	71	8.6	19	22.9	34
	1972					(no elections held)							
Madhya Pradesh	1967	40.1	167	2.6	7	28.3	78	1.3	1	10.0	19	17.7	24
	1972	48.4	220	0.6	0	28.5	48	1.2	3	6.3	7	15.0	18

Table 8.7 (continued)

State	Year	Congress[a] % votes	Congress No. seats	Swatantra % votes	Swatantra No. seats	Jana Sangh % votes	Jana Sangh No. seats	Communists[b] % votes	Communists No. seats	Socialists[c] % votes	Socialists No. seats	Other parties % votes	Other parties No. seats
Maharashtra	1967	47.0	202	1.1	0	8.2	4	6.0	11	8.5	12	29.2	40
	1972	56.3	222	0.1	0	6.3	5	3.6	3	4.6	3	28.0	37
Manipur	1967	32.5	16	0	0	0	0	6.1	1	12.5	4	48.9	9
	1972	32.6	18	0	0	0	0	10.1	5	5.4	3	61.0	34
Meghalaya	1967[d]												
	1972	10.1	9	0		0		0.6	0	0	0	89.3	51
Mysore	1967	48.6	126	6.6	16	2.8	4	1.6	2	11.4	26	29.0	42
	1972	79.3	189	0.6	0	4.0	0	2.1	3	1.7	3	12.3	21
Nagaland	1967	(no elections held)											
	1972												
Orissa	1967		30		49		0		8		23		29
	1972	(no elections held)											
Punjab	1967	36.6	48	0.5	0	9.8	9	8.5	8	1.2	1	29.0	38
	1972	43.0	66	0.1	0	5.0	0	9.8	11	0.9	0	41.2	27
Rajasthan	1967	41.4	89	22.1	49	11.7	22	2.2	1	5.6	8	17.0	15
	1972	53.2	146	12.3	11	12.2	8	2.5	4	2.4	4	17.3	11
Tamil Nadu	1967		49		20		0		13		6		146
	1972	(no elections held)											

State	Year						
Uttar Pradesh	1967	199	12	98	15	55	37
	1972						
West Bengal	1967	127	1	1	59	14	78
		41.1	0.8	1.3	24.6	28.2	4.0
	1972	218	0	0	49	0	13
		50.6	0	0.2	35.9	12.4	0.9
			(no elections held)				
Totals	1967	1659 (49.9%)	257 (7.4%)	268 (7.6%)	246 (7.1%)	286 (8.1%)	698 (20%)
	1972	1925 (74.6%)	16 (0.6%)	100 (3.9%)	126 (6.3%)	57 (2.1%)	352 (12.5%)

(no elections held)

aBoth wings of Congress are lumped together in the 1972 totals.

bCPI and CPI(M).

cPraja Socialists and Sanjukta Socialists.

dMeghalaya was created in 1972, out of Assam.

Sources: Marcus F. Franda, "India's 1972 State Elections," *Fieldstaff Reports*, American Universities Field Staff, South Asia Series, vol. XVI, no. 1 (1972); Iqbal Narain (ed.), *State Politics in India* (Meerut: Meenakshi Prakashan, (1967), pp. 658-59.

sition that India has been endowed with a very high order of top political officeholders. And leadership of great skill is certainly a prerequisite for orderly functioning of the system.

India began independence with a large and talented cadre, who had committed decades to nationally oriented political organization and agitation. Pessimists on India's future, such as Selig Harrison, have argued that this cohort is a wasting asset, that increasingly India's leadership will be regionally recruited and linguistically oriented.[60] The pathways to national leadership have certainly altered since independence; even if the new generation of leaders in the political realm win their spurs initially in the state arena, the cooptative force of a nationally oriented ethos may be sufficiently institutionalized so that there is a steady influx of new elites transferring their major locus of operation to the national level. The plaintive criticism voiced by a Gujarati political scientist at the transformation of Mararjee Desai when he shifted from the state to the national scene suggests this often occurs. "Gujarat," he wrote, "finds itself in an unenviable position of having a leader without being able to derive any worthwhile benefit from him."[61]

Although state powers are extensive and the currents of decentralization flow strongly in contemporary India, the central prerogatives in relation to the states are far-reaching. The national parliament can form new states by majority vote, without the consent of the territories involved. If state laws are repugnant to national legislation, the latter prevails. Residual powers belong to the center. By a two-thirds vote of the upper house, the Council of States, parliament may enact legislation in any field on the enumerated list of state powers. Most important of all, the president has emergency powers to suspend the constitution and take over direct central administration of a state if a threat to national security is deemed to exist, a financial emergency arises, or constitutional government has broken down.[62] In 1962, in reaction to the very strong electoral showing of the DMK in Tamil Nadu, then overtly espousing secession, a constitutional amendment was passed forbidding candidates or office-holders from advocating separation. This amendment had the desired "chilling effect" on the DMK, who immediately thereafter abandoned the secession objective (a decision also facilitated by the wave of patriotism provoked by the Chinese invasion of 1962).[63] Presidential intervention, first gingerly employed in Kerala, has be-

60. Harrison, *India: The Most Dangerous Decades.*
61. Narain, *State Politics in India*, pp. 122-33.
62. Marcus F. Franda, *West Bengal and the Federalizing Process in India* (Princeton: Princeton University Press, 1968), p. 201.
63. Barnett, "The Politics of Cultural Nationalism: The D.M.K. in Tamil Nadu," p. 205.

come an institutionalized process built into the expectations of all actors; at the time of the 1972 state elections, presidential rule was in force in no less than six states. Thus, the central arena remains the authoritative locus of power.

Two additional potent institutions with a strong national orientation deserve mention—the central bureaucracy and the army. The Indian Administrative Service, successor to the colonial Indian Civil Service, elitist to the core, mans the national bureaucratic establishment, both in the center and in the states. Small—only about 2000—highly selective, imbued with an administrative culture that has important continuities with the ICS, the IAS is a veritable nervous system for the polity. The armed forces likewise are a powerful instrument of unity, in spite of the tradition of very imbalanced recruiting developed by the British. The theory of "martial races," possessing communal values of courage and physical endurance, emerged in the late nineteenth century. Thereafter, recruitment was heavily concentrated in the northwest of India, with Nepāli Gurkhas, Punjabi Sikhs and Muslims, Hindu Jats and Rajputs, being favored groups. In order to maintain intact social rituals and controls, small units were homogeneously recruited among quite localized subcastes. But the principle of a communally structured army has been gradually diluted and recruitment made more representative of the country as a whole—although as late as the mid-1950s one-third of military academy entrants were Punjabis, while the four Dravidian states each had less than 5 percent, and West Bengal less than 1 percent.[64] The armed forces total 930,000, more than enough to leave no doubt where power lies. Our point here is that, through its constitutional prerogatives and through the capabilities of the national political elite, the central bureaucracy, and the army, the ultimate authority of the center and integrity of the state seems beyond challenge. This, of course, is in addition to the affective attachments which the idea of One India commands among the politically conscious segments of the population, and the legitimacy accruing to the central political institutions from the democratic processes through which their mandate to rule is validated.

POLITICAL CONFLICT IN THE STATES

At the state level, cultural conflict is much more intense and direct. However, as Weiner has cogently observed, it is almost always a web

64. Stephen P. Cohen, *The Indian Army* (Berkeley: University of California Press, 1971), p. 183.

of conflict whose boundaries are demarcated by the state frontiers. Very rarely does a moment of cultural tension in one state spill over into the next. The configuration of cleavage is invariably particular to a given state, and there would simply be no way for neighboring groups to relate themselves to it; cultural segments are not threatened by what happens in the neighboring states. Nor does the structure of politics provide the basis for a mutually advantageous alliance with a given participant in a contiguous battleground.[65]

Various cultural attributes may be noted which affect the pattern of conflict within states and their relationship with the center. Probably the most important differentiating factor, and greatest challenge to national integration, lies in the degree of cultural distance from the Hindi language, Sanskritic tradition of Hindu theological and cultural scholarship, focussed in north central India. Although India is a secular state and officially eschews any regional predominance in its cultural self-definition, yet there is an unmistakable center of gravity to its most cherished symbols of national identity. There is, however diffusely, a cultural heartland, in the Gangetic plain, symbolized in the location of the political capital in Delhi and more unambiguously affirmed through the choice of Hindi as the national language, even if its full coronation is indefinitely postponed. Degrees of tension in the relationship between the states and the national system bear some relationship to the cultural distance from the Hindu heartland; it has been most difficult with Tamil Nadu, the four small states of the eastern frontier, and Kashmir, all distinguished from the Hindi core on somewhat different cultural dimensions. However, linguistic tensions within states have largely disappeared with the virtual completion of state reorganization on linguistic bases.

State politics are the level at which caste becomes a factor. Electoral politics provide mobilized caste groupings the resources needed to enter the game; they do constitute credible vote banks and necessarily enter the coalition calculations of party leaders. The essential opportunism of caste affiliations in politics has made its role fluid and complex. The obvious riposte of a competing party is to make sure that no caste bloc of demonstrated performance as a vote bank—either through the horizontal mobilization of their followers or the vertical delivery of their dependent clientele from poorly politicized and socially vulnerable lower castes—is permitted to go unchallenged. The classic art of ticket balancing is the usual device. Thus in Andhra

65. Weiner has succinctly stated this argument in a frequently quoted passage, *State Politics in India*, p. 53.

Pradesh, the powerful Communist Party, initially linked with the Kammas, have a Reddi president, while Congress, well-supported by the Reddi rising cultivators, seeks to divide the Communist Kamma constituency. In Kerala, the CPI(M), largest party in the 1967 state elections, have an Ezhava base, but a Brahman, E. M. S. Namboodiripad, as leader. Castes as vote banks are free to change their deposits from one party to another; what is less clear is who within the group has the capacity to deliver the bank. Often it is only the elections themselves that will demonstrate who has the combination to the safe.

There can be no doubt that parties have become much more sophisticated in learning how to reckon with the caste factor. Universal suffrage elections with the overpowering Hindu-Muslim cleavage removed from the arena began only after independence. Initially, no one could be sure what the factors in voting behavior would be. Interesting testimony to that fact is that as astute a student of Indian politics as Myron Weiner, in his 1957 study on party politics, makes almost no mention of caste as a political factor. This partly reflects the national focus of the study, where caste is much less visible, but also is a faithful rendering of the state of the political art among the Indian political elite.[66] It was only after the second general elections, in 1957, that a fuller appreciation of the impact of caste as an orienting factor for mass publics became appreciated. In the meantime, elementary—and costly—errors were made in candidate selection; individuals were nominated from a caste only weakly represented in a constituency with a clearly dominant caste. This is the precise American equivalent of nominating a White candidate in a Black ghetto constituency or a Black in a White suburb or an Irishman in an Italian neighborhood.

Cultural pluralism in state politics overlays a pattern of intense factionalism, a phenomenon to be found at all political levels. One interesting theory of factionalism is advanced by Harold Gould:

Whether they are called "factions"—as political scientists like Paul Brass and anthropologists like Oscar Lewis have preferred to do—or something else, I would hold that the relatively small, intensely personalistic structures which abound at every level of Indian political life, and which so rarely assimilate themselves to large structures, are social manifestations of a largely unconscious "jati model" which governs group formation. Because the overwhelming majority of Indians are dominated in so many aspects of their individual and collective lives by *consciously formulated* caste structures *in being*, they rather inevitably and understandably seek to reproduce the *essential properties* sociologically and psy-

66. Myron Weiner, *Party Politics in India* (Princeton: Princeton University press, 1957).

chologically inherent in these structures in contemporary social spheres like politics and bureaucracies.[67]

Franda has observed that political leaders have an interest in sustaining factionalism, so that patronage flows through them rather than the impersonal institution of the party.[68] Each major leader has a personal following, bound to him through intimate, personalized ties, which themselves are relatively stable and persistent. A given faction is quite likely to have the personalized linkages reinforced by cultural commonalities; however, the total configuration of factionalism does not completely overlap cultural segmentation and, through the flow of alliances and animosities, partly cross-cuts it. As the largest party, Congress offers the most nourishing pasture for factionalism. An important structural factor is rivalry between Congress ministries in states where the party is in power (most of them most of the time) and the state party committee. Here the classical tension arises, well known to students of British political parties, between those deriving their authority from the elected assembly and those whose legitimacy accrues from the decision-making instances of the party.

Thus postpartition India, like postfirst-republic Nigeria, derives a degree of integrative strength from the very complexity of its cleavages. Cultural segmentation, within the present framework, is not aggregative. The linkages between conflict patterns within states are few, and spillover effect is very limited. Interactions between the state and national arenas are discrete and separate; groups of states do not share clear cultural commonalities, which dictate alliances between states. Aggregative politics and linkage functions have remained the domain of the political parties, which necessarily make use of cultural pluralism, but are not creatures of it—with the partial exception of the Jana Sangh.

India differs in cultural terms from Nigeria on one important count: there is a core set of national identity symbols, linked to the Hindi-Hindu-Sanskritic trinity and regionally seated in the Gangetic plain. Nigeria as a polity is culturally neutral; its national institutions are devoid of association with particular communal symbols and could only acquire such connotations in the now unlikely eventuality of their capture by one of the major ethnic configurations. There is both opportunity and peril in the core culture. If the elements of affective linkage gradually enlarge in a fashion which avoids cultural threat to the nonheartland states, then the rich sense of history and civilization can contribute power-

67. Harold A. Gould, "Toward a 'Jati Model' for Indian Politics," *Economic and Political Weekly* (Bombay), Feb. 1, 1964, p. 193, quoted in Franda, *Radical Politics in West Bengal*, p.246.
68. Ibid., p. 249.

fully to the ideology of nationalism. Conversely, if the heartland pursues policies which awaken linguistic or religious insecurities for outlying states, grave dangers can result. In the short run, the issue most calculated to activate the perilous alignment of heartland versus periphery is language. With patience and tact, the national role of Hindi may well be gradually enlarged to a point where it may gain broader acceptance as a national language. However, its most vigorous promoters are communalist interests within the heartland, represented politically by the Jana Sangh, whose strain of cultural exclusivism is little calculated to allay anxieties on the rimland. It proves very difficult to promote the development and modernization of Hindi without placing these responsibilities in the hands of a communal literati committed to the principle of Sanskritization, which removed the language from the verbal reach of even the mass public in the heartland, and diminished its utility as a lingua franca.[69] The cultural threat is felt most strongly by segments of the population whose interests and mobility aspirations are most immediately affected; young people, above all students, have provided the troops for linguistic riots. The doorway to an all-India career, above all in the prestigious IAS, is seen to be closed to the outlying linguistic zones by a Hindi-only policy. It is, in fact, a doorway through which relatively few will pass, but it remains nonetheless a consuming dream for a much larger number. It is no accident that Tamil Nadu, where the violence of anti-Hindi sentiment is strongest, had the highest fraction of entrants to the Indian Administrative Service during the 1948-60 period. No less than 24.1 percent of the new recruits were Tamils, although they are only 7.7 percent of the population.[70]

The pressures of resource scarcity on cultural fissures deserve mention. The 1967 electoral disaster for Congress and an upsurge in fissiparous pressures came on the heels of some bad monsoons and a phase of agricultural hardship. The era of good feeling which led to the 1971-1972 Congress sweeps would seem to have had some relationship to several good harvests and a growing sense of self-confidence over the apparent triumph of the "Green Revolution." Crisis returned in 1972 with another bad monsoon, and in a number of regions the economy became precarious. The extreme level of tension in Andhra Pradesh in 1972-73, although articulated in regional goals for splitting the province, had much to do with an intensifying struggle for employment opportunities, greatly sharpened by hard times in the economy. In Nigeria, on the other hand, the returns on the oil bonanza really began to

69. Das Gupta, *Language Conflict*, pp. 163-92.

70. Nayar, *National Communication and Language Policy in India*, p. 115. Punjab and Delhi were the only other regions significantly overrepresented.

flow on a lavish scale only after the civil war. To the structural factors we have argued in assessing the transformation of the parameters of pluralism must also be added the critical advantage of ample resources. The bitter edge of struggle is removed when the national institutions can manage distributive politics in such a way that something palpable is available for all.

Nigeria and India are both living experiments in human organization whose success as civil polities vitally affects the interests of all mankind. Mere survival is not enough; poverty as well as cultural pluralism must be confronted. Only the state can provide the essential direction in the unending struggle for development; should it be so paralyzed in its capacity to act by the suffusion of cultural conflict into all of its processes, prospects for a large segment of the human community would be dim. Such indeed was the vision implied in cultural conflict on a vast scale incorporated as a two- or three-person game—which, in the Indian case, did lead to partition. But the record does not support such a pessimistic view within the present framework of segmented cultural complexity. Nigeria, awash on a sea of oil, has been in a mood of confident development since the end of the civil war. India had had no such geological blessing, but the record of accomplishment over two decades of development planning, when set against the magnitude of the challenge, is remarkable.[71]

71. For a balanced assessment on this point, see John N. Mellor, Thomas F. Weaver, Ume J. Lele, and Sheldon R. Simon, *Developing Rural India: Plan and Practice* (Ithaca: Cornell University Press, 1968), and George Rosen, *Democracy and Economic Change in India* (Berkeley: University of California Press, 1966).

9 Indonesia and the Philippines: Integration and Cultural Pluralism in the Archipelago Republics

Indonesia and the Philippines, as nation-states, share a number of properties which make feasible a paired analysis of the politics of national integration and cultural pluralism.[1] Both polities are archipelago republics with a huge number of islands stretching over a broad swathe of Southeast Asia. Both have a single island which predominates as locus of political power, cultural core, and major concentration of population, respectively Java and Luzon. The Philippines, with 7100 islands, stretches for 1150 miles north to south; Indonesia, with 13,000 islands, extends approximately 3600 miles from east to west. In both cases, approximately half the population lives on the socially dominant island, which also contains the capital city (3 million for Jakarta, 1.5 million for Manila), a sprawling center which has given rise to a metropolitan culture of great importance for the integration of the states. Neither polity grew out of a historical kingdom; both are defined by the ambit of a colonial jurisdiction. In both cases, the ideology of nationalism has found a linguistic base, through the development of a national language uniquely identified with the national collectivity.

The differences, of course, are very great as well. Indonesia was in the mainstream of Southeast Asian history, and important areas were organized as precolonial kingdoms; the Philippines were on the

1. This chapter has been prepared with the invaluable assistance of Mohammed Kismadi, who served as my research assistant for 18 months. Scholar-teacher-journalist, Kismadi brought to his work the rich insights of his intimate knowledge of politics and society in his native land of Indonesia. He had taught for five years in a Filipino university in Mindanao. He is, of course, absolved from all errors which his best efforts could not enjoin; however, my debt to him is enormous. He produced a series of essays on specific aspects of integration and pluralism in these two countries, based on thorough coverage of published sources, filtered through the insightful *ferstehen* of his profound knowledge and understanding. These essays were then the subject of weekly conversations, to enlarge and expand upon them. In the footnotes to this chapter, where a specific reference is appropriate, it will be so noted; for facts or interpretations which are attributable to materials prepared by Kismadi, reference will be made to "Kismadi research notes."

periphery of these developments. The great traditions of Hinduism and Islam both had a profound impact on Indonesia, whereas the Philippines were only marginally touched by the latter. Spanish, then American colonial rule lasted for four centuries in the Philippines, with far-reaching effects on social structure and identity-formation processes; in the absence of competition from an established universal religion, Christianity, in its Catholic version, was thoroughly implanted. In Indonesia, although the operations of the private Dutch East India Company date back to the seventeenth century, colonialism became a serious undertaking only after the end of the Napoleonic wars in the early nineteenth century. Indonesia's independence was won by armed revolution; the Philippines achieved sovereignty by peaceful and constitutional processes.

But the commonalities nonetheless suffice to permit the parallel discussion of the two systems. After a consideration of the patterns of cultural pluralism in each country, we will examine the interaction of the national political arena and its cultural segments. Finally, the use of language as an integrative device deserves some special attention.

CULTURAL POLARITIES IN INDONESIA

Indonesia is commonly discussed in terms of a series of polarities of culture—Javanese aristocratic versus Islamic entrepreneurial, santri (devout) versus abangan (statistical) Muslims, prijaji (aristocratic culture) versus folk, modernist versus traditionalist. Each of these polarities may serve as a different prism, diffracting a particular facet of pluralism operating on a system-wide basis. Taken together, they provide a persuasive explanation for the initial postindependence party system.

The Javanese aristocratic/Islamic entrepreneurial dichotomy is attributable to Herbert Feith.[2] The former was the center of Hindu culture in Indonesia, had an agricultural economy, a shallow overlay of Islam, and long and intense colonial impact. The latter derives from the maritime Islamic sultanates based on the east Sumatran coast; commercially oriented, it has been less socialist, more anti-Chinese. Sumatran groups such as the east coast Malaya, Minangkabau, Achinese, and Buginese of Sulawesi (Celebes) would be included.

The explication of the *santri/abangan* duality derives from the seminal Geertz study, *The Religion of Java. Santri* are the pious followers of Islam

2. Herbert Feith, *The Decline of Constitutional Democracy in Indonesia* (Ithaca: Cornell University Press, 1962), pp. 31-32.

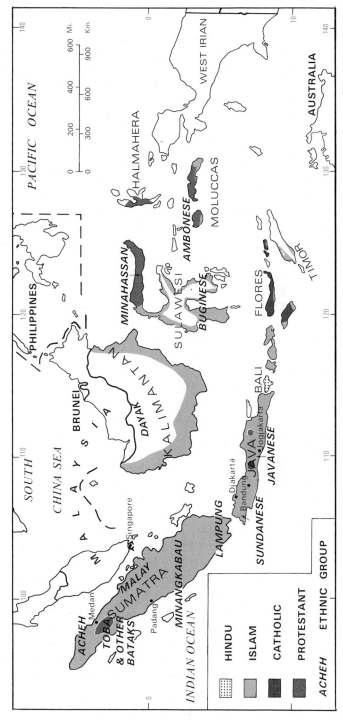

Map 9.1 Indonesia: Religion and Ethnicity

who have fully mastered its theological requirements, and faithfully follow the five pillars of Islam. *Abangan* are attracted by its external ritual, but little interested in its theology. External practices of Islam rest lightly on an older folk culture (Hindu in the Javanese case); the ritual as practiced by abangan is described by santri as utterly at variance with true Islam. The santri are more numerous among Sumatran Muslims than among Javanese.

The santri can be further divided into traditionalist and reform-oriented streams. The most important expression of the modernist trend was the Muhammidiya movement, founded in 1912, which was particularly influential on Sumatra.[3] Traditionalist interpretations of Islam were especially strong in Acheh on the northern tip of Sumatra and among segments of the Sundanese in West Java, reflected in the Darul Islam insurrection in the early years of independence. Traditionalist *santri* are wont to accord special deference to the views of *ulama* (religious teachers) in politics as well as to the Koran.

Yet another dichotomy is between the aristocratic culture and status, associated in the first instances with the traditional Javanese ruling class and the more particularistic folk perspectives. The *prijaji* term has been used in somewhat varying ways in the literature, and by extension has often come to refer to the Javanese bureaucratic class, or even the educated elite more generally. Linked to the *prijaji* concept is the metropolitan urban elite, identified by Hildred Geertz as a distinctive cultural category.[4] This group has been steeped in the Indonesian nationalist movement, operating within the central arena of politics, and correspondingly less closely linked to their ethnic origins.

At least in the *abangan* sense, the overwhelming majority of the populace are Muslims, with the proportion estimated at 90 percent. Despite its small size numerically, the Christian community has been important in cultural politics. Christian missionary activity was very selective, of necessity focused upon zones where Islam had not arrived first. Protestant evangelization was extensive among the Toba Bataks on Sumatra, the Minahassans (Menadonese) in Sulawesi, and the Ambonese in the Moluccas. Catholic efforts centered in the lesser Sunda islands. Christianity was linked with access to schools, and these in turn to mobility and status. Toba Bataks, Minahassans, and Ambonese are strongly represented in the elite in proportion to their numbers. The latter two groups were particularly relied upon by the colonizer as senior intermediaries and were also heavily used in the colonial constabulary.

3. On Muhammidiya, see Alfian, "Islamic Modernism in Indonesian Politics, The Muhammadiyah Movement During the Dutch-Colonial Period, 1912-1942," (Ph.D. diss., University of Wisconsin, 1969).

4. Hildred Geertz, "Indonesian Cultures and Communities," in Ruth McVey (ed.), *Indonesia* (New Haven: Human Relations Area Files Press, 1963), p. 36.

In terms of ethnolinguistic cultural groups, the most fundamental fact is the size and cultural characteristics of the Javanese. The last census to include a linguistic classification was that of 1930; at that time, Javanese totalled 47 percent. Feith estimates their present proportion as 52 percent, while Hildred Geertz ventures the much lower figure of 40 percent.[5] They are, accordingly, several times larger than the next most numerous group. They occupy the central and eastern provinces of the island of Java; although the capital of Jakarta lies in Sundanese country in West Java, ethnic Javanese are strongly represented in the city. Of the 645 ministerial level posts from 1945 to 1970, 61 percent were held by Javanese.[6] A very large proportion of the nationalist leadership was Javanese; in every respect, they are the primary, central group.

We may argue that the Javanese had the most firmly established ethnic identity historically. The Majapahit medieval empire was Javanese. The Javanese language was well developed and had a literary tradition. Javanese cultural pride certainly draws sustenance from this heritage, a self-confident sense of their leading role in Indonesia. However, modernization and political competition has not given rise to a strongly asserted Javanese cultural ideology, a fact of great moment in the integrative process. One set of explanations lies in the early commitment of the nationalist elite to Indonesian as a national language at an early date, a point to which we will return at the end of this chapter. Feith observes that there was no strong focus on the Javanese by others; most interethnic competition did not involve the Javanese.[7] Groups with the most explicitly developed identities, other than the Javanese, were on other islands. To this we may add the observation that neither social change nor political competition ever posed a cultural threat to Javanese. A leading place for Javanese did not require conscious assertion; it was there, without dispute. No other Indonesian group posed a challenge to the Javanese primacy, beginning with Sukarno and continuing with Suharto and his predominantly Javanese junta. We do not, of course, mean to suggest there is no current of anti-Javanese resentment on the outer islands. Nor should we overlook the important degree to which Javanese symbols did dominate state mythology, especially under Sukarno. However, the Javanese did not articulate a doctrine of domination, which might have bred anxieties among others.

Political sequences are no doubt relevant as well. The first nationalist political group, the Sarekat Islam, was founded in 1912 in the Java-

5. Feith, *The Decline of Constitutional Democracy in Indonesia*, p. 29; H. Geertz, "Indonesian Cultures and Communities."

6. Calculated by Kismadi.

7. Feith, *The Decline of Constitutional Democracy in Indonesia*, p. 29.

nese heartland, but catalyzed nationalist grievances through the medium of religious symbols of identity. Von der Mehden argues that, in its initial Javanese base, "the assumption of racial superiority by the Javanese" was an important source of the moral energy which fueled the movement.[8] Yet it was the lexicon of Islamic solidarity that gave voice to these sentiments, which permitted their extension to other Muslim communities. The social enemies of Sarekat Islam, apart from the colonial regime, were the Chinese commercial intermediaries. In the 1920s, the Nationalist (PNI) and Communist (PKI) parties were founded, creating a dialectic between secular, religious, and Marxist definitions of nationalism which did not become linked with patterns of ethnic pluralism.

There has been some migration both in and out of Java, but the pattern has not been symmetrical. Upward mobiles from socially competitive groups, endowed with good educational facilities or sustained by a mercantile tradition migrate to Jakarta: these are mainly Minangkabau, Toba Bataks, Minahassans, Ambonese, and, as traders, east coast Malays. The social medium in which most of these compete is dominated by the metropolitan urban culture, is linguistically Malay-Indonesian and not specifically Javanese. Thus, their problem tends to be their competitive relations with each other, rather than defining relationships of rivalry, dominance, or subordination to Javanese. Migration by Javanese, on the other hand, has mainly been peasants of the *abangan* category, who come stripped of the *prijaji* element from whom, in the deferential, clientage-oriented home environment, social and cultural leadership would have come. Many were recruited as plantation workers, who were often easier to induce into (low) wage labor than neighboring Sumatran groups, or as part of government-sponsored resettlement schemes in southern Sumatra or coastal Kalimantan (Borneo) or as demobilized army units. Socially decapitated, these peasant communities lacked the cultural spokesmen who might have given aggressive, and thus threatening, advocacy to ethnic claims of the Javanese immigrants.[9]

Javanese culture is by no means uniform or monolithic. The historic heartland of Javanese culture lies inland and to the south; it is embedded in the traditions of the princely states of Jogjakarta, Surakarta (or Solo), and Tjirebon, where the Hindu cultural substratum is most strongly preserved. An intermediate zone of smaller traditional principalities surrounds the princely states. Along the northern coast, in the Javanese linguistic zone, a quite distinctive cultural pattern obtained, with far greater incorporation into the world of Islam through its maritime interactions. One useful supplement to linguistic criteria

8. von der Mehden, *Religion and Nationalism in Southeast Asia*, p. 40.

9. R. William Liddle, *Ethnicity, Party and National Integration* (New Haven: Yale University Press, 1970), pp. 28-29; Kismadi research notes.

for establishing points of cultural discontinuity is through the use of *adat* law circles, or orbits of distinctive customary jurisprudence.[10] The Javanese culture area is divided into two *adat* law circles, reflecting the duality between coast and hinterlands. Linguistically, there is a marked gap between the heavily Sanskritized language of the court and the folk dialects spoken in the countryside. The comparative absence of cultural entrepreneurs demanding an integral Javanese subnationalism, as well as the commitment to Indonesian as the national language, have left these divergences within Javanese culture relatively intact.

Groups with a militant self-consciousness are almost exclusively those with marked social mobility on the outer islands. G. William Skinner has well expressed this point: "Ethnic awareness is intensified by inter-ethnic contact, and ethnic loyalties come to the fore only when the members of the group recognize common interest vis-a-vis others. It is notably those ethnic groups whose members during the last half century of Dutch rule were most mobile and most avidly in pursuit of scarce ends in the larger society which are outstanding today for ethnic loyalties bordering on chauvinism."[11]

Table 9.1 — Ethnic Distribution of Ministerial Officeholders, 1945-70

Ethnic Group	Number	%
Javanese	392	60.8
Sundanese	84	13.0
Minangkabau	90	14.0
Minahasan	25	3.9
Ambonese	20	3.1
Batak	16	2.5
All others	18	2.8
Total	645 [a]	

[a]The figure of 645 represents a total of ministerial postings, not separate individuals; some persons held a number of different cabinet positions during this period.

Source: Kismadi research notes.

The Minangkabau and Bataks are worth particular attention as socially and geographically mobile groups with a relatively high degree of cultural mobilization. The Minangkabau, an estimated 5 percent of the population, have nearly three times that number of ministerial posi-

10. B. ter Haar, *Adat Law in Indonesia*, trans, E. A. Hoebel and A. A. Schiller (New York: Institute of Pacific Relations, 1948), offers a comprehensive summary of customary law and a classification of *adat* law circles.

11. G. William Skinner, *Social, Ethnic and National Loyalties in Village Indonesia* (New Haven: Yale University Cultural Report Series, 1959), p. 7.

tions. Rapid change in their area of West Sumatra began at the end of the last century, with the forced imposition of coffee. Subsequently rubber was added, as a smallholder, not a plantation crop. Commercial talents have played a major part in the Minangkabau diaspora throughout the archipelago in this century; evidence of their mercantile capabilities lies in the fact that coastal West Sumatra is one of the few areas where Chinese merchants were not able to dominate indigenous trade.[12] Linguistically, they are very close to the east coast Malays, with near mutual intelligibility. However, their matrilineal kinship structure was quite distinctive. Islam is strongly rooted, along with a radical nationalist tradition during the terminal colonial period.

The Batak category is multilayered congeries of identities; the term Batak itself is more of a classifactory abstraction than affective reality, although a misty legend of an eponymous first Batak ancestor is found. Located in north central Sumatra, Bataks straddle several ecological zones. Using linguistic criteria, Hildred Geertz distinguished a northern group (Karo, Alas, and Pakpak Batak), the central group of Toba Batak, Simalungan, and the coastal Ankola and Mandailung.[13] It is these categories, rather than the Batak as a whole, which are the operative identity units. Christian mission activity had its greatest success with the Toba Bataks; it is this group which had developed the most numerous educated elite and has been the most mobile. The fact that most research in the Batak area has involved either the Toba or neighboring Karo Bataks, has tended to convey a model of the Batak cultural zone based on a rather particular sample. The coastal Mandailung and Angkola have had longer exposure to mercantile Islam, although it should be added that the sea lanes passed to the east side of the island and the west coast was much more isolated. To the east, the Batak area joined the east coast Malay Muslim complex; to the north lay the highly orthodox Islam of Acheh. Between lie areas where indigenous folk religions have not been overlaid with a universal faith.

The ambiguity of the comprehensive "Batak" term is suggested by the disaccord as to whether some frontier groups are Batak or not. One Batak scholar, Masgri Singarimbun, does not include the Alas among the Bataks.[14] Another Batak author, Harahap, includes not only the Alas but also the Gayo, farther north in Acheh province.[15] Crystallization of identity among the Batak groups has been a recent phenomenon. A recent study of ethnicity and politics among the Simalungan Bataks, which tends

12. Kismadi research notes.
13. McVey, *Indonesia*, p. 29.
14. Masri Singarimbum, "Kutagamber: A Village of the Karo," in Koentjaraningrat, *Villages in Indonesia* (Ithaca: Cornell University Press, 1966), p. 115.
15. E. St. Harahap, *Perihal Bangsa Batak* (Jakarta: Dep. P. P. dan K., 1960), p. 10.

to pit Simalungan against Javanese plantation workers and North Tapanuli Bataks, offers an interesting analysis of the identity formation process:

> Prior to the twentieth century the ethnic group as a self-perceived, coherent social unit did not exist in Simalungan or in North Sumatra. . . . Individuals had relations with individuals, lineage groups with lineage groups, and villages with villages, but few regular patterns of interaction existed above this level and there was little sense of belonging to larger social or political units. The Simalungun Batak kingdoms and the Malay sultanates of the East Coast provide a partial exception to this pattern, but they too were fairly small territorial units and it is uncertain to what extent the individual identified himself with their socially distant elites and primarily exploitative governments. . . .
>
> The sense of ethnic distinctiveness and ethnic community felt by members of the various ethnic groups in postrevolutionary Simalungun began to grow during the colonial period when economic change, improved communications, missionary activity, and other developments brought individuals of diverse cultural backgrounds into contact with each other for the first time. Simalungun Bataks, for example, resented the invasion of their homeland by outsiders who did not speak their language, did not follow their *adat*, and were not members of one of the four Simalungun clans. North Tapanuli Bataks, confronted by other groups, realized that they too possessed a common language and *adat* despite regional differences among them. Their sense of community was further strengthened by their common status as agricultural pioneers and by their ability to trace an assumed kinship connection with any other North Tapanuli Bataks.[16]

Along the eastern fringe of Batak country, in the east Sumatran lowlands, a fairly intensive zone of plantation agriculture had developed during the colonial period. Most of these plantations were abandoned by their European owners after the Indonesian revolution; Toba Batak, in particular, swarmed down out of their hills to settle these newly opened lands. Malays, Javanese formerly employed on the plantations, and Minangkabau also moved into these areas. This new agrarian frame made impossible the replication of the original village and kinship structures, thus requiring major social adjustments, as well as sharpening ethnicity.[17]

The Ambonese are an interesting case of unusually intense change. Initially, they were shifting cultivators with small, dispersed populations lacking centralized political structures. Their habitat, the Moluccas Islands, were the original "spice islands" and thus early attracted the mercantile attentions of the outside world. Malay Muslim traders came first, imposed their rule, and organized them as producers. Portuguese

16. Liddle, *Ethnicity, Party and National Integration*, pp. 57-59. On urban identity among Toba Bataks, see Edward M. Bruner, "Urbanization and Ethnic Identity in North Sumatra," *American Anthropologist* 63 (1961), 508-21.

17. McVey, *Indonesia*, pp. 89-90.

followed, then the Dutch; the spice islands were the first center of Dutch exploitation. The original Ambonese languages have long disappeared, being displaced by Malay and Dutch. The period of Malay dominance had left an embryo of Muslim villages; intensive evangelization superimposed a substantial Christian population. Ambonese culture is a complex composite, an identity which grows out of the impact of maritime Islam, Malay, Portuguese, and Dutch influences interwoven with the ancient culture, "Creole Moluccan."[18]

In the case of the Minahassans, who inhabit the long northern arm of Sulawesi (Celebes), the impact of the colonial system began much later, but was very intensive. In the mid-nineteenth century, the groups now called Minahassans were a collection of localized communities, outside the orbit of the great traditions of Southeast Asia. At that point, Dutch coffee planters and missionaries moved in. In a few decades, Minahassans became a settled, cash-cropping group, whose original clan-based social structure gave way to a territorial pattern of organization in which the church parishes became the most important social units. Minahassan also became an ethnic category, as a number of educated young men found their way to Jakarta or into the civil service ranks, and awareness grew of the distinctiveness of Minahassan identity in the broader arena of Indonesia society.[19] The identity formation process among the Batak groups, Ambonese, and Minahassans closely parallels the patterns we have described in earlier chapters for African groups which did not have precolonial kingdoms as identity foci.

Another set of ethnic groups may be distinguished who are bound to the national community through Islam and some degree of incorporation in the maritime networks of trade and cultural exchange, but who have not been successful competitors in the social mobility domain and have on the whole a lower degree of cultural mobilization; these include the Achenese and Lampung on the north and south ends of Sumatra respectively, the Buginese and Makassarese in Sulawesi. Of these, the Achenese of the northern tip of Sumatra are a somewhat special entity. Acheh was the last part of Indonesia to be brought under colonial control, about the turn of the century. Islam has the longest history in Acheh and is observed in a very orthodox form; Islamic reform movements, like Muhammadiya, have made little impact. Traditional leadership is exercised by religious notables, the *ulama*, rather than a political aristocracy. The Dutch never developed any major economic interests in Acheh and were content to leave the area to its own devices, a policy

18. Ibid., pp. 92-94.
19. C. van Vollenhoven, *Het adatrecht van Nederlandsch Indie,* 3 vols. (Leiden: E.J. Brill, 1906-1933), I, 326-52.

which has been largely continued after independence. An effort was made by the colonizer to neutralize the *ulama* by reinforcing traditional secular leaders; while some warmed to the Dutch solicitations, the net effect was to strengthen the role of the *ulama* in the anti-colonial response. Although not explicitly separatist, Achenese identity was an ideological world of its own, Islamic in idiom, out of tune with the secular currents which became dominant in the late 1920s.[20]

Much more diffuse is the ill-defined complex of south Sumatra groups to whom the collective label of Lampung is applied. There are wide differences of customary law and kinship structure and little self-awareness as a collectivity. The Lampung area has absorbed large numbers of Javanese resettled peasants. Also in Lampung territory are enclaves containing groups usually considered separate, whose identity relationship to a hypothetical Lampung community is unclear.[21]

Southern Sulawesi, unlike the Minahassan area, was well linked into the communication net of maritime Islam. Identity seems to have been structured by two rival kingdoms, the Makassarese and Buginese; the distinction was political, and not cultural or linguistic. Both were essentially maritime kingdoms, whose prosperity was based on their strategic location on the spice routes. The capitals were refuges for trading communities from other parts of the islands who have been forced out of their home bases. In turn, the kingdoms had established their own colonies on other islands, especially on the Kalimantan (Borneo) coast.

Most other groups were to all intents and purposes outside the system, integrated neither into the national arena nor into a broadened ethnic identity. Characteristic of this pattern are the many small, isolated groups in interior Kalimantan commonly labeled Dayaks. This is not at this moment a subjective identity, but an analytical category applied by outsiders to convey the notion of the similarities of social structure, language, and way of life. Such commonalities have served as the basis for ethnicity in other times and places; there may well be Dayaks in the future; but not today and probably not tomorrow. The direction of the future is suggested by the fact that in neighboring Sarawak, East Malaysia, culturally similar groups have been united around the political identity of "Dayaks." Relatively little is known about most of these groups; social science research has focused on the Javanese and other communities who have been prominent in Indonesian society. Most remote and isolated of all are the populations of West Irian, culturally, linguistically, and historically of a different world, whose only real point

20. J. M. Pluvier, *Overzicht van de ontwikkeling der nationalistische beweging in Indonesie in de jaren 1930 tot 1942* (The Hague: W. van Hoeve, 1953), p. 85.

21. Kismadi research notes.

in common with Indonesia was the shared subjugation to Dutch rule. The idea of Indonesia as coincident with the orbit of Dutch colonial conquest was a matter of passionate conviction, and after more than a decade of Dutch delay Indonesian determination on this issue carried the day. It is, however, safe to assume that the sparse populations of West Irian will remain utterly peripheral to Indonesian politics, lacking the minimum sense of cultural organization to articulate their interests within Indonesia or to lay claim to separate status.

Of critical importance in the relationship between pluralism and integration is what Hildred Geertz has called the "Pasisir culture" which joins a number of coastal groups; the concept overlaps the "Islamic-entrepreneurial" pole of the cultural dichotomy suggested by Feith, which we considered above.[22] This culture grew up around the spice trade from the fourteenth to eighteenth centuries and was closely tied to the diffusion of Islam. The core of this communications net is the coastal Malay culture of east Sumatra. It will be recalled from our discussion of the rise of Malay nationalism in Malaysia that the concept of Malayhood is of recent genesis and emerged in antithesis to the Chinese threat and the cultural requisites of the Malayan peninsula political setting. Malayhood is not particularly germane to cultural interactions in Indonesia; the coastal Malays are related to the Indonesian arena through more diffuse identity linkages, of which their nodal point in the Pasisir complex is perhaps the most important. In Indonesia, much more than in Malaya, Malays were a restless, mobile group, whose trading networks extended to coastal enclaves in West Java, south Kalimantan, and Sulawesi and into the lesser Sunda and Molucca Islands. Perhaps the most important integrative legacy of this network bequeathed to Indonesia was the lingua franca which has served as the basis for the national language.

To be complete, brief reference needs to be made to the Chinese minority, which numbers about 2.5 million. During the colonial period, the Chinese had carved out an important niche as commercial intermediaries; their very success in this role marked them as pariah entrepreneurs after independence, whose freedom of maneuver has been progressively circumscribed. The category is an ambiguous one, and the use of a Chinese surname is the only generally recognized indicator of Chinese identity. Many Chinese have been incorporated through intermarriage; others remain identified as Chinese even though they speak no Chinese dialect. No more than a third have Indonesian citizenship. Their social vulnerability, paradoxically, was defined both by their capitalist and Communist associations. They were an alien commercial com-

22 McVey, *Indonesia*, pp. 58-60.

munity, and the PKI provided one of the few channels open to them for political participation. Its liquidation in 1965 further jeopardized the Chinese minority. Although they remain significant in the economy, their situation is too precarious for them to play an active part in cultural politics.[23]

HISPANIZATION AND ETHNICITY IN THE PHILIPPINES

The Philippines presents a rather different pattern of identity formation. Although in the lexicon of the physical anthropologists the human stock of the Philippines is similar to the Indonesian, its cultural history diverges sharply. The cultural premises of Spanish rule were very different from the Dutch, and the precolonial societies offered a contrasting set of acculturative options; in particular, Islam had not pre-empted the evangelical field. Cultural outcomes were also quite distinctive from those resulting from Spanish colonialism in the western hemisphere; these differences as well deserve our attention.

Magellan first planted the Spanish flag on Philippine shores in 1521. In the centuries preceding, peoples of Malay antecedents had gradually settled along the coasts. As they did, an older population strata had retreated to the interior mountains, where they were able to escape the influence of the immigrants—and for that matter, the colonial rulers who followed. In so doing, they remained outside the framework of social change and, among other things, the demographic revolution which accompanied it. Their numbers are small, and their role vestigial.

The Malay immigrants formed coastal communities called *barangays*, each, according to social legend, marking the arrival of one set of canoe-borne migrants. In most areas, the *barangays* remained autonomous communities, pushing some distance inland up the river valleys if they prospered and grew. Only in the Sulu islands and southern Mindanao had this pattern begun to change with the arrival of Muslim Malay traders in the fifteenth century. These mercantile migrants brought Islam, and with it the concept of the sultanate, as well as the organizational capacity to derive the surplus necessary to support it. Thus, on the eve of Spanish conquest, a series of Islamic trading states were taking form in the southwestern Philippines. Those within the orbit of these states found conversion to Islam the easiest way to share the cultural prestige of the new state-builders; thus was implanted the Muslim community. Had European intervention not occurred at that moment, there seems every reason to believe that this pattern might have

23. G. William Skinner, "The Chinese Minority," in ibid., pp. 97-117.

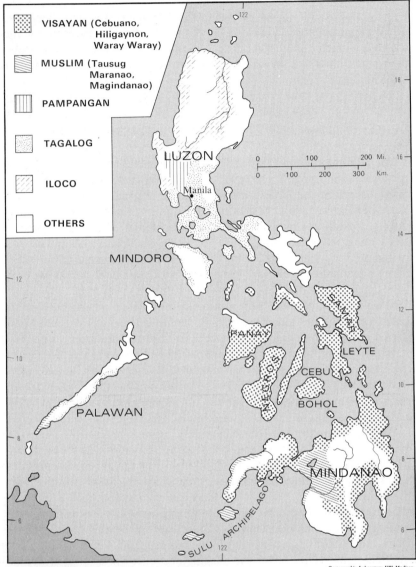

Map 9.2   Philippines: Major Ethnic Groups

Cartographic Laboratory UW-Madison

generalized through much of the archipelago in the next couple of centuries, with obvious consequences for the nature of cultural diversity.

However, in the course of events, a permanent Spanish bridgehead was established in 1565, and Manila was made the capital in 1572. The *barangay* lacked the capacity to resist the imposition of Spanish overrule, and Hispanic authority was swiftly established over most of the coastal region. Only the Muslim trading states of the southwest had the capacity for resistance; on the whole, Spanish policy aimed at sealing off Muslim expansion and its activities centered on Luzon and the Visayan islands in the northern part of the archipelago.

The Hispanization of the Philippines had as its motor elements the Christian mission orders, the galleon trade, and the eventual rise of an intermediary class.[24] It is worth noting that by the time Spanish administration was established in the Philippines, a well-articulated model had already developed in the western hemisphere. However, the Spanish did not find the centralized kingdoms with well-developed extractive authority for whose rule their own could be substituted, as in Mexico or Peru. Nor was there any immediately visible mineral wealth available for the confiscation, or mines which required the mobilization of large armies of servile labor.

The Philippine colonial economy was founded on the galleon trade, a four-cornered system linking Spain, Spanish America, China, and the Philippines. China provided tea, spice, and silk in exchange for Mexican silver, and Filipino rice, barks, and tobacco. The Chinese goods filled the galleon holds on the trip to Acapulco, and the return voyage carried mainly silver, as well as a few other New World products. The whole network was kept under careful regulation by the Spanish crown, which levied its own taxes upon it; only one yearly galleon sailing each direction was permitted, which kept profits high for those involved but also placed narrow limits on expansion.

Spanish rule over the *barangay* was institutionalized through the intermediary of the leading families. It would appear that the social structure of the *barangay* was conceptualized through the metaphors of Iberian feudal categories. The leading *barangay* families, presumed descendants of the *barangay* founders, were identified as a noble class, with an intermediate group of freemen and a lower class identified as "serfs." There was, no doubt, status differentiation within the *barangay*, probably rationalized within the kin-based metaphors of traditional society as a difference between founding families and newer arrivals, who accepted a dependent, clientage relationship in return for acceptance and security. But the degree of economic differentiation within the *barangay* would not seem to have offered sufficient surpluses to sustain a status system which deserved the Spanish labels. The Spanish institutionalized the three-class system, and in so doing no doubt in good measure succeeded over time in making it correspond more closely to their own image of social structure.

24. The best study of the Hispanization process is John Leddy Phelan. *The Hispanization of the Philippines* (Madison: University of Wisconsin Press, 1959).

The *barangay* heads were invested by the Spanish with responsibility for tribute and some forced labor; in return, their authority was reinforced by greater potential power than was available within the local *barangay* system. These persons became "political shock-absorbers and cultural middlemen"; to preserve their status with their subjects, they had to modify and soften the often harsh demands of the Spanish for tributary taxes and forced labor. To preserve their position in the colonial order, they had to cooperate with the Spanish.[25]

Initially, the Spanish did not interfere with land rights. However, as tobacco and rice became profitable crops in the galleon trade, grants of land began to be made to religious orders and Spanish settlers, on the encomienda formula developed in Spanish America. At first, the encomienda was merely a tax-farming system; however, after 1721 the encomienda itself was abolished, and the land rights gradually became equivalent to actual ownership. At the same time, the linkages of the galleon trade began attracting a growing number of Chinese immigrants, who soon outnumbered the Spanish in Manila. Filipino nobles and Chinese traders began to acquire land rights, in addition to the Spanish friars and settlers.

The Spanish population was never numerous in the Philippines and did not grow very much over the colonial years. In 1750, Spaniards numbered only 2000; in 1850, this figure had risen only to 5000.[26] Both Chinese and Spanish immigration was heavily male-dominated and formed many mixed unions with Filipino women; out of this came a mestizo community, many of whom were prominent in the land-holding aristocracy which had taken shape by the nineteenth century. This social class of Filipino and mestizo ancestry became known as the *ilustrados.* Christian, Spanish-speaking, economically rooted in land ownership, this Filipino elite was very different from the social groups which became the bearers of nationalist ideologies in Indonesia. The conflict of economic interest and social orientation between the Spanish crown and the *ilustrado* group developed swiftly in the nineteenth century; it was this milieu which provided much of the leadership in Filipino autonomist movements in the years just preceding the American conquest. Jose Rizal, who gave literary expression to the revendicative mood of the *ilustrado* class, was its most famous spokesman.[27] Another, much more radical revolutionary current which was founded upon

25. Onofre D. Corpuz, *The Philippines* (Englewood Cliffs, N.J.: Prentice-Hall, 1965), p. 28.

26. Frederic H. Chaffee et al., *Area Handbook for the Philippines* (Washington: Government Printing Office, 1969), p. 26.

27. His best-known novel, *Noli Me Tangere,* was translated by Leon M. Guerrero as *The Lost Eden* (Bloomington: Indiana University Press, 1961).

the discontents of dispossessed urban lower strata and rural tenants was led by Andred Bonifacio and Emilio Aguinaldo; however, this movement failed to command general *ilustrado* support, and did not have a permanent impact on patterns of social leadership.[28]

The crucial role of evangelization in the Hispanization process can be understood only in the context of the sixteenth century Iberian *Weltanschauung*. The wars against the Moors had only barely ended, and Catholicism was close to the innermost essence of Spanish identity. Postenlightenment colonialism operated in a far different cosmology. Magellan had barely set foot on Filipino soil when the conversion process was begun; in the few weeks before his death, he baptized 800. Within three decades of the establishment of permanent Spanish rule in 1564, the claim was made that half the Filipino population had entered into Christian communion.[29] The mission orders (Dominicans and Augustinians in particular) received extensive land grants in the interior, and the Spanish friars became a veritable feudal class. It is estimated that as much as 50 percent of the central Luzon agricultural land was in friar hands at the height of Spanish rule.[30]

For over a century, the Christian hierarchy was in the hands of the friars. Only in 1702 was the first Filipino seminary opened, and a secular Filipino clergy took form. A running struggle for ecclesiastical authority between the Spanish friars and Filipino secular priests developed not long after and was one of the subthemes of early nationalism. By the end of the Spanish era, in 1900, there were 2369 Spanish priests, belonging to one of the mission orders, and 675 Filipino secular priests.[31] Well over 90 percent of the Filipino population is Christian, and only 4 percent is Muslim, figures which are eloquent testimonial to the thoroughness of the Hispanization process.

Manila, as the colonial capital and economic center, was the focal point of Spanish influence; the Hispanic impact was felt most strongly by the Tagalog linguistic community who occupied the central Luzon core area. In the early years, the new Hispanic order found its most faithful supporters among the Tagalog. Many were regrouped in the Spanish reducciones, or settlement towns, generally located near Spanish fortifications. On two separate occasions, special royal praise was offered to the Tagalog for their fidelity to the Spanish crown, in 1636 and 1642.[32]

28. Kismadi research notes; Jean Grossholtz, *The Philippines* (Boston: Little, Brown and Co., 1964), pp. 20-22.

29. Kismadi research notes.

30. Cesar A. Majul, *Political and Constitutional Ideas of the Philippine Revolution* (Quezon City: University of the Philippines, 1957).

31. Kismadi research notes.

32. Phelan, *Hispanization of the Philippines*, p. 145.

Thus more than three centuries of Hispanization left a cultural legacy quite distinct from most of Africa and Asia. In the absence of competing centralized political structures or high religious traditions, nearly complete evangelization took place. An educated, landholding, partly mestizo upper class took shape, strongly influenced by Hispanic culture. Lower rural strata were tied to the *ilustrado* landholding class through linkages of patronage, which had become comprehensive webs of reciprocal obligation extending across a wide range of social transactions.[33] Although the zone of maximal Spanish impact was the Tagalog area, its cultural imprint was relatively uniform, save only in the Muslim southwest, a sphere of dissidence where Hispanization simply could not operate. Spanish administration was not founded on the metaphor of cultural segments; it did not seek out ethnic provinces, and its particular contours did not foster ethnic responses.

However, in identity terms, the outcome of the confrontation between Spanish colonialism and indigenous culture was strikingly different from the Latin American pattern, a fact which merits some speculative consideration. In Mexico or Peru, the self-concept of the new national culture was Hispanic at its core; in the Philippines, the idea of being Filipino was, with equal clarity, indigenous and not Iberian. The number of Spaniards was never large in the Philippines; probably only Paraguay was comparable in Spanish America—and Paraguay remains, to an important extent, bicultural. Further, Spanish colonialism was not the cultural shock in the Philippines that it was in the centers of high culture in Indo-America. In placing themselves at the top of a decapitated hierarchy in the Inca and Aztec kingdoms, a rather different pattern of cultural stratification was established, with Spanish culture enjoying the prestige of supremacy in a stratified social order. Relationships between the Spanish friars, soldiers, and merchants in the Philippines and the *barangays* were more diffuse, and mediated by the indigenous "nobility" discovered by the Spaniards in the *barangay*. In turn, when the hour of cultural choice came for the Sino-Spanish-Filipino mestizo class, who together with the *barangay* nobility had become the *ilustrados*, the option was Filipino.

The demographic factor may also have operated. Spanish intrusion does not appear to have produced the extraordinary devastation which attended epidemics of smallpox, syphilis, and other Old World diseases to which Indians had no resistance. Conquest itself involved little bloodshed in the Philippines, contrary to the carnage unleashed in establishing Spanish rule in Latin America. The early colonial economy did not

33. For a seminal analysis of the nature of patron-client ties and their social and political ramifications, see James C. Scott, "Patron-Client Politics and Political Change in Southeast Asia," *American Political Science Review,* LXVI, no. 1 (March 1972), 91-113.

have the harshly exploitative features of the Andes or Mexico. Neither mining for precious metals nor sugar plantations emerged with their insatiable demands for servile labor, worked in conditions which led to extremely high mortality rates in the western hemisphere. Rather the indigenous population in the Philippines, very sparse at the moment of colonial intrusion, grew steadily and expanded into previously unsettled inland areas. The Spanish population, which with no immigration and with few women could expand only through mestization, failed to develop the self-conscious Creole class which was subsequently to lead the independence movements in Spanish America.[34] The failure of the mestizo component to develop a Hispanic identity was probably the most pivotal factor of all. Possibly the conflict between Spanish friar and Filipino secular priest, reflected in the affirmation of difference as Spanish-Filipino rather than peninsular-Creole, was also influential. Finally, political sequences may have also played a part; had independence come in the beginning of the nineteenth century as in Latin America, won by a coalition of Spanish friars and mestizo *ilustrados* before the idea of nationalism in Asia had taken root, a different modal identity for the territorial collectivity might have been dominant, and consolidated itself.

The American interlude, from 1898 to 1946, did not fundamentally alter the cultural parameters but did provide a very particular sequence of political development. The Spanish friars were removed from the picture, and the church lands were purchased. Some aspects of the Hispanic impact were diluted; English supplanted Spanish as a language of education and administration. However, the *ilustrado* class was confirmed in its social hegemony by American commitment to a private property based economy. Very quickly, patterns which became deeply embedded in the Filipino political process became manifest. *Ilustrado* landowners learned to mobilize their clientele as vote banks and were able to make use of suffrage as a political resource. At the same time, the philosophy of mass education was applied and a very large educational system developed. Participation was readily accessible, but the early acceptance of the principle of independence meant that there was no phase of intense territorial mobilization, as occurred in Indonesia from the 1920s through the independence revolution, 1945-49.

In ethnic terms, four main clusters may be distinguished: Tagalog, Ilocanos, Visayans, and Muslims. The Tagalog we have already identified as denizens of the heartland of Spanish rule. Tagalog dominate Manila, and their language is the basis for the Filipino national language.

34. For a highly original analysis of the huge impact of epidemiology and demography over long time periods on population composition, see Curtin, *The Atlantic Slave Trade*.

Population densities are highest in the central Luzon plain, and the conflict sharpest between landlords and tenants. Tagalog mother tongue speakers are 21 percent of the population.[35]

If the Tagalog are the cultural core, the Ilocanos are the most mobile, the bearers of the stereotypes of industriousness, shrewdness and economic success which always seem to belong to one group in a multicultural setting. Initially, the Ilocanos were found in a coastal strip of northwestern Luzon; since, they have spread both along the coast and up into the hills. If we count heavily Ilocanized neighboring groups such as the Pangasinans, the Ilocanos are roughly 10 percent of the population. The Ilocano area has long been the center of tobacco cropping, an important export product since the days of the galleon trade. High population density and soil erosion have been inducements toward mobility. Institutionalization of migration as a norm for the restless young, as well, no doubt, as internalization of their own stereotypes have also been important. Filipino communities in Hawaii and California are predominately Ilocano or those who identify themselves as Ilocano in their emigrant situation.[36]

The Visayans occupy the islands lying between Luzon and Mindanao; they speak a number of closely related languages that are often separately classified but are largely mutually intelligible.[37] The Visayan label becomes an operative identity only among those who have emigrated, as urban migrants to Manila or as agricultural settlers to Mindanao; in their home areas, they are Cebuanos, Waray-waray, Ilongos, and others. The Visayan language group totals almost one third of the population. The most important Visayan migration has been into sparsely populated lands in Mindanao, a movement which probably began early in the Spanish period. Both under the American administration and since independence, the government has promoted major resettlement schemes encouraging the Visayan influx. The magnitude of the migration is suggested by the fact that there are more Cebuanos in northern Mindanao than on Cebu island.[38] As the Visayan migration has pressed deeper into Mindanao in recent years, it has come into active conflict with the Muslim inhabitants. The Visayans have had better access to government support, in particular in finding ways to secure title to new

35. Grossholtz, *The Philippines,* p. 80.

36. On Ilocano culture, see especially William F. Nydegger and Corriner Nydegger, *Tarong, An Ilocano Barrio in the Philippines* (New York: John Wiley & Sons, 1966.)

37. On Visayans, see Landa F. Jocano, *Growing up in a Philippine Barrio* (New York: Holt, Rinehart and Winston, 1969); and Ethel Nurge, *Life in a Leyte Village* (Seattle: University of Washington Press, 1965).

38. Socorro C. Espiritu (ed.), *Social Foundations of Community Development: Readings on the Philippines* (Manila: R.M. Garcia Publishing House, 1964), p. 205.

lands. To Muslim bitterness over what they regard as a land invasion by Christian immigrants is added resentment at the greater success and prosperity of the Visayans.[39]

The Muslim areas of southwestern Mindanao and the Sulu islands have never been well integrated into the Philippines, either under the Spanish or since; the outbreak of armed dissidence in this area in 1972 is the continuation of a pattern which began with the Spanish conquest. Isolation had as its cost the absence of an educational infrastructure and a very weak representation in the national political system. Filipino Islam was almost equally isolated from the major centers of Muslim theology; although the Spanish were not able to really occupy and acculturate the Islamic zone, they were able to seriously disrupt the mercantile, political, and cultural communications network which bound this far eastern frontier of Islam to the broader community of the Muslim faithful. A welter of status-creating legends are to be found, claiming that Arab missionaries were the vectors of Islam, a mythology frequent in Southeast Asia which functions to raise the prestige of the local Muslim community by projecting a direct link with the heartland of the great tradition.[40] In reality, Filipino Islam was carried by Malay intermediaries, and its remoteness left it to develop in relative isolation.

The contacts with Malayan Islam were most extensive on the Sulu Islands, inhabited by the Tausug linguistic group. At one time, this chain was united under a single sultan. Tausug vocabulary reflects a significant frequency of words of immediate Malay origin, an influence also observable in the lexicon of traditional political structures.[41] On Mindanao, there are two Muslim ethnic groups, the Maranao and Maguindanao. The latter have been most heavily affected by the influx of Visayan and other settlers. They did not, like the Tausug, develop a single sultanate, but a series of principalities. Among the Maranao, the concept of the sultanate was totally Filipinized, with every village leader laying claim to the title of sultan.[42] It should be noted that Muslims are an identity group only with relation to non-Muslims; among themselves, these three ethnic categories are the pri-

39. See Chester L. Hunt, "Ethnic Stratification and Integration in Cotabato," in Espiritu, *Social Foundations of Community Development,* pp. 202–31.

40. Kismadi research notes.

41. Wilfredo F. Arce, "Social Organization of the Muslim People of Sulu," *Philippine Studies,* XI, no. 2 (April 1963), 242-66; Najeeb M. Saleeby, *The History of Sulu* (Manila: Government Bureau of Printing, 1908); Cuthbert Billman, "Islam in Sulu," *Philippine Studies,* VIII (January 1960), 51-58; Alejo Santos, "The Sulu Problem," *Philippine Sociological Review,* VIII, no. 1 (January 1960), 34–38.

42. Manitua Saber, Manya Tamano, and Charles K. Warriner, "The Muratabat of the Maranaw," *Philippine Sociological Review,* VIII, no. 1 (April 1960), 10-55; Melvin Mednick, "Some Problems of Moro History and Political Organization," in ibid., vol. V. no. 1 (January 1957).

mary integrative identities. However, the distinction with non-Muslims is quite sharp; in this context, these groups describe themselves as "Muslims," while others are "Filipinos."

The strong hostility felt by the Spanish towards the Muslims was to an important degree internalized by the Filipino elite. The Spanish term "Moro" (Moor) continues to be used, although it is resented by Muslim Filipinos. Under American administration, the Muslim zone was given a special administrative framework, quite distinct from that applied in the Christian areas elsewhere. Until 1950, Manila appointed the governors for these areas, generally from among the Christian settlers. Government services have been meager; Mindanao roads are notoriously the worst in the archipelago, and until 1967 there was only one public high school in the entire Sulu island chain.[43]

Aside from the special case of Muslim separatism—in the last analysis a peripheral phenomenon, given the small size of the Muslim minority, the impossibility of its growth through the pre-emptive generalization of Christianity, and its marginality in cultural geography—ethnicity in the Philippines stands out by its diffuseness. Part of the explanation lies in the particular characteristics of Spanish colonial rule, which through the accidents of its acculturative premises, offered little inducement or opportunity for cultural mobilization on ethnolinguistic criteria. Another set of factors lie in the nature of the competitive political arena which grew up during the American period and was institutionalized after independence; to these we will return shortly. The time has now come to consider the impact of modern politics on cultural identities in Indonesia and the Philippines.

PARTIES AND PLURALISM IN INDONESIA

To situate our analysis of the interaction of politics and pluralism in independent Indonesia, a capsule synopsis of the major landmarks of postwar history is in order. On 17 August 1945, simultaneous with the Japanese collapse, Indonesian independence was proclaimed by two of its major nationalist leaders, Sukarno and Mohammed Hatta. The Dutch refused to recognize this verdict and tried to reimpose their authority, thereby triggering four years of bitter revolutionary warfare. The Indonesian revolution was most solidly implanted in Java, which led the colonizer to seek indigenous support by the appeal to regionalism; the Dutch tried to stitch together a federation, primarily out of outer island areas where they were able to re-establish control. Finally,

43. Kismadi research notes.

a peace treaty was signed by which the Netherlands recognized the independence of all Indonesia but West Irian on 27 December 1949. The concept of "federalism" was irretrievably stained by its association with the last gasp of colonialism; by 1950, Indonesia had become a unitary republic, with a powerful sense of nationalism sharpened in the years of armed struggle. Although the revolutionary period had produced a strong army, it did not give rise to a single political party. The new republic first sought legitimacy through constitutional democracy, whose high water mark was the national election of 1955. Although these elections were fairly conducted, they failed to produce the clear national consensus and stability which had been hoped. In late 1956, President Sukarno unveiled his concept of "guided democracy," which in its eventual form postulated a consensual linkage of the three main ideological currents—nationalism, Islam, and Communism. Parliament and parties lost their influence, and the army gradually eliminated a series of regionalist revolts. In 1962, faced with the prospect of an Indonesian invasion, the Dutch finally agreed to a lightly camouflaged transfer of authority over West Irian to the Indonesian republic. By this time, the main forces in Indonesian politics were the army, the Communists, and Sukarno himself. The uneasy coalition of these contenders broke down in late 1965, when in a confused crisis Sukarno was eased from power, and the army under General Suharto took over. A bitter struggle ensued between Communists on the one hand and the army and *santri* Muslims on the other. The PKI leadership was decimated, and hundreds of thousands of rural Communist followers were massacred; by 1968, at least for a long period, Communism as an organized force was eliminated from the Indonesian scene. A phase of depoliticized, technocratic rule by a civil-military bureaucratic duumvirate followed, which did yield some success on the development front and repaired some of the economic damage done in the final Sukarno years of flamboyant, solidarity-making politics. However, the problem of legitimation of power remained entire, and fears grew that institutionalized technocratic authoritarianism was the ransom of development. In an effort to restore a more political legitimation for the regime without placing in danger its continuity, national elections were held in 1971, with a new, military-sponsored national political movement entering the lists along with a number of the older vintage political parties.

During the Sukarno period, the impact of cultural pluralism is most clearly visible through the party system, the 1955 elections, and the stresses revealed in the welter of rebellion against the nationalizing authority of the central government; each of these will be considered before turning to the redefined rules of the game and political structures of the Suharto era. The four most important parties of the 1945-65 period were Masjumi, Nahdatul Ulama, PNI, and PKI. Together, these four garnered 77.9 percent of the 1955 vote; we will focus primarily upon them.

The first point to note is that each of these four parties had a national vocation. The symbols they wielded, the ideology which provided their language of political discourse was oriented toward the national arena, built on the bedrock doctrine of Indonesian unity. At the level of conscious debate, cultural pluralism was an illegitimate basis for politics, a betrayal of the political dream for which so many had sacrificed so much.

And yet, though unespoused, pluralism was very closely linked to the party system, both along the horizontal lines of division between *santri* and *abangan, prijaji* and commoner, and between ethnic, religious, and regional groups. Of the four major parties, two—Masjumi and Nahdatul Ulama—clearly represented the *santri*, or devout, stream in Islamic orientation. Within the *santri*, the reformist-modernist stream was embodied in the Masjumi, to which the Muhammadiya movement was closely tied. The orthodox-traditional current found its spokesman in the NU. The other two parties, PNI and PKI, were of secular, *abangan* hue. The PNI was closely tied to the *prijaji* elite, if we take that term in its contemporary usage. It will be recalled that the *prijaji* were originally the court aristocracy of the Javanese hinterland kingdoms; through their incorporation into intermediary roles in colonial administration and related access to Western schooling for their offspring, the *prijaji* class gradually underwent a metamorphosis into a modern administrative and political elite, whose power and status no longer was rooted in nobility of ancestry but rather in the capacity to play a bureaucratic role. The electoral strength of the *prijaji* lay in the capacity to transform patterns of deference and clientage related to the exercise of power and the patronage of the state into vote banks. The PKI, then, recruited its rural audience through aggregation of peasant discontents among those neither bound by affective *santri* ties to religious hierarchies of social influence nor incorporated in deferential dependency to the *prijaji* administrative class.[44]

A closer look at the nature of the social constituencies of the parties and the distribution of electoral support reveals the importance of cultural pluralism in shaping mass public responses to parties. The PNI, PKI, and NU all heavily concentrated in Java, while Masjumi found the great bulk of its support in non-Javanese areas. The PNI drew

44. The best account of the nature of Indonesian politics during the Sukarno period is found in the magistral study of Feith, *The Decline of Constitutional Democracy in Indonesia;* for a more succinct summary, see his chapter. "The Dynamics of Guided Democracy," in McVey, *Indonesia,* pp. 309-409.

85.97 percent of its total vote in Java, although Java is only two-thirds of the archipelago population (and ethnic Javanese, it will be recalled, roughly 50 percent, with most of the others being the Sundanese of West Java).[45] Further, the Javanese base of the PNI becomes even more impressive when its centers of strength in the outer islands are closely scrutinized; these are, very largely, areas of Javanese peasant resettlement or plantation labor, or in some cases represent the influence of Javanese administators. Of the 57 seats won by the PNI, 44 were in Java; of the remaining 13, all but 6 were in areas of Javanese migrant population.[46] This is not to suggest either that all Javanese migrants were PNI supporters (many also backed the PKI) or that the PNI appeal was restricted to ethnic Javanese, both of which propositions would be grotesque deformations of reality. At the same time, the PNI did have clear connotations as a Javanese heartland party, which affected perceptions of and orientation toward it by both Javanese and others.

The PKI received 88.6 percent of its vote and 35 of its 39 seats in Java, especially in the ethnic Javanese regions. The other 4 seats were in Sumatra, where PKI areas of strength were in plantation zones and the polyglot city of Medan, where ethnic conflict has been intense. As with the PNI, a significant fraction of its support on Sumatra comes from Javanese migrants.[47]

Nahdatul Ulama was almost equally concentrated in Java, winning 85.6 percent of its vote there. Like the PKI, within Java its appeal was strongest in the ethnic Javanese zone, where it won 31 of its 36 Java seats. NU was competing essentially for the *santri* vote with Masjumi. In the Javanese areas, NU won 31 seats to 13 for Masjumi, while in the Sundanese zone, Masjumi outdistanced NU by 13 seats to 5. Muhammadiya, in many ways the progenitor of Masjumi, had been founded in the Javanese heartland, but reached its fullest flowering in Sumatra.[48] This found expression in the election returns; Masjumi won 16 of the 35 Sumatra seats, compared to 2 for NU and only 5 and 4 for the PNI and PKI respectively. Of the 43 seats in the other outer islands, the *santri* parties did far better, taken together, than the secular nationalist movements; Masjumi took 13, and NU 6, with PNI winning only 7 (3 in the Bali-centered district), and PKI none at all. The centers of *santri* strength were the Buginese and Makassarese areas of South Sulawesi and the coastal fringes of Kalimantan dominated by migrant Buginese, Javanese, and Malays. PNI success bespoke the in-

45. Feith, *The Decline of Constitutional Democracy in Indonesia,* pp. 434-37.

46. Kismadi research notes. For evidence on the PNI appeal to migrant Javanese in North Sumatra, see Liddle, *Ethnicity, Party and National Integration.*

47. Feith, *The Decline of Constitutional Democracy in Indonesia,* pp. 434-37.

48. Alfian, "Islamic Modernism in Indonesian Politics."

Table 9.2—1955 Indonesian Election Results

Region	Main ethnic groups	Religion	PNI	PKI	NU	Mas-jumi	Other	To-tal
East Java	Javanese, Madurese	Muslim	14	14	20	7	8	63
Central Java	Javanese	Muslim	19	15	11	6	11	62
West Java	Sundanese	Muslim	11	5	5	13	15[a]	49
Jakarta	Javanese, Sundanese **Minangkabau,** Toba Bataks, Ambonese	Muslim, some Christian	1	1	1	2	0	5
South Sumatra	Lampung, Javanese migrants	Muslim	2	1	1	4	1	9
Central Sumatra	Minangkabau east coast Malay	Muslim	0	1	0	6	4[b]	11
North Sumatra	Achenese, Toba & other Bataks, Java-nese migrants	Muslim, Protestant (Toba Bataks)	3	2	1	6	3[c]	15
West Kāli-mantan	Dayak, Malay	Muslim (coast), folk (interior)	1	0	0	1	1[d]	3
South & East Kaliman-tan	Buginese, Javanese settlers	Muslim	0	0	3	2	0	5
North Sulawesi	Minahassan	Protestant	1	0	0	1	3[e]	5
South Sulawesi	Makassar, Buginese	Muslim, some Christian	1	0	2	5	3[f]	11
Moluccas	Ambonese	Christian, some Muslim	0	0	0	1	1[g]	2
East Lesser Sundas	diverse	Christian some Muslim	1	0	0	1	7[h]	9
West Lesser Sundas	Balinese, diverse	Hindu, some Muslim	3	0	1	2	2[i]	8
West Irian	diverse	folk	(no elections held)					
Totals			57	39	45	57	59	257

Table 9.2 (*continued*)

[a]Two by the socialist party, three by the army-backed I.P.K.I., which won only one other seat in the rest of the country, and three by a splinter Muslim party, P.S.I.I.

[b]Three by Perti, a local Sumatra Muslim party.

[c]Two by a Protestant party in the Toba Batak area.

[d]By a local Dayak party.

[e]Two by P.S.I.I., one by a Protestant party.

[f]One by P.S.I.I., two by a Protestant party.

[g]By a Protestant party.

[h]Two by a Protestant party, four by a Catholic party.

[i]By the socialist party.

Source: Kismadi research notes.

fluence of the administrative class above all.[49] Table 9.2 summarizes the 1955 election results by region.

Of the 59 scattered seats not won by one of the big four, 22 were accounted for by the Protestant party (Parkindo), the Partai Katolik, and the socialist party (PSI); 12 others went to two additional Muslim parties (P.S.I.I. and Perti). The Christian parties captured a substantial fraction of the votes of their potential constituencies, reflecting the cumulated effect of both religious identity and ethnicity. It will be recalled that the Christian population is heavily concentrated among the Toba Bataks, Minahassans, and Ambonese, plus groups of the lesser Sundas. The Catholic party did particularly well, receiving approximately 700,000 votes, with only a little more than one million Catholics in the country. The socialist parties had their support primarily among the national elite oriented toward the "metropolitan urban culture." Thus their influence was much greater before the elections than after. Within the framework of political elite interactions, they appeared quite significant; however, they found no basis of establishing a linkage with the mass public, either through cultural or ideological mobilization.

CRISIS AND INTEGRATION IN INDONESIA

Some further insight into the fissures in Indonesia society may be derived from an examination of some of its major crises which reached the point of armed confrontation. In crisis, some of the innermost tensions and stresses wtihin a society are laid bare; polarization reaches a point where neutrality becomes a problematical social option, where security in evasion of alignment is difficult to sustain. In the first two decades

49. Kismadi research notes.

after the 1945 proclamation of independence, a number of such occasions may be noted.

The integrative crisis was most severe in the immediate aftermath of independence, and then again in the 1956-58 period when a series of regional revolts occurred. The first wave of dissidence had two main variants: (1) regions which had firmly committed themselves to the Dutch-sponsored federation, and for whom Indonesian independence under the aegis of the revolutionary republic represented a potential cultural (and political) threat and (2) fundamentalist Islamic movements, whose conception of the obligations to theocracy were threatened by the predominantly secular views of nationalism and Islam in the revolutionary leadership. The most important example of the first type was the 1950 Ambonese revolt, culminating in the proclamation of an independent Republic of South Moluccas in April 1950. The Ambonese were the most vulnerable of all cultural groupings as a result of the exceptional intimacy of their relations with the Dutch and high degree of acculturation. It will be recalled that a large fraction of the old Dutch East Indies army was Ambonese; many Ambonese had adopted Dutch as a mother tongue. Indicative of Dutch acculturation was the emergence in the late colonial period of an Ambonese-dominated organization bearing the name of Door de Eeuwen Trouw (Loyal through the Ages); such an association could not have gained much support anywhere else in the archipelago. However, by September 1950 the Indonesian army had ended the secession. Many thousands of Ambonese, presumably those who felt most threatened by Indonesian rule, emigrated to Holland. Not all Ambonese were pro-Dutch; there was also a strong nationalist current.

More difficult to cope with were the Muslim fundamentalist uprisings, of which the most important was Darul Islam in West Java. This began in 1947 and continued until the middle 1960s; it was not until 1959 that it was safe to travel the Jakarta-Bandung road, which passed through the zone of Darul Islam, by night. Led by S. M. Kartosuwirjo, the main constituency was among *santri* Sundanese. Kartosuwirjo, who described himself as an *imam* (religious ruler), led an essentially theocratic movement; its intermediate leaders were the *ulama*. An administrative apparatus was created, and remained in existence in the mountain strongholds of Darul Islam for more than a decade. It was not till 1959 that the government succeeded in capturing Kartosuwirjo. Although Darul Islam was quickly sealed off—it only briefly spilled over into some Javanese adjacent areas—and was not a real threat to the survival of Indonesia, the ability of the movement to last so long, isolated, thrown back upon its own resources, is suggestive of the mobilizing force of *santri* Islam among the orthodox. More than simple identity is involved; the structural capabilities of the rebellion constituted by its *ulama* backbone were substantial. The social constituency to which it could appeal was too narrow for its objectives of creating the earthly kingdom of God; yet the cultural energies which it could tap were portentous and provide part of the explanation for the dimension of the rural massacres of Communist followers in 1965. Brief note may be taken of two rather similar Muslim revolts, one in Makassar in 1950 and one beginning in 1953 in Acheh. They appealed to similar kinds of Muslims; in the Acheh case, the continuing theme of regional dissidence was also present.

The most serious threat to the survival of the republic came during the regional military revolts of 1956-58. The Indonesian army had faced an integrative crisis of its own after independence; as part of the Dutch peace settlement, it had been agreed to incorporate parts of the regional forces recruited by the Dutch. Also, the revolutionary army itself had come into being through local recruitment of young nationalists. Thus many of the army units garrisoned in the outer islands were heavily drawn from the local populace, both officers and men. Particularly outside Java, the army was the main source of power and became drawn into the regional administrative problems. In Sumatra and Sulawesi, resentment grew at the inability of the cumbersome, inefficient central machinery in Jakarta to provide services or support to the outer islands. Sumatra and Sulawesi were well aware that most of Indonesia's export earnings came from their agricultural and petroleum production; it was easy to believe that Java was, through accident or design, monopolizing the benefits. Beginning in 1955, a number of regional army commanders in Sumatra and Sulawesi-generally indigenous to their areas of command—took matters into their own hands by smuggling the exports themselves and using the returns to finance administrative services for their areas.

When the 1955 elections failed to produce the anticipated rejuvenation of Indonesian political life, restlessness among the regional military commanders grew. In late 1956, a number of commanders in Sumatra and North Sulawesi simply announced that they no longer recognized Jakarta's authority. Later, in February 1958, under the protective cover of one of these dissident commanders (and apparently with some covert American encouragement), a number of Masjumi and socialist leaders fled Jakarta and proclaimed in West Sumatra the formation of a provisional revolutionary government to be led by Sundanese Masjumi leader Sjafruddin Prawiranegara. However, garrison leaders in Kalimantan and south Sulawesi sat on the fence, and south Sumatra only briefly joined. A long stalemate followed; neither side was eager to send army units into action against the other. The two centers of dissidence, Minahassa and the northern part of Sumatra, were separated by 1000 miles. Although separatism was latent in their composition and circumstances, the official debate was always confined to a more viable formula for directing the destinies of Indonesia. A cautious invasion of a dissident zone in Sumatra proved to be almost unopposed in March 1958, which naturally gave rise to others. The north Sulawesi campaign did encounter serious resistance, but by mid-1958 the end of regional military autonomy had come.

In its wake some major alterations in the cultural parameters of the system occurred. Masjumi, the main outer-island political party, was wholly discredited and, along with the socialist party, declared illegal in 1960. The power of the bureaucracy had increased, while parties other than the PKI had dwindled in significance. Although during the rise of nationalism and the revolutionary period regionalism had been overshadowed by the debates between radicals and moderates, secularists and *santri*, the regional military dissidence had given dramatic focus to a range of issues arising in the relationship between Java and the rest, particularly the politically conscious areas of Sumatra and Sulawesi. Writing not long before the overthrow of Sukarno, Herbert Feith identifies the mood: "Dissatisfaction is found among numerous non-Javanese of various social groups, who see the government as one of Javanese, founded on a Javanese military victory over other ethnic groups. Because the Javanese have provided a disproportionally large number of government officials, the power shift favoring the bureaucracy at the expense of other groups has tended to benefit ethnic Javanese to the detriment of others. Moreover, within the group of government employees there are many non-Javanese persons who believe they cannot rise higher because they are not Javanese or culturally Javanized."[50]

On three occasions, armed civil conflicts involving the Communist movement have occurred. In 1926, a Communist insurrection against the Dutch occurred, with participation mainly localized in West Java (Sundanese) and West Sumatra (Minankabau). In 1948, coincident with a wave of Communist revolts in South Asia, Communist forces took arms against the "bourgeois nationalist" leadership of the revolutionary republic. Finally, in 1965 there was the cataclysmic confrontation between the Indonesian army, *santri* Muslims, and the Communists, with the struggle quickly becoming a generalized massacre of those identified as Communists in Java and the plantation zones of Sumatra.

POST-SUKARNO: THE CIVIL-MILITARY COALITION

Out of this came the technocratic era of civil-military administration. The PKI and Sukarno were eliminated, effectively removing from

50. Feith, in McVey, *Indonesia*, p. 407.

politics the ideology-spinners, solidarity-makers, and symbol-wielders. The Islamic component of Indonesian identity received some nurture from the patronage of the army, which is far from a *santri* agency but much less flamboyantly secular than Sukarno. That part of regional resentment fueled by the sheer economic mismanagement of the Sukarno solidarity-building days had perhaps subsided; Sumatra and Sulawesi are prime beneficiaries of economic technocracy, as sites of the most readily exploitable agricultural and mineral resources. Ample time has now been available to the military leaders to restructure their forces so that the regional military revolts of 1956-58 are less likely to recur. And, as in Zaire, ethnicity, within the technocratic-authoritarian frame of the Suharto regime, has no institutional channel to make itself manifest. It is unlikely that the resentment of Javanese domination which Feith described has disappeared—Suharto is also Javanese—but the political system provided no structured occasions for cultural mobilization.

In 1971, national elections were held for the first time since 1955, which offer some interesting evidence as to the alteration in the structure of politics during that sixteen-year period.[51] Although neither the technocrats nor the military wanted to restore party domination, much less parliamentary democracy, they did seek some mechanism by which a degree of participation could occur without fundamentally altering their ultimate control of the system. The formula developed retained three safeguards for the civil-military coalition: (1) 100 of the 460 members of parliament would be nominated by the president, with 75 being military personnel; (2) parties deemed disloyal were screened out, PKI was excluded, and Masjumi, tainted by its association with the 1956-58 regional army revolt, was permitted to participate under a new name only after purging its leadership; (3) the army sponsored its own "non-party" electoral list, under the name of Sekber Golkar (Joint Secretariat of Functional Groups).

The results were a sweep for Golkar which far exceeded the expectations of informed observers and the regime itself. It won 62.8 percent of the vote, 227 seats, and a majority in all but three electoral districts (Acheh, Moluccas, Jakarta). Only Nahdatul Ulama remained a significant competitor, slightly improving on its 1955 vote percentage. Tables 9.3 and 9.4 summarize the results.

In suggesting some explanations for the magnitude of the Golkar sweep, we may first note some factors greatly weakening PNI and Parmusi,

51. For two useful reports on the elections, see Donald Hindley, "Indonesia 1971: Pantjasila Democracy and the Second Parliamentary Elections," *Asian Survey,* XIII, no. 1 (January 1971), 56-68; R. William Liddle, "Evolution from Above: National Leadership and Local Development in Indonesia," *Journal of Asian Studies,* XXXII, no. 2 (February 1973), 287-309.

Table 9.3—Indonesian Parliamentary Elections, 1955 and 1971, National Totals

Party	1955		1971	
	% votes	No. seats	% votes	No. seats
Masjumi/Parmusi	20.9	57	5.4	24
Nahdatul Ulama	18.4	45	18.7	58
PSII and Perti [a]	4.2	12	3.1	12
PNI	22.3	57	6.9	20
Christian parties	4.7	14	2.4	10
PKI	16.3	39	(banned)	
Sekber Golkar	(not in existence)		62.8	227
Others	13.1	33	0.7	0

[a]Small Muslim parties.

Source: Donald Hindley, "Indonesia 1971: Pantjasila Democracy and the Second Parliamentary Elections," *Asian Survey,* XII, No. 1 (January 1972), 58.

successor to Masjumi. Under government tutelage, the PNI had been carefully purged of its old leadership of the Sukarno period. The PNI had been, in Hindley's words, "the party of government, of patronage, of non-revolutionary, non-*santri* people."[52] These functions were largely assumed by Golkar, which further coopted the PNI's key instrument of clientage, the bureaucracy, especially its rural capillaries in face-to-face contact with the populace at large. In a stroke, the PNI had lost its functions and its activities in the Javanese heartland, and it had never been strong outside.

Parmusi was permitted to rise from the ashes of Masjumi on severely limited conditions. It faced the continuing hostility of important segments of the officer corps. The *sine qua non* of recognition was elimination of prominent Masjumi leaders; thus Parmusi had to win visibility for a whole new set of leaders. Further, it was beset by factionalism, with the dominant group accepting an essentially client role in relation to Golkar and the military regime and joining them in their denunciation of the former Masjumi leadership. Parmusi was thus a pale shadow of its predecessor, had no natural structure of rural organization to fall back upon, and made only a limp impact on the balloting.

NU, in contrast, had both constituency and structure intact. Its communication network depended upon the *ulama,* the Muslim religious teachers, and the orthodox predispositions of the rural *santri.* Although it maintained its strength, it did not notably improve it, and its real influence remained largely confined to Java. It does not appear to have picked up significant numbers of former Masjumi supporters, and

52. Hindley, "Indonesia 1971: Pantjasila Democracy and The Second Parliamentary Elections," p. 66.

Table 9.4 Indonesian National Elections, 1955 and 1971, by Region

Party	Year	N. Sum.	C. Sum.	S. Sum.	W. Java	Gtr. Jak.	C. Java	E. Java	Kal.	N. Sul.	S. Sul.	L. Sun.	Mo-luccas	W. Irian
Masjumi/ Parmusi	1955	37.8%	51.5%	43.1%	26.5%	26.1%	10.0%	11.2%	31.7%	25.9%	41.8%	17.9%	37.6%	(no elections in 1955; indirect elections in 1971)
	1971	10.5	15.2	9.4	4.0	7.7	5.0	2.7	6.1	4.6	4.7	2.0	14.9	
Nahdatul Ulama	1955	4.2	4.6	8.0	9.7	15.7	19.7	34.2	30.9	3.0	14.9	5.2	--	
	1971	6.4	4.5	10.4	13.1	23.7	21.9	35.2	17.9	4.8	8.3	5.6	6.6	
PSII and Perti	1955	5.0	24.8	13.2	5.7	3.1	0.7	0.5	1.2	23.7	10.8	1.4	3.6	
	1971	8.0	6.0	5.7	3.6	3.5	1.0	1.4	1.4	12.1	4.2	2.3	3.5	
PNI	1955	15.8	2.7	14.7	22.1	19.8	33.5	22.8	10.8	14.1	4.3	22.5	9.7	
	1971	4.8	0.7	4.3	1.7	11.6	18.5	5.0	2.0	4.2	0.3	6.6	4.2	
Christian Parties	1955	15.3	0.6	0.5	0.3	3.0	0.8	0.5	1.4	22.1	12.0	28.3	40.9	
	1971	4.6	0.9	1.3	0.7	5.9	1.4	0.5	4.1	6.7	1.6	11.5	22.5	
PKI	1955	12.4	5.8	12.1	10.9	12.6	25.8	23.3	2.4	4.5	1.7	3.0	1.5	
	1971	(banned)			(not in existence)									
Sekber Golkar	1955													
	1971	64.5	72.0	68.1	76.1	46.7	51.6	54.9	66.5	66.4	80.0	71.1	47.7	
Others	1955	9.5	10.0	8.4	24.8	19.7	9.5	7.5	13.0	6.7	14.5	21.7	6.7	
	1971	1.2	0.6	0.8	0.8	1.0	0.5	0.3	2.0	1.3	0.9	1.0	0.7	

Source: Donald Hindley, "Indonesia 1971: Pantjasila Democracy and the Second Parliamentary Elections," *Asian Survey,* XII, no. 1 (January 1972), 67.

indeed made no particular effort to redefine its cultural orientation to appeal to modernist *santri*.

The nature of Golkar, as a natural reflection of the new realities of power in Indonesia, also explains much of its success—a triumph which went far beyond the 30-40 percent of the vote which the government expected as the quasi-party swung into serious operation in mid-1970.[53] Civil servants were required not only passively to back, but actively to support Golkar; the administration is a formidable machine, assured of financing, secure against reprisals. Although the government was pledged to a free election, it also prohibited campaigners from "slander, contempt or disrespect of the government or government officials," a concept susceptible of elastic interpretation by the neighborhood garrison commander. It is interesting to note that, on the whole, Golkar made its weakest showing in Java; here the NU remained a live alternative for *santri* Muslims, and the residual PNI received most of its backing. Here, too, the new party had the task of trying to absorb the frightened and passive former supporters of the PKI. Elsewhere, with Masjumi emasculated, outside the Christian areas there was simply no alternative to Golkar, and overwhelming majorities were rolled up. To the extent that Golkar is an agency of affirmation of central power, which to outer island constituencies has a Javanese flavor, there is some poignancy in the proportions of the triumph.

After a fashion, Indonesia has passed through an integrative crisis in its first three decades of independence, without having fully resolved it. The nationalist revolution in Indonesia had, on the whole, left an integrative heritage; although the nationalist movement was never wholly united, its most salient divisions could be situated on secular-religious and Marxist-to-moderate spectrums. Significantly, the best-known—and ably done—study of the rise of nationalism, by George Kahin, has almost nothing to say on the question of cultural pluralism; this is a commentary on the visibility of ethnicity and not on the perspicacity of Kahin.[54] After independence, the sprawling republic faced stress along all its main lines of cleavage, although some important factors served to limit the disintegrative pressures. The party system grew out of the earlier ideological cleavages and the politization of the *santri-abangan* line of division—a metamorphosis which was above all Javanese. Aside from the outer island center of gravity of Masjumi, the party system did not divide Indonesia along its most dangerous cleavages. Neither did political competition lead to the explicit politization of ethnicity in the

53. Liddle, *Ethnicity, Party, and National Integration,* p. 293.

54. George M. Kahin, *Nationalism and Revolution in Indonesia* (Ithaca: Cornell University Press, 1952).

manner in which this occurred in Uganda, Nigeria, or Zaire. Javanese domination, by sheer weight of numbers and geopolitical centrality, is to some degree inevitable, and the post-1965 tendencies toward centralization of power inevitably will enhance this tendency. However, its impact is somewhat tempered by the relatively mild assertion of Javanese identity as cultural ideology. Javanese culture has its devotees and even entrepreneurs, but for the most part they have not claimed exclusive Javanese title to the state in a manner which would catalyze intense cultural insecurities among other groups. Like Zaire, Indonesia since 1965 has been through a depoliticizing period; the two pillars of power, administration and army, have increased their coherence and capacity, while its competitors are dispersed and demoralized. Golkar, which has some similarities in origin and purpose to the MPR in Zaire, had now been developed as the political arm of the regime—to date, only as an electoral instrument with some limited competition, rather than with the decreed monopoly accorded to the MPR.

ETHNICITY CONTAINED: TWO-PARTY FLUIDITY IN THE PHILIPPINES

In the Philippines, ethnic politics have been less significant than in Indonesia. Part of the explanation lies in the particular features of colonial experience which we have discussed above. However, the most powerful factor inhibiting ethnic mobilization has been the unusual structure of the political arena, a pattern which has no real parallel. As the basic parameters of politics remained quite stable from independence in 1946, until the abolition of constitutional democracy by President Carlos Marcos in 1972, we need not review in detail the sequence of events within that period, but can treat it as a single analytical frame. The implications of the Marcos authoritarian formula have not, at the time of writing, worked themselves out in actual practice; we will comment only briefly on postcoup politics.

Electoral politics have a relatively long history in the Philippines, and a bipolar party system took shape almost at once with the first national elections in 1907. Initially, the point at issue was whether statehood (backed by the Federalista party) or independence (supported by the Nacionalista party) should be the goal of political development. One can almost say that this was the last significant difference separating the two major parties, which, with some changes of nomenclature, have been a constant. Within a couple of decades, the statehood issue had disappeared from the scene, after which time the major parties had become virtually indistinguishable in terms of issues.

The second great constant has been the close linkage of the party system and Filipino social structure. We have suggested earlier that the liberal economy premises of American colonialism permitted the *ilustrado* class to secure its title to rural land and consolidate its social privilege. In Filipino parlance, the world was divided into "big men" and "little men." They become bound to one another in a seamless web of patron-client networks. The little man needed a patron who could offer a measure of physical security, a reserve of emergency material support, a channel through which any unavoidable transactions with officialdom could occur, and possibly an avenue of personal advancement, and the big man had need of clients; their numbers were an affirmation of his status. Also, they helped enlarge his control over rural resources; they cultivated his land, and turned back a generous portion of the crop. They were available, as an army of retainers, to perform numerous small services. And, with the coming of electoral politics, they became a critical political resource.

Electoral competition had important effects on the patron-client system. A new dimension of exchange and reciprocity entered the relationship. For the client, his vote represented a direct claim on some redistributive benefit. For the patron, his clientele was a vote bank, whose size affected his bargaining power with the party brokers whose task it was to stitch together a winning coalition. The Filipino party system thus politicized the pre-existing welter of patron-client networks into vertical chains of patronage extending into the chambers of Filipino congress, and the national ministries.[55]

The pattern emergent from interaction of the patron-client ordered countryside and the national bipolar party system is aptly summarized by Carl Lande: "The two rival parties in each province are structured by vertical chains of dyadic patron-client relationships extending from great and wealthy political leaders in each province down to lesser gentry politicians in the towns, down further to petty leaders in each village, and down finally to the clients of the latter: the ordinary peasantry. Thus both parties contain among their leaders and supporters members of all social strata, of all occupational groups, and of all regions."[56] Parties from the outset made use of the vote banks repre-

55. This process is given cogent exposition in Scott, "Patron-Client Politics"; see also Rene Lemarchand, "Political Clientelism and Ethnicity in Tropical Africa: Competing Solidarities in Nation-Building," *American Political Science Review*, LXVI, no. 1 (March 1972), 68-90.

56. Carl Lande, *Leaders, Factions, and Parties: The Structure of Philippine Politics* (New Haven: Yale University Southeast Asia Monograph Series No. 6, 1966). Lande has made a major contribution towards making comprehensible the confused factionalism of Filipino politics.

sented by the patronage nets; indeed, there was no other ready basis of mass appeal when the party system was born. In the process, the parties took on the characteristics of their clientele. The ties of reciprocal obligation and mutual advantage which bind patron and client together have nothing to do with issues, much less ideology; indeed, dogma and doctrine are irritants, even threats to the smooth functioning of the relationship. Translated to the next level of coalition formation, ideological positions are unlikely to improve the aggregative capacity of a party and may actually do some harm. The calculus of coalition building thus commands relegation of ideology to the dustbins of empty rhetoric.

In turn, the fact that parties were vertical chains of patron-client nets, essentially indistinguishable in terms of social composition, meant that there were no reasons why the parties should differ in social goals or economic philosophy. The bipolarity of the party system is also of critical import in structuring political perceptions and calculations. From the perspective of the patron investing his vote bank, the choice was between two contenders, and the game was won by selecting the winning side. From the viewpoint of the party-builders, the object was, in the most classical validation of the Riker theorem, the construction of a minimum winning coalition sufficient to gain command over the patronage resources of incumbency, but not too large as to require the division of the spoils among such a sizable following that its impact was diluted below the minimum threshhold of gratitude.[57] There have been short-lived third party movements, but these have, for the most part, been tactical maneuvers in faction formation designed to improve the bargaining position of a cluster of political brokers. Outside the system there was the option of radical or revolutionary dissent, represented in central Luzon by the Hukbalahup movement. For the average peasant, involvement in such an enterprise was a desperate adventure, contravening the prudential instincts of most; such undertakings were unlikely to yield short-term returns of security or material rewards, and only the advanced decomposition of the patronage system and sharp deterioration of economic circumstances of the "little men" could make this alternative attractive. Such, indeed, was the case in densely populated areas of central Luzon, but not in most of the archipelago.

Thus, externally viewed, Filipino politics had the appearance of remarkable stability. Two national parties locked in vigorous electoral combat at constitutionally prescribed intervals. The rituals of electoral

57. William Riker, *The Theory of Political Coalitions* (New Haven and London: Yale University Press, 1965), pp. 32-46.

politics were well observed; campaigns were carried on with much fanfare and a heated, albeit contentless, partisanship. Election years were moments of redistributive politics on a grand scale: roads were suddenly built; long dormant public works projects came off the shelves; large amounts of money percolated through the system, reflected in foreign exchange crises inevitably associated with the national elections. [58] Probably to an increasing extent, lower class voters, especially in urban areas, viewed their ties to patrons as short run and instrumental. Thus, the maintenance of networks required ever-increasing amounts of capital for payoffs with each successive election.

To fully grasp the internal dynamics of the electoral process, we need to take one further step and examine the essential fluidity of alignments. At the patron-client base of the system, this occurs at the margins of networks; although there is a stable core, there is also a floating group of more episodic clients, who may change sides in the course of a given electoral campaign. This process becomes more pronounced as we move up the scale to examine factions which are alliances of patronage nets put together by a political broker. At the heart of such a faction are an inner cluster of followers bound to the factional leader by enduring affective personal bonds; around its periphery are a larger number whose relations are more ephemeral and whose factional attachment is conditional and dependent upon particular patronage transactions associated with the short-term goals of a given election. The difference between the inner and outer circles is analogous to the distinction between outright purchase and a rental arrangement.

At the aggregative level of the national parties, there was virtually nothing to assure the perennity of attachments. As the parties were indistinguishable in program and social composition, there was almost no constraint on switching allegiances. Party identification by mass publics was, in reality, insignificant; vote banks moved at the dictates of the brokers, in anticipation of redistributive benefits; affective ties were there, but to patrons and not to parties. Indeed, on close scrutiny, it becomes clear that party-switching was not only a possibility, but a necessity for patrons and faction-leaders. The claims levied by factions on party brokers bidding for their vote banks could be enforced only by the credible threat of taking these votes elsewhere unless reasonable terms were met. As the system became institutionalized, it became a built-in expectation of party and faction brokers that party-switching was not merely a desperate expedient which could

58. Interesting data on this point may be found in Harvey A. Averch, John E. Koehler, and Frank H. Denton, *The Matrix of Policy in the Philippines* (Princeton: Princeton University Press, 1971). p. 109.

be indulged only in extreme circumstances, but was a readily available alternative.

Not only could party-switching occur, but it did on a stupendous scale. No stigma attached to switching, as long as it served the basic purpose of maximizing reward flow. Rural voters, in particular, looked upon voting, not as expressing a political choice, but as the fulfillment of a personal obligation to a faction leader.[59] One recent study of members of the House of Representatives suggests that party-switching is a very efficacious strategy for incumbents; of those who switched, 81 percent were re-elected, while only about 60 percent of those remaining with their previous party were returned to congress.[60] This process helps explain the fact that in every national election from independence until 1969 the party in power was defeated.

This system, with a fluid bipolar competition extending from the top right down to the local level, makes clear why cultural mobilization did not occur. The intricate web of shifting alliances, revolving about two parties, made impossible the creation of monolithic regional blocs. At the local level of patron-client vote banks, there was no cultural pluralism. Ethnicity as a factor in coalition formation could only have entered at the regional level, but was constrained by the predominance of a bipolar, national competition, whose duality was replicated at each echelon of politics. The immediate competitive alignment at the regional level was with a fluid set of socially and culturally identical factions, which were not distinguishable in ethnic networks. This being the case, the regional brokers could not bargain with national coalition-builders on the basis of their command of an ethnic clientele. Even the most culturally differentiated group, the three Muslims linguistic communities, were linked into the network of bipolar party factionalism.

REBELLION AND PLURALISM IN THE PHILIPPINES

The two major armed uprisings since independence, the Hukbalahap insurrection and the Muslim rebellion, are suggestive of the different solidarity requirements of violent resistance. The Huk movement (the acronym stands for "Peoples' Army to Fight the Japanese") had begun during World War II and waxed and waned in central Luzon as an antigovernment insurgency after independence. Its Marxist ideological

59. This point is well verified in an interesting survey by Hirofumi Ando, "Voting Turnout in the Philippines," *Philippine Journal of Public Administration*, XIII, no. 4 (1969), 424-41.

60. Steve Frantzich, "Party Switching in the Philippine Context," *Philippine Studies*, XVI, no. 4 (1969), 750-68.

affinities typed it as a Communist revolt, a characterization which, while not wholly false, removes too many of the subtle shadings of ideology and affiliation. The core of its armed support, careful analysis has shown, is in the Pampangan linguistic area, an enclave lying between the Tagalog and Ilocanos and totalling 3.2 percent of the population.[61] The Pampangans are closely related linguistically to the Tagalog but have a distinctive identity. During the Katipunan nationalist revolt against Spanish rule (1882-96) and again with the agrarian radical Sakdalista movement of the 1930s, participation was overwhelmingly Tagalog, and the Pampangans remained on the sidelines.[62] However, the heartland of Huk insurrection was in the Pampangan districts; conversely, the failure of most Tagalog in neighboring regions to join was a crippling setback for the Huks. It must immediately be stressed that none of these radical protest movements were explicitly founded upon cultural subnationalism. However, in a process very similar to that described for the Kwilu phase of the Zaire rebellions in 1964, a rising founded on the dynamics of rural discontent in a culturally plural environment became ethnically encapsulated. Although the impoverishment of the tenantry was quite general in central Luzon, once the response took on a Pampangan hue it became less attractive to the Tagalog. This cultural choice is operative under the conditions of very high risk associated with rebellion. Indiscriminate repression by the national army is a predictable response, and peasants are schooled by bitter experience to closely calculate their risks. For Pampangans, who might find a measure of cultural security within the movement to balance against the probable costs, the structure of choice was different from the Tagalog, who could not readily identify with the ethnic aspects. The encapsulation was more complete with the Ilocanos, who found the Huk alternative even less attractive.

The Muslim uprising which moved from a steady pattern of moderate dissidence to a more serious plane of armed insurrection in 1972 is too little documented to permit firm conclusions. The predisposing factors of impoverishment, Christian domination, and land conflict with settlers

61. The Pampangan base is clearly demonstrated by Edward J. Mitchell, "Some Econometrics of the Huk Rebellion," *American Political Science* Review, LXIII, no. 4. (December 1969), 1159-71. For some other studies relating to the Huk movement, see Frances L. Starner "Communism and the Philippine Nationalist Movement," *Solidarity,* VI, no. 2 (February 1971), 9-48; Alvin H. Scaff, *The Philippine Answer to Communism* (Stanford: Stanford University Press, 1955) (a very indulgent view of government responses to peasant discontent); Akira Takahashi, *Land and Peasants in Central Luzon* (Honolulu: East West Center Press, 1969); Ben Kerkvliet, "Peasant Rebellion in the Philippines: The Origins and Growth of the HMB," (Ph.D. diss., University of Wisconsin, 1972).
62. Mitchell, "Some Econometrics," p. 1167.

have been described above. One may speculate that the rupture of the links of vertical integration through the party patronage system by the Marcos coup of 1972 may have contributed to the expansion of rebellion. The cultural reference points of Indonesia and Malaysia and, through them, the broader worlds of Islam beyond suggest a frustrating contrast between polities where Muslims, however secular, hold power and the Filipino context where Muslims were regarded as a backward minority by the dominant Christians.

Both these cases suggest the proposition that armed confrontation requires a principle of solidarity which transcends the web of patron-client factionalism. Corollary to this is the premise that ideological formulation of discontent will not suffice in and of itself for peasant mobilization, although it may be of critical importance at the level of leadership. To date, this had been, on the whole, a marginal phenomenon in Filipino politics. However, the full consequences of the rupture proclaimed by President Marcos in 1972 have yet to make themselves felt. It has not escaped the attention of many that Marcos is an Ilocano and that many of the key operatives in his security apparatus belong to the same ethnic community. This fact was of much less significance during the era of bipolar factional parties, as "ethnic domination" could simply not occur within that framework. It is conceivable that cultural pluralism will become more salient in Filipino politics under the new authoritarian formula, as the devices which contained it no longer function. It represents, beyond any doubt, a profound mutation in Filipino politics. We have frequently argued that the political system itself was a major independent variable in shaping the pattern of cultural pluralism; from this it follows that the redefinition of the political arena will necessarily redefine cultural pluralism. This, of course, says disappointingly little until the march of events makes clear what the nature of the change will be.

NATIONAL LANGUAGE POLICIES: BAHASA INDONESIA AND PILIPINO

A final dimension of politics, common to both countries, is the development of a national language to replace the colonial linguistic legacy. This process has gone much further in Indonesia: the level of governmental commitment has been higher, and the natural advantages of the language are more evident. Also, in the Philippines the mass education policy pursued under American administration left in its wake a much larger elite with a stake in its command of English, while the lack of international standing and utility for Dutch limited its appeal.

There are many parallels in the development of the two national languages, Bahasa Indonesia and Pilipino. Both have as their primary base an indigenous language—Malay and Tagalog— which for different reasons appeared to enjoy a claim to primacy. Malay has been a lingua franca in the Indonesian archipelago for many centuries; its points of diffusion were the Muslim Malay trading state of Malacca (now in Malaysia) and the east Sumatra coast. One of Magellan's crew members, Pigafetta, made a list of Malay words encountered in the Moluccas which suggests that the trading lingua franca was already established in the spice islands by the early sixteenth century.[63] Malay rather than Arabic had also been the language associated with the diffusion of Islam. In the Tagalog case, its dominance was less due to any precolonial lingua franca role—the dispersed *barangay* settlements on the Philippine coast did not have a comparable mercantile network— than to the choice of Manila as the base for Spanish rule and trade. The Tagalog were most intensively affected by Spanish rule; they were correspondingly most numerous in the class of indigenous auxiliaries and intermediaries which grew up.

The colonial occupants went through a comparable sequence in their language policies. At first, the Dutch relied entirely on Malay as their medium of communication with their subjects, even with the Javanese courts. The colonial beachheads were first established in the coastal areas where the Islamic trading network with its Malay medium was well established. Similarly, the Spanish sought to find a single *lengua general* in which evangelization could be pursued and rule implemented. They believed that Tagalog was the most widely understood language and, indeed, that it was spoken by a majority of the inhabitants, although this perception doubtless reflected the concentration of Spanish occupation in the Tagalog zone.[64] However, with the establishment of a school system to produce subaltern personnel for the colonial system, the language question returned to the agenda. In 1850, the governor-general of the Dutch East Indies proposed that Malay be formally recognized as the official language; his proposal was eventually rejected in favor of Dutch, for reasons similar to those motivating Macauley's famous Minute on Education, enunciating the principle that a shelf of good English books was worth all the wisdom of India. Only through the use of the European language could the purported benefits of Western civilization be made accessible to the indigenous population, ran the reasoning. Although some Dutch

63. Kismadi research notes.
64. Ibid.; Ernest J. Frei, *The Historical Development of the Philippine National Language* (Manila: Institute of National Language, 1959), p. 6.

officials continued to argue the case for Malay or even Javanese, Dutch had won out by the turn of the century. The debate occurred rather earlier for the Spanish, and by the eighteenth century Spanish had replaced Tagalog in the seminaries and administration. After American occupation, Spanish was at once replaced with English.

In both cases, there was a significant linguistic component in the rise of nationalism. At a critical juncture, about the turn of the century, there was a general shift from the use of an Arabic to a Latin alphabet for Malay, which in turn facilitated the swift emergence of a Malay press; the number of Malay newspapers had reached 40 by 1918, and had swollen to 200 by 1925.[65] In the wake of nationalism came the emergence of Indonesian associations for cultural revival, the two most important being Jong Java (Young Java) and Jong Sumatra. The Javan body produced writing mainly in Dutch, while the Sumatran group used Malay as its medium; in using it, they developed a more contemporary idiom than the fairy tales and dynastic chronicles which constituted the bulk of Malay traditional literature. In 1928, a very important National Youth congress was held under the theme of "one nation, one people, one language"; Malay was rebaptised as "Bahasa Indonesia," and the Congress resolved that it should be developed as the national language. A national language congress was held in 1938, devoted to some of the practical issues involved in the transformation of Malay into a national language. During this period, rapid momentum was acquired in extending and modernizing the literary tradition of Indonesia.

In the Philippines, the national language issue arose somewhat later. There were some murmurs at the imposition of English, but the mass educational system made it available to many, and there was no initial consensus on an alternative. The *ilustrado* class clung for a time to Spanish; it was not until 1922 that the first speech in English was made in the Filipino House of Representatives. The language question reached the level of formal debate during the constitutional convention of 1934, which called for the establishment of a national language but without stipulating which it was to be. A National Language Institute was then established, with the mission of studying all languages spoken by more that 500,000 people, and developing from this is a general language. This commission, although it contained only one Tagalog member and its chairman was a Visayan, recommended in 1937 that Tagalog be chosen as the base of the new national language, Pilipino.[66]

65. Kismadi research notes.

66. Apolinar B. Parole, *Facts and Issues on the Pilipino Language* (Manila: Royal Publishing House, 1969), pp. 23-24. On the national language issue, see also Nobleza Asuncion-Lande, "Multilingualism, Politics and 'Filipinism,' " *Asian Survey,* XI, no. 7 (July 1971), 677-90.

The Japanese occupation in both instances gave important support to the national languages. Bahasa Indonesia and Tagalog were at once proclaimed as national languages, and use of the European language proscribed. This period was especially important for Indonesian, when much work was done in translating laws, setting up an array of special committees to coin terms for missing vocabulary, and composing Indonesian textbooks.

Thus, with the proclamation of the Indonesian republic in 1945, Bahasa Indonesia was already well established as a national language. After the end of the war with the Dutch, a period of rapid education development followed, with Indonesian now the language of instruction. It rapidly consolidated itself as the language of the metropolitan urban culture, as a predominant medium of modern literature as well as a pulp vehicle for popular expression. Particularly remarkable is the relative ease with which Indonesian outdistanced Javanese as a national language contender; Malay as mother tongue is spoken by only 6 percent, as against close to 50 percent for Javanese. At the time it was proclaimed as national language, Bahasa Indonesia was spoken by only 10 million persons, including three or four million native speakers; even today, only 30 million speak it, as compared with 60 million Javanese speakers.[67] The availability of an integrative language is an enormous asset; Malay had the advantage, not only of not being Javanese, but of being closely related to a number of Sumatran languages. Sumatran-Javanese relations would almost certainly have been very different had an effort been made to impose Javanese. Although a rare voice was raised in behalf of Javanese, the pressure was never serious. Over the long run, the sheer demographic weight of Javanese may be felt indirectly, with a measure of Javanization of Indonesian. But Indonesian appears securely established as national language and as a vehicle of identity formation.

Pilipino has not had such a clear pathway. Indeed, the name "Pilipino" was adopted in 1955 to diminish the opposition of non-Tagalog critics, who argue for the retention of English. An interesting court test was brought by Congressman Inocencia V. Ferrer in 1961 against the officials of the National Language Institute, charged with the development of Pilipino, for violating the constitutional requirement that the national language be a combination of existing languages; Pilipino, he claimed, is nothing but Tagalog. Although the case was lost, its argument still has some backing in non-Tagalog areas.[68]

Knowledge of Tagalog is spreading at an impressive rate. In 1939, census figures showed 25.4 percent of the population spoke Tagalog; the figure rose to 37.2 percent by 1948 and 44.4 percent in 1960. It should

67. Whiteley, *Language Use and Social Change,* p. 62.
68. Parole, *Pilipino Language,* p. 107.

be noted that the number of English-speakers also rose from 26.6 percent to 39.5 percent over the same period, placing the debate between Pilipino and English on very different grounds than in India, with its 2 percent of English-speakers. The relatively high literacy rates in the Philippines makes possible the diffusion of a vernacular culture facilitative of the spread of Tagalog; illustrated publications and literature of the comic strip genre in Tagalog have played an important part. There is also a thriving Tagalog film industry, whose movies are immensely popular in the countryside. Mass communication are highly centralized in Manila, a Tagalog-language city.[69]

Like Hindi, those assigned to the functions of developing the national language have an irresistible penchant for traditionalizing it. The National Language Institute has a proclivity for resurrecting unused or forgotten words from classic Tagalog, rather than legitimizing the actual vernacular usages. The real strength of Pilipino is the growing acceptance of vernacular Tagalog by ordinary citizens through the influence of the mass media, the impact of Manila culture, and its use in schools and administration. "Purification" is unlikely to increase the acceptability of Pilipino as national language, but appears to be an incurable professional disease of the language specialist.

Pilipino, or Tagalog in national disguise, does seem destined to play a significant integrative role. Despite the continued hostility of a certain number of non-Tagalog elites to Pilipino, at its present rate of expansion it now covers more than half the population; it spreads fastest among the young who are most likely to go to school, travel to Manila, or expose themselves to the media using Tagalog. The relative absence of ideological ethnicity in the Philippines dilutes the risk of linkage of Tagalog with any real cultural threat to other groups.

As multicultural polities, both Indonesia and the Philippines appear to have developed a secure sense of nationality. These two archipelago republics have largely completed the metamorphosis from artifact of colonial partition to nation-state. In both instances, underlying ethnic and religious cleavages would appear at first glance to contain the potential for a more salient pattern of cultural politics than actually has been manifest. In Indonesia, there is a major conflict potential in the relations between the ethnic Javanese and others. However, a number of factors have diffused this cleavage. The metaphors of nationalism did politicize religious differences but not ethnic ones. Among the self-aware ethnic communities, social competition was for the most part not directly with the Javanese. Neither the party system nor the civil-military bureaucracy has provided an arena for mobilizing ethnicity. The effectiveness of

69. Kismadi research notes.

Indonesian as a national language free of cultural threat has helped considerably. In the Philippines, the unusual depth of colonial impact, with its Hispanization and Christianization, was more notable for its cultural homogenization than differentiation. Spanish conceptualization of its colonized society did not employ the "tribal" map which so profoundly affected identity transformation in Africa. The images of modern politics were then embodied in the bipolar party system, which neither structurally nor metaphorically provided a place for cultural mobilization. The shifting alliances of patron-client networks related populace to politics in a manner which made ethnicity irrelevant. Aside from Muslims, latent communal identities are even less affirmed than in Indonesia. The wide diffusion of Tagalog-Pilipino and English has also facilitated national integration.

However, to achieve national integration and civil cohabitation with cultural pluralism is but one of the aims of political community. Both polities seem destined to undergo a phase of civil-military coalition rule, whose capacity to respond to other imperatives of equality and justice as well as development remains to be demonstrated.

10 Identity and Nationalism in the Arab World: The Struggle between State and Nation

In the view of political theorists, groups are entitled to the rights of nations if they possess unity of language and of race according to the German school; unity of history and of tradition according to the Italian school; and unity of political aspirations according to the French. If we are to consider the case of the Arabs in the light of these three schools, we will find that they have unity of language, unity of history and of traditions, and unity of political aspirations. The right of the Arabs to nationhood, therefore, finds endorsement in all schools of political theory.

        —1913 Arab Congress, Paris[1]

Who is an Arab? This may, at first sight, appear to be a simple question, but it is in fact of momentous importance to the Arab nationalist movement.
    An Arab is one whose "destiny" is, either by force of circumstance or intentionally, bound to the Arab world as a whole. . . . Whoever is descended from Kurdish, Negro, or Armenian stock but has inhabited an Arab country becomes an Arab by force of circumstances and by reason of the free association of his own destiny with that of the Arab world.

        —Clovis Maqsud[2]

When we find a man who disowns, and takes no pride in, the fact that he is an Arab, even though he is Arabic-speaking and belongs to an Arab nation, we must discover the reasons for his attitude. . . . Whatever the reason, we must not say he is not an Arab as long as he does not wish to be an Arab but disowns and despises his Arabism. He is an Arab, whether he likes it or not, whether he accepts it or not—at the present time. He may be ignorant, stupid, ungrateful, or treacherous, but he is an Arab all the same—an Arab who has lost his sensibility, his emotions, and maybe even his conscience.

        —Sati' al Husri[3]

1. Quoted in Hakam Zaki Nuseibah, *The Ideas of Arab Nationalism* (Ithaca: Cornell University Press, 1958), p. 49.
2. Quoted in Kemal H. Karpat (ed.), *Political and Social Thought in The Contemporary Middle East* (New York: Frederick A. Praeger, 1968), p. 59.
3. Quoted in ibid., p. 57.

WHO IS AN ARAB?

The question of who is an Arab under what circumstances, and what political obligations flow from that identity is indeed an important, even explosive question. The eighteen states which constitute the Arab world, stretching for nearly 5000 miles from Oman to Mauritania (with one more perhaps to come in the present Spanish Sahara) is probably the most problematic zone in the world state system. The idea of the Arab nation lives, even in the death of one effort after another to embody this dream in the state organization of the area. The convergence zones where Arab culture encounters its neighbors is a sphere of difficulty and tension—in Mauritania between Arabic-speaking Moors and Black populations of the Senegal valley, in Sudan as the basis for a bitter nine-year war of secession in the south, in Iraq as an apparently unending sequence of civil wars and short-lived truces between Arabs and Kurds. Transcending all else is continuous confrontation between the Arab world and the Jewish homeland state of Israel. Husayn and Faisal of the Hashemite house pass away, and Nasser arises to pick up the pan-Arab banner. The United Arab Republic ends in ignominious failure, and an unheard of young Colonel, Wanis Muammar al-Qaadafi, raises the Arab unity cry from Tripoli.

Pan-Arabism is the last of the multistate nationality movements, which were once an important part of the nationalism scene. Pan-Slavism has evaporated before the reality of Soviet domination of Eastern Europe. Pan-Turanism no longer stirs the Turkish heart. Pan-Africanism lives a modest existence, but its future seems limited to relatively amical interstate relationships; it was, in any event, not a nationality movement in the same sense as the others. The mobilizing force of Arab nationalism remains a passionate reality. At the same time, the state system which has emerged out of the wreckage of the Ottoman empire and colonial intervention by Spain, France, Italy, and Britain acquires a growing force and momentum of its own. The relationship between state and nation remains unresolved in the Arab world.

Add to this the constellation of external forces drawn into the Arab maelstrom by the near-continuous threat of war—indeed, actuality in 1948, 1956, 1967 and 1973—with Israel, and the waters are further muddied. This crisis has also spawned the territoriless nationality of Palestinian, whose Arab identity commands the solidarity of all others, yet is a further volatile factor in an equation of instability. Finally—as an astonishing new third world pattern, development with unlimited resources—in six of the Arab states, the magnitude of oil revenues has become such that there is virtually no financial constraint on decision-making. It is estimated that by 1980 the annual oil revenues in the Arab world will be

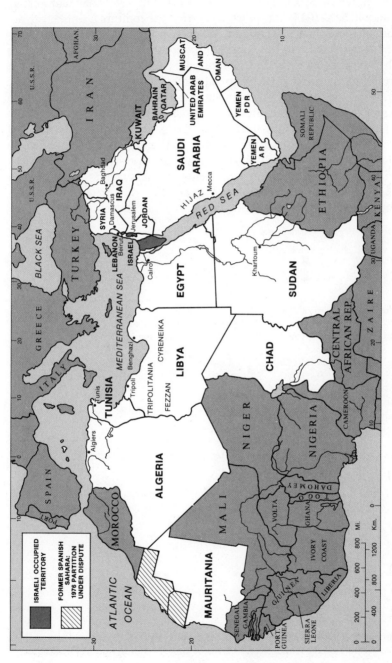

Map 10.1 The Arab World

ISRAELI OCCUPIED TERRITORY

FORMER SPANISH SAHARA: 1976 PARTITION UNDER DISPUTE

Cartographic Laboratory UW–Madison

on the order of $50 billion; between 1973 and 1980 their cumulative income will be $210 billion, of which current expenditure is unlikely to account for more than $100 billion. When free-floating sums of this magnitude are injected into the politics of inter-Arab relationships as well as Arab interactions with the international system more generally, the consequences become difficult to calculate. Throw into the balance the recently discovered energy crisis in the industrial world for which the Arab oil supplies will be the sole solution, and one has the makings of a very high order of involvement in the affairs of the Arab world by international actors. The likely impact of external determinants, when added to the basic volatility of the state system in the Arab world torn between conflicting principles of cultural legitimation, suggests an unusually wide range of possible outcomes.[4] Table 10.1 summarizes some pertinent data on the present constellation of Arab states.

Table 10.1—Profile of Arab States

Country	Population[a]	Ethnic diversity [b]	Religious diversity	Value of Oil Production ($billion)	
				1975 est.	1980 est.
Algeria	14,700,000	Kabyl (Berber)		1.1	2.3
Bahrain	220,000		Half Sunnite, half Shi'ite	c	
Egypt	34,130,000		Copts (7%)	(small output)	
Iraq	9,750,000	Kurd (15%)	Half Sunnite, half Shi'ite	1.2	6.4
Jordan	2,380,000				
Kuwait	830,000			2.2	5.0
Lebanon	2,870,000	Armenian (5%)	Maronite Christian (30%); Muslim (39%— half Sunnite, half Shi'ite); Druze (6%); Greek Orthodox (11%); Greek Catholic (6%)		

4. For an eye-opening analysis of the scale of the oil problem, see James E. Atkins, "The Oil Crisis: This Time the Wolf is Here," *Foreign Affairs,* LI, no. 3 (April 1973), 462-90.

Table 10.1 (*continued*)

Country	Population[a]	Ethnic diversity[b]	Religious diversity	Value of Oil Production ($billion)	
				1975 est.	1980 est.
Libya	2,010,000		Senussiya tariq in Cyreneika	2.2	3.1
Mauritania	1,200,000	Tukulor-Fulani (13%)			
Morocco	15,230,000	Berber (35%)			
Oman	680,000			.2[d]	
Qatar	115,000			c	
Saudi- Arabia	7,740,000		Wahabi tariq dominant	5.4	25.6
Sudan	16,090,000	Muslim: Fur (6%); Beja (5%); Non-Muslim: Nilotic groups (23%); Nuban (5%); Azande & related (5%)			
Tunisia				.1[d]	
United Arab Emirates				2.5[c]	8.2[c]
Yemen Arab Republic	5,900,00		Shi'ites (Zaidis and Ismalis) & Sunnites		
Yemen (People's Democratic Republic, former Aden)	1,470,000				

[a] 1971 United Nations estimates

[b] Non-Arab groups

[c] Figures for Bahrain, Qatar, and United Arab Emirates are lumped together.

[d] 1971 figures

Sources: Oil figures are from James E. Akins, "The Oil Crisis: This Time the Wolf is Here," *Foreign Affairs,* LI, 3 (April 1973), 479-80; Mauritania and Sudan data from Donald G. Morrison, Robert C. Mitchell, John N. Paden, and Hugh M. Stevenson, *Black Africa: A Comparative Handbook* (New York: Free Press, 1972), pp. 301, 344; Maghreb figures from Nevill Barbour (ed.), *A Survey of North West Africa* (London: Oxford University Press, 1959); Middle East data from Tareq Y. Ismael, *Government and Politics of the Contemporary Middle East* (Homewood, Ill.: Dorsey Press, 1970). It should be noted that the figures for the value of oil production were taken before the spectacular price rise following the October 1973 war.

GENESIS OF THE ARAB

The concept of Arabhood has a venerable history, which helps account for the diversity of contemporary usage. The word makes its first appearance in an Assyrian inscription dated as 853 B.C.[5] There were two quite different centers of Arab development in the ancient world. In southern Arabia, four prehistoric states of Arab linguistic base developed—the Sabbaeans, Hadramautians, Qatabanians, and Minaeans—apparently founded on a sedentary culture. In northern and central Arabia, the desert ecology imposed a quite different, nomadic social structure and made state formation more difficult; it was, however, out of this harsh environment that Islam and the universal Arab caliphate was born.

In the early seventh century, when the Prophet received his message, the meaning of Arab was specifically bedouin. The townspeople of Mecca and Medina spoke Arabic but were not identified as such; the settled Arabic-speakers of the Hijaz were of the Quraysh community, a group which has retained a special status because of its associations with Mohammed and the holy places. The northern dialect of Arabic appears to have become dominant throughout Arabia Deserta; in the century preceding the Prophet, a primarily oral literature of poems, proverbs, and mythologies had emerged, a heritage which provided the background for the Koran.

Around the inspirational message of the Prophet formed an army of conquest, a state, and, very quickly, a transformed concept of Arabhood. As bearers of the new revelation, Arab armies swept out of the desert, quickly overran the Levant, pushed across the northern shore of Africa to the Atlantic and on into Spain and to the east banks of the Indus in Sind (now Pakistan). The caliphate was founded as the earthly incarnation of the universal community of Islam. The Koran transformed the Arabs in the eyes of the settled civilizations contiguous to Arabia: Greco-Aramaic in the Levant, Sassanian in Iraq, Greco-Coptic in Egypt. Peoples who had a generation before regarded Arabs as unlettered, unruly barbarians who were a constant menace to settled civilization, now accepted, through the religious medium, Arabic as a language and culture of unique endowment. In less than three generations, although Islam was far from universally accepted, Arabic was firmly established as the language of state and rather swiftly displaced earlier languages. The last Greek document in Egypt dates from 709, suggesting that by this time linguistic Arabization was virtually complete in the lower Nile.

5. Bernard Lewis, *The Arabs in History* (London: Hutchison University Library, 1950), p. 11. For the early history of the concept of Arabhood, we have relied on this source, pp. 9-17, and Nuseibah, *The Ideas of Arab Nationalism,* pp. 3-41.

Thus within little more than a century an extraordinary alteration of cultural geography had occurred. Only a small fraction of the newly expanded Arab speech community consisted of the actual ethnic Arabs who had burst out of the desert. The numbers of original Arabs were relatively small; Mohammed, according to tradition, was able to assemble no more than 50,000 people on one of his triumphal processions, and the entire body of the original Arab hosts amounted to no more than a few hundred thousand persons.[6] The sphere of linguistic incorporation was stopped short at the frontiers of the Persian empire; the Persian view of Arabs at that time is probably well conveyed by the reaction of a Persian leader recounted by the great medieval Arab historian, Ibn Khaldun; astounded by the spectacle of the serried ranks of Arabs prostrate in prayer before the Caliph Omar, he asked how he could defeat a man "who can turn dogs into civilized beings."[7] Although Persia was briefly defeated, it was not really subjugated and certainly never accepted Arab cultural superiority. Persia was Islamacized, but in time it domesticated Islam into a Persian framework and made it virtually a national church. After the first wave, there was a much slower cultural diffusion process of Arab language and culture spreading up the Nile valley into Sudan and across to the southern fringe of the Sahara desert. In the Maghreb, linguistic Arabization was a much more gradual process than in Egypt, Mesopotamia, and the Levant; even today, an estimated 35 percent of the Moroccan population still claim some Berber dialect as mother tongue. Elsewhere, in both Asia and Africa, the subsequent spread of Islam was not linked to Arabization. Arabic as the language of the Koran, and thus of religious instruction, and Mecca as the goal of pilgrimage, gave to Arabic a special place and prestige, but the task of diffusion of the prophet's message was taken up by various non-Arab intermediaries.

In 750, the first Arab dynasty of the Ummayads came to an end, ousted by the Abbasids, a cultural change of great importance. The rise of the Abbasids was the triumph of an Islamic elite of cosmopolitan origins, not attached to the premise that the community of Islam was an Arab agency. Arabic remained the court language and the medium of theological debate and discourse, but the concept of the universal community was now religious, and not ethnic. With the entry of the Turks onto the Middle Eastern scene as a powerful actor, the Arab role became further diminished. The de-Arabization of the Islamic political community reached its final culmination in the founding of the Ottoman empire as successor to the title of the caliphate in 1517 and the ensuing Turkish conquest of the Arab lands, except for Morocco, and the hinterland areas

6. Joel Carmichael, *The Shaping of the Arabs: A Study in Ethnic Identity* (New York: Macmillan, 1967), p. 89.

7. Quoted in Nevill Barbour (ed.), *A Survey of North West Africa* (London: Oxford University Press, 1959), p. 16.

of desert Arabia, which had been the original cultural heartland. Further humiliation had come with the conquest of portions of the Holy Lands by the Christian crusaders and establishment of several Frankish kingdoms in the southern Levant. In this altered context, the once all-important distinctions between Arabs of the conquest and merely Arabized populations faded into insignificance. A fusion of identities gradually occurred; among the Arab people, confronted with the common experience of subjugation to the Turks, by silent and unconscious processes a common sense of Arabism took shape.

During this period—the dark ages of the Arab community in nationalist mythology—identity was not articulated in self-conscious form. Indeed, in many contemporary references of this period, the term "Arab" reverted to its earlier usages as a social rather than ethnic label; "Arabs" were the nomadic bedouin, and not the urban and settled population of the Levant, Nile Valley, or Maghreb coast. In the Levant, the term "Saracen" was in most common vogue at the time of the Crusades to refer to sedentary Arabic-speakers; Ibn Khaldun in his writings generally uses the word in this sense.

The duality between urban-sedentary and nomadic-bedouin Arab culture implied in these usages of the term is of fundamental importance. Bedouin groups are kindreds, segmented communities; their size is governed by the rigorous requirements of the desert environment through which they wander. Once a band exceeds an ecologically determined maximum, it must segment. Solidarity is defined in a series of circles, whose outer limit is a genealogically bound community commonly called a "tribe." Conflict binds to solidarity those enclosed within the circle of identity at which it occurs. For example, if the conflict occurs between two members of the lowest segmental units, the struggle will involve only these segments. If a segment is attacked by a group from another clan, then all other kin segments within the clan have at least a theoretical moral duty to lend their support. Loyalties are thus highly fragmented and localized; paradoxically, that part of the Arab linguistic community to whom the collective label was always applied by the cosmopolitan urbanites was the very one least likely to think in collectivities larger than the "tribe." The bedouin culture, it is said, is highly individualistic; this must be understood as referring to intense solidarity of small segments, and not literal individualism of an atomistic sort. The individual could only survive through the collective effort of the group; both physical security and material wants were satisfied by the segmental kindred. It was the community that assumed responsibility for redressing wrongs suffered by one of its members at the hands of an outsider; in return, the individual owed to the community unconditional loyalty. Bedouin Arabs shared the practice of an austere version of Islam; broader patterns of loyalty among nomadic Arabs came about primarily through the rise of Islamic brotherhoods, such as Senussiya in Libya or the Wahhabites in Arabia. From the time of the Abbasids to the rise of the Saud family, as the secular arm of the Wahhabis, bedouin Arabs of Arabia Deserta paid no heed to any imperial authority.

The urban culture was completely different, throughout the Arab-speaking world. It was the center of high Islamic culture, the fulcrum of centralized political organization, the nexus of trade. City and country-side eyed each other uneasily; for the rural Arabs, city-based dynasties cast out their long, tribute-collecting tentacles whenever their power permitted them to do so. City-dwellers saw their wealth as under the constant threat of desert marauders. [8]

Intercalary between the city and desert, along the river valleys permitting irrigated agriculture, above all along the Nile, and in coastal areas of the Maghreb and Levant and the Yemen mountains where rainfall sufficed for sedentary farming, the peasant village community existed with a culture and identity of its own. Although it was not possible for the village to escape political control by one or another sultan or royal governor, this authority was very lightly exercised; dynastic interest was limited to regular payment of taxes. The village had its own local leadership, both religious and political. It was a self-enclosed world, subject to a broader system, sharing its language and religion, but otherwise conceptually was bounded by its own narrow horizons. Exchange and communication .did not extend beyond the transactions of subjugation, a tribute payment. [9] For Egyptian peasants, before the contemporary mobilization of identity, "Arabs" were simply members of bedouin tribes in upper Egypt and the Arabian peninsula. As Carmichael suggests, they "could not have considered themselves 'Arabs' in any sense at all; indeed, it would have been impossible to put this question to them so as to make it meaningful."[10]

In the beginning of the nineteenth century, at the moment when modern Arab nationalism was about to be born, Arab culture had fallen very far from the glorious days of the Ummayads. The governors of the Levant, Egypt, and the Maghreb were Turkish in language and culture. Turkish was the primary language of administration. Arabic remained only the language of religion, but the great days of theological innovation were long over. The Levant was to be the cradle of the new Arab nationalism, the cultural workshop where the Arab heritage was reformulated in terms relevant to the challenge of modernization. At the base

8. For a useful analysis of desert, village, and urban modes of life, see Morroe Berger, *The Arab World Today* (Garden City, N.Y.: Doubleday Anchor, 1964), pp. 48-97.

9. On Egyptian village society, from a political perspective, see James B. Mayfield, *Rural Politics in Nasser's Egypt* (Austin: University of Texas Press, 1971), pp. 15-30.

10. Carmichael, *Shaping of the Arabs*, p. 279.

point, the resources for undertaking this mission were very meager. There was no Arabic printing press; books were very few, mainly devotional. Dialectical differentiation in Arabic had gone very far, with the centers of learning which had maintained classical Arabic moribund, and the classic literature buried in dust.

THE RISE OF ARAB NATIONALISM

A paradox bearing the seeds of a major contradiction in Arab nationalism lay in the important early role of Christian missions as the first intellectual link between the Arabs and the West. The missions had as their constituency the Arab-speaking Christian populations of what was then the Syrian province of the Ottoman Empire, including Lebanon and Palestine. Although mission activity among the Maronite Christians of Mount Lebanon dates from the seventeenth century, a significant impact dates only from the early decades of the nineteenth century. In the 1830s schools were established, an Arabic printing press was introduced, and work on rejuvenating the language began. Graduates of these schools were among the first to spread the message of Arabism as modern nationalism; a major landmark was in 1857, when at a secret meeting of the Syrian Scientific Society in Beirut a poem was delivered which "sang of the achievements of the Arab race, of the glories of Arabic literature, and of the future that the Arabs might fashion for themselves by going to their own past for inspiration."[11] But Islam was absolutely central to the Arab cultural heritage, and one of the most thorny issues in defining the concept of Arabhood has been the relationship of the Arabic-speaking Christian community. This question, it must be added, was relevant only in the Levant, and especially in Lebanon; Christians are significant nowhere else in the Arab world. Yet the pivotal geopolitical role of the Levant and the crucial historical role of Christian Arab intellectuals in the early development of Arab nationalism have given the problem an impact far beyond what numerical proportions would seem to suggest.

Arab nationalism, in the period between this first ode to patriotism and the Versailles Conference which set the basis for the contemporary state system, had to identify both "we" and "they" in the geography of identity. The concepts, of course, were interactive; who "we" are

11. George Antonius, *The Arab Awakening* (New York: Capricorn Books, 1965), pp. 49-54. Although this seminal work was first published more than three decades ago, it has not been surpassed as an account of the rise of Arab nationalism in the Levant, although some feel that he exaggerates the role of Christian Arabs.

implies different boundaries for "they," while the specification of the relevant other fixes "we" parameters. The great voice of Islamic reform was raised in the 1870s by Sayyed Jamaluddin al-Afghani; his focus was on Islam, not Arabism. A reformed, rejuvenated Islam, freed of foreign influences, could serve as the basis for restoration of the caliphate and as the basis for political unity of the world of Islam. Another major thinker, Abdul Rahman al-Kawakebi, added an Arab note by arguing that pan-Islam should be under Arab leadership and that the caliphate should return to Mecca, under the aegis of the Quraysh community. The pan-Islam proposition gradually dropped from the picture, and Arab nationalism before World War I came to focus mainly on Arab self-rule in the Levant and Mesopotamia; Beirut, Damascus, and to a lesser extent Baghdad were its main centers.

From 1830 on, "they" became a more complex issue; this date marked the French conquest of Algeria and the beginning of a process, which peaked just after World War I, of partitioning the former Ottoman domains among European powers. In 1881, Tunisia followed; in 1882, British troops landed at Alexandria, and in 1912 the Italians linked through conquest the two loosely held Turkish provinces of Tripoli and Benghazi. European powers thus became an important point of reference, although, for Christian Arabs, an ambiguous one. Tensions between the religious communities in the Levant had grown, in complex interplay between Muslim, Druze, and Christian; the first disorders broke out in 1841 and culminated in 1860 in a massacre of Christians in Damascus, on parts of Mount Lebanon; 11,000 Christian Arabs were killed in Damascus. This brought European intervention and cemented a strong tie of elements of the Maronite Christian community on Mount Lebanon to France.

For the Levantine Arabs, the Ottomans were the primary reference point. Political awakening was accompanied by a steady trend toward greater hostility to Ottoman overrule, although there were wide oscillations in function of the content of Ottoman Arab policy at any given time. In the immediate aftermath of the accession of Sultan Abd-al-Hamid to the Ottoman throne in 1876, there was a period of reduced tension. Abd-al-Hamid offered large subsidies for institutions of Arabic learning, refurbished the holy shrines in Mecca, Medina, and Jerusalem, and created a special elite Arab batallion of palace guards. In time, however, it became clear that the Sultan's statecraft was directed toward strengthening the Turkish hold on its remaining Arab provinces, not promotion of Arab autonomy in the Levant. The 1908 coup by young officers, whose motif was nationalism and modernization, also produced a moment of euphoria; many Arab officers played a leading part in this movement. This honeymoon was very brief; it soon became apparent that the Turkish component in the nationalism of the young officers was even more pronounced, that many were caught up in the spirit of the Pan-Turanian movement, and, like good jacobins, they soon turned to centralization and Turkification.

This set the stage for Allied exploitation of Arab nationalism in World War I and the formation of an Arab army to take part in the struggle to drive the Turks and Germans out of the Levant. The Arab legion, under the leadership of the Hashemite family and the legendary T. E. Lawrence, slowly fought its way up from the Hijaz to the conquest of Damascus in October 1918. The British army, under General Allenby, advanced along the coast and was thus in control of the most important areas. World War I eliminated the Ottoman-Turkish factor as a foil of Arab nationalism and introduced two new elements in Arab demonology. An extraordinarily duplicitous imperial diplomacy, operating under the pressures of wartime reason of state, had simultaneously promised an Arab Levantine state to the Hashemites, who then were generally accepted as the state-building vehicle for Arab nationalism, and made provision for a partition of the Arab Middle East between Britain and France and for the establishment of a Jewish homeland in Palestine. Imperialism and Zionism thus became the two identity-forming enemies for Arab nationalism, as the state system which now dominates the Arab world took shape out of the World War I partition.

In the period of gestation, some critical identity changes had occurred. Historically, the meaningful levels of identity were religious and local. The idea of Arab nationalism arose to claim precedence over religious community or clan, claiming that common language formed the moral basis for a united Arab political community. However, this galvanizing idea had to compete in turn with the loyalties attached to the more particularized state system which came to structure the Arab world, and conflicting identities which revolved around these new units. We turn now to the emergence of the contemporary state system, and patterns of cultural pluralism within it.

EMERGENCE OF THE STATE SYSTEM: SEVEN NODAL POINTS

The state system grew up in the twentieth century from several polity-forming cores; the Ottoman provincial system, the coastal sultanates of the Arabian peninsula, the Moroccan monarchy, the Nile Valley, the colonial partition, the Hashemite royal house, Islamic reform and purification movements, and the Jewish homeland. From these overlapping, competing, and interacting nodal points, came the contemporary state system. State formation was a complex dialectical process, which we will summarize by discussion of each of these nodal points.

The Ottoman empire had both a territorial and religious pattern of subdivision. In the Maghreb, Turkish rule established a territorial partition which was reflected in the subsequent states of Algeria and Tunisia, with Tripoli and Benghazi being separate provinces. A small ruling class grew out of the original Turkish garrisons, Turkish speaking but of rather diverse provenience. The Barbary States flourished through privateering in the sixteenth and seventeenth centuries, but this trade declined as European navies grew stronger in the Mediterranian. Algeria was the most unstable of these states, although it somehow remained in a piece, run by a Turkish elite which never numbered more than 15,000. In Tunisia, by the eighteenth century the office of governor had become a hereditary dynasty. From the seventeenth century on, Ottoman authority over its far western provinces was purely nominal. However, in 1835, some restoration of Turkish authority occurred in Tripoli and Benghazi.

In the Levant, Ottoman rule had to cope with complex religious pluralism; this was done through the institution of the millet, permitting communal autonomy and self-regulation in the matters of personal status in which religious laws differed. The last administrative reorganization, undertaken by Sultan Abd-al-Hamid in 1887, divided the Levant into the coastal provinces of Aleppo and Beirut and a hinterland province of Syria. Mount Lebanon was an autonomous region, and Jerusalem, comprising most of present Israel and Jordan, was also separate. However, the term "Syria" was frequently used to refer to the entire area.

Elsewhere, Iraq was formed out of three Ottoman provinces, Baghdad, Basra, and Mosul; the two former were frequently thought of as "Mesopotamia," while Mosul, Kurdish-dominated, was of another cultural world. Hijaz, an area along the Red Sea important particularly as seat of the holy cities of Mecca and Medina, Yemen, and an evanescent Persian Gulf province rounded out the Ottoman territorial organization.[12]

The second core of state formation came from the kingdoms and sultanates around the coastal fringe of the Arabian peninsula. The oldest of these, Yemen, traces its dynastic pedigree back more than 1000 years; the fertile soil and ample relief rainfall of the high mountain and plateau country of Arabia Felix permitted a much higher population than could occur in the arid zones. Oman, Qatar, Bahrein, Kuweit, and the seven sheikhdoms joined in the United Arab Emirates had retained their identity through periods of British and, for most, Ottoman rule.

12. Ibid., pp. 65-66.

The Nile Valley was a third nodal area. Here, Ottoman rule had long been exercised through Mameluke governors, an alien elite often of slave origins, usually taken from the Caucasian marches of the Ottoman empire. Egypt was a vast tax farm, generally leased to a given governor for a rather short term. The governor in turn relied upon an intermediary set of provincial overlords, also of Mameluke origin, to see to the collection of levies from the hundreds of villages lining the Nile. 1798 was a pivotal year; Napoleon landed and made a brief effort at conquest. When he was driven out in 1801, a wholly new era was ushered in. The villages were jolted by the cultural threat of Christian rule, made more tangible by the Napoleonic practice of naming Egyptian Coptic Christians as tax collectors. However, Ottoman rule was never really re-established. In 1805, a member of the military garrison, Mohammad Ali, led an uprising against the Turkish government which mobilized both the ulama and the villagers. Some 40,000 peasants joined in the assault on Cairo, an unheard of degree of rural mobilization.[13] The caliphate, out of necessity, had to endorse the *fait accompli* of Ali's coup, but was never able to exercise any influence over him. Mohammad Ali consolidated his rule through decimating the old Mameluke tax-fearing landholders and set about fashioning a centralized, secular state. From 1820, Egyptian authority was extended into the upper Nile, reaching its farthest point in 1872 through the annexation of the kingdom of Bunyoro, in Uganda.

For a time, Mohammad Ali and his son, Ibrahim Pasha, nursed the idea of an Arab empire under their leadership; they had extended their rule over the Levant by 1833. This was an ironic aspiration for Mohammad Ali, who was a Turkish-speaking Albanian, unable to communicate in Arabic. However, Ibrahim Pasha had learned the language and spoke of himself as an adopted Arab. The European powers were not enthusiastic about this new Arab state; British diplomatic pressure, in particular, was instrumental in forcing Ibrahim Pasha out of Syria in 1840. Had this state survived and consolidated itself, the course of Arab nationalism and nature of the Middle Eastern state system might have been totally different.

Morocco was a world of its own during the period of state formation. It can trace its ancestry as a distinctive political unit to the ninth century, although the real history of the state in roughly its present form begins with the rise of the Alawite dynasty in 1666. The Moroccan rulers had learned from the Turks the technique of recruiting certain communities as warriors for the throne by exempting them from taxation and providing them with good lands. These guich (army) communities were the backbone of the Moroccan throne. Geographically insulating

13. Mayfield, *Rural Politics in Nasser's Egypt,* pp. 24-26.

Morocco were the Atlas and Rif mountains, protecting the fertile plain of the Fez-Marrakech-Rabat/Casablanca triangle. Further protecting the kingdom was the zone of tribute-paying dissident mountain groups, largely Berber-speaking, who recognized their relationship to the throne but sought to minimize it. The degree of royal authority exercised over the *blad-as-siba* (zone of dissidence) dilated and contracted with the force and skill of a given monarch. But however tenuous its links to the Moroccan sultanate, it was a highly efficacious buffer zone.[14]

Fifthly, three state-forming religious movements affected the political geography of the Arab world, the Wahhabites in Saudi Arabia, the Senussiya in Libya, and the Mahdiya in Sudan. The first of these in time and importance was the Wahhabi movement in Arabia Deserta, which arose through the junction of a charismatic theologian, Muhammad ibn 'Abdul-Wahhab, and the house of Saud. From the man of piety came a doctrine of Islamic purification and austerity; from the house of Saud came a warrior community that could spread the message. The movement arose in the eighteenth century, just before the birth of Arab nationalism. Through this religious idiom of solidarity, a nomadic confederation under Saudi leadership arose, strong enough to challenge the Ottomans for control of the Levant by the early nineteenth century. Although they were pushed back, the Saudi confederation remained a powerful force in north and central Arabia and was able to gain recognition as a sovereign state after World War I. In the years following World War I, Saudi forces were able to expand the boundaries of their new state to the borders of the coastal sheikhdoms and, in 1924, to expel the Hashemites from the Hijaz and assume control over the holy places. It is to be noted that this new state, in its initial cultural self-concept, was Wahhabi and Saudi, and not Arab. The desert regions were outside the orbit of Arab nationalist thought which engaged Levantine and Egyptian intellectuals.[15]

The Mahdist state in the Sudan lasted for fifteen short years, but it probably deserved credit for changing the course of history on the upper Nile. From the annexation of much of Sudan by Mohammad Ali in 1821, a Turko-Egyptian administration had been established and relatively heavily garrisoned. Taxation was imposed, and a new class of prosperous merchants, many engaged in slave dealings, grew up in Khartoum. The imposition of Egyptian administration was attended by the resentments provoked by colonial rule elsewhere; in 1881 the son of a Dongola boat-builder, Muhammad Ahmed, received the divine message that he had been invested with the mission of the Mahdi, or God-

14. Clement Henry Moore, *Politics in North Africa* (Boston: Little Brown, 1970), pp. 12-22.
15. Antonius, *Arab Awakening,* pp. 21-22, 326-37.

guided one, to restore an earthly order more acceptable to God. By 1883, the Mahdi rapidly gained followers in the western Sudan; at the same time, the British were occupying Egypt, including Sudan. In 1885, in an epic battle, he defeated General Gordon, commander of the British garrison at Khartoum. Although the Mahdi himself died only a few months later, the state founded in his name survived until 1898. When British forces retook Khartoum, and the Madhist state collapsed, it was not Egyptian authority which was restored, but British, in the name of a condominium in which the Egyptian role was so minor as to be only barely perceptible. Five decades later, when a nationalist movement took form in the Sudan, the British had a strong interest in discouraging fusion with Egypt; this became, in effect, one of the major bargaining counters in the independence negotiations, and it was made very clear that the pathway that led to separate nationhood was strewn with many fewer obstacles than that which pointed toward the unity of the Nile Valley. Thus it was that Sudan assumed its place in the concert of nations as separate and sovereign state.[16]

The Senussiya was founded in the middle nineteenth century in Cyreneika (western Libya) by al-Sayed Mohamed bin Ali al-Senussi, who traced his descent from the Prophet's daughter, Fatima. Its doctrine bore the marks of the Wahibi movement, whose theology the founder had studied during a long stay in Mecca. It developed a string of religious lodges at the scattered oases of Cyreneika, and became a factor of common identity and unity among the highly independent bands of the Cryeneikan desert. Its hierarchy also provided a structure of political leadership, which the fragmented bedouin communities could not have generated on their own. Senussiya was considered a troublesome threat by the Turks in their last years in Benghazi. However, when the Italians invaded in 1911, Senussiya came to the aid of the Turks and made Italian conquest a very costly affair. Subsequently, when Libya after World War II was a ward on the hands of the United Nations which the organization was eager to set free, Senussiya in effect was the only organized force they could turn to. It was the grandson of the founder, Sayed Mohamed Idris al-Mahdi, then head of the Senussiya order, who was placed on the newly-created Libyan throne. Although Senussiya had only eighteen lodges in Tripolitania and fifteen in the string of southern oases known as the Fezzan, compared to forty-five in Cyreneika, nonetheless it provided a critical transitional structure for the new state. With the transformation of Libyan society by

16. Leon Carl Brown in Rotberg and Mazrui, *Protest and Power in Black Africa,* pp. 145-168; K.D.D. Henderson, *The Sudan Republic* (London: Ernest Benn, 1965), pp. 30-46.

the flow of vast oil revenues in the 1960s, the role of Senussiya diminished, and the monarchy was overthrown in 1969 by the military.[17]

The greatest impact of all on Arab state creation was the colonial partition. France and Britain were the major competitors, penetrating the Arab world from different directions and for divergent purposes. France acquired its first Arab foothold in 1830 in Algeria; in 1881, Tunisia was added. From its West African sphere of imperialistic expansion, the westernmost outpost of Arabic speech, Mauritania, was subjected about 1900 and organized as a very lightly administered appendage of the administrative federation of French West Africa, France and Spain divided the Moroccan kingdom in 1912. In the Middle East, French ambitions focused on the Levant, where a special relationship already existed with the Lebanese Maronite Christian community. In spring 1916 a secret Anglo-French treaty, the Sykes-Picot accord, was negotiated, which allocated to the French what are now Lebanon, Syria, the Mosul district of present Iraq, and a sizable chunk of Turkey itself. Mosul and the Turkish segment had to be abandoned in the peace settlement, but France was awarded as a single mandate tutelage over present Lebanon and Syria. Here decisions by the French in consolidating their mandate were crucial; many believe that a single Syria could have been maintained, with the support of most, at that moment in history. However, the French structured their territories in functions of degree of prospective loyalty from the different cultural segments. To the Ottoman autonomous district of Mount Lebanon, with its strong Maronite Christian population, was added the coastal strip from Tripoli to Sidon, a predominately Muslim zone. In Syria, the mandate territory was broken into four territories on the basis of religious and ethnic distinctions. In particular, the Druze (Jebel Druze) and Alawite (Latakia) areas were looked upon as possible centers of French support against the domination of orthodox Sunni Muslim Arabs. The lament of Antonius is a view widely shared among Arab nationalists on the partition of greater Syria after World War I:

> The country had a unity of its own in more ways than one. In spite of the great diversity of its physical features, it was geographically one and formed a self-contained unit enclosed by well-defined frontiers. In the economic field, it had developed its agricultural and commercial life on a foundation of natural resources, and the whole country was criss-crossed with a close network of interdependent lines of activity, linking region to region, the country side to the cities, and the coast to the interior. It had also cultural and historical traditions of

17. Among the sparse literature on Libya, see especially Majid Khadduri, *Modern Libya* (Baltimore: Johns Hopkins Press, 1963); Adrian Pelt, *Libyan Independence and the United Nations* (New Haven: Yale University Press, 1970); and the seminal work of E.E. Evans-Pritchard, *The Sanusi of Cyreneica* (London: Oxford University Press, 1949).

unity: ever since the Arab conquest, except for the interlude of the Crusades, it had formed one political unity and kept the language and customs which it had begun to acquire in the seventh century.[18]

This passage of Antonius was written about the time when the two mandated territories took advantage of World War II in 1943 to proclaim their independence. The identity-forming influence of separate state organization had already assured that their subsequent development would be as two units; since that time, their paths have further diverged.

British imperial expansion in the Middle East was largely shaped by the perception of the strategic requirements of the lifeline to India; in the expansive psychosis of the late nineteenth century, these exigencies were given quite elastic interpretation. British Indian naval forces became active in the Persian Gulf in the early nineteenth century, and beginning with Bahrein in 1820 a series of treaties establishing exclusive foreign relations with Britian were signed by the sundry sheikhs along the east Arabian coast. In 1839, India-based British forces stormed Aden, believed to be of value as an entrepot port on the route to India, as well as a strategic naval base. The logic of securing Aden called for a loose occupation over an extensive hinterland zone, which became part of Aden and, by succession, now constitutes the People's Democratic Republic of Yemen. Although Aden was developed as a base, the other coastal protectorates were left entirely to their own devices until the twentieth century, when political officers began to be posted at the courts of the sheikhs and sultans as advisers. However, the British impact was in no way comparable to other colonial domains in Asia and Africa where a thorough, British-directed administration was organized. British rule did, however, have the effect of freezing the status of the treaty-signing royal families, most of whom had claims to rule asserted only in the century or two preceding British intervention. The British role had the effect of pre-empting expansion into these zones by others—rival European powers at the apogee of imperial competition, Saudi Arabia, Iraq, or Iran in more recent years. In this sense, however slight its administrative impact, British rule was nonetheless decisive in shaping the basic frame of the contemporary state system.[19]

In Egypt, the modernizing state founded by Mohammed Ali became increasingly dependent on European powers. The impulse to transfor-

18. Antinius, *Arab Awakening*, p. 352.
19. Manfred W. Wenner, "The People's Republic of South Yemen," and A.M. Abu-Hakima, "Kuwait and the Eastern Arab Protectorates," in Tareg Y. Ismael, *Governments and Politics of the Contemporary Middle East* (Homewood, Ill.: Dorsey Press, 1970), pp. 412-49.

mation reached its peak under Khedive Ismael (1863-79), in whose reign the Suez Canal was completed. Ismael recruited many European functionaries, invested heavily in a wide range of development projects, but left Egypt heavily in debt to European financial interests as a result. Their influence, exercised through British and French diplomacy, forced the abdication of Ismael in 1879 and his replacement by a compliant successor, Tawfik. This in turn triggered a protonationalist revolt led by Colonel Ahmed Arabi, a native Egyptian of village origins, which represented both an Egyptian-Arab response to the continued recruitment of high-ranking officers among persons of Turkish or Caucusus ancestry, and to European interference. The following year, popular fervor led to riots in Alexandria, with forty European deaths, a fact which, at the high water mark of imperialism, called for occupation by the British army. The Egyptian adventure aroused bitter divisions in Britain, which were compromised in part by solidifying the British occupation while pretending that it was only temporary and provisional. Thus Britain retained the formal appearance of continuity in the Khedival administration and clung to the theory of residual Ottoman suzerainty, while proceeding in fact to organize its own administration. It was not until 1914, with the outbreak of war with the Ottomans, that Egypt formally became a British protectorate. The pressures of wartime mobilization bore so heavily upon the Egyptian population that murderous riots exploded in Cairo and elsewhere in 1919. By 1922, the British had conceded a nominal independence to Egypt. The fact of British rule during a critical period in the rise of Arab nationalism and in the definition of modern identity, placed Egyptian intellectual leadership before a very different set of problems than their counterparts in the Levant. In Egypt, the question was British rule, and revolt, as Egyptians, against it. In the Levant, Arab nationalism had Turkish domination as its orienting focus, and during the critical World War I period found support and stimulus from the British in overthrowing it.[20]

The establishment of Iraq, Jordan, and Palestine as separate entities under British mandate was a complex interplay between imperial lifeline considerations, the ambitions of the Hashemite family, and the Jewish homeland issue. Mesopotamia was viewed from British India as the capstone of control of the Persian Gulf, and British Indian troops invaded the Basra and Baghdad provinces of the Ottoman empire soon after the outbreak of hostilities in 1914. Although Turkish forces were ousted without great difficulty, when it became clear after the war

20. Of the voluminous literature arising from the Anglo-Egyptian relationship, see in particular Robert L. Tignor, *Modernization and British Colonial Rule in Egypt 1882-1914* (Princeton: Princeton University Press, 1966).

that the British intended to stay, disorders broke out in 1920 which claimed 10,000 lives, and cost the British Exchequer £ 40,000,000, or more than the total cost of the wartime Middle East campaign.[21] A *modus vivendi* was secured with nationalist forces in 1921, by the designation of the Hashemite prince Faisal, who had been military commander of the Arab forces during World War I, as king. The general acceptability of Faisal sheds interesting light on the nature of Iraqi identity at that juncture. Faisal had no particular connections with Iraq; his claim to leadership derived from his role as an Arab leader against the Ottomans. The Arab intelligentsia which had begun to take form in Baghdad was part of the same communication system as Arab nationalists of Damascus and Beirut; the premise of Iraqi distinctiveness was little affirmed. Faisal was acceptable as an Arab figure through whose agency immediate autonomy and relatively speedy independence could be obtained. To Iraq was added Kurdish Mosul; this new state was then incorporated into the British mandate system. A treaty providing for full independence was completed in 1930, but contingent on Iraqi admission into the League of Nations. The dramatically different attitude toward colonialism in League days from that of the United Nations was well demonstrated in the two year delay before Iraqi independence could be formalized in 1932.[22]

Jordan and Palestine were units constructed out of the wreckage of Ottoman domains by the British, trying to reconcile their contradictory wartime commitments to the Hashemites and the Zionists and at the same time to secure their Suez lifeline. During the secret wartime transactions, both the French and the Russians (before the Bolshevik revolution) had offered their imperial services in Jerusalem. Within the logic of the time, the best way for the British to keep both these undesirable neighbors out of Suez was to assume control of the area themselves. Thus Britain sought the mandatory power for Palestine and what became Jordan; the former rather closely resembled the Ottoman autonomous district of Jerusalem, while the latter included parts of the provinces of Syria and Hijaz. The Hashemites believed that the British had promised them all of Palestine as well as Syria. As a modest consolation for their inability to carry out the pledge of backing for an Arab National State of the dimensions that Hashemites had been led to expect, the British created the novel unit of Transjordan in 1921, with Hashemite Prince Abdullah as its head. Abdullah then settled at what was then a Circassian village on the Hijaz railway, Amman, to the unhappy role of a British-protected

21. Antonius, *Arab Awakening*, pp. 313-16.
22. Ibid., pp. 360-62.

ruler over what was then a truncated and desolate vestige of their dream of an Arab state. Artificiality and poverty kept this Hashemite state a British mandate until 1946.[23] Palestine became a separate territory, where the British between 1920 and 1948 exercised a mandate devoted to the utterly irreconcilable purposes of providing a "national home for the Jewish people in Palestine," while guaranteeing the "political and economic freedom of the Arab population."[24]

The other minor participants in the colonial partition were Italy and Spain. Italy's conquest of the Turkish provinces of Tripolitania and Cyreneika, and the extension of its authority to the Fezzan oases created the state of Libya. In the partition of Morocco in 1912, Spain obtained title to the northern strip, but maintained the fiction that it was a part of the Moroccan kingdom; independence in 1956 reunited the French and Spanish segments. In addition, Spain ruled four other Arab territories, the coastal towns of Ceuta and Melilla, the small desert enclave of Ifni, and the much larger, but barren and unpopulated, Spanish Sahara. Ceuta and Melilla, small fortresses on the north Moroccan coast, have been Spanish since 1580 and 1496 respectively; in 1950, Arabs were only 8 percent of the Spanish dominated population, although Morocco maintains a claim to sovereignty over them.[25] Ifni was claimed only in 1860, and occupied only in 1934; it was returned to Morocco in 1969. Spanish Sahara, with 60,000 people scattered over 106,000 square miles and with large phosphate and iron ore deposits, has been promised self-determination, but the legitimacy of its separate existence is open to contest by its three Arab neighbors of Algeria, Mauritania, and Morocco, especially the latter. It appears likely that in the next few years it will be the nineteenth Arab state.[26]

The Hashemite family was a seventh nodal point in the state formation process; in the linkage between their genealogical antecedents and role in the Arab national movement in the Middle East, they form an interesting transitional link between the Arab heritage and modern Arab nationalism. The patriarch was Husain ibn 'Ali, of the most noble of all Arab families, the Bani Hashem, of the Quraysh community associated with the holy places of Islam since the days of the Prophet. Many of this family had held the revered position of Sharif of Mecca.

23. William Sands, "The Hashemite Kingdom of Jordan," in Ismael, *Contemporary Middle East,* pp. 283-303.

24. The former statement was part of the 1917 Balfour Declaration, while the latter was a private promise given to Hashemite leader Husain, to reassure him as to the limited effects of the Balfour pledge. Antonius, *Arab Awakening,* pp. 258-70.

25. Barbour, *North Africa,* p. 185.

26. Rene Pelissier, "Spain's African Sandboxes," *Africa Report,* XI, no. 2 (February 1966), pp. 17-20.

Caliph Abd-al-Hamid made frequent use of the device of inviting prominent notables to reside in gilded surveillance at his court, as a means of forestalling possible opposition. Husain had become sufficiently visible by 1893 to merit one of these invitations to Istanbul, where he spent fifteen years of pious and genteel indolence. He did, however, stay in close contact with the developing ideas of Arab nationalism in the Levant; indeed, Istanbul was an important center of furtive debate on the Arab national idea. With him were three sons, Ali, Faisal (later king of Iraq), and Abdullah (subsequently ruler of Jordan).

With the overthrow of Abd-al-Hamid in 1908, Husain was able to return to the Hijaz, where he was named Grand Sharif of Mecca. From this base, contacts were established with the British in 1914, inquiring as to the possibility of British support if there were an Arab uprising against the Ottomans. Husain by this time nursed the dream of a grand Arab state, organized from the Hijaz, incorporating the Arab Levant, Mesopotamia, and, he hoped much of the peninsula. British interest in this proposal increased after the outbreak of World War I, and in 1915 a series of secret communications were exchanged between Husain and Sir Henry McMahon, which led to Arab entry into the war at the end of 1915 under the military leadership of Faisal. In these letters, the British agreed to recognize and uphold Arab independence in the area proposed by Husain, with the exception of coastal Syria, the Persian Gulf, and Iraq. A fatal ambiguity existed as to whether what became designated as Palestine was included in the promise, which was in any case incompatible with the sphere of domination promised to France in the Sykes-Picot accords.

The Arab revolt began in the Hijaz in June 1916. Faisal on missions to Damascus had made contacts with Arab secret societies among intellectuals and the al-Fatat league of Arab officers in the Ottoman army, with both groups willing to endorse the Hashemite credentials for Arab leadership. Faisal then turned to knitting together an Arab force from the fragmented and jealous bedouin communities. It was not until July 1917 that the Arab force had moved to the head of the Red Sea and taken Aqaba. From there the Arabs fought slowly northward, reaching Damascus in October 1918. In November 1916 Husain had proclaimed himself "King of the Arabs"; at war's end, the Hashemite forces occupied the hinterland from Damascus to the holy cities.

Bitter disappointment was soon to follow, as the nature of Anglo-French postwar intentions became clear. Faisal was driven from Damascus by the French in mid-1920, while British mandatory power over

Palestine was affirmed in 1920. The award of dependent domains in Iraq and Transjordan to Faisal and Abdullah was scant consolation to Husain. The final blow to the Hashemite dream came after Husain unwisely proclaimed himself Caliph of a restored community of Islam in 1924. Shortly thereafter, in 1926, the Hashemites were driven out of the Hijaz by expanding Saudi power. The Hashemite dynasty survived until 1958 in Iraq and lives yet in Jordan, but the moment when the Hashemites were symbols of Arab national aspirations is long past. For a brief moment, the intimate associations of the Bani Hasham family with the Islamic component of Arab historical identity, through their role as custodians of the holy places, could legitimate their claim to leadership of the Arab national movement. At that one moment, the Hashemite house would appear endowed with the state-founding mission of realizing Arab unity. Over time, the dynastic interests became tied to the survival of the vestigial state of Jordan, under assault after the rise of Nasser to wholly different, more secular and radical concepts of Arab nationalism.[27]

The final dimension in the state formation process was the Palestine-Israel phenomenon. The Jewish national homeland idea traces its origin to about the same moment as Arab nationalism; both ideas, soon to be locked in mortal combat, have the same philosophical basis, derived from the postulates of nineteenth-century European nationalism. A people had to discover its fulfillment through a national language and culture, politically expressed and territorially structured in an autonomous nation-state. Jews had a highly developed sense of identity and community, as a people of the diaspora, scattered in minority enclaves throughout the Western world, as well as in many Muslim lands. But the new standards of cultural prestige emergent in the nineteenth century made the links of the diaspora and shared experiences of oppression insufficient. Being a people was not enough; nationality and nationhood were required. The Old Testament was the central symbol of Jewish being; in the reformulation of Jewish identity as territorial nationalism, the Hebrew language of the Bible was revived and the ancient Holy Land became the territorial focus of Zionist aspirations.

Zionism was far from the dominant orientation among Jewish communities in the nineteenth century; indeed, many strongly opposed the national homeland idea, fearing that it would be used elsewhere as a pretext for withdrawing the precarious rights won by Jews as citizens in other lands. The wave of pogroms in Russia in 1882 forced the pace of events by triggering a very large Jewish migration; the great bulk went to America, but some took the more difficult path to the

27. Antonius, *Arab Awakening*, pp. 164-337.

Holy Land. Not long after, the World Zionist Organization was founded in 1897 under the impetus of Theodor Herzl, whose program was the organization of a Jewish homeland in Palestine.

At the beginning of the nineteenth century, there was a small Jewish community in Palestine, estimated at 5,000. It had been there at least since the Middle Ages, and some claim that a vestigial Jewish group had remained since Biblical times. It had increased very slowly to some 24,000 by 1882, when the first Aliyah, or immigrant wave, occurred, numbering 20,000-30,000. This immigrant group was very selective, ideologically motivated, strongly dedicated to the Zionist ideal. Those fleeing Russia and Eastern Europe who desired to better their material condition went to America. Those who chose the Palestine destination faced a precarious material existence, no absorbing society, and indifference or hostility from the dominant groups; only the power of the Zionist ideal drove them thither.

From 1904 to 1914, a second Aliyah flowed in, this time often composed of organized groups of Russian and Polish Jews, many of them socialists, with a more explicitly Zionist ideology as well as deep radical commitment. The second Aliyah brought the Jewish population in Palestine to 85,000 on the eve of World War I. Although the Jews were now numerous enough to make their presence felt and frictions over land began to arise, Arab political interest was focused upon the struggle with the Ottomans.[28]

World War I clearly portended a change in status of the Ottoman district of Jerusalem, and the World Zionist Organization deployed a far-flung diplomatic activity to win acceptance for the Jewish national homeland principle. Negotiations were undertaken on both sides to cover all contingencies, in Berlin as well as London. The wartime situation greatly increased the value of what the Zionists were offering, in Jewish backing; the war psychosis made each increment of potential backing seem much more crucial than it probably was, especially since the Zionist movement remained controversial within the Jewish community. Through channels quite separate from the ones which had undertaken the commitments to the Hashemites, the Zionists were able to secure the November 1917 Balfour Declaration, committing the British government to support of the homeland. The Zionists, in turn, were now anxious to see British protection over Palestine; the Balfour Declaration, at that time, engaged only Britain.

In 1922, at the time the mandate government was organizing itself, the Jews totaled 11 percent of the Palestine population, a figure which

28. On the history of Jewish immigration, see Judah Matras in Eisenstadt et al., *Integration and Development in Israel*, pp. 307-57.

increased to 28 percent by 1936. The British sought to found its administration on a dual structure, with each community having internal autonomy. However, its relations were stormy with both Jews and Arabs, and it never came close to creating the binational community which was the presumed political end. The Zionists sought massive immigration, with the object of achieving a Jewish majority, and wanted a wholly self-sufficient Jewish community, protected by its own paramiltary organizations. Arab goals were revocation of the Jewish national homeland edict; an end to Jewish immigration until a national government was formed, which would then decide its own immigration policy; and organic links between Palestine and neighboring Arab states. Animosities between the two communities built rapidly, and by the 1930s the British had lost control over the pace of events. A six-month Arab general strike in 1936, followed by two years of guerrilla attacks, led to the appointment of a Royal Commission to seek a course for the future. Their solution was partition, with an area substantially larger than those then dominated by Jewish settlers to become a Jewish state, the remainder to be annexed to Jordan. Indeed, there never was a moment when the interests of the two communities could have been compromised, so profoundly incompatible were their concepts of the state; in the words of one analyst. "The Zionists never dared to accept the idea of remaining a minority in a predominantly Arab area, and the Arabs in turn never dared to accept the legitimacy of the Jewish community, because they would have meant accepting Zionism and its implication of ultimate Jewish rule."[29]

In 1939, the British announced severe limitations on further immigration, with a ceiling of 15,000 per year for the following five years, then a complete ban unless the Arabs agree to accept more. Their policy statement pledged independence for Palestine as a single state within ten years, and also placed some limits on land acquisition. Both Jews and Arabs at once rejected this proposal; time, it turned out, was on the side of the Jews, and comparable terms were never again available to the Arabs.

The policy, moreover, collided immediately with the huge numbers of displaced Jews resultant from Nazi policies and World War II; in the event, another 153,000 entered from 1939 to 1948, many of them illegally. By 1947, the British concluded that the mandate was not only expensive but insoluble and turned the problem over to the United Nations. A UN Commission charged with making recommendations for the future was divided in its councils; a majority proposed separate Jewish and Arab states, with an economic union and international status for Jerusalem; a minority backed a single, federal state, an option then preferred by much Arab

---

29. Ann Mosely Lesch, in William B. Quandt, Fuad Jabber, and Lesch, *The Politics of Palestinian Nationalism* (Berkeley: University of California Press, 1973), p. 42.

opinion. In November 1947, the partition plan prevailed; the next month, a de facto provisional Israeli government came into being to ready itself for the day of British withdrawal, on 14 May 1948. Palestinian Arabs lacked the unity of purpose and organization of the Israelis. Since the Arabs did not accept the partition plan, Zionist forces felt freed of any obligation to restrict themselves to these areas allocated by partition. When the critical moment of independence came, warfare was already raging; despite the intervention of neighboring Arab armies, the Arabs were no match for the Israelis, and by the end of 1948 had to accept a ceasefire line which enclosed an Israel substantially larger than that of the 1947 partition plan. Of the 800,000 Arabs who had lived in the area which became Israel, all but 150,000 had fled or been driven out. The Jordanian state annexed the areas of former Palestine west of the Jordan River; the only remnant of Arab Palestine which retained its nominal status was the tiny Gaza strip, under Egyptian administration. Thus was born the Jewish state of Israel, the question of Palestine as an orienting focus for Arab nationalism, and the stateless nationality of Palestinians.

In this fashion, simultaneous with the growth of a sense of Arab nationalism predicated on the transcendant goal of a unified Arab state, the interaction of external participants in Arab politics, competing principles of state formation, the particularity of political sequences in different regions of the Arab world, and the rise of a vigorous Jewish homeland state in its Levantine core resulted in a state system profoundly at variance with the Arab unity ideal. The reality-shaping force of a state in the perspectives and political cognitions of its members, we have argued in chapter 3, is formidable. Arab unity was a passionate dream; the Arab state system was now an entrenched reality. To further elucidate the tension between these competing claims to solidarity and identity, we need to consider further the two main components in Arab identity—language and religion—and patterns of pluralism within the Arab states.

LANGUAGE AND ARABISM

Although Arabic language is the prime defining element in establishing the boundaries of the Arab world, its actual efficacy in establishing a single speech community is much less than might be supposed. The element of diglossia is very strong in the Arab world; although the classical Arabic of the Koran is one, the divergence of dialectical versions is very great.[30] Street dialects in Baghdad and Fez,

30. On the diglossia concept, with some Arabic examples, see Charles A. Ferguson, *Language Structure and Language Use* (Stanford: Stanford University Press, 1971), pp. 1-26.

for example, are sufficiently distinct to lose mutual intelligibility. The dark ages of Arab culture under the Ottomans accentuated this pattern, as the high, classical version fell into virtual disuse except as rote recitation of the Koran itself; the sheer scale of the Arab world, the different linguistic traditions with which it interacted at its periphery—Persian, Turkish, Berber, various African languages—all had their impact on popular speech, over a period of centuries when there was little save the Koran and the pilgrimage to Mecca for a few to hold the speech community together. The beginnings of modern Arab nationalism had linguistic revival as one of its first major components, but there was no authoritative center able to direct this process for the whole Arab world. Further, the introduction of a modern educational system frequently involved use of French or English as the medium of instruction. Thus language had come to be a unifying symbol, but was in many respects divisive as a means of communication.

Although differences remain, the effectiveness of Arabic as a medium of mass communication, administration, and education appears reasonably well-established in Egypt, the Levant, Iraq, and the Arabian peninsula. However, the problem remains severe in the Maghreb; the first Algerian foreign minister, Mohammed Khemisti, found there was no language in which he and Egyptian President Nasser could both communicate.[31] The French immigration into the Maghreb, which amounted to 10 percent of the population at its peak, was probably as large, proportionally, as the Arab influx twelve centuries earlier. Further, the French had far more powerful communication means for assimilation at their disposal. The dimensions of the Maghreb linguistic situation are summarized in Table 10.2.

Table 10.2—Language Use in Maghreb

Country	Estimated 1964 population	Dialectical Arabic speaking	Berber speaking	Classical Arabic reading	French speaking	French reading
Morocco	13,000,000	11,000,000	4,000,000	1,000,000	4,000,000	800,000
Algeria	11,500,000	10,000,000	2,500,000	300,000	6,000,000	1,000,000
Tunisia	4,500,000	4,500,000	very few	700,000	2,000,000	700,000

Source: Charles F. Gallagher, in Joshua Fishman, Charles A. Ferguson, and Jyotirindra Das Gupta (eds.), *Language Problems of Developing Nations* (New York: John Wiley & Sons, 1968), p. 134.

The educational system is a major source of circular dilemmas. Under French rule, this played a highly assimilative impact linguistically, and

31. Charles Gallagher, in Fishman, Ferguson and Das Gupta (eds.), *Language Problems of Developing Nations*, p.130.

in Algeria it produced an Arab elite that had lost its ability to use the mother tongue. In all three countries, a strong effort is made to expand the educational system rapidly. At the secondary and higher levels this means heavy reliance on French nationals as teaching staff, who generally do not know Arabic; thus the enlarged school system also expands the numbers of French speakers. While literacy in Arabic expands as well, most administrative routine continues to be carried on in French. The bilingual professionals, who predominate in the civil service and parastratal sector, may in fact conclude they have little interest in devaluing the unique asset they command. Charles Gallagher records a poignant interview with the director of the Arabization Bureau in Morocco, whose office prepares lexicons for spheres in which Arabic vocabulary is not equipped—tourism, sports, medicine, for example. Although careful distribution is given to the lists of new vocabulary established by the Arabization Bureaus, the director sadly concludes that nobody uses them, that at bottom Moroccan Arabs are "not serious" about Arabization.[32]

The diffusion of literacy through the school system and the extraordinary potency of oral mass media in the Arab world are certainly accelerating the linguistic integration at least within state boundaries. A study based on 1967 data on a representative Egyptian village showed that 95 percent of the adults listened to the radio regularly and that half the adult males either read a national newspaper or had one read to them. Parenthetically, the study offers some interesting data to suggest that political information does not flow to the periphery in the Lazarsfeld two-step model from media to opinion leaders, orally from leaders to followers, but is absorbed by most villagers directly from these highly accessible national media.[33]

THE AMBIGUOUS LEGACY OF ISLAM

Similarly, though the Arab role in the foundation of Islam is the primary source of the cultural prestige of the language and culture, it by no means follows that religion is a unifying heritage; indeed, in many respects, it is at the root of many of the most divisive hostilities. The most important of the divisions within Islam in the Arab world is between orthodox Sunni and Shi'ites. This schism, which began over legitimacy of the succession to the caliphate after the death of the Prophet's son-in-law

32. Ibid., pp. 134-43.
33. Iliya F. Harik, "Opinion Leaders and Mass Media in Rural Egypt: A Reconsideration of the Two-Step Flow of Communications Hypothesis," *American Political Science Review,* LXV, no. 3 (September 1971), 731-40.

Ali, subsequently acquired some doctrinal content, variable according to the Shi'ite sect in question. But in the political realm the Shi'ite-Sunnite division is far more a matter of identity than doctrine. This cleavage is of particular importance in Iraq and Yemen. In Iraq, it hews close to the natural social division between the folk Shi'ism of rural communities of the central Euphrates and the urban-based civilization of Baghdad, Basra, and other towns. In Yemen, it pits the Zaidi Shi'ites of the northern mountains, associated with the 1,000 year Imamate overthrown in 1962, and the Sunnite groups of the southern region and coastal strip.

The culminating point of diversity is found in the Levant. Islam in the first instance was superimposed upon Aramaic Christian communities. The interlude of the Crusader states found some deviant Muslim sects drawn into collaboration with the Frankish rulers, an alliance for which they paid a high price once the Christians were driven out, seeking refuge in the relative security of Mount Lebanon. During the long period of Turkish rule, the millet system of sectarian autonomy permitted the institutionalized encapsulation of the different religious communities. In the brief colonial period, the French sought out the Muslim minorities as natural allies, thus somewhat removing many of their educated members from the mainstream of Arab nationalism, and even placing them in a position where nationalism was a cultural threat. The two most significant are the Druze, found in present Syria and Lebanon, and the Alawites, in Syria. Both represent an element of synthesis of the Islam imposed by the Muslim rulers and the older religious traditions and particularistic heritages. Both Druze and Alawites are offshoots of the Ismailis, an extreme Shi'ite sect. The Druze hold that Hakim, a caliph of the Fatimid dynasty in Egypt (966-1020) is not dead, but will return; around this are woven doctrines of supernatural hierarchies and transmigration of souls which lead orthodox Muslims to consider them so heretical as to lie outside the community of Islam altogether. The Alawites nurture a cult of Ali, the fourth caliph, enshrouded in a ritual which appears to have Christian influences, as well as some folk beliefs particular to themselves.[34]

Other patterns of sub-Islamic solidarity attach to the brotherhoods, such as Wahhabis, Senussis, the Ansar (Mahdists) and Khatmiya in Sudan. In more contemporary idiom, the Muslim Brotherhood—which has been important in Egypt and Sudan, and to a lesser extent in the Levant—has also contributed to the diversity of political expressions of Islam. The Muslim Brotherhood is based upon a radical amalgam of nationalism and Islamic rejuvenation, propounds a moral regeneration by drawing upon the spiritual resources of Islam to make possible

34. A.H. Hourani, *Minorities in the Arab World* (London: Oxford University Press, 1947), pp. 7-8.

modernization without Westernization. It also mobilizes the frustrations, emotions, and hatreds which have attended the cultural humiliation of the encounter with Western doctrines, including Communism, which devalue the Arab heritage.[35]

Islam as unifier thus operates only in the diffuse sense of a collective recollection of an epic achievement in the classic age. As contemporary faith, it provides many different drummers for Arab nationalism; the sacred imperatives resounding through their different beats are an enduring source of division. Nor must we forget the significance of the Arab Christians in Syria, Palestine, and especially Lebanon.

The two most important Christian Arabic-speaking sects are the Maronite Christians and Greek Orthodox. Both are ancient communities. The Maronite church took form in the seventh century, through a fusion of the old Aramaic Christians and the followers of St. Maron; it became a rallying point for the other Christians as Islamization gathered momentum. The Maronites retreated to Mount Lebanon, where for a number of centuries their language remained Syriac. Although long considered heretical by Rome, the Maronites were key intermediaries for the Frankish kingdoms in the Holy Land; they re-entered Catholic communion in 1736, and subsequently were among the first Arabs to enter Western schools. The Greek Orthodox are followers of the Byzantine rite. The Maronites, by 1947 estimates, were 29.5 percent of the Lebanon population; the Greek Orthodox were 9.1 percent in Lebanon and 4.8 percent in Syria.[36]

NON-ASSIMILATING MINORITIES: THE KURDS

The state system as it took form in the Arab world gave rise to another form of pluralism, through the incorporation of important non-Arab minorities. In Mauritania, Sudan, and Iraq, cultural conflict with non-Arab communities has been sharp, with serious secessionist rebellions in Iraq and Sudan. An examination of these cases will yield useful insight into the conditions of integration through Arabization and the circumstances in which the cultural frontier between Arab and non-Arab produces differentiation and confrontation.

In Iraq, the primary non-Arab community are the Kurds, making up approximately 15 percent of the total population and located in the northern portion of the former Ottoman province of Mosul. Iraq was a cul-

35. For a concise summation, see Wilfred Cantwell Smith, *Islam in Modern History* (New York: Mentor Books, 1959), pp. 161-65; see also Nadav Safran, *Egypt in Search of Political Community* (Cambridge: Harvard University Press, 1961), pp. 231-44.

36. Hourani, *Minorities in the Arab World,* pp. 3-6, 12; Michael W. Suleiman, *Political Parties in Lebanon* (Ithaca: Cornell University Press, 1967), pp. 2-6.

Map 10.2   Iraq and Kurdistan

Cartographic Laboratory UW-Madison

turally flawed construct from the outset, and no enduring basis for incorporation of the Kurds has been found by an Iraqi government. The
nature of the dilemma is neatly summarized in a recent monograph
on the Kurds: "The Iraqis say:'You are Kurds, we are Arabs, but
together we are Iraqis. Iraq is a part of the Arab Nation, but as you are not
Arabs, we agree to granting you autonomy on our terms, on condition that
you continue to be a part of Iraq, without the right or the power of
secession.' What is the Kurdish answer?"[37]

The Kurds are today divided between Turkey, Iran and Iraq, with
smaller numbers in Syria and the Soviet Union. These are three main
dialect groups, of which only one has a written form. They occupy difficult mountain terrain in whose fastness they have found their security—
not until recently, however, as an ethnic community, but broken into

37. Hassan Arfa, *The Kurds* (London: Oxford University Press, 1966), p. 160.

much smaller identity groups, clans and principalities, divided by the jagged landscape. Indeed, some of their neighbors have denied their existence as a collectivity, claiming the languages are but a Persian dialect; a distinguished Arab scholar describes them in the following terms: "Kurdish is not a unified language but a group of dialects differing widely among themselves and akin to Persian. These dialects are spoken by a number of Moslem tribes, scarcely united enough to be called a nation . . .They have little written literature or national history, and have never possesed a national state, although powerful local dynasties have arisen at different times in various parts of Kurdistan."[38]

The Kurds have become a culturally mobilized community only in the present century. However, mythology of historical origin loses itself in the mists of ancient Near Eastern societies; one prominent view attaches Kurd ancestry to the Medes. The label "Kurd" appears to date from the Arab conquest, and was a designation applied to an array of linguistically similar clans by the Arabs. However, notes one leading student of Kurd society, "Most of the tribes of that time ignored the name 'Kurd' given to them by the Arabs and Iranians, and called themselves by their tribal or clan name, derived either from a prominent chief of clan, or from the name of the particular region or valley where they were living, or from the mountain chain along which they were nomadizing."[39] The Kurds quickly submitted to the Arab armies and accepted Islam; the Arabs left no military colonies, and Islamization was not accompanied by Arabization as it was for probably culturally similar peoples in the Mesopotamian plains to the south. A major hero in Kurd legendry was Salah-ed-Din (Saladin), the chivalrous twelfth century adversary of Richard the Lion-Hearted in romantic literature; this warrior-king evidently thought of himself as a Muslim and not a Kurd. His sphere of operation was entirely in the Arab lands, where he briefly united Syria, Egypt, and the Hijaz. For a time, the Kurds were participants in the Persian empire, from which they became culturally estranged in the fourteenth century, with the advent of a Shi'ite dynasty who made of this Islamic doctrine an Iranian national church, in which the predominantly Sunnite Kurds could not share. With the rise of the Turkish empire to their west, the Kurds became a buffer between Iran and the Ottoman empire.

At the turn of the twentieth century, the cultural arena for the Kurds was beginning to alter. Militant national ideologies were being forged

38. Hourani, *Minorities in the Arab World,* p. 11.

39. Arfa, *The Kurds,* p. 6. A similar argument is made by Israel T. Naamani, "The Kurdish Drive for Self-Determination," *Middle East Journal,* (XX, no. 3 Summer 1966), 279-95.

in both Turkey and Iran, as culturally diffuse dynastic empires were transformed into national states. At this critical moment in identity formation, the primary points of reference were Turkish and Iranian nationalism; it was these groups with whom the Kurds interacted most intensively and whose culture had a standing in the world not then enjoyed by the Arabs, just emerging from their long period of eclipse into a new age of imperial subjugation.

The idea of a Kurdish state first appears in 1880, apparently with Russian encouragement as a possible instrument of further Czarist expansion.[40] Until that time, although rebellion was endemic in the mountain reaches of the Kurd homeland, it was always carried out by clans and local communities, and never articulated in terms of general Kurd objectives. The collapse of the Ottoman empire, the aggressive claims being entered by Arabs and Armenians, and the emergence of a small Kurdish intelligentsia, many having been ranking servants of the Ottoman state, led to the bid for a separate Kurd state. High hopes were generated by the 1920 Treaty of Sevres, disposing of the Ottoman state, promising an autonomous state for the Kurdish areas, and holding out the possibility of independence. However, the swift resurgency of Turkey under Kemal Ataturk foreclosed the possibility that Kurds within the present Turkish borders might participate. Indeed, in the period from 1922-26, Turkish irregular forces pressed very hard against the former Mosul province, attached by the British to Iraq.

Iraq, as we have seen, was primarily a British creation. By the time of its actual implementation, the imperial idea in the Middle East was already bruised by the massive rioting in Egypt in 1919, the costly Arab revolts of 1920 in Iraq, the first indications of the severity of the Palestine dilemma, and the advent of mass nationalist agitation touching the Indian jewel in the imperial crown. In retrospect, it is curious that the attachment of the Kurdish districts of Mosul province should have commanded such priority, when the assumptions initially underlying the quest for Mosul, at least for the British, had come into serious question. But policy premises have their own momentum, and the British and King Faisal were unrelenting in their efforts, diplomatic and military, to guarantee the incorporation of the Kurd zones into the new Iraqi state during the years until 1926, when this outcome hung in the balance. Evil tongues whispered that the known oil deposits in the Kurdish region supply the missing pieces to the puzzle of motivations. The rejoinder to this charge by a former British officer deeply involved in securing the Kurd areas of Mosul for Iraq, and a lifelong student of Kurd affairs, offers revealing insight into the compulsions of the territorial imperative:

40. Ibid., pp. 23-24.

"That we were now engaged upon what was for Iraq a life-and-death struggle we none of us had any doubt, for we were convinced that Basra and Baghdad without Mosul could, for economic and strategic reasons, never be built up into a viable state. Although the world press was wont to represent the battle as part of a gigantic struggle for the control of oil it is interesting to look back and recall how very little oil figured in our calculations, at my level at any rate; I do not remember a single document in which oil was mentioned as a factor of outstanding importance, as distinct from the general pattern of trade, both import and export, which made the three wilayats a single and indivisible economic unit. . . the case was admirably summed up in a single sentence of an eloquent memorandum which King Faisal himself drafted and presented to the Commission: 'Therefore I consider that Mosul is to Iraq as the head is to the rest of the body, and it is my unshakeable conviction that though the question is only one of fixing a boundary between Iraq and Turkey it is nevertheless, and in fact, the question of Iraq as a whole; accordingly, the happiness or misery of four millions of human beings is placed in the hands of your honourable Commission.'"[41] A metaphor, of course, is not an argument, but can well be the source of unshakeable convictions; remove the oil, and the indivisibilities became singularly elusive, comprehensible only within the territorial pathology of state formation.

Thus was consolidated an Arab Iraqi state with an important and perennially dissident Kurd minority. Rebellion as an active state of armed conflict has waxed and waned; as a state of mind, it has been permanent. Arab nationalism has always surrounded the core of the Iraqi polity, in different ideological guises—from the moderate and pro-Western forms of the Hashemite line to the radical socialist modes which came into their own after the end of the monarchy in 1958. Kurd separatism is a threat to the Arab character of the Iraqi state, and it has proved exceedingly difficult to find a formula for Kurd autonomy that the Arab nationalist elites in Baghdad can accept; the ambit of Kurd cultural aspirations demands a degree of structural separation which clashes with the Jacobin centralizing perspectives of national leaders since 1958. Kurdish subnationalism could not concede cultural leadership to Arabism, and thus finds the Iraqi attachment at best uneasy. Even during moments of truce, the lurking suspicion of an unacceptable Arabization shrouds all interactions with a penumbra of distrust. But if Iraq is a cultural threat, the occasional opening towards a pan-Arab state looms as an ethnic catastrophe. As a minor linguistic atoll awash in a sea of Arab nationalism, prospects for cultural autonomy for the Kurds would be dim

41. C. J. Edmonds, *Kurds, Turks and Arabs* (London: Oxford University Press, 1957), p. 398.

indeed. Thus the Kurdish problem is a mortgage upon the Iraqi state, constraining its role in realizing the greater vision of pan-Arabism.[42]

EXPANSION OF THE ARAB WORLD: NORTHERN SUDAN

The Sudan as an Arab state is a particularly intriguing cultural compound, where processes of linguistic expansion of the Arabic community, completed centuries ago in most parts of the present Arab world, are visibly in progress. Indeed, of all the Arab states, the cultural attachment is most attenuated in Sudan; in the 1956 census, only 39 percent of the population identified themselves as Arabs. Yet Arabhood is a modal national culture, accepted as the basis for the state in the northern two-thirds of the country, and Arabic is rapidly spreading as a primary language, supported by the considerable assimilative resources of the state.

Although Arabic-speaking groups in small numbers have migrated across the Red Sea and up the Nile for a long time, the major influx dates only from the fourteenth century. In the fourth century, the upper Nile Valley came under the rule of the ancient kingdom of Axum, ancestor of Ethiopia; from Axum came Christianity in its Coptic version. During that time, the Nile from Khartoum north to Dongala was organized by Nubiyin kingdoms. Farther south, the Muslim Funj sultanate dominated from 1504 to the Egyptian conquest in 1821. During this period, there was a continuous process of cultural fusion, with an influx of Arab nomadic groups, and an incorporation of slave elements by the riverain populations, taken from the Nuba mountains or farther south.

The establishment of the Turko-Egyptian administration over much of northern Sudan from 1821 accelerated the slow diffusion of Arabic culture. Khartoum emerged as an important town during this period, and a significant inflow of Egyptian merchants and administrators occurred, helping to shape the cultural parameters of the Sudanese elite that would later develop. The Mahdist revolt was of great importance in shaping Sudanese identity, not only in the sense previously analyzed of detaching Sudan from Egypt, but also as a movement stitching together in protonationalist protest a culturally diverse coalition in northern and western Sudan. The Mahdi himself was an interesting recapitulation of this process; born in Dongala, in northern Sudan, revelation came to him near Gezira, well south of Khartoum; his message was received with great-

42. In addition to the sources cited, see also Richard W. Cottam, *Nationalism in Iran* (Pittsburgh: Pittsburgh University Press, 1964), pp. 65-74; I.T. Naamani, "The Kurdish Drive for Self-Determination," *Middle East Journal,* XX, no. 3 (Summer 1966), 279-95; M. Wenner, "Arab-Kurdish Rivalries in Iraq," *Middle East Journal,* XVII, nos. 1-2, (Winter-Spring 1963), 68;82.

est enthusiasm at first by the Baggara Arabs of western Sudan. Although his metaphor was religious, his medium was Arabic, and his achievement was a culturally Arab state which brought for a time all but the southern parts of Sudan under his rule. The idea of the Mahdist state became a significant historical aspect of later Sudanese nationalism, and the religious arm of the Mahdiya, Ansar, formed the basis for what was, in the 1958 elections, the largest single party, the Umma.

The question "What is an Arab?" is particularly complex in the Sudan. Many of the 39 percent who claim to be Arabs today are in reality Arabized Nubiyin, who have over the last four centuries adopted Arabic language and culture, and Islam. However, once a community becomes Arab in self-concept, it is important for it to secure status within the Arabic frame by devising a genealogical pedigree more impressive than mere Arabization. Thus it is that most riverain Arabic-speakers identify themselves Ja'aliyin, or of Abbasid origins, after the uncle of the Prophet. The other major division is the Juhayna cluster, including the Baggara and other pastoral and nomadic Arab communities of western Sudan; their descent is markedly less prestigious than the Ja'aliyin. As in the Middle East, the concept of Arabhood is a much more generalized and comprehensive notion among the urban Arab-speakers of the Khartoum connurbation, than among pastoral cattle Arabs (Baggara) or the camel-based nomads of the desert fringe. Even in the six northern provinces, Arabs totalled only 53.3 percent of the population.

Critical to the Arabization of the Sudan is the process of identity change among non-Arab populations of the north. Other major ethnic clusters in the north include the Beja (8.6 percent of the population), in the hills along the Red Sea coast; Nubiyin along the Nile in the northernmost area (4.4 percent), the Nubans, inhabitants of the Nuba mountain cluster to the west of Gezira (7.6 percent); and the Fur and other westerners (18.1 percent). Of these, incorporation is farthest advanced among the Nubiyin; well over 30 percent of those who still identify themselves as Nubiyin use Arabic as a first language.[43] Those who go to town adopt Arabic as a matter of course; within the urban social context, they are indistinguishable from Arabs. The complete Arabization of the Nubiyin is probably near at hand; there is no visible cultural resistance to this trend.

We have described in chapter 4 the Arabization process among the Fur; other western Sudan groups also quickly adopt Arabic if they move into a social setting where it is widely spoken. The Nubans, not to be confused with the Nubiyin, share a diffuse indentity only through common refuge on the mountain. The term describes a number of small linguistic groups, withdrawn into the Nuba mountains to avoid the slave-

43. McLoughlin, *Language-Switching in Sudan*, p. 50.

catchers, who long found them a prime resource. The upper reaches of the Nuban mountains are also a non-Muslim enclave. Nubans on the mountains retain a strong resentment against Arabs for the slave-raiding past. On the other hand, the mountain economy has very limited horizons; many young men must seek their fortunes elsewhere, in which case it is costly to maintain an anti-Arab attitude. A study in a Khartoum suburb found that persons of Nuban antecedents brought to Khartoum as slaves a century before were aware of their origins and slave background, but had become thoroughly Arabized; they spoke no Nuban tongue, no longer maintained kinship connections with the mountain, and were Muslims. A more recent Nuban influx had occurred after World War II, with the assimilation process at an earlier stage. They had become Muslims and knew Arabic, but continued to speak Nuban dialects among themselves and retained kinship linkages in the home area.[44]

The Beja are probably the most culturally resistant northern group. They are a very ancient group and have maintained a nomadic existence in their Red Sea hills for four millennia. Indeed, oral traditions suggest that the Beja have incorporated a certain number of Arab groups from across the Red Sea. Others have a very negative stereotype of them; an Arab traveller in the middle ages, Ibn Jubayr, wrote that they lived "like animals," and were a sullen, recalcitrant collection of thieves and liars, deserving of extermination.[45] A British view, expressed by a Sudan service administrator who long served among them, was not much more flattering: "of Beja indolence it is almost superfluous to speak. No nomad is fond of hard work, even in the service of his precious herds, but in this the Beja far surpass anything within my experience. Leisure is more to them than life; of manual labor they will have none, and they will starve rather than set their hand to tasks which with a little effort could ensure a certain degree of prosperity and freedom from want."[46]

The mystique of Beja impermeability has been somewhat overdone, although it is generally true that nomadic cultures are much slower to yield up their young men to urban migration and wage employment than sedentary agriculturalists. In fact, Beja were 5.6 percent of the Khartoum province population in 1956. Further, once removed from the homeland, they are linguistically adaptable. Of 2715 in the Khartoum area in 1956, not one customarily spoke Beja. Even in Kassala town,

44. Harold R. Barclay, *Buuri al Lamaab. A Suburban Village in the Sudan* (Ithaca: Cornell University Press, 1964), p. 95.

45. A. Paul, *A History of the Beja Tribes of the Sudan* (Cambridge: Cambridge University Press, 1954), p. 3.

46. Ibid., p. 7.

in the midst of a major irrigation scheme in their own area, one third of the Beja have switched to Arabic.[47]

One may suggest that within their home area, excepting the Kassala settlement scheme, there is a high degree of cultural self-sufficiency. The incorporative forces are very weak; there are few schools or administrative posts in the hills, nor any resources to encourage economic linkages. However, ethnic encapsulation is possible only within the framework of the isolated, nomadic way of life. The decision to leave for urban employment entails a choice for at least partial acceptance of the Arabic medium in which urban life occurs.

Thus throughout the north, social change appears to carry with it Arabization as silent partner. Arab culture and high prestige correlate on every status scale. Arabic in the unchallenged medium of high religious culture. It is the language associated with the power and majesty of the national state. It is the medium of social mobility, of the schoolhouse, of high status occupations, of the urban environment. Only the most isolated sectors of non-Arab communities remain outside the incorporative influence of Arabic. These are precisely the elements of society who are least likely to develop counter-cultural ideologies, as with Latin American Indians. The relationship between, say, Beja and Arab culture is wholly in contrast to the Kurdish pattern in Iraq. Beja have no alternative reference point against which to rank the competitive value of their culture, as the Kurds did in Turkish and Iranian nationalism. Although within the limiting frame of the Red Sea hills a Beja way of life can be maintained, it is beyond imagination that it could be put forward within the national arena as an identity competitive with the national Arabic culture.

Southern Sudan is a different world, which we will explore in more detail in chapter 12. For present purposes, suffice it to say that the Arabic cultural reference point was largely absent; in 1956, Arabs were only 0.2 percent of the population of the three southern provinces. Conversely, Khartoum was a very long distance from the south, and the number of southern migrants to Khartoum or other northern cities was relatively small (southerners were 2 percent of the Khartoum province population in 1956). The prestigious culture in the south was, during the colonial period, that of the Europeans; the channel of access to it was through the Christian missions and their schools. English and not Arabic had been used in the southern schools, and was the linguistic mark of the new elite. For these and other reasons to be

47. McLoughlin, *Language-Switching in Sudan*, pp. 50–51.

further elucidated, Arabism was not a prestigious incorporative frame, but a source of cultural anxiety.[48]

THE ARAB PERIPHERY: MAURITANIA AND CHAD

Mauritania has a different pattern of cultural stratification, owing to its artificial contours and colonial history. As the least developed and, until the recent discovery of large iron and copper deposits, most economically unpromising area of former French West Africa, it was only very lightly administered, from a seat not even located in the territory. What economic and social development did occur in the colonial era was mainly confined to the Senegal valley on the southern border, where dwelt the 13 percent of the populace that was not Arabic-speaking, the closely related Fulani and Tukulor. Political legitimacy was defined through the electoral process, however, which meant a government politically dominated by the Arabic-speaking Moors, with a senior civil service heavily drawn from the Senegal Valley, where educational infrastructure was far more advanced.

Accordingly, defining the place of Arabic in national culture has been a contentious matter. Command of French for the Fulani and Tukulor administrators was a key monopoly; a switch to Arabic in an economy with few occupational choices for the elite was a major status threat. The imposition of compulsory Arabic instruction in secondary institutions in 1966 led to major riots by schoolboys from the Senegal Valley. The level of conflict was somewhat subsided since, but it is very clear that Moors will continue to dominate politically and that their commitment to gradual implementation of Arabic as national language is unlikely to weaken. Further, as regional imbalances in education are somewhat altered in favor of the Moors, a growing number of Arabic-speaking educated elites will be not only available, but will find many senior positions blocked by an older generation of mainly Fulani and Tukulor French-speaking bureaucrats. Arabism seems a highly probable response to this situation.

The pattern of Arabization itself deserves brief commentary. In the years prior to the birth of Islam, Mauritania was populated by Berber-speaking groups. Conversion in Mauritania began only about the eleventh century and lasted for five centuries. At about the same time, in the eleventh century, Fatimid Egypt was invaded by two bedouin confed-

48. We have found particularly useful the doctoral dissertation of John Willis Sommer, "The Sudan: A Geographical Investigation of the Historical and Social Roots of Dissension," Boston University, 1968.

eracies, the Bani Hillal and Bani Soleim, reportedly driven from Arabia by exceptional drought. The Fatimids encouraged them to pass on to the Maghreb, where they were promised that a terrestial paradise awaited them. The Bani Soleim went only as far as present Libya, but the Hillalites, 150,000-200,000 strong, swept across the Maghreb like a swarm of locusts. One segment of them was finally driven into Mauritania about 1270. Over the next four centuries, a gradual symbiosis occurred, with the Berber groups finally adopting Arabic. It is this particular pattern of linguistic diffusion which explains the otherwise curious fact that Mauritanian Arabic is much closer to the Arabian peninsula variety than the vernacular dialects of Morocco or Algeria. What makes the linguistic assimilation particularly interesting is the enduring pattern of stratified relationships between the groups, which reflects not only different functions but unequal cultural prestige. The collectivities of Arab origin were warrior communities, to which Berber clans with a clerical specialization attached themselves as dependent members of a security community. Arab warriors assumed the tasks of protection, while the Berber groups were custodians of piety.[49]

Arabization, however, did not touch the sedentary populations, even though there was significant interaction through trade, religion, and, on occasion, through shared political institutions. The nomadic Moor culture neither exercised sustained political control nor enjoyed through conspicuous wealth or success a level of prestige which would have commanded emulation and linguistic assimilation. Incorporation became even less likely when the Fulani and Tukulor acquired a large edge in access to modernity through entry into the French educational system.

The only state with a large Arab population which is not politically dominant is Chad, where Arabic-speakers are 46 percent of the total. The next largest group are Sara, with roughly one-fifth of the population; however, they are situated in the heart of cotton country, where much of the very modest level of economic development has taken place. Despite their numbers, Chad Arabs are of nomadic culture and poorly equipped to compete in territorial politics. Education was almost wholly concentrated in the southern zone, or "Tchad utile" as it was known in colonial lexicon. Southern domination, however, has not been lightly accepted in the north. Five years after 1960 independence, revolt broke out in the north; by 1968, this insurrection reached a scale which led to intervention of French troops. In 1972, the Chad government at the price of a rupture of its Israeli relations deprived the rebellion of its Libyan patronage, and the scale of dissidence diminished. It is noteworthy that the insurgents invoked Islamic identity, but not Arab claims

49. Alfred G. Gerteiny, *Mauritania* (New York: Frederick A. Praeger, 1967), pp. 20-35.

per se. One may speculate that this follows the general bedouin pattern of identity, wherein Arabic speech is a matter of course but not generally the basis for an articulated identity. Religion, in the face of the Christian domination of the Chad government ranks, is a more natural definition of the differentiation between ruler and ruled.[50]

ARABS AND BERBERS: THE INCORPORATIVE SYMBIOSIS

The other pattern of stratified pluralism we wish to consider is the Maghreb, particularly Morocco, where Berber-speakers remain numerous. The interaction of Arab and Berber in Morocco now has a venerable history covering twelve centuries. Contrary to the relative facility of conquest in the Levant and Egypt, the first Arab wave in the seventh century met disaster in Berber country. However, by the early eighth century, nearly all of Berberland had been neutralized, followed by at least nominal acceptance of Islam. The profoundly segmentary, acephalous nature of Berber society made decisive encounters difficult, complete conquest impossible. Rather Islam was domesticated, blended with folk elements, rendered a syncretic expression of Berber culture. The coastal, urban centers were Arab central places, nodal points of Arab culture. The countryside remained Berber-speaking.

Over the years, there was a very slow expansion of the Arab zone, outward from its initial nodal points. This cultural flow was not structured, as in the Middle East, by periods of relatively strong central government; although the Moroccan monarchy had significant continuity, especially as a political idea, the zone over which it maintained strong control was quite limited. Also, there were dynastic moments when the concept of kingship in Morocco was under Berber direction, the most noteworthy of these being the Almoravids, whose point of genesis was in present Mauritania, in the eleventh century. Charles Gallagher suggests a persuasive conceptualization of the Arab-Berber polarity as a continuum. At one end, in long-established traditional cities like Tunis and Fez, the modal culture was carried by an urban bourgeoisie, speaking a dialectal but rich Arabic. In the fertile plains around the Arab towns, heavily exposed to urban influence, Arabic was clearly dominant. In the mountains, there is a transitional zone of Arab dialects heavily influenced by Berber; in the most rugged regions, there are large Berber-speaking pockets. The majority of Maghreb

50. Morrison, Mitchell, Paden and Stevenson, *Black Africa,* pp. 204-9. Literature on Chad is exceedingly meager; see especially Jacques le Cornec, *Histoire politique du Tchad de 1900 à 1962* (Paris: R. Pichon et R. Durand-Auzias, 1963).

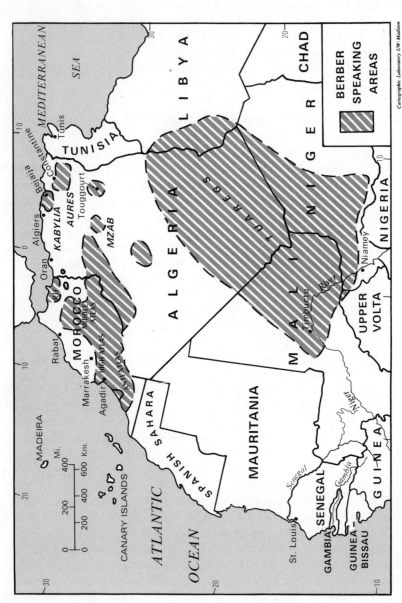

Map 10.3   Berber-speaking Zones

Cartographic Laboratory UW-Madison

Legend on map: BERBER SPEAKING AREAS

Arab-speakers must be of original Berber stock; there has been a gradual diffusion of Arabic, and a number of Arab-speaking clans can recollect the days when they used to be Berbers. But the initial Arab component was simply too small for total assimilation; an estimated 150,000 came in the first wave, then perhaps 200,000 arrived in the Hill-alite invasion, with a final influx of uncertain numbers of Andalusians expelled from Spain in the fifteenth century.[51]

The largest Berber enclaves are in Morocco—in the Rif mountains in the north, then in the Middle Atlas, High Atlas, and Anti Atlas ranges in the center and south. In Algeria, there are Kabyl pockets in the mountains behind Bejaija (ex-Bone), and the Aures mountains. The intriguing oasis towns of the Mzab, home of many of Algeria's most successful traders, and a broad swathe deep in the Sahara, extending down as far as the Niger Valley in Mali and Niger, sparsely inhabited by Tuareg groups, complete the picture.

In the Maghreb context, "Arab" and "Berber" are inescapable linguistic categories; they are not corporate groups, which perceive each other as exclusive collectivities in competitive interaction. Ernest Gellner elegantly captures the elusiveness of the Berber concept, in an outstanding recent collective inquest into the nature of Arab-Berber relationships:

It would of course be an exaggeration to say that Berbers and their language are an invisible social fact. You cannot ignore . . . something as conspicuous as that a man speaks, or even speaks exclusively, an unintelligible and difficult language. The urban Arab notes it with contempt, irritation or, sometimes fear. But the displeasure does not congeal around some permanent and central idea. The Berber tribesman is a menace *qua* tribesman, not *qua* speaker of a gibberish-sounding language. As a tribesman, he might also be an ally. . . .So, the difference which exists in linguistic fact and history is not underscored, for it lacks a connection with any of those ideas in terms of which men do see their world. . . .There are of course limits to what "our thinking can make so" or what it can obscure. But it can "make so" a good deal. For instance, a Berber who credits himself with an Arabic genealogy simply does not ask himself how he comes to be speaking Berber rather than Arabic. In particular, the fact that Berbers are the original population of North Africa, preceding Arabs and Islam, simply is not mirrored in the folk mind. The Berber sees himself as a member of this or that tribe, within an Islamically-conceived and permeated world— and not as a member of a linguistically defined ethnic group, in a world in which Islam is but one thing among others.[52]

51. Fishman et al., *Language Problems of Developing Nations*, p. 132.
52. Ernest Gellner and Charles Micaud (eds.) *Arabs and Berbers: From Tribe to Nation in North Africa* (Lexington, Mass.; D. C. Heath, 1972), p. 13. This magistral volume brings together a number of distinguished specialists in Mahgreb history and society; as the editors note, there is a remarkable congruence in their conclusions as to the "absence of a serious 'Berber problem.' " (Micaud, p. 433). This section relies heavily on the Gellner-Micaud study.

Berber as a collective designation has probably always been a label applied by outsiders. Under the analytical scalpel of the linguist, the commonalities in structure and vocabulary in the various Berber dialects are readily demonstrated; however, mutual intelligibility from one dialect to another is not to be assumed, and language similarities are utterly devoid of social relevance to the local Berber communities. Berber languages are solely oral media; although there is an Arabic alphabet for some Berber dialects, they are rarely written. Those who are literate, by definition, will know Arabic and possibly French as well. The language of the Holy Book is Arabic; the language of books in general is Arabic and French. To become an efficacious cultural ideology, a literate Berber tradition would probably be indispensable; there seems virtually no prospect that this will occur. There is neither an explicit demand for it nor any disposition on part of the national elite to promote Berber. Bilingualism is a well-established pattern; most Berber men can at least speak Arabic. Monolingual Berbers are mainly uneducated women, who remain strongly enclosed within rural society and highly unlikely to be the source of a cultural mobilization movement.

The concept of a sharp Arab-Berber dichotomy, however absent in the Berber mind, nonetheless came for a time to dominate French policy in Morocco. The French concluded that the central fact in Morroccan history was the continuing efforts of Arab-dominated central institutions to impose their will on Berber dissidents. Although French rule required domination of the central institutions, a way was sought to tie the perceived Berber zone of dissidence to France without necessarily passing through the monarchical structures. An admirable solution to this challenge to statecraft came through the premise of the Good Berber, which had earlier been developed in slightly different form for the Kabyls in Algeria. The Good Berber, it was held, was only superficially Islamicized. His traditional society was of democratic ethos, and his treatment of women far more free and equal. Equally slack was his linguistic commitment to Arabic. As the Berber languages obviously had no future, the Good Berber would readily accept French as his medium for modernization. Today's Good Berber was tomorrow's *français à part entier*. The high water mark of this policy was the famous Berber *dahir*, which was forced upon a very unwilling Sultan in 1930; this decree removed Berbers from the jurisdiction of Islamic law and created separate Berber tribunals, whose jural basis was supposed to be found in Berber custom.[53] Also, a special elite secondary school, the College d'Azrou, was set up as a

53. The intellectual history of French Berber policy is lucidly traced by Edmund Burke, "The Image of the Moroccan State in French Ethnological Literature: A New Look at the Origin of Lyautey's Berber Policy," in Gellner and Micaud, *From Tribe to Nation,* pp. 175–99.

Berber academy, entrusted with the formation of a Berber elite steeped in French culture, in an environment where Arabic influences were rigorously excluded.

The image of Moroccan cultural pluralism which undergirded the Berber *dahir* was flawed, and the consequences, from the French viewpoint, were disastrous. Rather than a mechanism for assimilation, this measure was an engine of nationalism, providing the catalyst for a swelling volume of protest. The dialectic of nationalism produced in its turn an equally false claim among Moroccan intellectuals that the Arab-Berber dichotomy was wholly a figment of a fevered colonial imagination.

In post-independence politics, there have been several junctures when particular happenings seemed to have a Berber visage. Just before independence, an autonomous Liberation army took form, mainly in the Berber Rif mountains; despite the claims of the then-dominant nationalist party, Istaqlal, to control it, this insurgent force was in fact an autonomous actor. In the immediate aftermath, several short-lived rural insurrections occurred, all in Berber mountain retreats. In 1957, a new political organization was founded, the Mouvement Populaire, mainly based in the Rif, and offered itself as a counter-weight to the urban-centered Istaqlal and other parties. Then in 1971 and 1972 the two attempted coups against King Hassan were led primarily by Berber officers.

Lending further credence to the Berber hypothesis was the appearance, at times, that the monarchy was refurbishing for its own uses the old French Berber policy. The Moroccan throne is at once secular and religious symbol; the ruling family are Sharifs, reputed direct descendents of the Prophet. The religious dimension of legitimation has been of particular importance in the strong affective attachments to the symbol of the crown in rural Morocco, including Berberland. The king, many believed, played the loyal, Berber countryside against the unruly elements in the large cities—unions, students, the at least rhetorically radical Union Nationale des Forces Populaires, which split from Istaqlal in 1960. The Royal army, established after independence, was at least 90 percent Berber both in officers and enlisted ranks. Many of the top officers had been trained in the French army, which had incorporated a number of promising sons of Berber notables.

What, then, are the limits to political Berberism? The most salient fact is the absence of a clear articulation of these events by participants as deriving from a Berber imperative. The Liberation army, the rural revolts, and the Mouvement Populaire were all rural responses to a perceived threat of urban domination in one or another form. It was the mainly Berber army that suppressed—without great difficulty—the revolts. The Mouvement Populaire carefully eschewed the use of Berberism as a platform; its party newspaper bore the name of *Le Maghreb arabe.*[54] In the 1971 and 1972 coups, the military participation necessarily meant that most actors would be Berber. At the same time, on both occasions, there were both Arabs and Berbers on both sides. At the point of crisis, neither Arabism nor Berberism was a moral principle capable of decisively affecting all alignments. There is a deep-seated cleavage between the swelling urban sector and the countryside; to the extent that the urban-rural cleavage also describes an Arab-Berber polarity, the terms became virtually interchangeable categories of macrosocial analysis, which would seem to assure their continuing currency.

The Algerian pattern of Kabyl politics is quite similar. During the revolution, Kabylia and the Aures were ecologically predestined as central places of insurrection; of difficult terrain, with only a rudimentary administrative control infrastructure, insurgent forces could readily build impregnable strongholds that would have been impossible to create on the settler lands. The dialectics of struggle then operated to totally commit the Kabyls to the revolution; their homelands felt the full weight of repressive operations by the French army, leading in turn to more complete mobilization. But when the war was won by a badly fractured Front de Libération Nationale in 1962, there was no Berberophone common front; Kabyls participated in all factions. One of the nationalist leaders, Ait Ahmed, did lead a revolt against the Ben Bella government in Kabylia in 1963-64; however, as Micaud observed: "Not only was it condemned by half the Kabyl deputies at the national assembly and not followed by a substantial fraction of local troops, but it petered out as soon as the border war between Algeria and Morocco had started. . . . In fact the revolt had had no separatist objective; Kabyl peasants were used by some Kabyl leader in Algiers as a power base to increase their authority in the central government."[55]

Arabism in the Maghreb has a rather different character than that of the Middle East. Arab culture is the symbol of national identity, in contra-distinction to French; the dignity of nationalism commanded an assertion of the centrality of Arabization as a riposte to the assimilative policies pursued by the French, above all in Algeria. The formation of the Arab self-concept in the crucible of French colonialism placed it in a quite separate arena from that of Middle Eastern Arab nationalism. While Arab intellectuals were certainly aware of the great figures in Levantine and Egyptian variants of Arab nationalism, the specific identity-shaping issues of the Middle East were quite remote:

54. Ibid., p. 271.
55. Ibid., p. 436.

the revolt against the Ottomans, the duplicity of World War I diplomacy, the collapse of the Hashemite dream, the relations between Christian and Muslim Arabs, and even the incandescent Israel question. The arena of nationalist struggle locked the Maghreb elite into a power conflict with the French state, and a running intellectual debate involving the French left, whose support was required to impose decolonization, and whose *Weltanschauung* had many points of tangency with the nationalists. Such interactions leave their mark on both parties; for the Maghreb nationalist intelligentsia, a legacy of tone, style, and substance distinctive from Middle East patterns remained. For Algeria and Morocco, the Kabyl and Berber phenomenon, however diffuse, imposed unspoken limits on Arabism as an integrative philosophy; although Arabic as national symbol was not in question, nonetheless Arabism in any exclusive form might conceivably create Berberism as its mirror image.[56]

But as yet cultural mobilization of Berberhood has not occurred and on balance appears unlikely to crystallize. Berber languages encounter the superior prestige and force attached to Arabic as the vehicle of Islam, the national language (albeit in uncertain partnership with French), and its place in the commanding heights of modernization—as the language of literacy (again, in tandem with French), as the language of the city and school. At this point in history, the linguistic resources for militant Berberhood would be very difficult to locate; it would probably require a unification of the Berber dialects around a generally accepted written version. But the social situation of Berber as a residual language of the most isolated elements in Maghreb society renders such a development highly improbable.

CONFESSIONAL PLURALISM

Finally, we need to consider the issue of confessional pluralism within the Arab framework to complete our survey of cultural politics in the Arab world. This mode of conflict has been of prime significance in Lebanon, Syria, Iraq, (North) Yemen, and Sudan. Nowhere is religious pluralism more crucial than in Lebanon, to which we turn first.

The basis of the Lebanese state is a "national pact," concluded in 1943 among the religious segments of the former French mandate as the

56. On Moroccan and Algerian politics, both the subject of an extensive literature, we would make particular mention, in addition to works already cited, of John Waterbury, *The Commander of the Faithful* (New York: Columbia University Press, 1970); David and Marina Ottoway, *Algeria: The Politics of a Socialist Revolution* (Berkeley: University of California Press, 1970); and Leon Carl Brown, *State and Society in Independent North Africa* (Oxford: Clarendon Press, 1963).

formula for the proclamation of independence. This unwritten but, in effect, entrenched constitutional accord concedes, on the one hand, that Lebanon has an "Arab face," but at the same time a distinctive identity arising from its confessional divisions, which require preservation in a separate state, with Western ties. A religious allocation of offices was established; the president is a Maronite Christian, the premier a Sunni Muslim, the speaker of the Chamber of Deputies a Shi'ite Muslim, and his deputy Greek Orthodox. Certain ministries also fall within the cultural partition; education and foreign affairs, for example, belong to the Christians. A religious allocation of parliamentary seats was also made, based upon the 1932 census, which recorded 30 percent Maronite Christian, 20 percent Sunni Muslim, 18 percent Shi'ite Muslim, 10 percent Greek Orthodox, 6 percent Greek Catholic, 6 percent Druze, and the rest scattered among smaller cultural segments.

There is considerable overlap between region and sect. On Mount Lebanon, which prior to the French mandate was all that the term "Lebanon" implied, Maronites and Druze dominate, with the Maronites on the more developed, northern part. Sunnite Muslims populate the coastal plain, attached to Lebanon by the French, while Shi'ites are concentrated in the south. Pluralism pervades every social domain. Names are almost always a reliable indicator of sect; upon introduction, new acquaintances can immediately place each other within the cultural map and define their interactions accordingly. Social intercourse between the sects is small; family relations and intimate friendships are almost wholly circumscribed by confessional lines. Communications media closely mirror this fragmentation; there are 49 daily papers for the 2,000,000 Lebanese, many externally financed, most closely associated with one of the confessional groups.[57] The school system is primarily operated by religious communities; 122 of 132 secondary schools are private.[58] Each sect maintains its own network of social and welfare organizations; the government participates very little in this domain.

In such a cleft society, it would be difficult to imagine a party system which did not reflect these divisions—and Lebanon has no such surprises in store. Perhaps more significant is the fact that, since independence, party members have never constituted more than one third of the total elected representation. Within the structural frame of confessionalism, the dominant pattern is patronage networks and cliques in fluid contention for such resources as are allocated through the formal political structures. At the summit, within the limits set by the national pact, a degree

57. Suleiman, *Political Parties in Lebanon,* p. 37.
58. Ibid., p. 31.

of consociational, interconfessional bargaining occurs. Ideology, as it may be readily guessed, plays virtually no role in this process. Thus the strong socialist tides which have swept over republican Arab states from Libya to Iraq in the last two decades have left Lebanon almost untouched. The politics of segmented confessionalism in Lebanon is that of the least common denominator. Cultural consociationalism tends strongly toward minimal policies. Christian elites, who dominate the entrepreneurial ranks, would certainly see in socialist policies an act of cultural hostility. Thus Beirut has become the major modern Arab capital where money is secure; with the fantastic influx of wealth in the peninsula states, Beirut has carved out a remunerative role for itself as an entrepot for capital. This process, needless to say, raises the stakes for the preservation of Lebanon as a separate state, whose confessional impasse is a cultural guarantee of a laissez-faire economy.

Lebanon as it has developed under the national pact thus has a highly ambivalent attitude towards Arab nationalism. While such sentiments are to be found among young intellectuals, especially Sunni Muslims, Arab unity is an obvious challenge to the patterns of confessional politics in which especially the Christian sects have found considerable security. Lebanon's most severe crises have arisen through the periodic summons to define its identity in the face of Arab imperatives—in 1957, when the Nasserite version of pan-Arabism seemed to be sweeping all before it, and in 1973 when a direct confrontation with Palestinian forces occurred. The national pact requires maintenance of Lebanon's Arab face; its insecurity would be high if a posture of implacable hostility to the greater Arab community were adopted. Thus in 1957 Lebanon needed to retreat from its exposed position of Western alignment, when this became wholly antithetical to an "Arab face." In 1973, a *modus vivendi* had to be found with the Palestinians; the Jordanian path of simple decimation of Palestinian forces would have risked unhinging the delicate cultural equilibrium.[59]

In Syria, unlike Lebanon, pluralism has become intertwined in complex ways with ideology. Under French mandate, the pale image of a Berber policy was visible in the regionalization of administration and creation of special provinces for the Druze (Jebel Druze) and Alawite (Latakia) Muslim sects. Sunni Muslims were dominant in Damascus and other towns, and the landowning and merchant groups that dominated Syrian politics until the mid-1950s. Christians, 14 percent of the population, were also well represented in the commercial classes. Druze and Alawite are primarily poor peasant communities, very susceptible to the radical

59. On Lebanon's intriguing politics, see also Michael Hudson, *The Precarious Republic* (New York: Random House, 1968), and Leonard Binder (ed.), *Politics in Lebanon* (New York: John Wiley, 1966).

appeal of Baath socialism. Pan-Arab nationalism, however, had its cultural center of gravity among the Sunni Muslims. Of some passing note in the intersection between cultural pluralism and ideological division was the fact that the founder and leader of the Baath Socialist party, Michel Aflaq, was a Christian, while the long-time leader of the Communist party, of some importance in the late 1950s, was Khaled Bakdash, a Kurd.

After the collapse of the union with Egypt, the Baath party came to power through military coup in 1963. Since that time, there has been a curious militarization of the Baath in both Syria and neighboring Iraq, along with a tendency to ascendancy of officers of Alawite and to some extent Druze origin. This came about partly through the relatively small role these groups played in the factional politics prior to that time, permitting them to escape the successive purges which shook the officer corps. Of rural origins, these officers were of radical bent and hostile to the urban bourgeoisie who had once dominated Syria. According to one estimate, Alawites now constitute 70 percent of the present officer corps, although they are less than 10 percent of the population.[60] However, the manifest lexicon of politics and military faction is ideological, and not sectarian. Nor should Alawite or Druze be seen as mobilized collectivities, participating as groups in the national arena. For example, the power struggle in 1965 pitted two Alawite generals, Muhammad 'Umran and Salah Jadid, against one another; the former is from a blacksmith clan east of Homs, while Jadid is from a tailor community in Latakia.[61]

In Iraq, the Shi'ite-Sunni division had had important political ramifications. Shi'ites, predominantly rural, incorporated in traditional structures, have resented their submergence by the urban-centered Sunnites. Shi'ite representation in cabinets under the monarchy never exceeded 26 percent, and until 1935 no cabinet included more than one. The educated Shi'ite, according to Abdul Raoof, finding himself faced with discrimination in government employment, "tends to be radical in viewing both the government and his political role—he suspects public policy and distrusts government authority."[62] The regime of General Abd al-Karim Kassim from 1958 to 1963 was a moment of brief entry into the sun of place and

60. J.C. Hurewitz, *Middle East Politics: The Military Dimension* (New York: Frederick A. Praeger, 1969), p. 153.

61. Eliezer Be'eri, *Army Officers in Arab Politics and Society* (New York: Frederick A. Praeger, 1970), p. 338. On the ideological dimension, see Karpat, *Political and Social Thought in the Contemporary Middle East.* For a well-done brief summary of Syrian politics, which are poorly covered in the literature, see the Suleiman chapter in Ismael, *Contemporary Middle East,* pp. 213-320. See also Moshe Ma'oz, "Attempts at Creating a Political Community in Modern Syria," *Middle East Journal,* XXVI, no. 4 (Autumn 1972), 389-404; Michael H. Van Dusen, "Political Integration and Regionalism in Syria," *Middle East Journal,* XXVI, no. 2 (Spring 1972), 123-36.

62. Ismael, *Contemporary Middle East,* p. 189.

preferment, for which they paid dearly after his overthrow, with thousands of Shi'ites killed, imprisoned, or dismissed from government service.[63] Shi'ites have tended to view Arab unity movements as altering their local circumstances to their further disadvantage.

In the Yemen Arab Republic, the Shi'ite sect of Zaidi established an imamate in the ninth century which lasted for a millennium. The Zaidis were organized as rural communities in north Yemen; their thousand-year domination was the more remarkable, in that it was exercised by a very small segment of the Zaidis, the Sayyids, whose fraction of the total Yemen population was 2-3 percent according to one source, 7 percent by another, 1 percent or less by a third.[64] The Sayyids were those who claimed direct descent from the Prophet and who by this token were eligible for high political office; the office of Imam itself was not hereditary, but was elective among the Sayyids based upon fulfillment of fourteen criteria of merit. Virtually all functions of rulership were the monopoly of the Sayyids, whose rule was enforced by tribal levies from the Zaidi communities. The eventual republic revolution was the result of an alliance between discontented Zaidi army officers, and non-Shi'ite Muslims. The Zaidi-Sunnite cleavage overlays once again the discontinuities between towns and countryside, with Zaidi communities dominating the rural areas, while urban merchants and tradesmen are mainly Sunni of the Shafi'ite rite. The downfall of the Sayyids may be attributed to a curious conjuncture of forces deriving from the gradual penetration of the idea of modernity to this isolated land. On the one hand, the penultimate Sayyid Imam Yahya in the interwar period was influenced by the normative model of the modern state; this led him to use the theocratic Sayyid oligarchy to enforce a far more thorough uniformity of legal observance and administrative regulation than had formerly obtained. Thus the medieval imamate, operating in terms of a borrowed model of the nature of the state, weighed much more heavily upon the subject population than had been its tradition. At the same time, ideas of secularism were making their mark, above all on the urban centers, and created a standard of evaluation against which the imamate appeared hopelessly retrograde.

Sudan is not only a vast laboratory of Arabization (in the north), but is also in the throes of vital transformations of religious identity patterns within Islam. The Turko-Egyptian period from 1820 to 1885 had produced, within the religious field, an integrative revolution of its own; the sufi orders and saint cults which had operated on a very local level

---

63. Ibid.

64. Hurewitz, *Middle East Politics,* p. 259, and Be'eri, *Army Officers in Arab Politics and Society,* p. 223, and Manfred Wenner, in Ismael, *Contemporary Middle East,* p. 383, respectively.

gave way to incorporative brotherhoods operating on a far wider scale. The most important of the new *tariqas* under Egyptian rule was the Khatmiyya, led by the Mirghani family, which flourished under the benevolent eye of the new administration. The Khatmiyya, as well as the Turko-Egyptian order, was challenged by the Mahdist state from 1883 to 1898; for the Mahdists, Khatmiyya was not only a rival for power and influence, but also contaminated by its Egyptian associations. After British rule was imposed in 1898; both the Mahdist movement, now known as Ansar, and Khatmiyya were treated with respect and prospered. When competitive nationalist politics came after World War II, the new elite quickly appreciated that the two brotherhoods were by far the most effective mass organizations in existence. Alliances were struck, and the *tariqas* were deeply enmeshed in the political party structure—Ansar with the Umma, Khatmiyya first with the National Unionist Party, then with the People's Democratic Party. In elections in 1954, 1958, and 1965, the brotherhoods demonstrated their capacities as vote-getting machines in the countryside. Indeed, it was precisely the electoral ritual which maximized their influence, as it was exceedingly difficult for any political movement to construct a national organization which could match the *tariqas*—who, moreover, had God on their side.

The Ansar also had on its side the image of its military past. The leaders of the sect were believed capable of raising a force of 200,000 armed followers to confront an army of less than 20,000, largely deployed in the south to fight the separatist revolt. Indeed, in 1965, an armed host of Ansar had appeared at the gates of Khartoum at a moment of crisis, and, without actually intervening, cast a shadow so long over the proceedings as to substantially alter the outcome. The political elite had concluded from the electoral campaigns that the primary loyalty of the rural masses, especially the Ansar, were to their religious leaders.

The army assumed power for a second time in 1969, this time under the banner of Islamic socialism. In 1970, a critical confrontation occurred, marking the end of an epoch in cultural politics. The Ansar leadership went into open revolt, sounded the call for the faithful to rally—but found that only a few thousand did—who were then subjected to a crushing defeat by the army, many of whose members (as well as President Nimeiry), were Ansar members. In 1968, Sayyid Ali al-Mirghani, Khatmiyya head since the beginning of British rule in 1898, passed away, removing from the scene a master manipulator of *tariq* politics and religious patronage. There seems reason to believe that an era has quietly passed, that the *tariqas* as intermediate agencies of cultural mobilization may have faded into the background. Certainly the national leadership no longer acts on the same assumptions as to the galvanizing force of the brotherhoods as did their predecessors a decade earlier.[65]

ARAB NATION OR ARAB STATES

What then, is the future of the Arab nation? Is Arab nationalism, as a pan-Arab unity concept, but an incandescent moment in the history of the identities and ideas in the Arab-speaking world, with Nasserism at its ascendant the shining hour? Or is it political revelation that will ultimately find an anointed messenger, that will reorder in its image the state system which now clamps its fragmenting frame upon the Arab community?

Our meanderings through the maze of identities in the Arab world make clear the magnitude of the barriers to be overcome. The appealing simplicity of the proposition that all are Arabs who speak Arabic and consider themselves such fades upon close scrutiny. Not all Arabic-speakers have the same self-concept; put another way, the cultural ideology of Arabism is by no means universally diffused. The multiplicity of arenas in which subjective identity as an Arab has been molded is a rich source of diversity. It made a considerable difference who "they" were with whom in hostile conflict partnership the "we" took shape and form. And when identity formation occurred without an external "relevant other" as conflict partner—as in the Arabian peninsula—for the most part, the nature of Arabism as identity symbol is far more diffuse. Religion has played a major part in defining social identities, as we have seen; here Islam can frequently be a divisive rather than integrative force—or, in other terms, sect rather than faith is the operative unit of social solidarity. The enclosure within the boundaries of several Arab-dominated states of substantial non-Arab populations creates acute and continuing tension between the pan-Arab idea and the exigencies of state-building. Arab unity can only be seen as a cultural calamity for groups such as the Kurds or southern Sudanese who will not find ultimate assimilation acceptable.

The state system, once established, acquires a powerful inertial force of its own, as we argued in chapter 2. The ubiquitous symbols of sovereignty—flags, coins, postage stamps, passports, identity cards, national airlines—are thrust daily before the citizenry, silently become an insep-

65. See the valuable and persuasive paper by John O. Voll, "Islam: Its Future in the Sudan," presented at the 15th Annual Meeting of the African Studies Association, Philadelphia, 1972. On modern Sudanese politics, see generally K.D.D. Henderson, *Sudan Republic* (London: Ernest Benn, 1965.)

arable part of the *gestalt* within which events are perceived. Specificity of political tradition, administrative practice, and policy choice becomes more pronounced. For example, at the end of World War I, very little except the confessional composition separated Syria and Lebanon—and yet today these two polities are utterly different worlds, whose policy incompatibilities extend practically across the entire gamut of state action. If the general thrust of our argument in chapter 3 be valid, then time is not on the side of Arab nationalism. That a simple association of sovereign states is likely to have precious little impact in advancing the Arab national idea is amply demonstrated in the meager accomplishments of the Arab League.[66]

And yet a funeral peroration would be premature. The capacity of the dream to waken a passionate commitment in men must not be underestimated. The basic regime instability of polities such as Jordan, Iraq, and Syria always leave open the possibility that a pivotal state could come under totally different leadership, in which the ideas and will of a few or even a single man could carry immense consequences. It was a handful of men who committed Syria to the union with Egypt in 1958. In Egypt, the commitment to an Arab identity became incomparably stronger under Nasser, when pan-Arabism tended to eclipse older views in some circles described as "Pharaohism," or sentimental emphasis on the uniqueness of the Nile past. Who five years ago would have guessed the somnolent Libya, basking in its golden shower of petroleum wealth, would come under the rule of a mercurial pan-Arab like Colonel Qaadafi? In a state system when the weekend harvest of coups can always produce a Qaadafi, then place in the equation must be left for a large random factor. Dynastic states must be considered a particular question mark. Hassan in Morocco had miraculous escapes in 1971 and 1972; when these conspiracies extended into the very antechambers of the king, implicating some of his most intimate collaborators, the perennity of the Alawite line cannot be taken for granted. Nor is the consummate skill of King Hussein in Jordan of outwitting an unending parade of plotters a certain guarantee for the future; all winning streaks come to an end. The peninsular monarchies in Saudi-Arabia, Kuweit, Bahrein, Qatar, Oman, and the Union of Arab Emirates are all spawning new social structures, modern civil bureaucracies and armies, whose fealty to kingship may not be perpetual.

To this must be joined the most explosive source of uncertainty—the Arab-Israel conflict and the growth of the diaspora nationality of Pales-

66. For a useful monograph which puts the accomplishments of the Arab League in the most favorable possible light, see Robert W. MacDonald, *The League of Arab States* (Princeton: Princeton University Press, 1965).

tinians. The many spectacular ramifications of this crisis need no re-counting here. It is, however, pertinent to recall what a novel phe-nomenon the idea of being Palestinian is. As a focus of Arab identity, the Palestinian self-concept dates no further back than the end of Ottoman rule over Syria, with which most Palestinian Arabs identified themselves at the close of World War I. The idea of Palestine took root in hostile symbiosis with the concept of Israel; had there been no Jewish national homeland, there probably would have been no Palestine either. The grow-ing conflict with Jewish immigrants, the tardy realization that Israel was to become an irreducible fact, the searing humiliation of 1948, the idle rancor of the refugee camps forged a sense of Palestinian nationality-in-exile which was an equally irreducible fact. In diaspora, the Palestinian identity was fed by its daily frustrations. Its desperation motivated an uninhibited terrorism which repeatedly demonstrated that a handful of determined persons, to whom the territorial imperative of Palestinian nationalism was a total and transcendant obligation, could create crisis situations of great magnitude. The diaspora had produced some important but little-noted social facts; in Kuwait, for example, a majority of the population are immigrants, with Palestinians being a major component. A substantial number of the technicians and skilled workers in Saudi-Arabia are Palestinians. In the broader frame of the impending period of energy shortage in the world, the key role that oil-producing Arab states will play in that, and the enormous revenues in prospect des-cribed at the beginning of the chapter, further vectors of uncertainty enter the calculus.

We would conclude that the verdict is far from in on the future state structure in the Arab world. Although the full realization of Arab unity appears improbable, there also seems far more potential instability in the state system as currently defined that in any other major region of the developing world. Many powerful forces are operating to entrench the state system in its present form. At the same time, the possibility of the cataclysmic disturbance in the whole equilibrium, the tempest which would sweep away a substantial fraction of the present states, is perceptible on the distant horizon, a cloud no bigger than a man's hand.

11   Latin American Indians:
Fugitive Ethnicity

Survey the best-known studies of Latin American politics, and the inescapable conclusion emerges that very little bearing upon the issue of cultural pluralism is to be found. There are, of course, many studies exploring the particular pattern of racial stratification peculiar to the non-Hispanic Carribean or continental enclaves such as Guyana which belong to the Caribbean world. A vigorous debate may be found on Gilberto Freyre's thesis on the nonracial character of Luso-Brazilian culture, in which the Freyre propositions have of late been badly mauled by empirical data.[1] A number of works have explored peasant organization and resistance in Andean politics where that term is synonomous with Indian, but the perspective is essentially one of social class rather than cultural pluralism. Significantly, two recent works which do explore the issue, both from a racial stratification model, are written by authors whose most extensive research experience has been in Africa and Asia.[2] One study by a Guatemalan scholar does reflect on the absence of nationalism among the Indians—but the nationalism at issue is Guatemalan nationalism, not Indian or Mayan self-affirmation.[3]

This is by no means some curious myopia on the part of the Latin Americanist; rather the answer to this apparent puzzle is that the question simply does not arise in the form we have been posing it in the present study. Indians *qua* Indians are not collective actors in the national political arena. They are actors on occasion as peasants, as in the Bolivian national revolution of 1952; more often they are acted upon by parties of populist ideology led by elites of middle class origin, who are committed to social mobilization and rural uplift. In many of the Latin American republics a very thorough mestization has occurred, often attended by a cult of *indigenismo*, glorifying the Hispanic-Indian

1. The classic statement of the Gilberto Freyre position is *The Masters and the Slaves* (2nd ed.; New York: Alfred Knopf, 1965); for rebuttals, see inter alia, Pierre L. van den Berghe, *Race and Ethnicity* (New York: Basic Books, 1970); John Saunders, in Ernest G. Campbell, *Racial Tensions and National Identity* (Nashville: Vanderbilt University Press, 1972), pp. 143-61; and the many references cited therein, including the works of Marvin Harris, Charles Boxer, Roger Bastide, and others.
2. Mason, *Patterns of Dominance;* van der Berghe, *Race and Ethnicity.*
3. J. Fernando Juarez Munoz, *El Indio Guatemalteco* (2 vols.; Guatemala City: 1931, 1946).

synthesis. But mestizo culture is essentially Hispanic, and *indígenismo* cannot be equated with cultural mobilization on a racial (Indian) or ethnic basis. Perhaps this contrast is most striking in the Caribbean; consider, for example, the Dominican Republic, where a White minority rules a substantial Black majority, yet where a cultural ideology of racial stratification is largely absent. Unlike the French (Haiti) or English (Jamaica) cases, there is very little Creolization of language, and protest has not openly been articulated in racial categories.[4]

However untoward, the cultural pluralism question nonetheless merits posing. Although close scrutiny will reveal some nuances, the absence of perception of deprivation in an ethnic idiom stands out in Latin America. And yet all the circumstances which have politicized ethnicity elsewhere would appear to be present. Indians are more than 30 percent of the population in Guatemala, Ecuador, Peru, and Bolivia and were a historic factor in most other Latin republics. They occupy the lowest rungs of the social scale; the new identity-forming resources of education, easier communication, urban migration, which have facilitated social protest through cultural mobilization in other settings, have not been directed to that purpose. The Indian, politically, remains a peasant, a *campesino*. What might be and is not, in social explanation, is equally worthy of our attention as the spectacularly visible pluralism of Africa and Asia.

Some of the factors which appear germane in considering the invisibility of the Indian as a culturally self-conscious group are the range of variation in the western hemisphere populations at the moment of Spanish conquest and the cultural premises of Spanish rule. We will then examine some specific situations, which will reveal some significant variations on the overall theme. Table 11.1 summarizes the racial composition of the Latin Republics.

COLUMBUS CREATES THE INDIANS

At the time of the footfall of Christopher Columbus in the Caribbean, there were, of course, no Indians; indeed, one can imagine the astonishment of the sundry Caribs, Arawaks, Mayans, Huastecs, Chibchans, Tupi, Inca, Araucanians, and many others to discover that they bore this strange classification, brought by one set of strangers from beyond the Atlantic and derived from another set beyond the Pacific. The populations encountered in many parts of the continent were quite sparse,

4. This point is well made in the contribution by H. Hoetink, in Campbell, *Racial Tensions and National Identity*, p. 24.

Table 11.1—Latin American Population, by Racial Group

Country	% Amerindian	% African	% White	% Mixed [a]	% Asian	% Unspecified
Argentina (1960) [b]	0.6	(overwheimingly White, but exact proportions unknown)				
Bolivia (1950)	63		37			
Brazil (1960)	1.5	11	61.7	26.5	0.6	0.2
Chile (1960)	3.2	(overwhelmingly mixed, but exact proportions unknown)				
Colombia (1961)	1.2	4	20	74.8 [c]		
Costa Rica (1962)	0.6	1.9	97.3	(included with White)	0.1	
Cuba (1953)		12.4	72.8	14.5	0.3	
Dominican Republic (1950)		11.5	28.1	60.4	0.0	
Ecuador (1961)	30.4	5	10	49.6		
El Salvador (1961)	0.4		5	94.6		
Guatemala (1959)	53.6			46.4 [d]		
Haiti	(overwhelmingly African, but exact proportions unknown)					
Honduras (1960)	5.5	2.1	1.2	91.1		
Mexico (1960)	8.8		10	81.2		
Nicaragua (1960)	2.9	10	17	70.1		
Panama (1960)	5.8	13.3	11.1	69		0.7
Paraguay (1960)	3.8	(overwhelmingly mixed, but exact proportions unknown)				
Peru (1961)	46.7	0.5		52.1	0.7	0.1
Uruguay	(overwhelmingly White, but exact proportions unknown)					
Venezuela (1961)	1.5	8	20	70.5		

[a]"Mixed" category includes Indian-White (mestizo), African-White (mulatto), and African-Indian (zambo).

[b]Dates refer to census year.

[c]Approximately 57% mestizo, 14% mulatto, 3% zambo.

[d]Ladinos

Source: Compiled from Statistical Abstract of Latin America, 1965 and 1971 editions, Center of Latin American Studies, UCLA.

but there were several zones of high concentration—perhaps 5-7 million in the Andean highlands[5] and 12-15 million in Middle America (Mexico and Guatemala).[6] Levels of social organization ranged from the most rudimentary in some of the remote rain forests of the Amazon basin and windblown barrens of Patagonia, to the remarkably centralized states of the Aztec and Inca. By far the greater part of the area was inhabited by groups practicing sedentary but shifting cultivation, whose political structures were quite localized; although linguists could

5. Julian H. Steward (ed.), Handbook of South American Indians, II (New York: Cooper Square Publishers, 1963), p. 81.
6. Eric Wolf, Sons of the Shaking Earth (Chicago: University of Chicago Press, 1962), p. 31.

classify families of closely related languages stretching over very broad areas, such as the Tupi-Guaraní from northern Argentina to the Amazon basin or the Carib from the northern coast of South America across the Antilles to the Bahama, these are analytical categories and not identity units.

The areas which could support with available technologies a population density and agricultural surplus requisite for bureaucratic empires to emerge were the central valley of Mexico, and the Andean highlands. Mayan kingdoms, in the forest lowlands of Yucatan and eastern Guatemala, had earlier achieved a high level of centralization; however, Mayan civilization had fallen on evil days before the conquest and was no longer a highly structured society at the time of its subjugation.[7] The Aztecs, at the time of Montezuma and Cortés, had recently established a precarious domination over several other powerful historical states of the Mexican highlands; their imperium was not linguistically integrated, nor had Aztec domination found a metaphor of empire reconciling its non-Aztec subjects to its permanence. It had, however, produced a highly stratified society, with a potent war-making capacity.[8]

The most remarkable political construction was the Inca, which stretched from Ecuador to northern Chile. Given the absence of a written language for record-keeping and communication and of wheeled vehicles, the scope and centralization of this bureaucratic empire was quite extraordinary. The system of imperial roads, constructed to standard specifications, and including some formidable engineering feats, stretched to all parts of the empire. Most interesting, from our perspective, is the well-conceived integration policy pursued. Quechua was the language of empire, and royal administrators were placed with the subordinate units created. Groups of Quechua-speaking settlers were sent to form colonies on the marches of empire; at the same time, groups from newly-conquered Indian communities were taken for resettlement in the Inca heartland, where they quickly became Quechuaized. The Inca dynasty was created only in about A.D. 1200; its phase of rapid expansion began in 1438, only a century before the Spanish conquest. When the Spanish arrived, linguistic assimilation was far from complete, especially in the zones conquered by Inca only decades before Pizarro. The assimilation process, ironically, was completed under the Spanish. Until well into the seventeenth century, the Spanish, especially the missionaries, made extensive use of Quechua in their dealings with the Indians, but none whatsoever

7. On the antique glories of Mayan civilization, see Elizabeth P. Benson, *The Maya World* (New York: Thomas Y. Crowell, 1967).

8. Wolf, *Sons of the Shaking Earth,* offers an excellent portrait of the political and social structure of the valley of Mexico at the time of conquest.

of other Andean languages. Thus, except in an Aymara enclave in Bolivia, Quechua became the sole Indian medium in the Andes. The idea of the Inca tradition remains alive, but memories of older divisions are entirely extinguished.[9]

In the fertile Cauca valley of the Colombian highlands, a Chibchan state appeared to be taking form, though it was aborted by the conquest. A caste system, suggestive of a political centralization process, was a conspicuous feature, and a relatively high population density had built up, variously estimated, but with 600,000 a median figure.[10] Altogether, it is estimated that the indigenous population from Mexico to Patagonia numbered 21-24 million.[11]

HISPANIC CONQUEST CULTURE

George Foster has remarked that one can journey in Spanish America from the Rio Grande to the Straits of Magellan and find the towns throughout this vast area of strikingly similar mode: the central plaza, facing the church; the substantial homes of the leading citizens in the streets leading out of the square; the humbler abodes of the poorer residents on the outskirts. Although Spain was far from a unified society in the sixteenth century, nonetheless a single conquest culture crystallized from the various regions of Iberia. The Spanish in Latin America, like the Arabs in the Maghreb, established themselves as the authority pole, geographically rooted in the towns. In the initial confrontation, Spaniards and Indians interacted directly, with the cultural shock pattern by the fact of political conquest. Subsequently, the relationship became institutionalized as a folk-urban continuum. A process of cultural interaction continued, followed the "familiar pattern of flow of influence downward and outward, from the urban-elite pole to lower classes and peasants. Spanish, Hispanicized, and partly Hispanicized peoples all along this continuum therefore continued to be exposed to new Spanish influences as they were passed along from the cities, and these people in turn became a point of diffusion of the items they accepted, to other populations less influenced by Spain."[12] The conquest culture was screened, with people accepting what they felt to

9. For a thorough compendium summarizing knowledge of the Inca as it stood two decades ago, see Steward, *Handbook of South American Indians,* vol. II; see also the remarkable 1846 classic of William H. Prescott, *The Conquest of Peru,* republished in abridged edition by Victor W. von Hagen (New York: Mentor Books, 1961).

10. Steward, *Handbook of South American Indians,* IV, 300-301.

11. Ibid., V., 665.

12. George M. Foster, *Culture and Conquest* (Chicago: Quadrangle Books, 1967), pp. 227-34.

be desirable and within their reach, while they rejected what they perceived as undesirable and within their ability to refuse.

In delineating the particular features of Hispanic cultures as an identity of conquest, it is crucial to recall not only the centuries over which it operated before the modern era of mobilized identities arrived, but also the historical circumstances of the fifteenth and sixteenth century Iberian peninsula, which formed the perspectives of the conquistadores. 1492 was a year of destiny—not only the first vision of the western hemisphere, but also the final expulsion of the Moors from the Iberian peninsula. What unified the Spaniards, aside from the intoxicating scent of pelf in the New World, was an intense sense of religious identity. Linguistic identity was not salient; three centuries would pass in Europe before the idea of nationality founded upon common language would come into its own. Territorial attachments were very local and rooted in the towns; Foster describes this pattern well: "The Spaniard's sense of attachment to his community is intense. . . whether one's native town be large or small, the same attachment to, love of, and fierce pride in it are found in each heart. This sense of community is not reflected in a local social structure that functions without major conflict and stress; the opposite is more nearly true: enmities may be strong, and antagonisms are deep and frequently long standing. At the same time against the world there is unity in local patriotism, and a genuinely strong belief that one's community is superior to all others."[13] Political unity was still precarious in Spain; only in 1479 was most of the peninsula brought under the same crown, through the dynastic union of Aragon and Castille. Dynastic rule knit the feudal domains of Spain together in personal union only; each retained its separate identity and privileges. The important genetic impact of the centuries of Arab and Berber residence in Iberia made skin color an ambiguous differentiator and was certainly not the basis for perception of the Moorish-Spanish cleavage. We and they in the Spain of the conquest was essentially a religious frontier, and it was this that was transposed to the New World. Conquistadores were motivated by a drive for status and honor, which found outlet in the quest for souls and gold: the former was an imperative of religious identity, and the latter gave the currency which could be converted into status in Spain.[14]

This dual theme of spiritual conquest and material exploitation provided the concept of colonial rule for Spain in the New World. And, as commodious vessels of domination, the Spaniards found the centralized kingdoms of Mexico and Peru. Cortes in 1521, Pizarro in 1532 seized the commanding heights of these two imperial systems, which offered

13. Ibid., pp. 34-35.
14. Mason is particularly persuasive on this point, *Patterns of Dominance,* pp. 234-39.

both the structures and symbols necessary for the establishment of their rule. The millions that were subordinated by these audacious military strokes had been well schooled in subjugation; the arrival of one set of rulers to replace another was in the natural order of the universe. The ruling class of the indigenous empires had been troubled by omens and prophecies of doom; a cosmology in which the inscrutable purposes of extraterrestial forces played a large part contributed to the demoralization which attended the initial defeats. The nobility was unable to effectively rally as a separate force once the central symbols of rulership had been captured. And the servile classes of the population operated within an ethos of docility. Indeed, within a feudal metaphor, the Indian nobility was absorbed into the Hispanic system, and the mass transformed into a peasantry.

The Spaniards were drawn to the main centers of Indian civilization by the accurate perception that not only power but wealth had been effectively centralized. It was these kingdoms whose extractive capacities had mobilized vast amounts of static wealth in their treasuries, a wealth which was certainly not to be found in the acephalous societies of the circum-Caribbean, the lowland forests, or the vast plains of the southern part of the continent. And it was here that spiritual conquest on a vast and exalting scale could be achieved. From these compulsions came the will to dominate, the impulse to embark on what could only have seemed a desperate adventure. Cortés set forth with 508 soldiers and 100 sailors, 14 cannons, 16 horses and 32 crossbows; Pizarro with 177 followers.[15] Although the horses and cannon certainly offered a technological advantage, the disparity of numbers was so great that only the psychology of the setting can explain both the expeditions and the outcome.

From the metaphors of feudalism, the Spanish developed an efficacious instrument of domination, the encomienda. Through this device, communities of Indians were allocated to conquistadores, who were entrusted with their welfare, while authorized to make use of them as an extractive resource. In practice, the encomenderos were able to make use of their Indian tributaries both for the produce of a salable agricultural surplus and for employment in the mines. With the gradual metamorphosis of social ideas, the feudal encomienda eventually became translated into the freehold hacienda by the nineteenth century. Not all Indians were absorbed into the encomienda system; some were organized into village settlements under a headman answerable to the

15. Wolf, *Sons of the Shaking Earth,* p. 152; Prescott, *The Conquest of Peru,* p. 223.

Spanish. These communities were liable to labor levies for roadway, mine, or factory. On the marches of empire, outside the main centers of Spanish exploitation, Franciscan, Jesuit or Dominican friars established mission settlements. Finally, by abandoning areas under Spanish occupation, Indians could avoid subjugation altogether. However, it should at once be added that this option was not easy to exercise for the highlands people of the valley of Mexico or the Inca empire; for the latter, in particular, it required descent into the tropical forest on the eastern slope of the Andes, a totally different ecological zone whose perils for the unadapted were perhaps more forbidding than the disabilities of subjugation.

Religion was not only central to the identity of the conquistadores, but also became a major nexus of incorporation. Highly elaborated religious cults were the supernatural concomitant of the centralized Indian systems; simultaneous with the decapitation of the empires was the destruction of the idols. Indeed, the friars had difficulty in containing the zeal of the conquistadores for the destruction of Indian religious artifacts. In the seat of the Aztec capital, the Spaniards ripped the idols from their pedestals, smote them to pieces, and cast them into the bottom of the lake—a scene repeated in the Inca capital and countless other times at lesser shrines. The rubble of the old temples served as landfill for the churches, which often rose on the same sites. Catholic hierarchy replaced the old priesthood of the sun cults. The pathway between the two was smoothed by some similarities of ritual and the syncretic possibilities within the village milieu, where the rigors of Catholic doctrine were mediated by local saint worship and a melange of folk belief. But spiritual conquest was all but completed in the first century of Spanish rule, despite the small size of the army of God; in Mexico and Guatemala, for example, the total number of friars probably never exceeded 1000.[16] Conversion could often be nominal and practice superficial. But Christianity was firmly established as the sole religious system operating beyond the level of the most localized community. It was a religion of the conquerer, helping to define the cultural continuum described by Foster; the Spaniard occupied the authority pole of this domain as well, a factor of signal import during the centuries in which the cultural relationships of the Indian populations and the broader society of which they were now a part became institutionalized. Here again the similarity in pattern with the Arab-Berber relationship in the Maghreb is intriguing.

16. Wolf, *Sons of the Shaking Earth,* p. 174.

DEMOGRAPHIC CHANGE: MESTIZATION AND MORTALITY

A process of enormous significance began at once with the arrival of the Spaniards: the genetic mingling of Spaniard and Indian, to which was added, in varying proportions, the involuntary influx of African slaves. Spanish women did accompany the early immigrants, but not in equal proportion; sexual gratification for the majority required liaisons with Indian women, producing the beginnings of the mestizo population which is today numerically dominant in more than half the Latin republics. In practice, the mestizo category was augmented by a steady stream of assimilated Indians, who moved to town, adopted Spanish as primary language and other external marks of Hispanic culture, and simply ceased to be Indians. In the coastal areas and islands of the Caribbean, where, generally speaking, indigenous populations either refused to serve as a servile labor force for the sugar estates or perished in the process, African slaves were brought to fill the gap. The most careful calculations on the dimensions of this demographic contribution, by Philip Curtin, suggest that 1.6 million Africans were landed in Spanish America and 3.6 million in Brazil between 1492 and 1870; in the later stages of the Spanish trade, Cuba, Dominican Republic, and Puerto Rico were the major destinations, but earlier substantial numbers were imported in what is now Columbia, Venezuela, Panama, Mexico, Ecuador and Peru.[17] Wolf estimates, for Middle America, that the number of Africans landed (250,000) was very close to the number of Spanish immigrants (300,000).[18] These have entirely disappeared as a distinctive group in Mexico, a result both of mortality rates and genetic incorporation bound to a concept of identity which treated the racially mixed as part of a Hispanicized continuum, rather than drawing a rigid line between White and all degrees of racially mixed ancestry. By way of digression, it may be noted that Curtin estimated the total number of African slaves brought to the United States at just under 400,000. A somewhat different mortality rate and conceptualizing of racial identity by Whites in a way which virtually excluded the Latin pattern of incorporation had produced a Black population of 22.7 million by 1970.[19]

The other demographic process of immense importance in fixing the cultural parameters of Latin America states was the catastrophic decline of Indian populations in many areas. The isolation of the western hemisphere had previously insulated them from an array of deadly micro-organisms against which partial immunities through long contact

17. Curtin, *The Atlantic Slave Trade*, p. 268.
18. Wolf, *Sons of the Shaking Earth*, p. 29.
19. Curtin, *The Atlantic Slave Trade*, p. 268.

had been developed in Europe. In Mexico, there were virulent epidemics of smallpox in 1520, 1531, and 1545; typhoid fever in 1545, 1576, and 1735, and twenty-nine subsequent periods; measles in 1595—and, from Africa, malaria and yellow fever ravaged the lowlands. Epidemiology was not the only explanation; the warfare which attended conquest, forced labor in the mines, alterations in the agricultural equilibrium by the introduction of cattle and sheep herds, and Spanish pre-emption of a good share of available irrigation water played their part. In Mexico and Guatemala, during the first century of Spanish rule, the Indian population fell to only one-seventh of its preconquest level. In 1650— the low point of Indian population—there were 1,270,000 Indians in Mexico and Guatemala, as compared with 120,000 classified as White, and 130,000 mestizos. By 1800, on the eve of independence, the Indian population had gone back up to 5,200,000, where it has remained quite stable since. However, the mestizo category increased seventeen-fold between 1650 and 1800, and then more than a hundredfold since the opening of the nineteenth century.[20]

On the Caribbean islands, Indian populations were virtually extinct within a generation. In the coastal zones, Indian populations were much reduced and either incorporated into the mestizo complex or pushed into inaccessible zones. The Chibchan culture, most highly developed of the Colombia-Venezuelan highlands, was swiftly decimated. After a lightning conquest of the Chibcha principalities in 1536 (Jimenez de Quesada subjugated an estimated 600,000 with 166 men and 59 horses), by 1600 only 1500 Chibchans remained.[21] By 1795, Chibcha dialects had completely disappeared.[22] In central Andes highlands, the population decline was not so steep; to this must be attributed in good part the greater cohesion of the Indian populations of Bolivia, Peru, and Ecuador today. The first census in Peru and Bolivia, in 1561, tallied 1,490, 137 Indians and is generally believed fairly reliable. In 1796 the figure had declined to 608,894. The preconquest population of this region is estimated at not much over 3,000,000. The Andes highlands were not so badly hit by disease; there were no major epidemics until the eighteenth century.[23]

In the Andes, there developed in the first two centuries of colonial contact an adapted cultural pattern, which then remained relatively stable in rural homogeneous Indian communities until the pulses of

20. Wolf, *Sons of the Shaking Earth*, pp. 196-99.

21. Steward, *Handbook of South American Indians*, IV, 300-301.

22. Orlando Fals-Borda, *Peasant Society in the Colombian Andes: A Sociological Study of Saurio* (Gainsville: University of Florida Press, 1955), pp. 236-37.

23 John Leddy Phelan, *The Kingdom of Quito in the Seventeenth Century* (Madison: University of Wisconsin Press, 1967), pp. 44-45.

modernization began to quicken in recent decades.[24] The western Guatemalan highlands were the other major center of self-contained Indian villages. Spanish overall control was unchallenged, and the assimilation of Christianity into the folk culture was a basic part of the colonial Indian cultural synthesis, encapsulated within the power and status hierarchy defined by Spanish rule.

ESCAPE FROM CONQUEST

For some, cultural autonomy was maintained through retreat from the zone of Spanish domination. Such sanctuary was available in much of the tropical low forest, in the recesses of the Amazon basis, the savannas of western Brazil and southern Argentina, the montane forests of Bolivia, Peru, and Ecuador, or the southern great plains of the United States (then Mexico). This was not without its price; the forest in particular was antithetical to the maintenance of complex societies. Indeed, many of the present tropical lowland forest Indian communities of the present day experienced a drastic deculturization, with the disappearance of class-stratified societies and highly ordered religions; in a number of cases, their agricultural technology, artistic expression, and artisanal activities are far less sophisticated than those of their forebears.[25]

Another form of reaction, rejecting subjugation, was the formation of rebel communities, often in collaboration with escaped African slaves; these *cimarron* bands were a major problem for the Spanish along the Peruvian coast north of Lima and along the Colombia and Venezuelan coasts. These culturally syncretic groups had to develop their own patterns of leadership and internal organization; they were not traditional communities. In Ecuador, the Esmeraldas coastal zone became the redoubt of Indian and Zambo (Indian-African) principalities until the nineteenth century, with the important effect of largely isolating the manorial society of the Ecuadorian sierra for three centuries.[26] In Venezuela, by 1570 *cimarron* rebel communities along the coast had become so numerous that travel by land was impossible. By the eighteenth century, the progeny of these communities had poured southward into the Venezuela llanos (plains), acquired horses and weapons, and become an unruly set of fierce horsemen who, under the leadership of regional

24. For a community study of such an Indian rural township, see Ralph L. Beals, *Community in Transition: Nayon-Ecuador* (Los Angeles: University of California at Los Angeles Latin American Center, 1966).

25. Steward, *Handbook of South American Indians,* IV, 15.

26. See the fascinating description of the failure of conquest in the Esmeraldes by Phelan, *Kingdom of Quito,* pp. 1-22.

chiefs, kept those areas out of effective central control until the twentieth century.[27] T. Lynn Smith has offered interesting data to demonstrate the importance of these groups in Colombia demography; the Colombian state has always been dominated by the Cauca valley and Antioquia, where the White and mainly White mestizo elements are predominant. In the Colombian periphery—coast and Amazonian lowlands—the Indian and African component, heavily mixed, are preponderant.[28]

Still another pattern of resistance to incorporation is represented by groups on the northern and southern flanks of the Spanish empire. The Spanish established an outpost at Buenos Aires in 1536, which was then abandoned in 1541 and not reoccupied until 1580. Some horses escaped at this period, became feral, and multiplied at an extraordinary pace. A similar process at about the same time occurred in the American southwest. In both the Argentine pampas and southern plains Indian groups learned to domesticate and utilize the horses, and transformed their way of life to incorporate this new factor of mobility. They also acquired firearms and became by the eighteenth century a major threat to the Spaniards. In the Argentine case, the linguistically-related Indian groups of central and southern Chile—called Araucanians by the Spanish, Mapuche by themselves—poured across the Andes in the eighteenth century, displaced or acculturated many of the existing Indian groups, and by the late eighteenth century were at the gates of Buenos Aires. In Chile, the Mapuche had horses by the mid-sixteenth century, developed a cavalry tradition, and were able to fix the Bio-Bio River as the effective southern frontier of Spanish rule. A Spanish governor in Santiago, 200 miles to the north, reported to the king of Spain that the campaign against the Araucanians had cost 29,000 Spaniards and more than 60,000 Indian and mestizo auxiliaries. Whatever element of poetry there might have been in these casualty reports, it is evident that pacifying the Mapuche was a different order of task than decapitating the Inca, Aztec, and Chibcha kingdoms.[29] In the nineteenth century, with a large new influx of European immigrants in both Chile and Argentina, the Indian domains became the scene of a frontier struggle, quite comparable to the one unfolding on the American frontier. It was not till 1879 that the Argentine army finally crushed the last Indian resistance, three years after Custer's last stand and twelve years before the Battle of Wounded Knee. In the American southwest, the small Spanish settlements in New Mexico were

27. Norman Gall, "Oil and Democracy in Venezuela," American Universities Field Staff, *Field Staff Reports,* South America, XVII, no. 2 (1973), 1-2.

28. T. Lynn Smith, "The Racial Composition of the Population of Colombia," *Journal of Inter-American Studies,* VII, no. 2 (April 1966), 212-35.

29. Norman Gall, "The Agrarian Revolt in Cautin, Part I: Chile's Mapuches," American Universities Field Staff, *Fieldstaff Reports,* South America, XIX, no. 4 (1972), 7.

increasingly vulnerable to the Comanches and Apaches, armed and horse-borne. The tide of White settlers in this instance, came not from Mexico but from the United States, to seize control in the 1846 War with Mexico of both the Spanish settlements and Comanches and Apaches.[30]

In all of these cases, the Indians, by rejecting and withdrawing from Spanish subjugation, remained outside the pattern of cultural stratification and incorporation which occurred in Mexico, Guatemala, Colombia, and the Andes. Those who found a bare subsistence in the deep recesses of the forest remained totally marginal to the national political systems which succeeded the Spanish empire—too small in numbers to count, too isolated to have access to the currents of change. Those who delayed conquest by matching Spanish military technology had made major adaptive changes in their material culture, and do have a separate identity. Although not much remains of the Araucanians of the Argentine pampas, the Mapuche survived as a compact and self-conscious group in Cautin province, in Chile. Their identity was sharpened by land grievances growing out of settlement by Germans and other immigrants in the late nineteenth century in this fertile area. The radical socialist government of Salvador Allende offered the Mapuche the opportunity to seize and occupy many of the estates in Cautin.

MEXICO: MESTIZATION AND INDIGENISMO

Of the historic centers of Indian culture and dense population, Mexico has gone farthest both in the incorporation of the Indians in the national identity, and in the uses of the myth of the Indian past as a basic component of Mexican nationality. Today 85 percent of Mexicans speak only Spanish, and about half the remainder are bilingual. In the urban core of Mexico, its capital city of Mexico City, only 2 percent are even bilingual in one Indian tongue and virtually none are unilingual Indians.[31] There was from the outset a choice for reliance upon Spanish as the sole linguistic instrument of rule. The most important Indian lingua franca, Nahuatl, did not have the orbit of languages such as Quechua or Tupi, that were utilized, especially by missionaries, as a *lengua general*. The remaining Indian language speakers are scattered in a number of linguistic islands. Even within these areas, it is rare that a compact area of unilingual Indians can be found; only in a few zones do Indian language speakers number more than 60 percent of the area population.

30. See the classic account in Walter Prescott Webb, *The Great Plains* (New York: Grosset and Dunlap, 1957), pp. 114-17.

31. Rubin, *National Bilingualism in Paraguay*, p. 47.

It has been estimated that at the present rate of linguistic shift, all Mexican indigenous languages will be extinct within a century.[32]

While the genetic and linguistic processes of mestization and Hispanization follow their now ineluctable course, *indigenismo* became a national cult. Wolf has described the process well: "Indian themes sounded again in the music of a Carlos Chavez, populated the murals of the Mexican Neo-Realists, guided the brush of a Roberto Ossaye in Guatemala, the hand of an architect designing the new university in Mexico City. Heroes of the Indian past became national archetypes; the bloodthirsty Mexico tyrants were transfigured into champions of the new united nations. Collective scorn and pity were heaped upon a Malinche, the Indian concubine of Cortés, for the betrayal into Spanish hands of her fellow Indians. In the murals of a Siqueiros, Cuauhtemec, the last Mexican king, tortured and put to death by Cortés, achieved a new transfiguration, rising from the dead to affirm a new and glorious future, while—in Diego Rivera's hands—his Spanish protagonist emerged as a hydrocephalic, syphilitic idiot."[33]

Indianism, paradoxically, has little to do with Indians; it is certainly not a cultural ideology developed or articulated by the scattered, rural Indian communities. The literati of Indianism are genetically mestizo, culturally Hispanic, nationally Mexican. Indianism is a philosophy of integration, not separation; Mexico is reconceptualized as the product of cultural fusion, not as the polity of the dominator. The elevation of the Indian component requires a role reversal; Montezuma becomes archangel, and Cortés the antichrist. But Indianism operates wholly in the domain of symbols; it is not a passionate voice of protest at the depressed and impoverished isolation of the vestigal Indian communities, much less a clarion call for the cultural mobilization of Taranean and Totonac, Mayan or Zapotec.

As a political force, the Indian is invisible. There has been one Indian president, Benito Juarez in the late nineteenth century; Juarez as president was a reformer of the classic liberal mold. He fought to circumscribe the role of the Church, and sought to extend the principles of the free market economy to all corners of the land—including the sale of former communal Indian lands. Although the political movement which has dominated Mexican politics since the Revolution, the PRI (Institutional Revolutionary Party) is a confederation of corporate groups; there is no Indian organ within it. The ideology of Mexico as the accomplished cultural fusion has a powerful grip upon the political elites;

32. Wolf, *Sons of the Shaking Earth,* p. 44.

33. Ibid., pp. 248-50. It should be added that, especially in ninteenth-century Argentina and Chile, but also to some extent in Mexico, a racist school of thought enjoyed some vogue, which blamed the Indian and mestizo elements for Latin American backwardness.

within this framework, there can be no "Indian problem." Nor is there any question of social exclusion, of systematic oppression; any of the residual Indians can join Mexico by leaving his Indian community, speaking Spanish, and modelling his external comportment upon the Hispanic model. But there does remain 8.8 percent of the population at the margins of the system who have not yet chosen the mestizo path. Remaining encapsulated within the Indian village is a choice for social isolation, political passivity.

INDIAN AND LADINO IN GUATEMALA

Neighboring Guatemala was a part of the viceroyalty of New Spain, with Mexico, but a colonial backwater containing little to excite strong Spanish interest. The Mayan world was long shattered, and there was no instant wealth to reward the roving conquistador. The Dominicans were able to establish a theocratic bastion and by the seventeenth century were strong enough to hold to a minimum the alienation of Indian lands to Spanish aristocrats. In the domain of identity lexicon, interesting reflection of the friar hegemony is found in the universal use of the term "Ladino" for the culturally Hispanic population of mixed or even full Indian blood which soon emerged. "Ladino" was a term formerly used in Spain for persons of African antecedents who had adopted Spanish speech and ways. Dominicans employed this, a cultural designation, to describe a successful product of their evangel—a Spanish-speaking Indian. In Mexico, under secular dominion, the racial term "mestizo" was employed.[34]

The customary classification of population is bipolar: the census lists Guatemalans as either Ladinos or Indians, despite a modest recent influx of European immigrants, especially Germans, who defy such labelling. Historically, there has been a steady trend toward Ladinoization: in 1774, Indians were 78.4 percent, which dropped to 64.7 percent in 1880, 55.7 percent in 1940, and 43.3 percent in 1964.[35] Guatemala City, the capital, lies at a cultural line of division: in the western highlands, Indians remain heavily preponderant, while to the east Indian enclaves are fewer, and the tides of Ladinoization run more strongly.

The Mayan concept remains the exclusive property of the archaeologist and historian; it is a scholarly kingdom, a living reality in the eye of the beholder, the excavator of the splendid temples overgrown by tropical forest, the tourist marveling at the museum artifacts. It is an extinct

34. Mason, *Patterns of Dominance*, pp. 262-65.
35. van den Berghe, *Race and Ethnicity*, p. 128.

identity for the descendants of the temple builders. Mayan languages have not been unified; they are a maze of dialects, which do not define a broader cultural idea. Loyalty is a relevant behavioral factor at the level of the family and village. Each local community has its own dialect, its special patron saint, often a costume and occupational specialization. To the outsider, the differences between them may appear small indeed. From the village perspective, they are a wall of isolation seldom breached. The villages are nearly endogamous; a stranger speaking another Mayan dialect is not a fellow Mayan, but a foreign Indian. The myth of the Mayan past stirs no memories, mobilizes no identities. One community study found the average Indian unaware that there was a precolonial, pre-Catholic period.[36]

We have argued at several junctures the impact of urbanization on identity-formation. But Guatemala cities are crucibles of Ladinoization; it is difficult to remain an Indian in a new town, precisely because identity was so particularized, family- and village-centered. An incorporative sense of collectivity, either linguistically defined as Mayan or racially defined as Indian, which could serve to congeal affective ties among urban migrants of Indian antecedents has not emerged. "Indian" is a Ladino category, labelling those whom Ladinos see as culturally distinctive and of lower status; differences among Indians are of neither interest nor relevance to Ladinos.[37] In the city, the particular community of the countryside cannot be reconstituted; the solace and security it provided cannot be found through reliance upon identifying marks of Indian affinity. Spanish is the language of the city; Indian dress or traditional hair style are ineffaceable signs of low status. The restless, ambitious young men most apt to make this journey are the most likely to be mobility-oriented and thus to adopt the external behavior of the Ladino. In the anonymity of the city, this cultural metamorphosis is instantly and painlessly accomplished.

Many of the small Indian towns have some Ladino component in their population; at this level, roles are very stratified and relationships between the two communities take on some of the attributes of a caste system. The Ladinos are bound into a nationally oriented class system, while the Indian communities remain self-enclosed. Locally, the name will usually be a reliable indicator as to cultural identity. The functioning of this racial stratification system has been well described in a community 100 miles east of Guatemala City by two social scientists, John Gillin and Melvin Tumin. There were some linkages, in the form of clientage bonds, between Indians and Ladinos; a few Indians would

36. John Gillin, *The Culture of Security in San Carlos* (New Orleans: Tulane University, Middle American Research Institute, Publication no. 16, 1951), p. 77.

37. van den Berghe, *Race and Ethnicity*, p. 148.

invite Ladinos to a social function, but never the reverse—and such functions were likely to generate commentary to the effect that "if so-and-so keeps on getting more ambitious, the *naturales* will think there is no difference between them and us."[38] Intermarriage was rare. Within the walls of the little community, mobility across the cultural line was not possible; to cease being an Indian, the individual would need to migrate elsewhere. Despite the apparent immutability of these barriers, the community was changing. In 1769, a church document records that the town had no Ladinos at all; by the time of these inquiries, the Ladino population was about one-third, and the Indians could generally speak Spanish. Change within the community was kept at a glacial pace by the paucity of communications linkages to the national system. Although the town was an administrative seat, in the early 1950s there were no wheeled vehicles. In the community of 5000, only five Ladinos received Guatemala City newspapers. There was one radio in town. In 1948, about 20 letters per week arrived at the post office. In 1941, 371 private telegrams were sent during the year, and 41 received. The public library consisted of one crate of books, never unpacked, whose most recent date of publication was 1896.[39]

The gradual process of Ladinoization may be seen at many different stages in the relatively abundant community monographs. Manning Nash described a small textile town in the western highlands, where the organization of a union in 1944 (70 years after the establishment of the mill) had provided a novel agency of articulation of common interest, which simple propinquity at the work place for seven decades had not produced. Union office had proved a vehicle of cultural mobility for the leadership; the three top leaders now had frequent occasions for travel to Guatemala City, and two had travelled abroad, one as far as Moscow. However, this cosmopolitan experience redefined them in the eyes of the community; they were now functional Ladinos, from the local community but not of it.[40]

In a community of the Guatemalan Yucatan, Norman Schwartz finds a nearly complete cultural Ladinoization, but a residual ethnic distinction which affects some aspects of social and political behavior. The cultural amalgamation has been only recently completed; in the late nineteenth century the ethnic segments were still sharply distinguished by a number of traits. The Indians remained bilingual, retained a distinctive costume,

38. Gillin, *The Culture of Security in San Carlos*, p. 26.

39. Ibid., pp. 4-7. See also Melvin Tumin, *Caste in a Peasant Society* (Princeton: Princeton University Press, 1952).

40. Manning Nash, *Machine Age Maya* (New York: Free Press of Glencoe, 1958), pp. 82-91.

were manual laborers, and almost exclusively maintained the *cofradía*, or association of the local patron saint, with an annual ritual ceremony then of signal importance to the Indian community. Today, only older persons and a recent influx of Indians from other areas still speak a language other than Spanish. Costume differences have disappeared, and the Indian *cofradía* crumbled in the 1920s; only shoelessness remains associated with Indian ancestry. Vestigial inequalities persist, and most remain aware of the ethnic derivation of established families in the town. This awareness, in a diffuse way, does enter into social relationships—marriages and consensual unions remain about 80 percent homogamous—and political factional alignments. The social atmosphere remains suffused with ethnicity, although overt reference to it is generally avoided.[41]

The other major instance where social mobility has occurred without attendant Ladinoization is in Guatemala's second largest city, Quezaltenango, in the western highlands. Here Indians have severed the moorings of the subsistence economy which enclose the archetypical Indian community and acquired a middle and upper strata component which retains an Indian identity. Within this group, children have passed through the strongly Hispanicizing educational system up through the university level, without becoming socially and functionally Ladinos. It would be such a community that could provide the indispensable intellectual resources for cultural mobilization, yet they have not, thus far, done so. Present evidence does not suggest they are likely to operate as an ethnic pressure group in the national arena.[42]

Over the last three decades, there has been a radical transformation in the power relationships between the Guatemalan national institutions and the rural periphery. In a first stage, Ladino political control over the countryside was augmented through the posting of central functionaries, invariably Ladinos, in local communities. Then, with the democratic revolution of 1944, competitive party politics seeped down to the rural level for the first time, and ideologies of radical transformation began to make some impact. However, as is invariably the Latin American pattern, populist and radical parties, even where their natural con-

41. Norman B. Schwartz, "Assimilation and Acculturation: Aspects of Ethnicity in a Guatemalan Town," *Ethnology*, X, no. 3 (July 1971), pp. 291-310.

42. Richard N. Adams, *Crucifixion by Power*, (Austin: University of Texas Press, 1970), pp. 166-67; van den Berghe, *Race and Ethnicity*, pp. 167-68. Other especially useful monographs dealing with Indian-Ladino relationships include Adams (ed.), *Political Changes in Guatemalan Indian Communities* (New Orleans: Middle American Research Institute, Publication 21, 1957); Sol Tax, *Heritage of Conquest* (Glencoe, Ill.: Free Press, 1952); Tax, *Penny Capitalism* (Chicago: University of Chicago Press, 1963); Robert Redfield, "Relations between Indians and Ladinos in Agua Escondida, Guatemala," *America Indigena*, XVI, no. 4 (October 1956), 253-76.

stituency of the impoverished and forsaken may be heavily Indian, do not employ cultural mobilization as a strategy. Indeed, they could not, as their leadership is Ladino and their social vision inspired by the cultural fusion and class conflict model: a modern Guatemala, led by peasants and workers, not a bicultural polity in which Indians recover their dignity as Mayans. The intensity of the national struggle sharpened in the 1960s, as the major actors benefitted from access to external resources; terrorism and guerrilla warfare on the one hand, ferocious repression on the other became part of the daily routine, with occasional elections leavening the scene. For our purposes, the significance of this struggle lies in the formidable increment of nationally oriented force. Insurgent challengers to the regime had to organize the countryside; the government, and above all the military, in repressing their radical opposition had to vastly increase their penetration of rural areas. Regime and revolution are both Ladino institutions, and their spiralling conflict can only have the effect of accelerating the incorporative process.[43]

THE ROLE OF THE INCA

Ethnic consciousness lies closest to the surface in the successor states of the Inca empire, Peru, Bolivia, and Ecuador. Here the cultural resources for ethnic mobilization are most extensive. Indeed, writing in the late 1940s, one distinguished scholar claimed that Indian sub-nationalism was an established social fact:

During the contact between Indian and Mestizo since the coming of the Spaniards, there has gradually developed a feeling of cultural and linguistic solidarity among the Indians which justifies the use of the term "Inca nation" to refer to the 6 million speakers of *Quechua* and *Aymara* in . . . Ecuador, Peru, and Bolivia. The *Inca* are a "nation" in the sense of being a group which shares a belief in a common culture, and which regards its language as the symbol of its separate existence. No political organization of any kind is implied, for the *Inca* nation exists without any national movement, without parties, and without a separate voice in any government. The feeling of solidarity is certainly present among the modern Indians, and can be traced back at least into the 19th century.[44]

Although we feel that the Inca nation is, in the long run, an unlikely vehicle for effective modern solidarity and political expression, nonetheless predisposing factors are far stronger than anywhere else in

43. The theme of the transformation of Guatemala through central aggregation of power is given important elaboration by Adams, *Crucifixion by Power*.
44. John Howland Rowe, "Inca Culture at the Time of the Spanish Conquest," in Steward, *Handbook of South American Indians*, II, 329-30.

Latin America. The historic myth of Inca has a more comprehensive appeal, both in its splendid achievements and its unifying impact. The Aztec kindgom was an imperfectly established military suzerainty over a congeries of collectivities, which retained both their political and linguistic specificity; Cortés was able to draw powerful support from Indian allies delighted with the opportunity of smashing the Aztec state and exploiting skillfully the endemic conflicts among Indian groups in the Mexican highlands. Although the Inca realm had only been unified during the century before the conquest, its policy of cultural assimilation had been well established and was completed under the Spanish except for the Aymara pocket around Lake Titicaca in Peru and Bolivia. To facilitate use of Quechua as a *lengua general*, the Spanish friars had unified it and equipped it with a written form, dictionaries, and grammars. This stands in sharp contrast to the dialectical chaos of the Mayan zone and lack of development of Indian languages in Mexico. In New Spain, the Spanish found no charm in the tropical humidity of Veracruz on the Mexican coast. The valley of Mexico, however, was not only fertile, but similar to the Iberian environment from whence they had come; thus the center of Hispanic power and influence was seated in the highlands. The rarified atmosphere of the much higher Andean *altiplano*, however, was far less appealing; Lima offered a coastal site where the equatorial sun was dehumidified and moderated by the cold Humboldt current offshore. The seat of empire became Lima, with relatively isolated *audiencias* established in the highlands in Quito and La Paz.[45] The central place of Hispanic culture was geographically separated from the areas of heavy Indian population in the mountains. In one of the rare community studies carried out in Ecuador, Beals found that the small Indian town which he investigated still maintained the legend that their ancestors had been Quechua settlers from the Cuzco Inca heartland, placed as a frontier colony for incorporative purposes—a stark contrast with the Guatemalan instance where conquest as a historical event had evaporated from social memory.[46]

The idea of Inca was invoked as a sanction for rebellion on a number of occasions. In 1742, on the eastern fringe of Quechua-speaking country, an Indian messiah of Cuzco connections, who had lived for a time in Spain, sounded the trumpets of insurrection, claiming that he was at once the son of God and a descendant of the Inca emperor Atahuallpa. This divine messenger, Juan Santos Atahuallpa Apo-Inca, revealed that he had been sent to restore the Inca empire and was endowed with the power to make mountains fall. The zone of his insurrection was mainly

45. This argument is well made in Mason, *Patterns of Dominance*, p. 258.
46. Beals, *Community in Transition*, p. 23.

under mission control; seventy to eighty friars were killed before his movement collapsed.[47]

The most legendary uprising was led in 1780-81 by José Gabriel Condorcanqui, whose memory is inscribed under the Imperial Inca title of Tupac Amarú II, descendant of the last crowned Inca emperor, Tupac Amarú, executed by the Spanish in 1571. His defiance of the colonial order at first won a string of triumphs, and many rallied to the cause of Inca rebellion. However, his ephemeral dominion could not withstand the onslaught of reinforced Spanish troops the following year. The revolt was taken seriously enough to provoke a furious uprooting of Inca symbols; a brief effort was made to suppress Quechua, and all surviving members of the Inca royal house were slain.[48] Although Condorcanqui may have been in the royal line, yet, two centuries after the dissolution of the Inca state, he was culturally mestizo. He had been educated in a Cuzco secondary school, spoke fluent Spanish, was clothed in the garb of the Spanish aristocracy: velvet breeches and beaver hat. From his Spanish visit, one may suspect that the messianic forerunner, Juan Carlos Atahuallpa Apo-Inca, was also Hispanicized. The Inca state that Tupac Amarú II would have created would have been Hispanic and Christian, and not a simple restoration of the old empire—although this vision was by no means shared by all of his followers.[49]

Rebellions in the *altiplano* continued to occur sporadically—in the 1870s, 1886, 1900—with occasional references to Inca symbols.[50] As in Mexico, however, the final resting place of the symbols of Indian identity is in the national pantheon. The radical military regime which assumed power in 1968 has coopted the great emblems of the Inca past; the statues of Pizarro are being removed from city squares, and the full-length portrait that had long hung behind the president's desk has disappeared.[51] While the master conquistador is in disgrace, the greatest rebel, Tupac Amarú II, has been officially designated as national hero. The symbol wielders are, of course, culturally mestizo—but then so was Tupac Amarú.

The first phase of Spanish rule in the viceroyalty of Peru closely resembled what later became known as indirect rule. Until 1571, the framework of the Inca state was Christianized and maintained under

47. Steward, *Handbook of South American Indians*, III, 512.

48. Philip Ainsworth Means, "The Rebellion of Tupac-Amaru II, 1780-1781," *Hispanic American Historical Review*, (II, no. 1, February 1919, pp. 1-25).

49. Steward, *Handbook of South American Indians*, II, 378.

50. Edward Dew, *Politics in the Altiplano* (Austin: University of Texas Press, 1969), pp. 27-28.

51. *New York Times*, 28 January 1973. On this subject, see also John D. Martz, "Formative and Philosophical Bases of *Indigenismo* in Peru and Ecuador," paper presented to 1971 annual meeting of the American Political Science Association, September 1971.

Spanish control at the top with Indian headmen at local levels. Thereafter, the Inca state was progressively dismantled, and its hierarchy disappeared. After the first century of Spanish rule, the Indian nobility as a distinctive social group had vanished. Many became Hispanicized, retaining a respectable status at the price of their identity; identity could only be preserved at the price of status. By 1650 Peru was essentially a mining economy, with Inca society destructured, levelled, and proletarianized. During the early period, the number of Spaniards was not very large—a mere 8000 in 1555, a figure equalled by the number of African slaves, although the latter have all but disappeared as a distinctive group.[52] An acculturated Indian class began to cluster about the Spanish settlements, forerunners of the assimilative wedges that would be driven into Indian society.

Hispanic culture was firmly established on the coast but was very thinly spread in the sierra. The very insecurity of Spanish supremacy in Bolivia, highland Peru and Ecuador may explain the institutional rigidity of the mechanisms which preserved it. Philip Mason, in his comparative inquest into patterns of domination, found that the social chasm between Hispanic landowner and Indian serf was greater in Ecuador, where he heard the most strongly expressed views of the incurable inferiority of the Indian.[53] The expulsion of the Jesuits in 1767 removed one paternal buffer for the Indians. Independence under Creole auspices at the beginning of the nineteenth century, followed by a free land market which led to the constitution of vast latifundia, whose property rights had the full backing of the state, reinforced Indian submergence.

All education and state business required the use of Spanish; mobility was available only through entry into the mestizo sector. An intermediate acculturative label came into general use, "cholo," the bilingual and socially mobile Indian. The political problem in the *antiplano* of Peru, concludes a recent study, "deriving from the castelike separation of mestizo and Indian cultural groups, is the feasibility of cholo assimilation in the mestizo cultural and social institutions, although this would lead . . . to the cholification of those institutions."[54]

A gamut of acculturative situations, as in Guatemala, is suggested in community studies. Lima represents a pole of Hispanicization; only 10 percent of its population speak an Indian language, and virtually all know Spanish.[55] In a small mining town not far from Lima, a former Indian community had become predominantly mestizo only in the pre-

52. James Lockhart, *Spanish Peru 1532-1560* (Madison: University of Wisconsin Press, 1968), pp. 12, 198.
53. Mason, *Patterns of Dominance*, p. 259.
54. Dew, *Politics in the Altiplano*, p. 86.
55. Rubin, *National Bilingualism in Paraguay*, p. 47.

sent century. Quechua was spoken by most of the older generation, especially women, but only about half of the younger people knew it. In 1905, 70 percent of the births were recorded as Indian, a rate which fell to 45 percent in 1940. After 1943, all births were recorded as mestizo; although in a strict sense this reflected the idiosyncracies of cultural conceptualization by the town clerk, it was still significant as evidence of transforming images. In an interesting inquiry into the visibility of identity, a panel of judges long resident in the town were asked to provide racial classification for 457 names of persons known to all of them. There was disagreement on 36.9 percent of the names, who for the most part were either relatively new arrivals or of recently mixed ancestry. Where inferences as to status are customarily drawn from this distinction, the degree of ambiguity is striking. All agreed that physical appearance today provides no decisive clues as to racial classification.[56] In the Ecuadorian community study by Beals, it was a strong-willed priest about the turn of the century who established the first school and applied heavy acculturative pressure. The legacy of his labors was nearly complete literacy in Spanish for those under 40, disappearance of the old long hairstyle for men, and atrophy of most distinctive aspects of dress. This servant of the Lord, as instrument of mestization, had valuable support from the vastly improved communications with Quito, not far away, which began to link the town into the commercial circuits of the capital through market gardening.[57]

The age of mass politics was very late in arriving in the Andes republics; Ecuador and Bolivia in particular have experienced a bewildering sequence of ephemeral dictatorships. However, the enlarging power of the state over its periphery, new currents of radical and revolutionary ideology which have entered the political arena, and the extension of political parties beyond the narrowly based cliques of the past have all made their impact. Ecuador has probably been least affected by the tides of change. In its early days of independence, the Creole elite manipulated the historic symbol of the Inca legacy, arguing that Ecuador was the successor state to Atahuallpa's domain, which had conquered the Inca throne from an Equadorian base shortly before the arrival of Pizarro. However, the reality was a political process in which the Indians played no part. A literacy requirement effectively barred the Indians on those occasions when elections were held. From 1830 to 1963, Ecuador had forty-eight presidents, of whom about 30 percent were army officers. Two decades ago, a leading student of Ecuadorian politics

56. Richard N. Adams, *A Community in the Andes* (Seattle: University of Washington Press, 1959).

57. Beals, *Community in Transition*, p. 25.

estimated that no more than 350 or 400 Ecuadorians were active in political parties, and all were White.[58]

Bolivia, with an even greater history of instability, lacked the coastal anchor of Hispanic domination which Ecuador and Peru possessed. The difference in census classifications is intriguing; Bolivia lists its mestizo-Hispanic component as "White," a term which Ecuador reserved for its upper social elite, and which has vanished entirely from Peruvian population taxonomies. Thus the 1950 Bolivian census listed 37 percent as "White," whereas in reality the genetically European component in Bolivia's population is exceeding small. But the use of the term as a conceptualization of cleavage is of great significance; it serves to magnify, through racial metamorphosis, the distinction between the Spanish-speaking elite and the Indian mass. The Bolivian Revolution of 1952 marked a far-reaching social transformation; for the first time in modern politics, the Indians were politically mobilized and enabled to expel the landlords from their haciendas. The national army was for a time abolished, and the arms were distributed to Indian peasants and mine workers to assure the survival of the revolution. Although a revolt of the impoverished, in racially stratified Bolivia, could be only an Indian revolution, the momentous social conflict was not seen in these terms. Of this alteration Robert Alexander writes: "One interesting aspect of this psychological change was an alteration in the popular vocabulary. Alexander explains this in the following words: 'From that moment the word "Indian" disappeared and was wiped from the language to become a relic in the dictionary. Now there existed the "peasant." The worker of the countryside had been given land and liberty in all of its aspects. "Indian," a feudal concept, was the serf of an epoch which had disappeared.' "[59]

With two decades of perspective on the enduring impact of the Bolivian Revolution, the full meaning of this assertion becomes more clear. It certainly does not mean the final cultural assimilation of the rural Aymara and Quechua populace. Access to land title, however small and unrewarding each piece of land, has for the moment stabilized the rural community. Although the social energies mobilized by the revolution were essentially Indian, the ideological categories in which it was formulated came from the Hispanic elite. Within the parameters of the 1952 social conflict, there was no tension of purpose. The goals which galvanized the participants were land for the rural folk, better returns for mine labor. No alternative conceptualization of deprivation had emerged from Indian milieux; there was no reason to quarrel with the social categories put

58. George I. Blanksten, *Constitutions and Caudillos* (Berkeley: University of California Press, 1951), pp. 5-36.

59. Robert Alexander, *The Bolivian National Revolution* (New Brunswick: Rutgers University Press, 1958), pp. 75-76.

452 THE POLITICS OF CULTURAL PLURALISM

forward by the revolutionary elites. But from there to conclude that the peasant category had been internalized fully as subjective self-concept was a vast—and, for Che Guevara, fatal—inferential leap.

The major alternative to the rural community for most Indians—since the seventeenth century—has been service in the mines. So long has large-scale mining been part of the social landscape that it seems to have existed from time immemorial. There is likely to be someone in the local community with experience in the mines. Recent studies have described in some detail the socialization process for Indian recruits to the mine labor force. Humble, retiring, uncertain of his Spanish, distrustful of strangers and authority-holders, the Indian laborer finds a new social framework with his work group and, above all, the union. The union makes its first contacts in Aymara or Quechua, but expects that in time the recruit will adapt to the Spanish-speaking milieu. The catechism of the union is learned—its part in a broader combat against capitalism and imperialism, its epic struggles, bitter defeats and magnificent triumphs—and its fraternal support is felt through the days of loneliness and anomie. The church, whose local ritual, festivals, and saints are so reassuring a part of the rural community, is bitterly attacked, and the folk way of life denigrated as retrograde and unworthy. In the course of time, the Quechua or Aymara recruit becomes a class-conscious cholo, who shifts to Spanish as a first language by imperceptible degrees, dresses like other workers, and diminishes his ties to the home community. While rural Indian communities are neither culturally mobilized Indians nor, subjectively, peasants, the mining system contains powerful socialization instruments which can make him a worker.[60]

In Peru, revolutionary leaders from urban backgrounds headed for the sierra in 1965, seeking to launch a peasant insurrection. The revolution was essentially a mestizo movement, which—inspired by legendry surrounding the Cuban Revolution, the writings of Guevara and Debray—was to bind itself to the dynamics of peasant discontent. The cosmology of the mestizo revolutionaries had no place for cultural pluralism. The self-criticisms by one of the participants after its failure are illuminating:

The guerrillas were in a difficult position in regard to the peasant masses. . . .
The man from the city discriminates against and feels superior to the man from the country, especially the Quechua peasant. And inversely, the latter distrusts the man from the city. The peasant has always seen him as the exploiter, the man who has come to take away his land, the master.

60. John H. Magill, "Labor Unions and Political Socialization in Bolivia," (Ph.D. diss., University of Wisconsin-Madison, 1972); John M. Hickman and Jack Brown, "Aymara Biculturalism and Sociopsychological Adjustment in Bolivia" (typescript, Department of Anthropology, Cornell University).

A very large proportion of our peasant population speaks only Quechua, and those who are bilingual prefer to speak their native language. They use Spanish only when they have to speak to the landowner. . . .
This may help explain why the process of recruitment of new guerrillas from the places where fighting was going on was very slow. . . .
There is a class factor at the bottom of all of this. The petty-bourgeois origin of the guerrillas gave them all the virtues and defects appropriate to this social sector of our country.
. . . The ideals proclaimed by the guerrillas necessarily appeared remote to the peasants, who were interested above all in their concrete and even local demands. While the guerrillas advocated social revolution, the peasants wanted more tangible things, the realization of small demands that the revolutionaries were not always successful in incorporating into their program. . . .
During his entire existence the peasant is separated from the life of the nation and is unaware of the great national problems, even though he suffers their consequences. In general, there is no developed national consciousness in Peru. . . . Naturally, this consciousness does not exist in the countryside either.[61]

A supplement to this analysis, from a recent study of radical agrarian movements in Peru, argues that what appeal the revolution was able to attract among Indian communities came from the most "traditional" areas, where participation was a collective response. The somewhat more prosperous farmer, bound into the commercial circuits of the modern sector, was more attuned to contemplate individualistic responses to perceived problems—land purchase, litigation, urban migration, use of party or local government channels.[62]

PARAGUAY: CULTURAL FUSION

Paraguay is an exceedingly interesting example of cultural synthesis. By most standards, it is a woebegone polity, forlorn in its poverty. It was certainly a great disappointment to its first Spanish settlers, who had voyaged to the ends of the earth for precious metals. Few ever followed in their footsteps; no huddled masses in Europe ever thought of Paraguay as the answer to their problems. Indexes of democratic political development

61. Hector Bejar, *Peru 1965: Notes on a Guerrilla Experience* (New York: Monthly Review Press, 1969), pp. 114–16.
62. Howard Handelman, "Struggle in the Andes: Peasant Political Mobilization in Peru," (Ph.D. diss., University of Wisconsin-Madison, 1971). The populist APRA party also deserves mention in this connection. Although *indigenista* in rhetoric, it was never really culturally Indian or Quechua, nor did it succeed in creating a real consciousness among Indian groups.

in Latin America inevitably place it at the bottom of the table.[63] No one has ever listed Paraguay among the economic miracles of the developing world. And yet, as an example of cultural integration, its very failures in other domains have contributed to a remarkable success. Every Paraguayan president has been able to speak Guaraní—whereas only one ruler in Mexico (Juarez) and Peru (Sanches Cerro) has been able to speak an Indian language. In the capital city of Asunción, 76 percent are able to speak Guaraní.[64]

A Spanish expedition with 350 men reached Paraguay in 1536. Their hopes were kindled by the sight of metal artifacts in the hands of the Indians; these had been obtained through raids on the fringes of the Inca empire. The Guaraní were receptive to their visitors and found very seductive the proposals for joint plundering expeditions to the places where precious metals could be taken. Several raiding parties did proceed through the arduous territory that separated Asunción from the Andes, but these were costly failures—and it ultimately became clear that Pizarro had beaten them to it. By this time, there was little choice but to settle down to a subsistence existence in the pleasant, fertile, well-watered plains surrounding Asunción.

The Indian hosts for the Spanish Paraguayan expedition were shifting cultivators, organized in small groups. Linguistically, they were part of the Tupi-Guaraní family, which stretched from the Amazon to northern Argentina. Effective social identity, of course, was far more localized; it was not until the seventeenth century that the term Guaraní came into general use to designate Paraguayan Indians. The Spaniards arrived without women; for both security and sexual reasons, marriage into Indian lineages was appropriate. Thus the formation of a mestizo community was immediate and complete, and very few new Spaniards arrived to alter the genetic stock.

After hope for precious metals was abandoned in the latter half of the sixteenth century, an encomienda system was established, with the usual disastrous results for the Indians. By the end of the sixteenth century, there were only 3000 Indians left in a 21-mile radius of Asunción, but a constantly increasing pool of mestizos, whose descendants form the principal stock of 2.5 million Paraguayans. There were some scattered Guaraní revolts in this period, but the small scale of Indian social organization made their defeat relatively easy.[65]

63. Russell H. Fitzgibbon and Kenneth F. Johnson, "Measurement of Latin American Political Change," reprinted in Peter G. Snow, *Government and Politics in Latin America: A Reader* (New York: Holt, Rinehart and Winston, 1967), p. 267.

64. Rubin, *National Bilingualism in Paraguay*, p. 47.

65. Steward, *Handbook of South American Indians*, III, 77.

From 1608 to 1767, in eastern Paraguay the Jesuits organized a series of theocratic Indian settlements, whose paternal order enjoyed striking material success. After the expulsion of the Jesuits in 1767, these communities dispersed, and the whole undertaking became only an exotic episode. The lasting contribution of the Jesuits came through their work in creating a standard Guaraní; an excellent grammar was produced in 1624.[66] This left the Asunción region the only zone of Hispanic impact, a pattern which has remained; 95 percent of the population lives within a 120-mile radius of the capital.

Within this community, the Indian mothers transmitted Guaraní to their children, who were linked through their fathers to the emergent mestizo community. This community had little in common with the Creole aristocracy which developed in the main centers of Spanish empire in America. Despite the depredations of the encomienda period, it was not sharply differentiated from the remaining Indians by language or status. Spanish cultural presence was sustained by a small outpost of the royal bureaucracy, the missions, and a very rudimentary school system—a modest infrastructure, but sufficient as the authority pole, the cosmopolitan medium.

It took little effort for the Asunción city council to depose the Spanish governor in 1811, but rather more vigilance to keep the expansive Argentinians at bay. During the rigorous dictatorship of José Francia, 1811-40, Paraguay was held in total isolation, and its already slight educational endowment further shrivelled. In 1864-70, Paraguay launched into one of the most suicidal wars of all time, taking on Brazil, Uruguay, and Argentina simultaneously. This adventure cost 50,000 square miles of territory, half the population, and six years of Argentine occupation. In the wake of the occupation, there was a period of strong Argentine influence, marked by assimilative cultural policy and downgrading of Guaraní. In 1894, a minister of education called it "a great enemy of cultural progress."[67]

The Chaco War with Bolivia (1932-35) marked a turning point. As a means of securing their communications, the Paraguayan army used Guaraní exclusively in the battlefield, building a new linkage between the language and Paraguayan nationalism; "use of Guaraní made the troops feel that they were defending the essence of what was uniquely Paraguayan and it helped mold them together against all opposition."[68] In 1944, a Chair of Guaraní was established at the National University. In 1950, an Association of Guaraní Writers was formed, and active government encouragement given to the Guaraní renaissance.

66. Rubin, *National Bilingualism in Paraguay*, p. 23.
67. Ibid., p. 28.
68. Ibid., p. 29.

An interesting division of function exists between the two languages. Guaraní is the language of popular songs, poetry, and informal, casual communication. Spanish is the medium for more formal transactions, all government business, most radio programs and films. Guaraní is not taught as a subject in most schools, although promoters of the language advocate such a step; thus, the habits and disciplines of the educational system serve to preserve Spanish as the primary written language. Guaraní is a language associated with national identity, which connotes the uniqueness of Paraguay. Although Spanish is clearly the higher status language, no particular emotional commitment attaches to it. No special defense of Spanish is required; its status is not in doubt. Guaraní devotees argue only for the extension of bilingualism. Only 8 percent of the Paraguayan population are monolingual Spanish-speakers; 52 percent are bilingual. Monolingual Guaraní speakers are exclusively rural, and at the bottom of the social scale.[69]

Paraguay is an unusually integrated polity in every respect; the compact nature of the settled part of the country brings Asunción and its politics within the communication orbit of all. Two community studies showed that virtually everyone gets to Asunción, at least occasionally.[70] The bilingual culture of Paraguay is essentially mestizo; the Indian component survives primarily through the language, while in other respects the modal traits are of Hispanic derivation. Whatever blemishes Paraguay as polity may bear, this little state, in its poverty and isolation, has fashioned a cultural synthesis rare in its harmony.

PEASANT OR INDIAN: THE ABSENCE OF THE ETHNIC METAPHOR

As we survey the Hispanic-American universe as a whole, the dominant fact is that the solidarity of the oppressed is not conceptualized in the lexicon of cultural pluralism. We may now return to the question posed at the beginning of the chapter, and suggest some general reasons why this should be so. The basic cultural quality of Latin America was instantly converted by conquest into a stratified relationship. Hispanic culture established an unambiguous supremacy, based upon its monopoly of power, its strategic locus at the urban terminus of the folk-urban continuum. Spiritual conquest as a dimension of Spanish colonial policy established a religious bond between the two cultures, but a bond

69. Ibid., p. 14.

70. Elman R. Service and Helen S. Service, *Tobati: Paraguayan Town* (Chicago: University of Chicago Press, 1954), pp. 16-18; Rubin, *National Bilingualism in Paraguay*, p. 31.

firmly rooted in the Hispanic heritage. Christianity, adapted to folk society, is as much a part of the social identity in Indian villages as
Islam is for Berbers in the Maghreb; in the same way, superordinance
acquired an implicit religious sanction. Demography and epidemiology
played a more important part than has been generally recognized. The
triumph of mestizo in Mexico could hardly have occurred with
its present completeness had it not been for the elimination of 6/7 of the
Indian population in the first century of Spanish rule, primarily through
the ravages of new diseases; to a lesser degree, similar impact was made on
other zones of high precolonial population densities. The sixteenth century
Spanish influx was not large numerically, and there was very little additional infusion of European stock until after 1840. Even then, the new
migration was strongly concentrated in the temperate zones. The
significance of this factor may be seen in the quite different identity
patterns emergent in the Philippines, occupied roughly at the same time
but never decimated. Time as a variable must also be given its due place.
The Spanish colonial period lasted for three centuries, in which time the
processes of cultural interaction and transformation could slowly work
themselves out, without external factors impinging. The idea of
nationalism was not abroad in the world. In areas where the social
hegemony of Spanish culture was made precarious by the numerical
imbalance, it could be institutionalized by a rigid, castelike system without
being brought before the bar of world opinion.

When independence came, it was the exclusive reserve of the Creole
elite, who laid sole claim to the new idea of nationalism and acquired
full control over the authoritative political institutions, however limited
their real influence over the rural periphery was in most states. By
this time, Indians had either been totally subordinated at the base of a
social caste system, retreated to the marginal subsistence existence of
remote forest areas, or, in the case of Argentina, Chile, and parts of
Mexico later seized by the United States, established themselves on the far
side of a hostile frontier on the basis of horse-borne mobility and possession of firearms. In the Chile instance, the Mapuche have remained
a culturally self-conscious group even after their subjugation in the 1880s,
and have exercised a collective pressure upon Chilean politics in the contemporary period.

But the large Indian populations of Guatemala and the Andes were
deprived of the cultural resources for a collective response to their
subordinated status. The highly structured Indian societies of Mexico
and Inca were both levelled and atomized. Social units were completely
localized, linked vertically by multiple bonds of dependence to the state,
the hacienda, and the church, but were wholly lacking in horizontal ties.

In Guatemala, where the atomization was most complete and where, it would appear, even the idea of a preconquest society was as remote as it was to the Maghreb Berbers, each community was endogamous, dialectically distinct, and habituated to viewing other Indians as "foreign Indians." In the Quechua-speaking zone, the historical myth of the Inca and linguistic integration offered a greater potential base for cultural mobilization; but this has not yet occurred and on balance appears unlikely.

The overwhelmingly Hispanic basis of the state, the urban sector, and the modern economy everywhere save in Paraguay creates a formidable acculturative machinery. Its pressures have become more ubiquitous in the twentieth century, as the power of the state and the national society has greatly increased, and the penetration of its infrastructure of cultural socialization into the countryside through the school system, the administration, and nationally oriented media has ramified and extended. Except in such rare cases as Quezaltenango in Guatemala, social mobility through the vehicle of Indian culture is simply not available. The pivot of Indian identity is the local rural community, whose economic horizons are severely limited. For the ambitious, the aspirant, the mobility-seeking among the young, there is no alternative but migration to town, education, wage employment—all of which require mastery of Spanish, and cultural adjustments which, with or without conscious choice, involve surrender of Indian identity to enter the mestizo world. Thus the very persons who, in other settings, have politicized ethnicity and forged cultural ideologies are continuously drained away from the Indian communities.

The availability of the mestizo channel of mobility is crucial and distinguishes the Latin American setting from most culturally plural environments. Although Indian subordination takes on the severity of a caste system in some times and places, in its actual operation it is localized. One may not be able to escape the identity ascribed by birth in the local community, but it is readily available by migration—which, for the rural young person, will probably be necessary in any case for real mobility. In the countries of high Indian populations, genetic mixing has been continuing for so long that the physical differences are slight; while an Indian migrant might be conspicuous racially in Stockholm or Montreal, he is not in Lima or Guatemala City, if he speaks Spanish and wears the clothing characteristic of urban people. The social situation, therefore, does not force the Indian to react as an Indian. Individual mobility through cultural migration is not an option open for the American Black. For most, this vehicle of individual choice is far less exacting than to contemplate ethnic mobilization and cultural confrontation—which, for the Black, is a necessity.

The structure of the political arena is likewise a potent factor. No Latin American political movement has ever operated on the national level through the mobilization of Indian racial or ethnic solidarity. Radical and revolutionary ideologies, which address themselves to the deprivation of the poor, do so through the metaphor of social class. These protest ideologies, heavily influenced by the Marxist tradition which developed in class societies, have an important impact in the shaping of social reality. To the mestizo intellectuals who are the manipulators and formulators of political ideologies, Indians are and must be peasants; they cannot be incorporated within the framework of protest as Indians, or Quechua. It is, of course, appreciated that they are in fact Indians, especially after Che Guevara's misadventures in Bolivia, and the failure of rural insurgency in Peru and Guatemala in the 1960s. But this can be seen as a problem of false consciousness; what is required is not the abandonment of the ideological premises, but the reshaping of rural consciousness in function of the categories of revolutionary thought. And history may well reward this revolutionary faith. The force of dominant paradigms of society in fulfilling their own visions should not be underestimated. The social categories into which mankind divides itself are, after all, human creations; Adam found neither class conflict nor cultural pluralism. The reality of any category comes from the general recognition and assent which it commands. In this sense, in the final analysis and in the long run, society probably does tend to become what men think that it is.

Lastly, the nature of Indianism as a political idea, where it occurs, deserves notice. In Mexico, Peru, and Paraguay, symbols drawn from the Indian past play an important part in the ideology of national identity. However, even in Paraguay, *indigenismo* is an instrument of mestizo symbol wielders and not a symptom of Indian cultural mobilization. The rehabilitation of Montezuma and Tupac Amarú as culture heroes is to embody the unity of the national culture, which is securely Hispanic. The very pre-emption of the symbols of Indianhood by nationally oriented elites epitomizes the cultural pathway on which Latin American states are embarked.

12 Biafra, Bangladesh, and Southern Sudan: The Politics of Secession

Things fall apart; the centre cannot hold;
Mere anarchy is loosed upon the world.

—W. B. Yeats

Separation might appear a ready solution for cultural pluralism; if one or more groups believe that ethnic security cannot be assured within the existing state or that their linguistic or religious aspirations cannot be satisfied, then what could be simpler than creating a territorial base which can be endowed with sovereignty. Communal safety, cultural fulfillment can then be assured by the new state which reflects the solidarity of the separating group. Yet the fact of the matter, as we argued in chapter 3, is that states rarely break apart voluntarily.

That in almost all situations the state may be counted upon to have the will and capacity to resist secession by force must enter the calculations of those contemplating separation. Far from being an easy solution, it is an option which can be exercised only at the cost of civil war. Secession is a costly adventure, which can only be contemplated when perceived cultural threat reaches an extraordinary level of immediacy. In the three cases we wish to examine, Biafra, Bangladesh, and Southern Sudan—the trigger events did raise fears of cultural annihilation; there was, of course, no such intent, but the atmosphere was so charged with anxiety that many among the seceding groups were able to place such a construction upon the flow of events. It is not our purpose to offer a detailed history of any of these secession attempts, but rather to inquire into their causes, assess their cultural basis, and evaluate the determinants of final outcome. More broadly, we seek further illumination of the themes of this study through comparative exploration of three instances of politics at moments of extreme cultural stress.

BEING IBO

On 30 May 1967, Lt. Col. Chukwuemeka Ojukwu, son of a Nigerian millionaire and then ranking Ibo officer in the Nigerian army, proclaimed "that the territory and region known as and called Eastern Nigeria together with her continental shelf and territorial water shall henceforward be an independent sovereign state of the name and title of 'The Republic of Biafra.' "[1]

Thus was born the ill-fated republic of Biafra, which lasted nearly a thousand days, until the flight of Ojukwu on 10 January 1970. Although the proclamation of independence contained no ethnic referents, from the outset the secession related essentially to the situation, the discontents, and above all the fears of the Ibo, who were the dominant group in the old Eastern Region of Nigeria. To understand the communal dynamics of the Biafran secession, we need first turn to the crystallization of Ibo subnationalism, and the Ibo situation within the Nigerian Federation.

Being Ibo, a concept for which unflinching sacrifice was made by millions, is a modern identity. First use of the term appears to date from the slave trade days, as a rough label for those originating in hinterland Eastern Nigeria and speaking related languages. There was neither a common political system nor a unifying myth of ancestry, around which identity could focus prior to colonial rule. Social units were village groups, of somewhat varying leadership patterns. The closest approximation to a shared communication system and common symbols which might have sustained transvillage identity was the Aro Chuku trading community. Their travellers were able to move with security because of supernatural protection provided by a powerful oracle (the "long juju") whose magical capacities were legendary in the region.[2] However, as late as the 1930s many Aro Chuku still denied that they were Ibo.

Iboland was the most difficult part of Nigeria to subdue. The centralized Hausa-Fulani emirates could be conquered from the top; in Yorubaland utter fatigue from the debilitating nineteenth-century civil wars and the intermediary role of distinguished Yoruba churchmen and coastal elites led to ready acceptance of British rule. But acephalous Iboland had to be subjugated segment by segment. In the process, very negative early stereotypes of "Ibo" developed; Ibo, to the British, compared most unfavorably with the aristocratic culture of the emirates of the Yoruba kingdoms and nascent Lagos elite. Doubtless this pejorative image explains the former eagerness of the Aro Chuku to dissociate themselves

---

1. Kirk-Greene, *Crisis and Conflict in Nigeria*, I, 451-52. This superb, annotated documentary record of the Nigerian civil war is an invaluable and comprehensive source.

2. Stephenson, in *Population and Political Systems in Tropical Africa,* argues in confronting the paradox of the high population density without political centralization in Iboland that the Aro Chuku were a protostate.

from the group, an attitude shared by Onitshans, who pointed to their historic connections with the Benin kingdom.[3]

By the 1930s, the Ibo image was beginning to change, with prejudicial views of the uncouth bush Ibo giving way to the aggressive, intensely competitive, modernizing new man. Some have argued that Ibo village society was unusually competitive, with leadership and recognition accruing to the strong achiever.[4] Another factor was the high population densities, virtually compelling many young men to seek their fortunes out of the village. A psychologist has argued that the initial negative stereotype itself may offer the explanation; recognizing that they were despised by the colonizer, Ibo developed a new self-image which incorporated traits more likely to win status respect, with material success in the forefront. This new value synthesis, it is argued, was transmitted to and internalized by the new generation.[5]

We need not further unravel this puzzle; whatever the causes, the consequences are beyond dispute. By the end of World War I, the idea of education spread rapidly in Iboland, conjointly with the proposition that the area lagged behind, had to "catch up." Competitive modernization was also internally measured; each community had the achievements of its neighbors as reference points and entered the race to "get up", individually and collectively. Tangible measures of community achievement and status lay in the artifacts of modernity—a school, a dispensary, a road, a church.[6]

Urbanization provided the competitive crucible in which active self-awareness was forged. Lagos was the prime cockpit; here the Yoruba had long dominated the elite ranks. In the Ibo challenge to their social hegemony, perceptible from the mid-1930s, ethnicity among both Ibo and Yoruba was sharpened and politicized. The first overt manifestations of an ethnic conceptualization of social rivalry came in the most prominent African organization of the epoch, the Nigerian Youth Movement, which became torn by ethnic factionalism on the eve of World War II. However, even at this point, Ibohood was a relatively novel and limited idea. Interesting testimonial to this fact is found in the commentary of M. M. Green, one of the first anthropologists to work in Iboland. Her field

3. Audrey C. Smock, *Ibo Politics* (Cambridge: Harvard University Press, 1971), p. 8.

4. Simon Ottenberg, 'Ibo Receptivity to Change," in William R. Bascom and Melville J. Herskovits (eds.), *Continuity and Change in African Cultures* (Chicago: Phoenix Books, 1959), pp. 130-42.

5. Robert A. Levine, *Dreams and Deeds: Achievement Motivation in Nigeria* (Chicago: University of Chicago Press, 1966), pp. 87-88.

6. On Ibo uplift, see Uchendu, *The Igbo of Southeast Nigeria;* Abernethy, *The Political Dilemma of Popular Education.* Many Nigerian scholars now prefer the *Igbo* spelling, but we retain here the more common usage.

work was in the early 1930s; however, it was only later that she recognized the potential social significance of the identity question:

There is no doubt that an increasing number of educated or sophisticated Ibo-speaking people are coming to use the name both about their whole people and their language and with a more or less clear idea of the unit to which the name refers. The name, in fact, is becoming a symbol of unity. . . .

As with most people, in fact, the Ibo feel the bonds between them most closely when they are confronted by foreigners. Two men from whatever part of Ibo-speaking country when they meet in Lagos or in London will call themselves brothers. Increasing sophistication is bringing a clearer notion of belonging to the whole unit of Ibo-speaking people. At home, however, people will count themselves as belonging to their village group, will recognize the neighboring village-groups as people with whom they trade and marry, and will say of the people beyond a radius of about seven miles: "The people of that place are very wicked."[7]

As Ibo communities developed in cities all over Nigeria, a rich fabric of ethnic associations, representing localities or regions in Iboland began to emerge. These bodies, dedicated to uplift, served as organs of self-help and mobility. They provided scholarships to promising young men, who could then be relied upon as spokesmen for the community; they founded many schools; they defended the status claims of the collectivities they represented.[8] In 1936 came the first attempt at pan-Ibo organization, when a convention was summoned of the Lagos-based ethnic unions representing Ibo sub-groups. The plea for the Ibo unity had one of its first public airings by a meeting organizer: "Brethren, this is the day and the hour when the Ibos of Nigeria should rally together . . . [and] sink all differences—geographical, lingual, intellectual, moral, and religious, and unite under the banner of our great objective—the tribal unity, cooperation and progress of all the Ibos."[9]

In 1944, organization on a more ambitious scale was endeavored, with the launching of the Ibo Federal Union. This body, as well as the more local ethnic unions, turned its energies to awakening the rural populace as to the urgent requirements of competitive modernization. The nature of the context could only be made clear by ethnic evangelization, by leading villagers to comprehend the larger solidarity unit whose fortunes they shared, as well as identifying the rivals who blocked the path. This task commanded the full energies of the ethnic associations, Ibo and other, in a process well described by David Abernethy:

7. M. M. Green, *Ibo Village Affairs* (London: Sidgewick and Jackson, 1947), pp. 6-7.

8. See the useful case study of these flourishing bodies by Smock, *Ibo Politics*; for a memorable novel describing a typical improvement association, see Chinua Achebe, *No Longer at Ease* (London: Heinemann, 1960).

9. Coleman, *Nigeria: Background to Nationalism*, p. 340.

What was the best course of action open to the urban migrant who was acutely concerned lest his ethnic group fall behind others in the struggle for wealth, power and status? Certainly the rural masses had to be informed of the problem. If the masses were not aware of their ethnicity, then they would have to learn who they really were through the efforts of "ethnic missionaries" returning to the homeland. These "missionaries" would also have to outline a strategy by which the ethnic group, once fully conscious of its unity and its potential, could compete with its rivals. . . . The gospel of ethnicity and the gospel of education were thus mutually reinforcing. Educational schemes sponsored by the tribal unions fostered ethnic consciousness in the rural areas; a heightened sense of ethnicity, in turn, facilitated the spread of education.[10]

For the Ibo, the magnitude of the challenge was confessed by Ibo Federal Union general secretary B.O.N. Eluwa, who travelled widely as "ethnic missionary" through Iboland in 1947-51; many rural folk, he notes, could not even imagine all Ibos.[11]

It was an Ibo, Nnamdi Azikiwe, who emerged in the 1940s as the stormy petrel of the new Nigerian nationalism. Ebullient, mercurial, extravagant in his rhetoric, indefatigable journalist, entrepreneur: his outspoken defence of African rights and flamboyance marked him for leadership. Azikiwe certainly did not regard himself as an ethnic politician; his 1937 book, *Renascent Africa*, vigorously denounces tribalism, develops an historical rationale for the cultural unity of Africa, and speaks of independence in a broader West African frame.[12] But these disclaimers did not satisfy his opponents, often irritated by the bumptious Azikiwe style. Many, especially Yoruba, began to complain that the new movement led by Azikiwe, the NCNC, was a thinly veiled instrument of Ibo domination. They noted that Ibo appeared to rally unanimously to the NCNC banners and that there was some overlap in leadership between the NCNC and the Ibo Federal Union. From an Ibo perspective, the NCNC and Azikiwe were attractive because they were the most vigorous voices of Nigerian nationalism on the scene; Azikiwe as leader was, of course, a matter of pride and helped bestow confidence in the movement. But there was every reason for the Ibo follower to repudiate with sincere indignation the allegations of diabolical Ibo intent; if it be true that Ibo are solid backers of the NCNC, went the reply, it is only because the Ibo are more fervent in their nationalism than other Nigerians. And it was precisely this occasional theme of the special role in nationalism entrusted to Ibo by virtue of their receptivity to modernization, their national outlook dictated by their diaspora to all major Nigerian cities, which others were wont to interpret

10. Abernethy, *The Political Dilemma of Popular Education,* p. 108.
11. Ibid., p. 110.
12. Nnamdi Axikiwe, *Renascent Africa* (Accra: published by the author, 1937).

as a disguised will to dominate. Chief Obafemi Awolowo, the leading pre-independence rival to Azikiwe, gives pungent voice to these views in his autobiography:

Besides, in spite of his protestations to the contrary, Dr. Azikiwe was himself an unabashed Ibo jingoist. And he gave the game completely away when he said inter alia in his presidential address to the Ibo Federal Union in 1949, as follows: "It would appear that the God of Africa has specially created the Ibo nation to lead the children of Africa from the bondage of the ages. . . . The martial prowess of the Ibo nation at all stages of human history has enabled them not only to conquer others but also to adapt themselves to the role of preserver."

It was clear from these statements and from the general political and journalistic maneuvers of Dr. Azikiwe over the years that his great objective was to set himself up as a dictator over Nigeria and to make the Ibo nation the master race. It would appear according to his reckoning that the only obstacle in the path of his ambition was the Yoruba intelligentsia, and these must be removed at all costs. . . . I am implacably opposed to dictatorship as well as the doctrine of *Herrenvolk* whether it was Hitler's or Dr. Azikiwe's.[13]

The 1950s were a decade of constant electoral activity and consolidation of political Ibohood. National or regional elections took place in 1951, 1953, 1954, 1956, and 1959; competition was keen and open, and great things were in the wind. It was during this period that ethnic perceptions of national politics became entrenched, and ethnic alignment became a self-fulfilling prophecy. Because political vocabulary became saturated with ethnic references, overt or implicit, popular cognitions were shaped accordingly. Anticipating an ethnic strategy by one's opponent, elemental instincts of self-defense dictated a comparable response.

Ibohood, it should be stressed, was not the only politically relevant level of identity. For many social and political purposes, identification with a given town, region, or clan might be the prime focus of loyalty. At the organizational level, the pan-Ibo body, the Ibo Federal Union (later Ibo State Union), was never as active or important as the matrix of local ethnic unions in Iboland. "Despite its grandiose self-image," Smock reports, "the Ibo State Union never effectively coordinated the activities of other Ibo ethnic unions and never exerted appreciable influence on the NCNC."[14] It was in these local bodies that individuals participated directly, and through which the uplift and self-help activities took place. Rivalries within Iboland were sharp and often bitter, and the dialectic of competitive modernization also operated between Ibo subgroups.

13. Obafemi Awolowo, *Awo* (Cambridge: Cambridge University Press, 1960), p. 172.
14. Smock, *Ibo Politics*, p. 17.

The first nodal point of change and new opportunity in Iboland was the Niger River port and trading center of Onitsha; it was the base for British penetration of Iboland, beginning in 1905. The missions, administration, and trading companies, as they unfurled across the Ibo countryside, brought with them Onitshan convert teachers and clerks, offering these new men an opportunity to acquire wealth on a scale previously unknown. The continuously expanding occupational opportunities drew Onitsha people from the home community in large numbers, and by the 1930s educated Onitsha men had become a significant component of the new permanent urban elite throughout Nigeria. "The number of Onitsha men who have attained great prominence in Nigerian affairs is remarkable in proportion to their total population," concludes a recent study, and "since they provided one of the first truly interlocally oriented elite strata of Nigerians, it is perhaps not surprising that some of the most active nationalistic Nigerian politicians (including Azikiwe) have been natives of Onitsha."[15] Onitshans, who numbered no more than 10,000, stressed their historic ties to the Benin kingdom, found dignity in their sacred chief, the *Obi*, and in many cases, as argued above, long denied their ethnic relationships with the Ibo. Locally, they were locked in bitter struggle, economic and political, with immigrants to Onitsha from elsewhere in Iboland.[16] A comparable political rivalry over social leadership in Umuahia between local Ibo clans is recorded by William and Judith Hanna.[17] Within the compass of Eastern Region politics, a sharp contest between Onitsha and Owerri was frequently discernable.

THREATS TO IBOHOOD

In 1945, an ominous event occurred in the northern Nigerian city of Jos. Without warning, a minor confrontation escalated into serious rioting directed against the Ibo immigrant community, with a number of lives lost.[18] In 1953, a graver outburst of mob fury, with Ibos the primary victims, erupted in the Hausa city of Kano.[19] Although they

15. Richard N. Henderson, in Melson and Wolpe, *Nigeria: Modernization and the Politics of Communalism*, p. 232.
16. See the account of this struggle in Richard L. Sklar, *Nigerian Political Parties* (Princeton: Princeton University Press, 1963), pp. 151-57.
17. Horace Miner (ed.), *The City in Modern Africa* (London: Pall Mall, 1967), pp. 151-84.
18. Leonard Plotnikov, *Strangers to the City* (Pittsburgh: University of Pittsburgh Press, 1967), p. 49.
19. John Paden gives a detailed account of the 1953 and 1966 Kano riots in Melson and Wolpe, *Nigeria: Modernization and the Politics of Communalism*, pp. 115-33.

seemed isolated outbursts at the time, they gave stark testimony to the vulnerability of the diaspora Ibo communities, in a period of sharpening political competition.

We have described in chapter 8 the rising fears and anxieties which mingled with the great hopes of independence, and the role of the federal elections of 1959 and especially 1964 in traumatizing ethnic insecurities. Other threatening trends heightened the sense of communal isolation and insecurity among Ibos. The efforts to conduct a national census in 1962-63, which everyone now recognized would largely define the cultural distribution of power, was profoundly unsettling. Suspicions that the southern regions had fraudulently dilated their figures led to cancellation of the first results and a costly retally. The second canvass again revealed some quite remarkable demographic trends. The Northern Region grew by 70 percent over the previous decade, the Western Region more than doubled, while the Eastern Region grew by only 50 percent. Ibo leaders believed they had been the victims of statistical surgery which amputated their parliamentary representation.

The Northern Region made clear that its vision of Africanization of the public service was Northernization, not Nigerianization, an exclusion particularly felt by Ibo civil servants. Expatriates—whose contracts were commutable—were preferred to southern Nigerians, who might lay claim to permanent employment guarantees. The federal civil service and public corporations became ethnic battlegrounds. The federal universities were torn by ethnic rivalry, mainly pitting Ibo and Yoruba against one another. The Ibo vice-chancellor of the University of Lagos was forced out by a Yoruba majority on its governing board; the distinguished Ibo historian and vice-chancellor of the University of Ibadan, K. O. Dike, cried out in despair at the paralysis of the institution that intellectuals were "the worst pedlars of tribalism."[20] In March 1964, the Western Regional government issued a white paper alleging Ibo domination of an array of public corporations; the Ibo director of Nigerian Railways was held responsible for the fact that 270 of 431 senior posts were held by Ibos; comparably, of 103 in the Nigerian Ports Authority, 73 were Ibos.[21] The noose appeared to tighten, as Ibo directors were placed on the defensive or, in a number of instances, forced out. East and north fought bitterly over the siting of the $75 million iron and steel complex; the Solomonic resolution of splitting it in two left both angry. The mood of the times is well captured by the remarks of the Northern delegation to constitutional talks in September 1966:

We all have our fears of one another. Some fear that opportunities in their own areas are limited and they would therefore wish to expound [sic] and venture

20. Kirk-Greene, *Crisis and Conflict in Nigeria,* I, 20.
21. Mackintosh, *Nigerian Government and Politics,* p. 559.

unhampered in other parts. Some fear the sheer weight of numbers of other parts which they feel could be used to the detriment of their own interests. Some fear the sheer weight of skills and the aggressive drive of other groups which they feel has to be regulated if they are not to be left as the economic, social, and possibly political, under-dogs in their own areas of origin in the very near future. These fears may be real or imagined; they may be reasonable or petty. Whether they are genuine or not, they have to be taken account of because they influence to a considerable degree the actions of the groups towards one another and, more important perhaps, the daily actions of the individual in each group towards individuals from other groups.[22]

The cynical rigging of the October 1965 Western Region elections was the final act of the decomposition of the First Republic. A cabal of army majors seized time by the forelock; on 15 January 1966 they put into operation a plan which appeared to include simultaneous capture of authority in Lagos and the regional capitals. Although the coup-makers did succeed in assassinating the federal prime minister and Western and Northern premiers, seizing temporary control of the Northern capital of Kaduna, in Lagos itself the putsch came apart, and the commander-in-chief, J.T.U. Aguiyi Ironsi, himself an Ibo, rallied the garrison. The surviving members of the federal government abdicated power to Ironsi.

JANUARY 1966: THE COUP OF THE IBO MAJORS

So totally discredited was the *ancien régime* that the new military government was at first received throughout the country with jubilation or, at the very least, benevolent toleration. The majors viewed themselves as instruments of liberation, dedicated to the very highest purposes of resurrection and unity of the Nigerian nation; the declaration by the leader of the putsch in the North, Major C. K. Nzeogwu, announcing the action conveys the flavor of the coup-makers' ideology—radical purification and cleansing of the sick and corrupt body politic, riddled with nepotists, tribalists, swindlers, and profiteers. His stiff warning to malefactors reveals at once the puritanism and the naiveté of the majors: "You are hereby warned that looting, arson, homosexuality, rape, embezzlement, bribery or corruption, obstruction of the revolution, sabotage, subversion, false alarm, and assistance to foreign invaders are all offences punishable by death sentence."[23]

22. Quoted in Kirk-Greene, *Crisis and Conflict in Nigeria*, I, 14-15.
23. Ibid., I, 125-36. It is worth noting that Major Nzeogwu was born and brought up in Kaduna, Northern Nigeria, and spoke Hausa better than Ibo; in this history we find reflected the intimate linkage of national and ethnic identities, and the relative lack of saliency of language as a basis for Ibo identity.

Only by bits and pieces did the public learn more about precisely what had transpired on 15 January; as a patterned perception began to emerge, elements of the composition and tactics of the coup gave rise to growing suspicions outside of Iboland as to its purposes. First, there was the jarring discovery that most of the conspirators were Ibo; this included 6 of the 7 majors and 19 of the 23 second-echelon ringleaders. There were certainly other important bonds linking the coup-makers: they were of an age-set within the army, had been trained together, and had come to know each other intimately and develop a high level of trust. Ibos were heavily represented in those particular rank levels of the army. But they were also embarked on an adventure which was revolutionary if it succeeded, and treasonous if it failed; there was thus strong reason to be circumspect in confiding details of the scheme to those who might be deemed likely to betray the plan to the officeholders.

Second, assassination within and without the army had the appearance of ethnic selectivity. The Yoruba western premier, S. L. Akintola, the Fulani northern premier, Sir Ahmado Bello, and the Hausa federal prime minister, Sir Abubakar Tafewa Balewa, were killed; the midwestern premier, Dennis Osadebay, and the eastern premier, Michael Okpara—both Ibo—were untouched. Within the army, at the time of the coup, there were twenty officers of the grade of lieutenant colonel or above, who outranked the majors. Seven of those were murdered in the coup; of the dead, only one was an Ibo—he was killed for refusing to hand over the keys of Lagos armory to the conspirators. Of the five northern and western senior officers who survived, two were abroad, one was vacationing in his home town, one (Gowon, now president) had a very lucky escape, and the fifth was believed in league with the coup-makers.[24] Five of the six Ibo officers of this rank escaped, although one or more may have been listed for assassination. None of these facts validate the communal conspiracy theory; however, they were more than sufficient to confirm suspicions by others in an inflamed atmosphere of fear and distrust.

Diffuse suspicion settled into hardened conviction in the months of the Ironsi regime from January to July 1966. General Ironsi was far from an Ibo chauvinist—indeed, he may well have been slated for execution. A series of acts with heavy symbolic connotations fed ethnic fears. The Ibo majors who carried out the coup, although arrested, were not placed on trial, a source of particular indignation to northern officers and men, outraged over the murder of four of the five ranking northern officers. Nor was there ever any official acknowledgment of their death, which

24. Robin Luckham, *The Nigerian Military* (Cambridge: Cambridge University Press, 1971), pp. 43-50. This meticulous and judicious reconstruction of the coup, read in conjunction with Kirk-Greene, *Crisis and Conflict in Nigeria,* and Walter Schwarz, *Nigeria* (New York: Frederick A. Praeger, 1968), offers the best insight into this turbulent period.

facilitated the circulation of rumors of miraculous escapes and super-natural deeds by the dead officers. In May 1966, 12 promotions were announced to the grade of lieutenant colonel to replace the murdered officers; although strict seniority criteria was used, 9 of the 12 were Ibo. Ironsi seemed to rely more and more upon an inner circle of four talented and dedicated public servants—all of whom were Ibo.[25] The catalytic spark came with the 24 May 1966 decree, abolishing the regions and pronouncing Nigeria a unitary state. In reality, this was largely a paper measure; there were no immediate means for implementation. But symbolic cues received in the North were of an imminent menace; the Ibo takeover, begun in January, was now to be completed. More mundane cues came from the exhibition in Ibo quarters of pictures of a smiling Nzeogwu or the murdered northern premier, Sir Ahmadu Bello, lying at the feet of an Ibo. Three days after the decree, anti-Ibo pogroms began in northern cities; the official death figure was 92, with unofficial estimates of several hundred, and many Ibo homes and businesses were razed. The ratchet of fear turned one level higher.

NORTHERN BACKLASH: TOWARD SECESSION

The rumor mill ground ceaselessly; by July tales were rife of a further Ibo coup to complete the "unfinished job" of January. The north was believed on the verge of declaring secession; relations between Ibo officers and northern enlisted ranks in the army were extremely tense. On 29 July, a second, loosely organized coup occurred, this time directed by northern officers. The furies of January were repaid with interest; General Ironsi was murdered, and assaults mounted on Ibo officers and men in garrisons up and down the country. Some 39 officers and 171 enlisted men were assassinated; of these, 27 of the officers and all but a handful of the other ranks were Ibo.[26] By this time, the integrity of the military structure was shattered. Surviving eastern members of the army made their way back to their home region, while northerners in the garrison in the Eastern Region were moved out. The ranking officer, Brigadier B. A. O. Ogundipe, declined to assume command; as a Yoruba, he felt that there was no way in which he could establish his authority over the now mainly-northern army—and he had been shocked at that moment to have an ordinary sergeant decline to obey his order till he could consult with his northern captain. Next in seniority was Yakubu Gowon, a Christian northerner from a small "minority" group, who was sufficiently acceptable to nor-

25. Schwarz, *Nigeria*, p. 204.
26. Kirk-Greene, *Crisis and Conflict in Nigeria*, p. 76.

therners to be able to assume command. His mission, many thought, would be merely to preside over the dissolution of Nigeria. How could a state survive when its coercive instruments had been pulverized into ethnic fragments and transformed into merely an armed mirror of the tensions within the society at large? One student of the Nigerian military states the dilemma well:

> We are then left with a situation where the officers of a certain tribal group become but the armed wing of a tribal political group, fighting against a similar combination of tribal group politicians and officers of the opposing tribe. The old political conflict is then fought out again, but the medium of conflict is no longer political maneuver, manifestos, votes, and speeches, but rather violence, with an immense advantage to the side which strikes first. This is a situation of lawless confrontation, analogous to some models of international affairs; it has its own inherent logic towards pre-emptive strikes and treacherous violence.[27]

At this juncture, the top leadership of what became Biafra became intellectually committed to secession.[28] All hopes of the regenerated, unified Nigeria which motivated the majors appeared gone. They had lost their foothold in the army, and a northerner was back in command in Lagos. There were also some unusual advantages. With the expulsion of northern troops, and regrouping of eastern troops at home, the Lagos government was not in control of the security forces in the Eastern Region; further, it had the embryo of its own army. Nor was Lagos in a position to exercise any real administrative control over the east. To these immediate factors may be added an underlying consideration, the financial confidence based upon the beginning of oil production in the Eastern and Midwest Regions. Throughout the history of Nigeria, the east had always been the poorest, the greatest beneficiary from inclusion in a broader polity. But now petroleum prosperity was on the horizon, and some could argue that the east could do better by keeping these resources for its own development.

It was not, however, until the following May, in 1967, that secession was proclaimed. In the interim, efforts were made to consolidate popular support, to seek a negotiated confederation so loose that sovereignty could be peacefully attained, and to acquire arms. In September and January, **agreements tantamount to dismantling Nigeria were virtually concluded**—averted by minority pressures in the first case and the subtle diplomacy of federal civil servants in the second. But in the immediate aftermath of the September discussions, the final cataclysm came, in the

---

27. M. J. Dent in Melson and Wolpe, *Nigeria: Modernization and the Politics of Communalism*, p. 368.

28. Persuasive argument on this point may be found in the memoirs of the former head of the Biafran civil service, Akpan, *The Struggle for Secession 1966-1970*, p. 71.

form of renewed and far more extensive anti-Ibo riots in the north. This time, estimates of the dead ran from 6,000 to 30,000. Perhaps 1,000,000 refugees poured back into the eastern homeland. Nearly every Ibo lineage had lost a member in the massacres; the diaspora, the last hostage to Nigerian unity, had now returned. Ethnic mobilization of the Ibo was virtually total.

BIRTH AND DEATH OF THE REPUBLIC OF BIAFRA

The proclamation of secession in May 1967 was greeted with en-thusiasm. The spirit of vengeance for the autumn pogroms was strong, and the air thick with illusions. Ojukwu was considered by his close associates to be a morbid pessimist for believing that three months would be required to secure the secession. Many thought the midwest might join them; others that the west would refuse to fight. All could hardly wait to crush the Hausa. Few had any concept of the dreadful cost of civil war.

On the federal side, many nourished comparable illusions. Military leaders maintained that a fortnight's blitzkrieg would see the end of Biafra. In the event, thirty months of costly struggle were required, from the time in July 1967 when the slow-moving federal offensive was initiated.

One costly miscalculation by the Ibo leadership was that eastern minorities would support the secession. Their voice had been still in the months leading up to the secession. They had, to a lesser degree, shared in the tragedies of the northern massacres and the intense emotion of the reaction to them. However, resentments smoldered over Ibo domination of the Eastern Region institutions, and the prospect of being a minority in an Ibo-dominated state was hardly reassuring. A chain reaction of distrust soon set in. Federal forces focussed much of the initial federal offensive thrust in the minority areas. Biafran leaders became persuaded that the federal advance was abetted by minority fifth columns. This led to suspicion of minority personnel in the Biafran regime and reprisals against minority zones within Biafran lines.[29] To make matters worse, from the Ibo perspective, the oil on which such high hopes were pinned was in the minority regions, not in Iboland. Further, Biafran access to the sea was through non-Ibo coastal areas.

Particularly interesting was the ambivalence of the Ibo of the Midwest Region. Initially, the midwest Ibo took the position that they were neutral; although not seceding, they did not wish either army to pass through their territory. However, a sudden Biafran invasion in August 1967 led to a

29. Abundant documentation on this point is supplied by Akpan, an Efik from Calabar, in ibid.

month of eastern occupation; Biafran forces were at one point at the gates of Ibadan. The midwest Ibo had always considered themselves somewhat distinct from eastern Ibo, a separateness sustained by their administrative location in a different jurisdiction, as well as their sense of historical relationship to the prestigious Benin kingdom. In August 1967, an assembly of "leaders of thought" of the midwest Ibo was called to debate the question as to whom they were and how they could relate themselves to the culturally polarized situation. Views on this issue were divided, but the conclusion was reached that their perception of identity did not command cultural alignment with the Biafran cause. Although they were Ibo and Biafra was recognized as an Ibo cause, yet the nature of their Ibohood was different, and fidelity to Biafra was not a proper inference.[30]

Within the first year, Biafra had been largely reduced to an Ibo redoubt, cut off from the sea. The initial passion for vengeance gave way to a gnawing fear that the grisly slaughters of the north would be repeated in the Ibo heartland, if they were overrun by federal troops. This chilling spector of genocide kept the struggle going long after there was any prospect of military victory. Only the flickering hope that world opinion might eventually bring about international intervention kept the war alive, against increasingly long odds.

The end, long in coming, arrived suddenly in January 1970, with the abrupt collapse of the Ojukwu regime. Two false prophecies had long cast their shadow over this moment, forecasting ethnic violence in different and even more brutal forms. On the one hand, many said, the Ibo solidarity which had supported so long a struggle against such overwhelming force simply could not be defeated. Although its regular army might be overrun, the Nigerian army would then face an interminable guerilla war against a tenacious and indomitable people. On the other, it was claimed, Ibo fears of genocide are no chimera; ethnic hatred was at so high a level and army discipline so slack that once northern troops were unleashed in Ibo country a bloodbath of genocidal proportions was bound to result. The prophecies were in fact interactive; the truth of one would make the other more likely. The predicted guerrilla resistance would draw the Nigerian army further and further along the path of indiscriminate repression; the Ibo populace, caught in a ferocious occupation, would be driven to guerrilla resistance as a matter of survival.

Although these forecasts had passionate advocates, they were to prove totally wrong. Once the Ojukwu regime fled, resistance stopped immediately. And, overall, the comportment of the Nigerian army was exemplary. By the time the secession collapse occurred, Nigeria had been restructured in such a way that the Ibo could not readily become a threat

30. I am indebted to Ebenezer Enwemnwa, who attended the conference, for this detail.

to other groups. The unifying impact of civil war on the rest of Nigeria had reduced the level of ethnic tension; the fearsome uncertainties of 1966 were long past. On the Ibo side, guerrilla struggle would have been continued ethnic disaster; once the very real fears of army brutality were allayed, the process of adjustment to the new situation began. Ibo government servants and traders with businesses in other regions had lost heavily. The competitive impulses quickly revived, and the spirit of uplift returned. Ibohood, obviously, has not vanished, but the fears which placed ethnicity at the center of all social transactions have receded. It is doubtful whether many Ibo are able to look at Nigeria in quite the way that Nnamdi Azikiwe did three decades ago, or even as Major Nzeogwu did in 1966. The fundamental fact is that there is simply no alternative to being Nigerian.

ORIGINS OF BENGALI NATIONALISM

While future generations of Nigerian school children will read about the war of Nigerian unity, Bangladesh history will record separatism as a triumphant struggle for independence. In both cases, the secessionist option was only pursued after years of participation within the system; the Bengali political elite did not become committed to independence until March 1971, in the wake of a savage repression by the Pakistan army, an event which played a role comparable to the July 1966 assaults on Ibo military personnel and the September-October pogroms in northern cities. Perhaps Bengal never felt so committed to Pakistan as Ibo elites did to Nigeria. An interesting dissertation by a Bangladesh student submitted only ten months before the Pakistani army onslaught, while chronicling in great detail the manifold grievances of Bengal, argues at the same time that there were no separatist movements in Pakistan comparable to those in Quebec or Biafra. He concluded: "Once an understanding was reached, and mutual suspicion, fear and hatred removed, the people of the two regions of Pakistan might again be hoped to treat themselves as members of one state with common hopes and aspirations. Regionalism in that situation is expected to lose its sharpness; for East Pakistanis, having their demands largely fulfilled or settled, will have little to fight for and will certainly give priority to issues of national rather than regional significance."[31]

How, then, were the dragon's teeth of cultural deprivation sown, which led to the sudden harvest of fully armed independence fighters in 1971, in a landscape where no separatists were to be seen only a year earlier? We

31. Safar A. Akanda, "East Pakistan and the Politics of Regionalism," (Ph.D. diss., University of Denver, 1970), pp. 309, 332.

need first to consider the dynamics of Bengali identity, before examining the immediate precipitants of withdrawal. A useful place to begin is a Kiplingesque passage from the autobiographical account of Ayub Khan, president of Pakistan from 1958 to 1969, whose perceptions may fairly be considered as representative of the West Pakistan elite: "East Bengalis . . . probably belong to the very original Indian races. It would be no exaggeration to say that up to the creation of Pakistan, they had not known any real freedom or sovereignty. They had been in turn ruled either by the caste Hindus, Moghuls, Pathans, or the British. In addition, they have been and still are under considerable Hindu cultural and linguistic influence. As such, they have all the inhibitions of down-trodden races and have not yet found it possible to adjust psychologically to the requirements of the new born freedom. Their popular complexes, ex-clusiveness, suspicion, and a sort of defensive aggressiveness probably emerge from this historical background."[32]

Bengali identity rests upon twin pillars: the Bengali linguistic-cultural heritage, shared with those of West Bengal state in India and with Islam. The first pillar sharply divided East Bengal from West Pakistan. Bengal was the first center of British empire in India; a new, educated elite had emerged by the early decades of the nineteenth century, under whose intellectual leadership a highly developed Bengali cultural ideology took shape. However, the gentry elite that fostered Bengali subnationalism, the *bhadralok* (respectable people), were primarily drawn from a small number of high Hindu castes; there were very few Muslims among them. According to 1901 census figures, male literacy among Bengal Muslims was only 6.8 percent, compared to 63.9 percent for Brahmans, 64.8 percent for Baidyas, and 64.8 percent for Kayasthas, to cite three of the castes who contributed heavily to the *bhadralok* ranks.[33] Thus Muslims shared only peripherally in the forging of Bengali identity; the great culture heroes are nearly all Hindu Bengali, including the most famed of them all, the Nobel prize winning poet Tagore.

The other identity pillar of East Bengal, Islam, dates from the thir-teenth century, when Bengal first came under Muslim rule. In the cen-turies that followed, Bengal history took a somewhat different course than that of the rest of northern India; the waves of invasion from the northwest and the constant influx of Muslim holy men from Persia and Arabia had a more dilute impact. There was, on British arrival, a Muslim ruling class in Bengal, but much fewer in numbers and much less powerful than in the north Indian heartland. Conversely, Islam had been a powerful

32. Ayub Khan, *Friends Not Masters* (New York: Oxford University Press, 1967), p. 187.
33. Broomfield, *Elite Conflict in a Plural Society: Twentieth Century Bengal*, p. 9. For other valuable studies, see Seal, *The Emergence of Indian Nationalism*, and Hardy, *The Muslims of British India*.

factor in Bengal peasant society; conversion occurred on a vast scale, particularly among the numerous depressed lower castes. Thus Bengal, which had over half of India's Muslim population, had a very distinctive configuration. Islam was rural, not urban; its traditional elite was very thin. Also, it was less of a church militant; it was not under the constant bombardment of the itinerant saints and religious teachers preaching mobilized piety and fervent religiosity.[34]

In Bengal, status deprivation for Muslim elites was swift and severe (in contrast to many other areas). The Bengal land settlement in 1786 had the effect of eliminating Muslims from the landed class. The early introduction of English to replace Persian and Urdu as administrative languages gave a decisive advantage to the new Hindu *bhadralok* class. Access to modernization was overwhelmingly determined by ranking on the traditional status scale; neither Hindu nor Muslim peasants had much chance of acquiring a modern education and a new social status. Thus, in twentieth century Bengal, the Hindu-Muslim cleavage strongly correlated with social stratification. The intelligentsia, the merchant class in Calcutta, the landlords throughout Bengal were Hindu; Muslims were poor peasants.

Accordingly, East Bengal was quite distinct from West Pakistan not just on one pillar of identity, but on both. Ayub Khan noted that Bengalis were still under Hindu "linguistic and cultural influence"; put another way, East Bengalis, although they played little role in creating the literary and poetic traditions associated with Bengali culture, did share in them. The stereotypes in which images of Bengali character are conveyed differ totally from those of West Pakistan. The list of traits cited by one Bengali Muslim as national attributes, if each characteristic were inverted to its opposite, would be a recognizable description of the archetypical West Pakistani; Bengalis, he wrote, are "nonaggressive and unwarlike, possessed of a dreamy and emotional temperament, prone to mysticism, art, music, erotic poetry and radical politics."[35] Not only were Bengalis removed from Punjabis, Pathans, and Sindhis by linguistic culture, but Islam was far less a common bond than might be assumed. Bengali Islam was the religion of the indigenous depressed peasant convert; in West Pakistan, Islam was the faith of the conquerors, the rulers, the courtiers. Or, as Ayub Khan had put it, Bengali Islam was a faith associated with the "downtrodden races."

In chapter 8, we have described the rise of political identities associated with the Hindu-Muslim cleavage and the circumstances making Pakistan inevitable. From this, it is worth recollecting that the proposition that Muslims in India were a nation far antedates any effort to give territorial

34. Broomfield, *Elite Conflict,* Seal, *Emergence of Indian Nationalism,* and Hardy, *Muslims of British India,* all document this point.

35. Akanda, "East Pakistan and the Politics of Regionalism," p. 144.

definition to that concept. Although the idea of splitting India on religious lines appears to have been first made in 1877 by John Bright, such amorphous speculation as on occasion appeared generally assumed the provincial lines of British India as a point of departure. The very acronym of Pakistan, dating from 1933, derives entirely from its West Pakistan components, *P*unjab, *A*fghania, *K*ashmir, *I*ran, *S*ind, *T*ukharistan, *A*fghanistan, Baluchista*N*.[36] The famous 1940 Lahore resolution of the Muslim League, containing the first public commitment to separate statehood, was ambiguous in its wording, demanding that, "geographically contiguous units are demarcated into regions which should be so constituted, with such territorial readjustments as may be necessary, that the areas in which the constituent units shall be autonomous and sovereign."[37] Although Muslim League leaders later claimed that only one state had been intended, the resolution was, to say the least, ambiguous. Many Bengalis found appeal in the separate state proposition; H. S. Suhrawardy, the Muslim premier of old Bengal province, 1946-47, proposed in early 1947 that an undivided Bengal seek separate independence.[38]

THE BIRTH OF PAKISTAN

However, the formula for independence was based upon a single Pakistan; such an outcome was inscribed in the logic of cultural polarization which led up to the 1947 holocaust. The images and cues of political identity related overwhelmingly to the metaphor of Hindu and Muslim; the political leadership of the Muslim League were passionately committed to the Muslim nation concept. But once this premise for sovereignty was accepted in early 1947, it also became inevitable that the partition had to occur at two levels. If Pakistan were to be granted self-determination as embodiment of the Muslim nation, it was unconscionable to attach to it areas of Hindu-majority population; accordingly, Bengal and Punjab provinces had to be divided, in order to divide India. Nearly all agreed that East Bengal, thus truncated, could not stand alone.

In this process, the cultural personality of Pakistan as a polity was defined in significant ways. The population exchange accompanying partition was far more lethal and complete in Punjab than in Bengal. Indeed, much of the Hindu exodus from East Bengal occurred in the years after independence, and even at the time of the last Pakistan census of

36. Khalid Bin Sayeed, *The Formative Phase* (Karachi: Pakistan Publishing House, 1960), pp. 110-13.

37. Ali, *The Emergence of Pakistan,* p. 38.

38. Sayeed, *The Political System of Pakistan,* p. 56.

1961 Hindus were nearly 20 percent of the East Bengal population (and Muslims a comparable percentage of West Bengal). Although Calcutta had been the scene of communal riots, rural East Bengal on the whole had not. Communal mob riots were generally an urban phenomenon, where the contenders faced each other as entirely impersonal collectivities, each fused into a single, integrated symbolized entity upon which fear mobilized as hatred could be decanted. But this depersonalization of relationships is less likely to occur between neighboring peasant families, even of different religion, between whom amicable interpersonal ties exist; it was such a pattern of religious intersticing that obtained in the Bengal countryside. The primary focus of anti-Hindu hostility was the landlords, of whom relatively few were Muslim. The Hindu landlord class was effectively dispossessed shortly after independence, and remaining rural Hindus were not economically differentiated from the Muslims. Thus, animosity to Hinduism and hostility to India were far less compelling sentiments in East Bengal than in West Pakistan. Further, the complex and almost irreconcilable issues dividing India and Pakistan in the wake of partition—Kashmir, the allocation of Indus waters—were matters which solely affected the western wing.

Paradoxically, the centers of most intensive Muslim League support lay in areas which could not be included in Pakistan. Jinnah and Liaquat Ali Khan, the best-known League leaders, were from Bombay. Many of the Muslim League elite came from the north central Indian heartland where, before partition, communal tensions had been highest. From these zones, the exodus to Pakistan was very selective and concentrated at the upper ends of the social stratum. For a poor Muslim in Uttar Pradesh, the flight to Pakistan was perilous, the distance was great, there was no reason to suppose he could have access to land and no obvious alternative means of livelihood. However alarming the wave of communal violence might be, exodus was, for many, simply not a realistic alternative. But the exodus did include two highly significant elites who came to play a crucial role in the formative phases of Pakistan: the Muslim League political leadership and the mercantile-entrepreneurial elites. The first provided the first generation of political leaders, and the second formed a major ingredient in the economic elite which rose to influence and power during the Pakistan "economic miracle" of the Ayub Khan era.[39]

The initial conceptualization of Pakistan, therefore, relied heavily upon the symbolic resources through which the idea of the Muslim nation had been politicized and diffused during the epic contest with Congress for the soul of India. Urdu, with its historic associations with the golden age of

39. This important point is well made by Rouna Jahan, *Pakistan: Failure in National Integration* (New York: Columbia University Press, 1972), pp. 24-25.

Muslim rule in India, was of central importance. Territoriality had played only a very modest part in political mobilization of Indian Muslims; much more important was the political status of Muslims in relation to their Hindu adversaries. Khalid Sayeed well summarized the motor forces in the demand for Pakistan: "Muslim had ruled India and they could not understand why under a democratic system they should be deprived of power and influence. Thus, it was this desire for power and unwillingness to live under those whom they have governed which largely explains the demand for Pakistan."[40] Islam as a political identity lay at the core; it was not a territorialized vision. Much less was it a yearning for a theocratic community, for the Islam of the *ulama, pirs*, saints, and holy men. There was, from the outset, a fundamental ambiguity in the cultural basis for the Pakistani state. Once conceded, the ideology of Pakistan had to become territorialized; in the process, its very basis was altered in ways whose profound implications were not visible to the founders of the state.

It is in this context that we may grasp the import of three major issues which, over time, drove a deep cultural wedge between East and West Pakistan: the national language, access to elite roles, and economic parity.

THE NATIONAL LANGUAGE QUESTION

The language issue was the first to emerge and the only one to be resolved. In retrospect, it is curious that this matter was ever permitted to degenerate into regional polarization. In its crisis stage, the language question was a landmark of Bengali cultural mobilization and helped create a frame of mind which persisted long after satisfaction had been given on the immediate issue. The will to impose Urdu as sole national language can only be understood in the context of the pre-independence cultural postulates.

Table 12.1 summarizes the linguistic situation in Pakistan in 1961, which is very revelatory of political stratification. Urdu was understood only by 1.34 percent of the East Pakistan population, whereas 99 percent knew Bengali. In West Pakistan, Urdu was known only by 14.7 percent, and only 7.6 percent spoke it as a mother tongue. One may reasonably assume that most of the latter group are refugees from north central India; the additional 7.1 percent of West Pakistanis who know Urdu are coterminous with the educated elite. By far the most important West Pakistani language is Punjabi, spoken by 66.4 percent in the region. Other West Pakistan regional languages include Sindhi (12.6 percent), Pushto

40. Sayeed, *Pakistan: The Formative Phase*, p. 194.

(8.5 percent), and Baluchi (2.5 percent).[41] Almost no one but mother-tongue speakers command any of these regional languages, which is also true of Bengali.

Table 12.1—Languages Spoken in Pakistan, 1961

Language	% of speakers		
	East Pakistan	West Pakistan	All Pakistan
Urdu	1.3	14.6	7.2
Bengali	99.0	0.1	55.8
Punjabi	0.0	67.6	29.5
Sindhi	0.0	14.2	6.2
Pushto	0.0	8.9	3.9
Baluchi	0.0	2.9	1.3
English	0.8	2.1	1.4

Source: Census of Pakistan: Population 1961 (Karachi: Government of Pakistan, 1961), VI, 32-33.

Urdu is, on the whole, accepted in West Pakistan as a medium of literate communication despite the small fraction of persons that speak it. The main script for Punjabi, Gurumukhi, is associated with the Sikhs and is thus culturally unacceptable to Muslim Punjabis. Only Sindhi of West Pakistan languages has its own script (based on Arabic) and literary tradition; Pushto and Baluchi are very little used as written languages. A modest move for official status for Sindhi did develop, but in general Sindhi elites, unlike their Bengali counterparts, did know Urdu. But the most passionate defenders of Urdu were the immigrants from north central India, where the status of Urdu had been a bitterly contentious issue since the 1870s, when Hindi movements first arose to demand its replacement in administrative usage by Hindi in Devnagari script.

Within a year of independence, clouds began to gather on the language question, as President Jinnah and Premier Liaquat Ali Khan made clear the determination of the new regime to establish Urdu as the sole national language. In a 1948 Assembly debate, the premier sharply retorted to a Hindu Bengali member who proposed Bengali as a parliamentary language: "Pakistan is Muslim State and it must have as its lingua franca the language of the Muslim nation. . . . Pakistan has been created because of the demand of a hundred million Muslims in this sub-continent and the language of the hundred million Muslims is Urdu. It is necessary for a nation to have one language and that language can only be Urdu."[42] At about the same time, Jinnah drove the same point home in Dacca itself, declaring in sharp tone, ". . let me make it very clear to you that the State lan-

41. These figures are from *Census of Pakistan, Population 1961*, IV, 33-37.
42. Akanda, "East Pakistan and the Politics of Regionalism," p. 72.

guage of Pakistan is going to be Urdu and no other language," adding that any who misled them on this score "is really the enemy of Pakistan."[43]

Bengali not only contravened the principle of a single national language, in the eyes of the Muslim League elite; its literary heritage was mainly Hindu, and its script was Devnagari (or Hindu) and bore the dangerous germs of pan-Bengali nationalism. This attitude, remarked a Bengali scholar, "seemed to be aimed at endangering the very existence of the Bengali cultural group within the state."[44]

Agitation on the language issue reached a crisis point on 21 February 1952, when the police fired into a student demonstration at Dacca University protesting the Urdu-only policy, killing three students. Thereafter 21 February was commemorated as Martyr Day, whose ceremonies invariably took on an anti-West Pakistan tone. The day following this tragedy, the East Bengal assembly, which had remained silent on the issue, passed a unanimous motion calling for equal status as a national language for Bengali. Students, it may be noted, were at the vanguard of Bengali cultural nationalism and subsequently played a major part in the guerrilla army. As in the Tamil case, the cultural threat was most severe for students. Government employment was the dream of many, even if it would be fulfilled for only a few. An Urdu-only policy would gravely disadvantage Bengali applicants in competition with West Pakistan, where the educated persons by definition had mastered Urdu. This anticipated deprivation affected relatively few people, but had a formidable mobilizing impact on those who were aroused. When joined to the relative absence of the constraints of family obligation, employment security, and generalized risk-aversion preferences which tend to ac-company age, students become an explosively volatile set of cultural activists. Students are also well equipped to elaborate and propagate an ideology of cultural protest, in the Bengali case around the richness of the language, "among the half-dozen most expressive and beautiful languages in the world,"[45] and the brilliance of its literature, with the poet Rabindranath Tagore the object of a particular cult of veneration.

The government delayed until 1956 before bowing to the inevitable and accepting Bengali as a second national language. The costs were high in integrative opportunities lost. The unifying memories of the common struggle for Pakistan independence were swiftly obliterated in East Bengal, and solidarities reformed around Bengali identity. The old Muslim League elites in East Bengal, whose commitment to Pakistan was strongest and whose Bengali sentiments were weakest, were the first

43. Jahan, *Pakistan: Failure in National Integration,* p. 37.

44. Akanda, "East Pakistan and the Politics of Regionalism," p. 73.

45. Akanda, "East Pakistan and the Politics of Regionalism," p. 82, quoting approvingly from a British biographer of Tagore.

victims. In regional elections in East Bengal in 1954, the Muslim League won only 9 of 309 seats, being crushed by the newly formed United Front, representing a coalition of new, culturally mobilized elites who did not bring to politics the fraternal sentiments of the League struggle of the 1930s and 1940s. Many of Pakistan's most fervent promoters in Bengal had been sacrificed on the altar of the Urdu-only policy.

ELITES AND POLITICS: THE MINORITIZATION OF BENGAL

A second arena of cultural struggle was over equal access to elite status, a partial correlate of the language question. We may conveniently divide the elite category into four sectors: military, bureaucratic, political, and economic. In the military sphere, Pakistan was at once saddled with the heavy burden of disparities deriving from deliberate recruitment politics in British India. The British believed the Bengalis utterly devoid of military qualities and recruited virtually none for the British Indian army in recent decades. Punjabis, on the other hand, enjoyed a splendid reputation and were heavily represented. In 1955, Bengalis numbered 14 of 894 officers in the army, 7 of 593 in the navy, and 60 of 640 in the air force.[46] The import of this particular disparity became more political when the army seized power in 1958, and it was clear that the military, as arbiters at least, were now an integral part of the power arena.

For different reasons, Bengalis were equally poorly represented in the bureaucratic elite. In the Indian civil service at the time of partition, there was only one Bengali Muslim, of the 133 ICS Muslims opting for Pakistan.[47] In 1958, in the top civil service ranks, 41 were Bengalis, and 690 westerners.[48] By the mid-1960s, some of the most irritating disparities within East Pakistan itself were rectified, and Bengalis held most key regional posts. But only two of the 17 central permanent secretaries were Bengalis.[49] The proportions of Bengalis in entering classes to the Pakistan civil service academy had gradually improved over the years; however, in the 22 classes from 1948 to 1969, Bengalis were a majority in only 6, while in 10 of these years they were fewer than 40 percent.[50] The historical origin of this disparity lies in the very small numbers of Bengali Muslims who broke the barriers of the status system during the colonial period, so heavily weighted in favor of the Hindu *bhadralok*. But this had

46. Jahan, *Pakistan: Failure in National Integration,* p. 25.
47. Sayeed, *Pakistan: The Formative Phase,* pp. 298-301.
48. Jahan, *Pakistan: Failure in National Integration,* p. 26.
49. Sayeed, *The Political System of Pakistan,* p. 195.
50. Akanda, "East Pakistan and the Politics of Regionalism," p. 132.

begun to change even in the late phases of the colonial period; there had, after all, been a Muslim government in control of old Bengal province from 1927 on. Punjabi Muslims, in contrast, had always held their own in the quest for mobility.

The economic elite had been radically transformed in the independence period. West Pakistan, at the dawn of independence, had an important landlord class, especially in Sind, but the urban mercantile elites in West Pakistan cities had been primarily Hindu. In East Bengal, as noted before, the landlords were 75 percent Hindu and effectively removed from the scene by a 1950 land reform. Three new economic elites emerged after 1947, and especially during the "economic miracle" decade of the 1960s. The most important was the new industrial entrepreneurial class—the "22 families"—so frequently cited as the *deus ex machina* which had combined its managerial skills with the large sums of public development capital which became available, to produce the beginnings of an industrial sector for Pakistan and fortunes for itself. This group was primarily drawn from four small, Urdu-speaking, mercantile castes—the Bhoras, Khojas, Memons, and Chiniotis—who had belonged to the Indian exodus.[51] This new group and its industries were based in West Pakistan. A second new entry into the economic elites was Punjabi large farmers who had enough capital and cultivating skill to prosper from the "green revolution." Thirdly, in East Bengal, economic leadership came from an immigrant community known as Biharis, which included not only persons from the province of Bihar, but others from northern India generally who had come to East Bengal after partition. Although this group was but a pale reflection of the industrial-mercantile set in West Pakistan, yet it did come to operate a large fraction of the very modest number of new economic enterprises in East Pakistan. Bengalis had not even a fingerhold in this sector. The powerful tradition of caste-allocated roles in the Indian subcontinent, though not immutable, had meant that a totally disproportionate number of entrepreneurs have come from a narrow range of mercantile or trading castes; in the rural sector, the most aggressive and successful green revolution farmers have been drawn from middle-to-upper-ranked cultivating castes. These categories were simply largely absent from Bengali Muslim society.

Only in the political elite did Bengalis count. Whatever the shortages of warriors, capitalists, and bureaucrats might be, Bengal was exceedingly rich in politicians. In the first decade of independence, three Bengalis served as prime minister—Kwaja Nazimuddin (who was also governor-general for a time), Mohammed Ali Bogra, and Suhrawardy—although none with much distinction or authority. Yet democratic politics were the

51. Sayeed, *The Political System of Pakistan,* p. 115.

main hope for Bengal; with 56 percent of the total Pakistan population, if power could only be defined by numbers, then Bengal would speak with a loud voice.

Both in East and West Pakistan an important generational difference must be noted. For the original, Muslim League political elites, political identity had been fashioned through the communal socialization of the Muslim-Hindu struggle over the creation of Pakistan. This generation had a totally different concept of Pakistan as a cultural polity than did those that began to emerge in both wings to challenge their leadership. The Urdu-speaking core group of this elite were still influential, although they came to realize they simply had no political base in Pakistan itself and would be eliminated by elections. As Sayeed observes, this Muslim League generation, "absorbed in the heat and excitement of the struggle for Pakistan, grossly underestimated the potency of regional and linguistic loyalties."[52] It was precisely around these cultural solidarities that a new generation of vernacular elites emerged, although their impact on the national scene was limited by the absence of openly contested, universal suffrage national elections until 1970. The surrogate parliament which sat in Karachi from 1947 to 1958 was a constituent assembly chosen by the provincial assemblies, which themselves had been constituted on a limited franchise prior to independence.

With this portrait of the politically influential elites sketched, the murky patterns of Pakistani politics during the first two decades come into clearer focus. In the first nine years of independence, a constitution was laboriously constructed, which did make provision for linguistic parity for Bengali and for democratic, universal suffrage elections to give issue to a new regime for Pakistan. These long-deferred elections were on the horizon for 1959, a conjuncture which decisively influenced the Ayub Khan coup in October 1958. In the first decade of independence, national politics were of an extraordinary fluidity, with ephemeral coalitions built upon shifting alliances in which cultural pluralism and personalistic factionalism intertwined in intricate patterns, with corruption and stagnation as silent partners. However, there were a set of Bengali politicians deeply immersed in these combinations and, at least in this fashion, integrated into the system. Although the cynicism of the endless maneuvers for a moment in the sun of office cast a pall over the entire politician class, yet the new constitution gave some hope for Bengalis that a government responsive to their grievances would emerge from elections.

The Ayub Khan coup fundamentally altered the cultural contours of power. The Punjabi-dominated military and bureaucracy were in power. The old Urdu-speaking and Muslim League political elite, by now well

52. Ibid, p. 66.

aware that elections would bring vernacular elites to power in both wings, was well disposed to a regime that would preserve their vision of Pakistan, if not their political status and functions. The technocratic, development oriented approach of Ayub Khan was enthusiastically supported by the economic elites, who were provided social order, public capital and a free hand for their entrepreneurial endeavors.

The Punjabi flavor of the new regime could hardly bring rejoicing in East Pakistan, though few could mourn the demise of the discredited old politicians. Ayub did make some genuine gestures toward East Bengal, in placing Bengalis in charge of regional administration and accepting the principle of parity in development. The adjournment of elections, however was a major disappointment, and the Ayub Khan formula of "basic democracies" (democracy focussed on local institutions, with indirectly elected tiers of representation diversified by appointed members, conducted without benefit of political parties) never caught the imagination of politically conscious Bengalis. This formula was designed to exclude the new vernacular elites on whom political Bengal counted for cultural salvation. Disenchanted East Bengal gave Ayub only a narrow majority of 53.5 percent over Fatima Jinnah, daughter of the old Muslim League leader and herself not a Bengali, in the 1965 presidential election, compared with his 73.5 percent vote in West Pakistan.

During the Ayub Khan era, the central issue in regional debate was developmental parity. An able new generation of Bengali economists began to assemble data on the distribution of benefits in Pakistan. In the first decades of independence, per capita income in East Pakistan actually fell from 305 rupees to 288, while that in the West rose slightly from 330 to 373. In the Ayub Khan decade, the East Pakistan figure went up to 291.5, while that of the West rose to 473.4.[53] Between 1959 and 1965, $282.8 million of United States development funds went to West Pakistan, against $100.3 million for the East.[54] Educational differentials appeared to be growing; in the first decade of independence, primary school enrollment per 100,000 population rose from 1,765 to 3,686 in the West, while remaining almost stationary in the East (6,349 in 1948-49, 6,361 in 1959-60); at the secondary level, the West ratio rose from 1,622 to 2,172, while that of the East fell from 1,189 to 1,061.[55] The energy which Bengali economists devoted to documenting disparities was matched only by the ingenuity of their indexes. Innumerable tables could be cited, but the point is really indisputable; East Pakistan had benefitted less, materially, from independence than had the West. In the latter phases of the Ayub

53. Jahan, *Pakistan: Failure in National Integration,* pp. 31, 79.
54. Sayeed, *The Political System of Pakistan,* p. 201.
55. Jahan, *Pakistan: Failure in National Integration,* p. 31.

Khan development decade, growing efforts were made to rectify the imbalances, but by now the disparity postulate was an article of faith with Bengalis. East Bengal, it was argued, produced most of the exports, but most of the imports went to the West. In return, East Pakistan was forced to purchase shoddy products from West Pakistan's new industries—a classic instance, in this view, of the colonial economy. With 1000 miles separating the two wings, they were, and should be, two economies; investments made in one wing had virtually no beneficial spillover effects upon the other. Although some figures from the late 1960s showed a fair equilibration of development expenditures, East Pakistanis quickly retorted that these calculations excluded three massive projects, involving huge outlays, which exclusively benefitted West Pakistan: the reconstruction of Indus River dams and irrigation infrastructure to take account of the partition of the headwaters between Pakistan and India; desalinization of the waterlogged Indus delta; and construction of the new capital of Islamabad.[56]

TOWARD SECESSION

In the 1960s, autonomist sentiment and cultural mobilization steadily increased in East Bengal. In 1962, the University of Dacca was closed for a year by a student strike against Ayub Khan's "basic democracy" constitution. The government riposted by setting up its own networks within the university, and the campus was a daily battleground of terrorist squads. The celebration of Tagore's birthday, the annual commemoration of Martyr's Day on 21 February became powerfully mobilizing symbolic events, invariably the occasion for mass demonstrations and mob actions. An increasing number of assaults upon police stations occurred, as well as widespread *gheraos*, where workers simply held their employers, often Biharis, captive in their offices until demands were met. The spiralling dissolution of public order, particularly in East Bengal, led to the ouster of Ayub Khan in 1969 by another West Pakistani general, Yahya Khan.

Bengali nationalism, up till this point, had lacked a leader, a program, and a party. After 1966 it acquired all three, sharpening its focus and unifying its purpose. Sheikh Mujibur Rahman emerged as the leader of the Awami League, a party formed in opposition to the Muslim League not long after independence. The Awami League had initially tried to function on an all-Pakistan level, but had always been primarily Bengali. In 1966, Mujibur and the Awami League captured the free-floating social

56. For a thorough study of the extraordinary scope and complexity of the Indus projects, see Aloys Arthur Michel, *The Indus Rivers* (New Haven: Yale University Press, 1967).

energies of Bengali nationalism with a Six Point Program, a platform for virtually complete autonomy, conceding to the central institutions only foreign policy and defense. East Bengal was to have a separate currency, sole powers of taxation, and its own militia. It is difficult to imagine that Pakistan would have long survived under such a regime, but Bengalis nonetheless insisted that their object was autonomy, and not secession.

Yahya Khan momentarily arrested the drift into confrontation with the pledge that parties would be given free rein in 1970 and that general elections would then be held. The capacity of power holders to underestimate the force of mobilized identities in polarized situations seems boundless; it would appear that the military-bureaucratic elite anticipated inconclusive results, with only a small majority for the Awami League in the East. Such an outcome, ran the argument, would leave the central elites in an arbitrating position. However, Bengali nationalism was now at flood tide, eclipsing the critical divergences of ideology and interest within East Pakistan. The Bengali middle class saw an end to Punjabi domination. The nascent commercial group saw new horizons of opportunity if the West Pakistan orientation of the economy ended. Radical socialists believed that revolution could be at the door if only the blocking force of West Pakistani mercantile capitalists and their Bihari intermediaries could be removed. The Awami League swept all before it, winning 160 of the 162 Bengal seats in the national legislature, enough for an absolute majority in the 300-seat parliament. In East Bengal, Awami League won 288 out of 300 assembly seats. In West Pakistan, the party of discontent, Ali Bhutto's People's Party, won 81 of the 138 West Pakistan parliamentary seats. The state for confrontation was set; a convening of the new parliament would raise the curtain.

The edge of Bengali bitterness was sharpened in November 1970, just before the elections, when catastrophic typhoon-borne floods took 200,000 lives. The reaction of Pakistan to this tragedy, Bengalis believed, was one of callous indifference. The clouds of distrust and suspicion which hung over the impending deliberations on the future shape of Pakistan darkened further.

The critical actors were now three: Mujibur, Yahya, and Bhutto. But the reactions of the audience were not controlled by the actors, and its volatile participation in the surge of events severely constrained the roles each could play. Bhutto tried to negotiate a power-sharing formula at the center with Mujibur; the latter, however, would not budge from the Six Point Program, which the Awami League now had the absolute majority to impose on its own. West Pakistan could not abide the prospect of Bengali control of the central institutions, while the autonomist demands were perceived as a poorly disguised separatism. Yahya tried fruitlessly to arbitrate, but had little influence with either party; he had only the Punjabi-dominated army as his leverage, a sledgehammer where only the most delicate scalpel could serve him. Postponement of the summons to parliament brought Mujibur under intensive pressure for a unilateral declaration of independence; by the beginning of March 1971, mob actions in East Bengal acquired their own momentum, and explosive clashes of Bengali demonstrators with security forces brought the hour of conflagration close. Mujibur tried to retain some influence over the course of events by declaring a noncooperation campaign, while rejecting the independence declaration. As the East Bengal administration was now largely staffed by Bengalis, it escaped the control of the Pakistan government. Yahya apparently reached a provisional agreement with Mujibur on the basis of the Six Point Program on 20 March, but this was at once denounced by Bhutto as a "massive betrayal of West Pakistan."[57] Constraining pressures now closed in on all sides and narrowly limited the options of the actors. Mujibur on 23 March declared that the Six Point Program had to be accepted by official proclamation within 48 hours, or the situation would be wholly beyond control. Yahya, faced with the choice between concessions that the West would not accept and the fatal course of repression, chose the latter. On 25 March, the Pakistan army struck. Its first targets included the bastion of cultural nationalism, the University of Dacca. The headquarters of the Bengali-manned East Pakistan Rifles and Bengali Police and its armory were seized, as were the communications centers—radio and newspaper. Mujibur was arrested and whisked to a West Pakistan prison.

The die was now cast. West Pakistani military sources appeared convinced that Bengalis would not fight, that the "swift surgical operation" so popular in army command posts would end the problem. However, the operation proved incomplete, and resulted in the total cultural mobilization of Bengal. Although the Pakistan army established its authority in the main cities, groups of *mukti bahini* (freedom fighters) soon emerged in the countryside. The communal nature of the struggle was sharpened by unleashing the mainly Punjabi army on the Bengal countryside; security operations by a force which felt itself in alien territory became ill-disciplined terrorism. Student leaders, personnel who had escaped the assault on the East Bengal Rifles, and police formed the nuclei of guerrilla bands. A segment of the Awami League political leadership fled to Calcutta to establish a government-in-exile. Ten million refugees streamed across the Indian borders, the largest such movement in a single time and place in history, placing an in-

---

57. Jahan, *Pakistan: Failure in National Integration,* pp. 185-204. Many West Pakistanis deny that an accord was reached.

tolerable burden upon a volatile area of India. The Pakistan army, seeking auxiliaries, found a number of willing recruits in the three-quarter million Bihari population, which gravely compromised its future, precarious at best, through the indelible stain of association with the repression.

The restoration of Pakistan, as it was known from 1947 to 1970, would in any event have been problematical, so total was the alienation of 56 percent of the population. Yet geopolitical factors were crucial in fixing the outcome. Unlike Biafra, Bangladesh insurgents had ready sanctuary in a neighboring state. Training camps for guerrillas were established in India, and arms supply circuits for *mukti bahini* were created. The *mukti bahini* alone were a significant nuisance, through ambushes and sabotage, and denied control of large areas of the countryside to the 80,000 man Pakistan army; however, they were far from able to mount a direct challenge to the Pakistanis. The intervention of the Indian army in December 1971 was the decisive stroke. Pakistan appears to have supplied the pretext for this well-prepared operation, through an ill-conceived and poorly executed effort at replicating the 1967 Israeli feat of immobilizing the opposing airforce with a preemptive strike at its air bases. Once the Indian invasion began, the Pakistan garrisons, completely cut off from resupply in wholly hostile territory, were caught in a gigantic trap and surrendered within a fortnight. The capitulation on 16 December 1971 marked the birth of the new nation of Bangladesh.[58]

SOUTHERN SUDAN: BASES OF DIVERSITY

The southern Sudan separatist movement is distinguished from the other two by the long duration of its struggle—nine years, as opposed to thirty months in Biafra—its isolation, and its internal fragmentation. The three southern provinces of Sudan—Upper Nile, Equatoria, and Bahr-al-Ghazal—are united only in their distinctiveness from the Arabizing north. With relation to northerners, southern Sudanese are Black, do not accept Arab culture as an assimilative pole, and use English as a medium of elite communication; through the mission schools, the elite are generally Christian. With relation to each other, ethnicity

58. For useful accounts in this period, see M. Rashiduzzaman, "Leadership, Organization, Strategies and Tactics of the Bangladesh Movement," *Asian Survey,* XII, no. 3 (March 1972), pp. 185–200; Louis Dupree, "Bangladesh," Parts I and II, American Universities Field Service, *Fieldstaff Reports.* South Asia Series, vol. XI, nos. 5–6 (June-July 1972). On Pakistan politics generally, in addition to sources cited, see also Karl von Vorys, *Political Development in Pakistan* (Princeton: Princeton University Press, 1965).

Map 12.1   Sudan: Ethnic Groups

Cartographic Laboratory UW-Madison

remains an important differentiator. The largest single linguistic cluster
are those of the Luo language family—Dinka, Shilluk, Nuer, Anuak, and
others—especially in the northern part. Closer to the Uganda border,
groups which can be classified linguistically as Eastern Nilotics (not
a subjective identity) include Bari, Mandari, Nyangbara, Pojulu,
Kakwa, and others. In the southwest, Azande-related groups are dominant, spilling into Zaire and the Central African Republic.

In sharp contrast to Biafra and Bangladesh, Southern Sudan is almost totally undeveloped. There was no town as large as 20,000; no mines or industrial development; only a very modest start in cotton as an export crop, mainly in Azande country. With 27.1 percent of the population, or about 4.25 million, in 1960 there were only three secondary schools in the south, compared with 65 in the north. In the same year, of 1,216 students in Khartoum University, only 60 were southerners.[59] It should be added that such development as did occur in the south was unevenly divided, being situated mainly in Zande country and Equatoria. Upper Nile and the bulk of Bahr-el-Ghazal provinces were the last areas "pacified" and the least touched by British administration. This modest degree of differential modernization between the northern Nilotic groups and the Equatorian peoples is a predictable basis of sociopolitical cleavage within the post-civil war Southern Region.

Southern identities were little politicized. There had been no contest among them for status and security in an urban sector, nor for power and prestige in a political arena. The elites were few in number, were not in competition with one another, had no social incentive to ethnic evangelization. Cultural anxieties came only in defining their relationship to northerners, who, from the southern vantage point, could all be considered as Arabs.

The north and south were first united under the nineteenth-century Turko-Egyptian regime of Mohammed Ali. For centuries, navigation up the Nile had been halted on the White Nile by the sudd, a vast, vegetation-choked, nearly stagnant stretch. In 1839, an Egyptian flotilla first pierced this barrier and established an administration further upstream, eventually extending into contemporary Uganda. Ivory dealers and slave traders quickly followed in the shelter of the embryonic administration, and very swiftly the human traffic reached a large scale. Even before the sudd was breached, an estimated 200,000 slaves were recruited from the south and the Nuban mountains for the Egyptian army. Egyptian governors forced Sudanese Arab communities to deliver a tribute tax in slaves; the Baggara Arabs of western Sudan became especially prominent in this role. By the middle of the nineteenth century, an estimated two or three hundred mainly Arab (and some European) trading firms were based in Khartoum. Although groups like the Azande or the Dinka, with a well-organized warfare capability, were not strongly affected, the smaller, acephalous, defenseless communities were simply decimated. Indeed, many of the communities hardest hit by Arab slave raiders no longer exist.[60] The Bari, occupying

59. Joseph Oduho and William Deng, *The Problem of the Southern Sudan* (London: Oxford University Press, 1963), pp. 46-47.
60. Sommer, "The Sudan," pp. 144-52.

the Nile banks south of the sudd, were also important trade intermediaries. The slave trade was still continuing in the southern Sudan as late at 1929.[61]

"SOUTHERN POLICY"

The British occupation of Egypt in 1882 had no effect on the south before contacts were cut off by the foundation of the Mahdist state. Though some Dinka for a time fought in alliance with the Mahdists, the latter never really succeeded in subduing the south. Under British administration again by the turn of the century, the south felt the colonial impact only very slightly in the first two decades of the century; although some missionary activity had begun, colonial order was not really secure in the south until the great depression broke—at which point there were no revenues available for development. In the interwar period a series of interrelated, half formed, often inarticulate premises concerning the south acquired the cumulative appearance of a "Southern Policy," later a source of bitter resentment by northerners, and blamed for the eventual secession.[62] The controlling postulate was that the south was fundamentally different from the north and required distinctive administrative organization. Administrative posts until the 1920s were almost exclusively manned by military officers; even later, district officers in the south were generally a special group, apart from the elite Sudan Service which ran the north.[63] Missionaries regarded Islam and Arabism as the two faces of Satan, to be rigorously excluded. Administrator and missionary joined in discouraging the wearing of the characteristic Arab white robe, the *jallabiya*, on the purportedly sanitary grounds that it would "harbour dirt and lice and so encourage disease."[64] Arab names were disapproved. The discovery of a slave ring in 1929 led to official closing of the three southern provinces to northerners; the commercial intermediary roles were filled instead by Greek and Levantine traders. Whereas Arabic was encouraged in the north as the lingua franca, in the south English was the sole medium of modernity. By 1940, notes a Sudanese journalist (with some exaggeration), Southern Policy was, in its own terms, a "great success"; Muslim influence "was

61. Henderson, *Sudan Republic*, p. 164.

61. For a systematic exposition of this view, see Mohamed Omar Beshir, *The Southern Sudan: Background to Conflict* (London: William Blackwood and Sons, 1968).

63. Robert O. Collins, "The Sudan Political Service: A Portrait of Imperialism," *African Affairs*, 71 (1972), 293-303.

64. Henderson, *Sudan Republic*, p. 162.

completely eliminated and the three southern provinces became to all intents and purposes a separate unit, closed to Northern Sudanese and widely open to the British, Greeks and missionaries of all nations."[65]

The most shadowy area of all in the penumbra of Southern Policy was the ultimate objective for the area. During the somnolent years of flood-tide colonialism in the 1920s and 1930s, absolutely nothing was urgent, least of all for Southern Sudan. There was occasional speculative talk about attaching the southern provinces ultimately to Uganda, possibly in the framework of a larger East African grouping. Needless to say, neither Ugandans nor southern Sudanese were involved in these discussions. Echoes of such talk carried to the north, where in a more politically sensitized arena they were seen as proof positive of the cunning duplicity which underlay Southern Policy.

Through the screen of Southern Policy, rather than through direct hostile interaction, southerners and northerners each had rather negative stereotypes of the other. For the north, the south was a vast and primitive region, whose people many habitually referred to as *abid* (slaves), a recurrent grievance of southerners. For the southerner, the northerner was avaricious and domineering, eagerly anticipating the impending opportunity to exploit the untapped wealth of the south, to force Islam and Arabism upon its inhabitants. The tales of the nineteenth-century slave traffic were preserved not only by the custodians of oral tradition, but also by the missionaries and administrators.

INDEPENDENCE AND CULTURAL INSECURITY

After World War II, growing nationalism in the north, as well as Egyptian pressure, forced the pace of political development; by 1947, the fateful decision had been taken that Sudan was to be developed as a single country. At a conference in Juba in 1947, involving northern, southern, and official representatives, the southerners were persuaded to take part in the proposed national assembly, which began operation in 1948. Subsequently, many southern leaders have challenged the bona fides of that agreement, but at the time it was made none could have foreseen that Sudan would be independent by 1956.

What little economic development the south had known occurred mainly between World War II and independence, with the launching of the Zande cotton scheme, a few sawmills, some schools and roads. North-

65. Beshir Mohammed Said, *The Sudan: Crossroads of Africa* (London: Bodley Head, 1965), p. 35.

ern traders streamed south, as for a time opposition to a united Sudan was latent and quiescent. A commission of inquiry subsequently observed that, at that moment, the main opposition came from a few British administrators, for whom "no opportunity was left without instilling into the people that northerners will dominate them; will treat them as their fathers did."[66]

The first national elections occurred in 1953; three parties competed in the south, the Southern Party, which enjoyed the backing of much of the southern elite; the National Unionist Party (linked to Khatmiya, then pro-Egyptian), mainly backed by northern traders; and the Umma (tied to the Mahdist Ansar sect). Curiously, the two northern parties competed for southern support by each portraying the other as the agency of the feared northern exploitation and domination. Arab communities linked to Umma, the NUP pointed out, were the lineal descendants of the nineteenth-century man-catchers. The northern merchants connected to NUP, Umma argued, chiselling, thieving exploiters. In 1954, the central government, now under Sudanese leadership, fearful of growing restiveness in the south, issued a provocative statement pledging "they shall use the force of iron in dealing with any Southerner who will dare attempt to divide the nation."[67] Not long after, the first list was published on new civil service appointments under Sudanization provisions; there were only four southern names out of 500 senior posts Sudanized, a confirmation of the growing suspicions.[68] On the heels of this announcement, the Southern Party, renamed Liberal Party, summoned a conference, at which the delegates agreed that only a federal formula could permit the south to remain in Sudan with acceptable cultural security.

In mid-1955, with independence only six months away, irritants accumulated for the south, as several minor incidents were maladroitly escalated by northern administrators into confrontations. In July 1955, redundancy forced the sudden layoff of 300 southern workers in small mills associated with the Zande cotton scheme; southerners believed this a shabby maneuver to permit their replacement by northerners.[69] Demonstrations ensued, leading to attacks on northern shopkeepers; security forces opened fire, killing eight, and the south crackled with tension.

66. Quoted from the Report of the Commission of Inquiry into Southern Sudan disturbances, August 1955, by Henderson, *Sudan Republic,* p. 171.

67. Ibid., p. 173.

68. Sommer, "The Sudan," pp. 75-76.

69. The Commission of Inquiry report, cited by Henderson, *Sudan Republic,* p. 175, makes no mention of hiring northern replacements. Nonetheless, Oduho and Deng, *Problem of the Southern Sudan,* p. 28, allege the northerners were hired.

The main security force in the south was the Equatoria Corps, with southern enlisted ranks and mainly northern officers. Word leaked to the administration that a mutiny was imminent, which led to frantic requests to Khartoum for the dispatch of northern troops. Some troops were sent, and orders were issued for the transfer of a portion of the Equatoria Corps to Khartoum. Southern troops firmly believed that they would be slaughtered on the arrival of the Corps, and the rumor spread throughout the south that there had been a massacre of southerners at Juba. In an atmosphere charged with cultural hostility, such rumors required no validation. Juba was far enough away so that there was no means of persuasive refutation. Mutiny broke out in Torit camp, in Equatoria, and seventy-eight northern officers and their dependents were killed; northern merchants came under attack in a number of small towns in Equatoria, generally triggered by the canard of the Juba massacre. It was worth noting that, at this juncture, the Dinka and other Upper Nile ethnic communities did not participate.[70]

The Equatoria mutiny was a critical turning point. The mutineers evaporated into the bush, many to reappear later as guerrilla fighters. Distrust between north and south was now sealed in blood. Southern security forces could not be trusted, and the south would have to be garrisoned with northern troops. The hunt for the vanished mutineers began the dreary cycle of punitive operations; the first recorded instance came in 1957, when the Ministry of Defence authorized burning 700 huts in the small Equatoria town of Yei in reprisal for purported harboring of fugitive mutineers.[71] This happened frequently in the following years, as the security situation gradually deteriorated, and the rural population became increasingly involved in resistance to northern rule.

The threat of status deprivation was hammered home to the most readily mobilizable group, young students, through educational policies developed in the wake of the mutiny. Many schools were closed the following year in the south, and a new Southern Policy began to take shape. Missionaries were believed to be the primary impediment to a policy of cultural integration, where it was hoped that Islam and Arabism could play the same assimilative role that we have described for the north. Arabic was to replace English as the medium of instruction, and northern schoolmasters were to be put in charge of the schools. Foreign missionaries were placed under increasing restrictions and finally excluded altogether in 1964. The effect of all these measures, in the eyes of aspirant southern youths, was to choke off their mobility opportunities

70. Henderson, *Sudan Republic*, pp. 176-78.
71. Ibid., pp. 185-86.

altogether—policies which appeared guaranteed to conscript a whole generation into rebellion.

In Khartoum, southern hopes were kept flickering that federalism might be accepted. In order to gain the support of southern M.P.s for independence on 1 January 1956, the Sudanese parliament unanimously committed itself to careful consideration of federalism. However, when it came time to consider implementation later in 1956, northern parties backed away from their commitment, and by 1957 had made clear their insistence on a unitary state with Arabic as national language and Islam as state religion. Elections were held in 1958 to establish a parliament based upon universal suffrage with seats allocated on the basis of the 1956 national census. The Umma (Ansar) party emerged as the leader, with 63 seats; the NUP (which had split in 1956, with the Khatmiya notables forming a splinter Peoples Democratic Party) was second with 45, while the PDP had 27. In the south, the southern party, the Liberals, won only 20 of 46 seats. Among the others were Arab merchants, who, southern intellectuals charged, were installed through administrative interference with the elections.[72]

Efforts to find a constitutional settlement opened up multiple fissures in Sudanese society of which the southern cleavage was but one. When in June 1958, northern members had definitively rejected southern federalist proposals, the southern bloc walked out. Within the north, rumblings of new support for federalism came from the Nuba mountains, the Beja on the Red Sea coast, and the Fur in the far west.[73] Other questions involving the Mahdist view of the state and relations with Egypt developed into a prolonged impasse; in November the army under General Ibrahim Abboud assumed power.

As in the Pakistan case (and Nigeria after the purge of Ibo officers in July 1966), military rule eliminated an important institutional nexus wherein bargaining and interaction, however frustrating, did continue. With southern parties (like others) now placed under sequestration, southern views were deprived of structural channels for expression. The army and civil service were now in full command; after Equatoria, the Sudanese army was not only overwhelmingly northern and Arab in its leadership and outlook, but nourished a particular grievance against the south. Under military rule, relations with the south descended into the maelstrom of civil war by 1963.

72. Oduho and Deng, *Problem of the Southern Sudan*, p. 35.

73. Southern spokesmen, whose political perceptions were governed by the image of Arabs culturally oppressing non-Arabs, attached great significance to these symptoms—see ibid., pp. 36-37. For reasons we have argued in chapter 10 we believe that the Beja and Fur restiveness was a distinctly secondary phenomena.

RISE OF THE ANYA-NYA

In 1960, a large number of southern politicians and intellectuals went into exile, apparently alerted by William Deng, a Dinka assistant district commissioner at Torit in Equatoria, that a number of them figured on a list of arrests ordered by the military government. Deng himself joined them, a major blow to the north, as Deng had just passed the Higher Arabic Examination and earlier in 1960 had penned a letter supporting integration.[74] Legal political parties in the south were suppressed with the military coup of November 1958. In 1961, under the leadership of Father Saturnino Lohure, the Sudanese Christian Association (SCA) was formed, with its principal base among the southern refugee communities which began to flee an increasingly repressive northern administration. Its primary locus was Uganda, and it served as the conduit for some flow of support through church and church-related channels. Soon after, other evanescent bodies began to appear—and submerge: the Mawaju Secret Movement, the Southern Sudanese Liberation Movement, the Sudanese Liberation Front. In late 1962, the Sudan African Closed Districts National Union (SACDNU) emerged in Kinshasa, with William Deng as prime mover. In 1963, the Sudan African National Union surfaced as the most conspicuous exile-based political movement, supplanting and incorporating the SACDNU, but not the SCA.[75] In 1961, as a conciliatory gesture, some eight hundred southern political prisoners, mainly former mutineers who had been captured, were released; many of these, finding no employment opportunities in the south, drifted into the guerrilla ranks. By autumn 1963, the phase of active military dissidence had begun in the south.

The complexity of the political-military struggle in the southern Sudan from 1963 to 1972 defies brief recapitulation.[76] A common fear of cultural annihilation was a unifying motif; Oduho and Deng note, in a booklet published on the eve of the armed phase of resistance, that, "From the present Northern Sudanese attitude and the policies applied to the South we are irresistibly led to the conclusion that their aim is to

74. Henderson, *Sudan Republic*, p. 186.

75. For many of the intricate details of southern organizations and personalities in the movements, I am indebted to an excellent undergraduate paper by Mark Francillon, "The Southern Sudan: A Political History 1958-1972," University of Wisconsin, Madison, 1972. Francillon also offered a detailed and invaluable critique of the draft version of this section.

76. In addition to sources cited above, useful although often conflicting data may be found in Alan Reed, "The Anya-nya: Ten Months Travel with its Forces inside the Southern Sudan," *Munger Africana Library Notes*, no 11 (February 1972); Oliver Albino, *The Sudan: A Southern Viewpoint* (London: Oxford University Press, 1970); Muddathir 'Abd al-Rahim, "Arabism, Africanism and Self-Identification in the Sudan," *Journal of Modern African Studies*, VII, no. 2 (July 1970), 233-50.

destroy the African negroid personality and identity in the Sudan and to replace it with an arabicised and islamicised South."[77] The insurgents did not have the unifying core or institutional resources of a regional governmental apparatus, as did the Ibo—and, to some extent, through Bengali staffing of the East Bengal public service, even the Bengalis. Their struggle was fought in almost total isolation; they lacked the sanctuary and support offered by India to Bangladesh insurgents and the access to international opinion which the skilled diplomatic machinery of Biafra afforded.

A rough portrait of the complexity of the movement emerges from a contemplation of the diversity of its components. Its most important element is also the least known, the Anya-nya, or guerrilla forces. Although at the 1972 peace talks, its numbers were said to be fewer than 10,000, when the opportunity for renumerated integration into the Sudan army as part of the peace accord arose, more than 20,000 self-identified Anya-nya appeared, a development reminiscent of the Algerian 1962 situation when the ranks of those claiming to have fought with the Armée Nationale de Libération ballooned enormously after the peace settlement. Its initial core appears to have been former mutineers of the Equatoria Corps, augmented by subsequent defections of southerners from the Sudan army, as well as schoolboys affected by the virtual closure of all schools in the south from 1964. Although their overall objects, name, and mode of operation was common, there was no overall military leadership until the very end. In 1970, Major General Joseph Lagu, a Madi from western Equatoria, acquired the reputation of foremost military commander, but it was only during the peace negotiations that his authority was consolidated. For a time, there were distinguishable Anya-nya clusters in Upper Nile, Eastern and Western Equatoria, and Bahr-al-Ghazal. In the late 1960s, the Zande group was arguing for a separate Sue River state, including Azande areas of Zaire and the Central African Republic. Through much of the period of rebellion, the various Anya-nya groups were the most intransigent in the demand for complete independence. Anya-nya leaders came from a rather different milieu than many southern politicians; they were less likely to be Christian, and hence were less tied to the missions. Indeed, a certain number were Muslims, especially those who had formerly served in the Sudan army.

A second important group were the exile politicians, who operated from neighboring countries under a bewildering succession of labels—SANU, Azania Liberation Front, Nile Provisional Government, and others. Neighboring states fluctuated in their degree of receptivity to the southern exiles and the amount of political activity they were disposed to tolerate. Operating from capitals as widely dispersed as Kinshasa,

77. Oduho and Deng, *Problem of the Southern Sudan*, p. 38.

Kampala, and Addis Ababa, factional cleavage among the exiles was inevitable, partly reflected in the shower of organizational titles.

Another segment of the political-intellectual elite remained in Khartoum. Reed claims that nearly all the southerners in Khartoum were secret sympathizers with the Anya-nya.[78] It would seem more plausible, during the long period of struggle when the outcome was uncertain, that loyalties were often ambiguous and that individual ties fluctuated with the waxing and waning of Anya-nya fortunes and labyrinthine web of factional conflict among the exile politicians. There was a degree of movement between Khartoum and the exile clusters. During moments of conciliatory overtures from Khartoum, some southerners would be wooed back; at other moments, offended or threatened by one or another development in Khartoum, others would slip into exile.

A fourth important group was the very large number of refugees who fled into Zaire, Uganda, and Ethiopia; at the time of settlement in 1972, these numbered an estimated 200,000. Many were young men determined to pursue their education. However poorly equipped the refugee settlements were in school facilities, they were at least better than the padlocked educational system in the southern Sudan.[79] Others were simply rural folk uprooted by the military operations in their homeland and terrified by the indiscriminate nature of repression in a culturally defined civil war. An additional 800,000 were internal refugees, who had fled from their homes into bush areas inaccessible to the Sudanese army.[80]

The actual scale of operations rose and fell with shifts of focus in Khartoum between a search for a political solution or all-out repression, and Anya-nya access to arms and supplies. The overthrow of the first military regime in October 1964 was partly motivated by a belief among some northern intellectuals, especially students, that the military policy of repression was bankrupt. In early 1965, some negotiations occurred; however, at the same time, the Anya-nya had a supply windfall when the Sudanese government, joining in the widespread African indignation at the American-Belgian parachute operation in Kisangani in November 1964 against Zaire rebels, agreed to permit the transit of arms from Algeria and China through the south to northeast Zaire. This involved a long overland transfer through Anya-nya zones; many truckloads of arms were ambushed and captured. Zaire rebels, fleeing the Zaire national

78. Reed, *The Anya-nya*, p. 18.

79. Ibid., p. 7. In a visit to a number of schools in eastern Zaire in 1969, I was struck to find the ubiquity of the southern Sudanese youth. The extraordinary tenacity of the young people of this diaspora, who, friendless and penniless, overcame innumerable obstacles to maintain a toehold in the educational ladder, was eloquent testimony to the power of the idea of education as gateway to a better life.

80. Sam C. Sarkesian, "The Southern Sudan: A Reassessment" (paper presented to the 1972 annual meetings of the African Studies Association, November 1972), p. 34.

army into southern Sudan, were also disarmed by Anya-nya units. Subsequently some arms became available through Ethiopia, in reprisal for Sudanese sanctuary and covert support for Muslim-led insurgents in Eritrea province. Israel also apparently provided some arms, presumably in retaliation for Sudanese solidarity with Arab states in the Middle East crisis.

The dialectic of conflict slowly enlarged the solidarity of the south. In the early stages, the north had placed high hopes in divisions within the south, and in particular the concentration of initial dissidence in Equatoria province. Numerically important groups such as the Dinka, Shilluk, and Nuer were not at first strongly involved. However, culturally threatening events followed one another in unending sequence, to render the polarization more complete. Under the Abboud regime, plans were unveiled to resettle 1.5 milion Arabs in Upper Nile province. Fraternal cohabitation, it was believed, would lead to harmony and amity and help diminish resistance to Arabic and Islam. Needless to say, Dinka, Shilluk, Nuer, and others whose lands were threatened by this proposal found it profoundly disquieting.[81] In July 1965, two separate massacres occurred, one involving 1400 Africans in Juba and another 76 in Wau; southerners believed these incidents demonstrated northern determination to exterminate the southern elite.[82]

Conflict lasted long enough to make it clear that neither side could win. The south was vast, its roads were few, and there was no way in which the Sudan army could control anything but the few administrative posts and perhaps daylight movement on the roads. As of 1967, the Sudan army numbered only 18,500, of which only two-thirds could be safely committed to the south.[83] On the other hand, Anya-nya could never rely upon meaningful help from outside; whatever informal sympathy the plight of the south generated in other African states, the commitment to the existing state system by the Organization of African Unity was overriding. Separatism had brothers and sisters in most African states, and the fear of the demonstration effect was universal.

Finally the exhausting civil war was brought to a negotiated end in 1972. An important immediate factor permitting settlement was, paradoxically, the growing unity of at least the military wing of the insurgent movement. The rise of Joseph Lagu as a leader of stature provided

81. Ibid., p. 25. Reed, *The Anya-nya*, p. 29, also mentions this hare-brained scheme.

82. In Juba, the African quarter was encircled and houses set afire; those trying to escape were shot, and it was claimed that army personnel made a tally of the intellectuals killed. In Wau, the scene of the massacre was a wedding party of a prominent member of the local elite, at which most of the Wau intellectuals were present. Whatever the precise details of these incidents, the forms in which they were recorded stressed the cultural threat to the southern intelligentsia.

83. Sarkesian, *The Southern Sudan*, p. 28.

a focal point for meaningful negotiations (which in turn strengthened his position). In previous conversations, usually involving the exiled or the Khartoum politician-intellectual class, not only were the southerners divided, but in the last analysis unable to speak for the military wing. Lagu, in contrast, became able to deliver peace if the terms were met. Sudan made generous concessions, in return for the maintenance of a single polity. Certainly the provisions guaranteeing the absorption of the Anya-nya as units into the Sudan army not only was an armed assurance for southerners, but also offered personal security for the guerrillas. Lagu became a deputy commander of the Sudan army and adjutant to President Gaafar al-Nimeiry. The south was to have autonomy, and be ruled by its own native sons; it could elaborate its own cultural policy, and thus end the anxiety of threatened cultural domination.[84]

THE IMPROBABILITIES OF SECESSIONISM

In what ways do the patterns observable in the causation, process, and outcome of secession instruct us? A full exploration of these complex dramas would have required far more space than we can indulge; all three are still so recent, at the time of writing, that many significant aspects remain obscure. Particularly is this so for the southern Sudan, the most poorly reported of the three. Each has been an epic struggle, in which the shape of the political community has been the object of armed conflict. In each, one important culturally defined collectivity concluded that communal safety could only be secured through total separation. From the causes and consequences of that choice, we may suggest several inferences, all of which will be subject to much greater refinement when these three crises have received the extended study which they deserve.

Firstly, even in its hours of greatest travail, the formidable power of the state system in compartmentalizing human groupings is verified. In all three cases, at the moment of armed struggle, there can be no doubt that the separation goal enjoyed overwhelming support from the solidarity community involved. Yet the central elites found a moral imperative in the idea of the state in its extant territorial frame, although during the conflict itself, if not always beforehand, there was general recognition that the seceding collectivity was solidary in its determination to separate. But there was very little doubt among central power-holders of their sacred obligation to oppose withdrawal with all force that could

84. On the Sudan settlement, see *Africa Report*, XVIII, no. 4 (April 1972), 4; David Roden, "Peace Brings Sudan New Hope and Massive Problems," *Africa Report*, XVII, no. 6 (June 1972), 14-16.

be mobilized. The sanctity of the territorial polity permitted of no Wilsonian speculation about the rights of nationalities to self-determination. The seceders, therefore, could not count upon any indulgence. In these interactions, force was the currency, and the eventual outcome in each instance depended upon the capacity to win militarily. In Biafra, the Nigerian army could overpower the secession, which had no contiguous zone of sanctuary and only limited external assistance. In the southern Sudan there was an exhausting stalemate, which forced a compromise settlement after nine bitter years (or seventeen, if we set the clock from the Equatoria mutiny in 1955). In Bangladesh, friendly sanctuary, substantial aid, and decisive armed intervention was available from India. From the separatist standpoint, Bangladesh benefitted from, not only total cultural mobilization, but also an extremely favorable set of geopolitical factors, which would only rarely be available to potential secessionists.

Secondly, the act of separation is well recognized as a risk-laden adventure and is only undertaken under circumstances of extreme cultural threat. For Biafrans, the attack on Ibo officers, followed by the pogroms in northern cities was a powerful shock. For Bangladesh, the repressive campaign by the Pakistan army marked the point of no return. In southern Sudan, the most traumatic single event was the Equatoria mutiny in 1955; the actual guerrilla campaign only gradually coalesced, and indeed it is not clear whether any identifiable group made a conscious decision for revolt. But the successive threats—rejection of federalism, northern domination of the Sudanized institutions, menaces of Arabization and Islamization, rumored massive detention of southern elites and resettlement of Arabs in the south—appeared to endanger cultural survival. In all three cases, the structure of politics at the center seemed wholly inaccessible to the alienated group. In each instance, a military regime held power in which the secessionists had no foothold.

In terms of the institutional resources of secession, the three secessionists form a continuum, with Biafra at one pole and southern Sudan at the other. Biafra undertook secession under full control of a well-developed set of regional institutions, with its own staff manning the hierarchy. The ethnic fragmentation of the Nigerian army left Biafra equipped with its own security force, although it was lacking in equipment. Bengalis occupied most of the public service positions, had a charismatic leader and political party. However, they were not in a position to prevent Pakistan from seizing control of the governmental machinery; their struggle had to be carried on by a loosely knit group of guerrilla forces and, diplomatically, by a government-in-exile. Southern Sudan began the struggle empty-handed. There was a southern party, but it was a loose-knit parliamentary and electoral coalition, with no real structure. The three southern provinces had been treated as a unique policy problem, but they had no regional institutions. The indirect-rule elites—the chiefs who administered the rudimentary local administration—had been the sole southern leadership until World War II, then had been completely eclipsed by the very small politician-intellectual class. Curiously, the very amorphous character of the southern Sudanese rebellion, structurally, made it inextinguishable. No decisive battle could be fought, no critical leader could be captured; the hydra-headed Anyanya were everywhere and nowhere. For Biafra, on the other hand, its very structural resources were in the end a weakness; once its institutional core had been defeated, nothing remained.

Fourthly the composition of the elite of the alienated cultural community and the distribution of its skills shape its perspectives to the national arena. In Biafra, the Ibo elite was very large and had established administrative and commercial leadership in a country-wide diaspora. With independence, regional elites had challenged the Ibo role and endeavored to use political institutions to reduce their role. Threatened in the domains critical to their status and mobility, Ibo elites were increasingly on the defensive and finally concluded they could find security only through a retreat into the cradleland. In Pakistan, Punjabis and Urdu-speakers completely dominated the military, bureaucratic, and economic elites. Only in the political sector did Bengali elites compete, the foreclosure of this sphere by military coup in 1958-71 and the ultimate unwillingness of West Pakistan power-holders to turn the system over to the vernacular political elites that had emerged after independence, meant that there was simply no way that the Bengali linguistic community could play a role in Pakistan commensurate with their numbers or expectations. In the southern Sudan, the small intellectual elite, English-speaking and Christian, saw only a paltry role for itself on the Sudanese stage, since the unitarian convictions of the northern elite precluded the establishment of a regional domain, with different cultural prerequisites, in which southerners might have found a reasonably satisfying outlet for their ambitions. It is precisely such an opportunity that is guaranteed by the 1972 settlement.

Fifthly, the importance of multiple identities is further underlined. In the Ibo case, pan-Ibohood is superposed upon more localized solidarities of particular impact in shaping political conflict within Iboland. In Pakistan, the independence elite, politically socialized in the transcendent struggle with Hindu India, believed completely in the integrative force of political Islam; they could neither foresee nor really understand the linguistic subnationalism which rose to the fore after independence. In

Bengal, the Muslim League elite was descredited in the first years after independence, with the idea of Bengali cultural solidarity of growing importance. In southern Sudan, the concept of southern solidarity, an artifact of missionary and administrative paternalism before World War II, became a reality only in the years of struggle. At the time of the Equatoria mutiny, ethinc groups reacted very differently; even in the early years of guerrilla warfare, ethnic divisions were a frequent source of tension, although this level of ethnicity had never been strongly politicized in Sudan.

Sixthly, the dynamic aspect of identity formation is well illustrated. The modernity of Ibohood was argued at length. Prior to World War I, Iboland had been a collection of local societies, pejoratively viewed by the colonizer and other Nigerians. Between 1920 and 1950, the Ibo had become a mobilized, partly urbanized collectivity, with a sharply altered social image; the "bush Ibo" had become the aggressive modernizer. In Bengal, one generation saw the alteration of the most salient identity from Islamic solidarity to Bengali cultural nationalism. In post-civil war Sudan, it is an open question whether the postulate of southern solidarity will be reinforced or whether ethnicity within the south will now become politicized. Initial evidence from postsettlement operation of the southern Sudan autonomous region suggests that ethnicity is becoming more salient, as groups compete for place and influence in the new regional government.

Lastly, the capacity of human communities for reconciliation must be set against their propensity for cultural conflict. During the Nigerian civil war, rare was the observer who dared forecast that a year after the war's end Ibo would be able to travel with security to most parts of the federation. In the postconflict psychology of fraternalism rediscovered, the former belligerents seem to acquire a sensitivity to cultural anxieties that could have easily averted civil war had it been present before. In southern Sudan, the world noted the 1972 settlement in skeptical disbelief. The triumphant tours of President Nimeiry through the south were astonishing in the scenes of enthusiastic affection. Nimeiry has become an embodiment of trust, a personification of cultural reassurance.

Somehow within the resources of statecraft there is surely a way in which cultural fraternalism is available at a lower cost.

13 Patterns, Trends, and Formulas

*As in an orchestra, every type of instrument has its special
timbre and tonality, found in its substances and form; as every
type has its appropriate theme and melody in the whole
symphony, so in society each ethnic group is the natural
instrument, its spirit and culture are its theme and melody, and
the harmony and dissonances and discords of them all make the
symphony of civilization, with this difference: a musical
symphony is written before it is played; in the symphony of
civilization the playing is the writing, so that there is nothing so
fixed and inevitable about its progressions as in music, so that
within the limits set by nature they may vary at will, and the range
and variety of the harmonies may become wider and richer and
more beautiful.*

—Horace Kallen[1]

*All nice people like Us, are We
And everybody else is They.*

—Rudyard Kipling[2]

Many analytical threads have been introduced in our exploration of a
selection of illustrative cases. The time has now come to draw many of
these together, as best we can, to return to our search for what is general
from the wealth of particular detail. The fabric which may emerge reveals,
alas, no simple design. The variables are many, and their interactive
patterns diverse. But all is not confusion. Regularities are discernible,
propositions do emerge. Cultural pluralism, at times, appears beyond the
ken of statecraft, but it is not beyond the reach of analysis. Indeed, it is our
conviction that, as its dynamics become better understood, the capacities
of statecraft to achieve harmonious civil order within a culturally plural
polity are thereby enlarged. In this final chapter, it is our purpose to
delineate some general patterns, specify trends, and consider political
formulas available for peaceful coexistence with cultural pluralism.

1. Peter I. Rose, *They and We* (New York: Random House, 1964), p. 56.
2. Quoted in Ibid., p. 74.

CULTURAL BASES FOR THE STATE AND DIVERSITY PATTERNS

In any polity, broad parameters are set by the cultural definition of the state and the specific type, number, and distribution of solidary entities within their territorial domain. The legitimating principles by which the power inhering in the institutions of the state is allocated and exercised are central to pattern establishment. It matters a great deal whether power is defined by universal suffrage elections, as in India or Lebanon; by traditional monarchy with specific cultural associations, as in Afghanistan, Saudi Arabia, and Ethiopia; by military-bureaucratic oligarchy, as in Egypt, Zaire, or Peru; by racial caste, as in South Africa. The dominant metaphors through which social conflict is politically conceptualized, through parties and ideologies, enter the equation. In some polities, the competition for scarce resources and values and the tensions born of unequal distribution of wealth and status are described almost exclusively in terms of cultural labels. In other instances, ideological divisions, which in the contemporary world usually have social-class derivations, are so powerfully dominant in fixing political discourse that cultural pluralism becomes distinctly secondary.

In chapter 3 we suggested a typology of states, in terms of their historical origin and cultural basis. These were:

1. Historically arbitrary, immigrant dominated
2. Colonial units, African or Asian immigrant power-holders
3. Homeland states
4. Arbitrary colonial units, indigenous successors to power
5. Colonial states with historical personality
6. Historical states affected by colonial phase
7. Traditional states
8. Cultural self-determination states

At the same time, we put forward a six-fold classification of cultural diversity:

A. Homogeneous
B. Single clearly dominant group, with minorities
C. Core culture, linked to central institutions, with differentiated groups in periphery
D. Dominant bipolar pattern
E. Multipolar pattern, with no dominant groups
F. Multiplicity of cultures, with more than one basis of differentiation

With these categories in mind, let us look at the dominant configurations in each region.

ASIA: CORE CULTURE AND MULTIPOLAR PATTERNS

In Asia, the state system, for the most part, has precolonial historical antecedents, mostly falling in categories 5, 6, and 7. This means that the nation-building process, through which the state seeks the sanction of nationality, frequently involved utilization of the symbol system associated with the historically dominant culture. At the same time, as the impact of the state on its periphery ramifies, the issue of relationships with culturally differentiated groups becomes critical for the several Asian states which fall in cultural diversity categories *B* or *C* (Burma, Thailand, Laos, Cambodia, Vietnam, Sri Lanka). National language policy is an inevitable issue arena in core culture states; the politically and historically dominant group will see in the promotion of its language through the vehicle of state power an indispensable instrument of cultural dignity and progress. The state has potent devices, of far greater import than anything associated with historical kingdoms, for implementing language policies. Even practices that may have existed previously are transformed in impact through their greater saliency to the population on the periphery; the state, for example, may have long required that transactions with it occur in the language of the core culture, but the significance of this fact is multiplied by the growing infusion of state institutions into everyday existence. The school system, allocator of mobility, through the language of instruction forces cultural choice into each village as it extends. The huge scale of the public sector—with or without benefit of socialist ideology—in the total matrix of modern institutions and the linguistic requirements for employment often link mobility opportunities and the core culture. For aspirant members of the young generation, this is a potent constraint toward acquisition of the state language. At the same time, it is a prime cause of cultural mobilization of the periphery; cultural policies which affect mobility opportunities affect the age group most susceptible to political organization and cultural mass movements. The propensity of this group for militant cultural solidarity is well illustrated in the Tamil and Bangali cases we have described. Although India has a cultural center of gravity in the Hindu religious tradition and Hindi language, it has pursued integration most successfully as a 5-*F* type polity. The non-Hindi zones are not prepared to see the imposition of Hindi as a national language; the resolute commitment to build India as a secular state is critical to harmonious communal relations with the large non-Hindu groups. In Sri Lanka, Malaysia, and Singapore, pluralism is essentially bipolar; we would suggest that the integrative outcome is very different if the political elite assumes a type *B* or *C* polity, as has been the case in Sri Lanka, or operates on the basis of type *D* postulates, as has occurred in Singapore and in large measure, Malaysia. In Sri Lanka, the endemic problem of the disaffection of the Tamil minority has been exacerbated by Singhalese insistence on elevating their language and religion to exclusive official status. Malays, on the other hand, have demanded an association of the state with their culture at the symbolic level, but have left a zone of cultural (and economic) autonomy to the Chinese population. Singapore has adhered to cultural neutrality, despite the large Chinese majority. Indonesia and the Philippines are both type 4-*F* states, with relatively successful cultural policies (with alienation of Filipino Muslims the main exception).

The idea of nation-building itself, so deeply embedded in the world culture of modernity, is likely to produce strains in core culture states in their relations with culturally distinctive zones. At the center, an unchallengeable corollary of nation-building is development of the cultural ideology of the dominant group: unification and modernization of its language, encouragement of its literature, shaping of a national history in terms of achievements of the core culture. Again, the resources of the modern state for this task are considerable; funds can be made available to the cultural literati for the pursuit of these great tasks, a group which, nurtured in a profound attachment to the virtues of their culture, is often disposed to classicalize it in ways which make it less serviceable as an integrative instrument. This has certainly been the case with Hindi cultural scholars, the National Language Institute in the Philippines, and Arabic literature bureaus in the Arab world. The linkage of the modern moral imperative of nation-building and a core culture is quite likely to render the national elites insensitive to the probable impact of certain nation-building strategies. Within the affective frame of core culture attachments, it seems both logical and right to require through state power that the core culture community be extended to be coterminous with the territorial bounds of the state, and that history be interpreted through the triumphs and calamaties of the dominant group. It was this type of process in Eastern Europe which made the Balkans a powder keg and led to extensive population exchanges to achieve a cultural homogeneity which forced assimilation failed to provide. So natural and right does this seem that policies quite provocative to the culturally distinct groups are often unwittingly adopted. In the United States, one need only recall how riddled were school history texts with ethnocentric interpretations, which came under fire only when politically mobilized minorities, Blacks and others, raised an effective challenge. The ethnocentricity was largely unconscious and passed quite unperceived by the dominant group. Comparable was the effort by the old Muslim League elite to impose Urdu as sole national language in Pakistan, or the extraordinary proposal developed by the Abboud regime in Sudan for resettling 1.5 million Arabic-speaking northerners in the south. In both instances, the elites of the dominant culture were unable to perceive these policies as cultural oppression; rather, they were merely pursuing the patriotic dictates of nation-building.

Overall patterns of cultural politization suggest the likelihood that core culture states can expect to face a challenge from peripheral cultures. Several factors may be identified in support of this proposition. There is likely to be an economic disparity between central core and periphery; certainly this is true of Burma, Thailand, Laos, both Vietnams. The logic of state-building will ineluctably lead to increasing administrative penetration of the periphery, along with schools and other social infrastructure. These institutions, in turn, are the agencies through which the periphery becomes more conscious of its material disparities with relation to the central core. The dominant group enters more directly into its line of social vision, which leads both to redefinition of one's own identity and resentment of the core culture group.

The nature of the process is affected by the type of cultural diversity, the capacity of political institutions to mediate and buffer the conflicts, the magnitude of differentiation between dominant culture and periphery, and the intensity of ideological articulation of identity. We argued in our chapter on India and Nigeria that two- or three-actor cultural conflict is particularly difficult to contain. This is the pattern in Sri Lanka, a communal drama whose last chapter has not yet been written.[3] More characteristic is a multiplicity of periphery cultures, distinctly less mobilized than the core culture. In Burma and Indochina, the hill groups are quite distinct from the dominant culture; with the exception of the Burma Karens and Shans, these identities are very little elaborated in ideological terms. However, they have been the object of political manipulation of various participants in the Vietnam, Laos, and Cambodian conflicts—of the United States in particular; ethnicity armed as a barrier against Communism has likely been intensified through the sheer necessities of survival. In Thailand, the cultural difference between the ethnic Thai of central Thailand, and the biggest minority, the Isam Lao of the northeast, is one of gradation rather than sharp linguistic and other discontinuities. A recent study has shown that the greatly increased interaction with a Thai-oriented national society has tended toward crystallization of an active Lao identity, superimposed upon the pre-existing, totally localized solidarities.[4]

3. The politics of communalism of Sri Lanka is well described in Robert N. Kearney, *Communalism and Language in the Politics of Ceylon* (Durham: Duke University Press, 1967).

4. Charles F. Keyes, "Ethnic Identity and Loyalty of Villagers in Northeastern Thailand," *Asian Survey*, VI, no. 7 (July 1966), pp. 362-69.

On the question of institutional capabilities, India perhaps ranks highest, with several tiers of elective bodies, and vital, if factionalized, political parties as arenas of bargaining, conflict within carefully regulated limits, and continuing interaction. Burma sets a pole of institutional atrophy; the strong commitment to nation-building through Burmanization of language, dress, and religion held by some national elites in the early independence period is emasculated by the incapacity of the Burmese state to accomplish anything of this order. In Afghanistan (as in Ethiopia), a core culture as a traditional state was associated with the monarchical institution until the coups of 1973 (Afghanistan) and 1974 (Ethiopia). In both cases, limited experiments with additional institutions, such as parliament, have not yet made a fundamental difference in the distribution of power. At the same time, change is coming to the periphery, and with it will inevitably follow a political awakening of other groups, who may come to resent the monarchy (and possibly the military which replace it) as identified with Pushtun or Amhara culture.

STATE, NATION, AND PLURALISM IN THE ARAB WORLD

Cultural pluralism in the Arab world is a three-dimensional interaction among the elusive idea of the Arab nation, a powerful force among some segments of opinion; the present state system, largely an artifact of imperial intervention in the Arab world; and ethnic and religious pluralism. We have examined at some length in chapter 10 the dialectic tensions between pan-Arabism, the state-nations, and the pluralism they contain. The idea of Arabhood has a powerful cultural ideology, which partly conflicts with state-oriented identities and creates particular problems for those Arab states of type *C* (Sudan, Morocco, Mauritania, Iraq). The homeland state of Israel, with its own integration challenge of Oriental Jews and Arabs, impinges upon most of the Arab world through the forging in opposition of the stateless nationality of Palestinians, bound to the solidarity imperatives of pan-Arabism. The apparent homogeneity of Arabhood, on closer examination, dissolves in the religious pluralism of polities such as Lebanon, Iraq, Yemen, and Syria; only a minority of Arab states, such as Tunisia and Libya, fall clearly in type *A*.

Arabism and the pan-Arab ideal are potent emotional forces which offer a role that seems to call forth a leader: the Hashemites Hussain and Faisal during World War I, then Nasser, and, most recently, Qaadafi have donned the mantle. The appeal of Arabism in politicized sectors cannot overcome the decisive impact which the existing state institutions have upon daily lives of people. It is the state that administers, that schools, and, for many of the elite, that employs. It monopolizes the symbols of sovereignty—stamps, coins, flags. In turn, the state and the national political arena which it defines serve as the transactional frame for plural patterns within it. Over time, conflict may become ritualized and circumscribed in ways which render it less threatening, as in Lebanon, and post-civil war Sudan. These delicate adjustments come under immediate threat in a larger Arab state, which make pan-Arabism a source of anxiety and fear for Iraqi Kurds and Shi'ite Arabs, Lebanese Christian Arabs, and southern Sudanese. On the other hand, in several states the incorporative force of Arab culture, with its prestigious bonds to Islam, provides some quite exceptional outcomes in northern Sudan and Maghreb. Here, periphery cultures, such as Fur and Beja, in Sudan, or Berber, in the Maghreb, do not congeal and politicize with social change; rather their modernizing edges break off and tend toward incorporation into a nationally oriented culture.

AFRICA: THE CULTURALLY NEUTRAL STATE

In sub-Saharan Africa, the state is differently conceived by its elites. The modal form of cultural basis is type 4, with a handful (such as Rwanda, Burundi, Lesotho, and Swaziland) as type 6, Ethiopia as type 7, Somalia as type 8, and South Africa type 1. In cultural diversity, pattern *E* and *F* are most frequent, again with a few exceptions. Somalia, Botswana, Lesotho, and Swaziland are homogeneous (at least at the level of linguistic identity); Gabon, Gambia, Rwanda, and Upper Volta have a single clearly dominant group (*B*); Ethiopia, South Africa, and Liberia have core cultures (*C*); and Burundi is bipolar (*D*). But despite these apparently numerous exceptions, yet there is a shared normative perspective as to the cultural neutrality of the state. This partly derives from the complete artificiality of most states, joined to the awareness of the multicultural basis of society. The ideology of nation-building, in this setting, involves suffusing the state with nonspecific African symbols, epitomized by Mobutu's "authenticity" campaign in Zaire, the negritude of Senghor, the utilization of Swahili as a nonethnic national culture in Tanzania. This has set important limits to the transformation of ethnicity into cultural ideology; while ethnicity has been a frequently utilized political weapon and charges have filled the air of ethnic domination of one or another state institutions, state power has never been placed behind cultural ideology-building, even when in the hands of a single group (with the exception of South Africa and Ethiopia). In some instances, such as the Kongo and Ganda, incipient trends toward elaboration of cultural ideologies withered on the vine. Thus, for example, in Kenya, where Kikiyu political elites are well entrenched in power, it would simply not occur even to those most determined that "the flag shall not leave Kikuyuland" to promote that aim through total identification of Kikuyu cultural symbols with the state of Kenya. This distingishes cultural politics from the Asian pattern in important ways. Although, as we have shown, ethnicity as a political role is quite important for Ibo or Luba-Kasai, it is inconceivable that it would be developed along the ideological lines of Tamil or Sikh subnationalism in India. Perhaps we might detect in this contrast the enduring impact of colonial images of society; Europeans looked upon Ibo, Yoruba, Kongo, and Ganda as "tribes," and not latent nationalities. No one would have dreamed of labelling the Tamil as a "tribe."

Indonesia and the Philippines are the only Asian states which parallel the African pattern. In these instances, nation-building has become identified with a state without historical or cultural antecedents, with the construction of an integrative national culture, separate from any sub-culture (although drawing from their cultural resources). This is particularly striking in Indonesian where the sheer demographic weight of the ethnic Javanese would almost certainly have led to grave strains if the history and language of Java had been postulated as core culture. The Indonesian language, whose cultural connotations are quite distinct from Javanese in both ethnic and religious domains, supplies an integrative metaphor which enjoys remarkably wide acceptance. In the Philippines, Pilipino, with its Tagalog derivations, has a more difficult task in dissociating itself with its subnational origins. Nonetheless, the self-concept of the collectivity from its first establishment through Spanish conquest in the sixteenth century has been nonethnic. The centrality, geographically and socially, of the Tagalog in other circumstances would have given the Philippines a very different, and far more difficult, nation-building task.

RACIAL SEGMENTATION IN THE CARIBBEAN

The Caribbean has inherited from its plantation past a series of racially segmented polities. Particularly in the British tradition, the type 2 states were founded on the premise of racial caste. Abolition and later democracy eliminated the numerically small white planter class as a significant category, but their concept of society endured; its reality-shaping power is underlined by the remarkable contrast with Cuba, Dominican Republic, and Puerto Rico, where racial divisions, although highly correlative with social class, do not serve as the lexicon for describing it. The color gradations within the population of African ancestry, involving degrees of genetic influence of the planter aristocracy, form the basis of sharp differentiation of status. Conflict is most intense in Guyana and Trinidad & Tobago, where plantation operators replaced freed slaves with indentured East Indian labor. Although differences of caste, language, and religion internally divide the East Indians, they, like Africans, were integrated through competition with the other racial community. The electoral arena was a decisive factor in converting social differentiation into solidary, mobilized political blocs. Although at first, both in Guyana and Trinidad & Tobago, parties were organized around ideological metaphors, the fires of partisan confrontation soldered the racial collectivities into cohesive blocs. Over time, parties inevitably came to reflect the most salient cleavages in society.

The African communities have developed a more self-conscious racial ideology, oriented towards the larger Black world. West Indian intellectuals played a critical role in the formulation of the idea of pan-Africanism and negritude; there is no really comparable philosophic elaboration of East Indian identity. Some have argued that ideologies of Black identity are analogous to *indigenismo* in Mexico or Peru, as middle class intellectual, mestizo-mulatto creations.[5] But whatever their social origins, doctrines of African racial solidarity, founded upon a history of bitter oppression and deprivation, have a powerful appeal to politicized sectors of society. Only in Haiti does the racial ideology appear to have become wholly incorporated into the concept of the state itself; here the particular history of the uniquely successful slave insurrection, followed by the legendary exploits of Toussaint l'Ouverture in defeating the Napoleonic army, conferred upon the state, through its act of genesis, a Black heritage. Elsewhere, territorial identities remained diffuse and for a time appeared on the way to absorption within a broader West Indian Federation; their affirmation came in reaction to this ill-fated experiment.

ETHNICITY IN LOW PROFILE IN LATIN AMERICA

Latin American states fall into category 1, by origin, and fall into a continuum from homogeneity to core culture with differentiated periphery (*A* to *C*) in diversity. The cultural postulates of Spanish and Portuguese colonialism, territorialized with the conquest of independence by the Creole elite, have created a powerfully assimilative frame. The historical trend has been from *C* to *A*. In polities such as Paraguay, Honduras, and Nicaragua, where there has been little addition through immi-

5. H. Hoetink, in Campbell (ed.), *Racial Tensions and National Identity,* p. 20.

gration to the population stocks long established, and neither European settlement nor Indian pre-Colombian numbers were large, cultural and genetic fusion is stable and complete.

In Mexico, scene of the largest original Indian populations, the unilingual, monocultural Indian is a residual sector and clearly on the path to complete incorporation in the predominantly mestizo population. The Indian survives through the mythology of *indigenismo*, a retroactive revalorisaton of the Indian heritage which, functionally, operates as the ultimate sanction of genetic mestization and cultural Hispanization. In Uruguay and Argentina, large-scale nineteenth-century European immigration gave an overwhelmingly White racial configuration, even though the Indian frontier in the latter case was not subdued until the late nineteenth century. In Guatemala, the Ladinoization pattern seems firmly established, although the peripheral Indian sector is still nearly half the population. In the three other republics with high Indian populations—Ecuador, Bolivia, and Peru—the potential resources for cultural mobilization of the periphery, through a unified language and potent historical myth, are far greater and mestization much less complete than in Mexico. In this context, the cultural policies of the mestizo Peruvian military regime in the early 1970s are of particular interest. The military elites were politicized by their successful campaign to suppress guerrilla insurrection in the Indian sierra in the mid-1960s. In power, they have sought to coopt both radical ideological symbols of the mestizo organizers of the abortive rebellions and cultural symbols associated with the Indian peasant mass: thus the canonization of Tupac Amarú and disenthronement of Pizarro as national symbol.

In former Spanish domains, although the magnitude of African importation in the Caribbean lands was very great, *indigenismo* does not have an analogous cultural mythology relating to Black incorporation. In Colombia and Venezuela, the coastal zones where the African genetic contribution is strongest have always been politically peripheral. Absorption of Indians without benefit of *indigenismo* is, to all intents and purposes, complete, while the African component has remained invisible in national mythologies. In Dominican Republic, the population that would be classified as Black in American racial conceptualization is 71.9 percent of the total, yet this proportion is not celebrated in national ideologies nor in philosophies of protest. There has been but one non-White president (Heureux), and White domination of the institutions of power has been comparable to that of the United States.[6] In post revolutionary Cuba, the Afro-Cuban heritage has been a rather muted theme in the Marxist-Leninist ideology of the Castro regime. As late as

6. Ibid., p. 29.

1841, Africans constituted an absolute majority over mulattos and Whites, but abolition of the slave trade and very substantial European immigration drastically altered population proportions; the most recent census lists 72.8 percent of the population as White.[7]

Only in Brazil has national myth-making turned its full energies to the African fact within the Brazilian amalgam. Nearly four million African slaves were landed in Brazil, or approximately nine times the number imported into North America.[8] 37.5 percent of the Brazilian population today is African or mulatto. A profoundly rooted sociology affirms that Brazil is a nonracial society, united by a culturally egalitarian Lusitanian personality. The national elites, predominantly White with some mulatto leavening, cling to the nonracial ideology as an article of absolute faith. Curiously, this unshakeable conviction is quite unsupported by empirical fact, as a number of inquiries have conclusively demonstrated.[9]

There has been a notable absence of visible Black racial movements or ideologies. There have, however, been more embryonic symptoms of racial mobilization than is generally recognized. Under the Getulio Vargas regime (1930-45, 1950-54), a Brazilian Negro Front became significant enough for the government to dissolve it. A Brazilian sociologist, L. A. Costa Pinta, who has contributed to the empirical challenge to the national ideology of nonracial society, recites a memorable experience when he was invited to chair a session of the first Brazilian Congress of the Negro, about 1950: "... a black member of the Congress affirmed that 'in Brazil racial prejudice does not exist.' The wave of protests that rose from the audience transformed the session into a tempest. There were boos and protests, proposals that the speaker be denied the floor, shouts and whistles that the president of the session quieted with great difficulty. . . . There there were speeches of protest spoken in every tone from revolt to pity that implied that the speaker was simply insane."[10] The importance of ideologies of Black racial solidarity in the world beyond Brazil, the fact that mulattos and Blacks in Brazil are not for the most part simply a rural cultural periphery, whose entry into the modern sector comes through the doorway of mestization, sets their situation apart from that of the Indian. The formidable influence of the nonracial national concept should not be

7. Ibid., p. 41. On the African component of the Cuban population see Frank Knight, *Slave Society in Cuba During the Nineteenth Century* (Madison: University of Wisconsin Press, 1970).

8. Curtin, *The Atlantic Slave Trade*, p. 268.

9. See, for example, Marvin Harris, *Town and Country in Brazil* (New York: Columbia University Press, 1956); van den Berghe, *Race and Ethnicity*; Charles Boxer, *Race Relations in the Portuguese Colonial Empire, 1415-1825* (Oxford: Clarendon Press, 1963).

10. Quoted in Campbell, *Racial Tensions and National Identity*, p. 149.

underestimated, but neither should the possibility of political mobilization of Black racial solidarity be wholly discounted in Brazil.

POLITICS AS INDEPENDENT VARIABLE

We have argued at many junctures that the political arena itself may be fruitfully seen as the independent variable in determining the nature and intensity of cultural mobilization. The locus of conflict within the political system delimits the possible contenders; we showed through the Zaire case the surprising differences in patterns of ethnicity in successive political phases, when conflict arenas shifted from the main cities, to political parties, to a new set of provinces, through rebellion to sharply centralized national institutions. As independent variables, electoral politics in a culturally plural environment are of particular importance in the conflict arena they provide. Campaign meetings are organized, with florid rhetoric denouncing the opposition. Rallies, marches, processions, libations are all public spectacles in a drowsy setting; the sheer entertainment value merits note and certainly attracts large audiences. The flood of messages pulsing through the social communications networks is likely to be heavily charged with overt ethnic references or ethnic cues so thinly disguised as to be transparent to all message recipients. Then comes the final dramatic act—the balloting itself. Hopes and fears, cultural expectations and anxieties have been brought to a tension point by the quickening pace of competition leading up to the moment of climax. The traumatization has likely produced some violent clashes and the fear of many more; the conspicuous deployment of police and perhaps army to protect the balloting underlines the gravity of the situation and the possible threats arising from an unfavorable outcome. Then comes the denouement—cultural triumph for some, congealing of anxieties for others, as the scene shifts, in the epilogue, to the division of rewards in function of the formulas prescribed by the voting. Cultural elections are ethnicity as guerrilla theater.

However, mitigating patterns deserve citation. Latent pluralism is not always activated by competitive elections; in Latin America, at those places and times where free elections have occurred, the potential cleavages of race and ethnicity have never been discovered. In the Philippines, despite the fact ethnicity there lay rather closer to social consciousness than in Latin America, the bipolar party competition which has obtained for much of this century served to inhibit politization of linguistic identity. The fluid factionalism which underlay the apparent bipolarity offered no structural possibility for cultural perception. This system had other defects which contributed to its demise in 1972, but cultural pluralism had no part in it. India is another vindication of the positive role democratic elections can play in a plural setting. Although cultural factors play an important part in Indian elections, they create an arena of bargaining and communal compromise which has been critical to the vitality of India. National parties compete on the basis of political, not cultural, ideologies (excepting the Jana Sangh). The party system, electoral machinery, and tiers of elected assemblies serve as transmission belt converting the particularistic energies of cultural pluralism into ideological inputs into the central political process. In the Pakistan case, West Pakistan elites could simply not have gotten away with the inequitable distribution of national resources had open elections been permitted in the early years of the republic. For these reasons, we cannot accept the Rabushka-Shepsle hypothesis that democratic politics are incompatible with cultural pluralism

INEQUALITY, EGALITARIANISM, AND PLURALISM

Short of the utopia which many have designed but none have realized, differential distribution of wealth, status, and power is an inevitable concomitant of organized human society. Also deeply rooted in modern political philosophy is the ideal of equality, the belief that the power of the state should be utilized to secure a redistribution of unequally shared resources.

As James Coleman has put it, "Whether viewed as a factual trend, a perceived technological possibility, or simply as the dominant aspiration underlying the drive for change, egalitarianism pervades all aspects of modern political life and culture and all forms of modern political ideology."[11] What may vary widely is the fashion in which inequalities are conceptualized and the identification of groups which ought to be beneficiaries of redistribution. Political philosophy, at one level, is worldwide intellectual tradition, in which causes and remedies of inequality and formulas for the governance of man are central themes. This debate is universalist in character and tends to be abstracted from the cultural particularities of specific polities. The categories of thought through which human inequalities are described do not derive from cultural pluralism; in one way or another, some concept of social divisions as classes, strata, or other functionally equivalent term enters in. The great ideologies which have dominated the third world—democratic left,

11. Leonard Binder et al., *Crises and Sequences of Political Development* (Princeton: Princeton University Press, 1971), p. 76.

Christian democracy, welfare state reformism, Arab or African socialism, Marxism-Leninism, Maoism, and the like—all embody universalistic metaphors in describing poverty and wealth. Within the inner temples of power, of course, ideologies carry less actual weight in concrete choice than official rhetoric might suggest; even here, however, we would argue that the patterns of thought imposed by dominant ideological images of society are subtle and pervasive in their effect. Further, social class theories are powerful explanatory tools of social inequality and conflict.

Cross-cutting ideological visions founded on universalistic stratification concepts is mobilized cultural pluralism. Although particular cultural identities may be ideologically conceived, as we have argued, cultural pluralism as a conceptualization of society lacks status as a philosophy; it is rather a social fact of compartmentalized solidarities, through which inequalities become perceived and measured by a different yardstick. The "national cake," through this prism, requires equitable division into proportionate pieces for each cultural segment; much less visible, from this perspective, becomes the issue of shares of each individual slice. The politics of communal distribution, as in Malaysia or first republic Nigeria, leaves little place for class-oriented ideologies. The converse, we have suggested, is true where universality ideologies wholly dominate, as in Latin America. One of the reasons why Indians do not perceive themselves as such politically is that available protest ideologies all identify them as peasants, who are only coincidentally Indians.

GROWING CAPACITY OF THE STATE

If we examine the broad course of political change in recent decades, set against the history of identity formation at national and subnational levels over a longer time frame and wider universe, what may be suggested by way of overall trend? First, we would like to recall the arguments advanced in chapter 3 concerning the increasing capacity of the state. The state system, in roughly its present form, is hardening into an iron grid fixing the most basic parameters of politics. The yearly increments of power of their coercive instruments, improving communications networks, ever more numerous public bureaucracies, new technologies of control—all of these strongly flowing currents merge into a powerful tide of central power. The idea of development and ideologies of socialism endow centralized authority with overriding moral purpose and sanction. The international system, fearful of the unfathomable and possible far-reaching disequilibrating effects of any refashioning of the state system, is at bottom committed to its maintenance. Significant resources flow from the international environment to the third world states, whose net effect is the strengthening of the state entities; conversely, for the most part resources are denied to those who would alter the system—as witness the loneliness of Biafra and the southern Sudan. Only in very special circumstances, short of a world-wide conflagration, is any alteration in the state frame likely, we have argued the exceptional geopolitical factors operating in the Bangladesh case, and have also suggested the possible liquidity of the state system in the Middle East, because of the uncertainties inherent in the Arab-Israeli conflict, the volatility of the Palestinian diaspora nationality, the continuing vitality of the pan-Arab ideal, and the uncertain identity of several states of the Arabian peninsula. Southern Africa also deserves mention as an area where the legitimacy of existing arrangements is under wide challenge, reflected in the controversies over the unrecognized state of Rhodesia, South Africa and its semisovereign apartheid Bantustan enclaves, South West Africa, and the Portuguese colonies. For the most part, the challenge lies not in the existing units, but in the racial caste system through which they are governed; the eventual dissolution of the latter could well bring with it a reshuffle of the former.

SPREAD OF AUTHORITARIAN FORMULAS

A second trend which affects the political arena within which cultural pluralism operates is toward authoritarian forms of power exercise. This usually involves some form of alliance between military and bureaucratic elites. Only a few polities stand out as conspicuous exceptions to the trend: India, Sri Lanka, Malaysia, Singapore, and Lebanon in Asia; the micropolities of Gambia and Botswana in Africa; Costa Rica, Mexico, and probably Columbia and Venezuela in recent years in Latin America. Elsewhere, we find entrenched politico-military rule in states like Burma, Indonesia, Egypt, Syria, Iraq, Algeria, Zaire, Nigeria, Brazil, and Peru; revolutionary authoritarian Marxist-Leninist regimes in North Korea, North Vietnam, Cuba; party-state oligarchies in many African states; monarchical regimes in Swaziland, Saudi-Arabia, Yemen, Kuwait, and Iran. In Latin America, there appeared a time, which roughly coincided with the Kennedy era in the United States and the launching of the "Alliance for Progress," when the traditional dictatorships seemed to be disappearing and democracy to be in an ascendant phase. From the perspective of the early 1970s, we may observe the rise of a new authoritarianism, technocratic in Brazil, radical in Peru, nationalist and modernizing, each after its own fashion, in both.

In Africa and Asia, once decolonization had been accepted as a goal by the colonizer, the successor state could only be fashioned according to the political norms obtaining in the mother country. Constitutional democracy was thus, in a sense, the ransom of independence. Nor should it be implied that this ransom was reluctantly paid; at the moment of independence, the nationalist elites were ready to accept a system which conferred prestige and respectability upon the exercise of new power. The transplanted institutions for the most part had shallow roots and only a short life span. Our discussions of Zairian, Nigerian, Ugandan, and Pakistani politics suggested some of the reasons for the atrophy. One after another, political impasse sparked a military takeover—or institutionalization of a single party system and interpenetration of party and state. Although the routes might vary, most political roads carried the polity to an authoritarian destination.

What then of the communal implications of the more powerful, more authoritarian state? The military-bureaucratic regimes offer a very different structure of access to politics. Incentives for cultural mobilization by political entrepreneurs are removed; numbers per se are no longer the name of the game. Indeed, strong disincentives are likely to be part of the operating principles of such regimes through the banning of parties and ethnic associations, prohibition of communally oriented publication, and like measures. "Tribalism" and "communalism" are sure of castigation by the central power-holders (except, of course, national cultures which are promoted in core culture states).

However, influence will now depend on the cultural balance within the governing elites themselves. In the praise occasionally extended to military elites as nation-builders in the developing world, insufficient note is taken of the possibility of major inequalities in representation within the military elites. "Martial race" theories, colonial security calculations, relative attractiveness of military service in poorer regions—these and other factors account for what is likelihood rather than mere possibility of disproportionate strength of some groups and the absence of others. Even though no favoritism was intended, it would be naive to imagine that policy outcomes and the distribution of rewards would be unaffected by the communal composition of the allocators, when they are not constrained by accountability to any other body. Perhaps more important than the actual inequalities is the probability that groups poorly represented among the power-holding elite will perceive that they are being shortchanged. Here we may recall the bitterness in Nigeria when General Ironsi announced the promotion of twelve lieutenant colonels in May 1966 by strict criteria of seniority; when nine were Ibo, the actual objectivity of the decision was totally obscured by the angry charges of ethnic chauvinism. In all three secessions that we examined, the advent of military regimes in which the alienated region was poorly represented shut off channels of access.

The same observations apply to the civil service elite. For quite different reasons, full cultural representativity is very improbable. Elite ranks of the bureaucracy have exacting entry criteria, which can only be met by those from areas relatively well endowed in educational infrastructure. For groups that find themselves outside the walls of these closed sanctuaries, an inevitable frustration and anxiety ensue, as there appears no way to communicate collective grievances effectively. The regional disparities in military and civil service ranks, resting upon different principles, may well not be the same. However, when a large group is excluded from both sectors in a military-bureaucratic coalition, trouble may be forecast.

We believe that there is a continuous process of broadening and consolidation of identities at the periphery. The state impinges increasingly upon the field of social vision of the individual. In so doing, the national polity becomes a relevant other, compelling a new self-definition. Through the prism of the broadened unit of self-awareness, conflict bounded by the territorial arena is likely to occur with other similarly extended communities, over scarce values within the broader system. Various aspects of change are reinforcing this trend. The phenomenal pace of urbanization is throwing new migrants into a setting where they must seek security through discovering social bonds of mutual obligation extending over a culturally defined, but broadened community; the city is also an arena of intense interaction and competition. Improving communication capacities enlarge message flows, which are shaped by the networks of communal solidarity. The expanded educational system throws out larger numbers of young people, with higher mobility expectations, that are likely to use channels of cultural solidarity to seek fulfillment. This generational set, acutely sensitive to opportunity structure and ethnic disparity issues, is also very susceptible to mobilization.

We believe there is also a trend toward the fixation of the broader identity labels. Particularly in Africa, many of the current ethnic labels are of quite recent vintage. However, as they become standard features of administrative classification and political discourse, they are institutionalized. In other words, the Naga, the Ibo, the Kiga, the Hutu, to mention but a few discussed in these pages, are probably here to stay.

LEVELS OF CULTURAL MOBILIZATION

This much is general; there are variable change patterns to report. We have argued, employing the distinction suggested by Joshua Fishman, that the institutionalization of cultural solidarity will vary according to the degree that it becomes ideologized. This occurs when a comprehensive cultural myth is elaborated, supported by a unified language (usually, an integrated interpretation of the collective past and vision of the shared future, equipped with an intellectual heritage in the form of a developed literature. When such a solidarity system is equipped with a comprehensive set of symbols to provide cognitive orientation and social cues, and has the cultural resources to ensure the socialization of the new generation, it is self-sustaining and an enduring social fact. This has clearly occurred for the major core cultures in Asia; for the more important linguistic groups in India, such as the Tamils, Bengalis, Marathis, and Telugu-speakers; for the Afrikaners in South Africa, for the Somali in Somali; for the Kurds in Iraq; recently, for the Blacks in the United States and non-Hispanic West Indies. However, it has not transpired for the hill peoples of Southeast Asia, for non-Arabic speakers in Sudan or Berbers in the Maghreb, for nearly all African ethnic groups, for Latin American Indians.

The intensity of cultural solidarity at any given moment varies according to the degree of political mobilization. Where access to political rewards occurs through direct cultural competition, where one self-conscious group perceived in the flow of events collective threat, through assault upon its symbols or through a curtailment of its access to social mobility or material rewards, then it is likely to respond through intensified awareness and mobilization.

In Africa and Asia, in the years of independence national elites have learned a great deal about the problems and perils of cultural pluralism. Accumulated experience is, of course, not equivalent to complete clairvoyance; nonetheless, a much more sophisticated level of statecraft is applied to the nation-building goal, and many of the structural incentives to cultural mobilization have been removed. Here the distinction between ideologized cultural systems and ethnicity becomes relevant; the latter will more readily lapse into a state of relative latency when mobilizing structural elements are removed and anxiety-arousing cultural policies avoided. In the African setting, the cultural neutrality of the state and the negative valuation attached to cultural mobilization serve as inhibiting factors for prospective cultural entrepreneurs.

We should add that the tendency toward enlargement of identity systems which attends penetration by the state institutions and other aspects of social change by no means implies a hostile reaction to the national system. This follows only in the special circumstances wherein the state institutions are identified with a dominant culture which is perceived as threatening; the Kurds in Iraq are a classic case in point. But in Nigeria, the Ibo awakening was associated with passionate commitment to Nigeria, until the point was reached where Nigeria appeared to be severely menacing for the Ibo as a collectivity. A survey by Fred Hayward in Ghana well documents this conclusion: little conflict was seen between local and national loyalties, and a surprisingly benign attitude toward the national government was found. The survey was done close to the 1969 elections, which themselves revealed an unmistakable pattern of ethnic impact upon voting choice. Taken in conjunction, these two measures of identity indicate that cultural pluralism was a significant determinant of political behavior, while at the same time contending groups shared a basically favorable orientation towards the national system—and found no incompatibility between ethnic solidarity and positive affective ties to the nation.[12]

COPING WITH CULTURAL PLURALISM

What is to be done? How can the developing state coexist with cultural pluralism? The answers to these question will mean the difference between social harmony and endemic civil war. We may exclude from the outset certain possible outcomes as impossible or undesirable. The application of the principle of cultural self-determination is beyond the pale of reality. The multiplicity of identities, the overlapping of various types of solidarity, the sheer numbers and small scale of many groups preclude such a solution except in extraordinary circumstances. The fate of Pakistan, one of the rare third world states initially constituted through cultural self-determination, illustrates the problem well: no sooner did the Muslim League win its goal of an Islamic state than an alternative basis of solidarity came to the fore in East Bengal. The international system is resolutely hostile to such an alternative, as are the national elites that control the machinery of the existing states; the most that seceders can achieve through armed rebellion is probably represented by the southern Sudan situation. At enormous cost in human suffering and a decade of development foregone, a stalemate was institutionalized which forced a compromise settlement, satisfying a number of cultural autonomy demands, but within the framework of Sudan.

12. Fred M. Hayward, "The Stability of Levels of National Integration: Projections from the Ghanaian Contest," and "Correlates of National Integration," forthcoming.

Coerced assimilation and cultural oppression are policies likely to incur high costs and yield minimal benefits. Cultural change is as old as human society and has often involved assimilation; we have suggested some of the conditions in which this may occur as a natural process in chapter 4. But the trends noted make this increasingly unlikely, except with the very localized social groups that must necessarily link themselves to a broader identity as they become bound within the circuits of the polity. But larger units of identity are becoming fixed and institutionalized, and less readily absorbable. A propensity to assimilate requires a view of the assimilating culture as of superior prestige, power, status and as conferring advantages of mobility or security. The politization and mobilization of ethnicity makes such a perspective much less likely. The very process of collective awakening, in the contemporary world, is permeated with the idea of equality; no cultural group has a just claim to privileged treatment. The crises which attended the politization of relationships in culturally stratified societies such as Rwanda, Burundi, and Zanzibar illustrate this point. The coming of collective self-consciousness to the African population on Zanzibar made unacceptable political and economic domination by the small Arab status group, whose hegemony was established without great difficulty in the nineteenth century.[13] In Rwanda and Burundi, the politization of horizontal solidarities of "Tutsi" and "Hutu" placed enormous strains on the vertical ties of clientage founded upon a premise of inequality. This conflict led to ethnic revolution in 1959 in Rwanda and to a series of crises in Burundi, the most recent of which was the massacre of 1972, whose human toll is variously estimated at between 100,000 and 200,000.[14]

As a cornerstone of cultural policy, security must be assured to identity groups as collectivities. In chapter 5, we have analyzed the galvanizing force of perceived threat to the symbol set which embodies identity. Judicious consideration of the cultural impact of contemplated policies is indispensable, above all in domains such as language and religion where identity is most intimately involved. The social cost of policies which generate acute anxieties—resistance, violent response, alienation, and impairment of trust—is very high indeed. Few choices can command such high priority on other grounds that they are worth pursuing if a high level of communal insecurity is a reasonable forecast.

This does not imply that nation-building must be abandoned, that a national language policy is impossible, that communal solidarity groups

13. For thorough treatment of the Zanzibar crisis, see Lofchie, *Zanzibar: Background to Revolution.*

14. See the outstanding study by Rene Lemarchand, *Rwanda and Burundi* (London: Pall Mall Press, 1970). On the 1972 Burundi crisis, see Warren Weinstein, "Conflict and Confrontation in Central Africa: The Revolt in Burundi 1972," *Africa Today*, XIX, no. 4 (Fall 1972), 17-37.

deserve a veto on all questions of public policy, or that the Lebanese model of confessional politics and a very limited role for the state is the sole pathway to cultural peace. Sensitivity in approach is central. Empathy of style, a visible effort to see the issue as it is perceived by various cultural segments, facilitates reassurance. The patient search for consensus is preferable to cultural fiat imposed by brute force.

A second foundation of threat-avoidance in nation-building is recognition that the principle of equality must be envisaged in terms of collectivities as well as individuals. This is so precisely because, in a plural framework, large numbers will evaluate their situation from a communal reference point. A frequent theme of French propaganda during the Algerian Revolution was that liberation should be accorded to the individual Algerian, and not to Algerians as a collectivity. Needless to say, such an argument made little headway in the war of liberation; Algerians were not prepared to look upon themselves in that way. Nor will mobilized cultural segments anywhere else; if a group reaches a level of awareness where collective calculations are made in politics, then to argue that opportunities are available to all individuals on an equal basis will not suffice if the counter-argument can be made that institutional disparities between groups exist. This, of course, will be recognized as the reasoning which lies behind the "institutional racism" argument in the United States. Blacks as a group are subject to disabilities which make the individual competition inequitable, and thus policies which provide confidence that collective equality is being provided are necessary to win trust that specific decisions involving individuals are fair. Thus, in India, Tamils cannot accept the argument that all applicants for the Indian Administrative Service are judged by objective tests, if the examinations themselves confer advantages on those speaking Hindi as mother tongue. A merit system in Nigeria which would have flooded the public service with southerners was found unacceptable by Hausa-speakers because of historical inequalities in the degree of development of educational systems. The examples could be multiplied *ad infinitum*, but the point is clear. Once cultural solidarity becomes a salient role for masses of citizens, then it will ineluctably become a measure of equality of opportunity in their eyes. Change and modernization will, in part, be reflected in communal competition for the enlarging resources of wealth, power, and status. Collective impediments, perceived discrimination are grave and mobilizing threats. This, of course, leaves unanswered the question of just how much weight should be placed on this factor. Rigid mathematical quotas have a poor historical track record. The formula in a given situation must above all be guided by careful sensitivity to collective sentiments of cultural segments.

Institutionalized access to processes of authoritative allocation at the national level for cultural sections is crucial. The trend to authoritarian formulas makes this question more critical, as significant groups may be poorly represented in dominant military and bureaucratic elites. There are, no doubt, diverse means by which this may be achieved; recognition of the problem is the prerequisite to its solution. One or another form of cultural representation within the power configuration of the system is the logical answer. Within the setting of electoral politics, the "balanced ticket" so well established in the political folklore of American cities and states where ethnic segments are salient is an obvious response; indeed, one of the great advantages of electoral recruitment of political elites is the likelihood that cultural solidarities will find reasonable reflection in the composition of the chosen representatives. But trend lines suggest that in many times and places, competitive elections will not play an important role; in these instances, alternative formulas for achieving the same purpose are required. The conspicuous presence of cultural delegates in authoritative institutions reduces anxieties and offers reassurance that the group views are being heard, if not necessarily followed. Regime empathy is thus institutionalized, if cultural segments are persuaded that the world as it appears to them is explained and that policies are adjusted in consequence of this understanding.

In certain circumstances, it may be desirable to guarantee access and representation through according cultural automony in certain policy spheres. In constitutional terms, this suggests that federal forms may at times be appropriate. This formula has worked poorly in a number of instances, as in first republic Nigeria, Zaire, Uganda, or the British West Indies federation. Constitutional formulas alone cannot suffice, nor can cultural issues be resolved by formulating them as judicial matters and referring them to the courts for arbitration and solution; this imposes far too high an institutional load upon the often weak judicial systems. Also, federalism is a scheme for areal distribution of power. When cleavages are not wholly territorial, they cannot well be captured by this device. In India, for example, a constitutional system which has important federal features while eschewing the term has continuing difficulties in stabilizing its component units. One wholesale transformation occurred in the 1950s when linguistic self-determination was, in fact, conceded as a principle for reorganizing states. A new wave of demands for realignment seems in prospect, with the violent pressures for dismemberment of the first linguistic state of Andhra Pradesh a probable omen of impending events. At the same time, Indian quasi-federalism has made important contributions to defusing pluralism by multiplying the arenas of negotiation and brokerage of competing claims.

In instances where conflict and cultural alienation reach a threshold where violent resistance is in prospect and secession is mooted, a large measure of autonomy may be the only way to offer cultural security. This was certainly the case in the southern Sudan, where northern political elites finally recognized that they were simply unable to govern the south, that southerners had to be placed in charge of their region in order for anyone to believe that deprivations were not to be exclusively laid at the door of Arab-Islamic cultural imperialism. In time, federalism or regional autonomy formulas may sufficiently allay anxieties and alter orientations so that autonomy may be quietly dropped. In Libya, distrust between Tripolitania, Cyreneika, and Fezzan was so pronounced at independence that a federal formula was indispensable. By the end of its first decade, regional fears had so diminished that a more centralized pattern could be adopted without controversy. Similarly in several of the larger Latin American polities federalism in the nineteenth century was an important therapy for a regionalism which has become very attenuated since.

Whatever the formula for access and representation, we believe that Arend Lijphart has identified a critical dimension of the politics of cultural accommodation in his analysis of pluralism in the Netherlands as consociational democracy. Some of the central premises of consociational politics are the recognition that the populace is structured in cultural segments, the agreement to disagree on questions of cultural ideology, proportionality in the distribution of rewards, avoidance of public debate of cultural issues, summit diplomacy by cultural elites to resolve differences.[15] Those operating at the national level share a commitment to the preservation of the state as the basic frame of politics, governance, and development. Leadership of exceptional ability, skill, and integrity is an absolute requisite of consociationalism. Their task is one of great delicacy; they must mediate between the conflicting requirements of national interests and the particular demands of their cultural segment. If they appear mere toadies for other groups, they will lose their legitimacy in the eyes of their following and thus their value as cultural delegates. If they pursue the interests of their solidary unit with exclusive and sectarian zeal, and mobilize their following in hostility to the state, then their contribution to national integration evaporates.

The tensions built into this process are obvious. But nation-building can only move forward through an ongoing consociational bargaining and compromise. There is simply no escape from the existing state system, as the political frame within which mankind must seek a better life. Conflict, some argue, is creative; that may well be, yet endemic civil strife along lines of cultural cleavage is surely not a pathway to either peace or

15. Lijphart, *The Politics of Accomodation,* pp. 123-38.

prosperity. There is no single prescription; each plural polity has its own unique configuration of diversity. The sensitive application of wisdom accumulated in the observation of the politics of cultural pluralism is not beyond the reach of statesmanship. There is, of course, no other choice.

Index

Judaism: religious and social identity, 56; fragmentation of, 57. *See also* Zionism
Justice Party, India, 118

Kabaka (king of Baganda), 150-51, 153-54, 225-26, 227, 249-55, 257-59, 264-65
Kabaka Yekka (KY, political party, Uganda), 150, 250-58
Kabarega (king of Bunyoro), 220-21
Kabyl: in Algeria, 418
Kachin: in Burma, 49
Kagwa, Sir Apolo (prime minister of Buganda), 227
Kahin, George M.: *Nationalism and Revolution in Indonesia* (Cornell University Press, 1952), 360
Kalamba, Mukenge (Zaire politician): alliance with Belgians, 175; mentioned, 176
Kalanda, Mabika: *Baluba et Lulua. Une ethnie à la recherche d'un nouvel équilibre* (Editions de Remarques Congolaises, 1959), 176, 187; *Tabalayi* (Imprimerie Concordia, 1963), 187
Kallen, Horace M.: in the *Nation* (1915), 16; *Culture and Democracy in the United States* (Boni and Liveright, 1924)
Kalonji, Albert (Luba-Kasai leader), 188
Kampala, Uganda: march on, 152-53; ethnicity, 242-43; mentioned, 155, 240
Kananga (Luluabourg): mutiny in Zaire (1944), 147, 178-79; terrorism (1959), 175, 177
Kann, Robert A.: *The Multi National Empire* (Columbia University Press, 1950), 24, 25, 53
Karen, Burma, 49
Kanuri: Ronald Cohen on, 306
Kanyinda-Lusanga, Theodore: "Pouvoir traditionel et institutions politiques modernes chez les Baluba du Sud-Kasai" (Mémoire de Licence, Université Lovanium de Kinshasa, 1968), 187, 188
Kariuki, Joseph Mwangi: *"Mau Mau" Detainee* (Oxford University Press, 1963), 130, 132
Karachi, 146
Karpat, Kemal H.: "Ethnicity and Community and the Rise of Modern Nations in the Ottoman State" (unpublished paper), 31; quoted on Ottoman ethnicity, 31; *Political and Social Thought in the Contemporary Middle East* (Praeger, 1968),

56, 373, 422
Kasavubu, Joseph (first president of Zaire): ethnicity of, 170, 194; political thought, 185
Kasfir, Nelson: "Controlling Ethnicity in Uganda Politics: Departicipation as a Strategy for Political Development in Africa" (Ph.D. diss., Harvard University, 1972), 35, 48, 49, 152, 239, 256, 268, 269, 270; 252N
Kashmir: 146-47, 313
Katanga secession, 81
Katz, David, and K. W. Brady: study summarized in Allport's *The Nature of Prejudice*, 148
Kearney, Robert: *Communalism and Language in the Politics of Ceylon* (Duke University Press, 1967), 509
Kedourie, Elie: *Nationalism* (Hutchinson, 1960), 13
Kelly, George Armstrong: "Belgium: New Nationalism in an Old World," *Comparative Politics*, I, no. 3 (1969), 9; on Belgium unity, 9
Kenya: ethnicity, 18; Kikuyu culture in, 125; Mau Mau movement in, 128-29; Kenya Peoples Union (KPU), 133; Kenya African National Union (KANU), 133; Kenya African Democratic Union (KADU), 133; Luos in, 246. *See also* Kikuyu
Kenyan African Union (KAU), 129, 135
Kenyatta, Jomo: *Facing Mount Kenya* (Vintage Press, 1962), 126, 127-28; on oaths, 130-31; political leader, 132-34;
Kerkvliet, Ben: "Peasant Rebellion in the Philippines: The Origins and Growth of the HMB" (Ph.D. diss., University of Wisconsin, 1972), 366
Keyes, Charles F.: "Ethnic Identity and Loyalty of Villagers in Northeastern Thailand," *Asian Survey*, VI, no. 7 (1966), 509
Khadduri, Majid: *Modern Libya* (Johns Hopkins Press, 1963), 389
Khan, Ayub: *Friends Not Masters* (Oxford University Press, 1967), 475; coup, 484; deposed, 486
Khan, General Yahya, 40, 486-88
Khartoum: Arab language in, 108-9; battle of, 388; mentioned, 407, 409, 410, 495, 496, 498, 499, 501
Kiambu, Kenya district, 134-35
Kiga: identity, 230

Paul, 1971), 126, 133

Marxist-Leninist ideologies in Africa and Asia, 41

Masai, 126, 134, 139

Mason, Philip: *Patterns of Dominance* (Oxford University Press, 1970), 287, 428, 433, 442, 447, 449

Mass media: in Third World, 80

Masson, P.: *La Bataille pour Bukavu* (Charles Dessart, 1965), 210

Mau Mau: uprising, Kenya, 128-34; oaths of, 129-31

Mauritania: peoples of, 411-12; mentioned, 402

Maya, 100, 429, 431

Mayanja, Abu, (Uganda intellectual), 254-55

Mayfield, James: *Rural Politics in Nasser's Egypt* (University of Texas Press, 1971), 381, 386

Mazrui, Ali A.: "Privilege and Protest as Integrative Factors: The Case of Buganda's Status in Uganda," in Rotberg and Mazrui, *Protest and Power in Black Africa*, 229; *Engineering and Nation-Building in East Africa* (Northwestern University Press, 1972), 263, 264

Mbala: ethnicity, 3-4

Mboladingua-Katako, Jules: "Conflict Ekona-Eswe au Sankuru de 1960 à 1964" (Unpublished mémoire de licence, Lovanium University, 1970), 193

Mboya, Tom, Kenya: assassination, 134

Mbundu: in Kwilu rebellion in Zaire, 145; mentioned, 4

McCoy, Alfred W., and Nina S. Adams: *Laos: War and Revolution* (Harper and Row, 1970), 87

McLaughlin, Peter: *Language-Switching as an Index of Socialization in the Republic of the Sudan* (University of California Press, 1964), 108, 109, 408, 410

McVey, Ruth (ed.): *Indonesia* (Human Relations Area Files Press, 1963), 330, 331, 334, 335, 336, 338, 339, 356

Means, Philip Ainsworth: "The Rebellion of Tupac-Amaru II, 1780-1781," *Hispanic American Historical Review*, II, no. 1 (1919), 448

Mednick, Melvin: "Some Problems of Moro History and Political Organization," *Philippine Sociological Review*, V,

no. 1 (1957), 347

Mellor, John L., Thomas F. Weaver, Ume J. Lele, and Sheldon R. Simon: *Developing Rural India: Plan and Practice* (Cornell University Press, 1968), 326

Melson, Robert, and Howard Wolpe: *Nigeria: Modernization and the Politics of Communalism* (Michigan State University Press, 1971), 18, 29, 37, 99, 278, 303, 306, 466, 471; "Modernization and the Politics of Communalism, A Theoretical Perspective," *American Political Science Review*, LXIV, no. 4 (1970), 240

Menelik II (king of Ethiopia), 91

Menon, V. P.: *The Transfer of Power* (Princeton University Press, 1957), 301

Mercier, Paul: "Remarques sur la signification du 'tribalisme' actuel en Afrique noire," *Cahiers Internationaux de Sociologie*, XXI (1961), 37

Merriam, Alan P.: quoted on Zaire independence, 159-60; *Background of Conflict* (Northwestern University Press, 1961), 160

Merton, Robert: *Social Theory and Social Structure* (Free Press, 1968), 39

Meru identity, 242

Mestizo in Latin America, 84, 436

Mexico, 440-41

Micaud, Charles, and Ernest Gellner (eds.): *Arabs and Berbers: From Tribe to Nation in North Africa* (D. C. Heath, 1972), 31

Michel, A. A.: *The Indus Rivers* (Yale University Press, 1967), 486

Migration: in cultural arena, 23; and identity changes, 100; effect on urban identity, 167-68; in pre-independence India, 301; significance in Indonesia, 332; in Philippines, 346; for Jews, 395-96, 397; of Bengali refugees, 488-89; of southern Sudanese refugees, 499

Military in nation building, 77-78, 520. *See also* Armed forces

Miller, A. H.: "Ethnicity and Political Behavior: A Review of Theories and an Attempt at Reformulation," *Western Political Quarterly*, XXIV, no. 3 (1971), 7

Miller, Eugene F.: "Positivism, Historicism, and Political Inquiry and its Rebuttals," *American Political Science Review*, LXVI, no. 3 (1972), 73

Minangkabau, 333-34